Werner Gephart / Jure Leko (Eds.)
In the Realm of Corona Normativities II

GEFÖRDERT VOM

Bundesministerium
für Bildung
und Forschung

Series of the
Käte Hamburger Center for
Advanced Study in the Humanities
»Law as Culture«

Edited by Werner Gephart

Volume 27

Werner Gephart / Jure Leko (Eds.)

In the Realm of Corona Normativities II

The Permanence of the Exception

VITTORIO KLOSTERMANN
Frankfurt am Main · 2022

recht als kultur
käte hamburger kolleg
law as culture
center for advanced study

Bibliographische Information der Deutschen Nationalbibliothek

Die Deutsche Nationalbibliothek verzeichnet diese Publikation in der
Deutschen Nationalbibliographie; detaillierte bibliographische Daten
sind im Internet über *http://dnb.dnb.de* abrufbar.

1. Auflage 2022

© Vittorio Klostermann GmbH · Frankfurt am Main · 2022
Alle Rechte vorbehalten, insbesondere die des Nachdrucks und der
Übersetzung. Ohne Genehmigung des Verlages ist es nicht gestattet,
dieses Werk oder Teile in einem photomechanischen oder sonstigen
Reproduktionsverfahren oder unter Verwendung elektronischer Systeme
zu verarbeiten, zu vervielfältigen und zu verbreiten.
Gedruckt auf alterungsbeständigem Papier ⊗ ISO 9706
Satz: mittelstadt 21, Vogtsburg-Burkheim
Umschlaggestaltung: Jörgen Rumberg, Bonn
Umschlagabbildung: Werner Gephart, Corona-Leviathan.
A Reverence to Thomas Hobbes (46 × 35,77 cm, digital collage
with the assistance of Michelle Chlup), 2021.
Druck und Bindung: docupoint GmbH, Barleben
Printed in Germany
ISSN 2193-2964
ISBN 978-3-465-04587-8

Contents

WERNER GEPHART
Preface: In the Absence of a Master Narrative? 9

Prologue

FRANÇOIS OST
Le Petit Prince au pays du Covid 19

I. The Shaking of System Worlds and the Intrusion of the Pandemic into the Lifeworld

DANIEL WITTE
Temporary Destabilizations: The Fragility of Normality and the
Normalization of the Fragmentary 29

MARTA BUCHOLC
The Quest for Herd Immunity: Coronavirus and the Two Global
Civilizing Offensives of 2020–2021 73

HANNA EKLUND
Law and Care 87

MAXIMILIAN MAYER AND KATHARINA C. CRAMER
Pandemic Disruptions and Transnational Care Relations: Towards
Closing the *Care Gap* in International Relations Theories 95

PETER GOODRICH
Mortem Instituere 119

UPENDRA BAXI
Suffering and Governance in Times of Death, Devastation,
and Desolation 129

GERD KRUMEICH
Corona und Krieg 147

II. Shifts in the Observers' Perspectives

MARIACARLA GADEBUSCH BONDIO AND BIRGIT ULRIKE MÜNCH
Long Covid – Unfortunately Not *Past*: Mapping (In)Visibility Perspectives from the Medical Humanities and Art History 157

BEATRIZ BARREIRO CARRIL AND KEVIN GRECKSCH
Reimagining Academia after Covid-19 173

CHIOMA DAISY ONYIGE
The Challenges, Complexities and Uncertainties of International Mobility for Global South Scholars in the Era of Covid-19: A Perception from a Nigerian Scholar 189

CHRISTA RAUTENBACH
The Many Colors of Covid-19 in South Africa: A Legal Perspective 197

SABINE N. MEYER
Covid-19 as a Magnifying Glass: Native America between Vulnerability and (Self-)Empowerment 223

PIERRE BRUNET
Le surréalisme juridique au temps du corona 251

III. Still in the Realm of the Normative

SAM WHIMSTER
Social Distancing and the Social Contract. Dual Normativities 257

KORNELIA HAHN
Love in the Time of the Covid Pandemic 271

ANGELA CONDELLO
Justice and (Sexual) Difference. Questioning Gender Inequality from a Feminist Perspective 291

BRIGITTE NERLICH
The Coronavirus and Covid-19: Verbal and Visual Metaphors 303

THERESA STROMBACH
From *Verbot* to *Gebot*? – A Linguistic View on Legal Phrasing in Infection Protection Law 319

HELGA MARÍA LELL
Persona, the Mask and the Anomic Person 327

VALÉRIE HAYAERT
Pestis and Anomia 337

SERGIO GENOVESI
Digital Rights in Times of Pandemic 345

FRANCESCA CAROCCIA
The Principle of Solidarity as Relational Dimension of the (Informed)
Consent: The Case of Covid-19 Vaccines 355

CHRISTOPH ANTONS
Intellectual Property Policies and *Vaccine Diplomacy* in Asia 369

JONAS GRUTZPALK
»Le réel c'est le cogne?« Über die Wechselwirkung von Corona-Virus und
polizeilichem Sanktionsregime 385

IV. Cultural Meaning of the Pandemic Crisis

STEFAN FINGER
Corona ist nicht das Ende 401

ANNE-MARIE BONNET
Art and Life in Pandemic Times 427

KATJA SPRANZ
Celebrities in Coronaland 443

HANNE PETERSEN
Re-Evaluation/Value of Nature under Conditions of Social Lock Down? .. 455

MAURIZIO FERRARIS
Coronavirus and the Education of Homo Sapiens 467

VOLKER KRONENBERG AND CHRISTOPHER PRINZ
Politics and Science: Greater, More Ambitious. Countering the
Temptations of (Post-)Pandemic Politics 491

About the Authors 499

Werner Gephart

Preface:
In the Absence of a Master Narrative?

This volume presents a second collection of essays dealing with the ongoing Covid-19 crisis.[1] But do the individual stories shared diverge here, or do they coalesce to create an overall narrative, a *Méta-Recit*? As is well known, Jean-François Lyotard posited the influential idea that the high times of narration have passed, with familiar master narratives losing their plausibility and persuasiveness in post-modernity.[2] But was he right after all, and does this apply to the pandemic era as well?

In fact, all contributions in this volume effectively concern one single topic: the profound *discomfort*[3] with the current crisis. *Daniel Witte* is not convinced of the often-claimed primacy of science during the pandemic, but rather confronts the discussion about a universal state of emergency with the remaining autonomies of party politics, as well as those of other social fields such as religion. *Marta Bucholc* grapples with the paradoxes of individuals creating a collective good, the community-building performance of which is supposed to consist precisely in the radicalization of antisocial distance.

Using the example of care work, *Hanna Eklund* examines to what extent a stronger sense of community coincides with structural changes to public life prompted by the fight against Covid-19. In doing so, she shows, especially for the European context, that care work, which was previously relegated to the private sphere and regarded as an individual practice, has now advanced to a collective experience in view of its omnipresence and its significance for the survival of modern societies – a shared experience that, in turn, has been or is essentially co-created by law. Regarding the global dimension, *Maximilian Mayer* and *Katharina C. Cramer* explain that the transnational care system has emerged as an extremely fragile structure, a development that state interventions (border closures, travel bans, etc.) alone cannot sufficiently explain, as the problem extends much deeper to a structural level. From a differentiation-theoretical perspective, they locate

---

[1] For the first volume cf. Gephart (ed.): In the Realm of Corona Normativities.
[2] Lyotard: *La condition postmoderne* (oddly translated into German as *postmoderne Wissen*, or post-modern knowledge).
[3] Armin Nassehi: Unbehagen, which offers a systems-theoretical explanation for this shared discomfort by building on theoretical motifs by Niklas Luhmann.

vulnerability in the incommensurability between the logics and rules of care work and the system of international relations.

Peter Goodrich struggles with a humanistic worldview that is all about promoting life rather than giving death an institutional face. What kind of *Danse Macabre* (Dance of Death) have we committed ourselves to? In his pointed analysis, *Upendra Baxi*, who sees suffering as the basis for human rights,[4] is likewise unable to make sense of the collective suffering from sickness, from death, from the fact that beloved ones could not be accompanied on their last journey, and from survivors who are apparently abused as test animals in the laboratory of humankind. *Gerd Krumeich*, however, is reluctant to elevate war experiences to communal experiences and project them onto the Covid-19 situation, his impetus for showing exactly where the limits of this metaphorical figure lie.

Mariacarla Gadebusch Bondio and *Birgit Ulrike Münch* familiarize us with the long-term effects of the virus, which, in line with reports on so-called *breakthrough* cases following double vaccination, do not help to reassure us. *Beatriz Barreiro Carril* and *Kevin Grecksch* describe the devastating effects the pandemic has had on academia; *Chioma Daisy Onyige* of Nigeria expounds upon this from the perspective of a globally oriented researcher, finding a significant increase in social inequality, for example, through deficiencies in digital infrastructures that render a steady stream of communication with the rest of the world practically impossible. In her nuanced contribution, *Christa Rautenbach* leaves no doubt as to who, in the end, will be hit hardest by the pandemic in South Africa, whereas *Sabine N. Meyer* shows us in all poignancy the harshness with which the virus – declared to be *democratic* at first – impacts Native Americans in particular, who react to this uncanny danger through impressive visualizations, including pandemic dances and powerful images. When *Pierre Brunet* summarizes the pandemic experience through the idea of *sur-realism*, we know that he is referring to both the aesthetic movement of the absurd as well as to an everyday understanding of a kind of *sur-reality* that cannot become more intense.

Sam Whimster devotes himself to entanglements in the realm of the normative, reminding us of the *normative paradigm* that Thomas P. Wilson developed with the help of Talcott Parsons, who is now seen as the progenitor of a Hobbesian-inspired normativism yet also failed to provide a satisfactory answer to question of normative behavioral control.[5] But at least the *Romantic Masterplot* par excellence can offer a way out, right? *Kornelia Hahn* introduces us to a figure that has emerged as we try to love in the time of Covid: the *Corona buddy*, with whom one shares an almost monogamous intimate relationship but, according to interviewees, does not show any kind of emotional feelings towards. *Angela Condello*,

---

[4] Baxi: The Future of Human Rights.
[5] For more on this, see Gephart: Gesellschaftstheorie und Recht, pp. 77 ff., pp. 179 ff.

on the other hand, analyzes the deterioration of women's social position in Western democracies — a setback for feminism triggered by the crisis of law in pandemic times. Here, she paradoxically suggests that a rehabilitation of difference feminism could open a space for more justice.

The fact that *Brigitte Nerlich* shows us the diversity of visual representations in which deficits of knowledge and power are articulated, however, is further proof of the extent to which the inexplicable and mysterious require figurative interpretation, i.e. metaphors. In the words of Hans Blumenberg: »Care crosses the river«[6] — and it does not find any peace or subside, but instead remains in a permanent state of restlessness, of changing crisis indices (from incidence to hospitalization rates), of behavior rules, of fleeting delusions of a return to *normality*, to times when we would play ball in the park or attend soccer matches in large stadiums. At the same time, we keep an eye on the number of hospitalizations to see how much further we can push the limits of such libertarian behavior. The linguistic means of expressing such ambivalence of the normative is the change from prohibitive to imperative norms, as *Theresa Strombach* thoroughly investigated using the example of the German rollercoaster of normative orders.

And what does it mean when societies of the West — as explored by Belgian artist James Ensor — transform into masked societies that are not celebrating the anonymity of the Venetian carnival. Such transformations demand the application of deep cultural-historical knowledge to discover the *persona* behind the mask, or even the role of masks in processes of identity building and identity management, as *Helga María Lell* demonstrates[7] — thereby simultaneously putting well-established forms of communication to a normative test, as numerous controversies about wearing a hijab in public institutions have shown us, for example. According to *Valérie Hayaert*, the artistic memorialization of forms of communication during the Corona crisis, and thus the construction of a collective memory of the current anomic state of society, has only just begun. The idea of also considering digital storage systems as a form of collective memory is not new; however, exploring how digital communication platforms and apps contribute to archiving social knowledge during pandemics and determining what role law plays in the fight against disinformation, in data protection, and in the protection against surveillance by (private) service providers is worth examination, which is what *Sergio Genovesi* has undertaken from a philosophical perspective.

Francesca Caroccia explores the extent to which the right to collective health conflicts with the right to self-determination by not only uncovering the knowledge-sociological foundations of this dualism, but also by identifying various governmental techniques (especially those used by European countries) that can help

---

[6] Blumenberg: Care Crosses the River.
[7] Cf. also Petri: Masking the Invisible / Segments of Political Space.

resolve the conflict of rights. *Christoph Antons*, in turn, uses examples from Asia to show the limits of law during the Corona crisis, as articulated in the relationship between property rights and a *vaccine diplomacy*, as well as in the resulting (geo)political distortions whose effects reach far beyond the region. With the fabulous development of vaccines, however, lamenting should have ultimately come to an end – because they are supposed to guarantee immunity against infection. Well, variants of SARS-CoV-2 are unpredictable, but what do you do when vaccination is ridiculed, populist politicians mock it, conspiracy theorists question its efficacy, and finally, the West's promises of salvation are thwarted, especially by postcolonial critiques of patent law? Should the now-established Leviathan then not at least save us as appears on the cover of this second volume? After taking a precise look at the regime of police sanctions, sociologist *Jonas Grutzpalk* cannot confirm that ...

But can't the great visions of science reveal more about the cultural significance of the pandemic crisis, such as what *Stefan Finger* pointedly asserts from the perspective of a political scientist, namely that Corona is not the end? Or, according to *Anne-Marie Bonnet*, that art continues even in times of Corona and has not reached its often-conjured premature end? Or, as *Katja Spranz* amusingly conveys, that even celebrities not only continue to walk their dogs in Beverly Hills, but also play their games of attention in *Coronaland*? Is the lesson to be learned that we need to seek to understand nature anew – that a new relationship to nature is virtually forced upon us – as I read *Hanne Petersen*? Or, in his systematic search for equivalents to the theodicy question, has *Maurizio Ferraris* not captured the focal point of all these futile attempts to ascribe the pandemic a sustaining cultural meaning? Should politics instead converse with science more intensely to always be aware of and counter the authoritarian and technocratic temptation, which lurks in states of emergency, as well as to provide assurance and meet challenges head on during times of Corona? *Volker Kronenberg* and *Christopher Prinz* reveal that this is a viable path, without losing sight of the autonomy, self-referentiality, and boundaries of the spheres in their argumentation – a separation of spheres that is of paramount importance for the continued existence of liberal democracies.[8] Marta Bucholc's approach could be driven further here to proclaim a new sort of societal figuration in which it is no longer a *royal mechanism* (Norbert Elias) that forces the taming of emotions through manners and using silverware,[9] for example, but in which handwashing, social distancing, coughing into elbows, limiting bodily contact, and virtualizing communication bear witness to a new, pandemic-induced level of the process of civilization – which, in turn, is tragically

---

[8] See also in the first volume of *Corona Normativities* Gephart: Introduction; Conclusion.

[9] Cf. Elias: Die höfische Gesellschaft. Bucholc promotes the reception of Norbert Elias's civilization studies, especially in Polish sociology, through translation and interpretation.

accompanied by a sense of powerlessness. Because if something really has come to an end – that should be clear by now to even the last skeptics – it is the idea of a controllability of the world,[10] the credo of Protestant ethics, to which Weber himself already fell victim when he died of the still understudied Spanish Flu. *In this sense, once again a master narrative has come to an end.*

The many tales told in this volume, however, come together precisely as a kaleidoscopic narrative absent of a commonly shared story. It becomes apparent that we, as scholars, must continue our work, counterfactually searching for meaning; participate in politics, in which also the perspectives and opinions of younger generations need to be heard; and actively support practices of democratic sustainability if we are really serious about taking responsibility for future generations. For Weber, this meant meeting the »demand of the day«[11] – as banal as this may be. In this respect, I actually believe that the pandemic perhaps demands more modesty and humility from us. And because the illusion of controllability has been permanently destroyed, would there not be a *vitam instituere* worth promoting?[12]

But please also seek the nuances in the contributions, which were miraculously contributed in a short amount of time, as with the first volume on *Corona Normativities*,[13] by friends, colleagues, and staff of the Käte Hamburger Center for Advanced Study in the Humanities *Law as Culture* and its supporters. The days of universally valid theses and claims of comprehensive theoretical powers of interpretation are obviously over.[14] The first part of this collection of stories concerns *the shaking of system worlds and the intrusion of the pandemic into the lifeworld* (I). Subsequently, we engage with *shifts in the observers' perspectives* (II) before taking up the initial idea of a *pandemic culture of validity* (III) – formulated in the first volume on *Corona Normativities* – in order to finally raise the question of the *cultural meaning of the pandemic crisis* (IV). To get started, *François Ost* takes us on a poetic journey to *Coronaland* with Saint-Exupéry's *Petit Prince*, where we encounter our planet in both a familiar and distanced way during the pandemic crisis.

---

[10] Wolfgang Schluchter has repeatedly emphasized with great persistence this leitmotif of Weber's analysis of occidental rationalism (see, for example, Schluchter: Die Entwicklung des okzidentalen Rationalismus).

[11] Weber: Gesammelte Aufsätze zur Wissenschaftslehre, p. 456.

[12] Cf. here also Esposito: Biopolitik wird nie aktueller sein als heute.

[13] Cf. Gephart (ed.): In the Realm of Corona Normativities.

[14] Plenty of this can be found in literature inspired by system theory. See Heidingsfelder/Lehmann (eds.): Corona; Volkmer/Werner: Die Corona-Gesellschaft. For a psychoanalytical point of view that builds on Giorgio Agamben, see, for example, Castrillòn/Marchevsky: Coronavirus, Psychoanalysis, and Philosophy. For a interpretative direction based on Durkheim's cultural sociology, see Alexander/Smith: COVID-19 and Symbolic Action.

I would like to thank to everyone who has passionately helped make this volume possible. Specifically, I am grateful to the proofreaders, including Isabel Pohl, Rika Elena Hünerbach, Cyrill Heinen, Lucas Lessenich, and Max Stötzel, who made all sorts of adjustments, added literature, and always offered a helping hand. A very special thank you also goes to my co-editor, Jure Leko, who so prudently managed this volume from the start and wisely corrected the contributions' order time and again. I am also appreciative of Candice Kerestan who lent us her precious knowledge of the English language as necessary. In this respect, I would like to express my sincerest gratitude for taking part in a *mission impossible*, now resulting in a book that at least hopes to trigger in readers a kind of recognition of our shared *condition humaine*.

Werner Gephart   Bonn, September 16, 2021

References

Alexander, Jeffrey C./Philip Smith: COVID-19 and Symbolic Action: Global Pandemic as Code, Narrative, and Cultural Performance, in: American Journal of Cultural Sociology, 10/2020, pp. 1–7.

Baxi, Upendra: The Future of Human Rights, third edition, New Delhi 2012.

Blumenberg, Hans: Care Crosses the River, Stanford 2010.

Castrillòn, Fernando/Thomas Marchevsky (eds.): Coronavirus, Psychoanalysis, and Philosophy. Conversations on Pandemics, Politic, and Society, London/New York 2020.

Elias, Norbert: Die höfische Gesellschaft. Untersuchungen zur Soziologie des Königtums und der höfischen Aristokratie, Frankfurt am Main 1983.

Esposito, Roberto: Biopolitik wird nie aktueller sein als heute: Was uns die neue Idee zur Corona-Gegenwart zu sagen hat, in: Neue Züricher Zeitung, May 16, 2020, https://www.nzz.ch/feuilleton/coronavirus-roberto-esposito-ueber-moderne-biopolitik-ld.1556128?reduced=true; last accessed September 20, 2021.

Gephart, Werner: Gesellschaftstheorie und Recht. Das Recht im soziologischen Diskurs der Moderne, Frankfurt am Main 1993.

Gephart, Werner (ed.): In the Realm of Corona Normativities. A Momentary Snapshot of a Dynamic Discourse, Frankfurt am Main 2020.

Gephart, Werner: Introduction: The Corona Crisis in the Light of the Law as Culture Paradigm, in: Werner Gephart (ed.): In the Realm of Corona Normativities. A Momentary Snapshot of a Dynamic Discourse, Frankfurt am Main 2020, pp. 11–28.

Gephart, Werner: Conclusion: »Communal« Dimensions of the Corona Crisis and the Rise of a New Validity Culture, in: Werner Gephart (ed.): In the Realm of Corona Normativities. A Momentary Snapshot of a Dynamic Discourse, Frankfurt am Main 2020, pp. 509–518.

Heidingsfelder Markus / Maren Lehmann (eds.): Corona. Weltgesellschaft im Ausnahmezustand?, Weilerswist 2020.

Lyotard, Jean-Francois: La Condition postmoderne. Rapport sur le savoir, Paris 1979.

Nassehi, Armin: Unbehagen. Theorie der überforderten Gesellschaft, Munich 2021.

Petri, Grischka: Masking the Invisible / Segments of Political Space, in: Werner Gephart (ed.): In the Realm of Corona Normativities. A Momentary Snapshot of a Dynamic Discourse, Frankfurt am Main 2020, pp. 375–407.

Schluchter, Wolfgang: Die Entwicklung des okzidentalen Rationalismus. Eine Analyse von Max Webers Gesellschaftsgeschichte, Tübingen 1979.

Volkmer, Michael / Karin Werner (eds.): Die Corona-Gesellschaft. Analysen zur Lage und Perspektiven für die Zukunft, Bielefeld 2020.

Weber, Max: Gesammelte Aufsätze zur Wissenschaftslehre, Tübingen 1922.

Prologue

François Ost

Le Petit Prince au pays du Covid

Imaginons le Petit Prince débarquant sur une planète bleue atteinte du Covid-19 ; que penserait-il de tout ce qu'il découvrirait ? Il chercherait à comprendre et rencontrerait tour à tour différents décideurs. En réponse à toutes ses questions, il ne se verrait opposer que des tautologies : à la guerre comme à la guerre, dura lex, sed lex, les affaires sont les affaires … Curieuse manière de raisonner, penserait-il sans doute …

Quinze mois après le déclenchement de la pandémie (plutôt une *syndémie*), il est possible, et nécessaire, de prendre du recul en vue de tirer certaines leçons pour les crises à venir. Une ample littérature s'y emploie. Parmi celle-ci, je retiens un ouvrage, écrit par des sociologues de l'organisation,[1] dont les conclusions sont intéressantes. Aux yeux des auteurs, les principaux dysfonctionnements qui ont marqué le traitement de la crise tiennent à la manière de raisonner des décideurs. Une manière routinière et quantitative, favorisant les savoirs stables et les certitudes. Des raisonnements sur le mode du « toutes choses égales par ailleurs » qui, après avoir ainsi beaucoup simplifié des problèmes complexes et évolutifs, aboutissent à la conclusion qu' « il n'y a pas d'alternative ». Et les auteurs de conclure à la nécessité de former les décideurs à la pratique du doute, de la critique, et de la discussion pluraliste. Nul doute que la fiction littéraire soit un bon exercice à cet égard. Si nous imaginions, par exemple, qu'un nouveau Petit Prince avait débarqué sur la planète bleue en février 2020, qu'aurait-il retenu ?[2]

Le politique

Le premier habitant que le Petit Prince rencontra (le pangolin qui l'accompagnait toujours avait été saisi et envoyé en fourrière, dès son arrivée dans le pays) était un politique.
— « Nous sommes en guerre », lui dit celui-ci, en relevant le menton.
— Mais il n'y a pas d'ennemi, juste un minuscule organisme vivant qui circule ; les virus ont toujours existé.

[1] Cf. Bergeron/Borraz : Covid-19.
[2] L'exercice que je tente ici à la faveur de la licence fictionnelle, je l'ai mené par ailleurs sur le terrain de l'explication documentée (cf. Ost : De quoi le Covid est-il le nom ?).

— Tu ne comprends pas, je veux dire que je décrète la mobilisation générale, tout sera mis en œuvre pour éradiquer le virus. À la guerre comme à la guerre. Il voulait dire que face à un événement exceptionnel, il fallait adopter des mesures exceptionnelles. Et il ajoutait : nous ferons cela quoi qu'il en coûte.
— Mais le pays n'est-il pas déjà très endetté ?
— Il faut ce qu'il faut, les banques centrales émettront plus d'argent, et les pays contracteront des emprunts.
— Cela coûtera très cher ; il faudra bien rembourser un jour ?
— La dette ne coûtera rien du tout : la Banque centrale européenne rachète les titres de la dette des États et leur reverse les intérêts qu'ils lui paient.

Tout de même, le Petit Prince se demandait comment il était possible de ne pas payer ses dettes, et comment ce qui était un délit pour les particuliers devenait une vertu pour les États.

L'épidémiologiste

Un peu plus loin, le Petit Prince rencontra un homme très affairé qui traçait de grandes colonnes de chiffres sur un tableau noir et dessinait des courbes impressionnantes.
— Je suis un épidémiologiste, expliqua-t-il : je construis des indicateurs à partir des chiffres que les autorités sanitaires me fournissent, et j'établis des modèles prévisionnels. Hier encore, nous étions sur un faux plat, mais aujourd'hui les courbes s'envolent.
— Alors, vous n'allez jamais sur le terrain ?
— Penses-tu, l'affaire est trop sérieuse pour être confiée aux généralistes. Dans deux semaines nous atteindrons le point de saturation des hôpitaux, alors nous confinons tout le monde. La santé n'a pas de prix, n'est-ce pas ?

Le Petit Prince pensait plutôt que tout, précisément, avait un prix, et que le pays avait sans doute beaucoup trop désinvesti le secteur sanitaire – il en payait le prix aujourd'hui. Mais l'expert, très en verve, reprenait :
— Mieux vaut prévenir que guérir ; ce virus est sournois : il tue et ne se déclare qu'après plusieurs jours d'incubation, alors le confinement général s'impose, nous ne pouvons prendre aucun risque.
— Le Petit Prince pensait que le risque zéro n'existe pas, et que vivre, c'est prendre des risques. Aussi se permit-il une question : si vous étiez confronté à un virus vraiment très dangereux, létal à 100 %, qui mettrait, disons, 70 à 80 ans à se déclarer, que feriez-vous ?[3]

---

[3] Cf. Mitchell : Méfions-nous du doux despote qui veut nous protéger de la mort à tout prix.

— Et bien, on confinera tout le monde le temps qu'il faudra. Tu ne comprends pas : la santé est le bien suprême : ne dit-on pas tant qu'on a la santé …

Le Petit Prince restait perplexe, se disant qu'on avait tous contracté le « virus de 70 ans » à la naissance. À nouveau, il risqua une question : « mais la santé mentale, qu'en faites-vous ? ».

— On s'en préoccupera plus tard, fit l'épidémiologiste. Dans l'immédiat nous traitons des données quantifiables, celles qui permettent d'élaborer nos modèles. Ce n'est pas le moment de couper les cheveux en quatre. Chaque jour de nouveaux variants, toujours plus dangereux, se présentent. Alors je dis : soyez responsables, restez chez vous !

Le Petit Prince prit congé, se demandant qui étaient ces habitants de la planète bleue : comment pouvaient-ils survivre, privés de contacts avec leurs semblables ? Il se remémorait aussi un autre voyage qu'il avait fait, au pied de la Montagne de la table : on y traitait la pandémie avec plus de sang-froid et moins de contraintes ; le système hospitalier était beaucoup plus décentralisé, et la prise en charge des malades plus communautaire – mais sans doute les pays plus pauvres étaient-ils plus proches des rythmes naturels et plus familiers de la mort.[4]

Le juriste

Devant le Palais de justice, le Petit Prince rencontra un juriste attaché au Ministère de l'Intérieur. Il lui signifie qu'il n'avait pas de temps à lui consacrer.

— Tu comprends, en ces temps exceptionnels, nous devons tout réinventer, toutes sortes de mesures dérogatoires au droit commun. Alors, du matin au soir, je fais des copier-coller entre tous ces arrêtés ministériels, ces règlements, ces circulaires, qui changent tous les jours.

— Mais je croyais que la Constitution ne pouvait jamais être suspendue ?

— En effet, elle ne l'est pas, puisque nous ne l'avons pas suspendue. Un état d'exception n'existe que quand on le décrète. L'État de droit est garanti puisque les citoyens peuvent introduire des recours et que nous appuyons nos arrêtés sur pas moins de trois lois.

— Mais on m'a dit que dans 148 cas sur 150 votre Conseil d'État avait rejeté ces recours.

— Tu vois, c'est bien la preuve que tout est en ordre ; nécessité fait loi, comme on dit.

Le Petit Prince se demandait alors pourquoi le gouvernement prenait tant de peine maintenant à faire voter une « loi pandémie » afin de donner une base lé-

---

[4] Sur le traitement du Covid en Afrique du Sud, cf. Goemaere : Des leçons à tirer du modèles de prise en charge venus du Sud.

gale certaine aux mesures prises depuis un an. Il pensait aussi qu'on disait plutôt : « nécessité n'a pas de loi », mais il n'osa plus déranger un homme aussi important et garda ses réflexions pour lui.

Le policier

Le Petit Prince s'était remis en marche. Au détour du chemin, il tomba sur un attroupement devant le parvis d'une église. La presse était présente, des cars de police aussi. Que se passait-t-il donc ? Un musicien a programmé un acte de désobéissance civile : il allait donner un concert dans l'église devant un public de quinze personnes.
— C'est interdit ?
— Les manifestations culturelles sont interdites, lui répondit le policier. Nous allons verbaliser l'artiste et mettre un terme à cette exécution.
— Mais les cérémonies religieuses sont permises au même endroit, avec quinze personnes ?
— Tu ne comprends pas, ce n'est pas la même chose.
— Mais le risque est le même, osa hasarder le Petit Prince.[5]
— C'est comme cela, dit le policier – dura lex, sed lex.

Le businessman

Un peu plus tard, le Petit Prince rencontra le businessman. Celui-ci était très content : on allait vacciner tout le monde, et sa société était la première à avoir commercialisé le vaccin. Son carnet de commandes comportait des dizaines de millions de doses.
— Bravo dit le Petit Prince, alors, vous allez divulguer votre technologie aux pays les moins avancés pour qu'on en sorte rapidement ?
— Tu n'y penses pas, cela ne marche pas comme cela, nous avons consenti des sommes considérables pour produire ce vaccin.
— Mais vos chercheurs ne sont-ils pas formés dans des universités subsidiées par l'État, et la recherche n'est-elle pas largement subventionnée ? Et puis n'êtes-vous pas déjà rentré dans vos frais depuis longtemps ?

---

[5] Dans un arrêt du 27 avril 2020, la Cour d'appel de Bruxelles décide qu' « aucune raison scientifique ne justifie cette discrimination » et écarte l'application de l'Arrêté ministériel concerné.

— Tu ne comprends pas, dit le businessman, qui considérait qu'il avait perdu beaucoup trop de temps dans cette conversation oiseuse : les affaires sont les affaires.
— Je crois que je comprends, dit le Petit Prince, mais quel sens cela a-t-il de vacciner un pays si le reste de la planète ne l'est pas ? Demain des variants …
— Précisément, dit le businessman, qui déjà prenait congé, il faudra mettre au point de nouveaux vaccins …

Le communicateur

Pour finir, le Petit Prince rencontra le communicateur ; très affairé, les écouteurs dans les oreilles et l'ordinateur sur les genoux, il préparait la communication du gouvernement pour la conférence de presse qui allait suivre le prochain Conseil de crise. Le Petit Prince était content : enfin, il allait comprendre comment raisonnent les habitants de la planète bleue.
— C'est très simple, dit le communicateur, nous utilisons la tautologie. Il suffit de tout répéter deux fois, sur le ton de l'évidence, pour qu'une thèse discutable ou probable devienne une certitude.[6]
— Mais en disant qu'une chose est ce qu'elle est, on ne progresse pas, on n'apprend rien ?
— Justement, il faut rassurer, réaffirmer avec force la normalité. Le grand public étant ce qu'il est, l'important n'est pas d'informer, mais de persuader. Par exemple, si je dis « la loi est la loi », évidemment, on le sait bien, mais le message qui passe c'est qu' il faut obéir à la loi.
— Mais alors, cette langue de bois permet de tout justifier …
— Tu ne voudrais tout de même pas qu'on ouvre la boîte de Pandore du débat, alors qu'il y a péril en la demeure ? Les choses sont ce qu'elles sont. Laisse la communication aux communicateurs, la politique aux politiques, et les vaches seront bien gardées.
— Évidemment, s'il est question de vaches à garder, alors je comprends, se dit le Petit Prince.
Le soir était tombé, et maintenant le Petit Prince se sentait bien seul, son pangolin lui manquait. Au cours de la journée, il n'avait rencontré que des gens importants ; ils occupaient le devant de la scène, sans doute parce qu'on avait décidé qu'ils exerçaient des tâches « essentielles ». Mais maintenant que la nuit était venue, le Petit Prince croisait des personnes bien différentes : tout un petit peuple de personnes invisibles, vouées aux tâches qu'on tenait pour inessentielles. Au coin d'une rue, aux abords d'un square verduré, il se joignit à un petit groupe qui écoutait la mélopée

---

[6] Cf. Gaudin-Bordes : La tyrannie de la tautologique : p. 55.

étrange d'une flutiste ; les accents de sa musique gagnaient jusqu'aux balcons des maisons avoisinantes où quelques silhouettes se laissaient deviner.
– C'est joli, dit le Petit Prince ; ta mélodie est entraînante, et tes notes sont claires. Le jeune fille s'interrompit un instant : tu sais, ce qui compte vraiment, c'est le rythme ; les silences sont aussi importants que les notes. C'est comme la respiration : tu inspires, tu attends un peu, tu expires. Pendant les silences, je reprends mon souffle et les gens autour de moi participent en imaginant la suite. A la fin, c'est la flute qui nous conduit, chacun a créé sa musique.
Plus loin dans la parc, le Petit Prince fut attiré par un funambule ; il avait tendu sa corde entre deux grands arbres, et maintenant il avançait sous la faible lumière des réverbères.
– Cela doit être très difficile, dit le Petit Prince ; heureusement ta corde est solide, et toi, tu dois être très musclé.
– Ne me distrais pas, répondit le funambule ; ce n'est pas la force qui compte, mais l'équilibre. J'avance en m'appuyant sur le vide autant que sur ma corde.
– Et pourquoi fais-tu cela, alors qu'il n'y a presque plus personne pour t'applaudir et que tout le monde est occupé par la maladie ?
– Je ne sais pas, répondit le funambule ; peut-être un jour les gens comprendront qu'eux aussi, ils marchent sur un fil tendu au-dessus du vide ?

Cette idée plaisait bien au Petit Prince ; et puis, il se disait que la musicienne et le funambule, eux au moins, ne s'étaient pas cru obliger de tout répéter deux fois ; au contraire, c'était comme s'ils parlaient à demi-mot, comme si le grand air soufflait entre les lignes.
Finalement, alors que l'obscurité s'était faite, le Petit Prince accosta une ombre à la sortie du dernier métro. C'était une aide-soignante qui avait terminé sa journée, commencée très tôt ce matin.
– Tu soignes les malades de la terrible maladie, dit le Petit Prince, alors tu dois être très compétente ?
– Oh, tu sais, je n'ai pas beaucoup de diplômes ; mais dans le home où je travaille, je donne aux gens ce que je peux : un peu de temps pour parler. Personne n'a jamais le temps, alors moi je donne du temps.
– Mais les gens, ils veulent être soignés, recevoir des médicaments ?
– Sans doute ; mais parfois, ils sont si seuls qu'ils attendent autre chose ; alors on parle ; on crée un peu de lien, et ils sont contents de me revoir le lendemain.
Je comprends, dit le Petit Prince, c'est comme avec mon pangolin, on s'attend tous les soirs…
Le Petit Prince déambula encore longtemps dans la nuit, songeant à tout ce qu'il avait entendu sur la planète bleue. C'est alors qu'on vint l'arrêter : il avait dépassé l'heure du couvre-feu, et ne disposait pas du corona pass. Circonstance aggravante : il n'avait pas rempli le Passenger locator form pour entrer dans le pays. Un arrêté

d'expulsion était pris contre lui. Le Petit Prince et son pangolin étaient envoyés dans le camp de Lesbos – « jusqu'au retour à la normale », lui avait-on signifié. Avait-il bien entendu : « retour à la normale » ou plutôt à « l'anormal » ?

Références

Bergeron, Henri / Olivier Borraz : Covid-19 : une crise organisationnelle, Paris 2020.

Goemaere, Eric : Carte blanche sur la pandémie de covid : Des leçons à tirer du modèles de prise en charge venus du Sud, in : Le Soir, 03.05.2021, consultable sur le site, https://plus.lesoir.be/369799/article/2021-05-03/carte-blanche-sur-la-pandemie-de-covid-des-lecons-tirer-de-modeles-de-prise-en; consulté la dernière fois 14.06.2021.

Gaudin-Bordes, Lucile : La tyrannie de la tautologique : l'évidence comme outil énonciatif et stratégie discursive, in : Langue française, n° 160, 2008/4, pp. 55–71.

Mitchell, Joshua : Méfions-nous du doux despote qui veut nous protéger de la mort à tout prix, Entretien au Figaro avec Laur Mandeville, consultable sur le site, https://www.herodote.net; consulté la dernière fois 09.07.2021.

Ost, François : De quoi le Covid est-il le nom ?, Bruxelles 2021.

I. The Shaking of System Worlds and the Intrusion of the Pandemic into the Lifeworld

Daniel Witte

Temporary Destabilizations: The Fragility of Normality and the Normalization of the Fragmentary*

> »Established risk definitions are [...] a magic wand with which a stagnant society can terrify itself and thereby activate its political centres and become politicized from within.«
>
> Ulrich Beck

Introduction: Sociology Going Viral

For a year and a half now, the world has been kept on tenterhooks by an impossibly small threat. The size of a SARS-CoV-2 virus is approximately 100 nm, or 0.0001 millimeter – about one-third the size of the smallest known bacteria, or 1/1,000th the diameter of a human hair. As we have learned (at the latest) in the meantime, this virus moves on a scale where colors no longer exist, and a now-familiar image points out that all SARS-CoV-2 particles in the world would fit comfortably in a Coke can.[1] Small as it is, however, a virus is an extraordinarily clever beast. It attacks in equally incredible numbers, it multiplies at tremendous speed and continuously adapts to its environment, and against the background of its inability to move under its own power, it uses the capacities of its hosts to continue its existence. The virus itself, which has spread so rapidly across the globe, is not actually moving anywhere – only the mobility of the human species itself turns a tiny pathogen into a threat to society as a whole, and only the interconnectedness of global society turns an epidemic into a pandemic threat of global proportions. This virus, which has paralyzed the world since 2020 and at the same time set it in motion, parasitizes not only the nature of the human organism but also the social structures of world society. This, in a nutshell, is the onto-logic of the pandemic.

This pandemic has become an all-encompassing world event – all-encompassing not only because of its global nature (which would be a tautological state-

---

* Parts of this paper have previously been published as Witte: Virologischer Imperativ oder temporäre Destabilisierung? All translations of quotations in other languages into English are by the author.

[1] Cf. Weaving: Scary Red or Icky Green?; Yates: All the Coronavirus in the World Could Fit Inside a Coke Can.

ment), but above all because of the scope of its impact. At the individual level, it is probably safe to say that it affects every single person on the planet in one way or another, presently and/or in the future. At the same time, and on a structural level, it affects all parts of society: The economy and politics, as well as the law and, of course, all kinds of scientific disciplines – not only the natural sciences, but equally the humanities; culture and the arts, as well as religion; and, as everyone has witnessed in the past year and a half, it has profoundly affected not least our private lives, the sphere of interpersonal communication, family life, friendships and intimate relationships, some of which have been brought to an almost surreal, dystopian standstill at times. While the virus itself is a purely biological entity, its pandemic spread is itself not a biological but a social phenomenon, and one that in turn threatens not only our biological existence, but also affects social life in its entirety. To be clear at this point, the virus does not close barbershops, restaurants, and shopping malls. It does not lock up populations, it does not prevent subjects from entering university buildings or having romantic relationships, and it does not threaten the arts or the fields of cultural production. Only social practices and their objectifications have the power to do all this: and they do so primarily in the form of political decisions and decrees, norms, regulations, and laws.

At the same time, the risks posed by zoonoses and the ensuing developments since 2020 represent both direct and classical »side-effects«[2] of modern societies' global interconnectedness, of the capitalist logic of exploitation, and of the political and social forms that go hand in hand with it. As Stephan Lessenich puts it exactly in this sense, crisis phenomena like the Covid-19 pandemic are »formation-characteristic phenomena«[3], which now (again *sensu* Beck) »strike back«[4] on these very formations. In fact, the spread of Covid-19 literally made petrified relations dance in a few days by singing their own tune to them:[5] In line with the theory of reflexive modernization is also the observation that the disruptive onset of the virus destabilized power balances between social fields and thus, in the long term, also created new scope for the politicization of social relations and debates about precisely these balances,[6] the outcome of which is not yet foreseeable at present. In this respect, large parts of our current problematic are social issues, both in their causes and effects. In other words: For the most part, we are not discussing

---

[2] Cf. Beck: Das Zeitalter der Nebenfolgen.
[3] Lessenich: Soziologie – Corona – Kritik, p. 220.
[4] Hartmann: Das kommt nicht von außen, cit. in Lessenich: Soziologie – Corona – Kritik, p. 219. In this sense, Klaus Dörre also explicitly speaks of a »repulsion of intensified globalization« and clarifies the social conditioning factors of the pandemic (in the form of, for example, »dwindling habitat for wild animals, closer human-animal contacts, widespread factory farming and climate change«) (Dörre: Die Corona-Pandemie, p. 174). Or, broken down to the essentials and in the words of Pierre Brunet: Nous sommes la raison du virus.
[5] Cf. Marx: Zur Kritik der Hegelschen Rechtsphilosophie, p. 381.
[6] Cf. Beck: Weltrisikogesellschaft, ökologische Krise und Technologiepolitik, pp. 64, 74f.

the effects of a biological entity, but the effects of social practices that respond to a particular situation caused by that biological entity and, in particular, its social dynamics. In the sense outlined here, and taking seriously this fundamentally hybrid nature of current events, we may draw on a classic notion of Marcel Mauss and speak of the Covid-19 pandemic as a total bio-social fact.[7]

I am writing these and the following sentences from a specific disciplinary perspective: that of sociology. Of course, sociology is not primarily concerned with the biological properties of the virus: for it, the social processing and social consequences of the pandemic are the focus of attention. This paper is thus concerned with the social dimension of the pandemic and its control, as well as with questions about the effects of the Covid-19 pandemic on society, many of which are no longer directly related to the virus itself. In this respect, the extraordinary situation over the past year and a half has indeed resembled a »laboratory«:[8] It has made things visible to sociology that otherwise elude its inquisitive gaze, or at least do not come into view with such clarity. The following chapter therefore addresses a number of seemingly heterogeneous questions: it is about the role of (non-)knowledge, about the fragility of social normality and constructions of reality, about the precariousness of critique in late modern societies and the role of the state in this context, about an at least temporary destabilization of social power-knowledge balances, and about the uncovering and normalization of the fragmentary and conflictive character of our form of socialization induced by this process. And, of course, the chapter also aims to some extent at the inner connections between all these facets of »Covid society« – in the hope that some of these connections may become a little clearer through this contribution. By combining both rather systematic and rather impressionistic observations to draw a preliminary picture of the pandemic, it will nevertheless inevitably remain as fragmentary as the current situation.

1. Non-Knowledge and the Pandemic as a Crisis of Information

If we direct our attention to the reactions to the Covid-19 pandemic as a social phenomenon, one thing quickly becomes clear: as far as its actual crisis character is concerned, this pandemic essentially represents an information crisis. In order to plausibilize this verdict, it may be helpful to consider the role and, above all, the impressive extent of non-knowledge in some relevant aspects.

---

[7] Similarly already, for instance, Chevé/Signoli: Les corps de la contagion.
[8] Cf. Condello: Immersed in a Normative Laboratory.

The first crucial point here is that the actual trigger of the crisis, the SARS-CoV-2 virus, was a largely unknown, unexplored actor in terms of its properties and behavior when the crisis began – and in many respects it still is. There was a widespread lack of knowledge about the most basic properties of the virus and the diseases it caused at the height of the so-called first wave (while it was not even clear at that time whether it was really a »first wave« to be followed by others): A lack of knowledge about its origin and its spread, about possible and typical symptoms, about typical and atypical courses of the disease, about mortality rates and, in general, about the dangers of infection, about possible vaccines (as well as about the possibility of vaccinating against Covid-19 at all), about possible forms of therapy, and so on. But even today (as of June 2021), we are not entirely sure about the extent of the initially invisible epidemiological threat, particularly about the critical number of infected people at any given time and in total to date (both globally and per country or region). A high number of unreported cases is suspected, and sociologists may be reminded of Heinrich Popitz and the question of what latent social function this lack of knowledge may have.[9] Many virus carriers do not become ill (or only asymptomatically), but how large this proportion really is remains the subject of competing estimates, projections and sometimes also speculation, and above all the role of children and adolescents in the epidemiological process and the chains of infection has been the subject of heated, often polemical debates for many months.

An obvious answer to some of these questions was found early on with »testing«, but once a testing infrastructure was in place and testing could be done on a larger scale, questions quickly arose about the reliability of these tests, the risk of errors in implementation (especially with privately conducted »rapid tests«), and the weight of the fact that no testing procedure is ever perfect, but always has error rates, i.e., can yield both false-negative and false-positive results. This accumulation of questions in turn created further uncertainties at the social level and with potentially serious interpersonal consequences: No one knows with certainty at any point in time who among his or her interaction partners might be a virus carrier (and thus potentially a danger), how dangerous which interaction is, where and at what time, and for whom it might become particularly dangerous. As a result, our interaction partners – each of our interaction partners – have begun to appear to us as potentially threatening, just as each of us is a potential threat at all times: indeed, an extreme (if you will, Hobbesian) scenario that makes it seem downright odd that social interaction has not been completely consumed by mutual distrust and a virally poisoned form of »double contingency«.[10]

---

[9] Cf. Popitz: Über die Präventivwirkung des Nichtwissens.

[10] And it would certainly be worth discussing again at a later point in time whether these experiences might not also have an impact on our basic social theoretical concepts (interaction, co-presence, etc.).

Moreover, a constitutive lack of knowledge has also characterized the entire field of societal responses and countermeasures from the very beginning. Which »measures« had any effect at all, and which really did or did have *significant* effects, could only be determined approximately and gradually over the course of many months, and is still subject to controversial debate. As we all know by now, the epidemio-logic of the pandemic is that these effects can only be estimated with a time delay, at the earliest about 10 to 14 days after the measures have been taken – a period, however, in which serious negative developments may already have occurred in the case of »wrong« decisions (whatever is to be understood by this); and it is precisely this time lag that makes it understandable why the structure of the pandemic situation tends to favor overcautious strategies. Accordingly, politics and society were (and partly still are) confronted with uncertainties about the appropriateness and correctness of any alternative course of action, which is exacerbated by a fundamental unreliability of figures and (comparative) values[11] – the months-long dispute about a »Swedish special path« being only one of the most obvious examples here.

However, the problem of incomplete knowledge is not limited to the epidemiological characteristics of the virus and the effectiveness of countermeasures either, but the latter's negative social consequences also hover like a sword of Damocles over the heads of decision-makers. One suspects and/or assumes that the economic damage caused by »lockdowns«, the impact of school closures on social inequalities in the education system, the consequences of increasing domestic violence, mental illness or even postponed (non-Covid-related) medical operations could be far-reaching – but at the time of the political intervention in the social machinery, all this could only be guessed at in a step-by-step manner. Reliable studies or unambiguous forecasts, which would have been necessary for a rational cost-benefit analysis, as rational choice theory has been trying to teach us for decades, were, however, sparse and, in contrast to rather diffuse fears and anxieties, by no means shaped the discourse. In this context, it is downright irritating that economists in particular, who have become so increasingly powerful and discursively influential over the years, failed to quantify the much-vaunted economic damage of lockdown measures at an early stage, so that public discourse and the political weighing process were largely dependent on dummy variables (»enormous damage«, »unimaginable unemployment figures«, »catastrophic market developments«, etc.).

Last but not least, we face a particularly pervasive, truly existential lack of knowledge about all those aspects of the pandemic that point to the future. Whether and when a vaccine could be developed and made available seemed unclear for a long time (and the speed with which this eventually happened surprised even proven experts), and to what extent drugs can be used to treat Covid-19 dis-

---

[11] See also Schmitz/Skokep (forthcoming) on the topic of pandemic-related »testing cultures«.

ease in the medium term (and which ones) remains uncertain at present. A constant source of surprises and new discoveries is also formed by the dynamics of mutations and resistances of the virus, whereby so-called »escape variants« are again suitable to disqualify the »knowledge« now gained about the success of the vaccination campaign as only provisional. Finally, this complex of questions becomes truly scary in the context of the meanwhile growing evidence that Covid-19 is not (only) a lung disease, but (also) a far more devastating systemic vasculitis, which can cause severe organ or nerve damage as well as post-Covid symptoms in the medium and long term, even in the case of so-called »harmless courses«, which is currently reinforced by the uncertainty to what extent children and adolescents (so far not protected by vaccination) might also be affected by this. Worst-case scenarios in which various of these fears, each with their own uncertainties, would come true in parallel, and this is only noted here in passing, could probably no longer be contained with the help of political measures or by disaster control qua hygiene measures, etc., but could at best be managed and processed at the cultural level.

Of course, and this is by no means to be denied with the previous impressions, the immense accumulation of non-knowledge on almost all relevant levels is contrasted with an equally impressive accumulation of knowledge and evidence. The race of the sciences against time thus became a project for society as a whole. In the spring of 2020, a development occurred in this context that also seems extraordinarily remarkable in terms of social theory, namely a far-reaching, albeit downright compulsory, transfer of trust to experts, especially virologists. Of particular interest for the development in Germany is the role of Christian Drosten in this context, a leading virologist in the field of coronaviruses, professor and institute director at the Charité in Berlin. With a regular, at times daily podcast that quickly became very popular, a truly remarkable talent for translating specialist scientific considerations for broader parts of the population, and reinforced by a mass media field that was only too happy to offer the charismatic scientist every conceivable stage, Drosten quickly became one of the most important and, for the time being, arguably also one of the most popular figures in German public life. At the same time, he became – along with other virologically and epidemiologically versed experts – an important advisor to the German government, which obviously depended in a fundamental way on the expertise of scientists – a dependence that quickly became clearly visible to all voters. The popularity and apparent influence of Drosten and others therefore immediately led to public speculation, polemics, and projections about whether it was not in fact the virologists who were determining policy (or whether Drosten might not even be a suitable candidate for the next chancellorship).

For a few weeks, politics and society actually seemed to follow and depend to a large extent on the knowledge and recommendations of scientists (a knowledge that, in light of the above observations, was quite incomplete, but crucial compared to all other actors) and to gratefully place themselves in the hands of these experts. Supplied by the media every half hour with »fresh« numbers and supposed news, but also a virtual reality of graphs and ratios, German society developed in parallel into a society of 80 million spare-time virologists and remedial students in the philosophy of science: Everyone quickly seemed to know that scientific findings always have only the status of temporary hypotheses, and terms like »reproduction rate« or »exponential growth« soon became part of the standard vocabulary of people who had never been particularly interested in scientific research or even epidemiological matters.

Against this background, the decisive caesura from my point of view then occurred just as quickly: the hobbyist virologically trained population had to be taught again and again by the actual experts. Developments were different from what had been expected, indicator X was no longer as decisive as it had been the previous week, and in addition, the now famous prevention paradox led to a part of the population being downright disappointed by the positive development of infection and mortality rates and dumping this cognitive dissonance on the alleged deficits of virological expertise. However, during this period, virologists still held tightly to the reins that policymakers had entrusted to them because of their own lack of expertise. The federal government appeared increasingly »controlled« by virological and other elites to some observers, to whom the relationship between consultation and decision-making, which is by no means unusual in the modern political system, was unfamiliar; the (natural) scientists, however, remained the »masters« of the situation and its interpretation, both vis-à-vis politicians and the 80 million laypersons in the scientific field.

According to my argumentation, this constellation was experienced by a not inconsiderable part of the population as a narcissistic affront, indeed as a kind of disenfranchisement never before experienced in this intensity and drasticness – and not at all because, for example, politics had developed to a considerable extent in the direction of an expertocracy within a few weeks, but simply because the intertwining of scientific knowledge and political decision-making, of expertise and government, but also the knowledge gap between »normal« citizens and experts became much more transparent and visible during these weeks, because it became more tangible and affected one's own life more directly and unexpectedly than usual; and it is this almost Freudian insult against the background of which conspiracy theories of the most diverse hues were to flourish in the coming weeks. The Corona crisis as a crisis of information and knowledge thus quickly became a crisis of reality itself.[12]

---

12 With wise foresight in this respect, the Director-General of the World Health Organization (WHO) warned as early as March 2020 of disinformation and an impending *infodemic* regarding Covid-19 (cf. WHO: Immunizing the Public).

2. Metaphysical Boredom and the Fragility of Normality

In recent years, the French sociologist Luc Boltanski has addressed the fragility of what is commonly called »reality« in various writings, but especially in his 2014 book *Mysteries and Conspiracies*.[13] For Boltanski, this »reality« is a fabric of causal relations, value standards, and normative postulates, in the establishment, stabilization, and preservation of which – quite in the sense of Pierre Bourdieu[14] – the modern nation-state, and state law in particular, play a central role.[15] Against this backdrop, a first of the many punchlines of Boltanski's seminal book consists in tying the emergence of the crime novel as a literary genre to the establishment of the Western nation-state: the disruption of state-guaranteed reality by crime is understood as an »irruption of the *world* in the heart of *reality*«[16] that constitutes the essence of any »mystery«. In the meta-narrative of the classic crime story, this riddle is in turn solved by agents of the state (classically: the Commissioner), thus restoring the social order of »reality«. The prior, state-guaranteed establishment of the very structure designated as (a certain form of) »reality« thus forms a central condition for the emergence and success of a genre that narratively effectively focuses precisely on the fragility of this reality (or normality),[17] on the uncovering of an »actual« reality hidden behind it, and on the »repair work« associated with it.[18] Underlying the crime novel, the detective novel, and in even clearer form the spy novel is thus what Boltanski calls the »conspiracy form«[19]:

»[S]ocial reality as initially perceived by a naive observer (and reader), with its order, its hierarchies and its principles of causality, reverses itself and unveils its fictional nature, revealing another much more real reality that it had been concealing. This second reality is inhabited by things, acts, actors, levels, connections and especially powers whose existence, indeed, whose very possibility, had not been suspected by anyone.«[20]

The state thus appears in this reversal and restoration of reality in an ambivalent way: on the one hand, it is itself subjected to a »test«, and on the other hand, it simultaneously stands up for the restoration of reality and control over it in the form of representatives or deputy agents.[21] This tension, however, is once again taken to

---

[13] Boltanski's book was first published in French in 2012. On the broader topic see also Boltanski: Rendre la réalité inacceptable; Boltanski: On Critique.
[14] Cf. Bourdieu: On the State.
[15] Cf. Boltanski: Mysteries and Conspiracies, pp. xv, 3, 15 ff., 47 ff., 230 ff.
[16] Ibid., p. 3; emph. in the orig.
[17] Cf. ibid., pp. 25, 57.
[18] There are, of course, analogies at this point (also addressed by Boltanski) to Goffman as well as to Garfinkel's ethnomethodology. On the general connection between the nation-state and the detective novel cf. Boltanski: Mysteries and Conspiracies, pp. 9, 18 ff., 56.
[19] Boltanski: Mysteries and Conspiracies, p. 13.
[20] Ibid., pp. 13 f.
[21] Cf. ibid., pp. 18 ff.

extremes by the spy novel, in which the state and its bearers themselves become the »principal instigator« of conspiracies and thus the starting point of an even more dramatic existential disquiet.[22] In these reflections of Boltanski, numerous motifs can already be found that can be made fruitful for the understanding of certain reactions to the Covid-19 pandemic. Of particular interest in this context is the figure of the detective (in the sense of the initially British variant of the genre), who, in contrast to the police commissioner (ideally: Maigret, dispatched from the French capital), is not bound to the law by protocol, but is able to solve mysteries as a »private eye« precisely by means of extra-legal tricks and even the temporary circumvention of the law: from this perspective, state law suddenly appears as »powerless to protect the state of law against subversion. Maintaining order implies suspending or sidestepping the law, resorting to a regime of exception«.[23] The logic of the state of exception thus congeals in the figure of the detective, namely in an actor who temporarily appears as the sovereign, who can take on the task of uncovering contradictions and deceptions, restoring order, and thereby cementing the fractures and cracks of a reality that has become fragile:

»Properly speaking, then, the figure of the detective is sovereign in itself because the detective has been given the ability to substitute for the state in order to achieve what the liberal state, in a democratic-capitalist society, cannot accomplish without bringing to light the contradiction that inhabits it, or at least what it cannot do all the time, not officially, not without danger of arousing criticism, opposition and rebellion – namely, in one and the same move, carry out the legal actions that belong to sovereignty and, by a sovereign act, exempt itself from them. The detective is the state in a state of ordinary exception.«[24]

At the same time, Boltanski, thinking clearly beyond the scope of the sociological question of literary genres, makes clear in the further course that such disturbances of reality are, on the one hand, systematically accompanied by certain, namely crisis-like, social events; but that, on the other hand, they also call not only the literary figures of the *detective* or the *commissar* to the scene, but also the *paranoiac* as a clinical figure and, this is the book's actual punchline, the *sociologist*, who in this respect is closely related to the aforementioned social figures. Crucial to the present context is the connection between crisis and paranoia, however, which in a sense shifts Durkheim's theory of *anomie* into the realm of the cognitive:

»Reality, when it holds together, presents itself first and foremost as a system of pre-established causalities that makes it possible to predict events, or at least to account for them. However, reality finds itself disturbed and even undone *in the face of a series of unfortu-*

---

[22] Cf. ibid., pp. 38 f., 163 ff.
[23] Ibid., pp. 30 f.
[24] Ibid., pp. 71 f.; see also ibid., pp. 52, 70.

nate events, situations (such as unrelenting poverty) or catastrophes, national catastrophes that can no longer be explained simply in terms of the causal factors recognized as valid for a given population on a given territory. A gulf is then created between the predictions and explanations supplied by the authorities and what is happening in fact, between the official descriptions and the unofficial versions of the stories that permeate the framework of reality and distort it. And it is indeed this gulf between ordinary causality and extraordinary phenomena that is filled by the interpretation according to which there is, lurking under the official, false power, another power that is real but hidden. The causes of what happens are not to be sought in surface reality. They lie elsewhere.«[25]

At this point, the clinical diagnosis of paranoia comes into view, which, for the reasons mentioned above, historically entered the social stage around the same time as sociology as a discipline and the detective novel as a literary form. Thereby, according to Boltanski, there is an underlying parallel not only between the paranoiac in the clinical sense and the conspiracy ideologies of the present, but also between the former and the »man of *ressentiment*« introduced via Nietzsche and Scheler.[26] According to Boltanski, however, *ressentiment* is a trait that is at the same time situated between (and closely related to) existential nihilism on the one hand and an experience of social »inability« and »impotence« on the other.[27]

In this interpretation we find a number of motifs — a deep experience of alienation from social reality, a fundamental doubt about the reality of this reality, furthermore the experience of one's own powerlessness as well as a diagnosis of decay inherent in this overall state — which can also be traced in a completely different context, namely in the fathoming of a »metaphysical boredom« as we encounter it in authors as different as Alberto Moravia and Martin Heidegger. Both Moravia's »noia« and Heidegger's »profound boredom« have nothing to do with being temporarily bored by something in concrete situations, but the boredom taken into account by both authors is of an existential and comprehensive nature: In his *Fundamental Concepts of Metaphysics*, Heidegger distinguishes being »bored by something« and being »bored with something« from a third form called »profound boredom«, a substantially deeper form of »it is boring for one«.[28] This »profound« form of boredom is boredom with existence as such, existential indifference, rendering »everything of equally great and equally little worth«,[29] including the individual ego, which in this way becomes an »undifferentiated no one«.[30] Crucial here is also the »overpowering nature« of this boredom, namely the way in which it already »transpose[s] us into a realm of power over which

---

[25] Ibid., p. 138; emph. added.
[26] Cf. ibid., pp. 177 ff.
[27] Cf. ibid., pp. 178, 183 ff.
[28] Heidegger: Fundamental Concepts of Metaphysics, p. 132 et passim.
[29] Ibid., p. 137; in italics in the orig.
[30] Ibid., p. 135; see also ibid., p. 138.

the individual person, the public individual subject, no longer has any power«.³¹ Profound boredom, according to Heidegger, is simultaneously characterized by »Dasein's being delivered over to beings' telling refusal of themselves as a whole« and »being impelled toward what originally makes Dasein possible as such«.³² At the same time, this powerful existential alienation opens a »moment of vision«, described by Heidegger as »the look of resolute disclosedness for action in the specific situation in which Dasein finds itself disposed in each case«,³³ it forces the I in this »moment of vision of genuine action«³⁴ to reach for what is possible (or what is thought to be possible).

A very similar conception of metaphysical boredom is found in the work of Alberto Moravia, especially in *La noia*.³⁵ I would like to leave it at this point to quote an excerpt from the protagonist's reflections on the first pages of the novel:

»For many people boredom is the opposite of amusement; and amusement means distraction, forgetfulness. For me, on the contrary, boredom is not the opposite of amusement; I might even go so far as to say that in certain of its aspects it actually resembles amusement inasmuch as it in fact gives rise to distraction and forgetfulness, even if of a very special type. Boredom, to me, consists, to be precise, in a kind of insufficiency or inadequacy or lack of reality. Reality, when I am bored, has always had the same disconcerting effect upon me as (to make use of a metaphor) a too short blanket has upon a sleeping man, on a winter night: he pulls it down over his feet and his chest gets cold, then he pulls it up on to his chest and his feet get cold; and so he never succeeds in falling properly asleep. [...] The feeling of boredom originates, for me, in a sense of the absurdity of a reality which, as I have said, is insufficient, or anyhow unable, to convince me of its own effective existence.«³⁶

With this reference to the »absurdity of reality«, the connection back to Boltanski is established via Heidegger's *Dasein* and, in an admittedly impressionistic manner, an interpretative frame is opened up that might help to understand how the information crisis of the pandemic could first become a crisis of reality and then also a mobilizing factor for the phenomenon that has become known as the »coronavirus deniers« or, in the German context, the »Querdenker« movement [literally meaning »lateral«, or »nonconformist thinkers«]. The argument, then, is that at this point two different elements have combined to create a highly problematic dynamic: On the one hand, there is the profoundly crisis-ridden experience of the

---

[31] Ibid., p. 134.

[32] Ibid., pp. 137, 140 (»Ausgeliefertheit des Daseins an das sich im Ganzen versagende Seiende« and »Hingezwungenheit an die ursprüngliche Ermöglichung des Daseins als eines solchen« in the German original).

[33] Ibid., p. 151 (the »Augenblick« of »Entschlossenheit zum Handeln in der jeweiligen Lage, in der das Dasein sich befindet« in the German original).

[34] Ibid., p. 295.

[35] *La Noia* was first published in Italian in 1960; English translations appeared first in 1961 under the title *The Empty Canvas*, later as *Boredom*.

[36] Moravia: The Empty Canvas, p. 5.

Covid-19 pandemic – which *normatively* pushes the social order in an anomic state, at the same time *cognitively* puts the reality of reality in the twilight and calls for narrative repairs of this damaged reality, thus bringing figures of the exception and the exceptional (of the most diverse hues, both state and extra-state) onto the scene. On the other hand, we encounter a metaphysical boredom and alienation that can be understood as a characteristic »fundamental attunement« of our time.[37] Together, these two elements formed a cocktail that provided the ideal nutrient solution for a culture of mistrust that had already been simmering for some time, as well as for conspiracy narratives through which, in this case, many actors found themselves forced into a »moment of vision of genuine action«, to use Heidegger's words again. It is not least this genuine link between the narrative structure of conspiracy ideologies emphasized by Boltanski[38] and the activist moment emphasized by Heidegger that can perhaps be made fruitful for understanding the current denialist movement, which is so massively politicized from the far right.

Against this background, it seems not at all surprising that the criticism of the coronavirus deniers and trivializers was quickly directed at the state and found expression in the form of *Maßnahmenkritik* (»critique of measures«). Beginning with the first restrictions in the spring of 2020, and then intensifying with each subsequent month of the pandemic, government decisions and measures to protect life and individual as well as collective health have been criticized as misguided, disproportionate, and excessive. In the most prominent exaggerations of this criticism in Germany, this quickly took on traits of the delusional: The Merkel government and its health minister Spahn were only looking for a (often: freely invented) reason for the equally arbitrary and permanent restriction of fundamental rights, wanted to put completely different plans into action behind the narrative of Covid-19, or even wanted to enslave the population in the service of even darker powers with the help of masks, curfews and microchips administered via vaccination. Some of the most virulent combat terms of this milieu from the past 18 months point in the same direction: the designation of the mouth-nose covering as a »muzzle«, the claim that the government wants to silence critics of the measures (»mundtot machen«), the talk of a »Merkel dictatorship« just dawning, and many more.

Interestingly, it seems to be precisely the rather unspectacular fact that a functioning state apparatus existed at all, that it seemed capable of acting in a crisis situation and that it was able to impose restrictions, enact laws and enforce them with recourse to the monopoly on legitimate physical violence in the shortest possible time, that drove critics onto the streets in droves. For example, images

---

[37] Heidegger: Fundamental Concepts of Metaphysics, pp. 157, 160.
[38] In a similar vein, see also Anne-Marie Bonnet's reflections on conspiracy theories as an art form in the first volume on *Corona Normativities* (Bonnet: Aren't So-Called Conspiracy Theories the Most Influential Art of Our Time?); furthermore Frode Helmich Pedersen's chapter in the same volume: A Pandemic of Narratives.

of demonstrators repeatedly circulated, loudly denouncing it as dictatorial interference in their fundamental rights when the police controlled the observance of distance rules and the wearing of face masks at gatherings or otherwise politely (for many observers far *too* politely) issued expulsions. The somewhat peculiar impression that had to impose itself in these weeks and months was that the very *existence* of a state capable of acting at all, and the fact that it resorted to its very own measures in an extreme situation, already appeared to some »Corona critics« as a scandalizable fact. In other words: the state itself – *as such* – and with it any measure of combating the pandemic was declared a scandalon. Boltanski's literary figure of the »conspiracy form«, in which it is precisely the state that appears as the author of those conspiracies, is taken to extremes here in a downright paranoid mode of existence.

But if it has now been said above that the sociology of the pandemic must essentially be a sociology of societal reactions to the pandemic, a sociology of how society deals with the pandemic and a sociology of its effects on societal contexts, then this sociology cannot be limited to looking at the reactions of radicalized milieus. A sociology with theoretical pretensions must paint a larger picture here, and the sociology of science, the sociology of the social sciences, and, finally, the sociology of sociology can by no means be excluded from this picture – that is, sociology is called upon to make its own discursive contributions, in turn, the object of analysis itself: The observations and positionings of the humanities and social sciences, indeed even the genuinely sociological reactions to the pandemic, are themselves without question also the object of sociological observation. On the one hand, sociology is interested in these objects because they represent an important component of the overall social discourse on social reality, because as perspectives on the social world they are themselves always positioned in this world and are influenced by various field effects. On the other hand, a sociology that considers itself reflexive is of course also interested in these objects because it must compare its own interpretation with them, sharpen it against them, and bring it into relation with them. This leads me to the next point.

3. The Marvels of Systems Theory and a Second-Order Amazement

We all knew it would happen eventually. We didn't see it coming. Nothing will ever be the same again. »Covid« will not change much in the structures of our coexistence. The pandemic will expose autocratic regimes as incapable of responding adequately to threats like the current one. The pandemic plays into the hands of those who rule with a particularly hard hand and have always propagated »law and order«. The current crisis is the end of the world as we know it, capitalism lies groaning in its last breaths, the age of globalization has come to its end. The current crisis will only reinforce existing inequalities and in the end leave global quasi-monopolists like Amazon as the only winners ...

It is quite impressive to see the self-confidence with which the community of scholars and, above all, of more or less public intellectuals came up with strong theses only a short time after the crisis began. Hardly anyone was ashamed to judge, hardly anyone even asked for a little time to reflect on an event of global significance and, in some respects, historical dimensions. Even moderate tones were rather the exception – instead, the discourse was largely dominated by pompous proclamations and a logic of maximum scholastic escalation: either/or, black or white, all or nothing. At the same time, the predictability of many of these crisis diagnoses was striking: as if on autopilot, many intellectuals clung to decades-old paradigms in order to present the most expected of the expected from the scripts of their respective scientific games, as has again been commented on many times. It would probably be wrong, and one would fall into exactly the same trap, to construct from this already now an equally strong thesis on the sociology of crisis intellectuals. However, one gets the impression that some colleagues have not done themselves any favors with such snap judgments. The enormous dynamics of the pandemic and the social reactions to it do the rest: The half-life of some diagnoses will prove to be soberingly short in retrospect and has already caused some of the steepest theses to fail in the face of the actual development of events.

In addition to the profession-specific socialization of intellectuals and their own role in the dramaturgy of the interplay between different social fields, there is another reason for this phenomenon: one of the main reasons why one could quickly get the impression of witnessing a game of »blind man's buff«, in which the participants navigate through a completely dark room and try to orient themselves and each other by shouting all the louder, is that this is actually a pretty good metaphor for the epistemic situation that formed a central part of the crisis. The self-confidence and the loudness with which particularly pointed interpretations were put forward particularly by the humanities, cultural studies and social sciences, the demand for contextualization of the events and even the much-mentioned renaissance of sociology in the face of Covid-19 merely complement the special significance that virology and epidemiology had in the course of the pandemic; they thus also point to the core of the pandemic crisis as a crisis of knowledge and reality.

In the following, I will concentrate very selectively on a few voices from German sociology in order to position my own field-theoretical account between these interpretations. To this end, I begin with three analyses presented from the field of sociological systems theory (broadly defined). Fabian Anicker, for example, from a perspective informed by sociological translation theory,[39] has presented an analysis of societal reactions to the Corona pandemic in which he diagnoses an »unprecedented *politicization* of society«[40] for the period following the outbreak of Covid-19. On closer inspection, however, against the background of a »strong influence of medical science on politics« and a »susceptibility of the political system to the scientific-medical definition of risk«, this represents at the same time a »medicalization of society via politics«[41] for Anicker, namely a »triumphal march of the medical code« in the form of an increasing »unilateralization of the value reference of politics«.[42]

With a very similar thrust, Rudolf Stichweh, who has been continuing Luhmann's theoretical project in Germany for many years, already stated in April 2020 that at least the first phase of pandemic management was characterized by the fact that »all [...] functional systems [of world society, D.W.] temporarily followed a single imperative«.[43] For the first time in the history of modernity, »the health system has become the whole of society, and specifically the health system in its most extreme form as a total institution, i.e., as intensive medicine«,[44] while the »whole of society remaining beyond the health system in all its activities [...] has been reduced to the peculiar sum formula ›flatten the curve‹, which actually says above all that one has to adapt the infection dynamics of society as a consequence of all societal activities to the processing capacity of the health system available at a given time and thus especially to that of intensive medicine«.[45] Quite similar to Anicker, Stichweh also diagnoses an at least temporarily »radically simplified political system that decides here, a system that knows an extremely sharpened hierarchy of decision topics, a hierarchy about which it does not believe itself to be able to decide and which it would therefore not put at the disposal of the democratic discourse. This hierarchy is dictated by the imperative of not overburdening the health care system, and this in turn is dictated by the ultimate importance of equal treatment and preservation of the life of the individual«.[46] A »key question«, Stichweh states, is therefore »whether and how it [the pandemic, D.W.] temporarily calls into question this social order of modernity [the functional differentiation of world society, D.W.]«.[47]

---

[39] The translation-theoretical approach draws heavily on assumptions of Luhmann's systems theory (cf. Renn: Übersetzungsverhältnisse), but at the same time goes beyond them.
[40] Anicker: Die Medizinisierung der Gesellschaft, p. 174.
[41] Ibid.
[42] Ibid., p. 175.
[43] Stichweh: Simplifikation des Sozialen, p. 197.
[44] Stichweh intentionally speaks of the *disease system* here (»Krankheitssystem«). I will stick to the more common term of the *health system* in order to avoid confusion due to the translation into English.
[45] Ibid., p. 199.
[46] Ibid., p. 200.
[47] Ibid., p. 198.

Finally, Armin Nassehi, one of the leading public intellectuals in the contemporary German debate, also emphasized several times in the spring of 2020 that »something is currently happening that seemed sociologically impossible, namely that the political system can virtually rule through, that is, intervene through political decisions in economic life, in the education system and in legally guaranteed standards«.[48] The basic structure of modern society, namely »[f]unctional differentiation«, Nassehi claims, would preclude this – »except in times that can be called a state of exception. For the most part, these were times of war, when the economic system, the educational system, the law, even religion could be put at the service of the collective cause«.[49]

What all three analyses have in common is that their authors show a profound astonishment. This is most obvious for Nassehi, for whom the first social reactions to the pandemic present themselves as a process that »seemed *sociologically* impossible« not only from a systems theory perspective but also more generally – as »something *we* always said: That is not possible«.[50] Anicker, too, understands the pandemic as both a »paradigm and problem case for the theory of functional differentiation«.[51] In the similarity of national political measures he sees »temporarily a factually largely coherent world policy« emerging, which he calls »astonishing«,[52] just as he considers the narrowing of political decision-making to the protection of individuals' lives »extremely unusual«[53] – both this narrowing and the »governing through« of politics (also emphasized by Nassehi) would make it »difficult« to justify »to continue speaking of ›autopoietically‹ operating systems«.[54] Likewise, Stichweh considers the focus on the protection of life to be as »striking« as it is »impressive«; the new order of function systems is called »peculiar« and historically without antecedents, and overall »the exceptionality and riskiness of the social experiment« of pandemic control is considered remarkable.[55] Finally, the reactions in the course of the »first wave« appear so singular to Stichweh that in a postscript written in June 2020, he still assumes that »everyone« would know »that it will not be possible to impose the same restrictions a second time«. For this reason, in the case of a second wave, »only decisive and, if necessary, brutal local measures« were conceivable, while »nationally generalized restrictions« would »not be possible a second time«.[56]

---

[48] Nassehi: Nicht Einzelne sind infiziert, sondern die ganze Gesellschaft.
[49] Ibid.
[50] Ibid.; Nassehi: »Es passiert gerade etwas, von dem wir immer gesagt haben: Das geht nicht«.
[51] Anicker: Die Medizinisierung der Gesellschaft, p. 174.
[52] Ibid.
[53] Ibid., p. 175.
[54] Ibid., p. 174.
[55] Stichweh: Simplifikation des Sozialen, pp. 198, 203.
[56] Ibid., p. 204.

Now, it would certainly be absurd to deny that we are living in extraordinary times in many respects, and it would be equally misguided to accuse colleagues of making incorrect predictions »on the running engine« of the pandemic in the spring of 2020. The amazement of systems-theoretically arguing authors about the fact that political reactions, as they have characterized this first phase of the pandemic, even seem to be conceivable and practically possible at all, may itself be astonishing as a social phenomenon. In fact, this is an amazement at the amazement of others, in systems-theoretical terms, therefore: a second-order amazement. Interestingly, the astonishment at the ability of the state in particular to act in the pandemic situation, at the ability of politics to »govern through« and »into« a large number of other systems, in a certain way resembles the reaction pattern described above, that has driven a large number of so-called »Maßnahmenkritiker« onto the streets. The reference to this parallel should not be misunderstood as polemic, if only because the sociological astonishment is theoretically and analytically motivated, while the indignation of the »lateral thinkers« is based on a supposed normative scandalon of the state. The impression remains, however, that also sociological observers, especially those trained in systems theory, were downright paralyzed by the nation-state's factual ability to act.

This astonishment, which is widespread in parts of sociology, is undoubtedly due to specific theoretical orientations, which is why I would like to base my further remarks on alternative assumptions. To be sure, I explicitly share Anicker's assessment that societal reactions to the Covid-19 pandemic can best be explored from a differentiation-theoretical perspective.[57] My starting point, however, is primarily field-theoretical assumptions that allow me to take a different look at what happened in 2020 and how the pandemic unfolded in society. In order to enable such a reassessment of the »measures« as well as their consequences from an alternative differentiation-theoretical perspective, though, it is first necessary to briefly recapitulate some of the decisions and developments of recent months.

4. *Huis clos?* A Selective Inventory

As far as the thesis of a »state of exception«[58] that is not only *social* but at the same time *theoretical* is concerned, the singular character of both the pandemic situation and the way it was dealt with, which this account assumes, must first be put into perspective.[59] To begin with, the fact that social practice in many differenti-

---

[57] Cf. Anicker: Die Medizinisierung der Gesellschaft, p. 173.
[58] Ibid.
[59] For theoretical as well as research pragmatic reasons, the following observations refer primarily to the social handling of the Covid-19 pandemic in Germany.

ated fields is strongly oriented by references to certain themes or values does not represent such an extreme singular case as some formulations suggest. In this context, of course, one should first think of war societies, although many authors, including the ones cited here, have rightly called for analytical caution in this regard – not least in view of the political use of this comparison – and pointed out parallels as well as differences.[60] Moreover, the fact that political discourse and media coverage (as well as other fields, depending on the case) were to a considerable extent determined by single issues could also be argued (albeit to varying degrees, as also in the case of pandemic control) for the counterterrorism heyday of the 1970s, possibly also for the »war on terror« following 9/11. In the long term, the Cold War had similar effects as well, determining doctrines, directives, and metastrategies, thus defining and shaping the overall framework of political debate. But similar effects can also be claimed for long-term processes of change: for example, the process apostrophized as »digitalization« has already determined large parts of pedagogical, political, economic or scientific action for several years, just as the climate crisis and the search for »sustainable« practices have become the subject of permanent reflection in all social fields, and sometimes already the central motif of far-reaching transformations. In this respect, the Corona crisis is unquestionably an extraordinary event, but by no means a singular one in every respect.[61] Rather, the thesis suggests itself that precisely »existential problems«[62] such as (civil) wars or nuclear threat scenarios, climate change or perhaps also terrorism[63] hold the potential to steer societal communication in specific directions to a considerable extent: they »put societies under pressure, challenge them«, and precisely through this »urge the concerted mobilization of all capacities for dealing with problems«; they »demand contributions from all sides« and »test the societal capacity« as a whole.[64]

Just as this cross-field focus on the issue is not an absolutely unique feature of the Covid-19 pandemic (*singularity thesis*), it is not possible to speak of a truly all-encompassing narrowing of social communication and social practices to this single topic and associated questions (or even to a »medical code«) (*simplification thesis*); nor do the social developments of recent months allow us to conclude that the temporary focus on the central theme of »combating the pandemic« – which,

---

[60] Cf. Anicker: Die Medizinisierung der Gesellschaft, pp. 179 f.; Stichweh: Simplifikation des Sozialen, p. 201; Nassehi: Nicht Einzelne sind infiziert, sondern die ganze Gesellschaft. Jens Greve sees the subordination of economic considerations to political ones as more of a parallel to the financial crisis of the 2000s (cf. Greve: Corona aus Sicht der Soziologie).

[61] Similarly, Klaus Dörre recognizes the »Corona pandemic as a historical caesura, but not as an event of secular uniqueness« (Dörre: Die Corona-Pandemie, p. 174).

[62] Scheffer: Existentielle Probleme, *soziologisch*, p. 3.

[63] At least according to Beck: Weltrisikogesellschaft, ökologische Krise und Technologiepolitik, pp. 62 f.

[64] Scheffer: Existentielle Probleme, *soziologisch*, pp. 22, 3, 17, 21.

incidentally, already lost much of its significance during the summer months (i. e., simultaneously with the decline in epidemiological indicators) – is a permanent phenomenon that must determine discourses in the long term and even lead to a »recoding« of function systems (*persistence thesis*). While this last restriction may surely be based on a certain hope, the second relativization requires us to take another look at the history of events in the year 2020. In fact, massive doubts arise about the simplification thesis outlined in this way, which in its pointed form states that social practice and communication in recent months have been determined by a single theme, or even: by the reference to a single binary code value (life / death).

In this context, differences between the authors rubricated here under a common thesis do emerge. Anicker understands the »medicalization« of society mediated by the political system as a process in which »the political discourse, relentlessly polytheistic in its value references, slipped into a temporary monotheism: in the firmament of the political system only [sic!] the medically defined value of the preservation of human bodies sparkled«.[65] The core of the thesis here is thus a »reduction of decision-relevant value references in the political system«, in which a »unifying narrowing of the view of ›the human being‹« as a »possibly sick body in need of healing« »radically suspended« the usual »drifting [of politics, D. W.] between different situational prioritizations of values«, leading to »[p]olitical decisions [...] [that] were *primarily* perceived as those that could cost or save human lives«.[66]

Stichweh initially makes a very similar argument at this point when he assumes that the importance of the individual in modern societies is demonstrated in the pandemic by the fact that »no other value point of view can compete with the highest value of the survival of as many individuals as possible«[67], which produced the supposedly »radically simplified political system« in precisely this question. However, where Anicker essentially limits the »medicalization« thesis to the political system (although a medicalization of society as a whole is at least predicted via this detour), Stichweh postulates an even more far-reaching disbalancing, in which temporarily »the health system has become the whole [sic!] of society« and this whole in »all [sic!] its activities« has referred to the flattening of infection curves.[68] In this sense, the thesis of an undermining of axiological pluralism in political decision-making practice – in favor of an »absolutization of medical value considerations«[69] – represents the more moderate interpretation, initially limited to the political system, while the dissolution of the whole of so-

---

[65] Anicker: Die Medizinisierung der Gesellschaft, p. 179.
[66] Ibid., pp. 174 f.; emph. in the orig.
[67] Stichweh: Simplifikation des Sozialen, p. 198.
[68] Ibid., p. 199.
[69] Anicker: Die Medizinisierung der Gesellschaft, p. 181.

ciety in medical communication (Stichweh) represents a more radical variant of the »simplification thesis«. I am convinced, however, that *both* interpretations overestimate the importance of the pandemic and the medical logic for the operation of other fields (including politics, and even during the various lockdown phases). This doubt should be briefly explained using the examples of the fields of politics and science.

Undoubtedly, the *political* debate in 2020 has revolved in particular around the consequences of the pandemic and appropriate strategies for its containment. However, it should not be forgotten that 2020 was also the year of the presidential elections in the USA, the decisive year of Brexit, and the year of the *Black Lives Matter* movement. Local and state elections took place along with the associated election campaigns, smaller and larger scandals came to light and were discussed, and there were extensive debates about anthropo-generated climate change, police violence in Belarus, the refugee camps on Lesbos, and drones for the German military. Now, many of these topics and debates may seem to some observers to have receded into the background in the current situation (and especially retrospectively), but on closer inspection there can be no question of a monothematic restriction of political discourse – or even of political communication in the narrower sense.

But even within the »Covid debate«, it is difficult to maintain the thesis that the medical »code« had started a »triumphal march« that was as unambiguous as it was comprehensive.[70] There is no doubt that some actors in the political field had to make decisions under uncertainty and great time pressure, which in terms of content were directed towards the containment of the pandemic; but on the one hand, this does not concern the entirety of all actors in this field, but strictly speaking only one of its segments (the part that is particularly visible to the public, consisting of government and opposition, especially at the federal and state level), and on the other hand there is much that speaks against the thesis that these decisions (and their criticism) were always made solely »in the sense of medical recommendations«.[71] One might think, for example, of the parallel competition for the chancellor candidacy between the German Union parties (CDU/CSU), which provoked many a criticism of the decisions (possibly also motivated by electoral strategy) of leading figures such as Markus Söder or Armin Laschet. In fact, these decisions at times resembled an »outbidding competition« of restrictive measures – a polemic cleverly used by Söder himself against his competitor, semantically hiding inner-party power calculations more or less virtuously behind the fig leaf of »medical recommendations«. In this respect, it should not come as a surprise that critical observation of pandemic policy by the mass media has repeatedly expressed doubts as to whether the »translation« of scientific (virological and epi-

---

[70] Ibid., p. 175.
[71] Ibid., p. 179.

demiological as well as sociological) expertise into legally binding measures was not in many cases »refracted« by genuinely political motives. However, the more moderate version of the »simplification thesis« must also be put into perspective to the extent that political decisions have been based on considerations other than medical recommendations (see below).

It is also true for the *scientific* field that one cannot speak of a complete focus on the pandemic topic across the board. Sociology is certainly particularly confronted with the challenge of providing interpretations of the current social situation (and its manifold consequences), and the self-assurance predicted by Stichweh for the scientific system as a whole as to whether the questions pursued in one's own research are still relevant in the future[72] will certainly have an effect here (although a comprehensive focus on the topic is not to be expected). In other parts of the scientific field, however, this »new beginning«[73] will be even less significant: Architectural science or space technology, Egyptology, geodesy or botany, for example, are unlikely to be affected by the pandemic in terms of the content of their research (and there are undoubtedly many others that could be mentioned, not least large subfields of medicine itself).

As far as everyday teaching and research practice is concerned, contact restrictions in particular have undoubtedly led to major changes, but it is by no means the case that remote work, for example, has brought about substantial restrictions for *all* actors in academia in equal measure. At this point, new social inequalities in the scientific field may emerge in the medium term (depending in particular on gender, marital status and the respective living conditions), but it would be completely wrong to assume that the pandemic would have led to a disruption of research and publication activity or even truly fundamental changes in scientific practice across the entire field. University teaching, too, has undergone a far-reaching change of form in a very short time as a result of the switch to digital formats (which occurred at too short a notice for most lecturers, was laborious, and is still fraught with numerous problems); but teaching as such has, by and large, continued with classic formats (lecture and seminar) and content (*Introduction to Sociology*, *Criminal Law I*, etc.).

Other social fields could be illuminated in a similar way: Even in the strictest »lockdown«, civil lawsuits were filed and judgments were rendered, cultural goods were produced and marketed, loans were taken out and investments made, education was provided, beliefs were practiced, and events were reported. Against this background, neither the systems-theoretical argument that functional differentiation has been undermined nor Hartmut Rosa's insofar similar thesis according to which »the state has largely overridden the inherent logic and dynamics

---

[72] Cf. Stichweh: Simplifikation des Sozialen, p. 203.
[73] Ibid.

of markets, as well as of the cultural, educational, and scientific spheres«[74] is particularly convincing. From a field-theoretical perspective, it could also be noted that the social struggles in the various social fields were by no means brought to a standstill or slowed down by the pandemic – or even by measures such as contact restrictions – but that sometimes the opposite may even have been the case.

In summary of this brief exploration, one can only caution against speaking prematurely at this time about the singularity, simplification, or persistence of »pandemic communication« in the medium of a medical code, or even drawing conclusions about the basic structures of modern society. However understandable such exaggerations may be, especially when the sociological observation takes place in a »pandemic atmosphere«, in a »state of emergency« also conjured up by the mass media, and under the »dense« life-worldly impression of rigid contact restrictions: There are good reasons to believe that much of this image, shaped by life-worldly experiences, will have to be relativized in retrospect.

5. The Incompleteness of the Virological Imperative and the Struggle for Systemic Relevance

However, an interpretation of the particular irritation that society's handling of the Covid-19 pandemic has caused among colleagues arguing from a systems theory perspective has yet to be offered. As is well known, sociological theories such as the theory of functional differentiation are at the same time world views and performative epistemological apparatuses that first produce their object »society« in a specific way, making certain aspects visible and allowing others to recede into the background (or even become invisible). Against the background of central assumptions of systems theory, the surprise of some sociologists therefore quickly becomes understandable: It is precisely a specific trademark of this theory that it assumes that modern society – as a functionally differentiated world society – no longer knows a place (»top« or »center«) from which direct intervention in the operations of the individual function systems would be possible. Accordingly, it is no coincidence that the central figure of »world society« is dramaturgically introduced in Luhmann's work from the very beginning via the demarcation from political theory and the dissolution of the »association of politics and society«[75]: The state can thus no longer be conceived as the central controlling instance of society

---

[74] Rosa: Pfadabhängigkeit, Bifurkationspunkte und die Rolle der Soziologie, p. 203.
[75] Luhmann: Die Weltgesellschaft, p. 4; cf. Luhmann: Die Unterscheidung von Staat und Gesellschaft.

as a whole,[76] but only as a self-descriptive formula and organizational form of the internally segmentally differentiated political system. Against this background, it seems clear at first glance why systems theory was initially perplexed by the events of spring 2020: the fact that politics not only somehow »has an effect« but could actually succeed up to a certain point in »determining system statuses [...] in the desired direction«[77] must appear from this perspective as a curiosity and an anomaly, even as something actually impossible.

On closer examination, however, even from a systems theory perspective, the situation is in principle not as extraordinary as assumed. One example of this is the temporary »closure of the retail trade«, which was probably considered one of the most rigorous lockdown measures: Not only is the wording inaccurate, since a large proportion of stores remained open on a regular basis – in addition to grocery stores and pharmacies, for example, car repair shops, opticians and Christmas tree sales. Moreover, temporary state restrictions on sales activities are not unusual *in principle*, but are an integral part of German (but not, for example, Italian or U.S.) labor and trade law in the form of store closing laws. Therefore, of course, it cannot already be considered a theoretically relevant anomaly if the state prohibits the sale of goods in stores at certain times (to be specified in more detail); it is first of all merely a »common« political ruling (although certainly unusual in its scope) that makes use of the legal system's performance (not: function) of »behavioral control«.[78] And it should be added that, in other cases, a wide variety of types of normative expectations have interacted with each other alongside »law« as functional equivalents (for instance, regular positive law as well as the law of exception, customs, manners, decency, tact,[79] and morality). In this sense, it was in fact often not law as such, but a more complex »pandemic validity culture«[80] that contributed in a broader sense to »behavioral control« in the direction of physical distancing, contact reduction, and so on; but the state nevertheless played a decisive role in the production and establishment of this normative fabric.

It is probably even more decisive for the systems-theoretically informed perspective, however, that *the political system* in no way made economic communication as such impossible, brought it to a standstill or even »forbid« it: The retail trade was (and still is) potentially free to deliver goods or to sell them by other means (e.g. via online platforms), the banks were just as open as the stock exchanges, and the major online mail order companies, as is well known, even prof-

---

[76] Or even as its »brain«, as Durkheim has put it (cf. Durkheim: Professional Ethics and Civic Morals, pp. 30, 53, 104; see also Witte: Passing the Torch; Witte: Ein ambivalentes Erbe).
[77] Luhmann: Die Politik der Gesellschaft, p. 110.
[78] Cf. Luhmann: Das Recht der Gesellschaft, pp. 156 ff.
[79] See also Suntrup: Corona: Biopolitical Models and the Hygiene of Tact; Hanske: Knigge in Times of Corona.
[80] Gephart: In the Realm of Corona Normativities; Gephart: Conclusion, pp. 513 f.

ited massively from the restrictions mentioned. Thus, it is not at all clear in what sense the economic system, to stay with this example, should have »temporarily followed a single imperative« of »flattening the curve« side by side with all other functional systems, or in what sense »the economy« should even have »predominantly ceased«, as Stichweh puts it[81] – and least of all if one bases this assessment on a systems-theoretical concept of »economic communication«. Likewise, on the stock exchanges and in the remaining businesses, in the banks and the countless offices and factories, agencies and large companies, which were by no means affected by closures to the same extent as part of the retail sector, interest continued to focus unchanged on payments and revenues, on profits and losses, not on the flattening of the infection curves.[82] To avoid any misunderstandings: Of course, alternative distribution channels were not or not readily available in many cases, the repeated closures of stores have already driven many owners into insolvency, and every single case is accompanied by dramatic individual fates and a worsening of social inequalities, just as the recent market and power gains of e-commerce giants like Amazon represent a massive problem that needs to be critically observed. However, a problem for the theory of functional differentiation or even the undermining of its basic principle cannot be constructed from this.

Field theory, following Pierre Bourdieu in particular, paints a completely different picture of society here, even if it is also based on differentiation-theoretical ideas. Two of the assumptions central to the present context are that, on the one hand, social fields are not conceived as units operating according to a single invariant functional principle, but rather as arenas of different practical strategies, in which autonomous and heteronomous poles simultaneously stand for different interpretations of what is »at stake« in a given field.[83] On the other hand, field theory also assumes contested balances of power *between* the different fields, which are competed for in a broader »field of power«.[84] These two basic assumptions now seem to me to be of particular importance for a better understanding of societal responses to the Covid-19 pandemic, if one wants to understand these as the dynamic result of conflicting interests, and the primary theoretically relevant

---

[81] Stichweh: Simplifikation des Sozialen, op. cit. and ibid., p. 201. As far as I can see, the formula of a »virological imperative« was introduced into the debate in the early stages of the pandemic by Gabriel: Die meisten liberalen Demokratien haben eine Ausgangssperre verhängt.

[82] In February 2021, the online portal *Statista* published an analysis by data journalist Matthias Janson, which put the share of economic sectors »not directly affected« by the lockdown measures at 87.2 % (measured by gross value added in 2018). Of the 12.8 % that were considered »directly affected«, 5.9 % were accounted for by education, arts, entertainment and recreation alone, with the remaining 6.9 % for retail, hospitality, motor vehicle sales and repair, and travel (cf. Janson: 13 Prozent der Wirtschaft direkt von Lockdown betroffen).

[83] Cf. Bourdieu/Wacquant: An Invitation to Reflexive Sociology, pp. 94–100, here: p. 97.

[84] Cf. Wacquant/Bourdieu: Das Feld der Macht und die technokratische Herrschaft; Bourdieu: On the State. For a more detailed discussion of this concept, see now also Schneickert/Schmitz/Witte: Das Feld der Macht.

effect of the pandemic itself – according to my main argument – as a temporary de- (and possibly re-) stabilization of field relations (understood as power relations).

The Covid-19 pandemic hit many countries in spring 2020 comparatively unprepared and with tremendous (infection) dynamics. Confronted with different epidemiological scenarios, with warnings of the effects of overburdened health systems and the first devastating images, especially from Italy, but not least also in view of a time lag effect between contagion, infectivity, disease outbreak and severe, possibly fatal courses of disease that should not be underestimated, political actors worldwide were forced to act in a very short time. This dynamic undercut any natural »inclination to not act, not yet to act, to act later«[85] and paired with classical conditions of decision-making under uncertainty in a »compulsion to have to act [...] under uncertainty«[86], which led to those packages of measures that culminated in the first so-called »lockdown« in Germany as of March 23, 2020.[87] However, at the latest with the first »relaxations« in mid- and late April 2020, a dynamic already set in that has shaped the public debate on the respective measures adopted to this day and is of particular interest both sociologically and especially in terms of social theory insofar as it involves the *weighing* of different measures, the direct *comparison* of their appropriateness, effectiveness, and reasonableness, and the always at least latently comparative discussion of the »systemic relevance« of different occupational groups and practices. From a field-theoretical perspective, a tangible conflict of interests becomes visible here, which refers to the balance of power between social fields and the chances of society-wide enforcement of the interests and strategies effective in each, i.e. the mutual »recognition of field-specific goods, practices and world views«[88] and the cross-field claims to validity attached to them.[89]

In this context, the attribution of the property of »systemic relevance« (already terminologically interesting for the sociological observer) is significant. In its March 2020 list, the German Federal Ministry of Labor and Social Affairs explicitly subsumed under this title industries such as information technology and telecommunications, parts of the financial sector, and parts of the mass media,[90] so it can by no means be said that the selection by definition refers only to sectors

---

[85] Minkmar/Beck: Über den Merkiavellismus.

[86] Schwering/Habermas: Jürgen Habermas über Corona.

[87] The terminological question of the appropriateness of the term »lockdown« will not be discussed further here. I follow (uncritically in this sense) the widely used distinction between a first lockdown starting in March, which was gradually relaxed in April and May, a »lockdown light«, which began on November 2, 2020, and a second (»hard«) lockdown starting on December 16, 2020, which was again gradually tightened from January 11, 2021.

[88] Schneickert/Schmitz/Witte: Das Feld der Macht, p. 27.

[89] A similar conflict could recently be observed in the debate about the »vaccination sequence« and the prioritization of certain occupational groups.

[90] Cf. Bundesministerium für Arbeit und Soziales (BMAS): Liste der systemrelevanten Bereiche.

directly related to the protection of human »life« (as suggested in the literature). Perhaps more interesting from a sociological point of view than this official definition, which was also expanded a few weeks later at the state level to include numerous occupational groups (such as security services, tax advisors and lawyers), however, are the debates that began in April 2020, driven by particular interests, about which other fields and occupational groups should also be considered »systemically relevant«. Corresponding proposals were made by freelance artists and building cleaners, the electrical and the funeral trade, the book trade and the association of land surveyors,[91] and other areas and professions could be added almost at will.[92] The concept of systemic relevance thus became a »contested concept«[93] in just a few weeks, and its contested nature also expressed the conflict over the assertion of different field-specific interests.

6. Equality of Fundamental Rights Revisited, or: The Episcopate's Laughter

The measures adopted and their relaxation often affect fundamental rights, so that the discourse on their »proportionality« and the question of where measures should be mitigated first often turns into a question of weighing legal interests. Affected by this were and/or are, for example, the right to freedom of assembly (Article 8 of the German Basic Law), the right to freedom of movement (Article 11) or even the freedom of the person (Article 2), which is restricted, for example, in the case of ordering quarantine. Relevant in terms of differentiation theory[94] here are in particular the right to freedom of occupation (i. e. in this case concretely: to freely exercise one's profession) (Article 12), which has been significantly restricted for various occupational groups (such as stage artists, gastronomes, or retailers), but also the right to freedom of religion (Article 4), when in the course of general or specific assembly bans, religious services and prayer events were prohibited. As is well known, such interventions must be »proportionate«, i. e., in this case, suitable, necessary and appropriate to combat the pandemic, and must be weighed

---

[91] Cf. Bund der Öffentlich bestellten Vermessungsingenieure e.V. (BDVI): Systemrelevanz der ÖbVI in der Corona-Krise.

[92] Not least from sociology, calls for recognition of the »systemic relevance« of both paid and unpaid care work increased once again (see, representative of the German discussion, Gather: Der Markt wird's nicht richten; Villa: Corona-Krise meets Care-Krise; Winker: Aufbau einer solidarischen und nachhaltigen Care-Ökonomie); and even if the connections between the »care crisis« and the »corona crisis« became clearly visible in 2020, it remains to be seen whether they will be remembered even after the pandemic has ended.

[93] Cf. Gallie: Essentially Contested Concepts.

[94] Certainly in the sense of Luhmann: Grundrechte als Institution.

against the protection of life and the right to physical integrity (also Article 2), which are likewise guaranteed by the Basic Law.

The case of religion is particularly interesting in this game of anticipated balancing of legal interests: Even if the Basic Law does not provide for an internal hierarchy of fundamental rights,[95] the comparatively restrained restriction of collective religious practices quickly caused some resentment and astonishment. From a virological point of view, there were numerous arguments against holding religious services and prayer meetings, since various factors came together here that, according to the available research, had to be regarded as accelerators of the infection dynamics and thus of the pandemic: not only the gathering of larger groups of people in closed, sometimes inadequately ventilated rooms, but also numerous aspects of liturgy (such as singing or praying together), which cannot be easily substituted or excluded, since they (like, incidentally, the co-presence of bodies themselves) are of constitutive importance for religious ritual dynamics and possibly also in theological terms.

In this respect – and also in view of the fact that, despite promised security measures on the part of the religious communities, violations and mass infections occurred again and again after their opening – it may be surprising from a purely epidemiological point of view that the churches in particular benefited from »relaxations« again very early on (namely as early as the end of April) »due to the special protection of the freedom to practice religion in the Basic Law«[96], while, for example, »emergency care« in schools and daycare facilities was successively extended again only in the course of May. And even during the »lockdown light« as well as the second »hard lockdown« at the end of the year, there was no renewed closure of places of worship, although now even more far-reaching measures than in spring (including the renewed closure of all schools in January 2021) were adopted. From various directions, but especially from the field of arts and cultural production in the broader sense, this treatment of religious communities was criticized, sometimes harshly, and a direct comparison was drawn between theaters, concert halls, etc. on the one hand and churches on the other. From the perspective of the cultural field, this criticism must seem understandable, since it constitutes probably one of the most endangered areas in the medium and long term and has suffered in a special way from state intervention (for which various reasons can be cited, such as the fact that stage programs, for example, are linked to seasons and/or advance ticket sales and therefore cannot be »restarted« at such short notice as, say, church services or most retail outlets).

---

[95] See, for instance, Alexy: Theorie der Grundrechte, pp. 79 ff., 138 ff.; Dreier: Dimensionen der Grundrechte, pp. 21 ff.
[96] Bundesregierung: Telefonschaltkonferenz, p. 4.

But how can this unequal treatment of churches and concert events, which has caused so much outrage, be explained? The viability of the sole reference to freedom of religion, which is opposed to encroachments on other fundamental rights also in this case (and does not enjoy priority over them), can certainly be questioned from a constitutional perspective.[97] From a sociological perspective, however, it seems obvious to point out that the church in Germany is still a powerful institution, especially where the preservation of its own autonomy claims is concerned. In this context, it should also be mentioned that numerous lawsuits had been filed against the bans on religious services in the run-up to the relaxations (as was also the case in France and the United States, for example), which occupied various administrative courts and even the Federal Constitutional Court (the latter having emphasized in its decision the need for a strict time limit on the bans).[98] Not least against this background, it therefore seems simply plausible that the churches and religious communities succeeded in exerting sufficient influence in the course of the joint preliminary talks on the aforementioned telephone conference of April 30, to which the corresponding resolution explicitly refers, to work toward a renewed permission of religious community practices. Field theory, by assuming a permanent struggle for influence and autonomy carried out in the field of power between different fields and field elites, at least provides a well-founded working hypothesis at this point. Sociologically naïve, however, it would be to assume that political decisions are *not* always the result of targeted lobbying, that they do *not* always come about under the influence of various (field-specific) interest groups, and that they are therefore *not* ultimately an expression of social power relations. On the one hand, an interpretation along these lines is reinforced by the fact that churches remained open and church services continued to be permitted when the second »hard lockdown« was declared in December 2020 and when in January 2021, among other restrictions, all schools and childcare facilities were even closed nationwide, which until then seemed to be *ultima ratio*, so to speak – »keeping schools open as long as possible« was still the motto until the turn of the year (and again in the spring of 2021), whereby their closure contrasts even more sharply with the still untouched religious services. On the other hand, the thesis also gains plausibility in the much-cited comparison with gastronomy and the cultural sector, whereby the latter in particular has a comparatively weak lobby or, in the case of the numerous »small« and solo artists, such a lobby is virtually non-existent. From a field-theoretical point of view, however, further arguments could be brought forward beyond the purely power-theoretical perspective: The political and the religious field of contemporary German society exhibit a greater degree of homology in questions of both capital distribution and the habitus affin-

---

[97] Cf., for example, Kingreen: Ist das Kunst?
[98] Cf. Bundesverfassungsgericht (BVerfG): Gottesdienstverbot.

ities of their actors than the political field and the field of cultural production; in field-theoretical terms, the »distance« of the political to the artistic field is thus significantly larger than that to the institutionalized pole of the religious field, which is a crucial factor in the »division of the work of domination« postulated by Bourdieu between different field elites.[99]

What is decisive in all of this, however, is that such a special role for the religious field in no way corresponds to the officially established pattern of differentiation of the local social formation and only became possible at all against the backdrop of a disruptive event in society as a whole; the destabilization of normative and cognitive order described above is thus complemented here by a destabilization of the socio-structural order of society: The »shock« of the onset of the pandemic in the spring of 2020 led to a temporary destabilization of relatively robust balances of power between the various social fields, which on the one hand plausibilized massive state intervention and on the other created the space for a process of selective renegotiation of (»systemic«) relevance and field relations in the field of power. In this context, the (nation-)state merely constitutes *one* relatively autonomous field in the field of power alongside others (science, religion, etc.)[100] – a field, however, whose autonomy was strengthened in a particular way in the first phase of the pandemic, before a second phase of continued »opening« and »lockdown« discussions simultaneously sparked a veiled debate about the autonomy relations of social fields in their entirety. In this way, the Covid-19 crisis opened up an arena for conflicts of interest and set in motion a process in which the social significance and worthiness of protection of certain spheres could be put up for debate and renegotiated to an extent that must be regarded as rather atypical in the »normal course« of society.

7. The Covid Society – Differentiated but Capitalistic

However, this temporarily limited renegotiation of power balances between social fields left one field largely untouched, which points to the flip side of the strengthened autonomy of the state. Not necessarily more surprising, but even more remarkable and instructive than the case of the religious field, is the fact that the *economic field* has not allowed its autonomy vis-à-vis other fields (including the state), and thus its dominant position in the field of power, to be significantly curtailed even by the shocks described above. As has been argued, the state did partially intervene in the dynamics of the economic field from spring 2020 onwards;

---

[99] Bourdieu: On the State, p. 247 f.; cf. Bourdieu: The State Nobility, pp. 371 ff.
[100] Cf. Schmitz/Witte: Der Nationalstaat und das globale Feld der Macht.

however, the focus on these interventions obscures the extent to which a large part of the field's actors were still able to pursue economic activities during the various »lockdowns« (and in some cases these activities were even explicitly protected). But even more importantly, the economic field succeeded in its usual sovereign manner in imposing its field-specific worldview on society as a whole, in asserting its interests across other fields, and in naturalizing them into universal ones.

As early as the spring of 2020, numerous business sectors in Germany were exempted from the retail closures; yet, even more significant are the many industries that were not directly affected by closure measures at *any* time (but at most via soft restrictions such as distancing rules): from manufacturing and processing to construction, from a majority of office and service businesses and agencies to the entire banking and financial market sector. There is no question that day-to-day professional practice in all of these areas carries the same risks of contagion, and much like churches, public transportation, where even during the »hard« lockdown in early 2021, mostly blue- and white-collar workers crowded to get to work, was the source of widespread anger and bewilderment. Moreover, the strong position of the economic field became even more apparent in the course of the »opening races« in April and May 2020: As Martina Franzen rightly notes, the hazardous situation had not changed significantly at all in this phase of the pandemic, so that one cannot avoid stating that the »political considerations of a gradual return to normality [...] were no longer in line with the advice of many virologists and epidemiologists«, but that »economic considerations came to the fore«.[101] The »simplification thesis« already criticized above thus seems even more questionable against this background.

Meanwhile, in this whole process, calls for shutting down a more significant part of the economy (and thus, in fact: social life as a whole) for a short period of time (e.g., 14 days or four weeks) have never risen above the status of critical journalistic interventions or campaigns like *#ZeroCovid*;[102] not even a binding »home office« (remote work) rule could be enforced at any time – and probably primarily because this usually clashes with the interests of corporate management (which cannot come as a surprise to anyone who also understands the institution of the office as a disciplinary control technique). Finally, against this background, the fact that schooling and daycare were maintained for so long despite a growing epidemiological certainty about the relevance of children and adolescents for the

---

[101] Franzen: Was heißt Systemrelevanz?

[102] Both the *No-COVID* initiative (to be distinguished from *#ZeroCovid*) and the high-profile call for a »pan-European strategy« published by a collective of authors in *The Lancet* were based, among other things, precisely on the argument that a shorter but more consistent lockdown would reduce economic costs (cf. Priesemann et al.: Calling for Pan-European Commitment, p. 92, with reference to Dorn et al.: The Economic Costs of the Coronavirus Shutdown; see also Baumann et al.: Eine neue proaktive Zielsetzung, here: pp. 5 f., 8).

incidence of infections, and the additional fact that this was justified in particular by reference to the educational mandate of the state and concern that pupils (not only from families with lower cultural capital) were in danger of losing out, seems either touching or cynical. Such sudden expressions of concern not only leave a bitter aftertaste in view of already dramatic social inequalities (and unequal treatment) in the education system, in the knowledge of a »traditionally« high number of hours lost at schools, and with a view to the health hazards also for children and young people. They should also not obscure the fact that childcare is, of course, an essential prerequisite for parents (not just »system-relevant« ones) to continue to be able to work (and, above all, to do so on the terms preferred by employers), i.e. in the debate about avoiding daycare and school closures, there is obviously a massive economic interest at work, which is all too often hidden behind supposedly well-meaning arguments and which, in the course of the controversy about the renewed closure of educational institutions in the face of a »third« and now also »fourth wave«, has asserted itself against all epidemiological evidence.

One must therefore conclude that pandemic control always reached its limits precisely where it touched and potentially restricted the autonomy of the economic field. Even the toughest measures of pandemic control cannot hide the fact that the »Covid society« remains a capitalist society in which – in field-theoretical terms – the economic field enjoys by far the greatest autonomy and is able to enforce its principles beyond its own field boundaries. Where, for example, the state took the traditionally strongly heteronomous field of cultural production[103] quite quickly and permanently on a short leash with its »right hand« (in order to then promise support with its »left hand«)[104], it granted the strongly autonomous economic field over long stretches a comparatively remarkable room for maneuver not covered by virology and epidemiology, which is not least due to the dependence of the »left hand« on tax revenues and thus the structural dependence of the state on the economic field.

8. The State and the Relative Autonomy of Social Fields: Toward a Comparative Sociology of Pandemic Management

The examples of the relation between the religious and the economic field on the one hand and the field of the nation-state on the other hand make it clear that the assumptions of a) an always only relative autonomy of fields as well as b) the accompanying contestedness and variability of their autonomy and corresponding

---

[103] Cf. Bourdieu: The Rules of Art.
[104] Cf. Bourdieu: La main gauche et la main droite de l'État.

power relations are capable of illuminating some peculiarities of German »Covid politics« that remain invisible from a systems-theoretical perspective or must simply appear as anomalies. The reading proposed here, however, also allows us to critically confront another group of positions that are, to a certain extent, diametrically opposed to the systems-theoretical perspective: I will classify these here somewhat crudely as »neo-Marxist« approaches and draw on two recent contributions by some of the central representatives in the German-speaking context, Stephan Lessenich and Klaus Dörre, as examples.[105]

For Lessenich, the pandemic policy since the spring of 2020 manifests a »*double bind* of democratic-capitalist state intervention«[106], in which »economic interests of production and social interests of reproduction«[107] must be mediated. In terms of this double logic, the state has deployed the entire range of its classical »governance resources«[108] – though by no means in order to thereby place human life *per se* above profit interests, but rather to save »*certain* lives«[109]. This »politics with life« turns out to be at the same time a policy of double exclusion, since the state as a democratic *nation*-state pursues a particularistic »protection of the natives« and at the same time as a *capitalist* state »aims at producing or restoring the working capacity« of the employed part of the population.[110] Similarly, Dörre describes the pandemic as an impact on an *interregnum* characterized by (quasi-)Bonapartist democracies, driving the state into a twofold crisis (»Zangenkrise«[111]), which is responded to with the help of two types of state intervention: by intervening in all spheres of society and enforcing rules of exception, on the one hand, and an »anti-recession interventionism« on the other, »aimed at stabilizing and rebuilding the economy«.[112] Dörre emphasizes more clearly than Lessenich that »the state in capitalism is not a mere committee of ruling classes« – in the spirit of Poulantzas: not a »homogeneous actor, but a social relation«[113], but precisely such a relation that is primarily based »on the material condensation of power relations

---

[105] This juxtaposition is similar to that made in Rosa: Pfadabhängigkeit, Bifurkationspunkte und die Rolle der Soziologie, whose contribution, together with the texts by Dörre and Lessenich cited here, forms a »controversy« in the *Berliner Journal für Soziologie*.

[106] Lessenich: Soziologie – Corona – Kritik, p. 221; emph. in the orig.

[107] Ibid., pp. 220f.

[108] Ibid., p. 223.

[109] Ibid., p. 221; emph. in the orig.

[110] Ibid., p. 222. As much as I agree with the first part of Lessenich's diagnosis – a nationalistic narrowing of the concept of life or of »life worth protecting« – this second assumption seems problematic to me. The article does not (as far as I can see) answer the obvious question of why the protection of the old and sick was paramount in pandemic policy – or whether Lessenich would already consider this an inaccurate (ideological?) description.

[111] Dörre: Die Corona-Pandemie, p. 167 et passim.

[112] Ibid., p. 175.

[113] Ibid., pp. 181f.

between classes and class fractions«[114]. This is exactly why the state under the sign of Covid-19 turns out to be a »hybrid« insofar as the »economic state [...] has to spoon out the soup that its unequal twin, the exceptional state, has made for it«.[115]

Whereas for systems theory the capacity of the state to act and to »govern into« other function systems itself becomes an explanatory problem, this potency of the state appears to neo-Marxist authors as an »everyday reality«[116], since through it the interests of the ruling class (and especially the interests of capital) are realized essentially or at least to a considerable extent. Despite all the differences in the details (within as well as between the two »schools«), however, both conceptions ultimately fail to recognize the always relative character of the autonomy of fields (and here: of the state). In one case, the state is denied the ability to act at all as a central governance instance and social »veto player«[117]; in the other case, even the »naturally« strong state appears merely as a stooge of capital (although that strength results precisely from this). With this opposing exaggeration of field-specific autonomies (here: the autonomy of the state *alone* and the capitalist economy watching behind it, there: the absolutely set autonomy of *all* function systems, also vis-à-vis the state and the economy), both perspectives are dealing with explanatory difficulties that clearly come to light in the present case: Systems-theoretical approaches cannot (satisfactorily) explain how politics was able to intervene in all areas of society at all, as the representatives of this school of thought themselves – surprisingly – had to admit at the beginning of the pandemic; neo-Marxist approaches, on the other hand, cannot (satisfactorily) explain why parts of the economic field could be restricted at all, why high economic costs could be incurred and why, for example, the religious field was so generously left out of the lockdown measures.

Thus the theoretical discussion of the Covid-19 pandemic – not surprisingly – varies patterns of argumentation and dichotomies that are already familiar from the general sociological discourse of global modernity: Here, the rash dismissal of the nation-state as a powerful actor in global society; there, an overemphasis on the nation-state's structuring of global sociality, which, where it is accompanied by the unreflective use of »state« categories and reference systems, leads into a sociological reproduction of »state thinking«[118] and methodological nationalism.[119] But a comparative perspective also reveals a second parallel to the globalization debate: as in its early days in the 1990s, sociology – across theoretical preferences –

---

[114] Dörre: Ausnahmezustand, p. 31.
[115] Dörre: Die Corona-Pandemie, p. 182.
[116] Ibid., p. 183.
[117] Nassehi: Das große Nein, p. 68.
[118] Bourdieu: On the State, p. 3.
[119] Beck/Grande: Jenseits des methodologischen Nationalismus; cf. Schmitz/Witte: Der Nationalstaat und das globale Feld der Macht.

seems initially fascinated by the *homogeneity* and *uniformity* of state responses on a global scale. For example, Anicker speaks of a »factually largely coherent world policy« against the background of »astonishingly uniform political preventive measures«;[120] Stichweh also emphasizes that in the first phase of the pandemic »all nation-states and territorial states make roughly the same decisions«;[121] but also Rosa, for instance, is surprised about »astonishingly similar reactions of nation-states worldwide«.[122] In view of the reliance of political actors on scientific expertise (also cited by Stichweh as an explanation), this similarity does not seem at all surprising; above all, however, the focus on similarities at the same time obscures substantial differences between these political reactions in a way that is reminiscent of widespread assumptions of homogeneity in the early globalization debate, in world society theory, or in neoinstitutionalism (in the sense of Meyer et al.). Nevertheless, these *differences* in pandemic management seem to open up the ultimately more interesting sociological research questions: Indeed, at this point, very different modes of dealing with Covid-19 can be observed, as shown not only by the now much-cited comparisons with many Asian societies or testing strategies in African countries, but already within the European Union by the equally widely debated Swedish »special way« or the particularly »tough« course of Spain; and in fact, the interim report of the 16-country *Comparative Covid Response* project reaches quite different conclusions here, namely that »policies were far from uniform, and countries with differing institutions, research traditions, cultural commitments, and routinized ways of decision making pursued their own directions«, which systematically led to »wide discrepancies in the efficacy of responses to the pandemic«.[123] From the perspective of a sociological research program that identifies the *variability* of patterns and cultures of social differentiation as the central problem of a theory of society that is also interested in comparative questions,[124] a fruitful field of research could be opened up here, in which questions of different cultures of measures and sanctions could be brought into focus, especially against the background of cultural specifics *and* differently developed settings of field relations. A prerequisite for this, however, would be a relativization of those still influential isomorphism assumptions – which were also dominant for a time in the discourse on globalization, but which have gradually receded into the background as a result of increasing interest in comparative research questions and pluralistic understandings of global modernity.

---

[120] Anicker: Die Medizinisierung der Gesellschaft, p. 174.
[121] Stichweh: Simplifikation des Sozialen, p. 200.
[122] Rosa: Pfadabhängigkeit, Bifurkationspunkte und die Rolle der Soziologie, p. 201.
[123] Jasanoff et al.: Comparative Covid Response, pp. 10, 24. Cf. also Lehmann: Legal System Reactions.
[124] As a first sketch cf. Witte: Schließungsverhältnisse und Differenzierungskulturen; for an elaborated research program see Witte: Differenzierung als Praxis (forthcoming).

Central from a field-theoretical point of view is then the question of how and to what extent *which* state succeeded in temporarily expanding its autonomy vis-à-vis other fields (including the economy) in the course of combating the pandemic. Indicators for this would be, for example, the extent of the (differential) restriction of fundamental rights, the acceptance and adoption of the genuinely political calculus of the »state of emergency« in other fields (for example, in legal practice), but also the degree of curtailment of economic freedoms. Moreover, short-, medium- and long-term shifts in the balances of power could be observed not only between but also *within* social fields. To give just a few examples: In Germany, for instance, autonomy gains of a specific *segment* of the political field could be observed in the medium term, when the Conference of Minister Presidents, which was largely decoupled from the parliamentary process and secured by the pandemic protection laws, discussed in a small leadership circle how to deal with infection figures, decided quasi-decretistically on new measures and subsequently »informed« its citizens. If lockdown measures put retailers even further on the defensive against large e-Commerce companies, shifts within the economic field can also be expected in the long run, and the uneven distribution of burdens, e.g., through »home schooling« and care work, is also likely to have implications for the distribution of capitals in a wide variety of fields (including academia, for example).

Outlook: The Normalization of the Fragmentary

Finally, it should be emphasized once again that field theory not only assumes that the autonomy of social spheres is always a relative measure, but it also conceives of the relations between fields as variable and changeable in principle, as dynamic outcomes of social struggles that can never be brought to a complete standstill. It thus insists (in contrast to the systems-theoretical perspective) that the relations between the various social fields can also be described as balances of power, but on the other hand denies (more strongly than neo-Marxist approaches) their unambiguity and immutability. Minor shifts within these balances thus appear as an aspect of the normal state of society, while major upheavals (or in extreme cases: »symbolic revolutions«) are rare but by no means impossible. Crisis-like shocks to doxic social self-understandings (as they manifest themselves, for example, in the social discourse of self-assurance about the »systemic relevance« of different occupational groups), however, constitute precisely a factor that is predestined to increase the intensity of these social struggles over field-specific resources, world views, and claims to autonomy, and thus also to call field relations into question.

Thus, there is no »corona determinism«[125] for a field-theoretical approach either, as Dörre puts it in another context; rather, the crisis has temporarily destabilized established relations and thereby also opened a door for political action in a sense that goes far beyond the role of state institutions, and thematically also beyond the handling of Covid-19 and other pandemics.

In this way, the pandemic simultaneously seems to underscore the »fragmentary character« of modern sociality that Georg Simmel discussed 100 years ago.[126] On the level of differentiation theory, a *general* shift of balances between social fields (even a »medicalization of society«) does not seem to me to be a taxable conclusion. Even if, in view of further challenges of the present (climate change, artificial intelligence, bioethics, etc.), it is possibly to be expected (and in some respects also to be hoped) that a process of »scientification« of various sub-fields (but especially of politics), which has already been diagnosed for decades, will gain further traction: What can be observed at present is perhaps rather the result of an as yet undecided confrontation between various social orders and forces, of a break-up of established relations and of a struggle for field-specific interests and interpretative sovereignties, which – conversely – manifests itself precisely in an increasing *politicization of the (natural) sciences*. The orientation of politics towards scientific knowledge, which was initially considered remarkable, now seems to have been pulverized between particular interests and clientelism and to give way to a pragmatic »cherry picking«. In this context, the »misuse of scientific arguments in political debate« that none other than Christian Drosten deplored and described as bordering on science denial,[127] could be described as an attempt at pseudo-scientification from various positions in the political field that merely parasitizes certain semantics of the scientific field, but places them in the service of genuine political interests. However, other shifts in power relations seem similarly likely, both between different fields in the field of power and within the respective social fields – for example, a resurgence of the nation-state field (quite paradoxical given the global nature of the pandemic) or fundamental transformations of the field of cultural production in favor of hitherto heteronomous forces.

At the same time, the overheating of public discourse and its fragmentation into sub-publics with not only different political positions but rather competing interpretations of »reality« underscores a process that has already been imposing itself on the sociological gaze for some years now and is being fueled not least by digitalization and social media. This process includes the comparatively banal fragmentation of society along interests and other, most diverse characteristics (poor versus rich, young versus old, liberal versus conservative, vaccinated versus unvaccinated,

---

[125] Dörre: Die Corona-Pandemie, p. 169.
[126] Simmel: The Fragmentary Character of Life.
[127] NDR: Coronavirus-Update (Podcast), episode 82.

etc.), but at the same time it goes far beyond this, revealing highly heterogeneous milieus and ways of life and thus at the same time a fissured epistemic landscape. The epistemic dimension of the crisis thus not only demonstrates the fragility of social normality, but also normalizes the existence of a plurality of fragmentary approaches to the world. The fact that these approaches increasingly include those who take the irritation of normality as an opportunity not only to repair a damaged reality, but also to escalate these irritations, in some cases to the point of completely losing touch with reality, must give pause for thought in terms of the sociology of knowledge, is already highly alarming politically, and will also represent an enormous challenge for the foundations of modern societies in the medium and long term – and especially with a view to the pressing issues of climate change.

Ultimately, however, if a prognosis can be ventured at all, at least an intensified *politicization* of social field relations and discourses seems likely – now understood in a broader sense of the questioning of the *status quo* and the temporary fragilization of field relations in the field of power. The fact that in this process the relative autonomy of *certain* fields could remain largely untouched (for example, that of the economic field), that for some fields (for example, the nation-state) a massive gain in autonomy is already becoming apparent, while others (for example, the fields of cultural production or individual scientific disciplines) are likely to be even more strongly characterized by heteronomous influences in the future, or that *certain* field relations could be stabilized and downright *depoliticized* in the long term as a result – all this is not denied, but on the contrary even seems likely. If the Covid-19 pandemic has brought one thing home, it is the fragility of our social reality, the constantly contested and thus also malleable nature of the relations between social fields, and the fragmentary and particularistic character of the world views and stakes with which the actors involved enter into these dynamics.

References

Alexy, Robert: Theorie der Grundrechte, Frankfurt am Main 1986.
Anicker, Fabian: Die Medizinisierung der Gesellschaft. Eine differenzierungstheoretische Skizze zur Corona-Pandemie, in: Zeitschrift für Theoretische Soziologie 9(2), 2020, pp. 173–183.
Baumann, Menno et al.: Eine neue proaktive Zielsetzung für Deutschland zur Bekämpfung von SARS-CoV-2, January 18, 2021, https://www.cassis.uni-bonn.de/de/dateien/strategiepapier-no-covid-plan; last accessed June 30, 2021.
Beck, Ulrich: Das Zeitalter der Nebenfolgen und die Politisierung der Moderne, in: id./Anthony Giddens/Scott Lash: Reflexive Modernisierung. Eine Kontroverse, Frankfurt am Main 1996, pp. 19–112.

Beck, Ulrich: Weltrisikogesellschaft, ökologische Krise und Technologiepolitik, in: Peter Massing (ed.): Gesellschaft neu verstehen. Aktuelle Gesellschaftstheorien und Zeitdiagnosen, 2. Aufl., Schwalbach/Ts. 2002, pp. 55–76.

Beck, Ulrich/Edgar Grande: Jenseits des methodologischen Nationalismus. Außereuropäische und europäische Variationen der Zweiten Moderne, in: Soziale Welt 61(3–4), 2010, pp. 187–216.

BDVI [Bund der Öffentlich bestellten Vermessungsingenieure e.V.]: Systemrelevanz der ÖbVI in der Corona-Krise, June 23, 2020, https://www.bdvi.de/de/forum/forum-artikel/2020-06-23-systemrelevanz-der-oebvi-der-corona-krise; last accessed June 30, 2021.

BMAS [Bundesministerium für Arbeit und Soziales] Liste der systemrelevanten Bereiche, March 30, 2020, archived at Wayback Machine: https://web.archive.org/web/20200524190221/https://www.bmas.de/DE/Schwerpunkte/Informationen-Corona/Kurzarbeit/liste-systemrelevante-bereiche.html; last accessed June 30, 2021.

Boltanski, Luc: Mysteries and Conspiracies. Detective Stories, Spy Novels and the Making of Modern Societies, Cambridge 2014.

Boltanski, Luc: On Critique. A Sociology of Emancipation, Cambridge 2011.

Boltanski, Luc: Rendre la réalité inacceptable. A propos de »La production de l'idéologie dominante«, Paris 2008.

Bonnet, Anne-Marie: Aren't So-Called Conspiracy Theories the Most Influential Art of Our Time?, in: Werner Gephart (ed.): In the Realm of Corona Normativities. A Momentary Snapshot of a Dynamic Discourse, Frankfurt am Main 2020, pp. 355–367.

Bourdieu, Pierre: La main gauche et la main droite de l'État, in: id.: Contre-feux. Propos pour servir à la résistance contre l'invasion néo-libérale, Paris 1998, pp. 9–17.

Bourdieu, Pierre: On the State. Lectures at the Collège de France, 1989–1992, ed. by Patrick Champagne, Remi Lenoir, Franck Poupeau and Marie-Christine Rivière, Cambridge/Malden, MA 2014.

Bourdieu, Pierre: The Rules of Art. Genesis and Structure of the Literary Field, Stanford, CA 1995.

Bourdieu, Pierre: The State Nobility. Elite Schools in the Field of Power, Cambridge/Oxford 1996.

Bourdieu, Pierre/Loïc J. D. Wacquant: An Invitation to Reflexive Sociology, Cambridge/Oxford 1992.

Brunet, Pierre: Nous sommes la raison du virus, in: Werner Gephart (ed.): In the Realm of Corona Normativities. A Momentary Snapshot of a Dynamic Discourse, Frankfurt am Main 2020, pp. 443–450.

Bundesregierung: Telefonschaltkonferenz der Bundeskanzlerin mit den Regierungschefinnen und Regierungschefs der Länder am 30. April 2020 (Beschluss), https://www.bundesregierung.de/resource/blob/975226/1749804/353e4b4c77a4d9a724347ccb688d3558/2020-04-30-beschluss-bund-laender-data.pdf?download=1; last accessed June 30, 2021.

BVerfG [Bundesverfassungsgericht]: Gottesdienstverbot bedarf als überaus schwerwiegender Eingriff in die Glaubensfreiheit einer fortlaufenden strengen Prüfung seiner Verhältnismäßigkeit anhand der jeweils aktuellen Erkenntnisse. Pressemitteilung Nr. 24/2020 vom 10. April 2020, https://www.bundesverfassungsgericht.de/SharedDocs/Pressemitteilungen/DE/2020/bvg20-024.html; last accessed June 30, 2021.

Chevé, Dominique / Michel Signoli: Les corps de la contagion corps atteints, corps souffrants, corps inquiétants, corps exclus?, in: Corps. Revue interdisciplinaire 5(2), 2008, pp. 11–14.

Condello, Angela: Immersed in a Normative Laboratory, in: Werner Gephart (ed.): In the Realm of Corona Normativities. A Momentary Snapshot of a Dynamic Discourse, Frankfurt am Main 2020, pp. 129–134.

Dörre, Klaus: Ausnahmezustand. Zur Politischen Ökonomie einer Seuche, in: spw. Zeitschrift für sozialistische Politik und Wirtschaft 43(2), 2020, pp. 26–32.

Dörre, Klaus: Die Corona-Pandemie – eine Katastrophe mit Sprengkraft, in: Berliner Journal für Soziologie 30(2), 2020, pp. 165–190.

Dorn, Florian / Clemens Fuest / Marcell Göttert / Carla Krolage / Stefan Lautenbacher / Robert Lehmann / Sebastian Link / Sascha Möhrle / Andreas Peichl / Magnus Reif / Stefan Sauer / Marc Stöckli / Klaus Wohlrabe / Timo Wollmershäuser: The Economic Costs of the Coronavirus Shutdown for Selected European Countries: A Scenario Calculation (EconPol Policy Brief 25), München 2020.

Dreier, Horst: Dimensionen der Grundrechte. Von der Wertordnungsjudikatur zu den objektiv-rechtlichen Grundrechtsgehalten, Hannover 1993.

Durkheim, Emile: Professional Ethics and Civic Morals, with a new Preface by Bryan S. Turner, London / New York 1992.

Franzen, Martina: Was heißt Systemrelevanz?, in: SozBlog. Blog der Deutschen Gesellschaft für Soziologie (DGS), April 30, 2020, http://blog.soziologie.de/2020/04/was-heisst-systemrelevanz/; last accessed June 30, 2021.

Gabriel, Markus: Die meisten liberalen Demokratien haben eine Ausgangssperre verhängt – doch ist sie, ethisch betrachtet, wirklich gerechtfertigt?, in: Neue Zürcher Zeitung, March 26, 2020, https://www.nzz.ch/feuilleton/coronavirus-warum-der-virologische-imperativ-auch-gefaehrlich-ist-ld.1548594; last accessed June 30, 2021.

Gallie, Walter B.: Essentially Contested Concepts, in: Proceedings of the Aristotelian Society 56, 1956, pp. 167–198.

Gather, Claudia: Der Markt wird's nicht richten – Löhne in der Care Ökonomie, in: SozBlog. Blog der Deutschen Gesellschaft für Soziologie (DGS), December

07, 2020, http://blog.soziologie.de/2020/12/der-markt-wirds-nicht-richten-loehne-in-der-care-oekonomie/; last accessed June 30, 2021.

Gephart, Werner (ed.): In the Realm of Corona Normativities. A Momentary Snapshot of a Dynamic Discourse, Frankfurt am Main 2020.

Gephart, Werner: Conclusion: »Communal« Dimensions of the Corona Crisis and the Rise of a New Validity Culture, in: id. (ed.): In the Realm of Corona Normativities. A Momentary Snapshot of a Dynamic Discourse, Frankfurt am Main 2020, pp. 509–517.

Greve, Jens: Corona aus Sicht der Soziologie. Alles wie im Krieg? (Interview), in: Münchner Ärztliche Anzeigen, April 09, 2020, https://www.aerztliche-anzeigen.de/leitartikel/corona-aus-sicht-der-soziologie-alles-wie-im-krieg; last accessed June 30, 2021.

Hanske, Theresa: Knigge in Times of Corona – Recognition, Attentiveness and Esteem, in: Werner Gephart (ed.): In the Realm of Corona Normativities. A Momentary Snapshot of a Dynamic Discourse, Frankfurt am Main 2020, pp. 215–219.

Hartmann, Kathrin: Das kommt nicht von außen, in: Der Freitag, March 19, 2020, https://www.freitag.de/autoren/der-freitag/das-kommt-nicht-von-aussen; last accessed June 30, 2021.

Janson, Matthias: 13 Prozent der Wirtschaft direkt von Lockdown betroffen, in: Statista, February 02, 2021, https://de.statista.com/infografik/24068/anteile-der-wirtschaftsbereiche-an-der-gesamten-bruttowertschoepfung-deutschlands/; last accessed June 30, 2021.

Jasanof, Sheila / Stephen Hilgartner / J. Benjamin Hurlbut / Onur Özgöde / Margarita Rayzberg: Comparative Covid Response: Crisis, Knowledge, Politics. Interim Report, January 12, 2021, https://assets.website-files.com/5fdfca1c14b4b91eeaa7196a/5ffda00d50fca2e6f8782aed_Harvard-Cornell%20Report%202020.pdf; last accessed June 30, 2021.

Kingreen, Torsten: Ist das Kunst? Dann kann das weg!, in: Verfassungsblog, November 04, 2020, https://verfassungsblog.de/ist-das-kunst-dann-kann-das-weg/; last accessed June 30, 2021.

Lehmann, Matthias: Legal System Reactions to Covid-19: Global Patterns and Cultural Varieties, in: Werner Gephart (ed.): In the Realm of Corona Normativities. A Momentary Snapshot of a Dynamic Discourse, Frankfurt am Main 2020, pp. 183–193.

Lessenich, Stephan: Soziologie – Corona – Kritik, in: Berliner Journal für Soziologie 30(2), 2020, pp. 215–230.

Luhmann, Niklas: Grundrechte als Institution. Ein Beitrag zur politischen Soziologie, Berlin 1965.

Luhmann, Niklas: Die Weltgesellschaft, in: Archiv für Rechts- und Sozialphilosophie 57(1), 1971, pp. 1–35.

Luhmann, Niklas: Die Unterscheidung von Staat und Gesellschaft, in: id.: Soziologische Aufklärung 4. Beiträge zur funktionalen Differenzierung der Gesellschaft, Opladen 1987, pp. 67–73.

Luhmann, Niklas: Das Recht der Gesellschaft, Frankfurt am Main 1993.

Luhmann, Niklas: Die Politik der Gesellschaft, ed. by André Kieserling, Frankfurt am Main 2000.

Marx, Karl: Zur Kritik der Hegelschen Rechtsphilosophie. Einleitung, in: Karl Marx / Friedrich Engels: Werke (MEW), Bd. 1, Berlin 1976, pp. 378–391.

Minkmar, Nils / Ulrich Beck: Über den Merkiavellismus, in: Frankfurter Allgemeine Zeitung, January 16, 2013, https://www.faz.net/aktuell/feuilleton/debatten/im-gespraech-soziologe-ulrich-beck-ueber-den-merkiavellismus-12027300.html; last accessed June 30, 2021.

Nassehi, Armin: »Es passiert gerade etwas, von dem wir immer gesagt haben: Das geht nicht« (Interview von Tobias Rapp), in: Der Spiegel, April 01, 2020, https://www.spiegel.de/kultur/soziologe-ueber-corona-ich-freue-mich-wenn-die-normalen-krisen-wieder-da-sind-a-72abdc71-b2a3-4bdf-9964-c34ff33e24b8; last accessed June 30, 2021.

Nassehi, Armin: Nicht Einzelne sind infiziert, sondern die ganze Gesellschaft, in: Der Tagesspiegel, April 11, 2020, https://www.tagesspiegel.de/politik/ueber-die-hyperkomplexitaet-der-corona-krise-nicht-einzelne-sind-infiziert-sondern-die-ganze-gesellschaft/25733056.html; last accessed June 30, 2021.

Nassehi, Armin: Das große Nein. Eigendynamik und Tragik des gesellschaftlichen Protests, Hamburg 2020.

NDR: Coronavirus-Update (Podcast), Folge 82: Die Lage ist ernst, March 31., 2021. Transcript: https://www.ndr.de/nachrichten/info/82-Coronavirus-Update-Die-Lage-ist-ernst,podcastcoronavirus300.html; last accessed June 30, 2021.

Pedersen, Frode Helmich: A Pandemic of Narratives, in: Werner Gephart (ed.): In the Realm of Corona Normativities. A Momentary Snapshot of a Dynamic Discourse, Frankfurt am Main 2020, pp. 409–417.

Popitz, Heinrich: Über die Präventivwirkung des Nichtwissens. Dunkelziffer, Norm und Strafe, Tübingen 1968.

Priesemann, Viola / Melanie M. Brinkmann / Sandra Ciesek / Sarah Cuschieri / Thomas Czypionka / Giulia Giordano / Deepti Gurdasani / Claudia Hanson / Niel Hens / Emil Iftekhar / Michelle Kelly-Irving / Peter Klimek / Mirjam Kretzschmar / Andreas Peichl / Matjaž Perc / Francesco Sannino / Eva Schernhammer / Alexander Schmidt / Anthony Staines / Ewa Szczurek: Calling for Pan-European Commitment for Rapid and Sustained Reduction in SARS-CoV-2 Infections, in: The Lancet 397(10269), 2021, pp. 92–93.

Renn, Joachim: Übersetzungsverhältnisse: Perspektiven einer pragmatistischen Gesellschaftstheorie, Weilerswist 2006.

Rosa, Hartmut: Pfadabhängigkeit, Bifurkationspunkte und die Rolle der Soziologie. Ein soziologischer Deutungsversuch der Corona-Krise, in: Berliner Journal für Soziologie 30(2), 2020, pp. 191–213.

Scheffer, Thomas: Existenzielle Probleme, *soziologisch*, in: Zeitschrift für Theoretische Soziologie 10(1), 2021, pp. 3–33.

Schmitz, Andreas / Daniel Witte: Der Nationalstaat und das globale Feld der Macht, oder: Wie sich die Feldtheorie von ihrem methodologischen Nationalismus befreien lässt, in: Zeitschrift für Theoretische Soziologie 6(2), 2017, pp. 156–188.

Schneickert, Christian / Andreas Schmitz / Daniel Witte: Das Feld der Macht. Eliten – Differenzierung – Globalisierung, Wiesbaden 2020.

Schwering, Markus / Jürgen Habermas: Jürgen Habermas über Corona: »So viel Wissen über unser Nichtwissen gab es noch nie« (Interview mit Markus Schwering), in: Frankfurter Rundschau, April 10, 2020, https://www.fr.de/kultur/gesellschaft/juergen-habermas-coronavirus-krise-covid19-interview-13642491.html; last accessed June 30, 2021.

Simmel, Georg: The Fragmentary Character of Life, in: Theory, Culture & Society 29(7/8), 2012, pp. 237–248.

Stichweh, Rudolf: Simplifikation des Sozialen, in: Michael Volkmer / Karin Werner (ed.): Die Corona-Gesellschaft. Analysen zur Lage und Perspektiven für die Zukunft, Bielefeld 2020, pp. 197–206.

Suntrup, Jan Christoph: Corona: Biopolitical Models and the Hygiene of Tact, in: Werner Gephart (ed.): In the Realm of Corona Normativities. A Momentary Snapshot of a Dynamic Discourse, Frankfurt am Main 2020, pp. 137–145.

Villa, Paula-Irene: Corona-Krise meets Care-Krise – Ist das systemrelevant?, in: Leviathan 48(3), 2020, pp. 433–450.

Wacquant, Loïc J. D. / Pierre Bourdieu: Das Feld der Macht und die technokratische Herrschaft. Loïc J. D. Wacquant im Gespräch mit Pierre Bourdieu anläßlich des Erscheinens von »La Noblesse d'État«, in: Pierre Bourdieu: Die Intellektuellen und die Macht, ed. by Irene Dölling, Hamburg 1991, pp. 67–100.

Weaving, Simon: Scary Red or Icky Green? We Can't Say What Colour Coronavirus Is and Dressing It Up Might Feed Fears, in: The Conversation, March 30, 2020, https://theconversation.com/scary-red-or-icky-green-we-cant-say-what-colour-coronavirus-is-and-dressing-it-up-might-feed-fears-134380; last accessed June 30, 2021.

WHO [World Health Organization]: Immunizing the Public against Misinformation, Augsut 25, 2020, https://www.who.int/news-room/feature-stories/detail/immunizing-the-public-against-misinformation; last accessed: June 30, 2021.

Winker, Gabriele: Aufbau einer solidarischen und nachhaltigen Care-Ökonomie. Ein Plädoyer in Zeiten von Corona, in: Michael Volkmer / Karin Werner (ed.): Die Corona-Gesellschaft. Analysen zur Lage und Perspektiven für die Zukunft, Bielefeld 2020, pp. 395–404.

Witte, Daniel: Ein ambivalentes Erbe: Von Durkheims (un-)politischer Soziologie zu Bourdieus Religionssoziologie des Staates, in: Berliner Journal für Soziologie 28(3–4), 2019, pp. 307–337.

Witte, Daniel: Passing the Torch: From Durkheim's Statism to Bourdieu's Critique of the State, in: Werner Gephart / Daniel Witte (eds.): The Sacred and the Law: The Durkheimian Legacy, Frankfurt am Main 2017, pp. 229–262.

Witte, Daniel: Schließungsverhältnisse und Differenzierungskulturen. Überlegungen zur relationalen Formatierung von sozialem Ausschluss, in: Stephan Lessenich (ed.): Geschlossene Gesellschaften. Verhandlungen des 38. Kongresses der Deutschen Gesellschaft für Soziologie in Bamberg 2016, 2017, http://publikationen.soziologie.de/index.php/kongressband_2016/article/view/536; last accessed June 30, 2021.

Witte, Daniel: Virologischer Imperativ oder temporäre Destabilisierung? Feldtheoretische Anmerkungen zur soziologischen Reflexion der Corona-Krise, in: Zeitschrift für Theoretische Soziologie 10(1), 2021, pp. 85–113.

Yates, Simon: All the Coronavirus in the World Could Fit Inside a Coke Can, With Plenty of Room to Spare, in: The Conversation, February 10, 2021, https://theconversation.com/all-the-coronavirus-in-the-world-could-fit-inside-a-coke-can-with-plenty-of-room-to-spare-154226; last accessed June 30, 2021.

Marta Bucholc

The Quest for Herd Immunity: Coronavirus and the Two Global Civilizing Offensives of 2020–2021*

Fast-spreading epidemic diseases bring to the fore two apparently contradictory tendencies in human societies. On the one hand, epidemics have a cruel way of reminding us about the fundamental fact of human interdependence, both in the micro- and in macroscale, exactly at the point at which some of us might wish to forget that whatever we do and wherever we are, we are never and can never be isolated from other people. The fundamental human sociability, which we usually perceive as unequivocally positive and valuable, displays its morose, threatening face in times when human encounter – any human encounter – is essentially bad news. On the other hand, while human touch and human encounter usually are the key mechanism for spreading the epidemic diseases and their resultant calamities, human solidarity, cooperation and mobilization are instrumental in minimizing the toll of the disease on human life, health, and well-being. Thus, by behaving less human, we are becoming more humane: by reducing our mutual interdependencies through limitations of our human sociability, we are serving the cause of our universal humanity.

It would still be premature to present a detailed chronology and periodization of the pandemic as a global phenomenon. Since early 2020 we have gathered plenty of evidence for the global community of fate, but also for exceptionalisms and idiosyncrasies, which have revived the old stereotypes dormant in intergroup perceptions, especially on the international level. We have seen small envies raise their ugly heads and black despair fall on hearts when our fellow humans in some other countries tended to fall sick or die less often than we did, we have seen blaming of some national governments and self-praise of some others, depending on whether their chosen strategies for dealing with the pandemic seemed to work or not. We have also seen the irony of it all, when some of those self-praising had to face their final impotence, and some of those declared incapable of action demonstrated resilience of which nobody would have suspected them. We have

---

* The author acknowledges the support of Polish National Science Centre (»National habitus formation and the process of civilization in Poland after 1989: a figurational approach«, 2019/34/E/HS6/00295). I am grateful to Marta Gospodarczyk for her kind assistance in editing the first version of this paper.

faced the unpredictability and the incalculability of the pandemic process which – we knew but forgot – should be associated with the expression *force of nature*. At the end of May 2021, the trajectory of the pandemic in some countries seems to be heading towards the end, while in some others the situation remains tragic with few portents of a change for the better. However, if any attempt at a periodization could be made, I would argue that the first phase of struggle against the pandemic, which I will call here the *social distancing phase*, is currently, since the beginning of vaccinations worldwide, being replaced with what I will call *the quest for herd immunity*.

In this chapter, I first offer a brief interpretation of the phenomenon of herd immunity in sociological terms in order to move on to elaborate on the current quest for herd immunity using Norbert Elias's theory of the process of civilization and in particular the concept of the *civilizing offensive* which has been developed in Dutch and British sociology since the 1970s. I will argue that both the social distancing and prevention campaign since early 2020 and the vaccination campaign since (roughly) December 2021 are civilizing offensives whose effect is hampered by the fact that each of them play out one of the two contradictory tendencies in our social lives which are both enhanced by the pandemic. It is my view that the social distancing campaign of 2020 was essentially a *self-protection* campaign, while the quest for herd immunity is essentially a campaign for the *protection of the other*. While the trigger to both of them is one and the same – the threat by the pandemic disease – the civilizational rationale behind them is entirely different. To argue the point, I will briefly characterize the goals and methods of the civilizing offensive in the two phases of the struggle against the pandemic, to demonstrate the contradictions in their respective message – and anticipated outcomes. It is my thesis that we had not one, but two global civilizing offensives since 2020, and that the effects of the first one, the social distancing campaign, had an adverse effect on the success chances of the second one, which we witness now while our populations struggle to cross the threshold of the herd immunity.

1. A Sociological View of Herd Immunity

According to Encyclopædia Britannica, herd immunity, which is also called »community immunity«[1], refers to

»[a] state in which a large proportion of a population is able to repel an infectious disease, thereby limiting the extent to which the disease can spread from person to person. Herd immunity can be conferred through natural immunity, previous exposure to the disease,

---

[1] Lee: Herd Immunity.

or vaccination. An entire population does not need to be immune to attain herd immunity. Rather, herd immunity can occur when the population density of persons who are susceptible to infection is sufficiently low so as to minimize the likelihood of an infected individual coming in contact with a susceptible individual. Herd immunity can prevent sustained disease spread in populations, thereby protecting susceptible individuals from infection. It is applicable, however, only to infectious diseases that can be spread by human contact.«[2]

Herd immunity to an infectious disease is, thus, a typical case for rational choice style of theorizing: some of us can be safe, because most of us have gained the immunity to the disease one way or another. Apart from individuals endowed with a natural immunity to a disease (something which must be fairly rare in the population in case of any disease which ever managed to spread enough to earn the epithet *infectious*), either previous exposure to infection or a vaccination must happen often enough in the population to provide with safety also those who have not made any of the two experiences. The Majority can protect the minority, and the minority can benefit by the majority's actions. However, even though we all know the saying *you are the traffic* it is only natural to perceive the others as the traffic and ourselves as those who must stand alone in jams for hours because of the others riding their cars, single occupancy, for no good reason. In thinking about herd immunity, it is only natural to think of ourselves as those to be protected.

But why is that so natural in the first place? Contrary to what might be expected, the reason requires no deep excurse in the domain of individual psychology, rational choice is quite enough. The mechanism of herd immunity divides people into three categories (leaving aside those lucky ones with natural immunity, as the synonym of lucky is *statistically negligible*): those who have been sick and got better, those who have been vaccinated, and the others. Let us take a simple view of things and assume that being sick or being vaccinated gives us reliable immunity protection for a certain, specified time. Now, in such a case, if I had been sick or vaccinated, I am protected anyway, so I do not care about herd immunity as something protecting myself. On the whole, it is a rare idea to get infected on purpose in order to gain immunity.[3] But, those of us who get the vaccine do it for that reason precisely. So, if I am vaccinated, it is for my own protection, and I do not need to rely on herd immunity. If I am not otherwise immune, I can only be protected by others, hence, herd immunity is only relevant to me as far as I (or, let us extend it a bit, my nearest and dearest) belong to the minority which will be protected by it despite not being immune themselves.

However, could I not get vaccinated for the protection of others around me? Do I really only consider myself as the member of the herd protected by others,

---

[2] Ibid.
[3] But it has been heard of: some parents deliberately expose their children to infection with *child diseases* such as chickenpox by having them participate in so-called *pox parties*.

and not as the individual protecting others by exposing myself to the protective behavior (the vaccine)? Now, here the rational choice theory comes in: my individual contribution to the protection of those around me is, statistically speaking, negligible. While I can ensure my own protection to a very considerable extent by getting the vaccine, it only helps those around me very little – unless a big enough fraction of the population decides to do the same. But why would any particular individual do it, if they may reasonably count that others will undergo the unpleasant and potentially risky ordeal of the vaccine and in that manner contribute to their protection?

I am, for the purpose of clarity only, not discussing the position of those members of the community which cannot opt for the vaccine for medical reasons or those, I think the saddest case of all, who cannot get the protection which the vaccine gives because they have been overlooked and excluded by the public health governance regimes, be it in the national or in the global scale. The ethical weight of herd immunity is, however, not in any way reduced by these considerations. First of all, herd immunity also protects those who really cannot be otherwise protected. Second, as soon as the herd immunity is achieved by the societies of the world which are privileged in terms of vaccine distribution, and always assuming that human nature, though possibly egoistic, is really *human* in any sense of the word, the probability should increase of the vaccines becoming available to those closing the global pecking order. However, in a nation state society which provides its members with reasonably reliable access to vaccination opportunities, those who do not take the vaccine will be those who could but choose not to. And, for each of them, their potential contribution to the society's herd immunity would be marginal, anyway. Of course, as a result of the marginal individual contributions, the herd immunity may not be achieved. But, accounting for the conditions which might be relevant for our choice whether or not to get the vaccine, it is beyond doubt that no single person can be identified who could influence the outcome in any direction.

I do apologize to my reader for this lengthy elaboration on the rational-choice interpretation of the concept of herd immunity. The goal of this chapter is obviously not to explore the limitations of human rationality, the chances of dying of thrombosis as a result of the vaccine, or the generational, economic, cultural, religious and other determinants of vaccine-related behavior. However, an understanding of the tension between the individual and communal dimension of an epidemic disease is crucial. Both individual and herd immunity can only be reached by individuals taking certain actions (unless, of course, individuals are forced to take them, which was, however, not practiced in most societies). But the reasons for protecting oneself and protecting others are very different in kind. This was clearly visible in the communication strategies adopted by many governments around the world during the Corona crisis.

2. One or Two Civilizing Offensives Against the Virus?

The term *civilising offensive* was first coined and then developed in the Netherlands in the circle of Bram de Swaan.[4] Initially, in the Dutch usage of the time it described »the deliberate, conscious attempts of powerful groups, including a historically paternalistic state, at altering the behaviour of sections of the population and inculcating lasting, ›civilised‹ habits«[5]. Stephen Mennell mentions the failed attempts of Fabian society ladies trying to persuade working class mothers to give their families porridge for breakfast as an instance of what he call the *emic* understanding of civilization: standards of behavior which a more powerful, established group strives to impose on the lower group perceived as less civilized in light of a particular standard, their own.[6] In this sense, the concept of a civilizing offensive has also been used to study

»contemporary, moralising government attempts at altering the conduct and behaviour of particular ›problematic‹ sections of the population […]. This development has coincided with the emergence of a more explicit and overt governmental and media discourse on what is perceived to be a social malaise, or de-civilising tendencies, within society […].«[7]

To this *emic* understanding of the concept of a *civilizing offensive* Mennell juxtaposes an *etic* version of it[8], which would refer to the theoretical meaning of the notion of civilization according to Norbert Elias.[9] The latter defined civilization as a process of pacification of society by way of consolidation of state (or: state-like) power corresponding to a structure of habitus in which the external constraints on individual use of violence are replaced by self-restraint, such change to be accompanied by changes in tastes, sensitivities and, crucially, in the scope of social identification and empathy of which typical individuals are capable as members of their respective social groups. The process of civilization entails a widening of the circles of identification: an expansion of the capacity to feel for others and with others beyond the boundaries of one's immediate social category.[10] For that reason, the process of civilization has been argued to be accompanied by a decrease in the barriers in interpersonal contacts resulting from deep differences of habitus manifest in the divergences of linguistic, esthetic, and emotional standards by which the behavior of individuals is judged by their environments. Civilization means more standardization, more unification of manners, but also more selective ways

---

[4] Cf. Mennell: Civilising Offensives and Decivilizing Processes.
[5] Powell: The Theoretical Concept of the ›Civilising Offensive‹.
[6] Cf. Mennell: Civilising Offensives and Decivilizing Processes.
[7] Powell: The Theoretical Concept of the ›Civilising Offensive‹.
[8] Cf. Mennell: Civilising Offensives and Decivilizing Processes.
[9] Cf. Elias: On the Process of Civilisation.
[10] Cf. De Swaan: Widening Circles of Identification, pp. 25–39.

of feeling, more attention to detail and more regard for another human being (or, indeed, another living creature in general).

A civilizing offensive in the etic sense would be an action aimed at and actually working toward an increase in civilization not in its social position-related normative understanding, but in the descriptive sense. At the first glance, the campaigns launched by the governments and supported variously by social organisations, churches and religious movements, celebrities and public intellectuals, etc. had all the traits of a civilizing offensive in the most basic etic sense of the term: their goal was to save human lives by influencing humans to refrain from behavior which might put it in danger, and to engage in behavior which required self-restraint and self-control.

2.1 Phase One: Social Distancing Campaign

I use the social distancing campaign as a general label for the stage in the struggle against the pandemic before a vaccine against Covid-19 became available. The goal of the campaign in this stage was to prevent the spreading of the disease as much as possible. The commonly advertised means of prevention included covering one's mouth and nose, which was initially discouraged, then encouraged, and the covering to be done with anything at hand, upon which the modes of covering evolved to exclude anything but a special type of a mask. Though most of research on mask-wearing is related to its medical and epidemiological aspects, some scholars raise the point of cultural significance of the practice and the insufficient sensitivity of public authorities to its implications.[11] While in some cultures wearing a face cover is more proliferate than in others, the sudden reduction of the means of facial expression by more than a half of the overall face surface (if not half of its expressive power) cannot but affect interpersonal communication (including verbal communication, with the general prevalence of mask-related mumbling), even though long-term studies of its effects have not, as yet, arrived. The means of prevention also included using disinfectants massively. This caused an ironic turn in attitudes towards disinfectant overuse prevalent in some circles, which had from time to time been censured heavily as contrary to reasonable immunity-building policy, especially in young children. But the crucial protective means from the point of view of the civilizing effect were those which affected the people's being together in one and the same place.

Arguably, the problems of being in one place were commonly framed as economic concerns, related to work organization, productivity, business survival, and the inequalities in the level of risk between various professional categories. Re-

---

[11] Cf. Timpka/Nyce: Face Mask Use During the COVID-19 Pandemic, pp. 1–4.

peated enraged narratives could be read of the well-paid white collars sitting comfortably at home (which frequently happened to be a rather large home with a garden) over their laptops and the *systemrelevant* classes, as the excellent German phrase went, who happen to earn rather less, enjoying their newly-gained system relevance travelling to their workplaces with public communication and spending hour and hour with shoulder to shoulder with other people in factories, hospitals and grocery stores. Not to mention the still others whose very livelihoods depend on people coming together, like performing artists, café and gym owners, etc. Another major framing was the educational one: the children and the youth not being able to get together in their respective educational institutions and suffering as a result, with the parents and other responsible persons suffering no less, and with gloomy predictions about the consequences of such a long-term deprivation.

If we consider the reactions to the prohibition for the people to come together, much of the media reports in the first phase of the pandemic were about people who are related (much less about those near and dear but unrelated, like teenagers in love) not being able to meet in flesh any more: children missing their grandparents, the elderly in the nursing homes missing their usual visitors, families not able to celebrate religious rites and traditional holidays together. A bit has also been said about the communities of choice, such as sport teams, kids' clubs, amateur choirs, and music bands: groups of people who used to do something together which required physical co-presence. However, interestingly enough, very little attention was given to the social relevance of the physical co-presence of strangers.

The difference between a stranger and a non-stranger is a crucial one for human societies, for a variety of reasons which have been discussed seminally by Georg Simmel in 1908 in his famous little essay on *The Stranger*.[12] To the Simmelian account Norbert Elias adds one important point: in proportion to the involvement of strangers in social lives of societies, the level of internal pacification of these societies increases. Which is the trigger and which is the result is less important for my argument than the fact the one of the markers of the process of civilization is the reduction of intergroup violence and, indeed, a reduction of groupness as such: individuals are getting more interdependent and social networks are getting denser and more inclusive. With the increase of the number of those with whom humans coexist and daily collaborate, the incidence of uncontrolled violence drops, and the size of the circles of identification rises.

What is the role of actual physical co-presence in this mechanism of civilization is not easily determined. On the one hand, self-restraint and self-control – just as external constraint and supervision – do have a strong physical component. Self-restraint means a certain molding of sensory perceptions, gestures and facial expressions, as well as the smells and the sounds produced by the body. The

---

[12] Cf. Simmel: The Stranger, pp. 402–408.

regard for others implied by the notion of the »*civilized behavior*« is reflected in the theoretical connection which Elias made between the formation of habitus and the figurations of a society. Humans behave in a way which corresponds to the way in which they are interconnected. While in each process of civilization there remain some dark corners which are not included in the general increase of self-restraint and where violence can be unleashed with relatively little sanction, those spheres would usually be delimitated rather clearly by way of what Bram de Swaan called »compartmentalization«[13]. If anything, civilisation enhances the difference between the general social sphere, which undergoes the process of »functional democratization«[14] (flattening of structures and growing interdependence). The reserves in which the standards of civilization are lowered or lifted altogether (such as the relations between parents and children, between men and women, or between the colonizers and the indigenous peoples). The compartments of lower standards may be huge and important in terms of their humanitarian, psychological, economic, environmental, and other significance. But the tendency over time would be for them to shrink, also as a result of external constraint, e. g. by law, but also by the simple expedient of more and more social spaces becoming freely available to strangers.

Let us now apply this reasoning to the social distancing in Phase 1 of the pandemic. The prohibitions to leave the house altogether (the furthest-reaching form of external constraint of physical co-presence), and the limitations of the number of persons and households which could be represented in a meeting immediately caused a reduction of contacts with strangers, and a shrinking of social spaces in which such interaction was possible. On the other hand, the uncontrolled sphere, inaccessible to strangers, grew to include everything which was not shown by the webcam device attached to their home computer and veiled by the virtual screen masking the background.

Many stories went viral in 2020 and 2021 of unexpected disturbances of the image produced by the digital communication media to which interaction migrated during the pandemic. Most of them, regardless of whether they would be about never getting out of the pajamas for months, only washing the front of your hair or sexual self-indulgence as a way of biding the time during an important meeting, show that the imposed privacy which could not be penetrated by strangers caused a relative reduction in the level of self-control related to physical appearance and forms of behavior. Other people – people from beyond one's immediate household – need not be regarded in any way beyond the range of the electronic interface. And let us remember that the number of single households is rising very

---

[13] Cf. De Swaan: Dyscivilisation, Mass Extermination and the State, pp. 265–276.
[14] Cf. Wouters: Functional Democratisation and Disintegration as Side-Effects of Differentiation and Integration Processes.

quickly in some parts of the world, as exemplified by the 19,5 % rise in the number of single households in the EU between 2010 and 2020. In 2020, in the EU the average number of people per household was 2.3.[15]

Much has been said about the rise of domestic violence under the pandemic and the exposure of the weaker members of our societies to the uncontrolled behavior of the stronger within the locked and impenetrable households.[16] I would argue that we should take the Eliasian line in interpreting the data on domestic violence: it is a part of the same phenomenon as lowering the standards related to physical self-presentation and limiting the possibility to go out and exercise self-restraint in behavior, speech and outlook alike when meeting strangers. Physical co-presence strengthens the disposition to show regard for others – and when there are no others to be regarded, the disposition wanes. Such was the state of our societies at the end of phase one: they were transforming into aggregates of semi-clause individuals or very small groups of individuals interconnected by electronic networks, with much fewer opportunities to collaborate, cooperate and orchestrate their behavior, and much fewer impulses pushing toward regard for others. The argument that the rationale for social-distancing was exactly the regard for others as potential victims of the pandemic is only partly valid: it lies in the nature of rational reasons that it is very difficult to bear them in mind constantly. Even though those social-distancing people were protecting the others, they were protecting them mostly by protecting themselves from getting infected. The strangers for whom we were social-distancing in the first phase of the pandemic became abstract and remote, pictures on the screen, figures in the graphs and statistics, bodiless and unattainable, defended from infection by our well-reasoned self-interest.

2.2 Phase Two: Quest for Herd Immunity

This was the state of our societies when the vaccine was finally there and the quest for herd immunity began.[17] The requirements regarding social distancing were not lifted, we were still from time to time called upon to stay at home, not travel, keep our distances when shopping, etc. But a new impulse was added to the list, to get vaccinated. Not as soon as possible, because the prioritization of age and other groups imposed order of immunization. But to get vaccinated at some point was the general imperative. It did not replace the imperative to distance from the oth-

---

15 Cf. Eurostat: Household Composition Statistics.
16 Cf. Boserup et al.: Alarming Trends in US Domestic Violence during the Covid-19 Pandemic, pp. 2753–2755; Bradbury-Jones/Isham: The Pandemic Paradox, pp. 2047–2049.
17 I disregard the sinusoidal movement of lockdowns and *returns to normality* in various countries and communities, even though they admittedly had an impact on how the phases of the pandemic played out locally.

ers: it was represented as a continuation of the same preventive policy, grounded by the same rationale. This was certainly true from the general bio-political point of view. But, sociologically speaking, the quest for herd immunity was governed by a very different principle than social distancing.

In the quest for herd immunity, the goal was initially to motivate the members of our societies most susceptible of infection or most relevant for the system to get vaccinated as soon as possible, in order to become immune themselves and to protect themselves and with them, the system, in particular the healthcare system on the verge of an overload. Up to a point, this was clearly an appeal to both egoistic motives (be safe yourself) and the altruistic ones (defend the system). But, from a certain point, when the vaccinations in the most susceptible groups were far advanced, the rationale changed. The egoistic motive was less and less relevant, and it became more and more problematic owing to the reports of medical complications following the injections with some of the vaccines. For many, protecting yourself by not getting the vaccine started to look like a rational strategy long before herd immunity was reached. At some point, the quest for herd immunity turned from being a *protect yourself* kind of campaign to a sheer *do it for the others* one. It could also be argued that this was a turning point at which the civilizing offensive of phase one, which was essentially aimed at eliminating certain forms of social behavior, turned towards the civilizing offensive aimed at evoking positive behavioral reaction: getting the vaccine.

To push for further progress of vaccinations, many individualistic arguments playing upon was to stress the altruistic, prosocial dimension of the action. Herd immunity was invoked to explain the need to protect strangers – those very same strangers who were largely eliminated from our lives in the first phase of the pandemic, who became icons on our screens. Now we were called to do harm to our own bodies in order to protect those strangers. It is either very small harm, the injection and maybe up to a few days of a fever, or very big harm, depending on the subjective perception of the risk of a thrombosis or other complications. Nonetheless, it is harm to our very real body, done to protect the bodies of others which were largely removed from our daily lives in phase one. So, the altruism applied exactly in the sphere which suffered the most in the pandemic: the physical, daily contact with others as a stimulus to show regard for them as flesh-and-blood creatures.

The social distancing phase of the pandemic reduced the need to identify with others as bodily, living creatures for obvious reasons of eliminating most of the opportunities to interact with them. We were left with our suddenly so individual bodies in our own compartmentalized spaces, and those bodies were now the object of campaigning aimed at using them to protect strangers.

The opposition against the vaccines for Coronavirus is in many ways similar to anti-vaccination movements known all over the world (possibly apart from the religious ones). The motive of individual harm was played against the collective benefit of having a population vaccinated, and societies and states were reproached for making individuals morally if not legally obligated to incur a risk in order to protect other individuals. The awareness of the obstacles which need to be overcome to ensure the success of the vaccinations was not lacking. In a 2021 *Lancet* comment, Rochelle Ann Burgess and colleagues wrote:

»In this new phase of the COVID-19 response, successful vaccine roll-out will only be achieved by ensuring effective community engagement, building local vaccine acceptability and confidence, and overcoming cultural, socioeconomic, and political barriers that lead to mistrust and hinder uptake of vaccines. [...] Globally, the COVID-19 pandemic has further marginalised historically oppressed and excluded groups, including people with disabilities and growing numbers living in precarity. These groups have suffered disproportionate economic and health consequences, and have been largely excluded from social protection and resources needed to minimise their contracting the virus. The widespread impacts of the pandemic have illuminated the structural violence embedded in society. Now these communities are being asked to trust the same structures that have contributed to their experiences of discrimination, abuse, trauma, and marginalisation in order to access vaccines and to benefit the wider population.«[18]

The gloomy picture of our societies in the second phase of the pandemic stresses the appalling fact that our societies again – as in the social distancing phase – expect their weakest members to show the most of the community spirit (and then complain if they do not). The inequality in the distribution of the risks and burdens of the struggle against the pandemic is undoubtedly one of the factors affecting the chances of the quest for herd immunity. However, the likelihood of general weakening of the community spirit as a result of the social distancing phase – though hardly measurable – should not be discarded easily.

3. Conclusion: The Hard Work of Inculcating Solidarity in a Social Void

The struggle for herd immunity in almost every country of the world is less successful than expected. The populations of these countries have been exposed to two deeply contradictory impulses of governmental biopolitics in a very short time. The first one of them, the social distancing campaign, included a number of means which intervened deeply in the basics of social habitus, suspending or, even, relegating the forms through which sociability was manifested and perpetuated. The second one relied on the human ability to identify with strangers and

---

[18] Burgess et al.: The Covid-19 Vaccines Rush, p. 8. References in the original omitted.

to make sacrifices in order to protect them, beyond the line of their own personal protection. The first phase thus reduced exactly those impulses which would be crucial for the success of the second phase. Any measures increasing groupness, inner-circle cohesion, isolation, and distrust of strangers are bound adversely to affect the capacity to identify with the community at large. The long-term effect of these measures is, of course, far from known thus far, but in the dynamic between two phases of the pandemic response, it is the short-term effect that is the most important. The social void created in the first place is not easily filled on a day to day basis with the abstract concept of social solidarity draped in the scientific costume of herd immunity.

Robert van Krieken in his seminal study of Covid-19 and the civilizing process was right to state that »a sustainable response to crises like pandemics will only be organized around rational reflection to a limited extent: in significant ways it will be constituted by shifts at the emotional and psychological level, in the realm of culture and habitus, by the formation of particular ways of being a person.«[19] This is certainly true, also because our ability to comply with the pandemic restrictions was indeed a function of how deeply we have internalized particular ways of being a person together with their respective standards of regard for others. But this *dictum* can also be reversed: an experience such as the pandemic, with a deep intervention in our habits of behavior, thinking and feeling about others, may also change our ways of being a person, even over a shorter period than usually assumed in historical sociology of social processes. In particular, the Coronavirus case shows that the civilizing offensives in the emic sense may converge with the civilizing offensives in the etic sense, aimed at changing human behavior so as to serve the cause of safety, interdependence, wider identification and more regard for others. The opposition against the emic civilizing offensives and their unexpected consequences can then hamper the success chances of the etic civilizing offensives, and thus the benefits of the process of civilization, especially for the weakest.

References

Boserup, Brian / Mark McKenney / Adel Elkubli: Alarming Trends in US Domestic Violence during the Covid-19 Pandemic, in: The American Journal of Emergency Medicine, 45(12), 2020, pp. 2753–2755.
Bradbury-Jones, Caroline / Louise Isham: The Pandemic Paradox: The Consequences of Covid-19 on Domestic Violence, in: Journal of Clinical Nursing, 29(13–14), 2020, pp. 2047–2049.

---

[19] Van Krieken: Covid 19 and the Civilising Process, p. 714.

Burgess, Rochelle Ann/Richard H. Osborne/Kenneth A. Yongabi/Trisha Greenhalgh/Deepti Gurdasani/Gagandeep Kang et al.: The Covid-19 Vaccines Rush: Participatory Community Engagement Matters More Than Ever, in: The Lancet 397(10268), 2021, pp. 8–10.

De Swaan, Abram: Widening Circles of Identification, in: Theory, Culture & Society, 12(2), 1995, pp. 25–39.

De Swaan, Abram: Dyscivilisation, Mass Extermination and the State, in: Theory, Culture & Society 18(2–3), 2011, pp. 265–276.

Elias, Norbert: On the Process of Civilisation. Sociogenetic and Psychogenetic Investigations, Dublin 2012.

Eurostat: Household Composition Statistics, June 01, 2021 in: Eurostat https://ec.europa.eu/eurostat/statistics-explained/index.php?title=Household_composition_statistics#Increasing_number_of_households_consisting_of_adults_living_alone; last accessed July 02, 2021.

Lee, Brian K.: Herd Immunity, in: Encyclopædia Britannica, December 30, 2013, https://www.britannica.com/science/herd-immunity; last accessed July 02, 2021.

Mennell, Stephen: Civilising Offensives and Decivilizing Processes: Between the Emic and the Etic, in: Human Figurations 4(1), 2015, https://quod.lib.umich.edu/h/humfig/11217607.00 04.109/--civilising-offensives-and-decivilising-processes-between?rgn=main;view=fulltext; last accessed July 02, 2021.

Powell, Ryan: The Theoretical Concept of the ›Civilising Offensive‹ (Beschavingsoffensief): Notes on Its Origins and Uses, in: Human Figurations 2(2), 2013, https://quod.lib.umich.edu/h/humfig/11217607.0002.203/--theoretical-concept-of-the-civilising-offensive?rgn=main;view=fulltext; last accessed July 02, 2021.

Simmel, Georg: The Stranger, in: Kurt Wolf (ed.): The Sociology of Georg Simmel, New York 1950, pp. 402–408.

Timpka, Toomas/James M. Nyce: Face Mask Use During the COVID-19 Pandemic – the Significance of Culture and the Symbolic Meaning of Behavior, in: Annals of Epidemiology, 59, 2021, pp. 1–4.

Wouters, Cas: Functional Democratisation and Disintegration as Side-Effects of Differentiation and Integration Processes, in: Human Figurations 5(2), 2016, https://quod.lib.umich.edu/h/humfig/11217607.0005.208/--functional-democratisation-and-disintegration-as-side?rgn=main;view=fulltext; last accessed July 02, 2021.

Van Krieken, Robert: Covid-19 and the Civilising Process, in: Journal of Sociology, 56(4), 2020, pp. 714–725.

Hanna Eklund
Law and Care

This text is a reflection on law seen through the prism of care. Our need for care forms life, most pronouncedly as children, when we get sick and when we are old. The pandemic period repositioned our human need for care in society from periodic to omnipresent. The demarcation between public and private shuffled: in terms of discussing care; seeing care; and evaluating the organization of care. Autobiographical realities of being ill conjured into a near collective experience of a disease, and concurrently the pandemic revealed the material state of caregiving facilities in different parts of the world at the same time.

While the Aids/HIV epidemic of the 1980s is memorably represented in art, the 1918 pandemic is rarely represented in literature, especially not by writers who lived through it.[1] Catherine Belling, writing on narrative medicine, ascribes this absence of fiction to a cultural context that discouraged the discussion of private suffering, and a biological condition that »bewildered the brain with fever.«[2] What is more, the 1918 pandemic was overshadowed by World War I, which provided a better narrative and stronger characters. Will we write novels about the Covid-19 pandemic? TV-series and films? If so, which stories, and whose, will we tell?

In the essay *Nomos and Narrative,* the American constitutional theorist Robert Cover wrote that »there is a radical dichotomy between the social organization of law as power and the organization of law as meaning.«[3] Law in pandemic times appears to enact that dichotomy in noteworthy ways. The power of law to restrict our lives has been well illustrated and felt. Angela Condello wrote that the pandemic has made us perceive »in depth what it means to have our existence regulated by legal norms.«[4] Yet, the difficulty of understanding the nature of a pandemic, who is right and who is wrong about the phases of the pandemic, the character of the virus, the effect of the vaccine makes the »organization of law as meaning« precarious. The vulnerability and uncertainty felt during the pandemic is shown in questions of whether we had too much law restricting movement and social gatherings, or too little. Law is collateral knowledge of our social world, and its insecurities.

---

[1] Cf. Jurecic: Illness as Narrative, pp. 3 f.
[2] Belling: Overwhelming the Medium, p. 58.
[3] Cover: Nomos and Narrative, p. 18.
[4] Condello: Immersed in a Normative Laboratory, p. 129.

It is further a question of perspective. From the perspective of the individual afflicted by illness the anthropologist Veena Das points us to the »reconfiguration of relations that are brought into view as an illness unfolds. The larger institutional complexes such as the state and the market are, from this perspective, folded into the biography of an illness rather than made to stand out as commanding entities that regulate policy, set prices, and monitor the quality of medical care, thus determining the outcomes of diseases for both individuals and populations.«[5] This perspective points to institutions as features of what it means to be ill, and in need of care, rather than understanding institutions as artefacts external to the illness.

Fundamentally, this text will seek to develop an account of the ways in which the uncertainties of pandemic times, with its manifold biographies of illness, may focus our attention on the relationship between law and the ethics of care. The moral philosopher Sandra Laugier has already pointed us to the ways in which the »perspective of the ethics of care, because it calls our attention to our general situation of dependence, is inseparably political and ethical; it develops an analysis of social relations organized around dependence and vulnerability – blind spots in the ethics of justice.«[6] This text will, in two short stages, relate to these blind spots, and the ways in which we may think of law when seen through the prism of care. First, as the carelessness of pre-pandemic times where law, and the state, retreated from its role as organizer and guarantor of access to good quality healthcare. Second, as a question of law's caretaking capacities.

1. Carelessness

The literary theorist Ann Jurecic points out that one of the essential, yet hopeless questions for the one who is ill is: Why me?[7] In pandemic times the question becomes rather, why all of us at the same time? This question – Why all of us? – might capture something more essential about the condition of our lives that was always there, but easier to neglect when there is no pandemic. As Das notes: »The boundaries of the human body are not the boundaries of the subject. So, the subject of illness or madness is not simply the individual but the web of relations.«[8] Illness is far reaching. While Covid-19 struck the elderly harder, the implications of illness – missing someone, worrying, living without someone – is not contained in one affected body.

---

[5] Das: Affliction, p. 203.
[6] Laugier: The Ethics of Care as a Politics of the Ordinary, p. 224.
[7] Jurecic: Illness as Narrative, p. 9.
[8] Das: Affliction, p. 205.

This understanding of illness pushes questions about whether *we will become* more prone to solidarity and communality because of the pandemic gently to the side. Illness carries an intrinsic connectivity in that it unfolds, rather than augments, a person's dependency on others. We may critique the ways in which we are connected to and dependent on others, but it is hard to escape from them. For Lautier, (and here I borrow from Das) our connection to reality is a question of accepting the flesh-and-blood character of others, rather than solving the intellectual puzzle of the existence of the other.[9] This ordinary realism of Laugier side-lines the grand theories of moral life and their abstract, yet colloquial, exemplifications. Illness, with or without pandemic form, is a non-containable experience and as such is part of our connection to reality. The pandemic revealed the way in which our current social organization of care does not account for how vulnerability and care give form to our lives, even when illness does not affect our bodies but the bodies of others. The pandemic is yet another indication of the implications of the corrosion of care as a collective concern.

In 2016 Nancy Fraser defined care work more broadly as social reproduction and described the current state of care as: »The result, amid rising inequality, is a dualized organization of social reproduction, commodified for those who can pay for it, privatized for those who cannot.«[10] Thus, with refence to what others have noted but which bears repeating, the Covid-19-pandemic has put a sharp light on the way in which the essentiality of care has been neglected. The specific modes of neglect have played out differently in different parts of the world during the pandemic, but the tendencies have been the same: the dismal state of elderly care; inadequately funded hospitals; shortages in medical equipment;[11] as well as the lack of adequate access to childcare for those who need to perform the care work desperately needed.

Herein lie several examples of the carelessness with which law has been detached from healthcare as a collective societal obligation. Gianmaria Ajani already observed how »the pandemic will question the retreat of the state.«[12] The function of law as guaranteeing the equal right to healthcare has corroded through privatization in multiple ways in Europe.[13] First, in terms of public services being abandoned and delegated to private actors. Second, through the development of private insurance schemes, i.e. transferring the cost of healthcare from the state to households. Third, introducing entrepreneurship in guidelines for public actors, and patients, rather than the ethos of public service.

---

[9] Cf. ibid., p. 209.
[10] Fraser: Contradictions of Capital and Care, p. 103.
[11] Cf. European Union Agency for Fundamental Rights: The Coronavirus Pandemic in the EU.
[12] Ajani: Possible Effects of the Pandemic Emergency, p. 163.
[13] Cf. André/Batifoulier/Jansen-Ferreira: Health Care Privatization Processes in Europe, pp. 3–23.

Francesca Caroccia developed a critique of private law in pandemic times, stating that as the pandemic hits different parts of the population harder the fiction of equality, which private law presupposes, is effectively unveiled.[14] The pandemic crystalized the state of a healthcare system, including elderly care, increasingly placed under (or never having left) the auspices of private law. A type of law that does not guarantee equal access to good quality healthcare, or, as Caroccia puts it, »offers neither sustain nor assistance.«[15]

During the financial crises of 2008 the European Commission, The European Central Bank (ECB) and the International Monetary Fund (IMF) set up an intricate »bailout« system, which functioned so that countries in sovereign debt received loans on the condition that they enacted political austerity reforms.[16] These conditions included cuts to public spending on health care, which deteriorated access to and quality of health care in these countries.[17] Claire Kilpatrick has written about how these debt conditionality measures were the *rule of law-crises* that should have received more attention.[18] Kilpatrick explains how these debt conditionality measures did not live up to minimum standards of legality. To put it simply, it remained unclear who created the debt conditionality measures, what they said, and even where to find them.[19]

Thus, one of the most sweeping alterations of access to care in the EU was ordained through measures that cannot be described as fulfilling minimal legality. By bypassing the EU's ordinary legislative procedure, different forms of care for people were erased from state's obligations with intentional legal formlessness.

This had a further important consequence, the Court of Justice of the European Union has in large part refused to perform judicial review of the debt conditionality reforms, stating that these are not to be considered EU law and as a result the Court does not have jurisdiction.[20] Thus the EU legal system could not review their legality, especially their compatibility with the EU's plethora of fundamental rights instruments and most notably the Charter of Fundamental Rights of the European Union, it just presumed they were not EU law. The signaling from the intricate constellation of authors of these measure – The European Commission, ECB, IMF, EU Member States' executives – is that access to care in the EU was not *worthy* of being erased by law (never mind sustained by law) and may as well be handled outside of the EU legal order.

---

[14] Cf. Caroccia: Searching for a Vaccine, p. 154.

[15] Ibid., p. 154.

[16] Hungary, Latvia, Rumania, Greece, Ireland, Portugal and Cyprus. Italy and Spain received instructions on how to reduce public spending.

[17] Cf. Karanikolos et al.: Financial Crisis, Austerity, and Health in Europe, pp. 1323–1331. This article discusses a broader group of EU countries than those which received loans.

[18] Cf. Kilpatrick: On the Rule of Law and Economic Emergency, pp. 325–353.

[19] Ibid.

[20] Cf. Poulou: Human Rights Obligations of European Financial Assistance Mechanisms.

The law of care in Europe has been watered down. Law is not used to construct a robust collective obligation to guarantee equal access to health care, rather, care is increasingly left to private law and versions of instruments that do not live up to standards of legality. Examining the place of our need for care on a more fundamental level, Estelle Ferrarese observes how »vulnerability has a tendency to be set aside so that the political can emerge.«[21] This, let us call it order of priority, underestimates the form vulnerability gives to our lives, not merely as a fragility but as an insight into what it means to be human. The pandemic has shown the already evident implications of such a careless approach to the human condition.

2. Taking Care

Veena Das, at the early height of the pandemic in May 2020, wrote that: »We should realise that people are not easily panicked by acknowledgements of uncertainty in scientific knowledge but they are crushed by the uncertainty generated by the kind of government orders that leave no room for them to sustain their already fragile arrangements for provisioning and social support.«[22] Das continues by describing that a particular problem arises when makers of law and regulations, such as policy and executive orders, do not acknowledge uncertainty, and pretend it is not there. In this pandemic period some governments have employed behavioral theory to construct law, often referred to as »nudging«[23]. This form of law-making relies on experts who believes that all human behavior is understandable to them and based on these insights they construct different forms of regulation. Veena Das points out that such law and policy making, especially in the area of global health policies, and now also during the pandemic, is constructed by people who do not know how poor people live, work, get sick and die and that their knowledge of human behavior more often than not is dangerously unaware.[24] Thus, not least in pandemic times, the idea of *behavioral insights* as a foundation for law-making relies on a self-assurance of the expert that should be self-doubt. This self-assurance, as Das observes, makes the people subjected to the regulation more panicked than an acknowledgement of scientific uncertainty.

How does law take care in a highly uncertain and unpredictable period? Robert Cover wanted to open up the closed spaced in which we guard knowledge about law, especially constitutional norms. He sought to account for how commitments

---

21 Ferrarese: Vulnerability and Critical Theory, p. 7.
22 Das: Corona Policy Must Factor in Scientific Uncertainty.
23 Derrig: Lockdown Fatigue.
24 Cf. Das: Affliction, p. 209.

to interpretation are created.[25] Following Cover's idea of jurisgenerativity we might have created knowledge about what the right to health should mean. For instance, the meaning of the right to health care within the EU as guaranteed in Article 35 of the Charter of Fundamental Rights of the European Union. This knowledge would come from different voices and different *worlds*, to quote Cover, being let in to formulate the meaning of law[26]. Nurses who worked on the frontlines, grandchildren who lost grandparents, husbands and wives of retired doctors who joined their old colleagues and lost their lives. All of these experiences should help us interpret the meaning of the right to health care.

The blind spots in the ethics of justice as we know it,[27] which Sandra Laugier described, are redressed if the quintessentially human experiences of needing care are accounted for, rather than dismissed as external to that which is legal. Our need for care is a certainty, which if properly addressed as such, might remedy the way in which we experience uncertainty in pandemic times, and ordinary times. Das has described how our forms of life domesticate crises and trauma; the ways in which illness descend into our lives and becomes its ordinary contours.[28] Crises lives on in our everyday, in recollections, changes to how we do things, the constellations of our social relations. Crises sink into the details and nuances of how we live.

Mindful of how our lives are given form, law's care taking capabilities lie in attentiveness – to detail, to the particular and to the vulnerable. More fundamentally, as Theodor Adorno wrote, »thinking of the other as a subject: the opposite of distraction.«[29] A calming stillness appears when we manage to focus on the individual in front of us, and accept the needs of others as well as of ourselves; an ideal starting-point for democratic law-making. Sandra Laugier, finally, reminds us that »care corresponds to an ordinary reality: the fact that people look after one another, take care of one another, and thus are attentive to the functioning of the world, which depends on this kind of care.«[30] Law should correspond to this reality, and be shaped so that the ethics of care is its justification.

---

[25] Cf. Cover: Nomos and Narrative, p. 46.
[26] Cf. ibid.
[27] Cf. Laugier: The Ethics of Care as a Politics of the Ordinary, p. 224.
[28] Cf. Das: Affliction.
[29] Adorno: Minima Moralia, p. 42.
[30] Laugier: The Ethics of Care as a Politics of the Ordinary, p. 219.

References

Adorno, Theodor W.: Minima Moralia: Reflection from Damaged Life, London 2005.

Ajani, Gianmaria: Possible Effects of the Pandemic Emergency on the Internal Coherence of EU Law, in: Werner Gephart (ed.): In the Realm of Corona Normativities. A Momentary Snapshot of a Dynamic Discourse, Frankfurt am Main 2020.

André, Christine/Philippe Batifoulier/Mariana Jansen-Ferreira: Health Care Privatization Processes in Europe: Theoretical Justifications and Empirical Classification, in: International Social Security Review, 69(1), 2016, pp. 3–23.

Belling, Catherine: Overwhelming the Medium: Fiction and the Trauma of Pandemic Influenza in 1918, in: Literature and Medicine, 28(1), 2009, pp. 55–81.

Caroccia, Francesca: Searching for a Vaccine. Rethinking the Paradigm of (Private) Law in Times of Pandemic Crisis, in: Werner Gephart (ed.): In the Realm of Corona Normativities. A Momentary Snapshot of a Dynamic Discourse, Frankfurt 2020.

Condello, Angela: Immersed in a Normative Laboratory, in: Werner Gephart (ed.): In the Realm of Corona Normativities. A Momentary Snapshot of a Dynamic Discourse, Frankfurt 2020.

Cover, Robert: Foreword: Nomos and Narrative, in: Harvard Law Review, 97(4), 1983, pp. 4–68.

Das, Veena: Affliction: Health, Disease, Poverty, New York 2015.

Das, Veena: Corona Policy Must Factor in Scientific Uncertainty, in: Deccan Chronicle, May 24, 2020, https://www.deccanchronicle.com/opinion/columnists/240520/veena-das-corona-policy-must-factor-in-scientific-uncertainty.html; last accessed June 6, 2021.

Derrig, Rián: Lockdown Fatigue: Pandemic from the Perspective of Nudge Theory, in: Verfassungsblog, May 26, 2021, https://verfassungsblog.de/lockdown-fatigue-pandemic-from-the-perspective-of-nudge-theory/; last accessed June 6, 2021.

Ferrarese, Estelle: Vulnerability and Critical Theory, Boston 2018.

Fraser, Nancy: Contradictions of Capital and Care, in: New Left Review, 100, 2016, pp. 99-117.

European Union Agency for Fundamental Rights: The Coronavirus Pandemic in the EU – Fundamental Rights Implications, Bulletin 6, November 30, 2020.

Jurecic, Ann: Illness as Narrative, Pittsburgh 2012.

Kilpatrick, Claire: On the Rule of Law and Economic Emergency: The Degradation of Basic Legal Values in Europe's Bailouts, in: Oxford Journal of Legal Studies, 35(2), 2015, pp. 325–353.

Karanikolos, Marina/Philipa Mladovsky/Jonathan Cylus/Sarah Thomson/Sanjay Basu, David Stuckler/Johan P. Mackenbach/Martin McKee: Financial Crisis, Austerity, And Health in Europe, in: The Lancet, 381(9874), 2013, pp. 1323–1331.

Laugier, Sandra: The Ethics of Care as a Politics of the Ordinary, in: New Literary History, 46(2), 2015, pp. 217–240.

Poulou, Anastasia: Human Rights Obligations of European Financial Assistance Mechanisms, in: Ulrich Becker/Anastasia Poulou (eds.): European Welfare State Constitutions after the Financial Crisis, Oxford 2020, pp. 24–48.

Maximilian Mayer and Katharina C. Cramer

Pandemic Disruptions and Transnational Care Relations: Towards Closing the *Care Gap* in International Relations Theories*

Introduction

The Covid-19 pandemic caused millions of deaths and a global health crisis. Following the initial outbreak in January 2020, most governments introduced non-pharmaceutical interventions (NPIs) to contain the spread of the novel respiratory virus SARS-CoV-2. Requirements of social and physical distancing, shielding, and cocooning strategies for risk groups, self-isolation regimes, travel bans, and border restrictions were maintained over weeks and months to contain the infectious disease, to reduce infection numbers, to protect lives and the functioning of national health systems. The impacts of these measures increased the pressure on the already delicate fabric of globalized care relations and reinforced the looming care crisis, a reality which did not receive sufficient theoretical and empirical attention at the nexus of international relations, global ethics, and global health studies.

In line with Sara E. Davies and Clare Wenham's arguments,[1] the side effects of Covid-19 and pandemic responses need to be seen through the lens of human rights.[2] NPIs had drastic, unintended consequences for many different care relations on which human dignity and daily well-being depend, such as routine fulfillment of basic needs, such as food, shelter, health care, and sanitation of individuals and communities worldwide. Closures of schools and child care facilities affected children's physical and mental health and put an immense burden on

---

* The research for this chapter was funded by the research project egePan Unimed (Development, Testing, and implementation of regionally adaptive health care structures and processes for pandemic management guided by evidence and led by university clinics). egePan Unimed is funded by the German Federal Ministry of Education and Research as part of the Netzwerk Universitätsmedizin (NUM) initiative (Grant-No.: 01KX2021). We are grateful for comments and feedback from Maike Voss, Mingyong Jacob Tong and the members of the project »Assessment of Evolving International Infrastructures and Pandemic Management« at CASSIS/University of Bonn, Janna Hartmann, Julia Holz, Kilian Knorr, Ga Young Lee, Anna Müller, Philip Nock, Annalena Pott, Miriam Siemes and Jan David Zabala Gepp.

1 Davies/Wenham: Why the COVID-19 response needs International Relations.
2 Colombo: Human Rights-inspired Governmentality: COVID-19 through a Human Dignity Perspective.

families that struggled to care for their children adequately.[3] Older people were shielded in care facilities and deprived of social contacts over long periods. Health professionals criticized those policies for their harmful consequences.[4] Many people were severely threatened by poverty and homelessness due to loss of income and employment and could therefore no longer secure basic needs and care for themselves and their families. People with special needs, chronic illness, or discriminated minorities were suddenly cut off from their supportive networks and necessary caring environments.[5] Care workers' commuting mobility and transnational parents' travel routines were limited by travel bans and border restrictions. As a result, experts, scholars, and care workers recurrently accused governments of inadequately acknowledging the effects of disrupted care relations, especially the impact on women who shoulder the majority of paid and unpaid care work. They warned of the harmful consequences of neglecting people's relational needs and vulnerabilities.[6]

In this light, we raise the question why international and national pandemic politics acknowledged only marginally the disruptive effects of NPIs on care relations. Why did policymakers do so little to protect relational care ties among societies and communities? This essay adopts a global perspective with a particular emphasis on the transnational reality of care relations. Such a view goes beyond immediate concerns of private hardships and individual coping strategies. Instead, the observation is a starting point that the organization and practice of care depend on fundamentally transnational relationships. National variations in welfare and family policies are often intimately connected to international political constellations, economic flows, and ethical considerations. The disruption of local and individual care arrangements during the Covid-19 pandemic, therefore, could translate immediately into concerns of international relation (IR) theories and the global health economy.

---

[3] Christakis/Van Cleve/Zimmerman: Estimation of US Children's Educational Attainment and Years of Life Lost; The Independent Panel: COVID-19; Baumann, COVID-19 and mental health in children and adolescents.

[4] British Society of Gerontology: Statement from the President and Members of the National Executive Committee of the British Society of Gerontology on COVID-19.

[5] Abuelgasim et al.: COVID-19: Unique Public Health Issues Facing Black, Asian and Minority Ethnic Communities; Smith/Judd: COVID-19: Vulnerability and The Power of Privilege in a Pandemic.

[6] The following publications exemplify the multitude of reports, statements, policy briefs and research articles that were published since the beginning of the Covid-19 pandemic and that claimed the lack of adequate governmental response to disrupted care relations. Cf. Royal Commission into Violence, Abuse, Neglect and Exploitation of People with Disability: Statement of Concern; Mor: In Developing Countries, Communities and Primary Care Providers – Not Hospitals – Hold the Key to Successful Pandemic Response; United Nations Human Rights Office of the High Commissioner: COVID-19: Who is Protecting the People with Disabilities?; Secretary of State for Health and Social Care: The Government's Response to the Joint Committee on Human Rights Report: The Government's Response to COVID-19: Human Rights Implications.

The pandemic powerfully demonstrated the inadequate conceptual understandings of care relations and their place within global governance. The manifold experiences of disruption and human suffering, related to border politics, migration, citizenship, or national security, reinforced the call for more attention, data and research.[7] The epistemic silence regarding the IR perspective on the globality of care relations seems to correspond closely with the marginalized role that care relations played in governmental strategies and responses to the pandemic. A confluence of four factors is noteworthy here. First, care issues remain invisible due to the persistent lack of systematic data and basic statistics that even concerns care within institutionalized facilities.[8] Second, the international institutional landscape for care-related policy coordination is fragmented. Responsibilities are scattered across many different international organizations. Third, care relations, in contrast to the burgeoning literature of international politics of (global) public health, seem to fall into the theoretical cracks between ethics, political theory, and approaches to global health security.[9] Fourth, there is a conceptual blind spot resulting from the incommensurability between the constitutive norms of modern states and rights-based international practices on the one side, and the mundane practicalities and ethics of caring relationships on the other.[10]

In the following, we firstly examine to what extent the implementation of governmental NPIs shattered local-global entanglements that sustain care relations. The disruptions during the Covid-19 pandemic lay bare the fragile legal-political arrangements. Secondly, availability of data and governance structures are discussed. Thirdly, we access the mismatches between the key concerns of care, international relations and political theory. Finally, drawing lessons from this chapter, we suggest 1) to address the lack of data and the absence of institutionalized authority to produce knowledge about care relations and 2) to revisit fundamental notions in international relations and political theory, such as law and rights, to create sufficient conceptual space for care and especially for transnational relationships of care.

---

7 Cf. Robinson: Resisting Hierarchies Through Relationality; Robinson: Globalizing Care; Duffy: Making Care Count; Lutz: The New Maids; Yeates: Globalizing Care Economies and Migrant Workers; Sevenhuijsen: Citizenship and the Ethics of Care.
8 Curiskis/Kelly/Kissane/Oehler: What We Know – and What We Don't Know – About the Impact of the Pandemic on Our Most Vulnerable Community.
9 Wenham: Feminist Global Health Security.
10 Cf. Robinson: The Limits of a Rights-Based Approach to International Ethics; Held: Morality, Care, and International Law.

1. Care Relations and Pandemic Disruptions

Contemporary care relations consist of local and global dimensions, which are indispensable to each other. For instance, scholarship highlights the connections between international flows of migrant care workers, domestic helpers, and transnational family networks and the organization of individual and local care arrangements; and these local arrangements were shaped and structured by national family policies, welfare arrangements, and cultural norms.[11] The growing commodification and marketization of care facilitated enormous global mobility of care workers. It gave rise to the worldwide care economy consisting of densely meshed webs of transnational care arrangements and mobilities.[12] The implementation of NPIs during the Covid-19 pandemic disrupted many of these *glocal* webs of care relationships.

The diversity and heterogeneity of webs of care and care practices they entail are crucial starting points to better grasp the subject. Communities and individuals share different and often implicit understandings of what care is, where it takes place and by whom it is provided – resulting in a wide variety of informal arrangements, hidden activities, and implicit meanings.[13] Subsequently, the pandemic led to various kinds of hardships within different communities and societies. The diversity of meanings and interpretations created difficulties for scholars and policymakers alike, because a common denominator to describe »the problem« and set a policy agenda at the multilateral level of collective action was unavailable.

To the extent that care work was historically associated with women's unpaid labor, (feminist) scholars provide a comprehensive framework to illustrate the all-encompassing role of care relations beyond gendered notions and a selective focus on private settings.[14] Nicola Yeates defines care as »a range of tasks and activities to promote the personal health and welfare of people who cannot, or who are not inclined to, perform those activities themselves.«[15] Mignon Duffy adopts a »nurturant care perspective« that includes »intensive relational work that is geared toward improving the personal well-being of others.«[16] Kathleen Lynch stresses the emotional aspects of caring as »love labour,« particularly within intimate care settings among families, relatives, and friends that require »affection, commitment, attentiveness and the material investment of time, energy and resources.«[17]

---

[11] Widding Isaksen/Näre: Local Loops and Micro-Mobilities of Care; Lutz: The New Maids; Yeates: Globalizing Care Economies and Migrant Workers.
[12] Yeates: Global Care Chains; Hochschild: The Commercialization of Intimate Life.
[13] Duffy: Making Care Count, p. 9.
[14] Tronto: Creating Caring Institutions: Politics, Plurality, and Purpose, pp. 102 ff.
[15] Yeates: Global Care Chains, p. 371.
[16] Duffy: Making Care Count, p. 9.
[17] Lynch: Love Labour as a Distinct and Non-Commodifiable Form of Care Labour, p. 557.

These different yet interrelated understandings of care accommodate the working experience and ethos of a wide range of professional and paid occupations such as nurses, physicians, psychotherapists, teachers, or social workers. But they also refer to unpaid, informal, and often invisible care work such as cooking, cleaning, and many »affective practices«[18] that are vital for humans as relational beings.[19] The Covid-19 pandemic severely affected most of these activities and the ways in which local and global contexts were (formally or informally) entangled by performing different care relationships.

Inequality occupies a central role as both a driving force and outcome of globally entangled care work. For instance, the lack of global social security frameworks or pension schemes leads to a significant vulnerability of care workers many of who are affected persistently by unequal and exploitative arrangements.[20] According to Arlie Hochschild, transnational care relations resemble »global care chains« that usually involve migrant care workers from middle and low-income countries providing care services in families and households in high-income countries.[21] As these care workers, who are primarily female, migrate for work, they tend to create a supply shortage of care in their home countries and within their own families. This shortage needs to either be filled by relatives, family members, or domestic helpers, thereby replicating the pattern of transnational care dependencies.[22] The global financial flows and dependencies, that are an essential part of the international economy of these care chains, grew considerably in recent decades. Care workers constitute a large group of those migrant workers. They try to escape the risks of poverty, climate change, and unemployment in their home countries while supporting their families and communities from abroad through remittances.[23] According to the World Bank, in 2019, migrant workers sent about $550 billion in overall remittances to their families in developing countries. That vast amount crucially contributes to the GDPs of countries in the Global South. Remittances are significantly higher than foreign direct investments ($342 billion) and official development assistance ($158 billion).[24]

The pandemic also impacted global pattern of care mobility. Relatively uncontrolled cross-border movements or flexible surveillance mechanisms enabled the flourish of transnational caring relationships in recent years within legal and organizational grey zones. For instance, transnational caring practices were common

---

[18] Lynch/Kalaitzake/Crean: Care and Affective Relations, p. 56.
[19] Held: The Ethics of Care, p. 10; Koggel: Perspectives on Equality.
[20] Lutz: The New Maids; Yeates: Globalizing Care Economies and Migrant Workers.
[21] Hochschild: The Commercialization of Intimate Life; Hochschild: Global Care Chains and Emotional Surplus Value.
[22] Palenga-Möllenbeck: Care Chains in Eastern and Central Europe.
[23] Clark/Bettini: »Floods« of Migrants, Flows of Care.
[24] Barne/Pirlea: Money Sent Home by Workers now Largest Source of External Financing in Low- and Middle-Income Countries (Excluding China).

at the borders between Germany and its neighbors, such as Poland and the Czech Republic, as well as among Southeast Asian countries such as Vietnam, Laos, Thailand, or Malaysia.[25] The sudden reintroduction of stricter border controls, mass testing, and vaccination requirements during the Covid-19 pandemic called transnational care chains into question.[26] Restrictions of international mobility greatly complicated travel routes, economic flows, communications for migrant care workers, and Live-Ins[27] that are critical for the maintaining of transnational family structures.[28] Grey zones became more limited because governments enforced more systematic surveillance and began to tie mobility possibilities more closely to citizenship status when it came to quarantine and visa regulations than pre-crisis settings.[29]

Yet, the international flow of remittances during the 2020 pandemic year decreased much less than expected, as migrant and foreign care workers continued their work under much more difficult and alarming conditions.[30] Leiblfinger et al. report that Live-Ins – who usually return to their home countries after a few weeks and rotate with another care worker – often extended their stays for weeks or month. As a result, Live-Ins had to suffer from additional burdens and pressures.[31] For instance, Vietnamese migrant workers abroad were confronted with harsh working conditions during the pandemic. They decided to send their babies and toddlers back to Vietnam onboard repatriation flights because they could no longer care for their children.[32]

In addition, NPIs affected the infrastructures on which daily and individual care arrangements rely. Decades of increasing marketization and outsourcing of care into public or commercial settings through expanded public and commercial provision of early child care and elderly care were testaments to gender equality policies, including maternal employment policies and the female share in the labor market.[33] But closures and restrictions of schools, childcare facilities, and elderly

---

[25] Yeoh/Huang: Family, Migration and the Gender Politics of Care.

[26] For instance, more than 100,000 movement restrictions with only 795 exceptions issued by 189 countries, territories or areas are estimated to have reduced the movement of roughly 2 million international migrants. For a discussion of more data: Cf. Migration Data: Migration Data Relevant for the COVID-19 Pandemic.

[27] Live-Ins are care workers that live in the same household as the persons they take care of and usually rotate after a few weeks with another care worker; Leiblfinger et al.: Impact of COVID-19 Policy Responses on Live-In Care Workers in Austria, Germany, and Switzerland.

[28] Brandhorst/Baldassar/Wilding: Transnational Family Care ›On Hold‹?

[29] Johnson/Lindquist: Care and Control in Asian Migrations.

[30] World Bank: Defying Predictions.

[31] Leiblfinger et al.: Impact of COVID-19 Policy Responses on Live-In Care Workers in Austria, Germany, and Switzerland, p. 145.

[32] Cf. Cramer et al.: COVID-19 Border Restrictions and Cross-Border Care Relations.

[33] Sevenhuijsen: The Place of Care; Lewis: Gender and Welfare Regimes; Fine/Davidson: The Marketization of Care.

care homes disrupted care infrastructures on which the societal organization of labor and economic value creation and emancipatory policies depend. While people began to work from home, individuals and communities struggled to provide adequate care to those who the public and commercial care providers left behind. Furthermore, border restrictions and travel bans aggravated the disruptive situation of care provision by restricting migrant care workers from traveling to their workplaces, burdening transnational families to receive foreign domestic helpers and to maintain their caring encounters, meanwhile limiting border-spanning medical travel and retirement migration.[34]

2. Lack of Data on Care Relations

The Covid-19 pandemic saw an unprecedented surge in research output. Researchers established various experimental and statistical data sets on epidemiological dynamics, treatments, and the impacts of policy choices. The Covid-19 dashboards by the Center for Systems Science and Engineering (CSSE) at Johns Hopkins University and the World Health Organization (WHO) were among the earliest and most comprehensive tools to track and visualize Covid-19 cases globally backed by gigantic amounts of automatically collected data.[35] Many governmental agencies worldwide began to issue regular reports containing up-to-date information on confirmed cases, deaths, positivity rates of tests or incidence rates, and the availability of intensive care beds, oxygen, or vaccines. The Blavatnik School of Government at the University of Oxford and the Technical University of Munich set up different projects that traced governmental responses to the pandemic.[36] The continued collection, monitoring, and evaluation of data showed how governments and researchers rendered the rapid dynamics of the Covid-19 pandemic as well as interventions to contain the virus legible and how epidemic measures and their effects got *datafied* and thus acknowledged and made actionable for public health policy makers across the world.

This kind of data-based governmentality that arose during the pandemic entails a »new biopolitical architecture« that expands preexisting surveillance technology and the reach of disciplining routines.[37] Besides, data and scientific evidence have come to support policymakers and reconfigure relationships among

---

[34] Cf. Yeates: Globalizing Care Economies and Migrant Workers.
[35] Dong et al.: Interactive Web-Based Dashboard to Track Covid-19 in Real Time.
[36] Hale et al.: A Global Panel Database of Pandemic Policies; Cheng et al.: COVID-19 Government Response Event Dataset.
[37] Kitchin: Civil liberties or public health, or civil liberties and public health? Using surveillance technologies to tackle the spread of COVID-19.

states and their citizens.[38] The central role of numbers, indicators and monitoring during the pandemic illustrated what scholars had pointed out earlier, that is, that political authority and expertise are very closely entangled. Modern state bureaucracies rely on statistical representations of the world to provide a basis for rational decision-making and buttress policy choices' legitimacy.[39] These data remain a selection though, always representing only some elements of a more complex reality. During the Covid-19 pandemic, indicators such as infection case numbers, mortality rates, ICU units, and positivity rates and so forth were at the center of data collection efforts. These health-related categories – the daily infection number perhaps most prominently – framed the main concerns and policy solutions of public health policy.[40] They also became the basis for measuring and visualizing country-specific indicator-based performances that resonated with the dominant policy narratives and enabled almost real-time comparisons within an ongoing global policy experiment.

Care was not among the priorities of pandemic policymaking. Of course, political emphasis on health-related indicators does not come as a surprise during a global pandemic. But such a narrow focus led to a serious underrepresentation of the far-reaching effects of disruptions beyond the health crisis. In fact, neither government agencies nor research institutes began to systematically collect and analyze data about care and caring relationships. This is in contrast to the great length in which infection-related statistics became generative for governmental responses to the spread of Covid-19.[41] The dearth of care data instead signals fewer interest and little political awareness of the care crisis. More than two years into the pandemic, comprehensive data to monitor and to evaluate care situations are still lacking. Health authorities have not gathered systematic knowledge in which ways governmental crisis management has affected different kinds of care relations among individuals, communities, and societies worldwide. Although scholarship pointed out the crucial role of family care, social work, and supportive networks to counterbalance socio-economic stress and maintain societal resilience,[42] disrupted care relations remained out of the public's eye and below the official radar.

Already before 2020, systematic data on care relations were rare and incomplete. Data collection suffered, among other things, from confusing terminolo-

---

[38] Cf. Rottenburg/Merry: A World of Indicators; Jasanoff: Virtual, Visible, and Actionable: Data Assemblages and the Sightlines of Justice.

[39] Bartl/Papilloud/Terrachr-Lipinski: Governing by Numbers; Rottenburg/Merry: A World of Indicators; Straßheim/Beck: (eds.): Handbook of Behavioural Change and Public Policy.

[40] Wenham: The Oversecuritization of Global Health.

[41] Curiskis/Kelly/Kissane/Oehler: What We Know – and What We Don't Know – About the Impact of the Pandemic on Our Most Vulnerable Community.

[42] Rogge: The Future is Now; Pfefferbaum/North: Children and Families in The Context of Disasters.

gies and incoherent definitions. Notions such as *care workers*, *domestic workers*, or *domestic helpers* were often used interchangeably.[43] The lack of data was particularly salient for people with special needs, unpaid care work, non-traditional care arrangements, and vulnerable groups such as children and older people. These groups and settings, consequently, lack visibility in political discourses and governmental action.[44] During the last decades, some progress was made in monitoring informal and unpaid care work, mainly through the compilation and analysis of time-use surveys, census data, and other micro-data formats.[45] Data gaps remained particularly concerning the availability, interoperability, and comprehensiveness of information from middle- and low-income countries and vulnerable groups. For instance, initiatives and expert groups argued that data on childcare arrangements, particularly those that live outside parental care and within non-family care arrangements, were rare or nonexistent.[46] Similar data shortcomings apply, especially to older people. In the US, at least 34 % of all confirmed Covid-19 deaths occurred in nursing homes or other long-term care facilities, while only 1 % of the entire population lived in these facilities.[47] More than 50 % of all confirmed Covid-19 deaths happened in long-term care facilities in some European countries.[48] Ad-hoc data collection efforts on care relations and arrangements was set up during the Covid-19 pandemic and promoted through non-governmental initiatives and international organizations. Yet, significant shortcomings remain due to incoherence and incompleteness of pre-crisis data collection frameworks and methods.[49] Similarly, global data on the pandemic impact on living arrangements, socio-economic contexts, and well-being of older people are incomplete.[50]

---

[43] Schwenken/Heimeshoff: Domestic Workers Count; Feige: Defining and Estimating Underground and Informal Economies; Duffy/Albelda/Hammonds: Counting Care Work.
[44] Addati et al.: Care Work and Care Jobs for The Future of Decent Work, p. 24; cf. SOS Children's Villages International/Development Initiatives: The Care of Children in Data.
[45] Martin/Zulaika: Who Cares for Children?
[46] Cf. SOS Children's Villages International/Development Initiatives: The Care of Children in Data.
[47] Curiskis/Kelly/Kissane/Oehler: What We Know – and What We Don't Know – About the Impact of the Pandemic on Our Most Vulnerable Community.
[48] European Centre for Disease Prevention and Control: Surveillance data from public online national reports on COVID-19 in Long-Term Care Facilities.
[49] Charmes: The Unpaid Care Work and the Labour Market, pp. 136 ff.
[50] Cf. United Nations Department of Economic and Social Affairs: Living Arrangements of Older Persons; Daoust: Elderly People and Responses to COVID-19 in 27 Countries.

3. Governance Arrangements

Arguably, incomplete data sets and missing political awareness were mutually reinforcing. Historically, both could be traced back to the low levels of institutional recognition by global organizations of health governance that were supposed to regulate care and caring relationships in multilateral contexts. For example, care related topics and concerns remain scattered across a wide variety of international organizations, such as the International Labor Organization (ILO), the International Organization for Migration (IOM), the World Health Organization (WHO), the International Monetary Fund (IMF), and the World Bank. Similarly, the immediate competencies and responsibility for care were delineated among a set of UN agencies and committees that encompassed, for instance, education (UNESCO) or women's rights (UN WOMEN). Moreover, it needs to be noted, that the WHO's founding documents' emphasis is put single-mindedly on health. WHO documents nearly exclusively used the notion of care with respect to medical care or health care regarding the prevention and treatment of illness and diseases.[51] Furthermore, international organizations' operations and their actions to coordinate and orchestrate often reflected the primary concerns of governments, such as security, economic prosperity, or individual freedom. In addition, international organizations tend to frame care as a commodity amenable to financial investment and monetary value to be distributed across societies aligned to national welfare and family policies.[52]

Against this background, the WHO's neglect of the pandemic's impact on care is unsurprising. During the Covid-19 pandemic, the WHO operated as the most critical international organization and coordination unit. The initial *Strategic Preparedness and Response Plan*[53], which guided the organization's pandemic policies from February to June 2020, emphasized the provision care in medical and clinical contexts. The updated plan that guides WHO's responses between February 2021 and January 2022[54] then began to include aspects of care. It regarded the provision of care as a critical, distinct aspect beyond immediate medical and clinical concerns.[55] The plan outlined, among other things, that women have been particularly affected by the socio-economic impacts of pandemic policies. WHO experts pointed to the »increased expectations to deliver unpaid care at home and in the community.«[56] They recommended that the future implementation of the preparedness and response framework »should be done to ensure linkages to

---

[51] Cf. the Constitution of the World Health Organization.
[52] Ungerson: Social Politics and the Commodification of Care.
[53] WHO: COVID-19 Strategic Preparedness and Response Plan, June 2020.
[54] WHO: COVID-19 Strategic Preparedness and Response Plan, February 2021.
[55] Ibid., p. 15 f.
[56] Ibid., p. 2.

other services, including safety and care, therapeutics and vaccines, with gender balance and inclusion approaches in participation and coordination structures.«[57] National expert committees and government advisory bodies on Covid-19 showed a lack of inclusiveness and interdisciplinarity.[58] They were therefore slow to effectively share care-related expertise to create awareness or guide policy decisions.

In June 2020, the WHO set up a framework to monitor and evaluate international and national performances during the Covid-19 pandemic. This framework included nine pillars: country-level coordination, planning, and monitoring; risk communication and community engagement; surveillance, rapid response teams, and case investigation; points of entry, international travel, and transport; national laboratories; infection prevention and control; case management; operational support and logistics; maintaining essential health services and systems.[59] In this context, relational aspects of other-directed care and self-care again remained marginalized aspects. As the evaluation framework simply translated pandemic responses into quantitative indicators, its statistical logic could not integrate properly concrete concerns of caring relationships due to the lack of data on care.

In sum, these observations indicate a mismatch: on the one hand, the Covid-19 pandemic has reminded billions of people of the centrality of care for human lives, safety, and dignity and revealed its intricate and fragile connections to the politics of local-global entanglements. On the other hand, care was almost absent from the official response of the international community. To close this »care gap« would at least require improved data collection and the establishment of a global institutionalized framework dedicated to care and caring relationships. However, suppose such actions reproduce current practices of data-driven governmentality and replicate dominant modes of neoliberal formations such as surveillance capitalism that regard care as a mere commodity. In that case, it remains questionable whether these efforts would be able to account for the human realities of care adequately.[60] Moreover, the care gap might stem from deeper roots: international institutions and the norms that underpin modern statehood and citizenship sit very uneasily with the practices and ethics of caring relationships.

---

[57] Ibid., p. 12.
[58] Rajan et al.: Governance of the Covid-19 Response.
[59] WHO: COVID-19 Strategic Preparedness and Response Plan, February 2021.
[60] Tronto: Creating Caring Institutions; Tronto: Moral Boundaries.

4. International Relations and Ethics of Caring Relationships

The scholarship on the ethics of care emphasizes the centrality of humans as relational beings. Selma Sevenhuijsen argues: »The guiding thought of the ethic of care is that people need each other in order to lead a good life and that they can only exist as individuals through and via caring relationships with others.«[61] Virginia Held mentions that care relations are constituted through particular senses of connection, encounter, and response, which carry moral value.[62] However, this element of relationality makes it complicated to integrate the ethics of care into broader, global governance and health diplomacy.[63] The main reason is the kind of ontology underpinning disciplinary perspectives on international relations that consider law and legislation as constitutive practices for both international society and the internal organization of nation states. International law as an primary international institutions puts interstate relations on a stable procedural basis. It ensures the pursuit of primary societal and political goals in national and international contexts despite anarchical conditions.[64] International law functions as a procedural reality that shapes, limits, and constrains the interests of states in international contexts and functions as a testament to a state's identity; the »social texture« of international society.[65]

Proponents of care ethics, in contrast, stress that abstract principles and procedures of international contractual law do not easily translate into the concrete and particular sphere and complex needs typical for care relations.[66] For instance, contractual aspects of impartiality, rationality, and rule-making underpinning practices of international law are in significant tension with requirements to develop a moral sense of obligation to comply with international law and rights and emphasize social relations.[67] What is missing in such instrumental interpretations of international relations is a bridge between foreign policy and modes of multilateralism based on international contractual law and the ethics of care. The latter requires recognizing the moral dimensions of rights and responsibilities and the roles of individuals, not only as citizens but also as relational beings. As Fiona Robinson argues:

---

[61] Sevenhuijsen: The Place of Care, p. 183.
[62] Held: The Ethics of Care, pp. 9–13.
[63] Cf. Robinson: The Limits of a Rights-Based Approach to International Ethics, p. 67.
[64] Watson/Bull: States Systems and International Societies.
[65] Reus-Smit: The Constitutional Structure of International Society and the Nature of Fundamental Institutions; Reus-Smit: The Moral Purpose of the State.
[66] Held: The Ethics of Care, p. 99.
[67] Robinson: The Limits of a Rights-Based Approach to International Ethics, p. 6.

»[a]n adequate approach to global ethics [...] must not be limited to the application of rational principles, universal codes, and impartiality in moral judgment; rather, it must be, at least in part, a morality of attachment and connection, which can help us to learn to respond adequately to particular others, rather than the universal, ›all others‹ in human rights theory.«[68]

This mismatch between the procedural qualities of rational international law as the modus vivendi for global governance and the moral responsibilities of states and individuals towards the often-informal practicalities of caring relationships is crucial to understand why governments have only marginally dealt with the disrupted realities of transnational care dependencies during the Covid-19 pandemic.

The securitization of the pandemic health emergency is another reason. Although the potential collapse of hospitals was the primary official concern of governments during the pandemic, it is important to note how the public debate framed the new infectious disease often as national security threat. In these discourses, eventually, state control triumphed over civil liberties and matters of health over care.[69] The concern with national security – understood as keeping the population safe and healthy – was reflected in the wartime rhetoric used in many countries, such as China, the United States, South Korea and France.[70] The preponderance of national security was evident from the implementation of border restrictions,[71] the announcement of export bans for medical equipment,[72] and the role that armed forces played in implementing NPIs. To legitimize those extraordinary measures, politicians framed the infectious disease as security threat, sometimes in strong resonance with growing patriotic or nationalist sentiments.[73] Under such conditions, governments allowed for exemptions for border crossings such as green lanes or commuting of (essential) workers to continue economic production and stability of the health care system. Cross-border flows were permitted not because governments acknowledged the vital webs of relational care among communities and families, but because they had to serve economic and health imperatives.

A broader critique from an ethics of care perspective, in addition concerns an individualist ontology inherent to liberal traditions in international relations theory. Liberal approaches privilege the principles of self-interest and individual autonomy. Such understandings regard humans as autonomous beings while failing to

---

68 Robinson: The Limits of a Rights-Based Approach to International Ethics, p. 6.
69 Cf. Rushton: Global Health Security.
70 Coatleven/Hublet/Rospars: Subsidiary Crisis Management in the COVID-19 Pandemic; Goodwin/Chemerinski: The Trump Administration; Dias et al.: The »Total Continuous War« and the COVID-19 Pandemic: Neoliberal Governmentality, Disposable Bodies and Protected Lives.
71 Kenwick/Simmons: Pandemic Response as Border Politics.
72 Hackenbroich/Shapiro/Varma: Health Sovereignty.
73 Woods et al.: COVID-19, Nationalism, and the Politics of Crisis; Kenwick/Simmons: Pandemic Response as Border Politics.

acknowledge the diversity of caring relationships and layers of responsibilities that tie humans as social beings together.[74] Joan Tronto remarks that recognizing the ties between and among individuals also means addressing the issue of dependency and power hierarchies among caring individuals, which »has been anathema to liberal notions of individual autonomy.«[75] She further argues, »[d]ependence, implying as it does that those who care for dependents can exercise power over them. But as many feminist theorists have observed, the conception of the rational, autonomous man has been a fiction, constructed to fit with liberal theories«.[76]

The tensions between individual autonomy, cost-benefit analysis, and the nature of caring relationships have important implications for the practices of international relations. Therein is a crucial lesson of the pandemic: the moral value of affective, non-atomistic relationships ought to be blended with current utilitarian modes and practices of multilateralism so that caring relationships and their inherent vulnerabilities can become a concern of international law and critical reference points for collective action during future health crisis. Our point here is not to argue against the essential role of rights, domestic and international law in international relations.[77] But individualism, if articulated as a binary ideology against collective interests and principles of precautionary collective action, does not help much in solving the policy riddles during a public health crisis in a responsible manner.[78] The Covid-19 pandemic illustrated the prevalence of classic public health dilemmas which influenced shifting public acceptance of preventive public health policy measures – from vaccinations and surveillance to mask-wearing and lockdown.[79] Overly individualistic approaches that prioritize personal freedoms were damaging to protect care relations from disruptions, as the failed protection of elderly persons in nursing homes in Sweden and the UK amply demonstrate.

Can the conflicting conceptual frameworks mentioned above be rendered complementary? Which type of governmentality should support public health policies during the next pandemic?[80] How can we connect alternative concepts, categories, and methodologies to translate concrete concerns of care into broader inter-

[74] Held: Morality, Care, and International Law, p. 176; Tronto: Creating Caring Institutions, p. 162.
[75] Tronto: Creating Caring Institutions, p. 162; Glenn: Utopian Visions, p. 85.
[76] Tronto: Creating Caring Institutions, p. 162.
[77] Cf. Robinson: The Limits of a Rights-Based Approach to International Ethics; Held: Morality, Care, and International Law, p. 176; For a discussion of liberal rights and law during the pandemic cf. Jasanoff: Pathologies of Liberty.
[78] Mickiewicz: Are Individualistic Societies Worse at Responding to Pandemics?
[79] Maaravi et al.: The Tragedy of The Commons; Yong: The Fundamental Question of The Pandemic is Shifting.
[80] For the debate on conflicting pandemic governmentalities see: Colombo: Human Rights-inspired Governmentality: COVID-19 through a Human Dignity Perspective; Kim: Bio or Zoe?: dilemmas of biopolitics and data governmentality during COVID-19; Dias et al.: The »Total Continuous War« and the COVID-19 Pandemic: Neoliberal Governmentality, Disposable Bodies and Protected Lives.

national political and legal contexts? This chapter merely raises these issues and offers a care-focused perspective without providing systematic answers. Three steps could provide a preliminary remedy for the neglect of care relations within international relations theories.

First, as feminist scholarship suggests, by emphasizing that the »inter-national« is, first and foremost, »inter-personal«, conceptual possibilities open up. To foreground relational aspects allows one to redirect analytical self-interested states, focus beyond the individual atomism and contractual interactions.[81] Second, it is worthwhile to acknowledge the limitations of current rights-based ethics for grasping the social and political dimensions of international and global moral concerns. As Fiona Robinson argues, traditional moral reasoning in international relations theory and political theory that stands behind human rights and states' rights is insufficient.[82] Rights in the liberal tradition represent abstract, impersonal, and rule-oriented discourses. They refer to autonomous rational individuals and are – given their fiction of equality among contractual parties – hard to reconcile with the typically asymmetric and dependent nature of care relations. The latter represent a kind of moral value that remains »after the law had spoken« and »cannot be legislated away.«[83] Third, the complexity and ambiguity of caring relationships do not easily translate beyond the private, personal sphere into international and global political decision making contexts – not to mention navigating care relations across different cultures and societies. The challenge for critical care ethics, according to Robinson, is that it »reveals the relational self, which resists the hierarchical binaries of Western modernity, and opens the door to ethics as plural, resistant of the dichotomies that divide us and are always open to revision.«[84]

Effective pandemic interventions and policies require collective modes of implementation, enforcement, and accountability which were clearly lacking during the pandemic. The tendency to push risks and choices down to the personal level of decision making, that is inherent to neoliberal discourses, is not helpful either, as it »creates a veil over the wounds inflicted by precarity and crisis while facilitating the unloading of responsibilities onto individuals and families.«[85] Such a notion of care invites a neoliberal reading that could prevent a more meaningful integration of caring relationships with IR theories. Indeed, the individualization of responsibilities was perhaps nowhere more evident during the pandemic than in the field of care relations.

---

[81] Wenham: Feminist Global Health Security. Cf. Enloe: Bananas, Beaches and Bases; Robinson: Stop Talking and Listen. Similar conceptual issues were raised prominently in the debate on »human security«. Cf. Adger et al.: Human Security.
[82] Robinson: The Limits of a Rights-Based Approach to International Ethics.
[83] Held: The Ethics of Care, p. 100.
[84] Robinson: Resisting Hierarchies Through Relationality, p. 14.
[85] Nguyen/Zavoretti/Tronto: Beyond the Global Care Chain, p. 210.

Conclusion

This essay explores the worldwide disruptions of care relations caused by the implementation of non-pharmaceutical interventions to curb the spread of SARS-CoV-2. The disruptions were considerable and, at the same time, demonstrated that care relations possess crucial international political dimensions – involving global care chains and dependencies that often arose within informal, illicit, and undeclared settings. Far from being a purely private burden or an issue of individual coping strategies, the global system of care dependencies came under immense pressure when countries started implementing border restrictions and travel bans. The insufficient governmental pandemic response put the fragility and (political) vulnerability of transnational care relations in full display. A possible explanation for why most governments failed to address the disruptions of local-global care entanglements seems obvious. Missing statistical data about care strongly correlate with governmental neglect. However, at a structural level it is important to look beyond inadequate knowledge. Although these issues cannot be fully resolved here concerning their theoretical and policy dimensions, this essay indicates a disjuncture between the social characteristics of care relations and the dominant understandings of individual rights and duties that underpin constitutive legal practices of modern states. In other words, at the core of the problem is an ontological incommensurability between the rational basis of international interactions of modern states and the relational characteristics of transnational care work. This *care gap* in political theory and international relations practices grew in significance during the Covid-19 pandemic. It calls for a broadening, and care-centered reorientation of, existing conceptual understandings, empirical analysis, and policy advice.

References

Abuelgasim, Eyad / Li Jing Saw / Manasi Shirke / Mohamed Zeinah / Amer Harky: COVID-19: Unique Public Health Issues Facing Black, Asian and Minority Ethnic Communities, in: Current Problems in Cardiology, 45(8), 100621, 2020.

Addati, Laura / Umberto Cattaneo / Valeria Esquivel / Isabel Valarino: International Labour Organization. Care Work and Care Jobs for The Future of Decent Work, June 28, 2018, https://www.ilo.org/wcmsp5/groups/public/---dgreports/---dcomm/---publ/documents/publication/wcms_633135.pdf; last accessed June 19, 2021.

Adger, W. Neil / Juan M. Pulhin / Jon Barnett / Geoffrey D. Dabelko / Grete K. Hovelsrud / Marc Levy / Ursula Oswald Spring / Coleen H. Vogel. Human Security, Cambridge 2014.

Barne, Donna/Pirlea, Florina: Money Sent Home by Workers now Largest Source of External Financing in Low- and Middle-Income Countries (Excluding China), World Bank Data Blog, July 19, 2019, https://blogs.worldbank.org/opendata/money-sent-home-workers-now-largest-source-external-financing-low-and-middle-income; last accessed July 08, 2021.

Bartl, Walter/Christian Papilloud/Audrey Terracher-Lipinski: Governing by Numbers – Key Indicators and the Politics of Expectations. An Introduction, in: Historical Social Research, 44(2), 2019, pp. 7–43.

Baumann, Menno: COVID-19 and Mental Health in Children and Adolescents: A Diagnostic Panel to Map Psycho-social Consequences in the Pandemic Context, in: Discover Mental Health 1(1), 2021, pp. 1–15.

Brandhorst, Rosa/Loretta Baldassar/Raelene Wilding: Introduction to the Special Issue: Transnational Family Care ›On Hold‹? Intergenerational Relationships and Obligations in The Context of Immobility Regimes, in: Journal of Intergenerational Relationships, 18(3), 2020, pp. 261–280.

British Society of Gerontology: Statement from the President and Members of the National Executive Committee of the British Society of Gerontology on COVID-19, March 20, 2020, https://www.britishgerontology.org/publications/bsg-statements-on-covid-19/statement-one; last accessed June 19, 2021.

Charmes, Jacques: The Unpaid Care Work and the Labour Market. An Analysis of Time Use Data Based on the Latest World Compilation of Time-Use Surveys, ILO, Geneva 2019.

Cheng, Cindy/Joan Barceló/Allison Spencer Hartnett/Robert Kubinec/Luca Messerschmidt: COVID-19 Government Response Event Dataset, CoronaNet v.1.0, in: Nature Human Behaviour, 4, 2020, pp. 756–768.

Christakis, Dimitri A./Will Van Cleve/Frederik J. Zimmerman: Estimation of US Children's Educational Attainment and Years of Life Lost Associated with Primary School Closures During the Coronavirus Disease 2019 Pandemic, in: JAMA Netw Open, 3(11), 2020.

Clark, Nigel/Giovanni Bettini: »Floods« of Migrants, Flows of Care: Between Climate Displacement and Global Care Chains, in: The Sociological Review 65(2), 2017, pp. 36–54.

Coatleven, Lucie/François Hublet/Théophile Rospars: Subsidiary Crisis Management in the COVID-19 Pandemic: Germany's Federalist Experiment in Transborder Perspective, December 01, 2020, https://legrandcontinent.eu/fr/wp-content/uploads/sites/2/2020/12/Subsidiary-crisis-management-en.pdf, last accessed June 19, 2021.

Colombo, Enzo. Human Rights-inspired Governmentality: COVID-19 through a Human Dignity Perspective, in: Critical Sociology, 47(4–5), 2021, pp. 571–581.

Cramer, Katharina/Maximilian Mayer/Janna Hartmann/Julia Holz/Kilian Knorr/Ga Young Lee/Philip Nock/Annalena Pott/Miriam Siemes/Jan David Zabala Gepp: COVID-19 Border Restrictions and Cross-Border Care Relations: The Cases of Germany and Vietnam, in: Working Paper Series: Politics of Pandemic Care, CASSIS/Bonn University, no. 2, May 2021, https://www.cassis.uni-bonn.de/de/ueber-cassis/prof.-maximilian-mayer/politics-of-pandemic-care/WP2_Border%20Restrictions%20and%20Care%20Relations_Cramer%20et%20al_20210527.pdf; last accessed July 01, 2021.

Curiskis, Artis/Conor Kelly/Erin Kissane/Kara Oehler: What We Know – and What We Don't Know – About the Impact of the Pandemic on Our Most Vulnerable Community, The COVID Tracking Project, March 31, 2021, https://covidtracking.com/analysis-updates/what-we-know-about-the-impact-of-the-pandemic-on-our-most-vulnerable-community; last accessed July 10, 2021.

Daoust, Jean-Francois: Elderly People and Responses to COVID-19 in 27 Countries, in: Plos One 15(7): e0235590.

Davies, Sara E./Clare Wenham: Why the COVID-19 Response Needs International Relations, in: International Affairs, 96(5), 2020, pp. 1227–1251.

Dias, Bárbara LCV/Jean-François Y. Deluchey: The »Total Continuous War« and the COVID-19 Pandemic: Neoliberal Governmentality, Disposable Bodies and Protected Lives, in: Law, Culture and the Humanities, 2020, https://doi.org/10.1177/1743872120973157.

Dong, Ensheng/Hongru Du/Lauren Gardner: Interactive Web-Based Dashboard to Track Covid-19 In Real Time, in: The Lancet, 20(5), 2020, pp. 533–534.

Duffy, Mignon/Randy Albelda/Clare Hammonds: Counting Care Work: The Empirical and Policy Applications of Care Theory, in: Social Problems, 60, 2013, pp. 145–167.

Enloe, Cynthia: Bananas, Beaches and Bases: Making Feminist Sense of International Politics, Berkeley 2014.

European Centre for Disease Prevention and Control: Surveillance data from public online national reports on COVID-19 in Long-Term Care Facilities, https://www.ecdc.europa.eu/en/all-topics-z/coronavirus/threats-and-outbreaks/covid-19/prevention-and-control/LTCF-data; last accessed July 10, 2021.

Feige, Edgar L.: Defining and Estimating Underground and Informal Economies: The New Institutional Economics Approach in: World Development 18(7), 1990, pp. 989–1002.

Fine Michael/Bob Davidson: The Marketization of Care: Global Challenges and National Responses in Australia, in: Current Sociology, 66(4), 2008, pp. 503–516.

Glenn, Evelyn N.: Utopian Visions: Engaged Sociologies for the 21st Century, in: Contemporary Sociology, 29(1), 2020, pp. 84–94.

Goodwin, Michele/Erwin Chemerinsky: The Trump Administration: Immigration, Racism, and COVID-19, in: University of Pennsylvania Law Review 169(2), 2021, pp. 313–381.

Hackenbroich, Jonathan / Jeremy Shapiro / Tara Varma: Health Sovereignty: How to Build a Resilient European Response to Pandemics. Policy Brief of the European Council on Foreign Relations, June 29, 2020, https://ecfr.eu/publication/health_sovereignty_how_to_build_a_resilient_european_response_to_pandemics; last accessed April 10, 2021.

Hale, Thomas / Noam Angrist / Rafael Goldszmidt: A Global Panel Database of Pandemic Policies. Oxford COVID-19 Government Response Tracker, in: Nature Human Behaviour, 5, 2020, pp. 529–538.

Held, Virginia: The Ethics of Care. Personal, Political, and Global. Oxford 2006.

Held, Virginia: Morality, Care, and International Law, in: Ethics & Global Politics, 4(3), 2011, pp. 173–194.

Hochschild, Arlie: The Commercialization of Intimate Life: Notes from Home and Work, Berkeley 2003.

Hochschild, Arlie: Global Care Chains and Emotional Surplus Value, in: Giddens, Anthony / Hutton, William: On the Edge. Living with Global Capitalism, London 2000, pp. 130–146.

Jasanoff, Sheila: Virtual, Visible, and Actionable: Data Assemblages and the Sightlines of Justice, in: Big Data & Society 4(2), 2017, pp. 1–15.

Jasanoff, Sheila: Pathologies of Liberty. Public Health Sovereignty and the Political Subject in the Covid-19 Crisis, in: Cahiers Droit, Sciences & Technologies, 11, 2020, pp. 125–149.

Kenwick, Michael / Beth Simmons: Pandemic Response as Border Politics, in: International Organization 74(S1), 2020, pp. 36–58.

Kim, Yeran: Bio or Zoe?: Dilemmas of Biopolitics and Data Governmentality during COVID-19, in: Cultural Studies, 35(2–3), 2021, pp. 370–381.

Kitchin, Rob: Civil Liberties or Public Health, or Civil Liberties and Public Health? Using Surveillance Technologies to Tackle the Spread of COVID-19, in: Space and Polity, 24(3), 2020, pp. 362–381.

Koggel, Christine M.: Perspectives on Equality: Constructing a Relational Theory, Lanham 1998.

Leiblfinger, Michael / Veronika Prieler / Karin Schwiter / Jennifer Steiner / Aranka Benazha / Helma Lutz: Impact of COVID-19 Policy Responses on Live-In Care Workers in Austria, Germany, and Switzerland, in: Journal of Long-Term Care, 2020, pp. 144–150.

Lewis, Jane: Gender and Welfare Regimes: Further Thoughts, in: Social Politics: International Studies in Gender, State & Society, 4, 1997, pp. 160–177.

Lutz, Helma: The New Maids: Transnational Women and the Care Economy, London / New York, 2011.

Lynch, Kathleen: Love Labour as a Distinct and Non-Commodifiable Form of Care Labour, in: The Sociological Review, 55(3), 2007, pp. 550–570.

Lynch, Kathleen/Manolis Kalaitzake/Margaret Crean: Care and Affective Relations: Social Justice and Sociology, in: The Sociological Review, Vol. 69(1), 2021, pp. 53–71.

Maaravi, Yossi/Aharon Levy/Tamara Gur/Dan Confino/Sandra Segal: The Tragedy of the Commons: How Individualism and Collectivism Affected the Spread of the Covid-19 Pandemic, in: Front Public Health, 9(627559), 2021.

Martin, Florence S./Garazi Zulaika: Who Cares for Children? A Descriptive Study of Care-Related Data Available Through Global Household Surveys and How These Could Be Better Mined to Inform Policies and Services to Strengthen Family Care, in: Global Social Welfare, 3, 2016, pp. 51–74.

Mickiewicz, Tomasz: Are Individualistic Societies Worse at Responding to Pandemics? in: The Conversation, October 13, 2020, https://theconversation.com/Are-Individualistic-Societies-Worse-At-Responding-To-Pandemics-147386; last accessed June 19, 2021.

Mignon, Duffy: Making Care Count. A Century of Gender, Race, and Paid Care Work. New Brunswick 2011.

Migration Data: Migration Data Relevant for The Covid-19-Pandemic, March 10, 2021, https://migrationdataportal.org/themes/migration-data-relevant-covid-19-pandemic; last accessed June 19, 2021.

Mor, Nachiket: In Developing Countries, Communities and Primary Care Providers – Not Hospitals – Hold the Key to Successful Pandemic Response, Brookings Institution, May 14, 2020, https://www.brookings.edu/blog/future-development/2020/05/14/in-developing-countries-communities-and-primary-care-providers-not-hospitals-hold-the-key-to-successful-pandemic-response/; last accessed April 02, 2021.

Nguyen, Minh T. N./Roberta Zavoretti/Joan Tronto: Beyond the Global Care Chain: Boundaries, Institutions and Ethics of Care, in: Ethics and Social Welfare, 11(3), 2017, pp. 199–212.

Palenga-Möllenbeck, Ewa: Care Chains in Eastern and Central Europe: Male and Female Domestic Work at the Intersections of Gender, Class, and Ethnicity, in: Journal of Immigrant & Refugee Studies, 11(4), 2013, pp. 364–383.

Pfefferbaum, Betty/Carole S. North: Children and Families in The Context of Disasters: Implications for Preparedness and Response, in: Family Psychology 24(2), 2008, pp. 6–10.

Rajan, Dheepa, et al.: Governance of the Covid-19 Response: A Call for More Inclusive and Transparent Decision-Making, in: BMJ Global Health 5(5), 2020, e002655.

Reus-Smit, Christian: The Constitutional Structure of International Society and the Nature of Fundamental Institutions, in: International Organization, 51(4), 1997, pp. 555–589.

Reus-Smit, Christian: The Moral Purpose of the State: Culture, Social Identity, and Institutional Rationality in International Relations, Princeton 1999.

Robinson, Fiona: The Limits of a Rights-Based Approach to International Ethics, in: Evans, Tony (ed.): Human Rights Fifty Years On: A Reappraisal, Manchester 1998, pp. 58–76.

Robinson, Fiona: Resisting Hierarchies Through Relationality, in: The Ethics of Care. International Journal of Care and Caring, 4(1), 2020, pp. 11–23.

Robinson, Fiona: Globalizing Care: Ethics, Feminist Theory, and International Relations, in: Alternatives: Global, Local, Political, 22(1), 1997, pp. 113–133.

Robinson, Fiona: Stop Talking and Listen: Discourse Ethics and Feminist Care Ethics in International Political Theory, in: Millenium Journal of International Relations 39(3), 2011, pp. 845–860.

Rogge, Mary E.: The Future is Now. Social Work, Disaster Management, and Traumatic Stress in the 21st Century, in: Journal of Social Service Research, 30(2), 2004, pp. 1–6.

Rottenburg, Richard/Sally E. Merry: A World of Indicators: The Making of Governmental Knowledge Through Quantification, in: Richard Rottenburg et al. (eds.): The World of Indicators. The Making of Governmental Knowledge through Quantification, Cambridge 2015, pp. 1–33.

Royal Commission into Violence, Abuse, Neglect and Exploitation of People with Disability: Statement of Concern – The Response to the COVID-19 Pandemic for People with Disability, March 26, 2020, https://disability.royalcommission.gov.au/publications/statement-concern-response-covid-19-pandemic-people-disability; last accessed May 15, 2021

Rushton, Simon: Global Health Security: Security for Whom? Security from What?, in: Political Studies 59(4), 2011, pp. 779–796.

Schwenken, Helen/Lisa-Marie Heimeshoff: Domestic Workers Count: Global Data on An Often-Invisible Sector, Kassel 2011.

Secretary of State for Health and Social Care: The Government's Response to the Joint Committee on Human Rights Report: The Government's Response to COVID-19: Human Rights Implications, December 2020, https://committees.parliament.uk/publications/4154/documents/41106/default/; last accessed June 20, 2021.

Sevenhuijsen, Selma: Citizenship and the Ethics of Care: Feminist Considerations on Justice, Morality and Politics, London/Routledge 1998.

Sevenhuijsen, Selma: The Place of Care: The Relevance of the Feminist Ethic of Care for Social Policy, in: Feminist Theory, 4(2), 2003, pp. 179–197.

Smith, James A./Jenni Judd: COVID-19: Vulnerability and The Power of Privilege in a Pandemic, in: Health Promotion Journal of Australia, 31, 2020, pp. 158–160.

SOS Children's Villages International/Development Initiatives: The Care of Children in Data. Evidence, Gaps and Opportunities for Change in the SDGS, Briefing Paper 2017, https://www.sos-childrensvillages.org/getmedia/881d3ec2-92a9-4a3b-9425-6d074be04c27/SOS-Children-s-Villages_The-care-of-children-in-data.pdf; last accessed March 15, 2021.

Steiner, Jennifer / Veronika Prieler / Michael Leiblfinger / Aranka Benazha: Völlig Legal!? Rechtliche Rahmung und Legalitätsnarrative in der 24h-Betreuung in Deutschland, Österreich und der Schweiz, in: Österreichische Zeitung für Soziologie, 44, pp. 1–19.

Straßheim, Holger / Silke Beck (eds.): Handbook of Behavioural Change and Public Policy, Cheltenham 2019.

The Independent Panel: COVID-19: Make it the Last Pandemic, 2021, https://theindependentpanel.org/wp-content/uploads/2021/05/COVID-19-Make-it-the-Last-Pandemic_final.pdf; last accessed June 19, 2021.

Tronto, Joan C.: Creating Caring Institutions: Politics, Plurality, and Purpose, in: Ethics and Social Welfare, 4(2), 2010, pp. 158–171.

Tronto, Joan C.: Moral Boundaries. A Political Argument for an Ethic of Care, New York / London 1993.

Ungerson, Clare: Social Politics and the Commodification of Care, Social Politics: International Studies, in: Gender, State & Society, 4, 1997, pp. 362–381.

United Nations Department of Economic and Social Affairs: Living Arrangements of Older Persons: A Report on an Expanded International Dataset (ST/ESA/SER.A/407), 2017, https://www.un.org/en/development/desa/population/publications/pdf/ageing/LivingArrangements.pdf; last accessed June 23, 2021.

United Nations Human Rights Office of the High Commissioner: COVID-19: Who is Protecting the People with Disabilities?, March 17, 2020, https://www.ohchr.org/EN/NewsEvents/Pages/DisplayNews.aspx?NewsID=25725; last accessed July 07, 2021.

Watson, Adam / Hedley Bull: States Systems and International Societies, in: Review of International Studies, 13(2), 1987, pp. 147–153.

Wenham, Clare: The Oversecuritization of Global Health: Changing the Terms of Debate, in: International Affairs, 95(5), 2019, pp. 1093–1110.

Wenham, Clare: Feminist Global Health Security, Oxford 2021.

Widding Isaksen, Lise / Lena Näre: Local Loops and Micro-Mobilities of Care: Rethinking Care in Egalitarian Contexts, in: Journal of European Social Policy, 29(5), 2019, pp. 593–599.

Woods, Eric Taylor / Robert Schertzer / Liah Greenfeld / Chris Hughes / Cynthia Miller-Idriss: COVID-19, Nationalism, and the Politics of Crisis: A Scholarly Exchange, in: Nations and Nationalism. Journal of the Association for the Study of Ethnicity and Nationalism, 25, 2020, pp. 807–825.

World Bank: Defying Predictions, Remittance Flows Remain Strong During COVID-19 Crisis, May 12, 2021, https://www.worldbank.org/en/news/press-re

lease/2021/05/12/defying-predictions-remittance-flows-remain-strong-during-covid-19-crisis; last accessed June 19, 2021.

World Health Organization: 2019 Novel Coronavirus (2019nCoV): Strategic Preparedness and Response Plan, February 04, 2020, https://www.who.int/docs/default-source/coronaviruse/srp-04022020.pdf; last accessed June 19, 2021.

World Health Organization: COVID19 Strategic Preparedness and Response. Monitoring and Evaluation Framework, June 05, 2020, https://www.who.int/docs/default-source/coronaviruse/who-ncov-me-framework-web.pdf?sfvrsn=656e430f_1&download=true; last accessed June 19, 2021.

World Health Organization: COVID-19 Strategic Preparedness and Response Plan (February 1, 2021 to January 31, 2022), 2021 https://apps.who.int/iris/rest/bitstreams/1335425/retrieve; last accessed June 19, 2021.

Yeates, Nicola: Global Care Chains, in: International Feminist Journal of Politics, 6(3), 2011, pp. 369–391.

Yeates, Nicola: Globalizing Care Economies and Migrant Workers. Explorations in Global Care Chains, London 2009.

Yeoh, Brenda / Huang, Shirlena: Family, Migration and the Gender Politics of Care, in: McGregor, Andrew / Law, Lisa / Miller, Fiona (eds.): Routledge Handbook of Southeast Asian Development, London 2017, pp. 173–185.

Yong, Ed: The Fundamental Question of The Pandemic is Shifting, in: The Atlantic, June 09, 2021, https://www.theatlantic.com/health/archive/2021/06/individualism-still-spoiling-pandemic-response/619133/; last accessed June 19, 2021.

Peter Goodrich

Mortem Instituere

I write as the bans, lockdowns, screenings, masks, closures and distancing of the pandemic are abrogated in New York State by gubernatorial decree and fireworks, the ludic and the legal. The *feux d'artifice*, dramatically playful fulminations are a nice touch as the doldrums and deflation of separation – of being in hiding – are replaced by a return to the viscera and vividness of the in person. The shift, which for common lawyers can usefully be designated as a move from *in rem* to *in personam*, from law to equity, designates a transition from exclusively machinic relay to the haptics and sensibilities of more immediate corporeal apprehension. Now we face the question of who returns, to what, after learning which lessons, how changed after the great fantasm and equally significant reality of death running amock the world of the living? What have we learned and how do we need to change before the happy relief of quotidian abnormality drowns the anguish of memory and the delirious politics of response to viral crises?

An absurdly inaccurate and bizarrely paranoid collection of essays by the philosopher Giorgio Agamben can form a point of entry. In *Where are we Now? The Epidemic as Politics* the principal argument is that a relatively minor viral threat to human life was used as an excuse for a state of exception, an abrogation of legal process of such magnitude as to exceed even wartime curbs on liberty and curfews of movement.[1] *Inter arma silent leges* becomes: amongst viruses laws are silent. There is of course some truth in that assertion. Laws were not used to equalize access to medications and treatments, nor were protective measures evenly applied. Race, class and sex were variables which meant that exposure to infection and likelihood of death were much more prevalent in low income communities and in low status jobs. Production lines, hospital emergency care, transportation and construction work all suffered much higher rates of death as also did those in minority demographics and associated counties with limited health care infrastructure. Politicians failed to act or acted improvidently, people died and the rituals of death could not be observed, the ceremonies of mourning abrogated by decrees that precluded the in person witnessing of the passage of the no longer in person.

There is no question that the delirious, unprincipled and poorly administered responses cost lives as well as imposed unnecessary restrictions and at times draconian mandates upon interaction as well as perambulation and burial. In the

---

[1] Cf. Agamben: Where Are We Now?

main, however, these were legal constraints and injunctions, the work of panicked parliaments and feverish executives. In a fashion not dissimilar to Agamben they seem frequently to have decided ahead of learning the facts, prior to evidence and in response to imaginal threats as well as real deaths. If law did not perform its historic function of requiring political reason to follow rules of procedure in such circumstances it was not because of the silence of the jurists so much as a product of the exponential excess of rules, the pluralization of delegations and administrative regulations. The errors lay in too much law, too unstable a set of promulgated norms, too impermanent or malleable a series of decisions in the face of the great and vanishing unknown of the unseen, the combustions and combinatorials of sub-atomic particles and invisible microbes. Law was not really the problem and it is certainly not the solution.

What is to be learned is a question of what did *not* happen, the failure of the legal system to require reason and restraint in the proliferation of norms. The birth and death of infection rates was inversely mirrored in the birth and death of novel promulgations in which the distance between science and political action, between medicine and law was much more of a problem than the lack of separation of powers that Agamben bemoans in his terror driven hostility to change. What is interesting, and here I proceed to my point, is not the critique of law, which is neither original nor novel, but rather the curiously reactive yet persistent theme of requiem, closure, funerals and death. A psychoanalytic reading of *Where Are We Now?* suggests a resonance of an unstated ciceronian question from the Cataline orations: *o di immortales, ubinam gentium summus? Quam rem publicam habemus*: *In qua urbe vivimus?* – »Where on earth, oh immortals, are we? What government do we have? In what city are we living?«[2] All good questions but they are directed somewhat unwittingly in Agamben's case to rituals of death rather than the larger questions implied, those of the theatrical character of the social, the opportunity presented by the mask, and the relation of the existent to the non-existent. Death came to visit, the scythe of sickness performed an unregulated yet predictable culling, non-existence became a social presence. The symbolic exchange of death entered the polity whose momentary task, in a change of venue, became more visibly and dramatically *mortem instituere*, that of instituting death in manageable or curtailed numbers, in taking the opportunity of passage to fill the void created by panic in the face of the unexpectedly virulent. Where *vitam instituere* was the coda of following past patterns, *mortem instituere* is the sign of instituting new beginnings, of the threat or embrace of death as the opening to novelty and the trigger of *poiesis*, the invention of theatres of social change, the installation of forms of being that reflect more directly where we are now, the environment we share, the bodies in common.

---

[2] Cicero: In Catilinam / Catilinarians, I, 9; transl. by the author.

Start with the theatrics, the masks and the newly thespian roles of acting from a social distance and staging institutional relations on Zoom, on Teams, on Skype on Google. It is hard to imagine a more ludic possibility, nor any more emblematic enactment of the social. If, as the jurist Pierre Legendre has lengthily elaborated and as other philosophers have recently taken up, the purpose of law is that of conveying structures, of *vitam instituere*, of instituting life in a theatrical mode that allows the quintessential legal invention, the visor and veil of medical integument is a conduit of the first category of institution, announcing the person who enters the social stage. Covid-19's first gift, if it can be termed such, meaning untaken opportunity and unentered opening was both ontological and epistemological. Suddenly everyone who could was charged with working online, staying at home, appearing on screen or performing in the social wearing a mask and appearing as an actor, from the traditional space of leisure or as an ambulant emergency, a necessarily in person operative. Masks, faces, *personae*, the thespian and terpsichorean aspects of the social were evident and visible in new ways. The paradox of Zoom is that it is the *dispositif* of the face, of the close up, of a theatrical intimacy, a ludic social presence and *desiderium* or affective longing that is staged to instruct in a play, the *serio-ludere* of a law which is classically driven by the aspect of justice and the prospect of truth.

Covid-19 accentuated the ceremony of the social, and the theatrics of social interaction have never been more evident as each and every player regularly put on a mask that not only disguises the proboscis but engenders a performance of presence, an enunciation and enactment of role and visibilization of discourse that should have had a greater degree of play, of ludic and comedic presence and presentiment. What after all was lockdown if not an opportunity to relate in different forms and by other avenues, coming as it did from the enlarged space of the *oikos*, from the domain of affect which made visible a different or indeed literal sense of *intimos recessus doctrinae*, the intimate interior space of doctrine. The mask was in other terms an incitement to the expression of desire, because of the novel conjunction of reaching out and of being virtually present, the instantiation of the presence of non-presence generating not only longing for sense, for touch, taste and smell, but also the fantasms of *mundus imaginabilis*, the spectacle of an imaginal life. Could this be the future, the *desiderium* of constant longing for what one cannot have, the infinite deferral of presence which appears only as image? And yet courtly love, *amour lointain*, seemed strangely absent, displaced perhaps by anxiety, deflected by a yearning, a nostalgia for normality as proximity.

The apparently proximate, what seemed near and larger than life was in fact only imaginal, the appearance on screen of untouchables, the vivid manifestation of virtuality as a vanishing sign of what was never present. The *zoomnambulant* relay generated the institution of a social modality of *amour lointain*, of distant, courtly love of others, of the unbearable force of desire that could not be sensorily sated. This constituted a sudden advenience of a social theatre of distant relations, of screens and masks intervening visibly to make each encounter a drama of presence and relation, a dance, a widdershin, of choreographed allure and separation. The key, the *clavis regni* of this peculiar and often desolate drama was its lack of script, its corporeal confusion, the novelty of this new mode of comedy of manners. It can be thought differently, reimagined as a radical occasion and an unprecedentedly visible event of the instituting of life, of presence becoming material and manifest because of precarity and because of the suddenly changed dynamics of interior and exterior, of *oikos* and polity. No one said that theatre should be easy or enjoyable so much as it should be instructive or to borrow from Legendre, the great and unacknowledged theorist of such unscripted scripting of the social, to institute is to project, to establish, to construct something in such a way that it holds up, so that it appears to be upright, to stand.[3]

Seldom has the theatrical process of constructing institutions or fabricating persons been more evident to the eye, more visibly on show and this despite the desiderata of distancing that catapulted the remediation of communication into scopic desires and the visuality of imaginal relays. It took the paradoxical form of separation, hiding from social life so as to foster social life: distance, deferment, delay, and frequently desipience, to trigger the unconscious in the most basic sense of the apparition of the not known. What was and still is to a great extent at issue is the most obscure object of desire, the quest to capture and sequence the microbes, to eradicate what cannot be seen by means of a process in which we simultaneously isolate from what we seek to discern and control. This is not to make the trivial point that protection is necessary when researching a threatening microbe but to enlarge upon a theoretical and theatrical prospect. The ontography of presence and absence, of visible and unseen has dramatically changed. Witness first the mediation of all relations which is simply made more evident by the near omnipresence of the masked subject which leads by lateral association to the admission that there is always a mask, a suit, a skin, a skirt, a scarf, a carapace, a robe, a habit and habitus that screens the entry to intercourse or interaction. This means we are always not seeing, our blindspots are far greater than our vision. Separation simply accentuated the sense in which the medium always negotiates the scope of distance and the degree of seclusion, the modality of masking. What is important, ontographically, and also politically, is not the tedium of regulations, the institution of restrictions upon relations, limitations on appearances, the reduction of bodies in spaces, but rather what was not seen and remained in the archipelago of the unsaid.

The mask also hides an absence, an unknown and occluded being, the other mask. Didn't Covid really teach us that there is always an unconsciousness, pat-

---

[3] Legendre: *Sur la question dogmatique en Occident*, pp. 106 ff.

terns of trauma and practices of repetition that lead to reaction rather than encounter? Separated from the combustive badinage and divagatory socializing, the distracting meetings and purgatorial conference liaisons, the individual escapes into the twilight zone of institutional encounters whereas in lockdown there is only the immediacy of the self in the poor theatre or post-dramatic scene of intimacy or at least the extimacy of interior relations. The great fear, the unconscious manifest in the closure of public space was in one sense a matter of hoping not to get what you were chasing. Now you did not have to go to work, did not have to leave the domicile, did not need to exit from loved ones or your loved self. The yearning for leisure, the cry for freedom seems to have rapidly become undesirable, too much, satiated indeed before it began. Less a question of a hero is hard to live with at home, although it is also that, than that utopian conditions, anarchic opportunities of mutual aid, are difficult to handle when they arrive without pretext or consideration.

There is another feature of the unconscious, expressed in symptoms, which relates to the triggering of fear and traumatic repetition. It may have been a partial exposure but tedium is the first sign of a wound in the fabric of the self and by extension in the projected sense of social equilibrium. Tedium, and play upon the *différance*, is phonetically and in some obscure etymological sense, *te deum*, an invocation of the divine, an instance of aperture and escape into another world. And so, it is waiting, the holding pattern, a circling desirous of another life, the looking out of the window wishing to open it, rather than looking in. Tedium is in part regressive, from adult to child, from public space to gynaeceum, from the putative goals of purpose to the anarchy of choice. The sensibility of the closed window, curtains drawn, skrim down upon the social stage moved between tedium and fear, the panic sense that the world as we knew it would disappear, would never be the same and with that affect comes the melancholy of unaccepted loss or in Agamben's case, *melancholia juridica* ironically emanating from a *soi-disant* anarchistic author.[4] A real instance of *iustitium*, of hiatus or chord and suspension of law in a time of tumult and moment of mourning leads from tedium expressive of the juridical silence, to crisis and critique declaring the bankruptcy of legal culture. In one piece on the epidemic and the failure of law it is the idiocy of an innominate law professor who in Agamben's view incorrectly distinguishes states of emergency and of exception that receives a verbal whipping.[5] As the invisible professor's distinction is stipulative the critique has to be more symptom of the author's *desiderium*, the melancholic longing for lost or unattainable love than it is of the error of the adversary. What both authors miss is that emergency is an emergence, a birth, something new.

[4] Cf. Agamben: Where Are We Now?
[5] Cf. ibid.

The window that is always open but still confines is tediously marked by the thwarted longing to escape, the sense of being trapped, behind bars, always looking out but never going out, either literally or in spectral abstraction. We cannot go there where we are not allowed is in Catholic terms mirrored in the philosopher's inversions of a non-existent conceptual space, another abstraction, the medial objective unconscious of a non-being merely longed for or railed against. Contrary to such fear of negativity, the denial of non-places, of silence and uncertainty there is also another sense of tedium as opportunity, as playful anticipation, and as creative drive. Law, and perhaps most evidently common law, is repetition that has become structural, that through longevity and use has demarcated the public sphere and political regimen of the city or other social space inhabited. It is habit and habitus of communal sense but not of course in a state of *iustitium* in which it is suspended in the face of danger, panic, fear and in our instance infection. To be a player you have to don a mask, as Grischka Petri so admirably adumbrates in Volume 1 (*In the Realm of Corona Normativies,* edited by Werner Gephart) of the current colloquy on Covid-19.[6] Is there not then a sense, a significant sensibility, an opportunity created by closure in which the unthinking – the unconscious – patterns of law and subjectivity are suddenly and expansively visibly disrupted, and in which ›we‹ become different, not least by virtue of the exposure of structure and law as fabrications that disappear when belief in them ceases to exist. What Legendre terms our fiduciary relation to law, our affective bond but also the unconscious pattern of following the emotional trail of trials, the nomos of normativity, is loosened.[7] Precedent, as I argued previously, has let us down. *Vitam instituere* in the old turn of phrase shifted to *vitam destituere* or indeed *mortem instituere.*

Implicit though largely unspoken, excluded, consigned both to out of the way spaces and strangely covert rituals, dark suits, black hearses, the practices of interment or incineration come most readily to mind as the tenebrous phantasm unleashed and to Agamben's dismay often stalled by pandemic.[8] This secreted unconscious facticity of death, the negativity that subtends the rituals, the *mortem instituere* of deathbound practices is precisely the reverse of extant legal structures, the wild card, the opening announced historically by the mask, the habitus of the face that lives on. How then did Western cultures, Italy, England, France, the European Union, the United States, South America, and I could go on, face the sudden proximity of the scythe, the increasingly omnipresent spectre of non-presence. Never was it clearer, save perhaps in war, that the instituting of life is a matter of negotiating its borders and intersections with death or more accurately nothingness. The pandemic shifted and highlighted that relation, that border and conflu-

---

6 Cf. Petri: Masking the Invisible / Segments of Political Space, pp. 375–407.
7 Cf. Legendre: God in the Mirror.
8 Cf. Agamben: Where Are We Now?

ence, the shadow that plucks at our coat tails. So the point and punctum emerges in the form of a sciography, a dance of shadows, the becoming visible of the intersection that manifests that we are and we are not. Instituting life is thus more than mere theatre: it is the drama of ontography that lockdown and pandemic released, the thespian opportunities and activist possibilities made available by the shifting sands of political and medical rescripting, the multiplication of stages upon which to play in virtual or actual and masked form the persona that we wish to become.

If I started by saying that restrictions had been lifted and masks abandoned in New York it was simply to mark another moment in the play of presence and absence, quotidian and extraordinary, that interpenetrate our pandemic days. I was not suggesting that seclusion was over or that the boundary between life and death was less visible. It is rather that a different stage and new performances become possible, the no more a person within the body of the living, the shadow – be it mask or face – that accompanies and manifests our presence in its various hues, blushes, colours, frowns, smiles and grimaces are the grimoire or enigma of our play. Witnessing and now living with the viral, with forces that can crash computers and persons equally, throws our subjectivity more immediately and viscerally upon itself. I become my own shadow, I play my part as I devise it, I have seen into the void, the unconscious realms of social abrogation, I have sensed the fear, intimate and extimate of open windows and masks that slip. It isn't over. Israel, the first state to open after fully vaccinating, has now closed again because of new variants. I must muster that sense of the poetic, that drive for a role and appreciation of the malleability of forms of connection, books, epistles, screen time, conversations, glances, gestures, indigitations that let me relinquish my longing by exposing my corporeal habitus. That is the function of ontographics, the inscription of the fact, the affect of being here. My unreal is real, my imaginal life can manifest, the hole at the heart of the social is the opportunity for which we have been waiting. New players. New game.

I am conscious finally that the ›do what you will‹ of *mortem instituere* can have catastrophic consequences, reactionary possessiveness, accumulative greed, wanton exposure and populist contagion. I can respond that no-one promised that the unconscious would be pretty but my point is a different one. What has become apparent or at least more visible and immediate is the sense in which the mask of the person and the theatricality of relations is an aesthetic and aesethical performance of role and play. It matters because it is our communal matter, it is our amicability and commonality, it is how we exist together, in the sciographic dance of virtual and corporeal connection and communication. The semaphore of the social is the enactment of parts, the semiotics of disposition, the waving over the parapet of closures or the rim of the self. It allows me to conclude that corona means crown and by extension corona virus is the illness of sovereignty, the death that the immortal brings to the living. Figure 1, an anonymous Spanish emblematist

Fig. 1: Anonymous, Emblem from the »Libro de las Honras« depicting death as a skeleton striking with a scythe at the crown hovering above it, Madrid 1603.

illustrates the simple Jesuitical point that death cannot touch that which lives on. The crown survives in the image as an overweening abstraction, as the governance of all, but it could be viewed differently. Death comes out to swing her scythe at the crown and so to demolish sovereignty, to be done with judgement. There is nothing else there, so it is the triumph of the crown that is to be terminated, whose time has come. In place of the apparent emptiness, air and smoke, one can rather see a canvas, spatial justice where mortals inscribe their time, build habitus and habits, masks that endure in the modality of belonging, of living in the collectivity of thought, in language, in art and in actions that in Nietzsche's diction require both their music and their dancing. Matterphorics supposes that all acts, each aesthetic matter and production, every mime, the last cry, all witness and express matter and that it matters when death's scythe, rising with the skeleton from the grave will fail to cull the thoughts that have already been and exist now in the perpetuity of having been said, played and done. They are the face we left, the mark we chiseled in the fabric of existence, seen or unseen, now and into the future. When the sovereign has actually to hide, the people can take to the stage without crowns, just with masks, to enact a poor theatre, a post-dramatic play, the matter, existential and aesthetic, poetic as well as politic of who we are.

In return or reprise of the opening questions: what have we learned, how are we changed upon return or as is equally likely, in continuation of living with con-

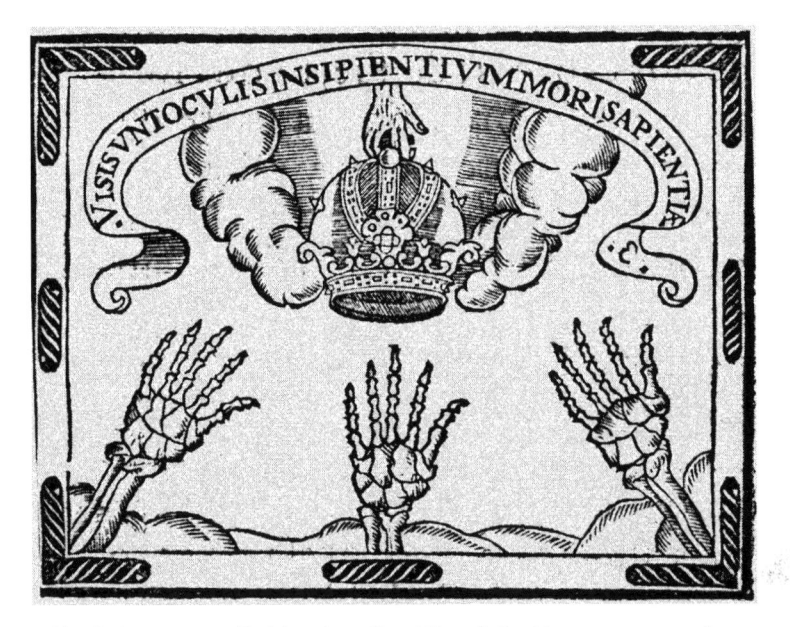

Fig. 2: Anonymous, Emblem from the »Libro de las Honras« representing skeletal hands reaching for the crown being raised to heaven, Madrid 1603.

tagion? In *Under the Rainbow*, the author James Attlee tells the story of a nurse in the English National Health Service who was perplexed by a young Covid-19 patient who despite potentially mortal illness kept trying to get out of bed and traverse the ward. Each time he was apprehended and returned to the bed, made to lie down and told to desist from life threatening activity. Finally, bemused and a little irritated the nurse asked him what he was doing. He replied that everyone working in the ward is wearing a green hat and that he could see green hats on one of the medical trolleys at the far end of the ward. He was getting up to get a green hat. He wanted to show that he was with them, that he supported the health workers, that he was a willing part of the scene, a member of the troupe, that he too was wearing a green hat even if only to die.[9] In that simple, colourist moment, beautifully relayed, there is a sense of the power of symbolic invention and amicable building of temporary communities. The anonymous emblematist (Honras) showed death with a scythe standing up from a grave to swing the sickle at the empty space created by corona, by a crown (fig. 2).

There is nothing in other words for death to take from the dominion of the sovereign, from that leviathan of abstraction that belongs so signally and chimerically to another world, to one that is not ours. The scythe hits only emptiness, not even

---

[9] Cf. Attlee: Under the Rainbow.

air, only air, because the medium of insufflation is neither visible nor tangible and so is not yet noticed. Like the infected patient yearning for a green hat we return or we continue in search of colour, in quest for the challenge of commonality and the paradox of belonging to a temporary community that we are a momentary part of creating. The green hat is what we make of ourselves, it is a mask, a semionautical medium, a relational aesthetic, a chapeau. In contradistinction to statues of conquerors, stellae of sovereigns, keep the hat on, soledad.

References

Agamben, Giorgio: Where are we Now? The Epidemic as Politics, London 2020.
Attlee, James: Under the Rainbow: Voices from Lockdown, Sheffield 2021.
Cicero, Marcus Tullius: In Catilinam / Catilinarians, Cambridge 2008.
Legendre, Pierre: God in the Mirror: A Study of the Institution of Images, Abingdon 2019.
Legendre, Pierre, Sur la question dogmatique en Occident, Paris 1999.
Nietzsche, Friedrich: Also sprach Zarathustra. I-IV, Munich 2007.
Nietzsche, Friedrich: Morgenröte / Idyllen aus Messina / Die Fröhliche Wissenschaft, Munich 1999.
Petri, Grischka: Masking the Invisible / Segments of Political Space, in: Werner Gephart (ed.): In the Realm of Corona Normativities. A Momentary Snapshot of a Dynamic Discourse, Frankfurt am Main 2020, pp. 375–407.

List of Figures

Fig. 1: Anonymous, Emblem from the »Libro de las Honras« depicting death as a skeleton striking with a scythe at the crown hovering above it, in: Libro de las Honras que hizo el Colegio de la Copañia de Iesus de Madrid, à la M. C. de la Emperatriz doña Maria de Austria, Hieroglificas, y varias poesias, Hebreas, Giegas, Latinas, y Españolas, fol 40r, Madrid 1603, Image: public domain.

Fig. 2: Anonymous, Emblem from the »Libro de las Honras« representing skeletal hands reaching for the crown being raised to heaven, in: Libro de las Honras que hizo el Colegio de la Copañia de Iesus de Madrid, à la M. C. de la Emperatriz doña Maria de Austria, Hieroglificas, y varias poesias, Hebreas, Giegas, Latinas, y Españolas, fol 45r, Madrid 1603, Image: public domain.

Upendra Baxi

Suffering and Governance in Times of Death, Devastation, and Desolation*

1. Agnotology: On How Much We Do Not Know When We Say We Know

Sapare Aude (*dare to know*) may well have been a Kantian motto for the European Enlightenment, but times have changed, and the apt motto furnished by *homo covidicus* is agnotology, the philosophy and sociology of ignorance.[1] We realize the contingency of all knowledge that leads us to a cascade or *convergence of catastrophes*.[2] Death and disease stalk us everywhere, but we do not know (except employing racist and xenophobic ways of *knowing*) where and how the pandemic originated or how long will it endure.[3] We do not know the causes, cures, and path (the global itineraries) of the pandemic. We know of biostatistics: the number of people tested, the number who recovered, and number who lost their life. We know that the healthcare systems in many countries have been stretched to their breaking points, and that cruel shortages of essential medicines, including a vital supply of oxygen, especially during the second phase of the pandemic, caused much death and reckless distress. And although some resist, the four imperatives of Covid-appropriate behavior are flouted – wearing masks, washing hands, maintaining distance, and getting vaccinated. We have also learned from experiencing

---

* I remain grateful to (Dr.) Pratiksha Baxi for her careful reading of, and comments on, the pre-final draft and for furnishing a correct citation of the name of poet for footnote 5.

[1] Cf. Proctor/Schlesinger: Agnotology; Peels: What Is Ignorance? Regarding references to the vidya and avidya (knowledge and ignorance respectively) in an insightful analysis of a judicial decision, see Singh: Constitutional Right to Vidya or Privilege for Avidya?

[2] Cf. Faye: Convergence of Catastrophes.

[3] President Joe Biden has now ordered a full investigation into the causes of the pandemic, whether it was natural or industrial. In a retaliatory response, the People's Republic of China has suggested that all security labs must be similarly investigated (cf. Biden: Statement by President Joe Biden on the Investigation). The World Health Organization (WHO) speaks in varying voices. Its chief scientist Soumya Swaminathan predicted that it would take four to five years before the pandemic was under control. However, in August 2020, WHO Director Tedros Adhanom Ghebreyesus said that the pandemic might end within two years (cf. BBC News: Coronavirus Pandemic Could Be over within Two Years). In contrast, Microsoft co-founder Bill Gates has now said that the pandemic will be over by the end of 2021. Similar uncertainties surround questions of the best therapy, healthcare systems, infection and fatality statistics, questions about co-morbidity, etc. (cf. The Economist: The Covid-19 Pandemic will be over by the End of 2021).

enforced isolation, alienation, banishment, and abandonment produced by periodic lockdowns and partial containment.

The second year of a raging global pandemic is now upon us – a new phase. Many theoretical and lived reflections abound. As the poet Benjamin L Pérez writes, we live in a »Wilderness of whys/ Labyrinth of I's«[4] and »Discover to remember/ Devastate to flower/ Break to repair/ Put together to shatter«[5]. Amid this disaster turned social catastrophe (or rather series of these), we must know that actual human and social suffering is central to all knowledge production, or more aptly called today *knowledge industries*. As research on health becomes capital-intensive, especially in the *natural* sciences, we may justly dub it an epistemic-military complex that specializes in the production of new social truths based on expertise and an abundance of states of the *new normal*.

It is trite to say (albeit necessary) that a pandemic is a disaster/catastrophe of global dimensions that entails new forms of knowledge and multi-level action, calling above all for epistemic and social humility. However, epistemic arrogance – the disposition that says we know the causes and effects, as well as affirms that it remains possible to give one right answer – is far from being a good response to a runaway pandemic. Epistemic humility does not, however, signify an absence of dissent or free speech. Certainly, it does not constitute any unfair dissent, sedition, or treason as insisted by some states and rulers out of strategic interest. Rather, it only means socially responsible (that is, response-able criticism, a Derridean idiom),[6] based always on the premise that there is no one right answer but the struggle for peaceful coexistence of many, equally reasonable and well-reasoned approaches.[7] Social responsibility, or response-ability, of either the rulers or the ruled is the hallmark of epistemic humility.[8] Responsibility in the contexts of a pandemic means the prevention of preventable individual harm or social suffering in a given situation – that is, the message of contemporary human rights, and human rights discursivity, as we know it.[9]

---

[4] Pérez: Epicycle(s).
[5] Ibid.
[6] Cf. Derrida: Specters of Marx. This conception has been developed further by physicist-philosopher Karen Barad. Developing the concept further, in the context of *ethico- onto-epistem-ology*, Barad writes: »Responsibility – the ability to respond to the other – cannot be restricted to human-human encounters when the very boundaries and the constitution of the ›human‹ are continually being reconfigured« (Barad: Meeting the Universe Halfway, p. 90). See also Campbell: The Deterritorialization of Responsibility.
[7] Cf. Baxi: The Future of Human Rights.
[8] This comes closer to John Rawls's notions of *overlapping consensus, reasonable pluralism*, and *constitutional essentials* (cf. Rawls: Political Liberalism).
[9] Cf. Baxi: The Place of the Human Right. The *impertinence* of this contribution is in the insistence that understanding justice theories remain both desirable and necessary for the development of the human right to health. Our troubles lie in the scrupulous allergy to the *J-word* (justice) in right to health discourse. See also Daniels: Justice, Health and Healthcare; Fleck: Just Health Care; Buchanan: The Right to a Decent Minimum of a Health Care.

Covid-19 adversely affected, and afflicted, human beings; and it demanded that policymakers and the political class take human suffering seriously and accentuate the core human rights to life, liberty, and health in the struggle against a global pandemic. Covid-19 has prompted the reassertion of these human rights, as well as the search for a correlative right to a better human future – a non-discriminatory and non-violent horizontal human right – namely the human right to healthcare for all, and access to a just and equitable healthcare system against state and corporate governance entities exacerbating the mismanagement of health crises. The insistence is on a new pandemic disaster ethic: an ethic of care.

Humankind knows that an epidemic, like all mass disasters, is an ineluctable aspect of governance and development. International relations studies have pointed out that studies of *mistakes* and policy *failures* are a staple of the pedagogy of international relations, though it is a different matter that these analytical categories have only now been subjected to rigorous scrutiny.[10] For our purposes, mistakes and failures – even of catastrophic proportions and dimensions – are special markers of epistemic humility. The question that arises is one concerning the relation between response-ability and mistakes. If mistakes in governance, healthcare (diagnoses, therapies), near and median predictions of viral behavior and mutants, vaccine research, and high technology are unavoidable in the trial-and-error situation of a pandemic, those who suffer have at least a *core human right to transparency*. To err may be human but there is no human right to commit an error, by the same token when it costs life, health, or liberty. There is also no human right not to admit to one's errors in handling a pandemic situation, and to cover these up by any political party, mass media, or scientific propaganda, thus inflicting inhumane suffering. It must be recognized as such – as a malfeasance and human wrong which now ought to create some human rights obligations of justice.

It is eminently arguable that such behaviors occurring as state governance or business conduct can be regarded as wilful harms attracting both global and national criminal law and civil liability. Almost all legal systems of the world regard intentional affliction of harm or injury – whether as simple or serious injury, an attempt to harm, or other allied offenses like attempt to commit homicide – as

---

[10] Cf. Krucks/Oppermann/Spencer (eds.): Introduction: Political Mistakes and Policy Failures in International Relations. As the learned editors say in their introduction, »[t]he study of situations in which something has gone wrong has, at least implicitly, always been a part of IR. Political events and decisions usually attract much greater scholarly attention if they are seen to be a failure than if they are considered a success […]. Mistakes such as the appeasement of Hitler, the Bay of Pigs invasion, the catastrophic mismanagement of diseases and pandemics (e.g. AIDS or Ebola) or the failure of banking regulations in the run-up to the recent financial crisis have always preoccupied scholars of IR. It is hardly a stretch to say that mistakes are omnipresent in IR research and that we do research and teach our students IR by studying mistakes. However, mistakes have rarely been the subject of systematic conceptual and comparative analysis in IR« (ibid. p. 2).

such. They also consider the conspiracy to do so as such offenses. Failure to observe Covid-inappropriate behavior under declared disaster law is, for example, punishable and often prosecuted under domestic law. What is more, in certain situations (such as with outright Covid denialism, or the headlong and heedless pursuit of research and use of chemical warfare agents prohibited under international law), heads of governments and international institutions ought to be held morally blameworthy and legally liable. One may even read into the International Criminal Court's definitions and categories of elements of crimes against humanity a certain warrant for international investigation and prosecution.[11] Aside from such issues, wider questions of human rights violations in pandemic situations require both ordered consultation and urgent remedial action by all state and non-state actors and networks. One such area is *disaster profiteering*, where, as seismologist John Mutter shows, patent holders and businesspeople plunder the world, putting profits over people. When »no one is looking«[12], Mutter writes, disasters become a »means by which the elite prosper at the expense of the poor.«[13] Disasters demonstrate how unjustly unequal our world has become. The elite prosper while the plight of the impoverished and the vulnerable steadily worsens.

If there is one message arising out of any contemplated post-Covid milieu, or at least long-term Covid context, it lies in the state's accelerated ethical evolution and business duties of preservation, protection and promotion of contemporary human rights norms, principles, standards, doctrines, and especially human rights to health and just healthcare institutions.

2. Are There Many Crises or Just One?

Understandably, virologists, epidemiologists, and other health scientists regard pandemics holistically as unified disasters, though unfolding with many unpredictable consequences. This monist view also persists in viewing pandemics as *natural disasters*, with a *dangerous supplement* of political practices of the catastrophization of evil. When we understand the Covid-19 situation as an avalanche of evils,[14] the question of disasters becoming catastrophes (as, for example, in Bho-

---

[11] Already, Irene Khan, the Special Rapporteur on the promotion and protection of freedom of opinion and expression, expressed certain anxieties about Covid *hostile propaganda* against some states (cf. Khan: Disinformation and Freedom of Opinion and Expression; Akrivopoulou/Garipidis: Human Rights and Risks in the Digital Era).

[12] Mutter: The Disaster Profiteers.

[13] Ibid.

[14] Cf. Ophir: The Politics of Catastrophization; And as relates the Indian judicial suo motu action nudging governance (cf. Baxi: The Accelerating »Avalanche of Evils«).

pal when 47 tons of methyl isocyanate gas were released) becomes and remains acutely pertinent.[15]

Already, we have a thesis about a convergence of catastrophes, to which Covid-19 has been added. Philosopher Ewa Plonowska Ziarek draws our attention to *triple pandemics* in her mediations on Covid-19: Alongside the pandemic is the resurgence of racism and the recrudescence of digital capitalism, which likewise constitute global crises.[16] As to the former, she recalls Levar Stoney, an African-American serving as Mayor of Richmond, Virginia, who said that »taken together these events constitute ›two pandemics‹ of Covid-19 and systemic racism: One is six months old, the other 400 years old. And as the events of the last month and the last two weeks have made it painfully clear, both are lethal,«[17] especially for people of color worldwide. The lethal sovereignty of the dominant classes is here writ large. Although complete statistics are not yet available, it is indisputable that Covid-19 fatalities have disproportionately risen across the racial divide.[18] Evidence also shows that discriminated and marginalized peoples have suffered around the world – and continue to suffer a great deal in the pandemic.[19] While most national disaster laws and policies within democracies forbid discrimination on any ground, regimes' societal prejudices and stereotypes do recur in many situations. Inequality justifications reign even in times of Covid-19.[20]

Algorithmic governmentality constitutes a third pandemic. What Ziarek adds to this couple of *computational capitalism*[21], or *algorithmic governmentality*[22],

---

[15] Cf. Baxi: Human Rights Responsibility of Multinational Corporations; Baxi: Disasters, Catastrophes and Oblivion; Romero: Punishment for Ecological Disasters.

[16] Cf. Plonowska Ziarek: Triple Pandemics.

[17] Ibid., p. 1.

[18] Cf. Gee/Ro/Rimoin: Seven Reasons to Care About Racism. Their concluding lines are: »Although prejudice and fear may be common reactions to outbreaks such as COVID-19, they should not be seen as justifiable or even natural ones. Now is the time for solidarity, not slurs« (emphasis added by UB, p. 955).

[19] Cf. United Nations Department of Economic and Social Affairs: Covid-19 and Indigenous Peoples; United Nations: Policy Brief; World Health Organisation: Disability Considerations; United Nations: Child Rights and the 2030 Agenda; United Nations News: Migrants Left Stranded and without Assistance.

[20] Cf. Ray/Rojas: Inequality during the Coronavirus Pandemic; Berkhout et al.: The Inequality Virus; Major/Eyles/Machin: Generation COVID. As is common knowledge, the number of billionaires in the world has grown in Covid times; as to the Covid-19 vaccine billionaires (cf. Tognini: Meet the 40 New Billionaires Who Got Rich Fighting COVID-19).

[21] Cf. Stiegler: The Age of Disruption; Stiegler: Nanjing Lectures.

[22] Cf. Rouvroy/Berns: Algorithmic Governmentality and Prospects of Emancipation. They rightly insist that this anormative governmentality does not mark increased public space but rather its reverse: »the algorithmic governmentality era one is rather witnessing a colonization of public space by a hypertrophied private sphere. So much so that there are fears that new forms of information filtering will result in forms of informational immunization conducive to a radicalization of opinions and the disappearance of shared experience« (ibid. p. v.). The older, though recent, way of putting this insight was that of Jürgen Habermas who spoke about the »colonization of lifeworld« (Habermas: Die Theorie des kommunikativen Handelns.). This form of governance »focuses not on

is the continual *datafication* of social realities and understanding of how »algorithmic governmentality works in tandem with digital capitalism«.[23] What Shoshanna Zuboff has accurately described as *surveillance capitalism* is also relevant here.[24] Certainly, it raises questions about distributive social justice and the nature of communities in the future.[25] And Covid-19, while occurring in the heyday of this new mode of production, enhances many anxieties for post-Covid futures of human rights, social suffering, and terrestrial futures.

3. Continuities

Although criticized rather severely,[26] Giorgio Agamben traces some important continuities between Covid-19 realities and post-Covid futures. In a short clarificatory note, Agamben said that the »problem is not to give opinions on the gravity of the disease but to ask about the epidemic's ethical and political consequences.«[27] Writing about the »wave of panic that has paralyzed the country«[28], he insists that »our society no longer believes in anything but bare life. Italians are disposed to sacrifice practically everything – the normal conditions of life, social relationships, work, even friendships, affections, and religious and political convictions – to the danger of getting sick.«[29] However, bare life is not »something that unites people but blinds and separates them. Other human beings [...] are now seen solely as

individuals, on subject, but on relations«, and »relations themselves are transformed, to the extent that they are paradoxically substantivized and represent an extraction from the becoming, and therefore an obstacle to the individuation process – rather than being strongly embedded in that process. The becoming and the individuation processes are a matter of ›disparation‹, in other words the processes of integration of disparities or differences into a coordinated system« (Rouvroy / Berns: Algorithmic Governmentality and Prospects of Emancipation, p. v.)

[23] Plonowska Ziarek: Triple Pandemics, p. 927.

[24] Zuboff: The Age of Surveillance Capitalism; Plonowska Ziarek summates Zuboff analysis as follows: »such capital is driven by the imperative of accelerated accumulation of data from all computational operations and its conversion into profits through the production of prediction products, ranging from advertising to predictive policing. Invented first by Google and now perfected by all digital giants, surveillance capitalism extracts ›collateral‹ data, the by-product of billions of users' online interactions, not only for matching advertising with user profile information (UPIs) but primarily for the fabrication of new prediction products which anticipate our actions coordinated as a ›system‹. What we then have is a ›government without a subject‹ but not ›without a target‹« (Plonowska Ziarek: Triple Pandemics, p. 4.).

[25] Cf. Yeung: Five Fears about Mass Predictive Personalization; Alanoca et al.: Digital Contact Tracing Against Covid-19. Concluding that »it is our collective responsibility to build solid ethical and governance frameworks to make informed choice« (ibid., p. 17).

[26] Cf. Caldwell: Meet the Philosopher; Christaens: Must Society Be Defended from Agamben?

[27] Agamben: Clarifications.

[28] Ibid.

[29] Ibid.

possible spreaders of the plague whom one must avoid at all costs and from whom one needs to keep oneself at a distance of at least a meter.«[30]

It is this predilection to regard the *other* merely as an epidemiological subject/object, rather than as a human being, and to regard the neighbor/stranger as a threat, that distinguishes the Covid era. The dread of dying and death, of being forlorn in funerals, the terror of loneliness in lockdowns and micro-containment and any negation of any form of sociability as a potential or actual *superspreader* event, alienates us from the concrete others. In fact, it not only *abolishes* the other, but impoverishes the self and the soul. In trying to understand the very possibility of human face and politics, Agamben wrote that »face is the place of politics«[31]. Communicating merely information »would never be politics properly speaking, but only an exchange of messages.«[32] For politics to happen, humans »must first communicate their openness to each other, recognise themselves in the face of another, the face is the very condition of politics, what is based everything that men say and exchange.«[33] In this sense, we behold the face as »the true city of men, the political element par excellence.«[34] Health regulation during Covid has ushered in a new *order* of a faceless world »without deaths. If the living lose their faces, the dead become only numbers«[35] and »as they had been reduced to their pure biological life, must die alone and without funerals.«[36] Agamben concludes: »The planetary project that governments are trying to impose is, therefore, radically impolitic. On the contrary, it aims to eliminate from human existence any genuinely political element, to replace it with a governmentality based only on algorithmic control.«[37] And face erasure, the removal of the dead, and social distancing are »the essential devices of this governmentality, which […] must be maintained even when the sanitary terror is eased.«[38] The permanent state of exception that pandemics create, and carry forward, is that of »a faceless society, a society without a past and without physical contact«[39], a »society of ghosts and as such doomed to a more or less rapid ruin.«[40]

»What is worrisome«, Agamben says, is »not only the present, but what comes after.«[41] This is indeed a justified anxiety about intuitions concerning a post-Covid world; this appears to some critics as a little overdrawn. The face/mask relation, for

---

[30] Ibid.
[31] Agamben: On the Government of the Faceless and the Deathless.
[32] Ibid.
[33] Ibid.
[34] Ibid.
[35] Ibid.
[36] Ibid.
[37] Ibid.
[38] Ibid.
[39] Ibid.
[40] Ibid.
[41] Agamben: Clarifications.

example, is not binary but may well be dialectically related. Further, free choice veiling practices are supported by even some ardent Islamic feminists. My own bewilderment at masked fellow passengers in Tokyo around Christmas was dispelled when these were deemed justified, both to protect one's health from the flu and in the Japanese people's interest of economic productivity! I have also noted the dialectic of the *face* and the *mask* of judicial activism in India as expressing a particular form of constitutional politics that I now call *demosprudential co-leadership* and *judicial co-governance* of the nation.

Concerning executive-led governance, however, Agamben is surely right to draw our attention to the historical and juridical permanence of things that are initially put in place as the *temporary* and the *transitional*. Absence of sunset clauses, legisprudence teaches us signifies that what stands declared as transitional is in fact a quasi-eternal state of affairs! The repeal of old laws is considered a marginal enterprise, especially when laws in the aggregate augment the already vast powers of governance and the de-subjectification of those governed. Thomas Hobbes's imagery of the commonwealth or state as a *mortal god* readily comes to mind,[42] even though many may wish to emphasize the word *mortal* rather than the term *god* (who by definition never dies).

Wars have left, as Agamben says, as »a legacy to peace a series of inauspicious technologies, from barbed wire to nuclear power plants.«[43] And so, may many Covid-19 scars continue »even after the health emergency experiments – closing universities and schools and doing lessons only online, putting a stop once and for all to meeting together and speaking for political or cultural reasons and exchanging only digital messages with each other, wherever possible substituting machines for every contact – every contagion – between human beings.«[44]

It is true that Agamben said this only in the early phases of the pandemic. Since then, the virus's global itineraries, and the histories of its mutant resilience, have betrayed the expectations about the pandemic's possible short life span and brought dire forebodings about the temporariness of social isolation and state control over community mores of being together. But the exceptional powers to treat ordinary citizens as epidemiological objects of contagion, to declare general or partial lockdowns, to declare the suspension of the internet, and to pronounce and punish contravention of pandemic appropriate norms will continue for as long as general disaster management cultures of power endure. How much will humanity suffer from the chilling effect on freedom of speech and expression, media freedom, and practices of civil society resistance or disobedience? However, the core of Agamben's general insight cannot be gainsaid: States will continue to

---

[42] Cf. Piasentier/Tarizz: ›The Government of a Multitude‹.
[43] Agamben: Clarifications.
[44] Ibid.

be armed with even greater, higher biopolitical power and a power to organize a *democratization of* disempowerment (to borrow a phrase from Ghanaian thinker Claude Ake). This augmentation of state necrophiliac power stands aggravated by the seventh decade of the Sixth Great Extinction now underway in this era of anthropogenic harm (to which Agamben's Covid thesis is deeply relevant but to which he pays so little direct attention).[45]

4. Biocultural Legitimacy, Alienation, and Solidarity

As against the *thanatopolitical* perspective emphasizing the negative face of biopower where the measure of population's protection »transforms itself into a killing machine«,[46] we have the alternative of affirmative *biopolitics*, mainly developed by Robert Esposito.[47] We are all familiar with the debate over the biophilic and necrophiliac potential of the biopolitical. Even so, other practices must be noted. Stalinism discourse emerges on this register, as Sergei Prozorov demonstrates, as a case of an extremely productive or positive biopolitics that turned into an equally extreme thanatopolitics. It is precisely »this extremity, whereby the paradox that arguably characterizes all biopolitics collapses into a paroxysm, that makes the case of Stalinism indispensable for understanding the potentiality for violence immanent to biopolitics as well as the limits that restrain this potentiality within various modes of biopolitical government.«[48]

Biopower/biopolitics are much studied, and some of their benign as well as cruel aspects are for all of us to see and feel during this pandemic. At the same time, we also need to understand how bio-legitimation of power is both accomplished and challenged respectively under the titles of good governance and ethics of just resistance. In a biopolitical age, political legitimacy everywhere rests on the ability of the state institutions to display care and compassion in extremity. However, we know that while states know how and whom to command, they do not really know how to care; while good at work with the ambivalent ethics of human rights, states are ill at ease with the ethics of the duty to care. The latter, however, typically forms a central task of governance in pandemic situations. Perhaps this duty can be articulated though the old Roman law doctrine of *parens patriae* or

---

[45] Cf. Agamben: Homo Sacer.
[46] Agamben: State of Exception, p. 86.
[47] Cf. Esposito: Bios.
[48] Prozorov: Biopolitics and Socialism, p. 2. This study concludes that the insight that urging us to overcome the reciprocal blind spots, and learn to ask »why socialism cannot be subsumed under the naturalist orientations of Western biopolitics, but rather remains the prime site for a critical engagement with biopolitical constructivism« (ibid., p. 16.)

primum non nocere (above all, do not harm.). The new languages, logics, and paralogics of human rights may well express and expand this role further. Also, in competitive democratic societies (where there exist some conditions of circulation of elites, as Vilfredo Pareto long ago speculated), biolegitimacy will entail issues concerning the very role-responsibility of political parties, whether forming the ruling party or political opposition groups. Questions now arise, for example, concerning the legitimacy of uncertain nature of the lockdowns, exclusion of public participation in redesigning healthcare systems, ordering of priorities making urgently available the essential medicines, supply of oxygen, and equities of vaccine distribution, Issues not commonly routine in public discourse now assume a centrality, such as funerals and cremation spaces, as well as the plight of orphans and other marginalized peoples, including indigenous peoples, disabled peoples, disorganized workers (I do not use the more common expression of *unorganized labor*), and rural and far-flung peoples not reached by governance at distance.

There is much talk about even judicial *overreach* in the management of the pandemic – but this rather facile *overreach* indictment may also extend to old and new media, domestic and transnational networks of social and human rights movements, and the emergent universal global middle class. Such talk about *overreach* is piquant, even poignant, when a pandemic carries too many marks, and the masks of the global fact of executive/political *underreach*. At a more reflexive level, we also need to extend the idea of contradictions propounded notably by David Harvey in his remarkable work on the seventeen contradictions of capitalism. What remains most germane to *Covid Normativities* is the third category of Harvey's last three *dangerous* contradictions (others being *foundational* and *moving* ones); I focus here on the very last one which concerns universal *alienation*.[49] The threshold question is: Are forms of alienation encountered differently in Covid-19 situations than in other types of contradictions, whether Marxian or Neo-Marxian experiences? Is there a continuity or break now in the unfolding forms of alienation thus produced?

We know three facts already. We have come to know that extensive alienation is rooted in the moral epidemiology of Covid- appropriate behavior. It is not a real or concrete utopia that is a good place to live. Covid-19 is not an example of ›isocracy‹ – of a kind of society where people do not rule or obey, a place where there is order without power, and a non-hierarchical cooperation. It does not seem to share, or make possible, isocracy's ›main conscious aim‹ which is »to level out relationships of power in whatever realm they might appear.«[50] It does not present a »state of affairs in which ›shared freedom‹ is made possible by endeavours to reject and dismantle any equal kind of power«.[51] Yet, the ethics of Covid-appro-

[49] Cf. Harvey: Seventeen Contradictions and the End of Capitalism.
[50] Bellanca: Isocracy, p. v.
[51] Ibid.

priate behavior foster both social isolation and distancing. Alienation seems to be the core of therapy, and even the goal of therapeutic justice. Exclusion is normalized as the most expeditious and effective therapy, not even some shared freedoms among social isolates. Social exclusion also provides an index of solidarity within alienation. Absence of solidarity appears to be a societal resource to combat the pandemic. The only ideal of good life is the ideal of life under containment and confinement, punctuated in some hyper-real ways by cyber-solidarity.

Even before the Covid pandemic, David Harvey showed that »[w]idespread alienation from a state system«[52] prevails, in contrast to the historical task »of trying to manufacture consent and social cohesion (usually out of an appeal to a constructed fiction about national identity and unity)«[53] which often founders. Now, this contradiction aggravates the already present »hegemonic practices of neoliberalism in both the economic and the political arenas«[54] which have given rise to »decentralised and networked oppositional forms«.[55] And the politics of the far right and the extreme left (for example, of the Tea Party as well of the *autonomists and the anarchists* in United States). These forces have converged in placing »limit or even to destroy the state«,[56] though under different rubrics – in the »name of pure individualism on the right«[57] and some kind of »individualistically anchored associationism on the left«.[58] These factors have been further escalated in the Covid-19 pandemic by the distrust of people in government systems, expert individuals and institutions, and captains of trade and industry. At the same time, humans violated by Covid-19 have been growingly appreciative of role of civil society and the media (to some extent even of the judiciary). Much work remains to be done to grasp the double movement of solidarity and alienation.

5. Concluding the Inconcludable

In what may post-Covid futures subsist? One may not even venture to approach an answer without looking at the intransigence of the ›business as usual‹ paradigm (BAUP). The resilience of the BAUP marks the presence – one may even say the immanent co-nesting-- of the ordinary within the extraordinary. The BAUP is most notable in the pandemic resilience shown by politics and the use offered in

---

[52] Harvey: Seventeen Contradictions and the End of Capitalism, p. 280.
[53] Ibid.
[54] Ibid., p. 281.
[55] Ibid.
[56] Ibid.
[57] Ibid.
[58] Ibid.

international relations as well as in economic diplomacy. It is the BAUP all the way from campaigning for elections (now also considered superspreader events) to the *circulation of elites*. Legislative assemblies and other public institutions function in a restricted manner political events and happenings, some of great magnitude (as the WTO's protection of pharmaceuticals companies, even amidst adversity of such a magnitude as the Covid pandemic) continue as before. Courts go digital; and digital acts of education, foreign relations, and global diplomacy have replaced traditional ways of conduct. Military conflicts and events occur, and so do terrorist acts, violent cross-border, disputations and conflicts, belligerent occupations, and violent acts of social exclusion within and across borders continue. Many more instances and histories that can be cited; however, the main point of the BAUP is that the business of doing politics, diplomacy, armed conflicts, and injustice continues as before, even during the Covid-19 pandemic. We again see the emergence of the *dual state*[59] (the chilling analogy of the Nazi state comes vividly before some minds) – but the *ordinary* and *extraordinary* seem etched forever in the acts of power, and the performances of state as well as corporate sovereignties. This reminds one of Agamben's thesis on the *state of exception* always becoming the rule.

Examining how these forms of action are affected by, and in turn affect, the pandemic must remain a deep subject of study. But it is certain that Covid-19 vulnerabilities will continue even when we further empower representational powers to govern in the very name of protecting human rights. The human right to health/healthcare render, subservient entire portfolios of all other core human rights. It is on the platform of the collective human right to health and life for all that justifications for their suspension of all other rights prevail.

But even so, the right to property, especially of the private property rights of mighty pharmaceutical corporations, seems to prevail over the right to health and life! These are congealed in the current state of discourse triggered by South Africa and India, which have asked the WTO for a temporary TRIPS waiver (October 2, 2020). Since then, the WTO has received support from 100 developing countries for waiving certain provisions concerning copyrights, industrial designs, patents, and protection of undisclosed information. This move, recently endorsed by 175 former world leaders and Nobel laureates, is not quite buttressed by one new

---

[59] Cf. Fraenkel: The Dual State. Nazi regime this exemplified two distinct states – one normative, the other prerogative. In the first, the administrative and judicial bureaucracy operate according to rules; in the second, the Party, and more particularly the Gestapo, operate free of any ultimate legal restraint. The second, of course, possesses complete power arbitrarily to supersede the first at any or all points. Alok Sheel has recently argued that »by controlling the outcomes of only a few cases, the prerogative state captures all state power. Populist dictatorships have proliferated across the world's democracies, from Latin America to Eastern Europe and Asia, even as cult-based rightist parties have gained sway in the US and Western Europe. Whether they will prove more durable than dictatorships of 20th century remains to be seen« (Sheel: Fraenkel's Theory of the Dual State May Need an Update).

initiative undertaken by the U.S. President for a wider trade negotiation.[60] Yet the European Union, and other developed countries, have blocked specific discussions despite detailed explanations given for TRPS – IPR measures for suspension (as pointed out by South Africa's TRIPS negotiator Mustaqeem De Gama). It has been argued that Covid-19 *vaccines would not exist* without governmental funding totalling around $ 100 billion globally in *vaccine development*. Significant procurement policies have also ensured *massive corporate* profits in any event.

At the WTO meeting on April 30, 2021, Washington showed some signs of cooperating towards a *global solution*. The U.S. Trade Representative was in July 2021 in Geneva negotiating a new deal to make Covid-19 vaccines available to all. However, the embedded ideology of *disaster* or even *toxic* capitalism prevails in times of pandemics. Light at the end of the tunnel still eludes, now on the ground a new mutant – Omicron – said to make a WTO meeting too unsafe to consider the matter. The BAUP continues as *disaster profiteers* tend to grow both in terms of the size of their profit margins and overall lobbying power, as recently shown in Covid-19 vaccine diplomacy acts concerning indemnification to pharma multinationals for vaccine production for India. The otherwise most welcome humanitarian response to combat phase two of Covid-19 does not mitigate but rather invite pandemic reflexivity about a permanent state of economic aggression, especially by the Global North against Global South nations and peoples (and within all nations against marginalized and vulnerable peoples). The BAUP may thrive on rampant denialism, conspiracy theories, and uncontrolled aggression against political rivals and conscientious citizens, of which the reign of former U.S. President Trump was an arch exemplar.

However, pandemic times require states everywhere to take people's suffering most seriously and heighten the need for accountability and justification of social action. They require us never to conflate the rule of law with the rule by experts – and demand only the performances of responsible sovereignty.[61] If anything, the pandemic must help us learn to keep apart, in the immortal phrase-regime of Professor Judith Shklar, *situations of misfortune* from *acts of injustice*.[62]

---

[60] Announcing a new global vaccine policy, President Biden has very recently provided some deals. The export ban of raw materials for vaccines has been lifted. Also, at least 75 % of these doses – nearly 19 million – will be shared, including approximately 6 million doses for Latin America and the Caribbean, approximately 7 million for South and Southeast Asia, and approximately 5 million for Africa. Important also is his remark that: »We are sharing these doses not to secure favors or extract concessions. We are sharing these vaccines to save lives and to lead the world in bringing an end to the pandemic, with the power of our example and with our values« (Biden: Statement by President Joe Biden on Global Vaccine Distribution).

[61] Notably developed in the Right to Protect (R2P) discourse (cf. International Commission on Intervention and State Sovereignty (ICISS): The Responsibility to Protect; Colamedic: Responsible Sovereignty).

[62] Shlkar: The Faces of Injustice.

References

Agamben, Giorgio: Homo Sacer: Sovereign Power and Bare Life, Stanford 1998.

Agamben, Girogio: State of Exception, London 2005.

Agamben, Girogio: Clarifications, in An und für sich, March 17, 2020, https://itself.blog/2020/03/17/giorgio-agamben-clarifications/; last accessed July 27, 2021.

Alanoca, Sacha / Nicolas Guetta Jeanrenaud / Isabela Ferrari / Nyasha Weinberg / R. Buse Ceti / Nicolas Miailh: Digital Contact Tracing Against COVID-19: A Governance Framework to Build Trust, in: International Data Privacy Law, 11(1), 2021, pp. 3–17.

Akrivopoulou, Christina M. / Nicolaos Garipidis: Human Rights and Risks in the Digital Era: Globalization and the Effects of Information Technologies, Hershey 2012.

Barad, Karen: Meeting the Universe Halfway: Quantum Physics and the Entanglement of Matter and Meaning, Durham 2007.

Baxi, Upendra: The Future of Human Rights, Oxford 2022.

Baxi, Upendra: The Accelerating »Avalanche of Evils«: Towards Covid-19 Constitutionalism? in: India Legal, May 10, 2021.

Baxi, Upendra: Disasters, Catastrophes and Oblivion: a TWAIL Perspective, in: Yearbook of International Disaster Law, 2(1), 2019, pp. 72–86.

Baxi, Upendra: Human Rights Responsibility of Multinational Corporations, Political Ecology of Injustice: Learning from Bhopal Thirty Plus? in: Business and Human Rights Journal, 1(1), 2016, pp. 21–40.

Baxi, Upendra: The Place of the Human Right to Health and Contemporary Approaches to Global Justice: Some Impertinent Interrogation, in: John Harrington / Maria Stuttford (eds.): Global Health and Human Rights. Legal and Philosophical Perspectives, London 2010.

BBC News: Coronavirus Pandemic Could Be over within Two Years – Who Head, in: BBC News, August 22, 2020, https://www.bbc.com/news/world-53870798; last accessed July 27, 2021.

Bellanca, Nicolò: Isocray. The Institutions of Equality, London 2019.

Berkhout, Esmé / Nick Galasso / Max Lawson / Pablo Andrés Rivero Morales / Anjela Taneja / Diego Alejo Vázquez Pimentel: The Inequality Virus. Bringing Together a World Torn Apart by Coronavirus through a Fair, Just and Sustainable Economy, in: Oxfam Digital Repository, January 25, 2021, https://oxfamilibrary.openrepository.com/bitstream/handle/10546/621149/bp-the-inequality-virus-250121-en.pdf; last accessed July 27, 2021.

Biden, Joe: Statement by President Joe Biden on Global Vaccine Distribution, in: Briefing Room of the White House, June 03, 2021, https://www.whitehouse.gov/briefing-room/statements-releases/2021/06/03/statement-by-president-joe-biden-on-global-vaccine-distribution/; last accessed July 27, 2021.

Biden, Joe: Statement by President Joe Biden on the Investigation into the Origins of Covid-19, in: Briefing Room of the White House, May 26, 2021, https://www.whitehouse.gov/briefing-room/statements-releases/2021/05/26/statement-by-president-joe-biden-on-the-investigation-into-the-origins-of-covid-19/; last accessed July 27, 2021.

Buchanan, Allen E.: The Right to a Decent Minimum of a Health Care, in: Philosophy and Public Affairs, 13(1), 1984, pp. 55–78.

Caldwell, Christopher: Meet the Philosopher Who Is Trying to Explain the Pandemic, in: The New York Times, August 21, 2020, https://www.nytimes.com/2020/08/21/opinion/sunday/giorgio-agamben-philosophy-coronavirus.html; last accessed July 27, 2021.

Campbell, David: The Deterritorialization of Responsibility: Levinas, Derrida, and Ethics after the End of Philosophy, in: Alternatives: Global, Local, Political, 19(4), 1994, pp. 455–484.

Christaens, Tim: Must Society Be Defended from Agamben? March 26, 2020, https://criticallegalthinking.com/2020/03/26/must-society-be-defended-from-agamben/; last accessed July 27, 2021.

Colamedic, Julian: Responsible Sovereignty: R2P and the Protection of Human Rights, in Academia, 2021, https://www.academia.edu/45071655/Responsible_Sovereignty_R2P_and_the...; last accessed July 27, 2021.

Daniels, Norman: Justice, Health, and Healthcare, in: The American Journal of Bioethics, 1(2), 2001, pp. 2–16.

Derrida, Jacques: The State of the Debt, the Work of Mourning, and the New International, London 1994.

Esposito, Roberto: Bios: Biopolitics and Philosophy, Minneapolis 2008.

Faye, Guillaume: Convergence of Catastrophes, London 2012.

Fleck, Leonard M.: Just Health Care (II): Is Equality Too Much? in: Theoretical Medicine 10, 1989, pp. 301–310.

Fraenkel, Ernst: The Dual State, Oxford 1941.

Gee, Gilbert C. / Marguerite J. Ro / Anne W. Rimoin: Seven Reasons to Care About Racism and Covid-19 and Seven Things to Do to Stop It, in: American Journal of Public Health, 110(7), pp. 954–955.

Habermas, Jürgen: Die Theorie des kommunikativen Handelns, Frankfurt am Main 1981.

Harvey, David: Seventeen Contradictions and the End of Capitalism, Oxford 2016.

International Commission on Intervention and State Sovereignty (ICISS): The Responsibility to Protect: Report of the International Commission on Intervention and State Sovereignty, Ottawa 2001, in: Global Centre for the Responsibility to Protect, December 01, 2001, https://www.globalr2p.org/resources/the-responsibility-to-protect-report-of-the-international-commission-on-intervention-and-state-sovereignty-2001/; last accessed July 27, 2021.

Khan, Irene: Disinformation and Freedom of Opinion and Expression. Report of the Special Rapporteur on the Promotion and Protection of the Right to Freedom of Opinion and Expression, A/HRC/47/25, Human Rights Council, 47th session June 21, July 09, 2021, Agenda Item 3.

Krucks, Andreas / Kai Oppermann / Alexander Spencer (eds.): Political Mistakes and Policy Failures in International Relations, London 2018.

Major, Lee Elliot / Andrew Eyles / Stephen Machin: Generation COVID: Emerging Work and Education Inequalities, London October 2020, https://cep.lse.ac.uk/pubs/download/cepcovid-19-011.pdf; last accessed July 27, 2021.

Mutter, John: The Disaster Profiteers. How Natural Disasters Make the Rich Richer and the Poor Even Poorer, New York 2015.

Ophir, Adi: The Politics of Catastrophization: Emergency and Exception, in: Didier Fassin / Mariella Pandolfi (eds.): Contemporary States of Emergency. The Politics of Military and Humanitarian Interventions, New York 2010, pp. 59–88.

Peels, Rik: What Is Ignorance? in: Philosophia 38(1), 2010, pp. 57–67.

Pérez, Benjamin L.: Epicycle(s), in: Merion West, April 25, 2021, https://merionwest.com/2021/04/25/poem-epicycles/; last accessed July 27, 2021.

Piasentier, Marco / Davide Tarizz: ›The Government of a Multitude‹: Hobbes on Political Subjectification, in: Sergei Prozorov / Simona Rentea (eds.): The Routledge Handbook of Biopolitics, New York 2016, pp. 36–49.

Plonowska Ziarek, Ewa: Triple Pandemics COVID-19, Anti-Black Violence, and Digital Capitalism, in: Philosophy Today, 64(4), 2020, pp. 925–930,

Proctor, Robert N. / Londa Schlesinger: Agnotology: The Making and Unmaking of Ignorance, California 2008.

Prozorov, Sergei: Biopolitics and Socialism. Foucault, Agamben, Esposito, in: Sergei Prozorov / Simona Rentea (eds.): The Routledge Handbook of Biopolitics, New York 2016, pp. 94–112.

Rawls, John: Political Liberalism, New York 1993.

Ray, Rashawn / Fabio Rojas: Inequality during the Coronavirus Pandemic, in: Contexts Sociology for the Public, in: Contexts, April 16, 2020, https://contexts.org/blog/inequality-during-the-coronavirus-pandemic/; last accessed July 27, 2021.

Romero, Leo M.: Punishment for Ecological Disasters: Punitive Damages and/or Criminal Sanctions, in: University of St. Thomas Law Journal, 7(1), 2009, pp. 154–181.

Rouvroy, Antoinette / Thomas Berns: Algorithmic Governmentality and Prospects of Emancipation: Disparateness as a Precondition for Individuation Through Relationships? in: Réseaux, 177(1), 2013, pp. 163–196.

Sheel, Alok: Fraenkel's Theory of the Dual State May Need an Update, in: Mint, September 23, 2020, https://www.livemint.com/opinion/online-views/fraen

kel-s-theory-of-the-dual-state-may-need-an-update-11600873439960.html; last accessed July 27, 2021.

Shlkar, Judith N.: The Faces of Injustice, New Haven 1990.

Singh, Mahendra pal: Constitutional Right to Vidya or Privilege for Avidya? in: Journal of the Bar Council of India, 8(251), 1981.

Stiegler, Bernard: Nanjing Lectures 2016–2019, London 2020.

Stiegler, Bernard: The Age of Disruption: Technology and Madness in Computational Capitalism, Cambridge 2019.

The Economist: The COVID-19 Pandemic Will Be over by the End of 2021, Says Bill Gates, in: The Economist, August 18, 2020, https://www.economist.com/international/2020/08/18/the-covid-19-pandemic-will-be-over-by-the-end-of-2021-says-bill-gates; last accessed July 27, 2021.

Tognini, Guacomo: Meet the 40 New Billionaires Who Got Rich Fighting COVID-19, in: Forbes, April 06, 2021, https://www.forbes.com/sites/giacomotognini/2021/04/06/meet-the-40-new-billionaires-who-got-rich-fighting-covid-19/; last accessed July 27, 2021.

United Nations, Department of Economic and Social Affairs, Indigenous Peoples: Covid-19 and Indigenous Peoples, in: United Nations, https://www.un.org/development/desa/indigenouspeoples/covid-19.html; last accessed July 27, 2021.

United Nations News: Migrants Left Stranded and without Assistance by Covid-19 Lockdowns, in: United Nations News, April 08, 2021, https://news.un.org/en/story/2021/04/1089302; last accessed July 27, 2021.

United Nations, Office of Human Rights: Child Rights and the 2030 Agenda for Sustainable Development in the Context of the Covid-19 Pandemic, https://www.ohchr.org/Documents/Issues/Children/ChildRights_2030Agenda.pdf; last accessed July 27, 2021.

United Nations: Policy Brief: The Impact of Covid-19 on Women, April 09, 2020, https://www.unwomen.org/-/media/headquarters/attachments/sections/library/publications/2020/policy-brief-the-impact-of-covid-19-on-women-en.pdf?la=en&vs=1406; last accessed July 27, 2021.

World Health Organization: Disability Considerations during the Covid-19 Outbreak, March 26, 2020, WHO/2019-nCoV/Disability/2020.1.

Yeung, Karen: Five Fears about Mass Predictive Personalization in an Age of Surveillance Capitalism, in: International Data Privacy Law, 8(3), 2018, pp. 258–269.

Zuboff, Shoshana: The Age of Surveillance Capitalism, London 2019.

Gerd Krumeich

Corona und Krieg

Als 1918 die Spanische Grippe wütete, verglich niemand sie mit einem Krieg, auch wenn man sehr wohl wusste, dass sie mit dem Großen Krieg zu tun hatte. Es wurde vermutet, dass die generelle Erschöpfung in den kriegführenden Ländern, vor allem aber an den Fronten, der Krankheit Tür und Tor öffnete. Wobei der Virus allerdings in den Armeen, die am Rande der Niederlage standen, erheblich stärker wütete und mehr *Verluste* nach sich zog als bei denen, die in der siegreichen Schlussoffensive des Jahres 1918 vorankamen und einfach mehr *élan vital* hatten.[1]

Aber es gab auch schon das an heutige Theorien der asymmetrischen Kriegführung erinnernde Argument, dass die *Bakterien* von den Feinden eingeschleppt worden seien, um die Bevölkerung zu zermürben. Dieser Gedanke lag übrigens insofern nahe, als damals sehr stark mit chemischen Waffen experimentiert wurde. Seit den ersten Gasangriffen vom April 1915 hatte sich der *Gaskrieg* absolut perfektioniert, war 1918 zum vermeintlich unverzichtbaren Bestand des inzwischen fast totalen Krieges geworden.[2] *Bakterien* sollten via Spanien eingeschleppt worden sein. Es gab auch die Meinung, dass der jeweilige Feind die Grippe als Kriegsmittel eingesetzt habe. Doch niemand wäre auf die Idee gekommen, der Spanischen Grippe den Krieg zu erklären, war man doch mitten in einem sehr echten Krieg.

So liegt die Vermutung nahe, dass die Häufigkeit der Kriegsmetapher in der aktuellen Corona-Diskussion auch damit zusammenhängt, dass wir alle nicht mehr genau wissen, was Krieg war, ist und sein wird. Zu diesem Problem habe ich mich näher in einem Interview mit der Frankfurter Allgemeinen Zeitung (FAZ) vom März 2021 geäußert.[3] Und meine Auffassung entspricht genau dem, was ein mir via Google zugänglich gemachter Leserbrief in der österreichischen Zeitschrift Meine Welt deutlich macht:

»Wenn im Zusammenhang von Corona, von Politikern und den Medien immer wieder von Krieg oder Kriegszustand die Rede ist, so ist das eine gefährliche Verharmlosung von

---

[1] Zur historischen Einordnung der Corona-Krise siehe Fangerau/Labisch: Pest und Corona; zur Bedeutung der Spanischen Grippe von 1918 siehe Vasold: Die spanische Grippe; Hieronimus: Krankheit und Tod 1918.
[2] Müller: Gaskrieg.
[3] Krumeich: Die Pandemie ist kein Weltkrieg.

Krieg. Diese Leute haben nie einen Krieg erlebt. Sie haben nie erlebt, was der 2. Weltkrieg alleine an der Heimatfront bedeutet hat: Wegen der Bombenangriffe tage- und nächtelang in Kellern zu verbringen und zu hoffen, dass man nicht getroffen wird. Städte die in Trümmern lagen und deren total zerstörte Infrastrukturen. Tote in jeder Familie. Hunger, Kälte, Mangel am Nötigsten. Menschen die vor dem absoluten Nichts standen. Das ist Krieg.«[4]

Der heute leider so häufig gebrauchte Vergleich von Corona und Krieg hat allerdings auch eine Reihe von Varianten, die wenig miteinander zu tun haben. Zunächst die harmloseste Form: Krieg als Sinnbild für *schwerer Kampf, entschiedener Kampf, gemeinsamer Kampf* u. a. m. Man zieht also in den *Krieg* gegen ein *Übel* und weiß, dass der Kampf gegen die Pandemie nur gemeinsam gewonnen werden kann. So berichtete das Domradio aus Köln im März 2021, dass der italienische Kardinal Zuppi den Kampf gegen Corona als einen zermürbenden *Krieg* nicht allein gegen das Virus, sondern auch gegen das Böse in uns, gegen die dem Lockdown folgende und überall herrschende *Müdigkeit* im Kampf gegen dieses Leid bezeichnet habe.[5]

Im Rahmen dieser harmlosen Variante gibt es dann auch noch die Assoziation *wie im Krieg*. Vieles, was wir in den letzten anderthalb Jahren mitgemacht haben, hat die Generation, die den 2. Weltkrieg und die Zeit nach 1945 erlebt hatte, an Restriktionen und Verhaltensweisen *während und nach diesem* Krieg erinnert.

Jens Greve, Soziologe mit den Schwerpunkten gesellschaftliche Differenzierung und politische Soziologie, hat das wie folgt beschrieben:

»Viele haben den Vergleich dieser Krise mit einem Krieg zu Recht kritisiert. Nicht die Gleichsetzung, aber der Vergleich, ist allerdings lehrreich. Wenn man genau hinsieht, zeigen sich aktuell ja durchaus Anzeichen dessen, was sich auch in Kriegsgesellschaften findet: Die ausgeprägteste Parallele ist natürlich die Einschränkung der Bewegungs- und Versammlungsfreiheit. Es gibt aber auch andere Momente, z. B. Rationierungen bestimmter Lebensmittel im Supermarkt oder Eingriffe in Eigentumsrechte wie der Beschluss, dass Mietschulden nicht zur Kündigung führen dürfen.«[6]

Es war in der Tat für viele Menschen in den Gesellschaften der westlichen Welt ein absolutes Novum, dass sie wegen der Epidemie mit Nahrungsmittelknappheit zu kämpfen hatten und sich in eine geradezu irrsinnige Kaufwut von nicht nur zig Dosen weiße Bohnen, sondern auch hunderten von Klopapier-Rollen steigerten. Die so agiert haben, werden ihr Verhalten wohl schon heute selber nicht mehr verstehen. Aber diese Panik war symptomatisch für die allgegenwärtige und von den Verantwortlichen immer weiter geschürte Angst vor Ansteckung durch Be-

---

[4] Kransteiner: Leserbrief. Zur Frage, wie die Corona-Krise die Kriegsgeneration an die Kriegszeit erinnert, vgl. Nann: Krieg und Frieden in Zeiten von Corona.
[5] Katholische Nachrichten Agentur: Kardinal nennt Kampf gegen Corona »Krieg« gegen das Böse.
[6] Münchner Ärztliche Anzeigen: Corona aus Sicht der Soziologie. Alles wie im Krieg?

rühren von irgendwas und irgendwem. Solche Verbote und Gebote hatten einen guten sachlichen Grund, denn das Virus war durchaus real und höchst aggressiv. Aber diese so ungewohnte Situation forderte von allen ganz neue Formen des Sich-Verhaltens und des Miteinander-Umgehens. Keine Umarmung mehr, das Gesicht unter einer Maske halbverborgen − der Mund des anderen nicht mehr sichtbar, was selbstverständlich auch die Verständigungsprobleme enorm verschärfte. Für Schwerhörige − wie ich es bin − bedeutete das eine weitgehende Ausschließung, man braucht ja die Mundbewegungen des Gesprächspartners, um diesen *überhaupt verstehen zu können*.

Solche Erschwernisse mussten aber für den *Krieg* gegen das Virus in Kauf genommen werden, und man konnte sich sogar ein wenig daran gewöhnen. Unbeholfen, aber nicht unbedingt arglos, war hingegen die Reaktion so vieler Regierungen weltweit, die zum *Krieg* gegen das Virus aufriefen, bzw. diesem direkt den Krieg erklärten. Das war und ist eine hochgefährliche Denk- und Verhaltensweise, weil es gemeinhin nicht bei der freundlichen Metaphorik bleibt, dass man gemeinsam und entschlossen das Virus bekämpfen müsse. Angefangen hat diese radikale Kriegsmetaphorik mit dem Angriff auf das World Trade Center von 2001 (*Nine-Eleven*), wo die Regierung Bush sofort den Taliban den Krieg erklärten. *America at War*, blieb dann Monate lang der Fließtext in allen US-Nachrichtensendungen, die man hierzulande sehen konnte. Ich habe damals versucht, gegen diesen Strom anzuschwimmen und argumentiert, dass es Krieg nur zwischen Staaten geben kann, dass es dafür Regelwerke gibt, insbesondere die Haager Konvention von 1907.[7]

Aber genutzt hat dieser Einwand selbstverständlich nichts, zumal sich durch die in den Folgejahren radikal zunehmenden kriegerischen Interventionen insbesondere der Islamisten eine neue Qualität der Auseinandersetzung ergab. So stark wurden ganze Regionen dann etwa vom *Islamischen Staat* beherrscht, dass diese Milizionäre eine durchaus staatliche Qualität gewannen. Das mag strittig bleiben, aber mir ist nicht bekannt, dass in diesen aktuellen Konflikten gefangene Djihad-Kämpfer so behandelt würden, wie vor 100 Jahren die *Franktireure* in Belgien oder Frankreich, die schlicht an die Wand gestellt oder aufgehängt wurden. Ausnahmen sind wohl die ausländischen IS-Kämpfer (und leider auch Kämpferinnen), die nach ihrer Heimkehr mit Gefängnis bestraft werden können, wie soeben geschehen.[8] *Vor Ort* aber, in den Krisen- und Kriegsgebieten, werden sie durchaus als normale Kriegsgefangene verwahrt bzw. ausgetauscht. Auch wenn diese Bedeutungsverschiebung des Soldaten-Status völkerrechtlich noch nicht kodifiziert ist, so ist sie doch die konsequente Folge des effektiven Machtzuwachses dieser Formationen, die heute einen zumindest halbstaatlichen Charakter haben,

---

[7] Krumeich: Dies ist kein Krieg.
[8] Agence France-Presse (AFP): Berliner Gericht verurteilt zwei IS-Mitglieder.

wie das Beispiel Hamas zeigt. Ein interessantes Beispiel für diese neue Situation ist, dass die türkische Regierung 2019 beschloss, die auf ihrem Territorium gefangen gesetzten IS-Kämpfer in ihre Heimatnationen zurückzuführen.[9]

Wir haben also in den letzten 20 Jahren gelernt, dass *Krieg* ohne Weiteres seine staats- und völkerrechtliche Exklusivität als Form eines Konflikts zwischen souveränen Staaten abgelegt hat. Die Verschleifung der Wortbedeutung ist nichts als die Folge der faktischen Umwälzung der zugrunde liegenden Verhältnisse. Und so konnte es geschehen, dass heute jeder und alle Welt vom *Krieg* gegen das Virus sprechen kann, ohne dass dies notwendigerweise eine sehr kriegerische Bedeutung hat. Ein gutes Beispiel hierfür ist eine Rede des gerade gewählten US-Präsidenten Joe Biden vom 26.11.2020 in seinem Heimatort Wilmington, wo er sich zum ersten Mal offiziell an die gesamte Nation richtete: »Ich weiß, dass das Land des Kampfes überdrüssig geworden ist. Wir dürfen nicht vergessen, dass wir uns im Krieg mit dem Virus befinden, nicht miteinander, nicht untereinander. […] Wenn Sie auf unsere Geschichte zurückblicken, sehen Sie, dass die Seele unserer Nation unter den schwierigsten Umständen geschmiedet wurde.«[10] Biden war sich also bewusst, dass die Angst vor der Pandemie auch zu innerer Zerrissenheit, zu Schuldzuschreibungen aller Art führen konnte, die ja sein Vorgänger Trump schon offen angesprochen hatte, wenn er immer wieder vom *China-Virus* sprach, oft verbunden mit der Vermutung, dass die Chinesen den Erreger absichtlich auf die Menschheit losgelassen hätten. Brasiliens rechtsextremer Präsident Jair Bolsonaro hat ebenfalls mit Äußerungen zum Coronavirus für Aufsehen gesorgt. In Anspielung auf China spekulierte er, ob derzeit »ein neuer Krieg« geführt werde.[11]

Ob Trump oder Bolsonaro, ob Netanjahu oder Orban, alle rufen den Krieg gegen das Virus aus. Das ist mehr und weitaus schwerwiegender als die umgangssprachliche Kriegs-Metapher, die weiter oben analysiert wurde. Hier geht es bereits um Krieg als Fortsetzung der Politik mit anderen Mitteln. Es werden konkrete Verantwortliche für das z.T. *hausgemachte* Desaster der unzureichenden Corona-Bekämpfung gesucht und gefunden. Bei Trump ging das nicht allein mit sprachlichen Entgleisungen ab, sondern mit konkreten militärischen Maßnahmen. Im Mai 2020 trat der Kommandeur des *Global Strike Command* der US-Luftwaffe, General Timothy Ray, mit der folgenden Erklärung hervor: »Seien Sie versichert, wir haben die notwendigen Schritte unternommen, um sicherzustellen, dass unsere Bomber und Interkontinentalraketen bereit sind und jedes Ziel auf dem Planeten jederzeit erreichen können. Wir sind voll einsatzbereit und

---

[9] La Depeche: La Turquie décide de renvoyer ses prisonniers, membres de Daesh, dans leur pays d'origine.
[10] Deutsche Presse-Agentur (DPA): Biden ruft zur Einheit im Kampf gegen Corona auf.
[11] Westdeutsche Allgemeine Zeitung (WAZ): Bolsonaro spekuliert über Corona-»Krieg«.

Covid-19 wird daran nichts ändern.«[12] Um was es geht, hat am deutlichsten wohl der französische Staatspräsident Macron ausgesprochen, als er sich angesichts der explosiv steigenden Fallzahlen und der überfüllten Intensivstationen eines Vokabulars bediente, das nur wenig entfernt war von den Aufrufen zur *Heiligen Einheit (Union Sacrée)* des August 1914. In seiner Rede an die Nation vom 16.03.2020 sprach er gleich sechs Mal vom notwendigen *Krieg* gegen die Pandemie. Mehr noch: *Nous sommes en guerre* wurde von Macron in dieser langen Rede geradezu leitmotivisch eingebracht:

> »Nous sommes en guerre, en guerre sanitaire certes. Nous ne luttons ni contre une armée ni contre une autre nation, mais l'ennemi est là, invisible, insaisissable, et qui progresse. Et cela requiert notre mobilisation générale. Nous sommes en guerre. Toute l'action du gouvernement et du Parlement doit être désormais tournée vers le combat contre l'épidémie, de jour comme de nuit. [...] Nous sommes en guerre. J'appelle tous les acteurs politiques, économiques, sociaux, associatifs, tous les Français à s'inscrire dans cette union nationale qui a permis à notre pays de surmonter tant de crises par le passé. Nous sommes en guerre et la Nation soutiendra ses enfants qui, personnels soignants en ville, à l'hôpital, se trouvent en première ligne dans un combat qui va leur demander énergie, détermination, solidarité. Ils ont des droits sur nous.«[13]

Zwar hat der französische Präsident seinen Kriegsruf anfänglich eingeschränkt, indem er erläuterte, es handele sich *gewiss* (nur?) um einen Krieg für die Gesundheit. Aber die in den folgenden und oben zitierten Absätzen gebrauchten Begriffe haben z.T. hochsymbolischen historischen Wert: er spricht von »mobilisation générale«, von einer *nationalen Einheit* wie im August 1914 angesichts der deutschen Kriegserklärung an Frankreich. So befindet sich das Pflegepersonal der Krankenhäuser »en première ligne«, also im Schützengraben. Und das abschließende »Ils ont des droits sur nous« ist nicht etwa nur eine schlichte Mahnung, die Verdienste der am Limit arbeitenden Ärzte und Helfer zu würdigen, sondern eine direkte – geradezu freche – Wiederaufnahme eines Ausspruchs von Georges Clemenceau. Als der *Tiger* im November 1917 an die Macht gerufen wurde, formulierte er nicht allein die berühmten Sätze, dass Frankreich sich im totalen Krieg befinde und dass man keine Verräter mehr dulden werde, sondern er erklärte auch, dass man sich besser um die Soldaten kümmern müsse, die täglich ihre Haut für Frankreich hinhielten: »Ils ont des droits sur nous.« Dieses Versprechen des Regierungschefs wurde dann in den 1920er Jahren von den Organisationen der *Anciens combattants* immer wieder aufgerufen, wenn es darum ging, die mangelnde Fürsorge für die Kriegsverwundeten u.a. zu beklagen. Der Historiker André Loez, Spezialist für die französischen Soldaten des Ersten Weltkriegs, hat dann auch sofort auf diesen schäbigen Versuch Macrons hingewiesen, sich mittels der Corona-Pandemie

---

12 van Auken: Die Corona-Pandemie und der globale imperialistische Krieg.
13 Le Monde: »Nous sommes en guerre«.

mit dem in Frankreich immer noch stark verehrten Georges Clemenceau, *Père la Victoire* von 1918, auf eine Stufe zu stellen.[14] Nota: Von Angela Merkel sind keine Kriegsmetaphern bekannt. Sie verabscheut jede Form von Krieg, auch jede nachträgliche Heroisierung, wie ich von ihr erfahren habe, als ich sie 2016 durch das Memorial von Verdun führen durfte.

Die Vergleiche von Corona mit Krieg und die Aufrufe zu einer nationalen Einheit, die ohne weiteres in wie auch immer fokussierte Feindschaft umschlagen kann, sind die eine Seite der Krisenrhetorik bzw. der Krisenbewältigung. Es gibt aber auch eine humanere Variante, die besagt, wie der Kampf gegen Corona auch weit über die Eindämmung der Krankheit hinaus Frieden in der Welt stiften kann. Diese Dialektik erinnert im Übrigen an die Darwin-Diskussion um 1900: während auf der einen Seite der Darwinismus und sein Topos vom *survival of the fittest* zu aggressiver imperialistischer Politik und sozialer Ausdifferenzierung ausgenutzt wurde – bis hin zu den verbrecherischen Varianten des NS – konnte es auf der anderen Seite durchaus gelungene Versuche geben, dieselbe Auffassung der Evolution für eine Humanisierung der Welt einzusetzen. So stellte etwa die populäre naturwissenschaftliche Zeitschrift *Kosmos* ihre Artikel unter das Motto, dass die Entwicklung der Menschheit nicht etwa auf Vernichtung des Schwächeren, sondern auf gegenseitige Befruchtung zum Fortschritt der Menschheit ziele.

Ganz ähnlich humanistisch argumentiert heute auch die brillante Analyse von Michael Nann, Referent für den Friedensbeauftragten des Rates der Evangelischen Kirche in Deutschland, im Informationsblatt der Evangelischen Arbeitsgemeinschaft für Kriegsdienstverweigerung und Frieden (EAK). Nann erinnert daran, dass UN-Generalsekretär António Guterres im April 2020 die »bewaffneten Akteure« aus der ganzen Welt aufgefordert habe, die Waffen niederzulegen, »um den Menschen in Konfliktgebieten eine bessere Chance zu ermöglichen, das durch Covid-19 verursachte Leid zu bekämpfen«. Er zeigt im Weiteren, dass dieser Appell auch bereits einige Früchte getragen habe, etwa in Kamerun, im Jemen oder auf den Philippinen. So habe die Regierung der Philippinen einen Stopp ihrer Offensive gegen kommunistische Rebellen angeordnet und in Afghanistan habe die Taliban ihren Kämpfern befohlen, das Gesundheitspersonal während der Krise zu schützen. Ingesamt, so Nann, ist »der Kampf gegen eine Pandemie das Gegenteil von Krieg. Es geht nicht um Mensch gegen Mensch, sondern um Mensch für Mensch. Wir haben es mit unserem Verhalten selbst in der Hand, die Zahl der Infizierten und der Toten zu verlangsamen und die Krise zu überwinden.«[15]

Die Pandemie kann also bestehende Krisen verschärfen und zu bewaffneten Konflikten ausufern lassen. Sie kann aber auch das Gegenteil bewirken. So zeigt eine von Tobias Ide an der Technischen Universität (TU) Braunschweig durch-

---

[14] André Loez: Twitter-Post, 16.03.2020, 08:15.
[15] Nann: Krieg und Frieden in Zeiten von Corona.

geführte Studie, dass es in Krisengebieten inzwischen schon in mehreren Fällen strategische Entscheidungen gegeben hat, die Kämpfe für die Dauer der Pandemie herunterzufahren.[16] Die Pandemie hat die gesamte Menschheit vor ein neues Problem gestellt und viele Staaten und Regionen bis in ihre Grundfesten erschüttert. Es kann also nicht verwundern, dass die Kriegs-Metapher so mächtig in Umlauf gekommen ist. Aber man wird wohl schon jetzt festhalten dürfen, dass im Unterschied zu früheren Zeiten, wo aus Krisenkonstellationen immer wieder Kriegspsychosen und schließlich auch Kriege entstanden, die Reaktionen heute doch insgesamt moderater ausfallen. Jedenfalls ist es in der Weltgesellschaft mit ihrem Corona-Problem nicht mehr so einfach wie früher möglich, die Menschen davon zu überzeugen, dass man den Schuldigen kennt, ihn benennt und durch einen gerechten Krieg vernichten kann und wird.

Literatur

Agence France-Presse (AFP): Berliner Gericht verurteilt zwei IS-Mitglieder, in: Badische Zeitung, 05.06.2021, https://www.badische-zeitung.de/berliner-gericht-verurteilt-zwei-is-mitglieder--202366504; letzter Zugriff am 17.08.2021.

Deutsche Presse-Agentur (DPA): Biden ruft zur Einheit im Kampf gegen Corona auf, in: Die Zeit, 26.11.2020, https://www.zeit.de/news/2020-11/26/biden-ruft-zur-einheit-im-kampf-gegen-corona-auf?utm_referrer=https%3A%2f%2fwww.google.de%2f; letzter Zugriff am 17.08.2021.

Fangerau, Heiner/Alfons Labisch: Pest und Corona. Pandemien in Geschichte, Gegenwart und Zukunft, Freiburg 2020.

Hieronimus, Marc: Krankheit und Tod 1918: zum Umgang mit der Spanischen Grippe in Frankreich, England und dem Deutschen Reich, Berlin/Münster 2006.

Ide, Tobias: Wenn Corona Kriege befeuert Studie zu Folgen von COVID-19 auf bewaffnete Konflikte, 18.12.2020, Technische Universität Braunschweig Presseinformationen, https://magazin.tu-braunschweig.de/pi-post/wenn-corona-kriege-befeuert/; letzter Zugriff 28.07.2021.

Katholische Nachrichten Agentur: Kardinal nennt Kampf gegen Corona »Krieg« gegen das Böse, 17.03.2021, Domradio.de, https://www.domradio.de/themen/corona/2021-03-17/muedigkeit-und-leid-kardinal-nennt-kampf-gegen-corona-krieg-gegen-das-boese; letzter Zugriff am 28.07.2021.

Kransteiner, Georg: Leserbrief: »Corona-Vergleich mit Krieg ist gefährliche Verharmlosung«, 30.03.2020, https://www.meinbezirk.at/wels-wels-land/c-loka

---

[16] Ide: Wenn Corona Kriege befeuert.

les/corona-vergleich-mit-krieg-ist-gefaehrliche-verharmlosung_a4012932; letzter Zugriff am 28.07.2021.

Krumeich, Gerd: Die Pandemie ist kein Weltkrieg, 19.01.2021, Frankfurter Allgemeine Zeitung, https://www.faz.net/aktuell/gesellschaft/gesundheit/coronavirus/historiker-krumeich-zu-kriegsanalogien-pandemie-ist-kein-weltkrieg-17152543.html; letzter Zugriff am 06.06.2021.

Krumeich, Gerd: Dies ist kein Krieg. Weshalb man Terroristen nicht zu Kriegsgegnern aufwerten soll, in: Süddeutsche Zeitung 17.09.2001, S. 16.

La Dépêche: La Turquie décide de renvoyer ses prisonniers, membres de Daesh, dans leur pays d'origine, 09.11.2019, https://www.ladepeche.fr/2019/11/09/la-turquie-decide-de-renvoyer-ses-prisonniers-membres-de-daesh-dans-leur-pays-dorigine,8532098.php; letzter Zugriff am 28.07.2021.

Le Monde: »Nous sommes en guerre«: le verbatim du discours d'Emmanuel Macron, 16.03.2020, https://www.lemonde.fr/politique/article/2020/03/16/nous-sommes-en-guerre-retrouvez-le-discours-de-macron-pour-lutter-contre-le-coronavirus_6033314_823448.html; letzter Zugriff 04.06.2021.

Loez, André: Twitter-Post, 16.03.2020, 08:15, https://twitter.com/andreloez/status/1239631476049788930; letzter Zugriff am 04.06.2021.

Nann, Michael: Krieg und Frieden in Zeiten von Corona, 24.06.2020, Redaktion Feinschwarz, https://www.feinschwarz.net/krieg-und-frieden-in-zeiten-von-corona/; letzter Zugriff am 28.07.2021.

Müller, Rolf-Dieter: Gaskrieg, in: Gerhard Hirschfeld/Gerd Krumeich/Irina Renz (Hrsg.): Enzyklopädie Erster Weltkrieg, Paderborn 2014, S. 519–522.

Münchner Ärztliche Anzeigen: Corona aus Sicht der Soziologie. Alles wie im Krieg?; https://www.aerztliche-anzeigen.de/leitartikel/corona-aus-sicht-der-soziologie-alles-wie-im-krieg; letzter Zugriff am 04.06.2021.

van Auken, Bill: Die Corona-Pandemie und der globale imperialistische Krieg, 12.05.2021, https://www.wsws.org/de/articles/2020/05/12/vana-m12.html; letzter Zugriff am 28.07.2021.

Vasold, Manfred: Die spanische Grippe: Die Seuche und der Erste Weltkrieg, Darmstadt 2009.

Westdeutsche Allgemeine Zeitung: Bolsonaro spekuliert über Corona-»Krieg« in: WAZ, 06.05.2021, https://www.waz.de/politik/bolsonaro-spekuliert-ueber-corona-krieg-id232224943.html; letzter Zugriff am 17.08.2021.

II. Shifts in the Observers' Perspectives

Mariacarla Gadebusch Bondio and
Birgit Ulrike Münch

Long Covid – Unfortunately Not *Past*: Mapping (In)Visibility Perspectives from the Medical Humanities and Art History

Long Covid (or post Covid) is a secondary disease that is difficult to detect with the usual diagnostic parameters, such as measurable laboratory values. The associated symptoms can impair vital functions such as breath, smell, taste, sleep, as well as motor and cognitive performance, but remains ›invisible‹ to others. Patients, especially those who are not acutely ill with Covid-19, are often not tested, and thus are placed in a precarious position through the lack of evidence. Even being correctly diagnosed proves to be a lengthy process as is receiving appropriate care and rehabilitation. This particular configuration of problems in a society thrown into a state of emergency by the pandemic has led to rapid networking, grouping and the mobilization of those affected worldwide. In the meantime, a variety of works of art has emerged on the subject of long Covid, some of which have been developed in close collaboration with patients. The medium of photography is often used to visualize the individual suffering of the *long haulers*. This visualization of the invisible puts the protagonists and their stories in the foreground, offering access to sufferers' altered perception of their own bodies or environment.

This paper analyzes the particularities of a disease that has triggered innovative forms of evidence generation in the face of a prevailing lack of clinical evidence, thanks to digital communication and information flow, as well as to the engagement of various groups of stakeholders. With regard to the different contexts in which the consequences of Covid-19 are discussed, we show which strategies for dealing with the disease are currently being negotiated. Long Covid narratives and images circulate alongside and sometimes even in response to scientific and programmatic writings. The long Covid phenomenon is marked by great diversity in the context of multimedia, where being affected and involved is at the same time accompanied by epistemic awareness. Images of long Covid lend themselves to critical and interdisciplinary reflection: Visualization of the individual suffering stands in a longer iconographic-iconological pictorial tradition, as demonstrated in the visualization of migraine. The similarities, but also the differences, with regard to varying constellations of origin for example, are here outlined. The potential in visualizing diseases through realistic and fictional images has only just begun to be exploited. In the following, this potential will be explored both epistemically and art-historically with regard to long Covid.

1. Mapping the Long Covid Framework

On February 25, 2021, the World Health Organization (WHO) published a document combined with an appeal to health-care workers and patients[1]: The target groups were asked to systematically collect information on Covid-19 and to contribute to a clinical platform created by the WHO. The goal stated is »to expand our knowledge on post Covid-19 condition, and support patient care and public health interventions.«[2] The *Global Covid-19 Clinical Platform Case Report Form (CRF) for Post Covid condition* – abbreviated to *Post Covid-19 CRF* – marks a turning point in several respects. Firstly, it demonstrates that the chronic condition that has been spreading since the spring of 2020 as a result of or in connection with Covid-19, initially referred to as »long Covid«, though later renamed, is being taken very seriously; it also shows that internationally coordinated efforts are being made to expand medical knowledge based on uniform documentation; and lastly it demonstrates that not only physicians and health care workers but also patients are being consulted as sources of information. When, in the spring of 2020, the first reports of long Covid sufferers appeared in the media, the WHO propagated a distinction between »mild cases« with a recovery time of about two weeks and »severe cases« sometimes taking up to six weeks to recover.[3] At this time, WHO estimated that about 80 percent of people infected with novel coronavirus would experience a mild or moderate course of disease.[4] Although the distinction between *mild* and *severe* cases is problematic given the long-term consequences, the WHO website continues to state: »Most people infected with the Covid-19 virus will experience mild to moderate respiratory illness and recover without requiring special treatment. Older people, and those with underlying medical problems like cardiovascular disease, diabetes, chronic respiratory disease, and cancer are more likely to develop serious illness.«[5] For those affected, the

---

[1] Cf. World Health Organization: Global COVID-19 Clinical Platform Case Report Form.
[2] Ibid.
[3] Cf. World Health Organization: Coronavirus; Löwensteil: We Need to Talk About What Coronavirus Recoveries Look Like; cf. Garner: For 7 Weeks I Have Been Through a Roller Coaster of Ill Health, Extreme Emotions, and Utter Exhaustion.
[4] Cf. Callard/Perego: How And Why Patients Made Long Covid.
[5] World Health Organization: Global COVID-19 Clinical Platform Case Report Form.

WHO distinction was and is frustrating. As the first cases of protracted sequelae, which were or were suspected to be related to Covid-19 manifested themselves, clinicians also began dealing with the consequences of Covid-19. The first medical studies came from countries such as Italy, where the pandemic had seen drastic developments in spring 2020.[6] As early as May 2020, a group of clinicians from Rome[7] pointed out the multi-organ consequences of Covid-19. This complicated by a lack of knowledge or sometimes by the too hasty circulation of information, but – according to the authors – on the basis of these first documented observations, the complex phenomenon should henceforth be researched systematically and in a highly interdisciplinary manner: »Without larger prospective observational studies that are only now being started, clinicians can retrieve information just from case reports and or small studies. This is the time to understand how Covid-19 goes forward and what consequences survivors may expect to experience.«[8]

This and other studies published in the spring and summer of 2020 report on persistent symptoms in a large proportion of patients who had overcome the acute Covid-19 phase: »Common symptoms include cough, fever, dyspnea, musculoskeletal symptoms (myalgia, joint pain, fatigue), gastrointestinal symptoms, and anosmia/dysgeusia.«[9] A growing interest in the post acute care needs of recovered Covid-19 patients is evidenced by publications in international medical journals as of early summer 2020, but the focus was initially directed toward the group of survivors, i. e., people who had contracted acute Covid-19, received clinical care and were monitored after hospitalization. The larger percentage of those suffering from the consequences of Covid-19 was neglected. Alongside these scientific publications, reports by patients have appeared in a wide variety of popular print media and blogs.[10] Thus, Paul Garner, a non-hospitalized Covid-19 patient writing in the British Medical Journal blog, describes his agonizing calvarium after what was in itself a »mild« illness.[11] For him and many other patients, and on top of the distressing symptoms, the lack of medical recognition and clinical evidence, often combined with misdiagnosis, psychosomatization, and trivialization, was a painful experience. The fact that many long Covid sufferers have become incapacitated, but have not initially had the right to appropriate care due to the unrecognized pathology of the illness, it is not hard to imagine the individual, family, and so-

---

[6] Cf. Gemelli Against COVID-19 Post Acute Care Study Group: Post COVID-19 Global Health Strategies; cf. Carfi/Bernabei/Landi: Persistent Symptoms in Patients After Acute COVID-19.

[7] Cf. Gemelli Against COVID-19 Post Acute Care Study Group: Post COVID-19 Global Health Strategies.

[8] Ibid.

[9] Carfi/Bernabei/Landi: Persistent Symptoms in Patients After Acute COVID-19, p. 603.

[10] Cf. Löwensteil: We Need to Talk About What Coronavirus Recoveries Look Like; cf. Callard/Perego: How And Why Patients Made Long Covid.

[11] Cf. Garner: For 7 Weeks I Have Been Through a Roller Coaster of Ill Health, Extreme Emotions, and Utter Exhaustion.

cietal consequences of their situation. For these patients and their families, long Covid presents a multi-faceted challenge. The clustering of difficult diagnosability, lack of knowledge, intermittent symptoms, and lack of therapeutic approaches are just some of the reasons. There are currently three coexistant theories on the aetiology of long Covid symptomatology, which for patients tends to increase the uncertainty. These theories postulate a) persistent viruses at immune-privileged sites, b) an aberrant immune response and/or c) autoimmunity.[12]

However, the palpable disorientation has also triggered initiatives whose impact has manifested itself on four levels: firstly, at the ontological level, primarily through the definitional-terminological decision by patients to label their condition as long Covid rather than post Covid; secondly, at the epistemic-normative and ethical levels through the the advocacy of a »symptom-based approach and the de-psychosomatization of symptoms«[13] that does not discriminate against long Covid patients and through the hard-won participation in the development of recommendations[14]; thirdly, at the health policy and global level, in which WHO revised its initial typology and developed data collection and documentation strategies directed at health-care workers and patients; and fourthly, at the aesthetic-artistic level, in which artists, as well as patients, post texts and images (including memes) on social media and networks with each other, draw attention to the problem in public spaces, for example through graffiti, deal with the complex of topics in a variety of ways, especially in the field of photography, and often include the biography of those affected in their works or photo stories.

Visual evidence of long Covid can thus be created from out of the most diverse artistic positions. The mobilization of long Covid sufferers has led to the generation of of experience-based narrative andvisually-supported evidence, which would have been unthinkable digital networking. The various groupings of long Covid sufferers have resulted in a diversification of public appeals, where they report their experiences in the media and even occasionally scientific journals. The robust involvement of laypersons has led to increasingly broad social and scientific attention to the phenomenon and the participation of stakeholders in processes such as guideline development, and in general to what can be called ›epistemic awareness‹ in a wide variety of populations. All these efforts have accelerated development: the WHO has recognized post Covid as a disease, guidelines have been developed in rapid succession. Publications in which physicians have collaborated closely with patients and not least, the large number of actively engaged physi-

---

[12] Cf. British Society for Immunology: Long Term Immunological Health Consequences of COVID-19.

[13] Cf. Siegelman: Reflections of A COVID-19 Long Hauler; Atkinson et al.: Seeing the Experimental Knowledge Through COVID-19.

[14] Cf. Gorna et al.: Long COVID Guidelines Need to Reflect Lived Experience; cf. Alwan et al.: From Doctors As Patients.

cians and health-care workers suffering from long Covid, betokens a new kind of inclusivity and a revised understanding of patient experience. For example, Felicity Callard, professor of human geography at the University of Glasgow, was also one of the first long Covid sufferers to mobilize in her dual role as researcher and patient. She published several essays raising awareness of the fact that people are being abandoned to their »invisible« suffering: »the significant suffering and labor that has been unfolding in people's homes, often at some distance from the support of NHS services [in the UK], remain, to date, largely invisible«[15]. The invisible suffering is reinforced by the fact that non-hospitalized patients who have had to overcome so-called mild Covid in home isolation continue to suffer the severe consequences without medical care. Callard describes introspection »from the sickbed« in a paper where she explores medical historian Charles Rosenberg's idea that epidemics have a dramaturgical-temporal form.[16] The horizontal body, Callard argues, shifts and condenses the temporal and spatial axes used to comprehend and narrate an epidemic event by, for example, epidemiologists. Unlike other epidemics, in the case of long Covid it was not medical professionals but patients who were the first to manifest and name their collective experience and knowledge of the consequences of Covid-19. With the gesture of naming and with the choice of prepositions, this group consciously included the temporal component of suffering in the name.[17] That the designation preferred by many patients is an ontological dimensioning of the disease expressed in this way has also been emphasized by physicians and nurses suffering from long Covid.[18] The term post Covid, which is preferred in medicine and also by the WHO, remains controversial.[19] It is misleading because it suggests – according to the authors of a manifesto by health care workers suffering from long Covid – a temporal caesura, a *before* and *after*.[20] Yet between the state of being sick with Covid-19 and the supposed *after* is an unidentifiable dividing line that presupposes Covid-19 has been cured. It is precisely this purported dividing line that sufferers reject. The language politics involved in these discussions have already been the subject of reflections in the sociology of science and medical ethics.[21] What has barely been reflected upon so far, however, is the visualization of this inherently invisible disease. Charles Rosenberg tied the visibility of an epidemic to the visibly sick and dying, and to the dead. For Rosenberg, »a true epidemic […] is highly visible«.[22] Since in long

---

15 Callard: Very, very mild: Covid-19 symptoms and illness classification.
16 Cf. Callard: Epidemic Time; cf. Rosenberg: What Is and Was an Epidemic?
17 Cf. Callard: Epidemic Time, p. 729.
18 Cf. Alwan et al.: From Doctors As Patients.
19 Cf. Perego et al.: Why the Patient-Made Term ›Long COVID‹ is Needed.
20 Cf. Alwan et al.: From Doctors As Patients.
21 Cf. Roth/Bruni: Participation, Empowerment, and Evidence in The Current Discourse on Personalized Medicine; cf. Roth/Gadebusch Bondio: The Contested Meaning of ›Long COVID‹.
22 Rosenberg: What Is an Epidemic?

Covid we are not dealing with the acute, contagious infection, but with a direct or no (longer) provable consequence of it, Callard's engagement with Rosenberg's visibility theory is at first surprising. But what is of interest in this context is her reflection on the (in)visibility of long Covid. For Callard, writing from a sickbed, the making visible of long Covid is linked to a political struggle: »What becomes clinically or sociologically visible often depends on multiple actors, tools, and media: to make something visible often requires political struggle and brings political consequences.«[23] The question arises whether the temporal aspect of long Covid that is emphasized and terminologically fixed by its naming contributes decisively to its invisibilization. The state in which an ongoing, intermittent symptomatology persists as a consequence of a no longer acute infectious illness cannot be easily recognized from the outside; it also cannot be measured and recorded by any biomarkers so far and is thus difficult to quantify and represent.

2. The Visualization of Long Covid

In particular, social media shows manifold attempts by long Covid sufferers to deal with the disease. In memes, which are usually characterized by images with short text – although the media can vary[24] – and reflect a topic in a humorous, ironic or even sarcastic to highly critical way, long Covid is widely received. On Instagram, the powerlessness of those affected and the ignorance of medicine and politics are portrayed in comic strips, in images taken out of context.[25] In one cartoon, for example, a genie appears, similar to Aladdin's magic lamp, who fulfills the patient's wish (»I wish that vaccines worked«). To the person's realization (»Nothing's changed«), the genie succinctly replies: »Correct.« Very often in the memes, one's own portrait is juxtaposed with a picture of a very old person in the sense of a before-and-after double portrait in order to make visible the inner state experienced as decrepit, while paralyzing fatigue is also a common theme, for example when the same picture of a sleeping person is entitled me doing work as well as me after work. The problem of a disease taking place inside the body with little or no symptoms visible to the outside world is in common to a wide variety of diseases. Likewise, many of these diseases have had to struggle with social acceptance for a very long time. In the case of long covid, there are two additional complicating aspects that do not apply to all diseases in this category: Firstly, the medical readings show no abnormalities. Secondly, that the disease as a new dis-

---

[23] Callard/Perego: How and Why Patients Made Long Covid, p. 733.
[24] Cf. Shifman: Memes in Digital Culture; cf. Kien: Communicating with Memes, pp. 1–12.
[25] Cf. Instagram: Longcovidmemes.

ease ›with a thousand faces‹ suddenly appeared in the past year among the group of survivors as a global phenomenon and emerged parallel to the coping efforts of the first lockdown and the search for a vaccine.

As such, it was pushed into the background by the urgency of the in the acute crisis and threat of the pandemic. The artistic positions which attempt to make visible, by means of altered or retouched or newly created images, the symptoms of the disease or the conditions caused by the disease are numerous. Above all, migraine symptoms have been taken up many times as a central social issue. The subjectivity of aura symptoms could be shown in pictures, and those affected could recognize their individual experience in these pictures or add their own symptomatology to them. Visual disturbances, especially as they appear in long Covid as well as in the migraine aura, can be depicted much more vividly by a picture than merely by a description of what is seen or the deviation of what is seen in contrast to the normal state. Illustrations, however, also allow the visualization of concrete or diffuse sensations, emotions and fears, for example by correcting or adjusting the color scheme or choosing a monochrome color scheme for the surroundings. How is altered image perception during a migraine attack representable? Gattnar – herself a migraine patient since the age of eleven – placed the visual field as it presents itself to a healthy person in parallel with the image seen during a migraine attack. She chose graphic interpretations and representations of neurological phenomena for this purpose, making the different forms of a migraine aura visually experienceable in an artist's book.[26] It is remarkable that the book follows a classical migraine attack in its structure and that this dramaturgy is also explained in concise texts. In an additional internet portal (https:g43punkt1-wixsite.com/aura), individual patients have the opportunity, starting from a motivically simple initial image – a left hand resting on the right thigh of a person dressed in jeans pants, to show how the image changes under the influence of the migraine. Gattnar has the possibility to query the most important symptoms, as well as to download the original image and to change it in the image editing program in a way that corresponds to the own personal visual migraine aura. The publication, which is based on a bachelor thesis (G43.1.-Aura Phenomena of a Classic Migraine), is thus continuously expanded and supplemented digitally. The results are anonymously juxtaposed to create a more holistic picture of the aura. Despite the anonymity, short statements of the affected persons are added to the pictures, which are placed next to each other in a square format, such as: »My aura looks like a flashing halo in the fog«, or: »It is like a shadow world. The environment and one's own perception changes. I don't feel some parts of my body and I see flashes and jags.«

---

[26] Cf. Gattnar: Phänomene und Darstellungen der (Migräne)Aura.

However, the text is only visible in the virtual format when the cursor is moved over the image. This initially enables direct comparison of the individual images without being distracted by the underlying text, and the heterogeneity of the individual auras becomes effective. The images on the website are supported by film and especially sound sequences, which explore the aesthetic representability of migraine and aura in their intermediality. Artistic positions on the subject of migraine and aura in particular can be found in music, such as Richard Wagner or Gustav Mahler, and in literature, texts by the author Siri Hustvedt, who contrasts the treatment of the topic in her novels and essays[27] with a non-fiction book related to psychoanalytical and neuroscientific findings, in which she describes the struggle against and the acceptance of the disease, but also the long path to this end, on which »philosophical resignation«[28] serves her as proven means. Artists such as Marina Abramovic or musicians such as Alwa Glebe, who have chosen *pain* as their main field of negotiation, also address the aura in various forms.[29] And already Lewis Carroll's *Alice in Wonderland* describes in micropsia and macropsia perceptual changes that occur within a migraine attack and can lead as neurological deficits to hallucinations that make one perceive one's own body as huge or tiny – for example, when Alice grows to gigantic size so that she no longer fits into the house, or the cat's head, characterized by a broad grin, begins to wander and hangs in the tree as a giant balloon. Carroll himself was demonstrably a migraine patient, so that the syndrome was also called *Lewis-Carroll-Syndrome* or *Alice-in-Wonderland-Syndrome.*[30] It is interesting to note that Gattnar's work was submitted in 2020, the website was launched in 2021, thus at a time when the Covid-19 pandemic was already underway and a very similar artistic conception would also be possible for long Covid. But in comparison to the most diverse artistic and medial confrontations of the entire Covid-19 image cosmos, the phenomenon of long Covid has so far still been accorded surprisingly little importance. One exception is the photographer Susana Vera, who works in Madrid. In her work, she has repeatedly made clear how she sees herself as a photographer: »The camera fulfills my need to express myself, but most importantly it's a tool that allows me to tell the stories of people whose voices might not be heard otherwise. It's a privilege and a great gift.«[31] In this sense, the images she produced in connection with long Covid can be integrated into her earlier works. In these, she sought to make the blind spots visible through her art as well, such as a documentary about two-year-old Mariam Mitn Ahamed, who suffers from hunger in Mauritania, the

[27] Cf. Hustvedt: Living, Thinking, Looking.
[28] Hustvedt: The Shaking Woman or a History of my Nerves.
[29] Cf. Podoll et al.: Obligatory and Facultative Symptoms of the Alice in Wonderland Syndrome.
[30] Cf. Todd: The Syndrome of Alice in Wonderland; Podoll et al.: Obligatory and Facultative Symptoms of the Alice in Wonderland Syndrome.
[31] Pinedo: The Faces in the Fog of ›Long COVID‹.

expulsion of a Madrilenian Roma community from their residential area or, entitled *Gabriel's Journey*, the path of gender reassignment of the trans-man Gabriel Diaz de Tudanca, who was declared a girl at birth. In the series *The faces in the fog of long Covid* Vera attempts to stage the symptomatology through portrait photographs, which can notably be arranged as a type of diptych: The left shows the portrait of the person looking frontally into the camera, made by blue foil (fog) mostly against a bright background, whilst the picture on the right, which is about half as wide, depicts an equally altered section of an object. For example, a child's blackboard lying in the light blue-white fog, stands for Susana Matarranz, a 44-year-old elementary school teacher, who was infected twice and therefore could not work for months.[32] She misses the children very much. The blackboard also represents her own account in which she was barely able to hold her arm, and therefore unable to perform the simple activity of writing with chalk on a blackboard, one of the basic manual skills of the teaching profession.

However, the blank slate of the photograph also stands metaphorically for the emptiness she feels: »The part of me that is profession is empty, like the blackboard. A piece of my heart, which are my students, whom I love dearly, feels empty and I feel like at this moment there's nothing I can do to fill it in.«[33] The image is photographed through a mid-blue plastic sheet, a technique which connects all the photographs in the series and simultaneously associates the nebulous, the impaired sharp vision, and the diffuse that characterizes the disease. The blurred, diluted vision, the tired eye that can no longer focus, simultaneously evokes associations with the *blue hour* through the choice of color. *L'heure bleue* is often used to describe the moment when the sun is below the horizon and the blue in the spectrum of light in the sky comes to the fore. Although the phenomenon can also be applied to the morning, the term *blue hour* is almost exclusively applied to the evening twilight. The melancholic context[34] of the blue hour, as it often appears in literature and art, fits long Covid just as well as the often-described exhaustion (fatigue) of the patients. Another photographic work was created in Italy in a *Post Covid-19 Day Hospital* of the Gemelli Polyclinic in Rome. The photographer Marco Carmignan visited the day hospital, which opened in April 2020, and visualized not only the symptoms of the patients like Vera, but also the setting of long Covid: such as »a doctor who takes a break in front of the Polyclinic's entrance, a doppler ultrasound device which is used to examine the veins' functionality, a hair lock of a female mid-30s long Covid patient, also a teacher (fig.1) or a photograph of a chest CT scan at the Day Hospital to check the lung status.

---

[32] Cf. ibid, Photography No.4 (by Susana Vera).
[33] Ibid.
[34] Cf. Hoeppe: Why the Sky is Blue.

Fig. 1: Marco Carmignan, Lock of hair, 2020.

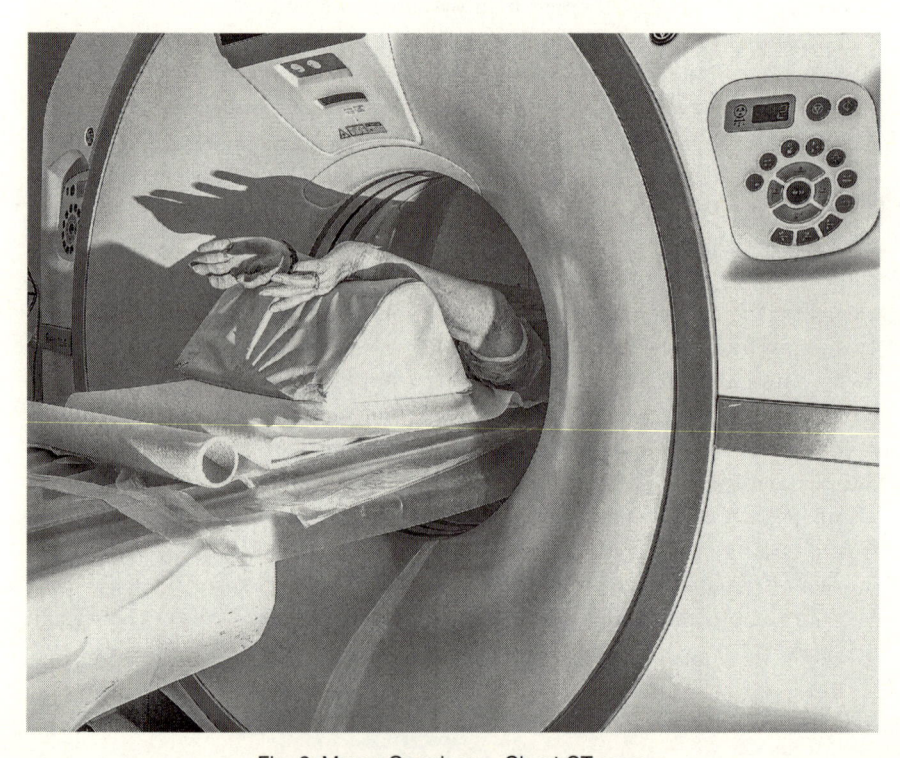

Fig. 2: Marco Carmignan, Chest CT scan
(Stefania, 68, undergoes a CT scan at the Day Hospital Post-Covid-19
of the Gemelli Polyclinic), 2020.

Fig. 3: Marco Carmignan, Portrait of Marta
(Marta 32, researcher and teacher), 2020.

This image just shows the arms and hands of the patient«[35] who is just positioned in the device, the hands cast a shadow, face, gender and physicality are not visible, only the turquoise hospital clothing is a little recognizable (fig. 2).

The teacher, whose tuft of hair is staged in one of the photographic works, is also represented within a half-figure portrait in Marco Carmignan's oeuvre:[36] In a darkly shadowed room, into which a single light beam enters from the left alone, she sits with a naked upper body and covers her eyes with both hands. Her half-length blond curly hair and several colorful ribbons adorning her wrists identify her as »Marta, 32-year-old scientist and teacher« (fig. 3). And Carmignan continues: »As early as begin of March 2020 she fell ill in Paris and returned to Italy. Even after 9 months she has not recovered, as the text describes: low-grade fever, pain in the legs, tiredness, memory problems and, as already mentioned, hair loss.«[37]

[35] Carmignan: Long Covid.
[36] Ibid.
[37] Ibid.

Both Vera and Carmignan contribute with their works to making the invisible disease visible. In Carmignan's work, there is a stronger reference to the direct connection to Covid disease, since the images from the clinic and the patient without a face are also reminiscent of works by those acutely ill with Covid-19. Both are united by the close reference to the affected persons, the sketching of their life situation and their individualization by mentioning their first names. In both cases, the persons portrayed are mostly female, also corresponding to the actual situation: young women in particular suffer from the late effects of corona. Women under fifty have a five times higher risk, also because they are immunologically stronger than men. Giving a biography to the diseased, or more specifically the diseased with the presented photographic works, even with a covered face as with the portrait of Marta, is a vital function of this art. The loneliness and helplessness portrayed in the shadowed room or in diffuse blue glow is also broken up in the various portals of the digital world, even sometimes employed sarcastically, as proven by the memes. The idea of dealing with the visualization of an invisible illness is not new and could already be exemplified in large numbers on the basis of illnesses such as migraine or depression. It becomes apparent that here, as with long Covid, identified as a disease for less than 15 months, a decidedly interdisciplinary approach must be found in order to do justice to the phenomenon in all its complexity. The authors of the paper on long Covid from the Policlinico Gemelli, cited at the beginning of this paper, from which the pictures of Carmignan originate, recognized early the need for interdisciplinary efforts. Only through the collaboration of several clinical disciplines could the insidious clinical picture be grasped.

After more than a year, it can be concluded that a phenomenon like long Covid still requires much more than clinical interdisciplinarity. The many faces, facets, and consequences of long Covid have led to a worldwide mobilization and networking of patients that is decisively changing media, societal, and medical perceptions of this unsolved health problem. The artistic initiatives in this paper are presented in solidarity with the process of self-assertion of long Covid sufferers. They turn those affected into protagonists, using the image to transform subjective experiences of illness into perceptible, comprehensible states at the boundary between inner and outer worlds. Such manifestations of the individual and collective struggle with an illness for which medicine has no measurable evidence, thus call for decidedly multi- and interdisciplinary scrutiny. Long Covid requires a radical interdisciplinarity, which combines the potential of both clinical research with contributions from the arts and the humanities as well as the expertise of those affected by the disease.

References

Atkinson, Sarah/Hannah Bradby/Mariecarla Gadebusch Bondio/Anna Hallberg/Jane Macnaughton/Ylva Söderfeldt: Seeing the Value of Experimental Knowledge Through COVID-19, in: History and Philosophy of the Life Sciences, 43(85), 2021.

Alwan, Nisreen A./Emily Attree/Jennifer Mary Blair/Debby Bogaert/Mary-Ann Bowen/John Boyle/Madeleine Bradman/Tracy Ann Briggs/Sarah Burns/Daniel Campion/Katherine Cushing/Brendan Delaney/Chirs Dixon/Grace E. Dolman/Caitriona Dynan/Ian M. Frayling/Nell Freeman-Romilly/Julia Hammond/Jenny Judge/Linn Järte/Amali Lokugamage/Nathalie MacDremott/Mairi MacKinnon/Visita Majithia/Tanya Northridge/Laura Powell/Clare Rayner/Ginevra Read/Ekta Sahu/Claudia Shand/Amy Small/Cara Strachan/Jake Suett/Becky Sykes/Sharon Taylor/Kevin Thomas/Margarita Thomson/Alexis Wiltshire/Victoria Woods: From Doctors As Patients: A Manifesto for Tackling Persisting Symptoms of COVID-19, in: BMJ 370(3565), 2020.

British Society for Immunology: Long Term Immunological Health Consequences of COVID-19, August 13, 2020, https://www.immunology.org/sites/default/files/BSI_Briefing_Note_August_2020_FINAL.pdf; last accessed December 10, 2020.

Callard, Felicity: Epidemic Time. Thinking from the Sickbed, in: Bulletin of the History of Medicine, 94(4), 2020, pp. 727–743.

Callard, Felicity: Very, very mild: Covid-19 Symptoms and Illness Classification, May 08, 2020, http://somatosphere.net/2020/mild-covid.html/, last accessed April 26, 2021.

Callard Felicity/Elisa Perego: How And Why Patients Made Long Covid, in: Social Science & Medicine, 268(113426), 2021.

Carfi, Angelo/Roberto Bernabei/Francesco Landi: Persistent Symptoms in Patients After Acute COVID-19, in: JAMA, 324(6), 2020, pp. 603–605.

Carmignan, Marco: Long Covid, https://www.marcocarmignan.com/long-covid; last accessed April 26, 2021.

Gattnar, Anisha: Phänomene und Darstellungen der (Migräne)Aura, Hildesheim 2020.

Garner, Paul: For 7 Weeks I Have Been Through a Roller Coaster of Ill Health, Extreme Emotions, and Utter Exhaustion, May 05, 2020, https://blogs.bmj.com/bmj/2020/05/05/paul-garner-people-who-have-a-more-protracted-illness-need-help-to-understand-and-cope-with-the-constantly-shifting-bizarre-symptoms/; last accessed March 25, 2021.

Gemelli Against COVID-19 Post Acute Care Study Group: Post COVID-19 Global

Health Strategies. The Need for An Interdisciplinary Approach, in: Aging Clinical and Experimental Research, 32(8), 2020, pp. 1613–1620.

Gorna, Robin / Nathalie MacDermott / Clare Rayner / Margaret O'Hara / Sophie Evans / Lisa Agyen / Will Nutland / Natalie Rogers / Claire Hastie: Long COVID Guidelines Need to Reflect Lived Experience, in: The Lancet, 397(10273), 2021, pp. 455–457.

Hoeppe, Götz: Why the Sky is Blue. Discovering the Color of Life, Princeton 2007.

Hustvedt, Siri: The Shaking Woman or a History of my nerves, London 2010.

Hustvedt, Siri: Living, Thinking, Looking. Essays, London 2012.

Instagram: Longcovidmemes, https://www.instagram.com/longCOVIDmemes/; last accessed August 20, 2021.

Kien, Grant: Communicating With Memes. Consequences in Post-truth Civilization, Lanham Boulder / New York / London 2019.

Löwensteil, Fiona: We Need to Talk About What Coronavirus Recoveries Look Like, in: The New York Times, April 13, 2020.

Perego, Elisa / Felicity Callard / Laurie Stras / Barbara Melville-Jóhannesson / Rachel Pope / Nisreen A. Alwan: Why the Patient-Made Term ›Long COVID‹ is Needed, in: Wellcome Open Research, 5(224), 2020.

Pinedo, Emma: The Faces in the Fog of ›Long COVID‹, April 12, 2021, www.widerimage.reuters.com/story/the-faces-in-the-fog-of-long COVID; last accessed August 20, 2021.

Podoll, Klaus / Derek Robinson: Migraine Art: The Migraine Experience From Within, Berkeley 2008.

Podoll, Klaus / Hermann Ebel / Derek Robinson / Nicola Ubaldo: Obligatory and Facultative Symptoms of the Alice in Wonderland Syndrome, in: Minerva Medica, 93(4), 2002, pp. 287–293.

Rosenberg, Charles E.: What Is an Epidemic? AIDS in Historical Perspective, in: Bulletin of the History of Medicine, 94(4), 2020, pp. 563–577.

Roth, Phillip H. / Tommaso Bruni: Participation, Empowerment, and Evidence in the Current Discourse on Personalized Medicine. A Critique of ›Democratizing Healthcare‹, in: Science, Technology, & Human Values, 46, 2021 (forthcoming).

Roth Philllip H. / Gadebusch-Bondio, Mariacarla: The contested meaning of »long COVID« – Patients, doctors, and the politics of subjective evidence. Social Science & Medicine 292 (2022) 114619 https://doi.org/10.1016/j.socscimed.2021.114619.

Siegelman, Jeffrey N.: Reflections of a COVID-19 Long Hauler, in: JAMA, 324(20), 2020, pp. 2031–2032.

Shifman, Limor: Memes in Digital Culture, London 2013.

Todd, John: The Syndrome of Alice in Wonderland, in: Canadian Medical Association Journal, 73(9), 1955, pp. 701–704.

World Health Organization: Coronavirus, https://www.who.int/health-topics/coronavirus#tab=tab_1; last accessed February 08, 2021.

World Health Organization: Global COVID-19 Clinical Platform Case Report Form (CRF) for Post Covid Condition (Post COVID-19 CRF), February 25, 2021, https://www.who.int/publications/i/item/global-COVID-19-clinical-platform-case-report-form-(crf)-for-post COVID-conditions-(post COVID-19-crf-); last accessed March 16, 2021.

List of Figures

Fig. 1: Marco Carmignan, Lock of hair, 2020. Reprinted with kind permission of the artist.

Fig. 2: Marco Carmignan, Chest CT scan (Stefania, 68, undergoes a chest CT scan at the Day Hospital Post-Covid-19 of the Gemelli Polyclinic), 2020. Reprinted with kind permission of the artist.

Fig. 3: Marco Carmignan, Portrait of Marta (Marta 32, researcher and teacher), 2020. Reprinted with kind permission of the artist.

The photographs have also been published on The Washington Post (In Sight section) on January 08, 2020.

Beatriz Barreiro Carril and Kevin Grecksch

Reimagining Academia after Covid-19

1. Back to What Normality?

The first months of the Covid-19 lockdown starting in March 2020 marked the occasion for many academics and higher education institutions to put into question the model of *normality*. In different instances the idea that the world we want to go back after the pandemic is not the one, we thought to be the normal one, but a new one where solidarity, respect for nature or recognition of human vulnerability gain space in media and conversations. The awareness of the relevance of these values came suddenly and forced by the pandemic circumstances: It was not difficult to see the social relevance, for instance in the work of doctors, nurses or street cleaners and the importance of public services. Also, the decreasing economic activity and the reduction of mobility showed how the sudden reduction of traffic led to cleaner air and flourishing of biodiversity. More than a year later, when we start seeing the end of the pandemic there is a general feeling that such reflections about what normality we want to live in have become less and less relevant. Where is education and particularly universities in this picture? It seems that generally education has not been perceived as an »essential activity« in the same sense that health services, for instance were seen.[1] Maybe because of the transition from face-to-face teaching to online teaching there has not been the need to consider teachers as essential workers in the majority of countries. Has this fact hidden the relevance of our activity in society? Or was the lack of attention to teachers and professors somehow in relation to a crisis that existed already before the pandemic? In relation to schools, the general tendency has been trying to replicate the »normal« model under the new circumstances, as if nothing has happened. In April 2020, the Spanish writer Elvira Lindo wrote in El Pais:

---

[1] A special recognition was made to teachers who were in charge of children of *essential workers* but the global category of teachers had not generally such a social consideration. However, the Special Rapporteur of the United Nations on the Right to Education »pays special tribute to teachers, many of whom are women, who have demonstrated courage (in particular those who have taken care of the children of frontline workers), commitment, creativity in designing new teaching methods and in finding ways to remain in contact with learners and flexibility in adapting to the new context« (cf. United Nations Special Rapporteur on the Right to Education: Impact of the Covid-19 Crisis on the Right to Education, par. 19).

»While it is true that the new generation of teachers will be more adapted to the technological reality, there are teachers who gain from being present, just as there are musicians who improve live. This virtual education also shows us a reality that we should not ignore: there are homes without broadband, families that do not have a computer or there is only one for the parent's work. [...]. And I wonder if this inequality could not be taken into account in gauging how much can be demanded in an unusual situation. [...] I fail to understand why not simplify these days, why not devote the confinement to creating, playing, listening to music, writing, reading, drawing, reflecting. Let's remember our childhood, our sacred time to fantasize and play alone. Emma Cabal, poet and teacher, writes to me: ›What is the use of making a morphosyntactic commentary at this time? I am in contact by mail with those I can and we recommend books, poems, they write me their reflections, I ask them about those other pupils I know nothing about and they tell me about them. It matters that they are well. It matters that everyone is well. She is a dedicated, excellent teacher.‹«[2]

2. The Installed Logic of Productivity in Academia before the Pandemic

This tendency towards productivity, results and success in spite of the difficult emotional and psychological context could be related somehow to the less and less relevance of the Social Sciences, Humanities and the Arts in educational systems and lead to the question whether this situation was exacerbated by the pandemic.[3] If it is true that empathy has increased during the pandemic, for example, teachers and lecturers generally speaking have been quite open to the particular circumstances of students who could not for instance meet a deadline because of a Covid-19-related problem, the general framework continued to be the same, very often putting the burden on the teachers and lecturers, who were sometimes seen as a kind of heroes instead of vulnerable human beings facing as well a common difficult context. Regarding universities, some scholars have warned before the pandemic about the effects of the »increased speed and efficiency« demanded by universities »regardless of the consequences for education and scholarship.«[4] The book of Maggie Berg and Barbara K. Seeber, *The Slow Professor. Challenging the Culture of Speed in Academia*[5] offers a mirror in which many of us can see our own experiences when facing a system that is becoming more and more managerial. It is particularly the scholars of the Social Sciences, Humanities and the Arts that suffer more from this tendency.

[2] Lindo: Niños sin banda ancha.
[3] Bakare/Adams: Plans for 50 % Funding Cuts to Arts Subjects at Universities ›Catastrophic‹.
[4] Seeber/Berg: The Slow Professor.
[5] Another essential book is Collini: Talking About Universities.

3. The End of Leisure Time and the Temptation of *as if* Culture

The last decade has witnessed an exponential growth of programs for assessing the performance of academics.[6] These mainly quantitative assessment processes are increasing exponentially. Academics are demanded to pass an increasing number of hours in front of the computer fulfilling procedures assessing their results, both in the fields of research and teaching. The time demanded by these procedures is getting longer and longer, to the extent that in some countries we see the emergence of companies that offer services helping academics in the fulfilment of these procedures. It is an odd solution, since no one but oneself can give the most accurate narrative of their own work and trajectory. It is a partial and far from perfect answer to the dichotomy in which many academics find themselves: dedicating their working time to *real work*, i.e. teaching and researching, or to fulfill procedures justifying that work. We are aware that some management competences are relevant for academic work and that universities need their leaders to be good managers, but the extent to which managerial work is placed upon academics nowadays is in our opinion putting at risk the academic quality of both teaching and research. In order to maintain quality standards, there is a more and more common tendency to dedicate an important part of leisure time, weekends and holidays included, to *real work*: research and preparing of teaching or assessing students, since many working days are full of meetings, many of them of dealing with management issues and other obligations of this nature.[7] It is therefore not uncommon that very often the content of the conversation among colleagues is about how overwhelmed they are. Sometimes, even, these conversations seem to be a kind of competition about who is busier and more exhausted, as if being exhausted has a sort of merit. The personal story told by Berg and Seeber about a conversation with a colleague met by chance during a summer is paradigmatic of these kinds of conversations.[8] In spite of the proven fact that exhaustion diminishes creativity,[9] many scholars are stuck in a vicious circle of never-ending working weeks in spite of non-satisfactory results. Another consequence of this tendency where less and less time of the working hours can be dedicated to research and teaching, is to approach such activities with a kind of what could be

---

[6] Cf. Binswanger: Sinnlose Wettbewerbe.

[7] The description of the day of Professor H. by Philosopher of Law Professor García Amado in his story »Un día en la vida de los profesores« is paradigmatic of this situation.

[8] They tell us that »one of [them] recalls running into a colleague by the waterfront one late August day and asking how his summer was going. »What summer? He replied, »I've been writing eight hours a day«. She felt terribly guilty that she had just been swimming with her daughter. It wasn't until she wrote this that she realized her colleague was out by the waterfront also, though presumably not enjoying it« (cf. Berg/Seeber: The Slow Professor, p. 22).

[9] Ibid., p. 20f.

presented as a pragmatic approach that we call the *as if culture*. Here, the temptation would be, apart from that of dedicating whole weekends to do *real work*, to adapt the way one does research to the often poor and inadequate assessment indicators (at least in the field of Social Sciences and Humanities (SSH)).[10] As it has been noted, »the methods that are usually applied are ill-adapted to SSH research«. These »methods only [...] apply [...] and adjust [...] the methods developed for and in the natural and life sciences.«[11] They are not suitable for seeing the value of highly innovative ideas, including those related with the creation of a new discipline, or in the middle of two disciplines, for which, for instance, there would not be a journal to publish these ideas, which would meet the criteria foreseen in such assessments. Mediocre works can have very often more opportunities to have good results in such assessments in comparison with more transgressive, original and maybe brilliant ones, which are very often the basis of the advance of Social Sciences and Humanities but which can be disincentivized. Very often indicators foresee (and expect) »spectacular research findings« which »can lead [...] to unethical reporting of findings.«[12] The criteria of these indicators usually deal with the length, the language expressions, i. e. ›buzzwords‹, the number of bibliographical references, however, there is no way of evaluating the actual quality of it. As a consequence, it appears an easy temptation to do *as if* one is really doing research work. It is not hard to find published research work presented in a tidy, clear and structured way yet completely meaningless – publication for publications' sake. The growing number of predatory journals contributes to this tendency in a kind of vicious circle: As Grudniewicz et al. consider: »[e]fforts to counter predatory publishing need to be constant and adaptable. The threat is unlikely to disappear as long as universities use how many publications a scholar has produced as a criterion for graduation or career advancement.«[13]

Fighting against exhaustion and the »as if« culture demands a deep rethinking of academia, which before the pandemic was not really a priority. Many universities had started to offer free courses for research and teaching staff focused on combating stress or to learn how to successfully fulfill applications of their research assessments. However, it does offer some form of absurdity, if academics

---

[10] Ibid. Many of these procedures do not foresee that the evaluators belong to the same discipline of the scholar who is the subject of such an evaluation. Or the opposite, i. e. they belong to the same discipline, which becomes a problem in smaller disciplines where the evaluators from university A who are assessing university B will be the future evaluees of university B when it is their turn to evaluate university A. This creates the temptation toward a positive assessment since both universities want to continue their work with ideally the same share of funding. And, depending on which assessment procedures are applied, sometimes, even evaluators are not academics, but experts in management who do not have the tools and knowledge for assessing the relevance and the adequacy of the assessed work.

[11] Ochsner/Hug/Galleron: The Future of Research Assessment in the Humanities, p. 9.

[12] Ibid., p. 3.

[13] Grudniewicz et al.: Predatory Journals, p. 212.

are to attend courses telling them how to de-stress from work, courses which are offered during normal working hours, hence taking yet again time away from research and teaching. As Lashuel said:

»When it comes to faculty burnout and mental wellness, most universities have chosen to delegate these issues to their human-resources departments, which are increasingly offering workshops and online resources to help faculty members to improve their skills in managing their projects, teams, stress and other issues. This is an important first step, but it is not a substitute for direct engagement and open, community-wide discussions on work-related stress and mental-health.«[14]

This led us to a broader topic of reflection: *agency*. Impossible deadlines and being continuously subject to evaluation processes can easily affect and damage one's self-esteem. Academics can be very easily felt as mere objects of constant assessment. Being always alerted of what it is missing in our CVs, we tend to overlook our achievements and there is neither time nor energy for thinking whether such assessment procedures actually make sense. The very »exercise of agency«[15] is at risk. This dynamic evokes the theory of Mark Hunyadi in his book about *Tyranny of the Ways of Life*: »the expectations of behaviour that are permanently imposed by the system on individuals and groups, and which are imposed independently of the will of the actors.«[16] Even when these kinds of assessments are not compulsory but voluntary, it is not very common to renounce to be part of them. It is in this sense that the exercise of agency can be said to be at risk. In addition, the fact that the hours dedicated to the fulfilment of these time demanding procedures are mostly individual work contributes to the isolation from our colleagues. Time spent on this is time not spent for reflecting together about common research topics or about the pertinence of such systems of evaluation, which reason and survival rests in the competition among scholars. There are little chances that academics can reflect in political terms about their situation.[17]

4. Academia during the Pandemic

Academics not only needed to face the challenges of passing from face-to-face teaching to online teaching but also to the need of keeping up with many deadlines for publications or research proposals. Not much attention has been placed on the fact that after spending many hours in front of the computer doing online

---

[14] Lashuel: The Busy Lives of Academics.
[15] For using the expression, cf. Berg/Seeber: The Slow Professor.
[16] Hunyadi: La tyrannie, p. 43; transl. by the author.
[17] Cf. Berg/Seeber: The Slow Professor, p. 57.

teaching, it is really difficult – and not healthy at all – to add more hours in front of the screen for doing research and on top of that the managerial work. Some university leaders have shown more empathy than others factoring in these circumstances and in the way they communicated. However, very rarely vulnerability and the possibility that we can commit mistakes because of the difficult global situation was recognized. Yet on a less official level it was not uncommon to receive emails or automatic reply emails, where highly prestigious and competent scholars »confess« to not being able to answer a mail soon or to fulfil the deadline because of the effects of the pandemic on their mental health. These kind of *confessions* of human vulnerability offer hope and the possibility for thinking more about these kinds of issues. They can contribute to follow a path already initiated by some academics who increasingly recognize that research, particularly in Social Sciences and Humanities is not only something related with successful results but also with processes. Very often, these processes do not offer an immediate and successful result but they are necessary, because the results can very often come in the future and sometimes in unexpected ways. This is why some scholars have already started to include *failures* in their CVs. For example, the case of Princeton Professor in Psychology Johannes Haushofer who published his *CV of failures* including in it, for instance research funding he did not get and papers rejected by academic journals.[18] Related to this approach is the determination of trying to publish less. As the researcher Giorgio Kallis wrote on Twitter: »Talking of limits, my good friend Erik Swyngedouw [a Geography professor at Manchester University] had an excellent idea for a limit that would liberate all of us academics, and make the world a better place :-) 100,000 words career-limit for each academic. No pressure to publish, no bogus journals, more thinking, less writing.«[19]

This would not only contribute to a more honest[20] research but also to its sustainability (and that of the life of academics!). It seems paradoxical that universities around the world are engaged in collaborating to achieve the 17 Sustainable Development Goals (SDG) of the United Nations but the approaches are focused »outside« (by instance encouraging lecturers to speak about the SDGs in their lectures to the students)[21] but not »inside« (in order to do a critical assessment of their performance in terms of sustainability).

[18] The Guardian: CV of Failures.
[19] Kallis: Twitter-Post from November 19, 2019.
[20] Fonseca: The Pitfalls of »Salami Slicing«; Tolsgaard: Salami-Slicing and Plagiarism.
[21] Grund: How Can Universities Meaningfully and Effectively Use the SDGs?

5. Academia after Pandemic

While preparing this chapter we searched for the words *Academia* and *Pandemic* in Web of Science, an academic search engine. The results showed 209 academic articles on the topic. We consider that very probably it was going to be difficult for us to add something new to this discussion, at least from the approach of a traditional academic text. This is why we decided to draw on humor. We wrote a one-act play, which starts below.[22] We thought of this as a complementary method to think about the current challenges of academia. We firmly believe in the power of humor for change. We hope that very probably many of us see themselves reflected in this piece and we hope it can contribute, even if only a little bit, to be more aware about some things that ask for a change in academia. As Berg & Seeber we think that little changes among some groups of academics within an institution can create larger changes. We »Don't given up hope.«[23]

Any Other Business

Characters[24]
VICE DEAN FOR IMPACT *(has worked his way through the upper echelons of university management, last published paper 15 years ago)*
PROFESSORIAL TEACHING FELLOW *(teaches a lot, likes feedback and evaluations)*
RESEARCH PROFESSOR 1 *(male, lead author on at least 12 journal articles per year, supervises 12 PhD students)*
RESEARCH PROFESSOR 2 *(female, recently appointed as part of the university's equality strategy)*
PROFESSOR FOR DIGITALIZATION [joining the meeting online] *(musicologist, most cited publication: ›The benefits of vinyl over mp3 files in dodecaphony‹)*
POSTDOC *(completed their PhD in Classics five years ago, is on their eighth fixed-term contract)*
STUDENT CONSUMER *(studies Business Administration but contemplates transferring to a degree in University Management)*

---

[22] We are not the first ones presenting a reflection on the universities challenges through theatre. The Professor of Philosophy of Law, Manuel Atienza has already done this himself in Una apologia del Derecho.
[23] Berg/Seeber: The Slow Professor, p. 84.
[24] All characters and actions are purely fictional and bear no resemblance to real life.

Europolis, Tuesday 20 October 2030
The Committee On Values, Innovation and De-stress is holding its meeting on Integral Management, Productivity, Assessment, Careers and Teaching (IMPACT)
Meeting agenda

1. *Apologies*
2. *Minutes from last meeting*
3. *Discussing the evaluation results for the degree in University Management*
4. *Face-to-face-distant teaching*
5. *Assessment of research assessment*
6. *Any Other Business*

The Vice-dean for IMPACT opens the meeting. Apologies were received from the Vice-dean for Innovation who can't make it to the meeting due to childcare responsibilities. In her apology she stressed that the time of the meeting goes against the university's own child friendly policies, which were a result of the university subscribing to the Sustainable Development Goals. Research Professor 2 is away in her role as an external reviewer for a degree at another university.

VICE DEAN: Does anyone have comments on the minutes from the last meeting?

STUDENT: Our complaint, voiced during the last meeting, that some professors lack Zoom-charisma, has not been sufficiently minuted.

VICE DEAN: Let me get back to the minutes … *[he reads aloud]* ›The student feedback surveys show that some professors lack Zoom-charisma‹ I think this is adequate. Don't you think so my dear colleagues?

STUDENT: From our point of view, this is too general. As I said in the last meeting, the data from the feedback surveys show that 97 % of the students said that 4 out 5 professors lack Zoom-charisma. We feel this relevant data is not represented in the minutes.

PROFESSOR FOR DIGITALIZATION: *[can't be heard by the others because he forgets to unmute himself]*

VICE DEAN: You need to unmute yourself!

PROFESSOR FOR DIGITALIZATION: Can you hear me now?

ALL: yes!

PROFESSOR FOR DIGITALIZATION: My opinion on the issue is … *[his video image freezes]*

VICE DEAN: Are you still there? Can you hear us?

[Silence]

VICE DEAN: Let's move on and get back to him when is back online. The next item on the agenda is discussing the evaluation results for the degree in University Management. As you all know, in our efforts to climb up the university rankings and to be on the cutting edge of research and teaching, we introduced a degree in University Management. The degree delivers an outstanding and world-leading program in university management. Managing a university, and this differentiates it from a private company, requires highly-skilled people who are able to deliver on Key Performance Indicators such as efficient human resources management, project management or resource allocation. This in our view justified a new degree. A degree that satisfies the need of universities for highly qualified people in order to fulfil the requirements and to face the challenges of higher education in the present and future.

POSTDOC: If I may interrupt. As I pointed out before in this committee, postdocs are concerned that more university management will lead to fewer positions in research. Already on one researcher come four managers, one for impact, one for development, one for research and one for careers outside academia.

VICE DEAN: But the new degree and its graduates would help you and your colleagues to be better researchers.

POSTDOC: Could you explain how. Do these managers know about my research topic?

VICE DEAN: Our efforts in this direction have already led, and we have discussed the data in this committee before, to more research income and improved our ranking.

POSTDOC: It's not a question of ranking. What I mean is how are these (makes air quotes) university managers helping me exactly with my research. Or do you mean they will help me to complete the application for the research assessment? I would like to bring this up under agenda point 5 again.

VICE DEAN: Thank you. Let's move on then, shall we. Would anyone else like to comment on this issue?

RESEARCH PROFESSOR 1: I highly welcome the introduction of this degree. Just recently I attended a management committee meeting where in fact the managers were not managers at all but academics. Managing should be left to those who know how to manage.

PROFESSORIAL TEACHING FELLOW: May I suggest we make the Introduction into University Management a compulsory lecture for all new students. It is vital we lead them onto the right path early in their studies.

PROFESSOR FOR DIGITALIZATION: (his camera is turned-off now, but we can see the clapping hands emoji)

VICE DEAN: Thank you for this point, which I second. Let me finish this agenda item by saying that the global pandemic ten years ago was proof that a strong and well-equipped university management helped us to steer the ocean liner that our university is through rough waters. I vividly remember our Gold, Silver and Bronze group meetings, the thrill of the latest government data and the first in-person sandwich lunch after the end of lockdown. I hope you all agree when I say that we have become world-leading in university management.

The next item is face-to-face-distant teaching. Professor for Digitalization please go ahead.

PROFESSOR FOR DIGITALIZATION: *[has lost the connection to the video call and is now trying to call into the meeting from his phone. His voice keeps breaking up]*

VICE DEAN: We cannot hear you. Professorial Teaching Fellow could you introduce us to the issue instead.

PROFESSORIAL TEACHING FELLOW: *[surprised and not prepared]* Oh! Yes, mhhh, as you may remember we are the second university in the whole country which started the implementation of what was called in 2021 »face-to-face-distant« teaching learning. The concept, coined by the University Psychomanagerialist Nick Farrow, answered to the need of supressing the negative aspects of distant teaching. More specifically, several universities registered a high amount of student complaints in that year, stating that the stress the professor felt during online teaching, linked to Zoom fatigue, was transmitted to them. As you know, even if there has not been another pandemic until today, universities – and this one would not be an exception – cannot renounce to distant teaching. Having the possibility of reproducing the same lecture for different groups of students has enormously contributed to the reduction of costs, meaning less academics are needed, allowing to hire more managers. So, the solution proposed by Nick Farrow includes training lecturers with a whole set of competences enabling them to do distant teaching as if *[emphasizing these last words]* they are doing face-to-face teaching. This is what he called the »face-to face-distant« teaching.

POSTDOC: If I may, I am wondering where is the face of the student, since none of my students switch the camera on. Besides, I find the Farrow method quite unrealistic. Am I the only one in this room who did the course offered by the University?

[Silence in the room]

VICE DEAN: Clears his throat nervously.

STUDENT CONSUMER: I have the right to privacy. The student union has issued us with legal advice and the law is pretty clear on when and why I have to turn on my camera or not.

POSTDOC: Well, then we shouldn't call it face-to-face distant teaching.

PROFESSORIAL TEACHING FELLOW: Nick Farrow is a well-known expert in his field and may I remind you that all postdocs are required to take this course which his offered by PEST – the Postdoctoral Evaluation and Standardization Trainingcenter.

VICE DEAN: I propose that we establish a new working group to create better understanding of the face-to-face-distant teaching method. May I suggest my niece to chair this working group who after finishing her PhD in Ancient History with summa cum laude has recently been appointed Head of Teaching Innovation at this very institution. She underwent extensive training and has made several internships with Nick Farrow.

ALL EXCEPT THE POSTDOC: [with admiration] Aaah!

VICE DEAN: Let us finally talk about the assessment of the research assessment. Research professor 1, please go ahead.

RESEARCH PROFESSOR 1: My dear colleagues, the assessment of our research is the most important evaluation of our research every five years, commonly known as REF. Many countries have followed our great example ...

PROFESSOR FOR DIGITALIZATION: *[finally has a stable connection and interrupts]* Yes, in Spain they call it SEXenio *[he starts giggling]*

RESEARCH PROFESSOR 1: Thank you for this contribution. I am also proud to say the from next year we will not only have an assessment of our research – REF, but of our teaching – TEF, and our knowledge exchange – KEF. REF-TEF-KEF will be a state-of-the-art assessment of our broad range of research and teaching activities. It will also create new employment opportunities for our University Management graduates.

POSTDOC: But what about jobs in research?

PROFESSORIAL TEACHING FELLOW: Will these new people help us with the filling in of the forms for these assessments?

RESEARCH PROFESSOR: No, my dear colleague. The forms are best filled in by those who know best about their work – you! The new employees in administration will however monitor your progress and send you reminder emails.

POSTDOC: So this will mean more non-research or non-teaching related work for us?

RESEARCH PROFESSOR: No, REF-TEF-KEF will provide you with the skills and expertise you'll need in the job market of the future.

POSTDOC: By filling in forms?

VICE-DEAN: Excuse me, I think your sarcasm is inappropriate in this discussion. You should instead learn to value the benefits of assessment. We will be able to provide you with a personal score based on your research, teaching and impact.

RESEARCH PROFESSOR: Exactly! Fill in and score high!

VICE DEAN: We are running late and I would like to bring this Committee On Values, Innovation and De-stress meeting to a close. Any items for Any Other Business? [he waits a couple of seconds] No one? Well, then I wish to thank my colleagues and we'll see each other at the next C.O.V.I.D. meeting.

[People start chatting and leave the room]

PROFESSOR FOR DIGITALIZATION: *[Struggling again with his internet connection]* I would like to raise the point of better IT equipment. ... Hello, can anyone hear me?

END

Concluding Remarks

The attentive reader will have noticed that much of what we describe in our little one-act play is not so far from reality if not reality already. We, as academics, have all been in meetings where we felt out of this world due to their absurdity. What worries us is the tendency to not questioning these practices anymore. Stoically, most of us accept what is burdened upon us also because at the end of the day we love our profession and are committed to research and teaching. Most of us are pretty resilient. Rejected papers or funding applications are the normality, not the exception, yet we tend to talk about the positive things, those aspects of our work that give us truly pleasure. But this positive attitude should not prevent us from being critic and »exercise our agency«[25] with relation to situations that, as we saw at the beginning of this chapter, are not beneficial neither for scientific progress nor for the wellbeing of academics. Coronavirus has led some us to be more honest with ourselves and our profession. Caring responsibilities – those related with children such as home schooling included, – are now much more accepted *excuses* for not attending a meeting, as is not sending emails after normal working hours. Many departments even went as far as prohibiting sending emails between six in the evening and eight in the morning, so that recipients do not feel pressured to answer immediately. The explicit mention of the need of rest and the recognition of our vulnerability is something that many academics have started to do. Whether these emergent practices are here to stay or are going to disappear once the pandemic is (hopefully) over remains an open question, the answer in fact depends on our common awareness and determination to maintain such concerns alive. Expressing these concerns and questioning established working practices and norms should be the new norm in academia. After all that is what we do in our research, yet we have become complacent for reasons of job insecurity, avoiding conflicts. Hence, the next time we sit in a meeting and we feel that a new task, committee or exercise requires us to spend an irrational amount of time away from research or teaching without any meaningful use, we should not ask how we are going to find time for doing it, hence being the willful enablers, but instead we should ask *Why?* In an editorial for Nature, the author said: »(...) the dynamics of science are no different from those of the arts: success in both depends on resonance between the individual's imagination and the shifting moods and desires of audiences.«[26] Alas, billions were pumped into vaccination research last year and this year, for all the right reasons, and with considerable if not overwhelming success. But the moods and desires will shift once the pandemic is under control. It also shows how apparently simple it is to come to a solution if you just throw a lot of money and

---

[25] Berg/Seeber: The Slow Professor.
[26] Nature: Form Is Temporary.

working hours at it. Yet with the success of the vaccine rollout an irony came to light as well: vaccines save our lives, however, the dispute about sharing of vaccines across the world shows none of this matters if we cannot figure out how to fairly share a resource. Social Sciences, Humanities and the Arts are essential for looking for answers for the most relevant problems and needs of humanity. They are as well those who mainly suffer from the managerialist approach of research assessing procedures as opposed to other disciplines like engineering or science, which never seem to be under the same pressure of imminent closure or funding cuts. The Corona Pandemic has also seen an at least partial return of expertise. Virologists who lived a quiet laboratory life were suddenly catapulted into the spotlight. In the age of post-truths and fake news this was a welcome return.[27] Scientific data mattered and continues to matter. Whether politicians follow the scientific advice is a whole different issue, but the lessons we can learn from this is that sound and rigorous science trumps dangerous half knowledge. On the other hand, we must make sure all disciplines are equally represented. Of course, virologists and epidemiologists should be at the helm of pandemic research but it should be undergirded by Social Scientists, Humanities and Arts scholars. This is what the British Academy has done in a large report, but our fear is that it is drowned in the noise of our current race back to *normality*. We all too easily became fixated by numbers (infections rates, deaths, etc.) but rarely did we see a psychologist or sociologist talking about the long-term consequences of for example lockdowns for the individual and societies or a policy researcher who explains how we could overcome some of the inequalities that were laid bare open during the pandemic. In many countries, the daily government press conferences did not include any kind of concern or advice on these issues. What can we do as academics in the future? As mentioned before, we should ask why we spend so much of our time on tasks that are only remotely related to our actual research and teaching instead of what we are supposed to do – pushing the boundaries and finding solutions for the long-term problems we face and actively engaging in the debate through teaching, influencing the political debate and activism. It is with Berg and Seeber that we vindicate both the pleasurable and political of such a process.[28] As Alfonso Calvo Caravaca, Professor of Private International Law,[29] told us recently: »University teaching is a very beautiful profession. I still think it is one of the most beautiful in the world. It also has the advantage that you get paid for doing what you like: studying and learning.« All of this, however needs time. And »time for reflection and open-ended inquiry is not a luxury but is crucial to what we do«.[30]

[27] A return, which of course had its backlash from self-appointed virologists and conspiracy theorists.
[28] Berg/Seeber: The Slow Professor, p. 11.
[29] Carols III University, Madrid, Spain.
[30] Berg/Seeber: The Slow Professor, p. x.

References

Atienza, Manuel: Una apología del Derecho y otros ensayos in Una apología del Derecho y otros ensayos, Madrid 2020, pp. 17–34.

Bakare, Lanra / Richard Adams: Plans for 50 % Funding Cut to Arts Subjects at Universities ›Catastrophic‹, in: The Guardian, May 06, 2021, https://www.theguardian.com/education/2021/may/06/plans-for-50-funding-cut-to-arts-subjects-at-universities-catastrophic; last accessed June 13, 2021.

Berg, Maggie / Barbara K. Seeber: The Slow Professor. Challenging the Culture of Speed in the Academy, Toronto 2016.

Binswanger, Mathias: Sinnlose Wettbewerbe. Warum wir immer mehr Unsinn produzieren, Freiburg 2010.

British Academy: The COVID Decade. Understanding the Long-Term Societal Impacts of COVID-19, London 2021.

Collini, Stefan: Speaking of Universities, London 2017.

Fonseca, Marisha: The Pitfalls of »Salami Slicing«: Focus On Quality and Not Quantity of Publications, November 04, 2013, https://www.editage.com/insights/the-pitfalls-of-salami-slicing-focus-on-quality-and-not-quantity-of-publications; last accessed June 12, 2021.

García, Amado Juan Antonio: Un día en la vida de los profesores (universitarios) H. y J., July 19, 2014, https://www.garciamado.es/2014/07/un-dia-en-la-vida-de-los-profesores-universitarios-h-y-j/; last accessed: June 12, 2021.

Grudniewicz, Agnes / David Moher / Kelly D. Cobey, Gregory L. Bryson / Samantha Cukier / Kristiann Allen / Clare Ardern, Lesley Balcom, Tiago Barros, Monica Berger, Jairo Buitrago Ciro, Lucia Cugusi, Michael R. Donaldson, Matthias Egger, Ian D. Graham, Matt Hodgkinson, Karim M. Khan, Mahlubi Mabizela, Andrea Manca, Katrin Milzow, Johann Mouton, Marvelous Muchenje, Tom Olijhoek, Alexander Ommaya, Bhushan Patwardhan, Deborah Poff, Laurie Proulx, Marc Rodger, Anna Severin, Michaela Strinzel, Mauro Sylos-Labini, Robyn Tamblyn, Marthie van Niekerk, Jelte M. Wicherts & Manoj M. Lalu: Predatory Journals: No Definition, No Defence, in: Nature 576, 2019, pp. 210–212.

Grund, Lydia: How Can Universities Meaningfully and Effectively Use the SDGs? IISD SGD Knowledge Hub, July 06, 2020, https://sdg.iisd.org/commentary/generation-2030/how-can-universities-meaningfully-and-effectively-use-the-sdgs/; last accessed June 13, 2021.

Hunyadi, Mark: La tyrannie des modes de vie, Lormont 2015.

Kallis, Giorgio: Twitter-Post, November 19, 2019, https://twitter.com/g_kallis/status/1196853572224372736; last accessed June 12, 2021.

Lashuel, Hilal A.: The Busy Lives of Academics Have Hidden Costs – And Universities Must Take Better Care of Their Faculty Members, in: Nature, March

05, 2020, https://www.nature.com/articles/d41586-020-00661-w; last accessed: June 12, 2021.

Lindo, Elvira: Niños sin banda ancha., in: El País, April 04, 2021, https://elpais.com/elpais/2020/04/04/opinion/1585990755_241346.html; last accessed June 14, 2021.

Nature: Form Is Temporary. Analysis of Career-Long Impact Offers Renewed Hope for Scientists Waiting for Success, in: Nature, 559, 2018, pp. 151–152.

Ochsner, Michael/Sven Hug/Ioana Galleron: The Future of Research Assessment in the Humanities: Bottom-up Assessment Procedures, in: Palgrave Communications, 3, 17020, 2017, pp. 1–12.

The Guardian: CV of Failures. Princeton Professor Publishes Résumé of His Career Lows, April 30, 2016, https://www.theguardian.com/education/2016/apr/30/cv-of-failures-princeton-professor-publishes-resume-of-his-career-lows; last accessed June 12, 2021.

Tolsgaard, Martin G./Rachel Ellaway/Nikki Woods/Geoff Norman: Salami-Slicing and Plagiarism: How Should We Respond?, in: Advances in Health Sciences Education, 24, 2019, pp. 3–14.

United Nations Special Rapporteur on the Right to Education: Impact of the Covid-19 Crisis on the Right to Education; Concerns, Challenges and Opportunities, June 30, 2020, https://undocs.org/A/HRC/44/39; last accessed June 14, 2021.

Chioma Daisy Onyige

The Challenges, Complexities and Uncertainties of International Mobility for Global South Scholars in the Era of Covid-19: A Perception from a Nigerian Scholar

The Covid-19 pandemic turned out to be the biggest disaster of the century, not only in terms of the high mortality rate but also in terms of the overall impact on the lives of the people of the world. For international scholars like me, who are from a global south country, the Covid-19 pandemic brought on a whole new meaning to the complexities and uncertainties we face in our daily lives in the world of scholarship and research. The pandemic exposed and exacerbated the glaring inequalities across races, gender and socioeconomic status. For the mobile scholar from the global south, this situation becomes even more disturbing, as he or she has to find ways of connecting with the outside academic community for academic collaboration despite all the challenges associated and brought on by the pandemic situation. The combination of lockdowns, mobility restrictions, changes in visa rules and regulations, unequal access to life-saving vaccinations, non-access to good health care facilities, technologies, and disaster preparedness, just to mention a few examples, may all have a long-term impact on the participation and engagement of global south scholars with their counterparts in the global north. I fear that the promotion of diversity and inclusion in scholarship may not be feasible in the near future, especially when there is no more access to underrepresented scholars due to the bottlenecks and complexities surrounding the mobility of global south scholars.

This paper intends highlighting the many ways in which the ongoing pandemic hinders the mobility of global south scholars using my perspective, the perspective of a Nigerian scholar. I will start by shortly introducing the Covid-19 pandemic situation in Nigeria. Then I will discuss the concept and context of academic mobility from a Nigerian scholar's perspective. Here, I will describe the motivation for engaging in academic mobility from the global south to the global north; the process a scholar has to undergo in order to get the necessary documentation to engage in this academic mobility. I will discuss the reality of the Covid-19 pandemic and its effects on education and academics in Nigeria. We may not see the last of pandemics in the future, however, I conclude this piece by emphasizing the need to understand the implications of the impacts of such pandemics on the mobility of academics from the global south to the global north, particularly reflecting on how the current global health crisis and future health crisis intensify social and economic inequalities across different academic mobility schemes and opportunities.

1. The Covid-19 Pandemic Situation in Nigeria

The new coronavirus was introduced to Nigeria on February 25, 2020, by an Italian engineer traveling from Milan to Lagos. As a way of controlling the viruses spread, screening procedures were quickly established at ports of entry in all the international airports in the country. The media started broadcasting public health announcements, such as the need for hand-washing and social distancing, as very large numbers of victims could overwhelm the weak medical facilities of the country.

Prior to the arrival of the first index case of the coronavirus, journalists and media practitioners from Nigeria were trained by the World Health Organization (WHO) in workshops organized in many African countries to inform media professionals on the facts about Covid-19. According to Dhamari Naidoo, the WHO emergency officer who conducted the training, »journalists and media are critical to getting the right messages to the community.«[1]

Communicating risks in Nigeria had generated diverse responses and outcomes. There had been a lot of misinformation and disinformation about the coronavirus. Fake news about the pandemic was rife on social media. People in Nigeria were getting their daily Covid-19 news and information from any source on the internet. The fake news around the coronavirus had ranged from claims that millions of people have died; to faux science suggesting that drinking boiled water can cure you of Covid-19. While fake news is a global problem, it is especially so in Nigeria, where false information on social media can quickly end up on legitimate news outlets.[2]

In a bid to contain the spread of the coronavirus, the Nigerian President Muhammadu Buhari first ordered the lockdown in the Federal Capital Territory and a few other states on March 29, 2020. This was later extended to other states with flight restrictions that lasted until September 2020. The impact of the lockdown stifled economic activities in the country, restricted freedom of movement and

---

[1] World Health Organization (WHO): Supporting Media to Bust Harmful Myths on Coronavirus Disease.
[2] Cf. Gikandi: Nigeria Fights Fake News about Coronavirus.

affected all educational institutions and businesses alike. Measures were put in place by the Nigerian government which included, among others, a 14 days quarantine for people coming from countries with a high incidence of Covid-19 infection. Despite such measures, citizens deliberately flouted such orders even when they were at risk of contracting the Covid-19 infection.[3] These types of incidents were all consequences of the miscommunication and the misinformation that the people in the country were grappling with at that time. Nigeria is currently experiencing a third wave of Covid-19 that has seen the country experience relatively high figures, despite the introduction of Covid-19 vaccination.[4]

2. The Concept and Context of Global Academic Mobility from a Nigerian Scholar's Perspective

On the foreign scene, countries all over the world were locking down and locking out. A number of mobility restrictions were enacted in most countries to slow down the transmission of the Covid-19 virus and to flatten the curve of the growing infection cases. These mobility restrictions also included temporary shutdowns of Embassies and Consulates in countries around the world. For those Embassies providing skeletal services, there are restrictions on the types and number of visa and consular services provided. There has also been a temporary restriction for visa issuance to students who had been admitted into institutions in countries located in the global north. Such students and scholars have been requested to stay in their home country and join classes online due to the pandemic. For example, in 2020 the United States extended and expanded immigration restrictions, citing the need for protecting the country's own workforce.[5] Decisions such as these, and prolonged uncertainty about changing visa and green card rules and regulations had a significant impact on the socio-economic and mental wellbeing of admitted students, postdoctoral fellows and faculty members from foreign countries who had plans of getting quality education.[6] Due to the Covid-19 pandemic, we

---

[3] A story carried in the newspaper THE PUNCH of April 12, 2020, tells a story of some Nigerians leaving their quarantine centers (cf. Abioye: Chinese Doctors' Flight: How Three Airline Crew Members ›Disappeared‹ from Lagos Quarantine Centre).

[4] For more information about Covid-19 in Nigeria, see the data from the website of the Nigerian Centre for Disease Control (NCDC).

[5] For immigration-related policies issues during the Covid-19 pandemic, see the July 2020 Migration Policy Institute (MPI) report (cf. Pierce/Bolter: Dismantling and Reconstructing the U.S. Immigration System: A Catalog of Changes under the Trump Presidency), a list of executive actions created by the National Immigration Forum (NFI) (cf. Zak: Immigration-related Executive Actions During the COVID-19 Pandemic).

[6] Cf. Subbaraman/Witze: Trump to Suspend New Visas for Foreign Scholars, p. 19; Dah-

have seen a swift move from face-to-face communication and learning to online communication and learning. From an organizational point of view, curfews and other social distancing measures have forced academic institutions to make a rapid transition to videoconferencing and other online education tools, though student satisfaction with this situation is generally not high, as most students and scholars from the global south do not have access to a functioning internet or equitable access to high-quality remote learning.[7] As a scholar from the global south, during this ongoing pandemic, I have had many cases of my students both at the undergraduate and postgraduate levels not having a laptop, and those who have laptops and or phones to use for online learning, have to deal with and grapple with the problem of poor internet connectivity or no internet connectivity depending on where they are trying to access the internet from in Nigeria.

I have always known that there are vast inequalities between the countries of the global north and those of the global south, but during the Covid-19 pandemic this became even more apparent as the pandemic unearthed massive inequalities even within our societies. Already existing inequalities were further exacerbated, which I think was particularly evident in the educational sector. In my country it was very difficult to quickly move to the use of digital technology for online and virtual learning. During the national lockdowns, the educational sector was particularly affected: with children not being able to go to school and, in most cases, there being no realistic way for them to move to online learning, they often stayed at home and were idle. Apart from access to learning, all around the world, the social institution known as school was also a potential safety net for children, but in the wake of the pandemic and the school closures that soon followed, school children lost this oftentimes vital safety net.[8]

As a mobile hybrid scholar and researcher who would travel several times in the year for meetings, conferences and fellowships, I was hit very hard by the effects of the pandemic as I couldn't participate effectively during video conferences due to bad internet connectivity. I had to subscribe to several internet providers at the same time, so that if one connection failed me, I could switch to the other one. This proved to be a costly venture, but I didn't want to be left behind when important information was being discussed, and I also wanted my presence to be registered by my colleagues in the global north, as I knew very few of my colleagues in the global south would be able to still engage with scholars from other countries during the pandemic. These kinds of inequalities have serious social and economic consequences in terms of North-South academic collaborations, and widening the

---

douh-Guebas/Vandebroek: Impacts of the COVID-19 Pandemic on International Academic Study Exchange and Research Mobility Programs.

[7] Dost et al.: Perceptions of Medical Students Towards Online Teaching during the COVID-19 Pandemic.

[8] Cf. Sharma: Torn Safety Nets.

opportunity gap between social groups. For students from Nigeria who were given admissions to institutions in the global north but are now victims of the current visa restrictions, I am worried about how they can cope since they absolutely need digital access to join their online classes in the interim and to be able to compete with their counterparts in the global north.

This brings me to the issue of the motivation for engaging in academic mobility from the global south to the global north. Prior to the pandemic, when I applied for a fellowship abroad, one of my motivations was to take off time from domestic and office duties and instead to focus on researching and analyzing of data already gathered in the field. Going abroad also opened up an opportunity to gain access to the best scholars and students in my field, to gain knowledge in the state of the art in my field of study. The best part however was having access to the well-equipped libraries and library facilities which are lacking in most Nigerian Universities.

According to Başak Bilecen and Christof Van Mol students and faculty members involved in academic mobility are expected to acquire more knowledge and academic culture which in turn would lead to prestige, credibility, and specific skills that would be valued by employers.[9] In other words, being a mobile scholar gives you a leverage for advancing you career in a competitive labor market both in the source country and the destination country. For researches in the global north, one advantage is that having access to mobile scholars from the global south allows for easy collaboration in projects involving local communities in the global south. All of this collaboration and mobility is not without its own challenges for the scholar from the global south. Here I talk specifically about the hurdles and challenges associated with obtaining a visa to travel to all these countries. As for visiting mobile scholars, the administrators from the global north oftentimes do not realize or consider the significant efforts and time commitment required from foreign mobility scholars when moving to a new country, applying for a visa, preparing to travel, learning a new language, and living in a different culture. I can categorically tell you that in the area of acquiring a visa, be it for a short stay or a long stay, is a very stressful and costly venture to say it mildly. In the part of Nigeria where I live, in the city of Port Harcourt, there are no embassies of the countries of the Global North. I therefore have to fly domestic flights to Lagos or Abuja to apply for a visa. I fly in rickety planes to Lagos in bad weather and pray that I reach my destination in one piece. My prayer is even more intense when I fly back home because one wants to see their family alive again.

The visa application process takes weeks to gather all the necessary documents requested by the consulate, and of course you have to come with two or three copies of all documents. Getting an appointment can be another challenge, but when that is sorted out, you have to book your flight ticket well in advance to get

[9] Bilecen/Van Mol: Introduction, pp. 1241–1255.

a good discount, as well as book a hotel room close to the consulate because almost none of these expenditures are refunded by the institution you will be visiting in the Global North. You may be lucky to get a refund for your visa fee, after presentation of a receipt. Yet, the worst part about applying for a visa is that you don't know if you will eventually get the visa or not. If you are not granted the visa, imagine the time and financial loss you must have incurred? Visa problems present an obstacle for many researchers in the global south to participate in the broader scientific community according to Connie Nshemereirwe, as she advocates that if we are to encourage diversity and inclusion in academia, then, academics from the global south must be able to meet freely.[10] There have been calls for a global passport for scholars. The idea of a global passport for scholars is a noble suggestion, but with the current situation presented in the form of the a global health crisis and ongoing future health crisis, this idea might not seem feasible at the moment since the world is as a whole still experiencing extreme restrictions which can be very unpredictable.

Conclusion

The rapid spread of the Covid-19 pandemic and its aftermath have severely impacted the ability of mobile scholars from the global south to achieve their scholarly feats and endeavors. There are momentous hurdles that scholars in the global south tended to face pre-pandemic. With the present pandemic situation, these hurdles have become insurmountable. There is no doubt that Covid-19 and its aftershock is here to stay. In order to be able to make the best out of a bad situation, and in order to bridge the social and economic inequalities across different academic mobility schemes and opportunities, international students, mobile scholars from the global south and their administrative hosts in the global north, should find adaptive solutions to collaborate with each other by proactively addressing important challenges faced by international students and mobile scholars. The world is a global village. Whatever affects one part of the globe will eventually affect the other part of the globe. The Covid-19 pandemic has taught us this big lesson. Locking up and locking out is not the solution to the problem.

---

[10] Cf. Nshemereirwe: Tear Down Visa Barriers That Block Scholarship.

References

Abioye, Oyetunji: Chinese Doctors' Flight: How Three Airline Crew Members ›Disappeared‹ from Lagos Quarantine Centre, in: THE PUNCH, April 12, 2020, https://punchng.com/chinese-doctors-flight-how-three-airline-crew-members-disappeared-from-lagos-quarantine-centre/; last accessed September 08, 2021.

Bilecen, Başak / Christof Van Mol: Introduction: International Academic Mobility and Inequalities, in: Journal of Ethnic and Migration Studies 43(8), 2017, pp. 1241–1255.

Dahdouh-Guebas, Farid / Ina Vandebroek: Impacts of the COVID-19 Pandemic on International Academic Study Exchange and Research Mobility Programs, in: Ethnobiology and Conservation 10(1), 2021, https://ethnobioconservation.com/index.php/ebc/article/view 513; last accessed September 08, 2021.

Dost, Samiullah / Aleena Hossain / Mai Shehab / Aida Abdelwahed / Lana Al-Nusair: Perceptions of Medical Students Towards Online Teaching during the COVID-19 Pandemic: A National Cross-Sectional Survey of 2721 UK Medical Students, in: BMJ Open 10(11), 2020, https://bmjopen.bmj.com/content/bmjopen/10/11/e042378.full.pdf; last accessed September 08, 2021.

Gikandi, Halima: Nigeria Fights Fake News about Coronavirus, in: Public Radio International (PRI), March 06, 2020, https://www.pri.org/stories/2020-03-06/nigeria-fights-fake-news-about-coronavirus; last accessed September 08, 2021.

Nigeria Centre for Disease Control (NCDC): Covid-19 Nigeria, https://covid19.ncdc.gov.ng/; last accessed September 08, 2021. / Nigeria Centre for Disease Control (NCDC): An Update of COVID-19 Outbreak in Nigeria, https://www.ncdc.gov.ng/diseases/sitreps/?cat=14&name=An%20update%20of%20COVID-19%20outbreak%20in%20Nigeria; last accessed September 08, 2021.

Nshemereirwe, Connie: Tear Down Visa Barriers That Block Scholarship, in: Nature, Oktober 30, 2018, https://www.nature.com/articles/d41586-018-07179-2; last accessed September 08, 2021.

Nunn, Michelle: 5 Things We Can Do to Help Fight Coronavirus in the World's Neediest Countries, in: TIME, April 10, 2020, https://time.com/5818863/help-fight-coronavirus-worlds-neediest/?utm_source=newsletter&utm_medium=email&utm_campaign=the-brief&utm_content=20200413&xid=newsletter-brief; last accessed September 08, 2021.

Pierce, Sarah / Jessica Bolter: Dismantling and Reconstructing the U.S. Immigration System. A Catalog of Changes under the Trump Presidency, Washington 2020.

Sharma, Nikita: Torn Safety Nets: How COVID-19 Has Exposed Huge Inequalities in Global Education, in: World Economic Forum, June 05, 2021, https://www.weforum.org/agenda/2020/06/torn-safety-nets-shocks-to-schooling-in-developing-countries-during-coronavirus-crisis; last accessed September 08, 2021.

Subbaraman, Nidhi / Alexandra Witze: Trump to Suspend New Visas for Foreign Scholars, in: Nature 583(7814), 2020, p. 19.

World Health Organization (WHO): Supporting Media to Bust Harmful Myths on Coronavirus Disease, February 13, 2020, https://www.afro.who.int/news/supporting-media-bust-harmful-myths-coronavirus-disease; last accessed September 08, 2021.

Zak, Danilo: Immigration-related Executive Actions During the COVID-19 Pandemic, in: National Immigration Forum (NIF), November 18, 2020, https://immigrationforum.org/article/immigration-related-executive-actions-during-the-covid-19-pandemic/; last accessed September 08, 2021.

Christa Rautenbach

The Many Colors of Covid-19 in South Africa: A Legal Perspective

When the pandemic struck, I had plans in place. Projects that included extensive academic exchanges and excursions internationally. Those plans came to an abrupt halt when South Africa and the rest of the world closed their borders. I accepted my fate willingly because everyone faced similar dreadful circumstances, and we all (silently) agreed that we would weather the storm until normality returns. But weeks turned into months and months into years, and, as I write this, South Africans still struggle with the consequences of the pandemic, and there is no indication when or if we will ever return to the lives we had before. The ripple effect of the pandemic is all around us and, as we all try to move forward, we struggle to understand the diverse effects of a pandemic that came to rule our lives. In a short period, South Africa produced a stream of laws to deal with the pandemic, and the courts have been flooded with applications to challenge some of these laws as abuses of human rights. This contribution is a humble account of the many faces of the coronavirus as seen from the eyes of a South African law academic.

1. Into South Africa: The Beginnings

When the rest of the world became aware of the new coronavirus, initially detected in Wuhan, China, in December 2019, there was no indication that it would influence every possible aspect of daily life on a global scale. But it has. South Africa and its inhabitants have not been spared. On March 5, 2020 the South African National Institute for Communicable Diseases (NICD) confirmed the first positive Covid-19 case. The patient was a 38-year-old male who had travelled to Italy with a group of ten people.[1] Within a week South Africa had seventeen confirmed cases. Sixteen cases were people who had travelled abroad, but the seventeenth one marked the beginning of the local transmissions. South Africa took instant action.

---

[1] Cf. Mkize: First Case of Covid-19. All ten people were traced and isolated to prevent a further spread, cf. Wiysonge: South Africa's War on COVID-19.

On March 15, 2020 it classified the pandemic as a national disaster and declared a state of disaster. The disaster declaration is the centre of power to the executive and newly established structures created in terms of the Disaster Management Act 57 of 2000 (DMA). One such structure is the newly established National Coronavirus Command Council (NCCC),[2] headed by President Cyril Ramaphosa and nineteen Cabinet Ministers, the National Defence Force, the National Police Commissioner, and a secretariat.[3] Within a matter of days, an arsenal of statutes, regulations, guidelines, and directions followed, all aimed at curbing the virus.[4] A five-level Covid-19 risk alert system was introduced whereby the reach of South Africa's restrictive public health measures was graded according to the spread of the virus and the ability of the health system to cope with it. Alert Level 5 represents a high Covid-19 spread with low health system readiness and thus involves drastic measures. Alert Level 1 represents a low Covid-19 spread with a high health system readiness and less extreme measures. The country went into so-called *hard lockdown* – Alert Level 5 – at midnight, March 26, 2020. Alert Level 5 eventually lasted until April 30, 2020.[5] The drastic measures seemed to work initially but, after a slow start, the numbers of infections began to grow and the first wave peaked on July 24, 2020, with a total of 13 944 daily new cases, 173 587 infections and 7067 deaths. The infections slowed down to below 900 in September 2020 but steadily increased again to create a second wave that peaked in January 2021 with 21 980 daily infections. The number came down significantly over the next three months but then gradually increased again. We experienced the tip of the third wave in June 2021. On June 1 the daily new infections were 21 584. The total number of deaths was 61 029, representing 1016 deaths per 1 million population.[6] A positive sign is that the numbers are already in decline. Since July 25 the daily new infections have been below 10 000 a day, which prompted the President to adjust the lockdown level to Alert Level 3, with less restrictive measures to curb the

---

[2] The legality of the NCCC was questioned in Esau v Minister of Co-operative Governance and Traditional Affairs 2020 (11) BCLR 1371 (WCC), at para 5. However, the Court dismissed the contention, upholding the President's argument that government should arrange itself as it deemed fit, and that the NCCC was a legitimate committee of government.

[3] Cf. Ramaphosa: Statement by President Cyril Ramaphosa.

[4] For a detailed list, cf. South African Legal Information Institute (SAFLII): Newsroom COVID-19 Materials.

[5] Alert Level 4 was introduced on May 1, 2020 and lasted until May 31, 2020. Alert Level 3 was from June 1 to August 17, 2020, and Alert Level 2 from August 18 to September 20, 2020. Alert level 1 commenced on September 21, 2020 until June 28, 2021. South Africa returned to Alert Level 4 on June 29, 2021 to try and curb the third wave, cf. Government Notice R567 in Government Gazette 44778 dated June 29, 2021.

[6] All the statistics are available on the website of the South African Department of Health, the National Institute for Communicable Diseases and Worldometers. Reliable statistics regarding South Africa's population do not exist but it is estimated that it has a population of about 60 million people, cf. World Population Review: South African Population 2021.

spread of the virus. According to statistics, South Africa has the highest number of Covid-19 infections in Africa but not the highest in the world. It ranked 17th on the global scale on July 16, 2021.[7] However, considering the fragile state of South Africa's public health care system and its generally bleak economic outlook, these numbers are way too high to manage successfully. There is no denying that the coronavirus has not only been infecting people but has also permeated every aspect of everyday life fueled by social, economic, political, and human rights discourses. It has exposed the good in people and the bad, and it has uncovered the inadequacies of and inequalities in leadership in South Africa and elsewhere. The politics of the pandemic has been used and abused by the social media on an unprecedented scale, and it has challenged legislatures and executives globally. As I am a lawyer, the legal response to the Covid-19 pandemic is my forte, but I am not oblivious to the socio-economic impact of the pandemic. The signs are evident in a struggling economy such as South Africa, where there are enormous economic disparities between people and communities and where the divide between the public and private health systems is particularly noticeable. The virus does not discriminate but social circumstances do. While rich countries celebrate vaccinating millions of their citizens, South Africa and other African countries lag far behind. Against this background, this contribution gives a small glimpse into the many faces of the coronavirus in South Africa. In this country, political and social challenges are already the norm instead of the exception.

2. A Legal Response to the Corona Pandemic[8]

South Africa is a young democracy bound to a supreme Constitution[9] containing a comprehensive, justiciable Bill of Rights.[10] To prevent past injustices and inequalities, especially under the hands of the former government with its segregation policies, the Bill of Rights confirms that it is the »cornerstone of democracy« that »enshrines the rights« of everyone in South Africa«, and it »affirms the democratic values of human dignity, equality and freedom«.[11] The state has

---

[7] Cf. Worldometer: Homepage.
[8] A useful summary of the legal framework within which responses to the corona pandemic operate is provided in the Oxford Compendium of National Responses to Covid-19, cf. Kruger et al.: Republic of South Africa: Legal Response to Covid-10.
[9] Constitution of the Republic of South Africa, 1996 (hereafter the Constitution) that came into operation on February 4, 1996. It was preceded by a transitional Constitution of the Republic of South Africa 200 of 1993 that was in operation from April 27, 1994 to February 3, 1996. It contained a Bill of Rights in chapter 3.
[10] Cf. chapter 2 of the Constitution.
[11] Cf. section 7 of the Constitution.

the responsibility to respect, protect, promote and fulfil the rights in the Bill of Rights and they may be limited only in terms of the limitation clause.[12] It sanctions limitations that are *reasonable and justifiable*, taking into account several factors, such as the nature of the right, the purpose of the limitation, the nature and extent of the limitation, the relation between the limitation and its purpose, and whether there are less restrictive means to achieve the purpose of the limitation. The corona pandemic posed and continues to present unique challenges to some of these constitutional guarantees. Governments worldwide, including that of South Africa, adopted measures to mitigate the spread of the virus across and between borders by restricting movement and contact among people. South Africans do not respond well to any measure that restricts movement. They do not have fond memories of bygone years when apartheid and state of emergency laws determined your movement and kept people apart every step of the way. Also, the prevailing socio-economic situation makes it extremely difficult to restrict movement, especially in extremely dense areas where informal public transport is the only mode of travel. Given the circumstances, how has South African law responded to the pandemic?

The South African Constitution requires state institutions to act in concert with the law, and they may not exercise more power than is permitted in terms of the law. This limitation of state power is contained in the well-known principle of legality. According to the case of *Fedsure Life Assurance v Greater Johannesburg Transitional Metropolitan Council*,[13] legality is »central to the conception of our constitutional order that the legislature and executive in every sphere are constrained by the principle that they may exercise no power and perform no function beyond that conferred upon them by law.« Thus, even though Covid-19 required extraordinary measures, the government's response had to be shaped and constrained by law. The South African government had two options to respond to the pandemic; either to declare a state of emergency[14] or a state of national disaster.[15] There are essential differences between these two responses, the most notable of which is the fact that the former allows the state to temporarily derogate (suspend) certain rights.[16] In contrast, a state of national disaster allows a limitation of

---

[12] Cf. section 36 of the Constitution.

[13] Cf. 1999 (1) SA 374 (CC) para 58.

[14] Cf. section 37 of the Constitution provides for the declaration of a state of emergency when the »life of a nation is threatened by war, invasion, general insurrection, disorder, natural disaster or other public emergency« and it is necessary to »restore peace and order«.

[15] A state of disaster is declared in terms of section 27 of the DMA.

[16] The state must pass legislation that declares expressly that it is suspending certain rights for a period of time under strict conditions. A few rights are non-derogable, namely human dignity and life. Other rights can be suspended only to a certain extent (cf. the »Table of Non-Derogable Rights« in section 37 of the Constitution for a complete list).

rights only subject to stringent constitutional imperatives.[17] Despite the severity of the pandemic, the state has not deemed it necessary to restore »peace and order«. Therefore, South Africa did not declare a state of emergency but opted to declare a state of national disaster under the framework of prevailing disaster management laws such as the DMA,[18] and the National Disaster Management Framework of 2005 (NDMF), including a growing list of regulations, guidelines and directives.[19]

The DMA provides several types of structures to manage the disaster,[20] but it is not clear if those structures are functional since the NCCC with input from the National Joint Operations and Intelligence Structure (NatJoints)[21] has overtaken the roles they were supposed to fulfil.[22] The effect of the disaster declaration is that all the provisions of the Constitution remain intact and the state is obliged to »respect, protect, promote and fulfil the rights in the Bill of Rights«.[23] However, it may limit those rights if such a limitation is reasonable and justifiable under section 36 of the Constitution. In addition, through the Minister of Cooperative Governance and Traditional Affairs (CoGTA) the executive has wide-ranging powers to make regulations or directions regarding a range of matters.[24] However, these powers must be exercised only to the extent that it is necessary to protect and bring relief to the public, protect property, prevent or combat disruption or deal with the effects of the disaster.[25]

Since the pandemic struck and the disaster was declared, the growing raft of laws have had a far-reaching impact on people's daily lives, some of them severe. The legal measures impose restrictions on various activities to slow down the spread of the virus. They grant exceptions to various state institutions to act differently than they usually do. The enabling provision that allows the Minister of CoGTA to make regulations and issue directives in this regard is section 27(2) of the DMA. However, as *De Beer v Minister of Cooperative Governance and Tradi-*

---

[17] Cf. section 36 of the Constitution.
[18] Section 1 of the DMA defines a disaster as »a progressive or sudden, widespread or localised. natural or human-caused occurrence which – (a) causes or threatens to cause – (i) death, injury or disease; (ii) damage to property, infrastructure or the environment; or (iii) disruption of the life of a community; and (b) is of a magnitude that exceeds the ability of those affected by the disaster to cope with its effects using only their own resources«.
[19] The first set of regulations was published under Government Notice R318 in Government Gazette 43107 of March 18, 2020.
[20] Cf. sections 4 and 5 of the DMA that make provision for an Intergovernmental Committee on Disaster Management, and a National Disaster Management Advisory Forum.
[21] Despite being a committee that coordinates security and law enforcement, NatJoints has been tracking the pandemic and has been advising the NCCC on Covid-19 regulations and directions (cf. Department of Planning, Monitoring and Evaluation: Covid-19 Country Report, Chapter 3.1, p. 11).
[22] Cf. Singh: How South Africa's Ministerial Advisory Committee on COVID-19 can be Optimised, p. 439.
[23] Cf. section 7(2) of the Constitution.
[24] Cf. section 27(2) of the DMA for a list of these matters.
[25] Cf. section 27(3) of the DMA.

tional Affairs pointed out,[26] section 27 was not initially promulgated with a pandemic such as a virus in mind but with other types of disasters, such as flooding. As explained by the Court, section 27(2):

»places the power to promulgate and direct substantial (if not virtual all (*sic*)) aspects of everyday life of the people of South Africa in the hands of a single minister with little or none of the customary parliamentary, provincial or other oversight functions provided for in the Constitution in place. The exercise of the functions should therefore be closely scrutinized to ensure the legality and constitutional compliance thereof.«[27]

In its struggle to flatten the corona curve, the South African government has focused its attention on preventing the collapse of the health system. It has neglected other important aspects such as public life, food and work security, economic stability, and poverty. The state of disaster has not changed the responsibility of the state to respect, protect, promote, and fulfil all constitutional rights. The onus remains on the state to justify any limitations to those rights. Several judicial attacks have already been launched against various decisions that limit rights in some or other way. I deal with some of the cases in the next section.

3. What the Judiciary Has to Say: Capita Selecta

Having a justiciable Constitution and the rule of law makes it easy to instigate litigation where people feel aggrieved by the government's actions and other such matters. However, the corona pandemic is unchartered territory for everyone, including for the judiciary. Judges had no precedent on which they could rely, and laws were being made up at the same speed as the virus was mutating. A quick search of the online database of LexisNexis (subscription needed) reveals that more than 50 judgments have already been handed down since the South African government declared a state of disaster. Since many cases are unreported, the number is probably much higher. It is impossible to discuss all the judgments in the confines of a single chapter such as this, but I will examine a few to illustrate the types of issues the courts are facing.

---

[26] 2020 (11) BCLR 1349 (GP), para 4.14.
[27] Ibid, para 5.4.

3.1 Testing the Constitutionality of the Declaration of Disaster and Other Lockdown Laws

As already explained, the national state of disaster did not alter the rule of law or the constitutional protection of rights and liberties. Over the years, the judiciary has become a renowned watchdog for protecting human rights, and South Africans who can afford it or have the backing of large organizations with the means to litigate are flocking to the courts to claim protection where they feel their rights are being infringed. The corona pandemic and the government's legal response to it opened the floodgates, and the cases soon began to line up. One of the first applications (the *Hola Bon Renaissance Foundation* (HBRF) case) concerned a failed application launched in the apex court of South Africa.[28] The HBRF[29] asked for direct access to the Constitutional Court to argue that the total lockdown – Level 5 announced on March 23, 2020 – was invalid and unconstitutional.[30] The foundation claimed that Covid-19 did not pose a serious threat to South Africa and its people since there was no proof that it was deadlier than any other known virus such as malaria, tuberculosis or HIV/AIDS. At the time of the application only a few people had been infected and there had been no Covid-19 related deaths. However, the foundation's application for direct access was denied because the Court felt the case had no reasonable prospects of success. Given the roller coaster effect of the virus ever since, the foundation would probably have reconsidered its application. Still, no one was to predict the full extent of the devastation the virus would eventually cause.

In another case, *Mohamed v The President of the Republic of South Africa*,[31] the applicants contended that the lockdown regulations were unconstitutional. They argued that the regulations prevented them from honoring their religious obligation to perform daily prayers in a mosque, which resulted in a severe violation of their freedom of movement, freedom of religion, freedom of religious association, and right to dignity. They argued that government should make an exception to allow for their daily prayers.[32] The Court agreed with the government's counter-argument that the lockdown regulations restricted everyone and that they were »both reasonable and necessary given the threat that Covid-19 poses to human life,

---

[28] Hola Bon Renaissance Foundation (HBRF) v President of the Republic of South Africa 2011 (10) BCLR 1009 (CC).

[29] Very little online information on the HBRF is available but from the founding affidavit of the *chairperson* of the foundation, it seems to be a non-profit voluntary and political association with the objective to »address and encourage the communities' transformation by creating a community that is skilled, self-sustained with a central economic opportunity« (cf. paragraph 4 of the HBRF's Founding Affidavit).

[30] Cf. HBRF's Notice of Motion.

[31] Cf. 2020 (7) BCLR 865 (GP).

[32] Cf. ibid., para 25.

dignity and access to healthcare.«[33] In the Court's view, again regarding *ubuntu*, everyone in South Africa:

»is called upon to make sacrifices to their fundamental rights entrenched in the Constitution. They are called upon to do so in the name of ›the greater good‹, the spirit of ›ubuntu‹ and they are called upon to do so in ways that impact on their livelihoods, their way of life and their economic security and freedom. Every citizen of this country needs to play his/her part in stemming the tide of what can only be regarded as an insidious and relentless pandemic.«[34]

In *Esau v Minister of Co-operative Governance and Traditional Affairs*,[35] the applicants again failed to convince the Court that the lockdown regulations were unconstitutional, even though there was no proper public participation in the drafting thereof, and some seemed irrational.[36] Some of the regulations imposed severe restrictions on the freedom of movement, economic activity, the right to human life and family life. In addition, there were several ostensibly nonsensical restrictions, such as the prohibition on the selling of clothing such as open-toed shoes; a ban on supermarkets to sell warm food; curfews on exercising and limitations on the types of exercises permissible[37] and the places where one could exercise. Nevertheless, the Court did not question the Minister's approach which under the circumstances involved issues of high policy that have to be made in a »polycentric manner« and held:

»I accept that the measures do not satisfy everyone and there is a great deal of criticism levelled against them. The inconvenience and discontent that the regulations have caused the applicants and others have to be weighed against the urgent objective and primary constitutional duty to save lives. That is the nature of the proportionality exercise which government has had to embark upon.«[38]

The Court was satisfied that the government acted in the best interest of everyone. It held that a rational link between the prescribed measures and their purpose existed, and the application failed.[39] The judgment was taken on appeal, where the Court dismissed it save for two exceptions.[40] The Court held that the limitation placed on the types of exercises, and when and where one could exercise (within

---

[33] Ibid., paras 32, 77.
[34] Ibid., para 75.
[35] Cf. 2020 (11) BCLR 1371 (WCC).
[36] Issued in terms of section 27(2) of the DMA published under Government Notice R480 in Government Gazette 43258 of April 29, 2020.
[37] The only exercises allowed were walking, running, and cycling.
[38] Esau v Minister of Co-operative Governance and Traditional Affairs 2020 (11) BCLR 1371 (WCC), paras 253 f.
[39] Cf. ibid., paras 255–258.
[40] Cf. Esau v Minister of Co-Operative Governance and Traditional Affairs 2021 (3) SA 593 (SCA).

a radius of five kilometers from home) was unconstitutional and invalid. And so was the prohibition on the selling of warm food.⁴¹

Why were the courts initially less critical of the government's approach to curb the spread of the virus? When the first salvo of judgments came, the coronavirus was an unknown phenomenon, and the judiciary was equally cautious of what its effects on South Africa were going to be. Understandably, the courts preferred to err on the side of caution as there was »no cure, no adequate treatment« and »no guaranteed prevention«. This was »a global disaster which humanity has not encountered before.«⁴² As time progressed, the judiciary accepted to a lesser extent the government's intrusion on constitutional rights. One example is *De Beer v Minister of Cooperative Governance and Traditional Affairs.*⁴³ The applicants challenged the validity of the declaration of a national disaster and all the regulations that followed. Like the HBRF application, they argued that the government's reaction to the pandemic was a gross over-reaction, considering the low mortality rate compared with those of other diseases that were already plaguing the country. The Court disagreed and held that South Africa had a responsibility to declare the disaster for two reasons: first, to curb the rapid spread of the virus, and second, to honor the pronouncements of the World Health Organization (WHO).⁴⁴ The Court also accepted the fact that measures to curb the spread of the virus were urgently needed. However, the measures – regulations and directives – are subject to two types of limitations. The first type is the statutory limitations listed in the DMA.⁴⁵ The Minister may issue the regulations and directives only after consulting the »responsible Cabinet member« and »only to the extent that it is necessary for the purpose of« protecting and bringing relief to the public, protecting property, preventing, or combatting disruption or dealing with the effects of the disaster.⁴⁶ Secondly, the measures to curb the spread of the virus must be constitutional. In other words, they must be employed to »achieve a permissible objective to be both rational and rationally connected to that objective.«⁴⁷ This process entails a rationality test. The question is whether »the means employed are rationally related to the purpose for which the power was conferred?«⁴⁸ And if they do not, there is a disconnect between »the means and the purpose«; »they fall short of the standard demanded by the Constitution,« and they are not permissible limitations in terms

---

⁴¹ Cf. ibid., para 161.
⁴² Ibid., paras 156f.
⁴³ Cf. 2020 (11) BCLR 1349 (GP). The name of HBRF popped up again as *amicus curiae*.
⁴⁴ Cf. ibid., para 4.12.
⁴⁵ The regulations and directions may only be made regarding a list of scenarios, but this list is quite wide and gives a wide discretion to the minister, cf. section 27(2)(a)-(o) of the DMA for the detailed list.
⁴⁶ Cf. section 27(2) and (3) of the DMA.
⁴⁷ Ibid., para 6.2.
⁴⁸ Ibid., para 6.

of the Constitution.⁴⁹ The state argued that the »South African population has to make a sacrifice between the crippling of the economy and loss of lives« and that the regulations cannot »be set aside on the basis that they are causing economic hardship, as saving lives should take precedence over freedom of movement and to earn a living.«⁵⁰ The Court agreed that the saving of lives is a constitutional imperative, but it was also mindful of the fact that South Africa had reached a level where the spread of infection could not be wholly prevented. Therefore, the objective should be to »at least attempt to limit the spread or the rate of infection whilst at the same time maintaining social cohesion and economic viability.«⁵¹

Against this background, the Court continued to test the rationality of some of the lockdown regulations and their connectivity to the stated objectives of preventing the infection.⁵² In applying the rationality test, the Court concluded that some of the regulations were indeed irrational. For example, up to 50 people could attend funerals across provinces, but individuals could not leave their homes to attend to their sick family members or loved ones.⁵³ Using the example of hairdressers and taxi drivers, where the former were prevented from working while taxi drivers could continue to work, the Court said:

»To illustrate this irrationality further in the case of hairdressers: a single mother and sole provider for her family may have been prepared to comply with all the preventative measures proposed in the draft Alert Level 3 regulations but must now watch her children go hungry while witnessing minicab taxis pass with passengers in closer proximity to each other than they would have been in her salon. She is stripped of her rights of dignity, equality, to earn a living and to provide for the best interests of her children.«⁵⁴

Other irrational regulations included the restricted hours of exercise,⁵⁵ allowing people to run on the promenade but not on the beach,⁵⁶ allowing long-distance travel and funerals but not properly regulated night vigils, and so on.⁵⁷ What emerged from the evidence before the Court was that once the state of disaster was declared, the government followed a »paternalistic approach, rather than a constitutionally justifiable« one, that gave scant regard to the

»extent of the impact of individual regulations on the constitutional rights of people and whether the extent of the limitation of their rights was justifiable or not. The starting

---

49   Section 27(2) and (3) of the DMA, paras 6.4–6.6.
50   Ibid., para 6.9.
51   Ibid., para 6.11.
52   Cf. ibid., para 7.
53   Cf. ibid., para 7.1.
54   Ibid., para 7.3.
55   Cf. ibid., para 7.8.
56   Cf. ibid., para 7.9.
57   Cf. ibid., para 7.7.5

point was not ›how can we as government limit constitutional rights in the least possible fashion whilst still protecting the inhabitants of South Africa?‹ but rather ›we will seek to achieve our goal by whatever means, irrespective of the costs and we will determine, albeit incrementally, which constitutional rights you as the people of South Africa, may exercise‹.«[58]

In another case, a political party was dissatisfied with the government's use of racial criteria to provide relief to struggling businesses during the lockdown. In *Democratic Alliance v President of the Republic of South Africa*,[59] the Democratic Alliance questioned the decision of the government to use criteria such as race, gender, youth, and disability to determine who should benefit from two funds created to dispense funds to small businesses during the lockdown. The Court held that the regulations were vague and legally non-compliant because they did not give any guidance on what weight was to be given to the criteria mentioned. Therefore, the apparent criteria fell short of basic principles of the rule of law requiring that the exercise of public power be sure, even if discretion to allocate funds was permissible. The Court set aside the criteria and referred the matter back to the Minister for a redrafting of the regulations. The role of race, gender, youth, and disability had to be reconsidered and adequately construed.

In an earlier case, two law students were dissatisfied with the fact that they had to vacate the University residences during the total initial lockdown. In March 2020 Wits University issued a directive that all residences were to be closed, and students had to evacuate their residences within 72 hours. Two students brought an urgent application against the University in *Moela v Habib*[60] to stop them from being evacuated. They argued that the University had to satisfy itself that the students had been tested for Covid-19 and that it was safe for them to go home without the threat of spreading the virus. They also claimed that their right to health care and other rights compelled the University to assume responsibility for testing students. If it refused to do so, these rights would be violated. The Court was not convinced that the University should deal with the matter as suggested by the two students, because

»the majority of people in the South Africa (and globally) are in the same situation as the applicants. We have all had meetings or been in contact with other people who may have been exposed to someone with SARS COV-19, or who may have it themselves. The suggestions by the applicants that the way in which the University should deal with this by testing all students in residences before they are sent home, is simply not feasible.«[61]

---

[58] Ibid., para 7.17.
[59] Cf. [2020] 3 All SA 747 (GP).
[60] (2020/9215) [2020] ZAGPJHC 69 (March 19, 2020) (Unreported).
[61] Ibid., para 54.

In the end the application failed, and the Court held that the University had followed all the protocols recommended by the WHO, the NCCC, the President and renowned experts in the field.[62] In its concluding words the Court appealed to all to remain calm in the spirit of *ubuntu*. The idea of *ubuntu* has been mentioned in several cases.[63] Although an African ethical philosophy of life, the concept of *ubuntu* has been introduced into the legal landscape. It was noted in the postamble of the transitional Constitution but was not incorporated in the final one. Still, it has developed into one of the most used concepts in South African jurisprudence. The first reference to it in a judgment of the Constitutional Court was in the highly acclaimed case of *S v Makwanyane*[64] that dealt with the abolition of the death penalty. Since then, the normative value of *ubuntu* has been praised and criticized by legal scholars, but it is now firmly entrenched in our legal literature.[65] One of the most cited explanations of its meaning was given by a former judge of the Constitutional Court, Justice Mokgoro. She said:

»Generally, *ubuntu* translates as humaneness. In its most fundamental sense, it translates as personhood and morality. Metaphorically, it expresses itself in *umuntu ngumuntu ngabantu*, describing the significance of group solidarity on survival issues so central to the survival of communities. While it envelops the key values of group solidarity, compassion, respect, human dignity, conformity to basic norms and collective unity, in its fundamental sense it denotes humanity and morality. Its spirit emphasizes respect for human dignity, marking a shift from confrontation to conciliation.«[66]

As the corona pandemic moves on without losing speed, South Africans – like everyone else – are slowly but surely losing their patience and *ubuntu*. They are losing patience with having to give up their freedom to move around when and where they want to, to visit premises such as shops, parks, churches, restaurants, and sport facilities, to visit friends and family members, and to smoke and drink.

3.2 No Smoking or Drinking

Two limitations that have been making South Africans hot under the collar are the banning of the sale of tobacco and vape products and the sale, dispensing and transportation of liquor. Their grievances also found their way to the courts. On March 25, 2020 the government announced a ban on the sale of all tobacco

---

[62] Cf. ibid., para 58.
[63] Also cf. the Mohamed case discussed at 3.1. above.
[64] Cf. 1995 (6) BCLR 665 (CC).
[65] For more on the concept of *ubuntu*, cf. Rautenbach: Legal Reform of Traditional Courts in South Africa, pp. 275–304, specifically pp. 289–294.
[66] S v Makwanyane 1995 (6) BCLR 665 (CC), para 308.

and vaping products because, amongst other things, people may share cigarettes and thus saliva that could spread the virus. Smokers were not happy with the decision. It is estimated that about eight million South Africans still smoke cigarettes.[67] About 700 000 people signed a petition calling on the government to lift the ban. They were supported by the tobacco industry, which was losing money in the process.

In May 2020, in *Fair-Trade Independent Tobacco Association v President of the Republic of South Africa*,[68] the applicant, representing Southern African cigarette manufacturers, lodged a court application for an order to have tobacco products declared as *essential goods*, and that the sale of tobacco products was lawful. It argued that there was no rational connection between the ban and the objective of curbing the spread of the virus. The government argued that the ban was necessary to protect human life and to reduce the potential strain on the health care system.[69] In the end the Court dismissed the claim and reiterated that

>»an important consideration that should not be lost sight of is that the means chosen by the Minister, i.e. the ban, need not be the most effective nor the best suited. Ultimately, the question remains whether there is a rational connection between the ban, as the means preferred, and the saving of lives through curbing infections and preventing a strain to the country's healthcare facilities. This, we are satisfied, the Minister has been able to demonstrate.«[70]

On July 24, 2020 the applicant's leave to appeal the decision was denied because nothing of substance or new was raised by it.[71]

The ban remained in place during Alert Levels 5 to 3. A few months later the British American Tobacco South Africa and nine other applicants involved in tobacco products again applied for a court order declaring the ban against tobacco products and vape products unconstitutional in *British American Tobacco South Africa (Pty) Ltd v Minister of Co-Operative Governance and Traditional Affairs*.[72] The applicants challenged the ban's constitutionality by invoking human rights violations such as the freedom of trade, the arbitrary deprivation of property rights, dignity, privacy and bodily and psychological integrity.[73] The matter was heard

---

[67] Cf. Department of Planning, Monitoring and Evaluation: Covid-19 Country Report, Chapter 6.5, p. 11.

[68] Cf. Fair-Trade Independent Tobacco Association v President of the Republic of South Africa 2021 (1) BCLR 68 (GP).

[69] Cf. ibid., at paras 29, 35, 41–49 and 70.

[70] Ibid., at para 70.

[71] Cf. Fair-Trade Independent Tobacco Association v President of the Republic of South Africa [2020] JOL 47868 (GP).

[72] Cf. British American Tobacco South Africa (Pty) Ltd v Minister of Co-Operative Governance and Traditional Affairs [2020] JOL 49180 (WCC).

[73] Cf. sections 22, 25, 10, 14, and 12(2) of the Constitution.

during August 2020, but the ban was lifted before a judgment could be delivered. In answering the question of whether the lifting of the ban rendered the application moot, the Court held that there were »exceptional circumstances of compelling public interest« that required it to determine the moot issue.[74] Three of the circumstances included: (1) the disaster was still not over, and the ban could be re-introduced in future; (2) people had already been criminally convicted while the ban was in place; and (3) the binding effect of the *Fair-Trade Independent Tobacco Association* case that declared the ban constitutional had to be determined.[75] The Court considered the facts before it. After a lengthy analysis it concluded that it could deviate from the *Fair-Trade Independent Tobacco Association case* because the latter used the rationality test whilst the proportionality test was relevant.[76] The proportionality test is more stringent than the rationality test. The Minister had the onus to prove that the limitation of rights (the tobacco ban limiting human rights) was justified. After a purposive interpretation of the enabling provision[77] that requires »necessary« steps to be taken to »prevent an escalation of the disaster«, the Court concluded that the tobacco ban indeed violated fundamental rights. It held that the government failed to convince the Court that the use of tobacco increased the risk of developing a more severe form of the coronavirus, which would increase the strain on the public health system.[78] Therefore, the ban was unconstitutional and invalid.[79]

It is interesting to note that the ban on tobacco had several unintended consequences, as pointed out in the *British American Tobacco South Africa (Pty) Ltd case*.[80] Both consumers, the tobacco industry and the receiver of revenue were severely affected. Individual witnesses provided affidavits in which they explained what effect not smoking had on their mental state and the extreme, illegal measures they had to take to find tobacco products to continue smoking.[81] Their statements concerning the emotional state of smokers addicted to nicotine were backed by evidence from a scientist with a PhD[82] and a survey based on the response of several users of tobacco products.[83] The survey revealed that the ban failed to support public health; instead it resulted in the booming of the illicit cigarette trade market. Cigarette prices soared while government revenue declined. In addition the stability of the tobacco chain, from the farmers to the manufacturers

---

[74] Ibid., para 27.
[75] Cf. ibid.
[76] Cf. ibid., paras 129–135, 156 f.
[77] Cf. section 27 of the DMA.
[78] Ibid., paras 156–163.
[79] Cf. ibid., paras 216 f.
[80] Cf. ibid., paras 39–59.
[81] Cf. ibid., paras 40–42.
[82] Cf. ibid., paras 43 f.
[83] Cf. ibid., paras 48–50, cf. van Walbeek et al.: Lighting up the Illicit Market.

and finally to the sellers, was under severe strain, and everyone faced financial hardships.[84] The government's bid to appeal the judgment of the *British American Tobacco South Africa (Pty) Ltd case* failed.[85] However, this was a small victory and the general view is that the tobacco ban did more damage than good in the long run.[86]

Although South Africans can finally smoke in peace, drinking their favorite alcoholic beverage remains a thorny issue. On March 18, 2020, during Alert Level 5, the government declared a ban on liquor sales, dispensing, or transportation.[87] The ban remained intact during Alert Level 4 except for export purposes.[88] The domestic sale of liquor was initially legitimized during Alert Level 3 on June 1, 2020 for home consumption, but alcohol could not be consumed in restaurants, overnight accommodation or places of entertainment.[89] On July 12, 2020 liquor sales, dispensing, and transportation were banned again except for export purposes.[90] The ban remained intact throughout Alert Levels 2 and 1. Still, the sale of liquor for consumption at home or on licensed premises was allowed under certain conditions, such as on limited days and during limited hours, provided the regulations related to the curfew were not infringed.[91] From December 29, 2020 onwards the country moved between Alert Levels 1 to 3, but the alcohol ban was not intensified, though the sale remained subject to a few manageable restrictions.

However, a total liquor ban was announced when South Africa moved back to Alert Level 4 on June 28, 2021. South Africans were once again prevented from buying or transporting alcohol or drinking in public spaces.[92] On July 25, 2021 the government announced that South Africa was on adjusted Alert Level 3 and, to the delight of almost everyone the alcohol ban was eased. Liquor may again be sold on specific days and during certain hours, the transportation of alcohol is permitted, and wineries and breweries may continue to offer wine and brew-tast-

---

[84] Ibid., paras 53 f.
[85] Cf. Fair-Trade Independent Tobacco Association v President of the Republic of South Africa (21688/2020) [2020] ZAGPPHC 311.
[86] Cf. Department of Planning, Monitoring and Evaluation: Covid-19 Country Report, Chapter 6.5, pp. 13–21.
[87] Cf. regulation 8 of Government Notice R318 in Government Gazette 43107 of March 18, 2020. Alert Level 5 lasted from March 26 to April 30, 2020.
[88] Cf. regulation 26 of Government Notice R480 in Government Gazette 43258 of April 29, 2020. Alert Level 4 lasted from 1 to May 31, 2020.
[89] Cf. regulation 44 of Government Notice 608 in Government Gazette 43364 of May 28, 2020. Alert Level 3 lasted from June 1 to August 17, 2020.
[90] Cf. regulation 9 of Government Notice 763 in Government Gazette 43521 of July 12, 2020.
[91] Alert Level 2 lasted from August 18 to September 20, 2020. Regulation 61 of Government Notice 891 in Government Gazette 43620 of August 17, 2020 dealt with the details of the liquor ban. Alert Level 1 lasted from September 21 to December 28, 2020, but the only restrictions on the sale and dispensing of liquor were the shortened selling days and times, and the curfew, which prevented people from remaining in places of drinking after hours.
[92] Cf. regulation 29 of Government Notice R565 in Government Gazette 44772 of June 27, 2021.

ings.⁹³ The government's motivation for the alcohol bans is to reduce the number of trauma cases to keep the emergency rooms open for Covid-19 patients. Studies have shown that this motivation is not without merit.⁹⁴ However, it is feared that the ban's impact on economic and social stability has severely impacted on other sectors. In general, the alcohol ban has affected the economic growth of the manufacturing industry quite considerably, which has resulted in job losses.⁹⁵ The wine industry was and still is severely affected. Not only have their supply chain and exports suffered severe losses, but also the income of wineries and restaurants. South Africa has suffered a significant loss in GDP and revenue,⁹⁶ and it will take years before the negative impact of the lockdown will be overcome.⁹⁷ Litigation to question the alcohol ban took remarkably longer to be instituted than the smoking ban. However, when the alcohol ban resurfaced with the declaration of Alert Level 4 in June 2021, a large brewery launched an urgent application to have the ban struck down in *South African Breweries (Pty) Ltd v Minister of Corporative Governance and Traditional Affairs*.⁹⁸ The brewery did not challenge the ban's constitutionality but instead followed a highly technical route based on the rules of administrative action.⁹⁹ On July 22, 2021 the Court held that given the circumstances and the limited time frame in which the Minister had to act to curb the third corona wave, it could not be said she acted in a procedurally unfair manner, and the application was dismissed. Three days later the alcohol ban was relaxed, but contrary to the previous times when it was lifted, people did not flock to the liquor stores to buy alcohol, and no spike in online sales was reported.¹⁰⁰ One can only speculate about the reasons why – people had either stocked up because they expected the ban or could no longer afford to buy alcohol.

3.3 Relief Measures and Labor Disputes

Every day since the pandemic struck and the lockdown began, I have realized my privileged position. I have relative job security and can continue paying my monthly bills. However, others are not so fortunate. South Africa's historical devel-

---

⁹³ Cf. regulation 44 of Government Notice R651 in Government Gazette 44895 of July 25, 2021.
⁹⁴ Cf. Moultrie et. al.: Unnatural Deaths, Alcohol Bans and Curfews: Evidence from a Quasi-natural Experiment During Covid-19.
⁹⁵ Cf. Department of Planning, Monitoring and Evaluation: Covid-19 Country Report, Chapter 6.5, pp. 8 f.
⁹⁶ Cf. Gross Domestic Product.
⁹⁷ Cf. Department of Planning, Monitoring and Evaluation: Covid-19 Country Report, Chapter 6.2, pp. 4, 8 f., 15–19.
⁹⁸ Cf. (10996/2021) [2021] ZAWCHC 135 (July 22, 2021) (Unreported).
⁹⁹ In terms of the provisions of the Promotion of Access to Administrative Justice Act 3 of 2000.
¹⁰⁰ Cf. Masweneng: No long queues or spikes in online sales as booze ban is lifted.

opment and social make-up filter through every aspect of daily life. The country is characterized as one of the most unequal societies in the world, with enormous disparities between people and groups.[101] These issues cannot be ignored when a disaster such as a corona pandemic strikes. The uniqueness of South African society and the challenges it brings to the fore were highlighted by the Court in *Solidarity obo Members v Minister of Small Business Development*:

> »At the level of principle and given the deep fault lines including those of poverty, race and exclusion that continue to exist in our society, the onset of the Covid 19 crisis has on the one hand united South Africans in dealing with and attempting to overcome the impact of the virus. On the other hand it has also sharply highlighted the fault lines in our society where it is so evident that more often than not the poor and the disadvantaged face the major brunt of the crisis. The response to the crisis must therefore recognize this uneven playing field and therefore calibrating such a response to deal with the impact of the crisis as well as the effect of historical disadvantage is not only permissible at the level of principle but warranted and necessary.«[102]

The case dealt with the government's decision to put economic relief measures in place to help the tourist industry, which had been hit hard by the corona pandemic. The Tourist Relief Fund provided a once-off grant to be administered in line with existing black empowerment criteria, excluding many businesses owned primarily by white people. The applicants sought an order setting aside the Minister's decision to use empowerment criteria to evaluate the emergency applications. However, the Court held that the criteria were flexible and that it could not be said that race was an insurmountable obstacle for white-owned businesses. Also, there was a rational connection between the fund's eligibility criteria and the government's objective in dealing with the corona pandemic, which meant that the application had to fail.[103]

The corona pandemic poses an immense threat to job security, and a great deal of the litigation deals with unfair dismissals and other challenges in the workplace. A few examples may be mentioned. Reduced working days was the issue in *Mqayi/City to City Doors*.[104] The employee said that he was unfairly dismissed when he was required to work only certain days of the week, even though the employer explained that it was only permitted to employ five workers at a time during the lockdown. The Commission for Conciliation, Mediation and Arbitration (CCMA) dismissed the claim and held that the lockdown regulations prevented the employer from conducting business. The failure of employees to report for duty has been the subject of several cases in the CCMA, but they all had different

---

[101] Cf. Schlemmer/Møller: The Shape of South African Society, pp. 15–50.
[102] [2020] 9 BLLR 948 (GP), para 36.
[103] Cf. ibid., para 45.
[104] Cf. [2020] 11 BALR 1195 (CCMA).

outcomes. One case, *Mahlophe/ETA College*,[105] was about a lecturer who failed to return to continue with her lecturing after the total lockdown was relaxed. The evidence revealed that she has been advised to return to work several times but had not returned and had not provided a compelling explanation for not returning. Her services were terminated. The CCMA agreed that she had abandoned her work and had not been unfairly dismissed, as she had claimed. Therefore, she was not entitled to be reinstated or to receive back-pay. The fear of contracting the virus at one's workplace came to the fore in *Mahlasela/Patensie Citrus Ltd*.[106] The employee was a seasonable worker on a farm. She was afraid of contracting the virus and had been told, in that case, to stay at home and not come back. She regarded these words as a dismissal and approached the CCMA to claim compensation for unfair dismissal. The CCMA evaluated the facts and concluded that she had not been dismissed but had been suspended for the period during which she had decided to stay away. She had not been given a hearing before the suspension, which entitled her to compensation of a month's salary. The refusal of an employee to attend work during Covid-19 was also the issue in *Botha/TVR Distribution*.[107] The employee refused to return to work when he was summoned to do so. However, during the hearing it turned out that the employee's refusal had been just the last straw and that he had been disrespectful to his superiors for a long time. After hearing the evidence, the CCMA held that the dismissal was substantially fair but procedurally unfair because he had not been given enough time to prepare his defence. He was awarded compensation equal to a month's salary. There are also examples where an employee reported for duty but was dismissed because he was still under quarantine, and the results of his Covid-19 test were still unknown. In *DETAWU obo Jacobs/Quality Express*,[108] the employee claimed that he had not known that he should stay at home and that his dismissal was unfair. The CCMA ruled that he could not hide behind his ignorance, given the seriousness of the virus. He had deliberately ignored the safety of his colleagues, and he had damaged the trust relationship that should exist between an employer and employee. Therefore, his dismissal was fair. The refusal to renew a fixed-term contract formed the basis of an unfair dismissal claim in *Qeqe/Ikhala Public Further Education Training (FET) College*.[109] The employee's fixed-term contract had been extended for two months after the lockdown was introduced to allow her to complete the project for which she had been appointed. When her employer did not renew the contract after the extended period, she approached the CCMA for

---

[105] Cf. [2021] 2 BALR 163 (CCMA).
[106] Cf. [2021] 2 BALR 153 (CCMA).
[107] Cf. [2020] 12 BALR 1282 (CCMA).
[108] Cf. [2021] 5 BALR 453 National Bargaining Council for the Road Freight Industry (NBCRFLI).
[109] Cf. [2021] 1 BALR 92 (CCMA).

compensation based on unfair dismissal. Her application failed because her contract had been terminated by law, which is not a dismissal as required by labor law. An employee's refusal to wear his face mask properly landed him in trouble in the *National Union of Metalworkers of South Africa (NUMSA) obo Manyike/Wenzane Consulting and Construction*.[110] He had been dismissed for pulling his mask below his chin while speaking on his cellular phone and because he had already received a previous warning. The CCMA found that the dismissal was too harsh and that a short suspension would have been more effective because it was more likely to bring about a behavior change. Other examples include: the dismissal of an employee who was unable to attend work due to the absence of public transport during lockdown, which was fond to be unfair, and she had to be reinstated;[111] the dismissal of a hotel receptionist for racially abusing hotel guests refusing to adhere to the Covid-19 regulations, which was found to be fair;[112] the dismissal of an employee working as a caretaker at a children's home for going home during lockdown against the instructions from management, who did it to avoid infecting children with the virus, was found to be fair; the dismissal of a doctor's assistant for a breach of confidentially because she informed the management of the hospital that the doctor might have been infected by the coronavirus and should be tested, which was found to be unfair because she was only following health and safety protocols;[113] and the dismissal of an employee who sold liquor from a store during the alcohol ban, which was fond to be fair.[114]

Given South Africa's high unemployment rate, job security is certainly at the forefront of everyone's minds.[115] Research done in 2020 gives a grim view of the impact of the corona pandemic on the labor market.[116] The authors observe a 40 per cent decline in active employment. Mostly vulnerable groups are being affected, such as those in lower levels of education and informal traders. It is estimated that 20–33 per cent of job losers have fallen into poverty since the pandemic started.[117] Given that poverty was already disproportionately common in South Africa, this number is alarmingly high. It does not bode well for the future employment rate and economic stability of the country. South Africa is also home to more than 60 000 waste pickers that recycle 80–90 per cent of garbage annually.[118] The daily earnings from recycling are their only income. Under strict lock-

---

[110] Cf. [2021] 5 BALR 479 Metal and Engineering Industries Bargaining Council (MEIBC).
[111] Cf. Mtshweni/Smollan Sales and Marketing (Pty) Ltd [2021] 1 BALR 66 (CCMA).
[112] Cf. Joubert/Wilderness Hotel (Pty) Ltd [2021] 7 BALR 745 (CCMA).
[113] Cf. Sliedrecht/Mathonsi [2021] 6 BALR 669 (CCMA).
[114] Cf. Wulana/Boxer Superstores (Pty) Ltd [2021] 1 BALR 109 (CCMA).
[115] The official unemployment rate was 32,6 per cent in the first quarter of 2021, Department of Statistics South Africa: Media Release, June 1, 2021.
[116] Cf. Jain et. al.: The Labour Market and Poverty Impacts of COVID-19 in South Africa.
[117] Cf. ibid., p. 2.
[118] Cf. Maleka/De Wet: Helping South Africa's Waste Pickers Face the COVID-19 Crisis.

down, their movement was restricted, and their daily income was affected. They fall outside the scope of the normal relief funds established by the government. Still, other projects funded by United Nations Industrial Development Organization (UNIDO) and local stakeholders brought some relief.[119] However, there is no telling if the programme has been successful or if everyone was reached.[120]

3.4 Excessive Force by Security Forces during Corona Times

The corona pandemic had and still has a sobering effect on the mood of the South African population. The relations between government forces and the populace have not always been positive. Socio-economic hardships faced by the majority of South Africans are causing frustrations, and tempers are running high. As explained by the Court in *Khosa v Minister of Defence and Military Veterans*:

>»During the last year or so international rating agencies classified the South African investment rating as being of ›junk‹ status which of course had its own consequence on the financial markets, on the value of the Rand, and the ability of the government to borrow money on international markets. Added to that was the fact that there is vast unemployment in South Africa, substantial inequality between various groups of our population, lack of basic facilities such as electricity and water, the supply of electricity, and very little foreign investment which could have alleviated the situation. Coupled to that are the problems that have been grabbled (*sic*) with for years, relating to State Owned Enterprises which by any definition were all insolvent, and unable to function either properly or at all from time to time. All of this obviously had an effect on the mood of the nation, if I could call it that, and especially the youth who were faced with limited employment opportunities and the lack of any hope to obtain a proper education. These are unfortunately the realities and they play a role in this application if it is read properly as a whole.«[121]

The government was aware of the negative *mood* of the nation and knew that the lockdown would exacerbate the situation. On March 25, 2020 the President authorized the South African National Defence Force (SANDF) to support the enforcement of the lockdown regulations and to assist with maintaining law and order. When the lockdown commenced, the social media were soon flooded with various accounts of brutality inflicted by the security forces. The *Khoza* case deals with one such incident.[122] Evidence revealed that members of the SANDF entered the home of Mr Khoza and another person and accused them of violating the lockdown regulations. In the presence of bystanders, Mr Khoza was forcefully pulled

---

119 Cf. ibid.
120 Cf. Chamane: After 10 Months of Lockdown, still no Covid-19 Relief.
121 2020 (7) BCLR 816 (GP), para 4.
122 Cf. Khosa v Minister of Defence and Military Veterans 2020 (7) BCLR 816 (GP).

out of his home, where he was assaulted. He later died of his injuries. Family members of the deceased approached the Court for relief on multiple issues, which the Court granted.[123] It declared that everyone is entitled, even during a national disaster, to the right to human dignity, the right to life, the right not to be tortured and the right not to be treated or punished in a cruel, inhuman, or degrading way. These rights must be respected, protected, promoted and fulfilled by all the security forces, including the SANDF, the South African Police Force (SAPS), and any Metropolitan Police Department (MPD). These forces remain bound by domestic law and may use only the minimum force that is reasonable to perform their official duty. The members involved in the brutal attack had to be placed under precautionary suspension pending the outcome of their disciplinary hearing. A code of conduct and guidelines on the enforcement of lockdown regulations had to be developed. In addition, internal investigations into the Khoza-incident had to be conducted and the reports furnished to the Court. However, when the investigation was finally completed the SANDF exonerated the soldiers from all wrongdoing,[124] an outcome that was widely criticized.[125] The *Khoza* case is not an isolated one. There have been other incidents where members of the SANDF and SAPS have been involved in misconduct, though these incidents have not made their way into the courts yet.[126] But all is not doom and gloom. Reports of how civil society has mobilized itself to soften the blow of the corona pandemic have been a beacon of hope.[127]

Conclusion

One cannot do justice in the confines of one chapter to the many colors of the coronavirus in a multifaceted country such as South Africa. We are faced daily with negative stories, but there are also positive ones. The government's vaccine rollout had a bumpy start, but it is now well under way. Statistics reveal that on July 28, 2021 more than seven million people had already received at least one vaccination.[128] Unfortunately, corruption in the public sector remains rife, and the corona pandemic has opened the doors for even more corruption. The new, streamlined tender procedure for pandemic-related products and services opened the door for

---

[123] Cf. ibid., para 147.
[124] Cf. Venter: Soldiers Cleared of Alexandra Man's Murder.
[125] Cf. Ngoepe/Wa Afrika: SANDF Report on the Death of Collins Khoza »a Sham«.
[126] Cf. Department of Planning, Monitoring and Evaluation: Covid-19 Country Report, Chapter 3.2, pp. 23 f.
[127] Cf. Department of Planning, Monitoring and Evaluation: Covid-19 Country Report, Chapter 8.
[128] Covid-19: Online Resource and News Portal.

already corrupt networks to strengthen and exploit their stranglehold on corruption.[129] The prices of essential goods such as masks were inflated, and although some of the culprits were called to justice, many excessive price hikes were never reported.[130] In the decade before the pandemic struck, the South African economy was already in trouble because of sluggish growth, severe unemployment, extreme poverty and inequality, and low levels of saving and investment. The pandemic and the lockdown measures have increased these challenges manifold.[131] The pandemic has hit the tourism and hospitality sector hard, and they are likely to struggle to recover even if tourism regains momentum worldwide.

During the lockdown the decline in business activities[132] has profoundly affected the generation of revenue for the South African government, which has already led to a budget deficit in 2021.[133] This deficit will probably filter through to the South African public soon. The travel bans on South Africa, especially Germany's, are exceptionally long and harsh. South Africa is currently listed as *Virusvariantengebiet* by the Robert Koch Institute.[134] The suspension of travel and the limited exemptions have left many stranded and frustrated. Of all the countries identified as *Virusvariantengebiet*, South African has remained on the banned list for the longest period.[135] South Africa always had close ties with Germany. Still, it seems there is no political will to have the ban relaxed, and everyone that needs to travel between South Arica and Germany will suffer the consequences.

People across South Africa and the world have been devastated by the Covid-19 pandemic through illness, death, or financial difficulty. The need for help has never been greater. In South Africa I am privileged, in comparison with many others. I live in a freestanding house and have freedom of movement. I have a car to travel in. I have job security and I can work from home. And I have private health insurance. Yet, all these privileges did not help me when the virus infected people close to me. All of them survived with mild complications. Others are not as privileged. Many live in shacks in densely populated areas, use public transport, are poor, and lack job security. And they must make use of the public health services,

---

[129] Department of Planning, Monitoring and Evaluation: Covid-19 Country Report, Chapter 3.2, pp. 25 f.

[130] In Competition Commission v Matus [2020] 1 CPLR 295 (CT) the Commission found that the gross profit margins for the essential products were unreasonable and the firm had to pay a settlement amount to the Commission. In another case, the Competitition Commission penalised Dischem Pharmacies for the excessive price hiking of face marks during the pandemic.

[131] Cf. Department of Planning, Monitoring and Evaluation: Covid-19 Country Report, Chapter 6.1, p. 1.

[132] Cf. Department of Statistics South Africa: Business Impact Survey of the Covid-19 Pandemic in South Africa.

[133] National Treasury: Budget Review 2021.

[134] Cf. Robert Koch Institut: Informationen zur Ausweisung internationaler Risikogebiete.

[135] Cf. Daniel: Germany's Travel Ban on SA is one of the Longest and Harshest.

which are shambolic.[136] The coronavirus does not discriminate; it infects everyone that comes in its path. However, the consequences of the pandemic and those affected by it are where the inequalities are most prevalent. All of us experience the pandemic differently, and context is crucial. The law is ineffective against the virus and its many colors, but it is a powerful tool for protecting and advancing human rights in a time where those rights are under threat.

References

Botha / TVR Distribution 12 BALR 1282 (CCMA), 2020.

British American Tobacco South Africa (Pty) Ltd v Minister of Co-Operative Governance and Traditional Affairs JOL 49180 (WCC), 2020.

Chamane, Musa: After 10 Months of Lockdown, still no Covid-19 Relief for SA's Waste Pickers. IOL, February 1, 2021, https://bit.ly/3iUIjR4; last accessed June 28, 2021.

Competition Commission v Matus 1 Civil Praxis Law and Rules (CPLR) 295 (CT), 2020.

Constitution of the Republic of South Africa 200 of 1993.

Constitution of the Republic of South Africa, 1996.

Covid-19: Online Resource and News Portal, https://sacoronavirus.co.za/latest-vaccine-statistics/; last accessed June 28, 2021.

Daniel, Luke: Germany's Travel Ban on SA is one of the Longest and Harshest – Hurting Couples, Students, Jobs, in: Business Insider South Africa, July 15, 2021, https://www.businessinsider.co.za/german-travel-ban-on-south-africa-faces-challenge-2021-7; last accessed June 28, 2021.

De Beer v Minister of Cooperative Governance and Traditional Affairs 2020 (11) BCLR 1349 (GP).

Democratic Alliance v President of the Republic of South Africa 3 All SA 747 (GP), 2020.

Department of Planning, Monitoring and Evaluation: Covid-19 Country Report, https://www.gtac.gov.za/Pages/COVID-Country-Report.aspx; last accessed July 28, 2021.

Department of Statistics South Africa: Business Impact Survey of the Covid-19 Pandemic in South Africa, https://bit.ly/2Vl4V4M; last accessed July 28, 2021.

Department of Statistics South Africa: Media Release, June 1, 2021, https://bit.ly/3ycrAyS; last accessed July 28, 2021.

DETAWU obo Jacobs / Quality Express 5 BALR 453 (NBCRFLI), 2021.

---

[136] Cf. Mbunge: Effects of COVID-19 in South African Health System and Society, pp. 1809–1814.

Esau v Minister of Co-operative Governance and Traditional Affairs (11) BCLR 1371 (WCC), 2020.
Esau v Minister of Co-Operative Governance and Traditional Affairs (3) SA 593 (SCA), 2021.
Fair-Trade Independent Tobacco Association v President of the Republic of South Africa (1) BCLR 68 (GP), 2021.
Fair-Trade Independent Tobacco Association v President of the Republic of South Africa (21688/2020) ZAGPPHC 311 July 24, 2020, (Unreported).
Fedsure Life Assurance v Greater Johannesburg Transitional Metropolitan Council 1999 (1) SA 374 (CC).
Government Notice 608 in Government Gazette 43364 of May 28, 2020.
Government Notice 763 in Government Gazette 43521 of July 12, 2020.
Government Notice 891 in Government Gazette 43620 of August 17, 2020.
Government Notice R318 in Government Gazette 43107 of March 18, 2020.
Government Notice R318 in Government Gazette 43107 of March 18, 2020.
Government Notice R480 in Government Gazette 43258 of April 29, 2020.
Government Notice R480 in Government Gazette 43258 of April 29, 2020.
Government Notice R565 in Government Gazette 44772 of June 27, 2021.
Government Notice R567 in Government Gazette 44778 dated June 29, 2021.
Government Notice R651 in Government Gazette 44895 of July 25, 2021.
Hola Bon Renaissance Foundation (HBRF) v President of the Republic of South Africa 2011 (10) BCLR 1009 (CC).
Hola Bon Renaissance Foundation (HBRF): Founding Affidavit, https://bit.ly/3BTFk3M; last accessed July 28, 2021.
Hola Bon Renaissance Foundation (HBRF): Notice of Motion, https://bit.ly/3BTFk3M; last accessed July 28, 2021.
Jain, Ronak/Joshua Budlender/Rocco Zizzamia/Ihsaan Bassier: The Labour Market and Poverty Impacts of COVID-19 in South Africa, in: SALDRU Working Paper Series, Number 264, 2020, http://www.opensaldru.uct.ac.za/handle/11090/980; last accessed July 28, 2021.
Joubert/Wilderness Hotel (Pty) Ltd 7 BALR 745 (CCMA), 2021.
Khosa v Minister of Defence and Military Veterans 2020 (7) BCLR 816 (GP).
Kruger, Petronell/Khulekani Moyo/Paul Mudau/Marius Pieterse/Amanda Spies: Republic of South Africa: Legal Response to Covid-19, in: Oxford Compendium of National Responses to Covid-19, doi:10.1093/law-occ19/e6.013.6; last accessed July 14, 2021.
Mahlasela/Patensie Citrus Ltd 2 BALR 153 (CCMA), 2021.
Mahlophe/ETA College 2 BALR 163 (CCMA), 2021.
Maleka, Tebogo/Petronella De Wet: Helping South Africa's Waste Pickers Face the COVID-19 Crisis and Beyond, https://www.unido.org/stories/helping-

south-africas-waste-pickers-face-covid-19-crisis-and-beyond; last accessed July 28, 2021.

Masweneng, Kgaugelo: No long queues or spikes in online sales as booze ban is lifted, in: Times Live, July 26, 2021, https://bit.ly/2TNh9Da; last accessed July 28, 2021.

Mbunge, Elliot: Effects of COVID-19 in South African Health System and Society: An Explanatory Study, in: Diabetology & Metabolic Syndrome, 14(6), 2020, pp. 1809–1814.

Mkize, Zweli: First Case of Covid-19 Coronavirus Reported in SA. Media Briefing, https://bit.ly/377ETEZ; last accessed January 01, 2021.

Moela v Habib (2020/9215) ZAGPJHC 69, March 19, 2020, (Unreported).

Mohamed v The President of the Republic of South Africa 2020 (7) BCLR 865 (GP).

Moodley, Clinton: SA Ship Crew Race to Get into Germany, but Travel Bans make it Difficult, in: IOL, https://bit.ly/3rJmAPL; last accessed July 28, 2021.

Moultrie, T A et al: Unnatural Deaths, Alcohol Bans and Curfews: Evidence from a Quasi-natural Experiment During Covid-19, in: South African Medical Journal, 111(9), 2021, http://www.samj.org.za/index.php/samj/article/view/13345; last accessed July 28, 2021.

Mqayi / City to City Doors 11 BALR 1195 (CCMA), 2020.

Mtshweni / Smollan Sales and Marketing (Pty) Ltd 1 BALR 66 (CCMA), 2021.

National Institute for Communicable Diseases, https://www.nicd.ac.za/diseases-a-z-index/covid-19/surveillance-reports/national-covid-19-daily-report/; last accessed June 01, 2021.

National Institute for Communicable Diseases: COVID-19, https://www.nicd.ac.za/covid-19/; last accessed July 28, 2021.

National Treasury: Budget Review 2021, https://bit.ly/3zJOLRB, last accessed August 07, 2021.

Ngoepe, Karabo / Wa Afrika, Mzilikazi: SANDF Report on the Death of Collins Khoza »a Sham«, in IOL, June 7, 2020, https://bit.ly/3iYGkuZ; last accessed July 28, 2021.

NUMSA obo Manyike / Wenzane Consulting & Construction 5 BALR 479 (MEIBC), 2021.

Promotion of Access to Administrative Justice Act 3 of 2000.

Qeqe / Ikhala Public FET College 1 BALR 92 (CCMA), 2021.

Ramaphosa, Cyril: Statement by President Cyril Ramaphosa on Measures to Combat COVID-19 Epidemic. Media Statement, March 15, 2020, https://bit.ly/3753ASB; last accessed July 01, 2021.

Rautenbach, Christa: Legal Reform of Traditional Courts in South Africa: Exploring the Links Between uBuntu, Restorative Justice and Therapeutic Jurisprudence, in: Journal of International and Comparative Law, 2(2), 2015, pp. 275–304.

Robert Koch Institut: Informationen zur Ausweisung internationaler Risikogebiete durch das Auswärtige Amt, BMG und BMI, https://bit.ly/3rIoaBz; last accessed July 28, 2021.

S v Makwanyane 1995 (6) BCLR 665 (CC).

SAFLII: COVID-19 Materials, http://www.saflii.org/content/covid-saflii-0; last accessed July 22, 2021.

Schlemmer, Lawrence / Valerie Møller: The Shape of the South African Society and its Challenges, in: Social Indicators Research, 41, 1997, pp. 15–50.

Singh, Jerome Amir: How South Africa's Ministerial Advisory Committee on COVID-19 can be Optimized, in: South African Medical Journal, 110(6), 2020, pp. 439–442.

Sliedrecht / Mathonsi 6 BALR 669 (CCMA), 2021.

Solidarity obo Members v Minister of Small Business Development 9 BLLR 948 (GP), 2020.

South African Breweries (Pty) Ltd v Minister of Corporative Governance and Traditional Affairs (10996/2021) ZAWCHC 135, July 22, 2021, (Unreported).

South African Department of Health: COVID-19 Online Resource & News Portal, https://sacoronavirus.co.za/; last accessed July 28, 2021.

South African Government, https://bit.ly/3yhwp9f; last accessed July 01, 2021.

South African Government: Newsroom, https://bit.ly/3yhwp9f; last accessed July 22, 2021.

Van Walbeek, Corne / Samantha Filby / Kirsten Van der Zee: Lighting up the Illicit Market: Smoker's Response to the Cigarette Sales Ban in South Africa. Research Unit on the Economics of Excisable Products, https://bit.ly/3yc3bcY; last accessed July 25, 2021.

Venter, Zelda: Soldiers Cleared of Alexandra Man's Murder, in: IOL, May 28, 2020, https://www.iol.co.za/news/soldiers-cleared-of-alexandra-mans-murder-48630266; last accessed July 28, 2021.

Wiysonge, Charles Shey: South Africa's War on COVID-19, April 20, 2020, https://www.thinkglobalhealth.org/article/south-africas-war-covid-19; last accessed January 01, 2021.

World Population Review: South Africa Population 2021, https://worldpopulationreview.com/countries/south-africa-population; last accessed July 28, 2021.

Worldometer: South Africa, https://www.worldometers.info/coronavirus/country/south-africa/; last accessed July 28, 2021.

Worldometer: Homepage, https://www.worldometers.info/coronavirus/; last accessed July 1, 2021.

Wulana / Boxer Superstores (Pty) Ltd 1 BALR 109 (CCMA), 2021.

Sabine N. Meyer

Covid-19 as a Magnifying Glass: Native America between Vulnerability and (Self-)Empowerment

Introduction

Covid-19 has taken a tremendous toll in Indian country and led to an enormous amount of physical and psychological suffering. As various recent analyses have demonstrated, Native communities have been affected disproportionately by the pandemic. Studies reveal that incidence rates among Indigenous persons are 3.5 higher than those of non-Hispanic/Latinx whites. And a recent report from APM Research Lab states that one in 475 American Indians and Alaska Native populations has died from Covid-19, compared to one in 825 for white Americans and one in 645 for Black Americans. Disproportionate mortality rates are particularly shocking in certain regions such as New Mexico where Native Americans account for 44 % of Covid-19 deaths despite merely constituting 11 % of the state's population. Native communities in Arizona have witnessed nearly 22 % of Covid-19 deaths even though they only make up 2 % of that state's population. And all these numbers, analysts suggest, are underestimates due to a lack of reliable and accurate Covid-19 data.[1] The most vulnerable group within Native communities has been the elder members, whose loss has caused not only great emotional pain but also immense anxieties concerning the future of Indigenous cultures and languages. Tribal elders are keepers of Indigenous languages, knowledge and history, which are passed down orally from generation to generation. As Monica Harvey (Navajo) has put it: »When you lose an elder, you lose a part of yourself. You lose a connection to history, our stories, our culture, our traditions.«[2]

Harvey's words, along with statistics such as the ones above, are good starting points for an article that endeavors to offer first reflections on the impact of Covid-19 on Native America, with a particular focus on the realms of law, politics, and culture. As I will show, the pandemic has functioned like a magnifying glass:

---

[1] Cf. Yellow Horse/Huyser: Indigenous Data Sovereignty and COVID-19 Data Issues for American Indian and Alaska Native Tribes and Populations; cf. O'Keefe/Walls: Indigenous Communities Demonstrate Innovation and Strength Despite Unequal Losses during COVID-19; Howard-Bobiwash/Joe/Lobo: Concrete Lessons, p. 3.
[2] Voice of America News: Native American Tribes Try to Protect Elders.

it has illuminated the legacy and enduring power of settler colonial policies and laws to create landscapes of disadvantage and discrimination and states of vulnerability. By throwing into relief deficient, unjust, and discriminatory structures, the pandemic has highlighted the necessity and inevitability of legal-political change: the implementation of robust structures of equality and Native self-determination and the consequent acknowledgment of Native sovereignty by federal and state governments. As their fight against the containment of Covid-19 has once again demonstrated, Native communities have the capacity and power to lead and manage their own affairs and to mobilize their members through arts, storytelling, and other Indigenous cultural practices. The comparative analysis of Native practices of resistance to Covid-19 in the realms of law, politics, and culture unearths the inextricable and efficient intertwinement of politics and aesthetics and the power of community in Native America.

1. Federal Indian Law and Its Creation of Landscapes of Neglect and Vulnerability

I would like to start my discussion of federal Indian law and its creation of landscapes of neglect and vulnerability in Native America with a work of art by J. NiCole Hatfield (Comanche and Kiowa) (fig. 1). Hatfield was asked to produce artwork in response to the pandemic by Illumi*Native*, a Native-founded and -led organizational network that seeks to work for the greater visibility of Native Americans by bringing together »Native storytellers, artists, youth, organizers, tribal and grassroots leaders as well as non-Native partners in entertainment, media and social justice.«[3] The group of works Hatfield created ended up playing a central role in the network's campaign Warrior Up, through which Illumi*Native* sought to mobilize Native peoples and artists to publicly stand up and speak out in the fight against Covid-19.[4] While being offered to activists for download and sharing, Hatfield's piece below was also chosen for the cover of a recently published report, *The Impact of COVID-19 on Indigenous People*, which was presented by Illumi*Native* and other Native organizations.[5]

Hatfield's artwork is suggestive of the complex ways in which law, culture, and community have interacted in precipitating as well as handling the Covid-19 crisis. At the center of the piece, we see two Native women with masks and gloves, who hug each other in tight embrace. Notably, these two women are drawn on the page

---

[3] Illumi*Native*: Homepage.
[4] Cf. Illumi*Native*: Warrior Up.
[5] Unbound Philanthropy: The Impact of COVID-19 on Indigenous People.

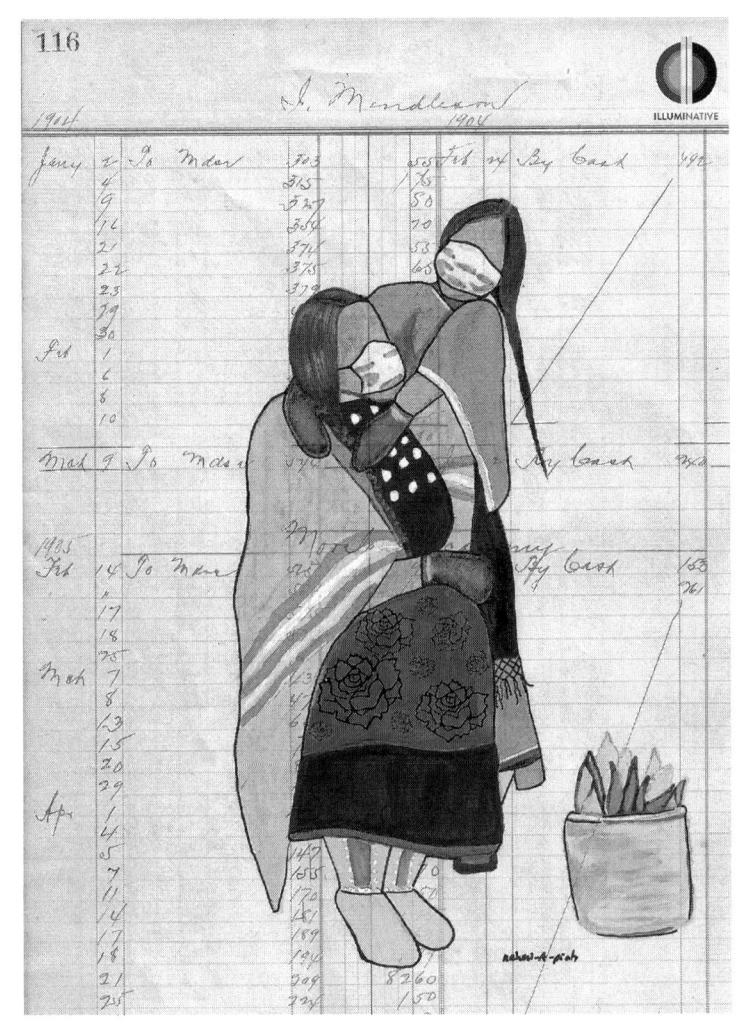

Fig. 1: J. NiCole Hatfield, *Keep Them Safe*, Ledger Art, 2020.
(Original color artwork reproduced in black and white for publication)

of a historical ledger dating back to the year 1904, with the original handwriting shining through the bright colors of their clothes. In the history of settler colonization, ledger books were used by government agents to make Native lands and lives legible and quantifiable within settler colonial taxonomies and regimes of knowledge. The data collected in these books provided the statistical foundation on the basis of which federal Indian laws and policies such as Removal, Assimilation and Allotment, or Termination were designed. They also served to document how laws and policies were put into action, that is, how *thoroughly* officials and settlers on the ground realized the federal government's objectives to expel and dispossess Native individuals and communities, to assimilate them to settler colonial ways of living – in short, to extend its administrative and regulatory control over Native bodies, lands, and lives. Hence, rather than being mere historical documents, many of these ledgers have, until the present day, maintained their efficacy – they are still consulted, often by Native Americans themselves, to determine Native forms of belonging in the contexts of struggles over tribal citizenship or land rights.[6]

Drawing two Native women in their attempt to protect themselves and each other against Covid-19 on the page of a historical government ledger containing federal administrative data, Hatfield encourages us to view the pandemic through the lens of history – to analyze it in light of settler colonial bureaucracy, laws, and policies. Native lives have unfolded themselves against the backdrop of a settler colonial legal-political order, which has determined Native subjectivities, forms of social organization, governance, and health. Hatfield's artwork encourages viewers to reflect on the relation between the drastic impact of Covid-19 on Native American communities and past and present workings of the settler state. These workings may be illustrated best by focusing on federal Indian law.[7] Federal Indian law, as Native and non-Native scholars, activists, and politicians have pointed out, has been responsible for creating the inequitable structures and disadvantages that have made Native Americans one of the populations most vulnerable to Covid-19. Through federal laws and policies, Native Americans were decimated, deprived of their tangible and intangible property, separated from their kith and kin; such laws and policies also sought to suppress Native culture. The structural and direct violence emanating from these laws and policies has exerted a tremendous psychological toll on Native individuals and communities and has had a devastating impact on their forms of social organization, governance, and landholdings. And even in the era of so-called Indian Self-Determination, which was inaugurated in the 1970s, the federal government has greatly neglected its special trust relation-

---

[6] The Cherokee Nation, for instance, determines tribal citizenship on the basis of the Final Rolls that were compiled by the Dawes Commission in the context of allotment (cf. Ray: A Race or a Nation?). Much more could be said about these ledgers and the tradition of using these ledgers by Native Americans. For recent scholarship on Native ledger art as a practice of resistance; see Fuller: Critical Hermeneutics and the Counter Narrative of Ledger Art; see also Pearce, Richard: Women and Ledger Art: Four Contemporary Native American Artists.

[7] Federal Indian law is the body of law developed to govern and define the legal relationships between Native tribes, federal and state governments with respect to treaty rights, issues of real property, jurisdiction, administrative law, criminal law, issues of economic development, health care, etc. The body of laws that constitute the field of federal Indian law encompasses select provisions of the U.S. Constitution, treaties between the United States and Native nations, Congressional statutes, executive orders, and a great number of court decisions reaching back to the early 19th century; see also Duthu: Federal Indian Law; Fletcher: Federal Indian Law; and Hoss/Tanana: Upholding Sovereignty and Promoting Tribal Public Health Capacity during the COVID-19 Pandemic.

ship with the Native nations. Anchored in the U.S. Constitution and specified by numerous treaties between the federal government and Native nations, Supreme Court decisions, regulations, laws, and executive orders, this trust relationship obligates the federal government to advance tribal self-government, to provide services and support to Native Americans, to promote the welfare of Native American communities, and to protect their lands and resources. It is Congress's duty to fund this special trust relationship appropriately via legislation.[8] As Native Americans have repeatedly pointed out and as the U.S. Commission of Civil Rights has highlighted in its 2018 briefing report *Broken Promises*, the U.S. government has reneged on its trust obligations, having not »provid[ed] adequate assistance to support the interconnected needs of Native Americans such as local infrastructure, self-governance, housing, education, health, and economic development.«[9] The end result of such failure is »that Native Americans face significant inequities among major criminal and public safety, health, education, housing, and economic measures compared to the rest of the nation and non-Native people.«[10] In the area of health, for example, the government-funded Indian Health Service (IHS) spent $3,332 per person in 2017 compared to $9,207 per person in federal health care nationwide. Native lives and communities have been systematically »degradated,« to use the Commission's own words.[11]

As in other pandemics in the past,[12] Covid-19 has thrown into stark relief the past and present failure of the United States to live up to its trust obligation. Tribal health infrastructure is highly deficient, homes are overcrowded, broadband is missing, and Native communities have poor access to transportation, electricity, and water, and hence are easy prey to the virus.[13] In a hearing before the Committee on Indian Affairs United States Senate on February 24, 2021, representatives of Native communities and organizations from across the country drew a direct link between the utter vulnerability of Indian country to Covid-19 and the »centuries of colonial violence and neglect.«[14] »Covid-19,« it is said in the statement by the United South and Eastern Tribes Sovereignty and Protection Fund (USET SPF), »is exposing the ever-widening gap between the trust obligation owed to Tribal Nations and the execution of that obligation [...]. The nation and world are witnessing the deadly consequences of [federal] neglect, as Covid-19 spreads

---

[8] Cf. U.S. Commission on Civil Rights: Broken Promises.
[9] Ibid.
[10] Ibid.
[11] Ibid., pp. 66–67, 203.
[12] See Doshi et al.: The COVID-19 Response in Indian Country, for further examples such as the 1918 flu and the H1N1 virus, which hit Indian country hardest.
[13] Ibid., para. 43; Howard-Bobiwash / Joe / Lobo: Concrete Lessons, p. 7.
[14] Ibid., para. 1; see the speeches by Fawn Sharp, President of the National Congress of American Indians and the statement of the United South and Eastern Tribes Sovereignty and Protection Fund, in: United States Congress: A Call to Action, pp. 4, 67.

through Tribal communities [...].«¹⁵ »The health of American Indians and Alaska Natives,« Hoss and Tanana argue in a similar vein, »is intrinsically tied to federal law and reliant upon the federal government fulfilling its treaty obligations and trust responsibilities.«¹⁶

The inextricable connection between the vulnerability of Native American communities, the workings of federal Indian law, and the U.S. government's neglect of trust responsibilities became blatantly obvious in the first year of the pandemic, particularly in three areas of federal-tribal interaction: conflicts over the degree of Native sovereignty in the context of tribal efforts to contain Covid-19, the federal government's setting up of the Coronavirus Relief Fund, and the issue of data collection for governmental purposes.

After the outbreak of the pandemic tribal governments were quick to implement measures against the further spread of the virus. Some of these measures, in particular the enforcement of travel restrictions, curfews, and the setting up of checkpoints on roads entering reservations, evoked resistance from non-Natives and their political representatives, who were skeptical of the right of tribes to exert regulatory power over nonmembers. Their skepticism has been fed by countless federal court rulings over the years that express doubts of such tribal authority over nonmembers or restrict such authority to situations in which the conduct of the nonmember »threatens or has some direct effect on the political integrity, the economic security, or the health or welfare of the tribe«¹⁷ – a formulation leaving it to the courts to decide whose lives matter most. In response to the checkpoints put up it by Cheyenne River Sioux and Oglala Sioux in April 2020, South Dakota Governor Kristi Noem threatened them with litigation and asked the White House and the Department of the Interior to end »these unlawful tribal checkpoints/blockades« on state and federal highways. The Bureau of Indian Affairs then reprimanded the Cheyenne River Sioux for not having consulted with the state and »threaten[ed] the Tribe's Public Law 93-638 law enforcement contract through an unlawful emergency reassumption – imperiling Tribal public safety as well as public health,« as tribal leaders point out in the lawsuit they then filed in June 2020. The plaintiffs also claim that the White House Chief of Staff threatened the security of the federal government's relief fund for the tribe if it was used for such containment measures.¹⁸ The actions of Noem and the Trump adminis-

---

15 United States Congress: A Call to Action, pp. 67, 72.
16 Ibid., p. 78.
17 Cf. *Montana vs. United States* (1981), qtd. in Fletcher: Indian Lives Matter, p. 41; for further information and examples of court rulings on the issue of tribal civil jurisdiction over nonmembers, see Fletcher: Tribal Civil, Criminal, and Regulatory Jurisdiction.
18 Cf. United States District Court for the District of Columbia: *Cheyenne River Sioux Tribe v. Donald J. Trump et al.*; United States Congress: A Call to Action, p. 69; for other examples of states undermining Native efforts at containing COVID-19, see Doshi et al.: The COVID-19 Response in Indian Country, para. 16.

tration, as the complaint argues, did not only undermine Native sovereignty and jurisdiction over tribal lands, but also thwarted tribal efforts to contain the pandemic. In the eyes of federal and state governments, Native lives seem to matter less than those of non-Natives.

The power of federal Indian law to determine Native health and degrees of vulnerability became also visible in the federal government's handling of Corona-relief funds. Of all the Covid-19 bills passed by Congress in the first year of the pandemic, the Coronavirus Aid, Relief, and Economic Security Act (CARES Act), which was signed into law by President Trump on March 27, 2020, was the most significant one. While tribal governments were relieved to receive funds at all, the CARES Act only allocated 5 percent of the $2.2 trillion in aid to them. Through the Coronavirus Relief Fund that the act established, tribal governments were supposed to receive $8 billion in direct assistance. In addition, the IHS received $1.032 billion to fund IHS, Tribal, and Urban Indian Organization programs.[19] Besides pointing out the insufficiency of the funding,[20] Native leaders and nonpartisan policy institutes criticized the government's management of the allocated funds. Neither did the Treasury Department disburse any money until well after the deadline determined by Congress. Nor did it allocate the full amount of funds (instead only $4.8 billion). »Data leaks, legal challenges, and inexcusable delays have marred the entire process, forcing tribes to spend money that they don't have to run basic services,« a report of the Center for American Progress summarizes federal government's distribution of CARES Act funds.[21] Tribal leaders also complained that Native communities were not included in the national vaccine strategy, which resulted in a lack of test kits, protective and medical equipment, and vaccines. In addition, access of tribal governments and the IHS to the Strategic National Stockpile, a stockpile of vaccines, medicines, and medical equipment reserved for public health emergencies, was restricted and not guaranteed.[22] Even worse, Native nations had to choose whether to receive vaccines from the IHS or the state; *wrong* decisions could have dramatic consequences.[23] Similar to historical examples of pandemic relief legislation, such as the Indian Vaccination Act of 1832,[24] the CARES Act was set up without proper input from and consultation with Native Americans. Federal legislation, critics of the act argued, should be

---

[19] Cf. United States Congress: A Call to Action, p. 4; Hoss/Tanana: Upholding Sovereignty and Promoting Tribal Public Health Capacity during the COVID-19 Pandemic.

[20] The representatives of the NCAI demanded $15 billion for tribal health and $20 billion in direct aid to tribal governments, cf. United States Congress: A Call to Action, p. 4.

[21] Doshi et al.: The COVID-19 Response in Indian Country, para. 6.

[22] Hoss: COVID-19 and Tribes: The Structural Violence of Federal Indian Law, para. 6.

[23] Cf. United States Congress: A Call to Action, p. 6; Doshi et al.: The COVID-19 Response in Indian Country, para. 10.

[24] For more information on the history of the Indian Vaccination Act, see Pearson: Lewis Cass and the Politics of Disease.

grounded in Native sovereignty and allow tribal governments more self-determination in how to use funding.²⁵ And if we believe the transcript of the aforementioned trial, then the Corona-relief funds of the CARES Act were also used, at least in some occasions, to whip tribal governments into compliance with federal ideas about the extent of Native sovereignty. While the act was presented by government officials as a noble gesture, as a sign of responsibility, generosity, and care on the part of the federal government, such praises must not hide the fact that the act was also a demonstration of federal power over Native nations that – as the checkpoint episode suggests – not rarely, and perhaps not accidentally, brought with it the infringement of Native sovereignty and self-determination.

Hatfield's Covid-19 artwork (cf. fig. 1) also draws our attention to the historical significance of numbers for the incorporation of Native lands and lives into settler colonial bureaucratic regimes and the conception of settler colonial law and policy, in particular during pandemic times. By placing the two Native women on settler colonial data and administrative information, which shine through their clothes, Hatfield alludes to the complex relationship between the (in)visibility of Native lives and state systems of bureaucratic representation. By having their lives translated into numbers and recorded, Native Americans become visible and are rendered intelligible to the state and its representatives and may reap the beneficial aspects of the trust relationship with the government. This visibility, however, comes at a price. The sober numerical representations and well-ordered tables on the ledger page stand in stark contrast to the Native women's multi-patterned and -colored clothes and their uncontainable emotions. And the amount of »baskets,«²⁶ counted to account for economic output and possibilities of trade, does in no way capture the meaning of corn for the lives of the two women. Being represented via the state's bureaucratic and administrative registers entails the risk of being made legible on the state's own terms that, more often than not, contradict Indigenous self-perceptions and self-understandings. By integrating Native lives into Western regimes of bureaucracy and administration, the state exerts its sovereign power over them; it defines what it means to be *Indian*.

In the legal-political debates about the federal government's response to Covid-19 in Indian country, its use of bureaucratic registers and data has been a highly controversial issue. »Government actions,« as Fawn Sharp has argued before the Committee on Indian Affairs United States Senate, »are often data-driven.«²⁷ When determining the distribution of the Coronavirus Relief Fund, the Department of the Treasury chose to rely on census-based data rather than on the enrollment data provided by tribal governments, even though it is common

---

²⁵ Cf. Doshi et al.: The COVID-19 Response in Indian Country, para. 7.
²⁶ I read »By bask« as an abbreviation of »by basket«.
²⁷ United States Congress: A Call to Action, p. 6.

knowledge that Native Americans have historically been the most undercounted group on the U.S. census.[28] As a consequence, several tribes barely received any funding or received far less funding than they were eligible for according to their own tribal enrollment numbers.[29] The Center for American Progress has even argued that state and federal governments »deliberately exclu[ded]« Native Americans from their collection of demographic data relating to Covid-19. In May 2020, nearly half of the states that had published racial demographic data relating to Covid-19 infections did not identify American Indians and Alaska Natives as a distinct group, instead grouping them under the category of »Other.«[30] The Centers for Disease Control and Prevention (CDC), the major player in the national fight against Covid-19, refused to give out Covid-19 related data to tribal epidemiologists but readily made this data available to state agencies.[31] Tribal leaders also complained of »data leaks,« that is, »the unauthorized public release of tribal data during the Coronavirus Relief Fund« and of government agencies transferring tribal datasets amongst each other, using tribal data out of the context they were designed for and without tribal consent.[32] State and federal governments' collection and use of data has distorted and downplayed the severity of the Covid-19 crisis in Indian country and occluded existing health disparities and inequalities. It has negatively impacted U.S. policymaking and government action, as well as tribal crisis management. Lack of health data or flawed datasets have made it difficult for state, federal, and tribal governments, as well as Native organizations, to trace and interpret the development of the pandemic in Indian country and to come up with appropriate policies and actions.[33] Lacking or flawed data have thus directly impacted Native lives: the failure of the federal and state governments to produce reliable data reflecting outbreak, development, and the impact of Covid-19 on Native communities and individuals has rendered them, to a great extent, invisible in public health discourse. It has greatly downplayed Native rates of infection and deaths and left unseen the extent to which Native vulnerability to Covid-19 is inextricably tied to the inequities and disadvantages that federal Indian law and policies have produced over the past centuries. The federal government's refusal to respect — what has become known in scholarly jargon as — »Native data sovereignty,«[34] that is, its refusal to work with data collected and certified by the tribes themselves, has led to severe underfunding of tribal

---

[28] Cf. Kesslen: Native Americans, the Census' Most Undercounted Racial Group, Fight for an Accurate 2020 Tally.
[29] Cf. Doshi et al.: The COVID-19 Response in Indian Country, para. 4.
[30] Ibid., para. 4.
[31] Cf. Yellow Horse/Huyser: Indigenous Data Sovereignty and COVID-19.
[32] United States Congress: A Call to Action, p. 12.
[33] Cf. Hoss: COVID-19 and Tribes: The Structural Violence of Federal Indian Law, para. 8.
[34] Cf. Kukutai/Taylor: Indigenous Data Sovereignty: Native data sovereignty is here defined as »the inherent authority of Tribal Nations to govern data about their peoples, lands, and resources.«

governments during the pandemic and has left Native communities ill-equipped to contain the pandemic and to shoulder the breakdown of their economies.[35]

If federal agencies did produce Covid-19 related datasets of Native Americans, these datasets often delivered distorted images of Native American personal and communal efforts to counter the pandemic. Thus, the reports on vaccine series completion rates among demographic groups that the CDC regularly issues during the pandemic stated in March 2021: »The lowest series completion rate (83.7 %) and the highest prevalence of missing the second dose (5.1 %) was among AI/AN persons.«[36] Reported without further comment and without any contextualization, this data suggests the availability of vaccines for Native Americans, on the one hand, and the lack of capability/responsibility among those receiving them, on the other. Read in light of the discourse of »vaccine hesitancy« that has been prominent in American political discourse[37] as well as the media, emphasizing that Native Americans are more hesitant to get vaccinated than the rest of the population, such data creates images of Native Americans as adverse to modern science, ignorant, backward-oriented, and unable to manage their own affairs, including their health.[38] The CDC's numbers also cover up Native Americans' often limited access to vaccines and the mismanagement of vaccination campaigns by the federal government. As late as April 2021, Congressmen Mike Garcia and Raul Ruiz addressed in Congress the lack of »Covid-19 vaccination equity,« stressing that vaccine access is a far greater problem than vaccine hesitancy. »Communities of color,« Ruiz emphasized, »are receiving vaccines at a lower rate than their White counterparts.«[39] Native-led surveys have highlighted other structural barriers to access vaccines, such as distance to clinics and vaccine cost.[40] Numbers signifying *vaccine incapacity*, together with the discourse of *vaccine hesitancy*, shift the blame for the severity of Covid-19 in tribal communities to the victims themselves and render invisible the enormous efforts and contributions of Native governments and organizations in the vaccine rollout as well as the willingness of individual Native Americans to get vaccinated in order to protect their commu-

---

[35] Cf. Yellow Horse/Huyser: Indigenous Data Sovereignty and COVID-19; United States Congress: A Call to Action, p. 11.

[36] Kriss et al.: COVID-19 Vaccine Second-Dose Completion and Interval between First and Second Doses among Vaccinated Persons, p. 389.

[37] See the question concerning »vaccine hesitancy« among Native communities asked by the Committee Chairman in the hearing of tribal leaders in February 2021, in: United States Congress: A Call to Action, p. 44.

[38] Cf. Coburn: Contrary to Sensational Reporting, Indigenous People Aren't Scared of a COVID-19 Vaccine.

[39] United States Congress: Encouraging Cosponsorship of Tri-Caucus COVID-19 Vaccination Equity; United States Congress: Memorializing the Intent of the Tribal Portion of the Coronavirus Relief Fund in the Coronavirus Aid, Relief, and Economic Security Act.

[40] Cf. Urban Indian Health Institute: Strengthening Vaccine Efforts in Indian Country, p. 7.

nities.[41] The settler state's production and distribution of Native-related Covid-19 datasets thus comes at a high price in that it presents Native communities as desperately in need of federal intervention. As Hatfield suggests in her artwork and as the Covid-19 pandemic demonstrates, being represented via the state's bureaucratic and administrative registers means being represented on the state's own terms. From the point of view of the Indigenous who are represented, state representations are, more often than not, misrepresentations, reinforcing existing hierarchies and power structures.

2. Native Leadership, Managerial Capacity, and Self-Determination during the Pandemic

I would like to begin the second part of my article with a piece of Native art that was also produced for the Warrior Up campaign by Illumi*Native*. In his work of street art, Steven Paul Judd (Kiowa-Choctaw) returns to history, too. While Hatfield reminds her viewers that Native suffering during the pandemic can only be understood against the backdrop of a long history of colonization and oppression, Judd's art focuses on Native acts of survival and resistance in past health crises, such as the smallpox pandemic in the 1830s, with the aim to instill hope that tribal communities will once again persist by fighting Covid-19 with their own Indigenous weapons, which are embodied by the arrows shot by a traditionally clothed warrior.

As shown above, the Covid-19 pandemic has thrown into relief existing landscapes of vulnerability in Indian country that have resulted both from a long history of settler colonial violence and oppression and from ongoing federal mismanagement and neglect. Yet at the same time, the pandemic has enabled the world to see tribal governments' and organizations' effective crisis management and hence Native capacity for leadership, resistance, and survival. Native suffering and tribal measures taken against the spread of the virus have led to heightened coverage by major media outlets and have sparked public interest in the issue of tribal sovereignty. The pandemic and its representation in the media have thus opened up a discursive space Native leaders have been using effectively to demand the expansion of tribal self-governance and – what has been called – the overhauling of the trust relationship. Finally, the pandemic has provided fertile ground for Native digital activism. What is most noteworthy about the online campaigns against Covid-19 is their moving far beyond the medical and educational spheres. Native individuals, networks, community organizations, and activist groups have turned

---

[41] See, for instance, the results of the survey conducted by the Urban Indian Health Institute: Strengthening Vaccine Efforts in Indian Country.

Fig. 2: Steven P. Judd, Street Art, 2020.
(Original color artwork reproduced in black and white for publication)

to Indigenous artwork, comedy, and storytelling to empower Native Americans across the United States.

Native efforts of curbing the spread of the virus have included the implementation of laws and policies as well as public health measures by tribal governments, such as incident command systems, call centers, stay-at-home orders, road blockades, and curfews.[42] In addition, tribal health organizations, community centers,

---

[42] For more examples of the COVID-19 management of tribal nations, see Native Governance Center: How Does Tribal Sovereignty Operate during COVID-19?

and nonprofits have been playing a critical role in stopping the spread of the virus by providing information, distributing educational materials, and hosting informational events.[43] Native political representatives and organizations have also worked hard to replace the discourse of Native vaccine hesitancy by one of Native vaccine acceptance. In the hearing before the Committee on Indian Affairs United States Senate, Native leaders emphasized the high vaccination rates among their constituents. In Alaska, for instance, Julie Kitka from the Alaska Federation of Natives argued, the »tribal health system leads the nation in vaccination rates.«[44] In January 2021, the Urban Indian Health Institute (UIHI), one of twelve Tribal Epidemiology Centers in the United States serving urban Indigenous health programs nationwide, presented the results of a survey titled »Strengthening Vaccine Efforts in Indian Country,« which it had conducted in December 2020. While the UIHI grants that »historic distrust, rooted in the legacy of colonialism, genocide, and medical experimentation, *may* contribute to vaccine hesitancy,« its survey results emphasize »Covid-19 vaccine acceptance.«[45] UIHI emphasizes that seventy-five percent of all Native survey participants positioned themselves in favor of getting vaccinated out of responsibility for their community and due to their wish to preserve Native culture:

»Participants shared that vaccination was a way to protect Native communities and preserve cultural ways. Many shared that their decision to be vaccinated stemmed from a sense of duty, respect, and love for community. Some even thought of vaccination as a form of resistance to longstanding colonial and racist violence. Many participants felt or understood others' hesitancy towards getting the vaccine. Despite systemic injustice and skepticism of vaccine development, their love for Native people and wish to prevent unnecessary deaths and illness ultimately outweighed potential risks from the vaccine.«[46]

Participants who declared unwilling to receive the vaccine, the survey points out, expressed their great trust in tribal clinics and doctors. Thus, they were not against vaccination per se but rather skeptical of the vaccine efforts of federal government organizations, such as the CDC, Food and Drug Administration, and the National Institutes of Health.[47] What is most noteworthy about this study, however, is its employment of an »Indigenous research methodology,« which combines qualitative data analysis with Native »stories of strength and resilience.«[48] By creating

---

[43] As one of many examples, see the activities of the National Council of Urban Indian Health as described on their website; National Council of Urban Indian Health: Coronavirus Resource Center.
[44] United States Congress: A Call to Action, p. 42.
[45] Urban Indian Health Institute: Strengthening Vaccine Efforts in Indian Country, p. 7; italics by the author.
[46] Ibid., p. 34.
[47] Cf. ibid., pp. 2, 22–24.
[48] Ibid., p. 34.

a visual contrast between the abstract, sober numbers on the ledger page and the Native women's colorful clothes and their emotional embrace, Hatfield's artwork (fig. 1) points viewers' attention to the way in which data alone is unable to create an understanding of the actual suffering of Native people and their lived experiences during the pandemic. By embedding its datasets in personal stories, UIHI contributes to such understanding. One survey respondent, for instance, describes their attitude toward the vaccine as follows:

»It [the vaccine] is the only real precautionary and preventative step the US Federal government is providing the people. Although the US government should have and could have done so much more for all people living here, if we turn down the vaccine, we not only risk our lives and the lives of others [...] we undermine all the struggles our tribes have gone through to keep our people safe. Even when the US government has directly worked against our tribal checkpoints and safety efforts. To not get vaccinated, is to say the US government's failure to protect the people is right, and our tribal efforts, wisdom, and courage is wrong.«[49]

This response, as well as many others, demonstrates that being vaccinated means much more to a great number of Native Americans than protecting one's own or one's family's health or being able to return to one's professional or social lives. Getting the vaccine serves to protect entire communities: their members, culture, language. It is seen as an act of resistance against past and ongoing acts of colonization and oppression and as the only way to make possible Indigenous futures.[50] From the respondent's viewpoint, to refuse the vaccine is a slap in the face of hundreds of years of Native resistance to settler colonial violence and oppression and a nod to past and ongoing federal Indian laws and policies. By referencing the smallpox (fig. 2), Judd's art similarly conceptualizes vaccination as an act of survival and resistance: for the smallpox could only be uprooted by Native Americans' acceptance of the government-administered vaccines. Overall, Native-led vaccine campaigns, such as that by UIHI, have supported the vaccine effort in Native communities and have demonstrated that getting vaccinated is, for many Native Americans, both medical and political praxis. Native vaccine rollout campaigns have not only worked against the further spread of Covid-19 but also against allegations of Native vaccine hesitancy. They have sought to replace assumptions of backwardness, irresponsibility, and ignorance by evidence of tribal leadership, self-governance, and sovereignty.[51]

The media's frequent reports about pandemic exercises of tribal sovereignty, in combination with those about the federal government's continuous infringement

---

[49] Ibid., p. 37.

[50] Not incidentally, UIHI's Vaccination survey is part of a greater survey called Indigenous Futures.

[51] See also Jones: COVID-19 Vaccine Rollout among Indigenous Communities Seen as a Model for Others.

of rights of Native self-governance and its neglect of the trust relationship, have created a discursive space for representatives of Native nations and organizations to voice their demands for greater federal responsibility, the recognition of tribal sovereignty, and the expansion of tribal self-governance. For instance, in its statement prepared for the hearing before the Committee in Indian Affairs United States Senate in February 2021, the USET SPF stated:

»The time is long overdue for a comprehensive overhaul of the trust relationship and obligations, one that results in the United States finally keeping the promises made to us as sovereign nations in accordance with our special and unique relationship. This change is urgently needed, as the global pandemic exposes for the whole word to see the extent to which generations of federal neglect and inaction have created the unjust and untenable circumstances facing Tribal Nations in the fight against COVID-19 [...]. Tribal Nations are political, sovereign entities whose status stems from the inherent sovereignty we have as self-governing peoples, which pre-dates the founding of the Republic. The Constitution, treaties, statutes, Executive Orders, and judicial decisions all recognize that the federal government has a fundamental trust relationship to Tribal Nations, including the obligation uphold [sic] the right to self-government. Our federal partners must fully recognize the inherent right of Tribal Nations to fully engage in self-governance, so we may exercise full decisionmaking [sic] in the management of our own affairs and governmental services, including jurisdiction over our lands and people. However, the full extent of our inherent sovereignty continues to go unacknowledged and, in some cases, is actively restricted by other units of government, including the federal, as well as state and local governments.«[52]

This statement once again demonstrates that the Covid-19 pandemic has worked like a magnifying glass, having made visible health disparities, federal neglect, and the ongoing curtailment of Native sovereignty by federal, state, and local governments. USET SPF takes Covid-19 as an opportunity to lay out broad areas of governmental reform: first, the federal government should »provide full and guaranteed federal funding to Tribal Nations in fulfillment of the trust obligation« and implement – what USET SPF calls – a »Marshall Plan for Indian Country« through which tribal infrastructure is rebuilt and restored. Because federal funding has resulted from »clear legal and historic obligations,« the trust obligation »exists in perpetuity.« Hence, USET SPDF emphasizes, federal funding cannot and must not be viewed as a grant and tribal governments not as grantees, who need to prove that federal investment is justified. Second, the move away from government paternalism can only succeed through changes in federal Indian law itself, through the passage of laws that remove the »limiting language« of current law and comprehensively expand tribal self-government. Tribal self-governance needs to be expanded »to all federal programs where Tribal Nations are eligible.« Third, USET SPF speaks out in favor of a »Tribal Nation-defined consultation

---

[52] United States Congress: A Call to Action, p. 68.

model with dual consent as the basis for strong and respectful diplomatic relations between two equally sovereign nations.« And the requirement of such consultation must be implemented via statute and not via executive order, as it has so far been practiced.[53] USET SPF and other critics of federal Indian law argue that such changes in federal Indian law and policy would also have a positive effect on the evolution of the Covid-19 pandemic in Indian country. They would enable Native nations to determine themselves how to use Covid-19 relief funding – an approach that also caters to the diversity of Indian country.[54] They would encourage federal, state, and local governments to respect Native data sovereignty. Such data sovereignty would entail the use of tribal enrollment data for distributing (relief) funding; the production of datasets that highlight the effect of the pandemic on Native communities; and the empowerment of Native communities to control the use and spread of their own data.[55] Finally, improved forms of consultation, in particular, would guarantee tribal involvement in the conceptualization of laws and programs affecting Native communities. This would not only give them a meaningful voice in their own governance but it would also heighten the quality and efficiency of these programs. USET SPF even resorts to international law, to the language of Indigenous rights, to strengthen its demands for sovereign equality and tribal consent to government actions: »In the long term, we must return to the achievement of Tribal Nation consent for federal action as a recognition of sovereign equality and as set out by the principles of the United Nations Declaration on the Rights of Indigenous Peoples.«[56] On July 20, 2020, UN Special Rapporteur on the Rights of the Indigenous Peoples, José Francisco Calí Tzay, had already explained to the international community what the standards and principles of the United Nations Declaration on the Rights of Indigenous Peoples meant during the Covid-19 crisis:

»The essential element for an efficient State response to the pandemic for indigenous peoples is to respect the autonomy of indigenous peoples to manage the situation locally while providing them with the information and the financial and material support they identify as necessary. Coordination between indigenous and non-indigenous authorities as equals is essential to the overall effort to respond to the pandemic. Unfortunately, indigenous peoples appear to have been largely left out of the COVID response. While the level of preparedness for the pandemic was low around the globe, indigenous peoples were even less likely

---

[53] United States Congress: A Call to Action, pp. 71 f.

[54] Cf. ibid., pp. 68–71.

[55] Cf. Doshi et al.: The COVID-19 Response in Indian Country, para. 4, 5; cf. Yellow Horse/Huyser: Indigenous Data Sovereignty and COVID-19 Data Issues for American Indian and Alaska Native Tribes and Populations.

[56] United States Congress: A Call to Action, p. 71; during the Obama presidency the United States eventually signed the Declaration. Even though it is not a legally binding document, this signature expresses a commitment to its principles and standards for the treatment of Indigenous peoples.

to be included in any form of national pandemic contingency plan. Nationwide measures to stop the pandemic were applied to indigenous territories without their free, prior and informed consent and did not take into account the systemic barriers faced by recipients.«[57]

It cannot be assessed to what degree Tzay's appeal has strengthened Native American demands for greater participation, inclusion, and self-determination during the pandemic. Neither can it be gauged to what degree the changes in federal Indian law and policy that we have witnessed since the beginning of the year 2021 are a result of the Covid-19-magnifying glass and the ensuing Native domestic interventions or of the Biden administration taking up work. What can be assessed with certainty, however, is that the American Rescue Plan, the $1.9 trillion economic stimulus bill passed by Congress and signed into law by President Joe Biden on March 11, 2021, is »a momentous step forward,« to cite Nick Tilson, Oglala Lakota.[58] For this Rescue Plan differs from the Coronavirus Relief Fund in various ways that can, within the scope of this article, only be sketched out: Its investment of $31.2 billion into tribal communities represents »the single largest investment in the tribal nations in U.S. history.« Such investment can be viewed as — what Senate Indian Affairs Chairman Brian Schatz has called — »a down payment on the federal government's trust responsibility to Native communities [that] will empower American Indians, Alaska Natives, and Native Hawaiians to tackle COVID-19's impacts on their communities.«[59] Of the overall sum, $20 billion is, at the moment of this writing, being distributed to tribal governments to fight the pandemic, with the allocations being, at least in part, based on tribal enrollment data.[60] Moreover, there will be funding, for instance, for Native health systems, including money for vaccines, testing, tracing; for education and housing programs; Native language preservation; and tribal community efforts to combat domestic violence.[61] While Native representatives are, of course, excited about »the comprehensive nature of federal funds« allocated through the Rescue Plan, they endow the act with a meaning transcending the monetary realm: pieces of legislation such as this, they emphasize, have the potential to inaugurate a new era in the relationship between tribal communities and the federal government. Not only does the federal government, for the first time in the pandemic, fulfill its trust responsibility but it also treats Native nations as sovereign entities and equal partners.[62] This is why Tilsen, full of optimism and hope, sees this financial in-

---

[57] Tzay: Report of the Special Rapporteur on the Rights of Indigenous Peoples, pp. 13 f.

[58] Sy / Kuhn: Why Native Americans Are Excited about the American Rescue Plan, and their Future.

[59] For this and further information of the allocation methods used by the federal government, see Indianz: American Rescue Plan Act.

[60] Cf. ibid.

[61] Cf. American Indian Policy Institute: An Overview of the American Rescue Plan for Indian Country.

[62] Trahant: $31 Billion Represents ›a Massive Opportunity.‹

vestment as »begin[ning] to open a conversation about entering into a brand-new policy era« – an era he tentatively calls »an era of consent.«[63]

3. (Self-)Empowerment as a Path Forward

In the course of the Covid-19 pandemic, the language of empowerment has been increasingly used by Native politicians and activists in their interactions with the federal government. In the Hearing before the Senate Committee, Carmen *Hulu* Lindsey from the Office of Hawaiian Affairs framed her demands for greater self-determination for Native Americans in terms of empowerment. Thus, she asked the federal government »to empower all Native Americans [...] with the same opportunity to choose their own path – understanding that each tribe, band, nation, pueblo, village, or community is best-served through their unique, self-determined means.«[64] The language of empowerment has also been used outside the legal-political arena. Rather than waiting to be empowered by the federal government, Native American individuals and communities have worked toward empowering themselves, both by effectively managing the pandemic through legal-political and medical interventions, geared particularly to protect the elders, and by engaging in Indigenous cultural practices. In fact, the coronavirus pandemic has spawned Native cultural production and storytelling to a massive degree. Using their own websites and social media channels to reach Native communities across the nation, Native networks, community organizations, and activist groups have through the production and distribution of Native artwork, film, and comedy sought to instill hope and to raise community spirit. Illumi*Native*, for instance, whose campaign Warrior Up I mentioned at the beginning of this article, has partnered with prominent Native artists to create Covid-19-related Indigenous artwork that can be freely downloaded throughout Native America and beyond to embolden Native individuals and communities to fight against the spread of the virus. The network also supported the production of a film including prominent Native Americans who emphasize the significance of Native community responsibility and the power of »standing together« in the struggle against Covid-19. Illumi*Native* also put up its own news channel, »Low Rez News,« in which the Native comedy group 1491 presents »coronervirus news« in four episodes, which, by means of humor, seek to alleviate existing anxieties and suffering.[65]

---

[63] Cf. Sy/Kuhn: Why Native Americans Are Excited about the American Rescue Plan, and their Future.
[64] United States Congress: A Call to Action, p. 36.
[65] Cf. Illumi*Native*: Warrior Up.

Fig. 3: Warrior Up campaign, Illumi*Native*, 2020.
(Original color image reproduced in black and white for publication)

Native Americans have also turned to the internet to continue engaging in cultural practices that require people coming together. Virtual beading circles, drum socials, along with other forms of online engagement, have been viewed as a means to promote the mental well-being of community members, which is inextricably intertwined with communal practices of Indigenous culture.[66] Some Native communities, such as the Mashantucket Pequot, have used virtual formats to host intergenerational gatherings where the elders tell traditional stories, or to host Pequot language bingo nights to work toward preserving both Pequot lan-

---

[66] Howard-Bobiwash/Joe/Lobo: Concrete Lessons: Policies and Practices Affecting the Impact of COVID-19 for Urban Indigenous Communities in the United States and Canada, p. 10; see also Allaire: How Virtual Beading Circles Are Empowering Indigenous Women; Therien: »Social Distance Powwow.«

guage and culture.[67] The Facebook group *Social Distance Powwow*, which was established on March 16, 2020, and which has more than two hundred thousand followers, is a particularly prominent example of Native online activism during the Covid-19 pandemic.[68] Created by Dan Simonds (Mashantucket Pequot) to alleviate the pain and fear the virus caused in Indian country, this Facebook initiative has allowed Native dancers of all ages, across and even beyond North America, to share photos and videos of themselves dancing in their regalia in their backyards, homes, on basketball courts, and has created a platform for Native vendors to sell their crafts and arts. Besides powwows, the group has also hosted theme weeks from Native communities across North America, centering on storytelling, Native history, and culinary practices. The Facebook group, Yvette Leecy (Confederated Tribes of Warm Springs, Oregon), a Native vendor and grandmother of two young dancers, said, is »a healthy connection. Instead of building fear, we're building faith. We're going to do our social dance for healing, for our lands, for our people, for the sick, for the people that can't dance. We hope that this helps everybody.« Whitney Rencountre, a Crow Creek Sioux tribal citizen and one of the administrators of the page, explains the reach and attractiveness of *Social Distance Powwow* in similar terms: »It's a way to connect with people, and it's a way for us to kind of pass time and maybe divert from the fear of this Covid-19. This is a way to express ourselves while social distancing.«[69]

The telling of Native »stories of strength and resilience«[70] has played a particularly central role in Native efforts of self-empowerment. Native health organizations have circulated Native stories that negotiate the experience of the pandemic in order to provide mental and psychosocial support to Native American individuals, particularly children. The children's storybook *Our Smallest Warriors, Our Strongest Medicine: Overcoming COVID-19*, published by the Center for American Indian Health and distributed via its website free of charge, »seeks to reach Indigenous peoples across Turtle Island and portray a sense of communal efficacy, strength and hope in the face of the Covid-19 pandemic.«[71] Covid-19-related stories of resilience and strength have also been shared during the online production of crafts and via the *Social Distance Powwow* Facebook group. Another prominent outlet of Native stories of coping with the pandemic has been the digital project »Indigenous Impacts: How Native American Communities Are Responding to COVID-19« (fig. 4). On the website of this project there can be found coronavirus stories contributed by Native Americans across northern Minnesota, rang-

---

[67] Cf. Voice of America News: Native American Tribes Try to Protect Elders, Their Knowledge from Loss to Coronavirus.
[68] Cf. Therien: »Social Distance Powwow.«
[69] Abourezk: »We're building faith.«
[70] Urban Indian Health Institute: Strengthening Vaccine Efforts in Indian Country, p. 34.
[71] Center for American Indian Health: Our Smallest Warriors.

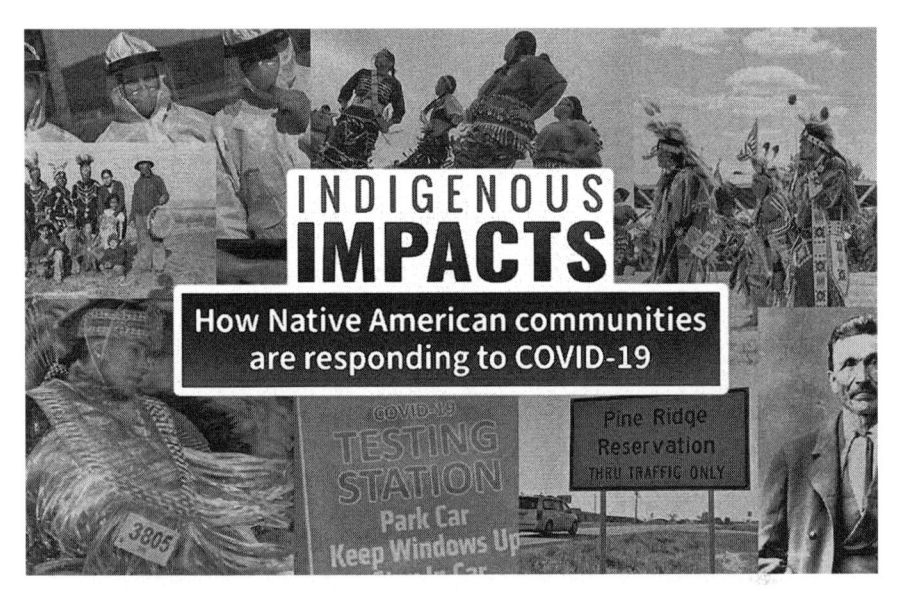

Fig. 4: Indigenous Impacts, Website, 2020. (Original color website graphic reproduced in black and white for publication)

ing from personal reports about Native community efforts against the pandemic, to poetry, essays, songs, and films.[72] The emotional depth and generic breadth of the stories assembled on this website cannot be done justice to within the scope of this article. It can be stated with certainty, however, that by assembling such a great variety of Native »voices«, as the website calls them, representing unique, and sometimes contradictory, views and experiences, *Indigenous Impacts* strives to make Native lives visible in their multifaceted nature and complexity. Just as the tight embrace of the two colorfully clad Native women in Hatfield's artwork embodies their refusal to be regulated, controlled, and understood via the reductive data of settler colonial administration (fig. 1), the Native voices and stories of resilience on this and other websites attest to the failure of settler taxonomies to grasp the emotions and suffering of Native individuals, the experience of vulnerability by Native communities, and their collective efforts of perseverance and resistance.[73]

As this article has suggested and as the photo montage of the *Indigenous Impacts* website illustrates so lucidly, Native *weapons* against Covid-19 have been manifold, ranging from legal-political and medical interventions to the use of

---

[72] Cf. Indigenous Impacts: How Native American Communities Are Responding to COVID-19.
[73] In the fall of 2021, another website featuring Indigenous »stories of strength and resilience« will be launched: Indigenous Stories of Strength.

Indigenous community work, cultural production, and the telling of stories about both past and present. What holds all these efforts together is the strong belief in Native empowerment. Native individuals and communities have used the Covid-19 pandemic to highlight the necessity of empowerment from without, that is, the empowerment of tribal communities by the settler nation. Through their interventions in the federal government's law and policy making during the pandemic, Native representatives and think tanks have consistently positioned themselves in favor of greater Native self-determination and have asked for the recognition of Native leadership and management. As a report of the Center for American Progress so succinctly puts it:

»The solution is, and has always been, to defer to the tribes themselves on how best to handle social issues in a culturally competent manner. Treaty obligations mandate that the federal government not only respect their ability to do so but also direct funding and resources toward that end. For too long, the federal government has been an aggressor when it should respect tribal sovereignty and absent when it has the responsibility to act. It has never been more apparent or urgent that this double-headed disaster be reversed and redressed. [...] In the long run, the federal government needs to acknowledge and internalize that the best it can do for Indian Country is to listen and work with tribes and tribal leaders. This is not only the most effective but also the lawful path forward.«[74]

These Native efforts to secure empowerment from without have gone hand in hand with Native efforts at empowerment from within. Such self-empowerment has taken on forms that extend beyond the realms of law, politics, and institutionalized activism to also encompass Native creativity, knowledge, and cultural practices, first and foremost storytelling.

To go back to where I started, the Covid-19 pandemic has thus functioned as a magnifying glass in a threefold manner. It has thrown into relief Native vulnerability in the face of past and present forces of settler colonial oppression, which have become manifest in federal Indian law and policy. The pandemic has also highlighted tribal governments' and organizations' effective crisis management and hence Native capacity for leadership, resistance, and survival. What is more, by posing a threat to the lives of Native elders – pillars of tribal knowledge and language – and by disrupting communal practices of Indigenous culture, Covid-19 has highlighted the tremendous importance of Native culture and community for the majority of Native individuals, irrespective of whether they live on reservation lands, or in urban or diasporic Native communities. During the pandemic Native culture and community have been the bedrock of Native self-empowerment. And community has in those past months been understood by Native Americans as a verb rather than as a noun, as ways of doing rather than a state of being. Engaging in Native cultural ways and working toward preserving these ways, the pandemic

---

[74] Cf. Doshi et al.: The COVID-19 Response in Indian Country, para. 14–15.

has shown, is essential for community health and resilience, and hence, ultimately for cultural, even physical, survival.

I would like to close with a quotation from the essay *Amidst Dark Times, Resilience* that Curtis E. Rogers, a community services officer with the White Earth Police Department in White Earth, Minnesota, contributed to the *Indigenous Impacts* website. For this quotation stands out in the way it captures the simultaneous sense of vulnerability and (self-)empowerment that has been prevalent in Native America in these pandemic times: »One thing that has not changed during these dark times has been the resilience of my people. We have survived boarding schools and removal from our lands. We have survived forced assimilation and genocide. We have survived and we will survive this.«[75]

References

Abourezk, Kevin: »We're building faith«. Social Distance Powwow Brings Indian Country Together despite Coronavirus, March 30, 2020, www.indianz.com/News/2020/03/30/were-building-faith-indian-country-share.asp; last accessed July 4, 2021.

Allaire, Christian: How Virtual Beading Circles Are Empowering Indigenous Women, in: Vogue, March 24, 2020, https://www.vogue.com/article/indigenous-virtual-beadwork-circles-tania-larsson; last accessed July 10, 2021.

American Indian Policy Institute: An Overview of the American Rescue Plan for Indian Country, July 1, 2021, https://aipi.asu.edu/blog/2021/03/overview-american-rescue-plan-indian-country; last accessed July 14, 2021.

Burris, Scott/Sarah de Guia/Lance Gable/Donna Levin/Wendy E. Parmet/Nicolas Terry: Assessing Legal Responses to COVID-19, July 31, 2020, https://papers.ssrn.com/sol3/papers.cfm?abstract_id=3675884; last accessed July 14, 2021.

Center for American Indian Health: Our Smallest Warriors, Our Strongest Medicine: Overcoming COVID-19, https://caih.jhu.edu/programs/strongmedicine; last accessed July 10, 2021.

Coburn, Veldon: Contrary to Sensational Reporting, Indigenous People Aren't Scared of a COVID-19 Vaccine, March 14, 2021, www.theconversation.com/contrary-to-sensational-reporting-indigenous-people-arent-scared-of-a-covid-19-vaccine-156444; last accessed July 08, 2021.

Doshi, Sahir/Allison Jordan/Kate Kelly/Danyelle Solomon: The COVID-19 Response in Indian Country. A Federal Failure, June 18, 2020, https://www.

---

[75] Indigenous Impacts: How Native American Communities Are Responding to COVID-19.

americanprogress.org/issues/green/reports/2020/06/18/486480/covid-19-response-indian-country/, last accessed July 01, 2021.

Duthu, N. Bruce: Federal Indian Law, in: Oxford Research Encyclopedia of American History, December 02, 2014, https://oxfordre.com/americanhistory/view/10.1093/acrefore/9780199329175.001.0001/acrefore-9780199329175-e-18; last accessed July 09, 2021.

Fletcher, Matthew L. M.: Federal Indian Law, St. Paul 2016.

Fletcher, Matthew L. M.: Indian Lives Matter: Pandemics and Inherent Tribal Powers, in: Stanford Law Review Online, 73, 2020, pp. 38–47.

Fuller, Katie: Critical Hermeneutics and the Counter Narrative of Ledger Art, in: Journal of Social Theory in Art Education, 41, 2021, pp. 123–136.

Hoss, Aila: COVID-19 and Tribes: The Structural Violence of Federal Indian Law, in: Arizona State Law Journal Blog, August 14, 2020, https://papers.ssrn.com/sol3/papers.cfm?abstract_id=367426; last accessed July 07, 2021.

Hoss, Aila / Heather Tanana: Upholding Sovereignty and Promoting Tribal Public Health Capacity during the COVID-19 Pandemic, August 01, 2020, https://dc.law.utah.edu/cgi/viewcontent.cgi?article=1235&context=scholarship; last accessed July 15, 2021.

Howard-Bobiwash, Heather A. / Jennie R. Joe / Susan Lobo: Concrete Lessons: Policies and Practices Affecting the Impact of COVID-19 for Urban Indigenous Communities in the United States and Canada, in: Frontiers in Sociology, 6, 2021, pp. 1–14.

Illumi*Native*: Homepage, www.illuminatives.org; last accessed July 15, 2021.

Illumi*Native*: Warrior Up, https://illuminatives.org/warriorup/; last accessed July 15, 2021.

Indianz: American Rescue Plan Act: Tribal Allocation Methodology, May 10, 2021, www.indianz.com/covid19/2021/05/10/american-rescue-plan-act-tribal-allocation-methdology/; last accessed July 05, 2021.

Indigenous Impacts: How Native American Communities Are Responding to COVID-19. Duluth News Tribune, September 27, 2020, www.duluthnewstribune.com/indigenous-impacts/6671542-How-has-COVID-19-affected-Native-American-communities-people-View-the-entire-Indigenous-Impacts-project-here; last accessed July 10, 2021.

Indigenous Stories of Strength, https://indigenousstrengths.com/; last accessed July 15, 2021.

Jones, Kristin: COVID-19 Vaccine Rollout among Indigenous Communities Seen as a Model for Others, March 24, 2021, www.coloradotrust.org/content/story/covid-19-vaccine-rollout-among-indigenous-communities-seen-model-others; last accessed July 15, 2021.

Kesslen, Ben: Native Americans, the Census' Most Undercounted Racial Group, Fight for an Accurate 2020 Tally, in: NBC News, December 29, 2019, https://

www.nbcnews.com/news/us-news/native-americans-census-most-undercounted-racial-group-fight-accurate-2020-n1105096; last accessed July 10, 2021.

Kriss, Jennifer L. / Laura E. Reynolds / Alice Wang / Shannon Stokley / Matthew M. Cole / LaTreace Q. Harris / Lauren K. Shaw / Carla L. Black / James A. Singleton / David L. Fitter / Dale A. Rose / Matthew D. Ritchey / Robin L. Toblin: COVID-19 Vaccine Second-Dose Completion and Interval between First and Second Doses among Vaccinated Persons – United States, December 14, 2020–February 14, 2021, in: Morbidity and Mortality Weekly Report, 70(11), 2020, pp. 389–395.

Kukutai, Tahu / John Taylor: Indigenous Data Sovereignty: Toward an Agenda, Canberra 2016.

National Council of Urban Indian Health: Coronavirus Resource Center, www.ncuih.org/Coronavirus; last accessed July 03, 2021.

Native Governance Center: How Does Tribal Sovereignty Operate during COVID-19?, https://nativegov.org/tribal-sovereignty-and-covid-19/; last accessed July 14, 2021.

O'Keefe, Victoria M. / Melissa L. Walls: Indigenous Communities Demonstrate Innovation and Strength Despite Unequal Losses during COVID-19, April 02, 2021, www.brookings.edu/blog/how-we-rise/2021/04/02/indigenous-communities-demonstrate-innovation-and-strength-despite-unequal-losses-during-covid-19/; last accessed July 14, 2021.

Pearce, Richard: Women and Ledger Art: Four Contemporary Native American Artists, Tucson 2013.

Pearson, J. Diane: Lewis Cass and the Politics of Disease: The Indian Vaccination Act of 1832, in: Wicazo Sa Review, 18(2), 2003, pp. 9–35.

Ray, Alan S.: A Race or a Nation? Cherokee National Identity and the Status of Freedmen's Descendants, in: Michigan Journal of Race and Law, 12 (2007), pp. 387–463.

Social Distance Powwow: Facebook-Group-Page; www.facebook.com/groups/832568190487520/, last accessed July 10, 2021.

Sy, Stephanie / Casey Kuhn: Why Native Americans Are Excited about the American Rescue Plan, and their Future, 23 Apr.2021, www.pbs.org/newshour/show/why-native-americans-are-excited-about-the-american-rescue-plan-and-their-future; last accessed July 14, 2021.

Therien, Eloise: »Social Distance Powwow« Group Celebrates Performers from Blackfoot Confederacy, April 26, 2020, https://globalnews.ca/news/6870412/coronavirus-social-distance-powwow/; last accessed July 10, 2021.

Trahant, Mark: $31 Billion Represents ›a Massive Opportunity‹, March 13, 2021, https://indiancountrytoday.com/news/31-billion-represents-a-massive-opportunity; last accessed July 08, 2021.

Tzay, José Francisco Calí: Report of the Special Rapporteur om the Rights of Indigenous Peoples. Annual Reports to the General Assembly, 20 July2020, https://undocs.org/A/75/185; last accessed July 01, 2021.

Unbound Philanthropy: The Impact of COVID-19 on Indigenous People, www.unboundphilanthropy.org/wp-content/uploads/2020/11/Illuminative_COVID_report_B1-1.pdf; last accessed July 14, 2021.

United States District Court for the District of Columbia: Cheyenne River Sioux Tribe v. Donald J. Trump et al., June 23, 2020, www.indianz.com/covid19/wp-content/uploads/2020/06/crstvtrump.pdf.; last accessed July 14, 2021.

United States Congress: A Call to Action: Native Communities' Priorities in Focus for the 117th Congress. Hearing before the Committee on Indian Affairs United States Senate, February 24, 2021, www.congress.gov/event/117th-congress/senate-event/LC65999/text?s=1&r=26; last accessed July 05, 2021.

United States Congress: Encouraging Cosponsorship of Tri-Caucus COVID-19 Vaccination Equity, April 21, 2021, www.congress.gov/congressional-record/2021/4/21/house-section/article/h2003-6 q=%7B%22search%22%3A%5B%22not+only+are+communities+of+color%22%5D%7D&s=4&r=1; last accessed July 03, 2021.

United States Congress: Memorializing the Intent of the Tribal Portion of the Coronavirus Relief Fund in the Coronavirus Aid, Relief, and Economic Security Act (CARES Act), March 26, 2021, www.congress.gov/congressional-record/2021/3/26/extensions-of-remarks-section/article/e314; last accessed July 03, 2021.

Urban Indian Health Institute: Strengthening Vaccine Efforts in Indian Country. Results from a National COVID-19 Vaccination Survey, January 28, 2021, https://www.uihi.org/projects/strengthening-vaccine-efforts-in-indian-country/; last accessed July 14, 2021.

U.S. Commission on Civil Rights: Broken Promises: Continuing Federal Funding Shortfall for Native Americans. Briefing before the U.S. Commission on Civil Rights, December 01, 2018, www.usccr.gov/pubs/2018/12-20-Broken-Promises.pdf; last accessed July 14, 2021.

Voice of America News: Native American Tribes Try to Protect Elders, Their Knowledge from Loss to Coronavirus, December 27, 2020, www.voanews.com/usa/native-american-tribes-try-protect-elders-their-knowledge-loss-coronavirus; last accessed July 15, 2021.

Yellow Horse, Aggie J./Kimberly R. Huyser: Indigenous Data Sovereignty and COVID-19 Data Issues for American Indian and Alaska Native Tribes and Populations, April 03, 2021, https://link.springer.com/article/10.1007/s12546-021-09261-5; last accessed July 03, 2021.

List of Figures

Fig. 1: J. NiCole Hatfield, *Keep Them Safe*, Ledger Art, 2020. Produced for the Warrior Up campaign by Illumi*Native*. Reproduced with the kind permission of Illumi*Native*.

Fig. 2: Steven P. Judd, Street Art, 2020. Produced for the Warrior Up campaign by Illumi*Native*. Reproduced with the kind permission of Illumi*Native*.

Fig. 3: Illumi*Native*, Warrior Up campaign, 2020. Reproduced with the kind permission of Illumi*Native*.

Fig. 4: Indigenous Impacts, Website, 2020. Reproduced with the kind permission of Forum News Service.

Pierre Brunet

Le surréalisme juridique au temps du corona

Que retiendra-t-on des très nombreuses mesures prises partout dans le monde pour tenter d'endiguer la pandémie ? À première vue, une forme de réalisme, incontestablement : les États ont mis en œuvre des moyens conséquents aussi bien financiers que juridiques, voire militaires parfois, pour lutter contre la pandémie ; ils ont aussi su faire évoluer leur droit et l'adapter aux circonstances. À bien y regarder pourtant, ce réalisme apparent, déclaré, intentionnel et mieux encore clamé haut et fort laisse place à nombre de propos, comportements et décisions incohérents, absurdes, contradictoires, qui n'ont de sens qu'en eux-mêmes mais en sont très vite dépourvus dès lors qu'on cherche à les mettre en relation les uns avec les autres. La vitesse avec laquelle les variants évoluent et les informations se contredisent frappe toute prescription juridique d'obsolescence quasi immédiate. Bien que – ou parce que – vivant à l'heure de la surinformation, nous sommes plongés dans un surréalisme juridique, contraint d'observer un droit surréaliste.

Je m'explique.

Le surréalisme désigne ce mouvement poétique, littéraire et artistique bien connu qui entendait laisser libre cours à l'imagination et à l'inconscient renversant au passage toutes les conventions de l'époque, sollicitant les associations les plus étonnantes voire absurdes, mêlant volontiers humour noir et nonsense. Passé dans l'usage courant, le mot a fini par désigner des situations inattendues, invraisemblables, dont on ne parvient pas à comprendre les causes ni à prévoir les conséquences. Le terme est parfois galvaudé lorsqu'il est employé pour qualifier des faits inhabituels. Sans doute que les productions surréalistes donnaient des représentations inhabituelles de la réalité mais elles ne se contentaient pas de cela. Le surréalisme avait pour ambition de faire apparaître ou de faire percevoir une autre dimension de la réalité y compris dans ce qu'elle avait de cocasse ou de grotesque. Les mesures prises par certains États pour tenter de lutter contre la pandémie ont des allures de constructions surréalistes. Le propos pourrait de prime abord paraître inutilement provocateur ou frappé de l'humour le plus noir. Pourtant, avec un peu de recul, le chaos normatif auquel on assiste depuis plus d'un an donne le vertige. Le seul moyen de lui donner sa cohérence est peut-être d'adopter un regard surréaliste sur cet enchevêtrement de normes. Le chaos vient d'abord de ce que face à une pandémie globale les réponses restent toujours nationales. Il y a à cet égard une certaine ironie à voir l'Organisation mondiale de la Santé (OMS) adresser des messages aux États et les États ne pas en tenir compte. Il ne s'agit bien évidemment pas de dire que les recommandations de l'OMS constituent des normes contraignantes pour les États mais au moins pourraient-elles être vues comme des normes pragmatiques. Or qui veut encore voyager doit naviguer entre les différentes règlementations qui ne sont nulle part les mêmes car elles tentent de tenir compte des situations des différents pays. Mais voilà : la situation de chaque État évolue à un rythme imprévisible de sorte qu'un État peut, du jour au lendemain, se voir inscrit sur la liste rouge des États dont les autres doivent se méfier. Et l'on assiste alors à des discours qui ne manquent pas d'ironie : les gouvernants de l'État inscrits sur liste rouge se plaignent de faire l'objet d'une discrimination tout comme le font les citoyens de ces mêmes États que l'on menace d'exclure de toute vie sociale voire professionnelle s'ils ne prouvent pas qu'ils se sont vaccinés. Inversement, les citoyens réclament que soit instauré un contrôle aux frontières de leur État et que les personnes à risque soient empêchées d'entrer sur le territoire national. Mais ces mêmes citoyens s'exaspèrent qu'on les empêche de voyager en exigeant d'eux qu'ils soient vaccinés ou en possession d'un test ou d'un document attestant qu'ils ne sont pas porteurs du virus. Afin de satisfaire la demande sociale autant que les exigences des scientifiques, les États ont effectivement imposé une *quarantaine* (dont la durée évolue en une à deux semaines) aux personnes qui arrivent sur leur territoire mais aucun État n'adopte la même forme de quarantaine. Mieux même : pour certains, dont la France par exemple, la quarantaine est laissée à la libre responsabilité de l'individu qui n'est donc ni contrôlé ni pris en charge... Le chaos vient ensuite de la combinaison de l'urgence et de l'incertitude. Les règles adoptées le sont parfois sur le fondement d'études scientifiques et d'évaluations statistiques. Le problème est qu'à peine adoptées, ces règles semblent inadaptées à la situation car les données scientifiques évoluent aussi vite que les variants du coronavirus. Inversement, certaines règles sont adoptées indépendamment des données scientifiques. Ce n'est donc pas sans ironie que l'on voit se multiplier les commentaires contradictoires qui ne sont pas sans rappeler des formes d'écriture automatique. Les uns dénoncent la tyrannie médicale ou sanitaire, la dépendance de la politique envers la science et rappellent avec force la nécessité d'une autonomie du politique pour préserver la démocratie. Les autres à l'inverse dénoncent l'irresponsabilité des politiques qui ne tiennent pas compte du discours scientifique en n'adoptant pas les normes que les scientifiques promeuvent et le risque, pour la démocratie, d'une société qui tournerait le dos à la science. Quant aux scientifiques, ils sont, comme toujours, divisés sur les normes en question et ravis de laisser aux politiques le soin de décider des normes juridiques – hormis quelques personnalités trop heureuses de bénéficier de leur moment médiatique. Quant aux politiques, ils assurent à la fois respecter scrupuleusement les avis scientifiques mais conserver leur autonomie de jugement en tenant compte de l'acceptabilité sociale des mesures prises. Ainsi, par exemple, le port du masque : dans le pays qui est le mien, au début de l'épidémie en février-mars 2020, le gouvernement s'est rendu compte que les réserves de masques étaient au plus bas et qu'il n'y en avait donc pas assez pour la population entière. Il fut alors dit que les masques n'étaient pas nécessaires et les pharmacies ont reçu l'ordre de ne pas en vendre. Puis des contrats ont été passés, des commandes ont été effectuées et les masques sont devenus disponibles. Dès lors, le port du masque a été déclaré non seulement nécessaire mais aussi obligatoire. Ce qui montre que le fondement de cette obligation n'était pas tant la donnée scientifique que la disponibilité de la ressource, si l'on peut dire. Le thème de l'acceptabilité sociale de la norme donne lieu à des discours qui ne sont pas moins surréalistes. Ainsi, de la vaccination : obligatoire ou non ? En France, dans un premier temps, le Président de la République a d'abord annoncé : « je l'ai dit, je le répète : le vaccin ne sera pas obligatoire » (27 décembre 2020). Puis quand il a été question de mettre en place un passeport sanitaire, le même déclarait : « le passe sanitaire ne sera jamais un droit d'accès qui différencie les Français. Il ne saurait être obligatoire pour accéder aux lieux de vie de tous les jours, comme les restaurants, théâtres et cinémas » (29 avril 2021). Il y avait quelque chose de surréaliste à entendre une telle déclaration car il suffisait de regarder un peu ce qui se passait ailleurs pour se douter que le discours présidentiel relevait du *wishful thinking*. Et il a suffi de quelques mois pour que le doute devienne réalité : le 12 juillet, le président français déclarait : « L'apparition du variant se traduit cependant par une augmentation des contaminations partout dans le monde. Pour lutter, une seule solution : le vaccin. » Et dès lors, conformément aux institutions que connaît la France, le Parlement a été saisi d'un projet de loi conforme aux volontés du Président et qui fut adopté dans une ambiance survoltée mais tout à fait inutile puisque la majorité parlementaire très confortable et fidèle au Président de la République peut aisément rejeter les demandes d'amendements de l'opposition. Le résultat est pour le moins étonnant : d'une part, le vaccin devient obligatoire pour certaines professions (les soignants, les sapeurs-pompiers ou les professionnels travaillant auprès des personnes âgées mais pas pour les policiers ni les gendarmes !) ; d'autre part, la loi prévoit l'obligation de présenter un *passe sanitaire* (parcours vaccinal complet, test négatif récent ou certificat de rétablissement) pour accéder à de nombreux lieux publics : les cafés et restaurants, foires et salons, établissements médicaux, mais aussi les avions, les trains et les cars dès lors que ces moyens de transport effectuent de longs trajets – en revanche, les trajets plus courts ne nécessitent pas ce *passe sanitaire*. Ainsi, plutôt que d'imposer la vaccination en la rendant obligatoire pour tout le monde ou, au contraire, de la recommander en laissant chacun libre de décider pour lui-même, la stratégie consiste à inciter la population à se vacciner en brandissant la menace d'une sanction non pas seulement juridique mais aussi sociale. C'est un euphémisme de dire que l'acceptation sociale d'une telle norme est, en France, plutôt faible … Il serait cependant vain d'imputer cette situation à une seule cause et il est évident que la contestation sociale sert plusieurs intérêts politiques. Mais au nombre des causes probables, on peut difficilement exclure la stratégie erratique du gouvernement faite à la fois de *stop & go* et de déclarations optimistes laissant croire à la population que tout serait bientôt fini et qu'elle pourrait retrouver la vie d'avant – autant de messages en décalage complet avec les discours des scientifiques qui n'ont jamais cessé d'alerter sur les dangers des variants, la nécessité de ne pas baisser la garde et d'encourager la vaccination le plus tôt possible. Or, la menace d'*exclusion sociale* que contient la loi française n'est elle-même que le résultat quasi mécanique d'une campagne de vaccination tardive qui a elle-même été précédée de discours lénifiants tenus par le Président de la République et les différents ministres lesquels espéraient ainsi renouer avec la croissance économique. Le cas français est loin d'être le seul : les dirigeants du Japon, pays organisateur des Jeux Olympiques (JO) de 2021, ont cédé au même double discours socialement incompréhensible : afin de justifier le maintien des JO, le gouvernement a levé l'état d'urgence et toute la population a progressivement repris une vie comme avant s'accoutumant très vite à l'idée agréable que la situation était devenue bonne. Or, la contamination est repartie à la hausse car le variant Delta est arrivé … le Premier ministre japonais a donc réinstauré l'état d'urgence tout en déplorant que ses concitoyens « ne ressentent pas la gravité de la situation ». Mais comment la population pourrait-elle ressentir cette gravité ? Et comment ne pas comprendre l'exaspération que ressent cette même population devant les changements de normes ? Le surréalisme juridique vient au fond de ce que le droit semble le reflet de l'inconscient de gouvernants dont le désir secret serait de faire plier la nature à leur désir et de la pandémie une parenthèse aussi brève que possible afin de revenir à la situation *d'avant*, comme si un retour en arrière était possible. Le droit qui en résulte n'est pas intrinsèquement irrationnel. Car toutes les règles produites en temps de corona le sont selon des procédures qui s'inscrivent dans une rationalité juridique bien établie, quand bien même on aurait recours à des procédures exceptionnelles. Mais ces règles procèdent d'une forme de dérèglement juridique provoqué par la combinaison de l'urgence, de l'incertitude et des différents intérêts contradictoires qui sont en jeu. Il est à cet égard fascinant de constater la similitude des réponses juridiques apportés et le chaos que produisent les divergences qui demeurent. À scruter les différentes réglementations prises par les États pour tenter de lutter contre un même virus, on a le sentiment de se trouver face à une composition surréaliste, mêlant le macabre, l'humour noir et le *nonsense*.

III. Still in the Realm of the Normative

Sam Whimster

Social Distancing and the Social Contract. Dual Normativities

> »Let observation with extensive view,
> Survey mankind, from China to Peru; [...]
> How rarely reason guides the stubborn choice,
> Rules the bold hand, or prompts the suppliant voice,
> How nations sink, by darling schemes oppress'd
> When vengeance listens to the fool's request.«
>
> Samuel Johnson

At the time of writing this (May 2021) scientific research indicates that the principal route of the Covid-19 virus is through air borne transmission: »When people cough, sneeze, sing, speak or breathe, they expel an array of liquid droplets formed by the shear-induced or capillary destabilization of the mucosal linings of the lungs and respiratory tract and saliva in the mouth. When the person is infectious, these droplets of sputum are potentially pathogen bearing, and represent the principle vector of disease transmission.«[1] The policy corollaries of this are numerous and include measures of physical distancing for inside and outdoor environments, new standards of ventilation and air filtering, and rules on the wearing of face masks. Rephrasing the scientific excerpt just cited, it is humans that are the vector of transmission, specifically their co-presence. To a health professional this is a banality, to a sociologist it is the heart of the question of what is sociality/sociation (*Vergesellschaftung*). The health professional, usually through the voice of the politician, recommends *social distancing*. For the sociologist the interesting question is what constitutes the social in *social distancing*. Policy driven *social distance* is in fact a recommendation placed on top of existing patterns of *social distancing* which are already embedded in the culture and habits of social groups. These are generalizable up to the level of whole cultures. The Japanese maintain a deferential space in face to face encounters, and many cultures practice versions of bowing and curtseying, again in south east Asia. In the West protocols of court society[2] have vanished in face of the merchant culture of the handshake and the egalitarianism of the modern global age. The Latin kiss on each cheek should be regarded

---

[1] Bazant/Bush: Beyond Six Feet.
[2] Cf. Elias: The Court Society.

as particularly lethal, as the evidence, in early 2020, from Lombardy shows.[3] Human interaction operates not just dyadically but *en masse*. Large sporting events and religious festivals are celebrations of solidarity, or what Durkheim called collective effervescence; or what Raja Sakrani in her survey of religious sociation calls *Holy April!*.[4] Even in April 2021 Indians en masse perform the rituals of bathing in the Ganges as intrinsic to the festival of Kumbh Mela. Evangelical sects in the United States refused to heed public health advice. Conversely, sharia forbids any tangible contact between genders. The British refused to ban high profile horse racing and football events until March 2020, even though the evidence of infection rates was by then well known. The political rallies of President Trump throughout 2020 and of President Modi in West Bengal, in April 2021, testify not only to the vanity of politics but also to the imperative of collective presence.

1. The Micro and Macro Sociology

The micro-sociology of this is termed Interaction Ritual Chains which analyze at the inter-individual level the forces of sociality that bring people into close contact. Following Randall Collins' exposition, there is a universal dynamic to this, which comprises: Co-presence where people can sense what other people are doing; people's focus on an object of mutual attention, such as a priest or singer; a commonality of emotion which can range from joy, excitement, anger, or any other emotion; a rhythmic entrainment where people are caught up in singing, chanting or dancing.[5]

Interaction rituals just as surely operate in mundane, everyday settings: talking to neighbours, meeting outside a pub or nightclub or an office entrance. Igbo culture, as Caroline Okumdi Muoghalu explains, involves the maintenance of intricate communal bonds through a register of *social distancing*, which overall demands some proximity in an encounter.[6] Micro solidarities are created through these more or less unconscious rituals, and involve learned behavior from the past and imitative behavior taken up from single cues. Time-wise many encounters are momentary, but they repeat according to a pattern whose underlying dynamic is to create some sociality through face-to-face interaction. Faces signal emotion

---

[3] Cf. Al-Sahamahi: The Handshake. For a contrast, Allert: The Hitler Salute. The contrast is also methodological, Tilman demonstrating the binding force of the phenomenological encounter, Al-Sahamahi preferring the reductionism of evolutionary biology despite her sharia upbringing.

[4] Cf. Sakrani: Religious Co-narration of Corona, p. 234.

[5] Cf. Collins: Social Distancing as a Critical Test of the Micro-Sociology of Solidarity. See also Savelsberg: Balancing Rights and Responsibilities, p. 317.

[6] Cf. Muoghalu: Igbo Culture and the Coronavirus Pandemic Social Distancing Order, pp. 261 ff.

through the complex of facial muscles, and the brain has neuron receptors dedicated to making unconscious reciprocal responses.[7] This pushes the analysis of *social distancing* towards micro-sociology and how encounters are inflected by culture and context.

Yet we also have direction from above as political leaders in China, Taiwan, South Korea, for example, legislate and enforce rules of isolation, mask-wearing, social contacts; and we have leaders who proclaim complete laissez aller, as in the example of Brazil's Bolsonaro, Trump in the United States and the President of Mexico, Andrés Obrador, who endorsed the continuation of hugging and kissing. The micro-sociology and culture of tribes residing far up the Amazon alongside a deliberate refusal to put in place country-wide measures to reduce the spread of infection resulted in the decimation of communities by the Covid-19 virus. It is as if the Spanish conquistadores had returned with their lethal germs. Micro-sociology is not impervious to exogenous dangers, especially in large federal countries where plebiscitary fed vanity triggers lethal public health risks.

This appears to return us to the sociological conundrum of top-down vs. bottom up theories, and the theorists who have sought to integrate the two.[8] The difficulties of integration of this two levels analysis is the nature of the bonding mechanism between humans. Micro-sociologists problematize it, quite rightly in my view. Macro sociologists, like Talcott Parsons, assume the integrative efficacy of norms, which many critics have found problematic. But Parsons's macro theories still reference the ambition that politics performs a steering role and that culture patterns the normative. If a society conformed to the precepts of full-blown structural functionalism, it would be well-placed to control a novel corona epidemic. The sort of society that did conform to this model was 1950s North America, but fundamental changes in that society as well as the rise of social movements from the 1960s onwards increasingly rendered structural-functionalist theory vulnerable to critique. That said, it is an interesting heuristic to consider. It is a way of interrogating the question of why some countries had a »successful« pandemic while others experienced a catastrophic pandemic.

Functionality matters, structures (*Gebilde*) are always determinative; however, norms bring us to the indeterminacy of normativity. The first two elements are a given, at the point when the pandemic struck. A Colombian city official, interviewed on British Broadcasting Corporation (BBC) television, says: »It lays it right there (smacks palm of his left hand with other hand) and tells you what society is.«[9] Citizens in the Colombian city were placed in lockdown. In poor areas this created an immediate problem of food supplies. Given the organization and resources

---

[7] Cf. Turner: Cognitive Science and the Social, pp. 86–88.
[8] Cf. Coleman: Foundations of Social Theory.
[9] British Broadcasting Corporation Two: Pandemic 2020.

of the society, people's needs simply could not be met. The point can be generalized across all societies: their prior organization determines their ability to react to the Covid-19 virus. And this to a degree explains the large variation in infection and death rates per 100,000 people across the globe. Certain societies have in-built advantages, for instance, in terms of citizen attitudes, civil and health defences, and political leadership; other societies were highly vulnerable to the virus precisely because of the different nature of those factors. The pre-Covid organization of society – in theoretical terms, its current degree of structural-functionalism – sets up a methodology of sociological determinants of success and failure. But normativity upsets this model. Citizens attitudes were not only different between advanced societies but varied during the pandemic within a country and over time.

The functionality of mask-wearing belongs to the universality of common sense. In South East Asian societies the normativity of this was accepted. In Western societies it was initially subject to, and held up, by the demand for experimental data. This scientization of policy was a bad mistake, failing to realize that the world had entered into a (global) natural experiment. Then, following Trump's example the mask became a political symbol of what divided the Republican base and the urban Democrat. At the time of writing, the Biden administration has announced that mask-wearing is no longer required for those who have been vaccinated. This introduces uncertainty, because the unvaccinated can chose not wear masks and they no longer stand out in any shared space as rule violators. The officials at the Centre for Disease Control and Prevention (CDC) may have assumed conformity to norms in the two populations of the vaccinated and the unvaccinated. But in an online comment to the Washington Post's medical columnist, Dr Leana Wen complains:

»How is it that the CDC thinks people will be truthful when it comes to vaccine status? Bogus vaccine cards were available within days of the vaccine rollout to the public. People have used the Constitution, of all things, to justify their selfishness. I have lost so much confidence in so many institutions since we all found ourselves in this pandemic last year. Any words of encouragement? BTW, I am fully vaccinated and will continue to mask indoors.«[10]

It is reported that Democrats persist wearing masks, even though vaccinated, as in the above comment, as a political signal. In the United Kingdom the necessity of masks is under explicit consideration, leading to discretionary behaviour in public. So, from personal observation (May 18, 2021), my local supermarket no longer enforces mask-wearing. Most customers do wear them, but non-mask-wearers are now conspicuous. In the milieu of a supermarket there is suddenly an indeterminacy. Attitudes are being struck, imitation à la Gabriel Tarde is primed.

[10] Wen: Should We Keep Wearing Masks?

2. Normativity: Conforming and Non-Conforming

Citizens' behaviour is the weak middle link in establishing an ordered response to Covid-19, and this seems to be applying also to the success and efficacy of vaccination programmes. In terms of sociological theory, Parsonian at this point, we require intelligent and effective leadership (*a steering mechanism*) which is accepted as legitimate by citizens, who model their behaviour according to public health information and legislation. Participative and cooperative citizenship is the cultural variable, that feeds into everyday norms, those of correct *social distancing*, mask-wearing, isolation and quarantine. In the United States and the United Kingdom, two of the richest countries in the world and with advanced health systems, the level of infections and deaths is completely out of line with many other similar countries. There have been failures at the political and public policy level, and failures of citizen compliance and cooperation. The latter is crucial in that the primary vector of Covid-19 virus transmission is face to face interaction. In the U.K. the government invoked powers given to them under the Public Health Act (Control of Diseases), which was legislated back in 1984 in respect to infectious diseases:

»The Public Health (Control of Disease) Act 1984 (as amended) protects the health of the public through a system of surveillance and action. Surveillance allows for the identification, investigation and confirmation of an outbreak of a disease or a case of contamination. Appropriate and timely intervention to control the spread of the disease including isolation and quarantine can be initiated.«[11]

This was the legislative authority for the government to initiate a series of lockdowns, drastically restricting freedom of movement of citizens and giving the police powers in law to enforce infringements. In Max Weber's term this legislation was a set of legal propositions (*Rechtssätze*). Weber allows that in a modern society there is a legal order (*Rechtsordnung*), but that there is no necessity that its legal propositions would be complied with by citizens. From the juristic perspective, legal propositions have normative force. They are part of the body of law, and law is cardinal to the order of a society. From the empirical perspective, individuals may choose to obey, conform, exploit, ignore or violate a legal proposition. In this latter case, a law has normative force by virtue of the validity of enacted law, but it does not follow empirically it will be conformed to in all cases. To quote Weber:

»*The Legal Order and the Economic Order*

When we speak of ›law‹, ›legal order‹ [and] ›legal proposition‹ (*Rechtssatz*), then the distinction between the juristic and the sociological perspective must be observed particularly rigorously. The first [the juristic] asks what counts as law in an ideal sense (*ideell*). That

---

[11] Griffith: Using Public Health Law to Control the Spread of Covid-19.

means: what significance, and with this in turn, what normative meaning ought to be placed in a logically correct way on a language-construct presenting itself as a legal norm. The second perspective [the sociological] in contrast asks: what in fact happens from being part of a community, since there exists the chance that the participants in communal action – especially among those who exercise a socially relevant degree of actual influence on this communal action – regard certain orders as subjectively valid and behave in practice such that those orders serve as a standard for their own action. The principal relation between law and economy defines itself according to this distinction. [...] [T]he economic order and the legal order stand in utmost intimate relations with one another, so this has to be understood not in a juristic sense but in the sociological sense, as one of empirical validity. The sense of the word ›legal order‹ then changes completely. It then means not a cosmos of norms that are logically intelligible as ›correct‹, but a complex of the factually determinative reasons of real human action.«[12]

Max Weber did not anticipate *influencers* on social media, but the sense is the same. Those in political and culturally significant positions can influence adherence or non-conformity to norms. President Trump and an army of *influencers* on social media sought to undermine, on libertarian grounds and other *darling schemes*, the legal regulations which authorized lockdowns. In the quoted passages Weber is discussing the relation of the legal order to the economic order. It can equally be applied to the political order. Certain legal norms, in a juristic sense, require both parties to come to an understanding, to an *entente* (in French), and what Weber terms an *Einverständnis*. Weber introduces this as a heading in his essay *Some Categories of Interpretive Sociology*, where it serves as a fundamental sociological category. In its broadest sense it is an agreement to reach consensual action. Modern power is predicated on legitimacy, the acceptance by citizens of the legitimacy of those who exercise power. This is never certain and there always the exist the chance, the probability, that normative acceptance of power can be withdrawn or challenged. Jean-Pierre Grossein writes:

»D'où le concept de ›validité par l'entente‹ (*Einverständnisgeltung*), que Weber étend à l'analyse du ›pouvoir d'imposition‹ en général et ainsi de la domination, laquelle implique nécessairement une ›entente relative à sa légitimité‹, dont l'analyse sociologique doit, selon Weber, mettre au jour les ›divers fondements possibles.‹«[13]

The majority of countries of the Organisation for Economic Co-operation and Development (OECD) are afflicted with such challenges to legitimacy, mainly because of their drift to plebiscitary leadership under conditions of economic insecurity and impoverishment. In these regimes the ability to contain and control Covid-19 – to flatten the curve of infections and deaths – is severely compromised. The crisis of legitimacy and trust manifests itself at the level of normativity.

---

[12] Weber: Recht, pp. 191 ff.
[13] Grossein: Concepts fondamentaux de sociologie, p. 85.

For Talcott Parsons norms are a control mechanism that deliver system integration. Parsons' social actor lives in a normative environment, which provides rules for conduct. Different environments – relevant here are the polity and economy – provide the rules and maxims for conduct. Both of these – polity and economy – are sets of institutionalized norms. The polity is a normative environment in which obligations and rights are defined by virtue of the individual's collective membership in that polity, so in a structural functional way able to manage resources and accomplish tasks.[14] An economy concerns the production of goods and services, the allocation of resources and the management of tasks. Occupational roles is one of the modalities of institutionalizing norms. People carry out tasks according to their occupational role and status. Social order, in advanced societies (implicitly 1950s America), is a matter of integration and social control. Each (sub-)system has its own institutional cues which translate into the normative regulation of actions. Parsons' achievement was to devise a sociological theory (of considerable sophistication and complexity) that explained how social order was achieved and maintained.

The large issue the Covid-19 pandemic has raised is dysfunctionality and disorder – and it has placed the focus on normativity, because virus transmission comes down, primarily, to face to face encounters (as Randall Collins has underlined). Weber's treatment of normativity allows its institutionalization, as in the legal order, but in parallel he insists on the empirics of how groups and societies chose to behave and what norms they validate. Weber's social actor is given options and discretion, Parsons' social actor follows normative rules. Juristically a *Rechtssatz* for Weber is a normative obligation, sociologically it is open to group determination. Parsons is theorizing how a whole system can function, Weber makes no presumption of system integration. For him each sphere of life has its own values, these spheres are in conflict because their fundamental values cannot be reconciled, and normativity itself is a labile quality. Weber's conception of the social world is pluralist, Parsons seeks an integrative unification. At this point the chapter has travelled rather far into the high seas of sociological theory. Delivering the correct normative micro-sociology is the key to the control of the virus, but the interesting question is how different societies and countries have achieved this. In posing the question, we (just about everyone rushing to print) are being rather premature, because the necessary empirical groundwork has yet to report. Attention has been focused on epidemiology but this a mathematical model, extrapolating from assumed rates of infections in myriad populations; technically the Susceptible-Exposed-Infectious-Removed (SEIR) model.[15] Researching face to face encounters has yet to receive close ethnographic study, though local pub-

---

14 Cf. Garfinkel: Parsons' Primer, pp. 279 ff.
15 Cf. Mainelli/Price: Post-Covid-19 Calcs Beat the SEIR in Forty Days.

lic health workers are, so to speak, one step away from providing these accounts. It is also probably the case that the analysis of video-footage will supply evidence on physical distancing in group situations of various kinds, and this data might reveal country and cultural differences. Social Network Analysis has yet to make its important contribution, because it has the capacity to map empirical patterns of actual transmission (but here it is dependent on local health data, especially test and trace operations, which have not been a conspicuous success to date).[16]

3. The Constitution of Societies

That noted, the nominalism of face to face encounters still has to be related to the overall sociological constitution of societies. Sociological theory has yet to break new ground here, and come up with new lines of inquiry. The recent publication of Harold Garfinkel's lectures on Talcott Parsons suggests ways of more accurately capturing the nature of the face-to-face interaction, which of course was Garfinkel's speciality; and is usually contrasted with Parson's overdetermination of control in matters of social interaction.[17] For Parsons stability and social order is secured through norms and shared values across a population. Garfinkel (in his newly published lectures from the early 1960s) highlighted that shared values in Parsons was a re-working of Hobbes' social contract. Hobbes' individuals – all passion and desire – are asocial and only by virtue of natural rationality do they accede to the authority of the sovereign. The social contract of an individualised population with a sovereign is a rational step in the regulation of self-interest. The Parsonian individual is already a social actor by virtue of membership in a community, where over the centuries from late medieval internecine war and conflict a general sense of social contract has emerged, becoming constitutive of a social order within which the social action framework can be conceptualised. The latter has been placed to the fore in the reading of Parsons, not the idea of a prior social contract.

Garfinkel elaborates the argument as follows: »In the Structure of Social Action Parsons treated Hobbes' statement of the problem of order as one that formulated with a force that, Parsons proposed, had never adequately been answered by those that conceived the possibility of a stable society in utilitarian terms […].«[18] One

---

[16] Cf. Saraswathi et al.: Social Network Analysis of COVID-19 Transmission in Karnataka, India. In the context of the state of Karnataka with its composite of advanced urbanism and traditional villages, the authors report: »Gender influences the morphology of clusters, with men seeding the clusters and women propagating them« (ibid., p. 15). The Japanese approach as reported by Masahiro Noguchi traces back each infection to a source, a »cluster-based approach« – or, in network analysis a »clustering coefficient« (Noguchi: Cluster-Based Approach and Self-Restraint, p. 297).
[17] Cf. Garfinkel: Parsons' Primer.
[18] Garfinkel: Parsons' Primer, p. 153.

such was J. S. Mill, in particular the utilitarian notion of pursuing the maximum of felicity, and the avoidance of harm, in a society. This does not take us very far, other than social theorists assume society to be (internally) in a state of peace and not civil war. Garfinkel continues: »The search terminated with the conception of action governed in its course by an order of moral expectations binding and enforceable upon all as constituent features of their common situations of action.«[19] If one offered up this question to Max Weber, I think the answer would be that Law was the constituent feature of a common situation; with the nation, in a time of war between nations, as constituent of shared community (the *pathos of community*). If offered to Alfred Weber the reply would be culture, and of course continuing from Alfred, Parsons' own pattern variables supplied an overarching cultural cue for social interactions in the various (sub-)systems. What you do not obtain is the Hobbesian necessity of law, which is a widespread apprehension across the volume of essays: In the Realm of Corona Normativities. Modern sociality, even in plebiscitary authoritarian states, forbids such a regress. This is a powerful idea, although it is quite difficult to nail down as an applicable argument. With reference to advanced societies Garfinkel notes, in relation to Parson, the importance of property and contract as constitutive, both of which involve claims in law and so Law itself as constitutive. This is a considerable step forward from Karl Marx's and Max Weber's more elemental conception of property (and management) as forms of appropriation and expropriation, which become sanctified and embedded in law. Garfinkel also highlights occupation, and its twin concept, stratification. Occupation and three sorts of division of labor provides the basis of class divides, in Max Weber.[20] In Parsons' hands occupation and vocation were worked up into one of the constituent ideas of the social order, the role of the professionals. They are so to speak the social contractors, able to conduct the delivery of goods and services within an economy and polity without any personal commitment to outcomes, i.e. they are the pacifiers and the neutralizers.

4. The Sociological Social Contract

We do not have to agree with Parsons' reverential respect of professionals; rather simply grasp the powerful idea that in different societies and countries some prior social contract is realized and delivered through the working parts of a society. Occupation, at its widest – not just professionals, is a marker of social status in

---

[19] Ibid.
[20] Cf. Weber: Economy and Society; cf. Whimster: Economics and Society and the Fate of Liberal, pp. 35–38.

the United States, and without that social classification, in its everyday usage and reflexive understanding, it would be hard to grasp how that country functions.²¹ As an act of sociological imagination, the question can be posed for any country or identifiable social group; (and in an *ethno* sense it can be posed within any society by any group). The answers would include kinship networks, religions and their ecclesiastical forms, officialdom, dominant forms of sociality such as egalitarianism, justice etc., which would sit alongside the generic modern division of labour, as outlined by Durkheim. This remains imprecise and somewhat nebulous, and it may be an admission that the determinants of the currents of social life cannot be identified in observable phenomena. But it allows us to ask the question of what happens when the (Parsonian) social contract breaks down and how to locate the components in such breakdowns. In theoretical terms, how does the social contract infuse social interaction at the micro level? Garfinkel thought that Parsons could not be ignored in this matter. Such an acknowledgement is important coming from the champion of ethno-methods. In his lecture, *The Program of Ethnomethodology*, Garfinkel says: »The prefix *ethno* [...] means ›seen from the point of view of the common sense interests of a member of society in the course of managing and coming to terms with his everyday affairs.‹«²² It involves becoming acquainted with the everyday understandings of the world that are held in common by participants in a given social situation, to follow Husserl. It is the common understanding (*Sinnzusammenhang*) to which participants are oriented, to follow Max Weber. »More particularly«, says Garfinkel, »[I] have borrowed from Parsons' work in which he delineated the constituent tasks that make up the problem of social order.«²³

The article *Notes on the Art of Walking* amuses by naming the everyday assumptions about not bumping into other people: social distance in its everyday facticity.²⁴ From this we require an ethno-method for explaining *social distancing* in everyday encounters. This is the vector of virus transmission and it is precoded in the instantiation of social behaviour. This is close to saying that it is an unconscious predisposition. In terms of health policy, the isolation of the single individual is effective in arresting the spreading of the virus. Keeping people two meters apart in their encounters with others is a policy aspiration that collides with the predispositions to proximity and social distance. So, following Garfinkel, social order, which in this context is taken as being able to reduce the infection and death rate in any society, is informed by a social contract and its instantiation in everyday situations. There is no one explanatory factor. The outcome lies in the

---

²¹ This is not a Weberian insight. He observed the socially cohesive force of sects, now a disuniting feature of American *mores*.
²² Garfinkel: Parsons' Primer, p. 327.
²³ Ibid., p. 336.
²⁴ Cf. Ryave/Schenkin: Notes on the Art of Walking.

common sense of face to face encounters, whose determination is multiple and will correspond to the real structures and embedded meanings of actual societies and countries. Supermarkets organize their space even prior to the pandemic according to the principle of what Marc Augé terms *non-space*. In Grischka Petri's interesting discussion supermarkets are also fighting the ethos of expressive consumerism; not Hobbesian anarchy but the aimlessness of *liquid modernity*. The postmodern social contract accounts for the latter, economic utilitarianism for the former. The check-out aisles of the supermarket have »organisational validity« as outlined by Werner Gephart.[25] The issue is how the higher level sense of social contract slides through and is instantiated in settings of everyday encounters. The same point can be argued for religious prescription as instantiated in gendered face-covering, or how ultra-orthodox Jewish teaching manifests itself in a sick household. Reluctance to leave the home for hospital is countered by a strong neighbourly ethic to supply oxygen in the home if required – a reminder that the altruism of medical care is itself a reflection of a social contract based on neighbourliness.[26]

The above paragraph may not read like a conclusion, but it is the endpoint of a theoretical consideration of normativity. What has been expounded and exposed are two normativities. Firstly, the implicit normativity of a social contract woven into the tapestry of social structural threads. This line of inquiry takes the sociologist back to the givenness of any one society or country or community, but with the additional task of delineating the social contract, or its lack, in a way that goes beyond the utilitarian. The second normativity is the taken for granted understanding held in common at the face to face level. This is more than a static norm, it is an activity that is constituted through understandings, which are ambient to the situation itself and to the society. Hence we are dealing with a dual normativity.

Faced with the enormity of the Covid-19 pandemic there is a huge pressure to produce a correct sociological analysis and its corresponding policy proposals. The compulsion is to follow Durkheim in classifying societies in terms of health and pathology and using mortality statistics as an indicator, like suicide rates, of societal morbidity. In Corona Normativities (volume one) I pursued this approach through the axes of integration and discipline as they were deployed by Mary Douglas and others: an analytic of rules and grids.[27] This showed an initial predictive power in identifying which countries were best, and worst, placed to deal with a pandemic. It was fairly obvious that the People's Republic of China was going to be overall more successful in containing the epidemic than the United

---

[25] Gephart: Conclusion, p. 514.
[26] Cf. Przybilski: Imagining Infection and Dealing with Disease in Jewish Law.
[27] Cf. Whimster: Discovering Society in a Time of Plague, pp. 241–249.

States of America. The value judgement is quickly reached that Asian societies prioritized the collective over the individual and that the incompetence of Western governments lay with the privileging of the individual. Maybe. Finland has a relatively low rate of deaths, held to follow from its egalitarian ethos, its social contract. In Japan self-restraint (*jishuku*), writes Mashiro Noguchi, leads people to follow »certain norms voluntarily rather than by force. Self-restraint is linked to weak leadership.«[28] Japanese citizens stayed at home by virtue of an outmoded Leviathan. Citizen compliance across China is too monolithic an explanation, and we await regional and local patterns.

It is still open season for blame, and viruses mutate just as change is always emergent in societies. Garfinkel, in milder times, warned off the rush to objectivity and judgement; or perhaps now: objectifying the social contract of a society. A »troublesome question remains«, he lectured: »What kinds of objective worlds result from the actual decisions that an inquirer must make in coming to terms with the actual circumstances within which his inquiry must be accomplished.«[29] This applies to the lead method in countering the virus, which is epidemiology. »Because we are allowing at the outset that every person who addresses inquiries to the events of human conduct operates with some solution to the questions of sensibility, objectivity and the rest, the very variety of human types and interests, actions and circumstances dictates the existence of a variety of solutions in use.«[30] There is more to be discovered, indeed whole social worlds we did not think needed discovering. The *we* here is not the royal *we* but the ethno *we* – us. How will the plurality of social scientists »hold each other to a knowledge and [its] use of within the constraints imposed by a respect for the socially organized character of their everyday activities«?[31]

References

Allert, Tilman: The Hitler Saltue, On the Meaning of a Gesture, New York 2008.
Al-Sahamahi, Ella: The Handshake. A Gripping History, London 2021.
Bazant, Martin / John Bush: Beyond Six Feet: A Guideline to Limit Indoor Airborne Transmission of COVID-19, in: medRχiv: The Preprint Server for Health Sciences, January 24, 2021, https://doi.org/10.1101/2020.08.26.20182824; last accessed June 10, 2021.

---

[28] Noguchi: Cluster-Based Approach and Self-Restraint, p. 298.
[29] Garfinkel: Parsons' Primer, p. 332.
[30] Ibid.
[31] Garfinkel: Parsons' Primer, p. 327.

British Broadcasting Corporation Two: Pandemic 2020, https://www.bbc.co.uk/programmes/p0993tmy; last accessed June 16, 2021.

Collins, Randall: Social Distancing as a Critical Test of the Micro-Sociology of Solidarity, in: American Journal of Cultural Sociology, 8, 2020, pp. 477–497.

Collins, Randall: Interaction Ritual Chains, Princeton NJ 2005.

Coleman, James: Foundations of Social Theory, Cambridge MA 1990.

Elias, Norbert: The Court Society, Oxford, 1983.

Garfinkel, Harold / Anne Warfield Rawls (eds.): Parsons' Primer, Berlin 2019.

Gephart, Werner: Conclusion, in: Werner Gephart (ed.): In the Realm of Corona Normativities. A Momentary Snapshot of a Dynamic Discourse, Frankfurt am Main 2020.

Griffith, Richard: Using Public Health Law to Control the Spread of Covid-19, in: British Journal of Nursing, 29(5), March 2020, https://doi.org/10.12968/bjon.2020.29.5.326; last accessed March 13, 2021.

Johnson, Samuel: The Vanity of Human Wishes. The Tenth Satire of Juvenal, London 1749.

Mainelli, Michael / Henry Price: Post-Covid-19 Calcs Beat the SEIR in Forty Days: Naively Modelling Covid-19, in: Long Finance, April 11, 2021, https://www.longfinance.net/news/pamphleteers/beat-the-seir-in-40-days-na%C3%AFvely-modelling-covid-19/; last accessed June 11, 2021.

Muoghalu, Caroline Okumdi: Igbo Culture and the Coronavirus Pandemic Social Distancing Order, in: Werner Gephart (ed.): In the Realm of Corona Normativities. A Momentary Snapshot of a Dynamic Discourse, Frankfurt am Main 2020.

Noguchi, Mashiro: Cluster-Based Approach and Self-Restraint: Japan's Response to Covid-19, in: Werner Gephart (ed.): In the Realm of Corona Normativities. A Momentary Snapshot of a Dynamic Discourse, Frankfurt am Main 2020.

Przybilski, Martin: Imagining Infection and Dealing with Disease in Jewish Law, in: Werner Gephart (ed.): In the Realm of Corona Normativities. A Momentary Snapshot of a Dynamic Discourse, Frankfurt am Main 2020.

Ryave, Alan / Jim Schenkein: Notes on the Art of Walking, in: Roy Turner (ed.): Ethnomethodology, Harmondsworth 1974. pp. 265–274.

Sakranaik, Saraswathi / Amita Mukhopadhyay / Hemant Shah / Hebbale Ramakrishnaiah Ranganath: Social Network Analysis of COVID-19 Transmission in Karnataka, India, in: PubMed 2020, https://dx.doi.org/10.1017%2fS095026882000223X; last accessed June 11, 2021.

Sakrani, Raja: in Gephart, Werner (ed.): Religious Co-narration of Corona, in: Werner Gephart (ed.): In the Realm of Corona Normativities. A Momentary Snapshot of a Dynamic Discourse, Frankfurt am Main 2020.

Savelsberg, Joachim: Balancing Rights and Responsibilities during a Pandemic, in: Werner Gephart (ed.): In the Realm of Corona Normativities. A Momentary Snapshot of a Dynamic Discourse, Frankfurt am Main 2020.

Turner, Stephen: Cognitive Science and the Social. A Primer, New York 2018.

Wen, Leana: Opinion: Should We Keep Wearing Masks? Leana S. Wen Answers Your Questions about the Latest CDC Guidance, in: Washington Post, May 18, 2021, https://www.washingtonpost.com/opinions/2021/05/18/masks-cdc-guidance-covid-live-chat/; last accessed June 11, 2021.

Weber, Max: Concepts fondamentaux de sociologie, Paris 2016.

Weber, Max: Economy and Society. An Outline of Interpretive Sociology, New York 1968.

Weber, Max: Wirtschaft und Gesellschaft. Recht (Max Weber-Gesamtausgabe: Volume I/22-3; edited by Werner Gephart/Siegfried Hermes), Tübingen 2010.

Whimster, Sam: Discovering Society in a Time of Plague, in: Gephart, Werner (ed.): In the Realm of Corona Normativities. A Momentary Snapshot of a Dynamic Discourse, Bonn 2020.

Whimster, Sam: Economics and Society and the Fate of Liberal Capitalism, in: Lawrence A. Scaff / Edith Hanke / Sam Whimster (ed.): The Oxford Handbook of Max Weber, New York 2019.

Kornelia Hahn

Love in the Time of the Covid Pandemic

> »The only thing that would allow them to bypass all that was a case of cholera on board.
>
> The ship would be quarantined, it would hoist the yellow flag and sail in a state of emergency [...].
>
> If such things were done for so many immoral, even contemptible reasons, Florentino Ariza could not see why it would not be legitimate to do them for love.«
>
> Gabriel García Márquez

A number of preliminary questions occurred to me when I was first invited to contribute an essay under the still exciting and intellectually adventurous theme of ›Love in the Time of the Covid Pandemic‹, including the general question of whether falling in love and conducting love relationships now plays a more *minor* role than in pre-pandemic times. Does love even contribute at all when it comes to analysing social changes during a pandemic? Or could love perhaps be one of the *key* ways by which to conquer at least some of the impacts of a global health crisis? Focusing on *performing love*, i. e. on the multiple performative practices of embodied and non-embodied communications ascribed and interpreted within a cultural model of romance, a further question that arises is whether and to what extent loving relationships and the possibilities of such relationships have necessarily been distorted by the fact that some of the key measures adopted to mitigate the pandemic entail limiting physical contact as much as possible. This in turn leads to the question of whether the practices we perform for the sake of love must now be considered among the most dangerous of all aspects of social life in terms of the potential risks they pose for contagion. In addressing this task, moreover, there also exists what at first sight might seem an apparent blueprint for a literally essayistic – in the sense of tentative – reflection on this same topic, namely Gabriel García Márquez's famous novel *Love in the Time of Cholera*. First published in Spanish in 1985, this novel narrates the love story of a couple that starts in the 1870s but has been suspended almost over their lifetime. It is quite remarkable that this novel does not deal with any of the preliminary questions set out above, nor with any other currently widespread reflections on love in the time of the Covid pandemic. Instead, Márquez's novel interestingly entwines the connection between love and a health crisis in a way that depicts love as a risk to the bodily condition of the lovers comparable to the threat posed by the plague. As Michael Peters has aptly commented: Marquez's title is based in this systematic ambiguity – cholera as both disease and passion. Love is a sickness comparable to cholera and creates physical symptoms and effects as lovesickness.[1]

As evident in the quotation with which I open this essay, *Love in a Time of Cholera* also depicts another connection between the practices performed due to plague and those performed due to love. This connection lies in how the measures introduced to mitigate infection can be co-opted by lovers as a means of self-quarantining themselves, thereby enabling them to evade or mitigate any unwelcome societal expectations that might be imposed on them. In the fictional world of Márquez's novel, love is an immaterial cargo borne along and protected by nautical technology. By grasping the opportunity to signal that there is a health crisis on board, the passengers are able to take advantage of the legal requirements for physical and social distancing that demand the ship have an uninterrupted passage, sailing on without making any scheduled calls at harbours to pick up new passengers. While such practices of distancing are typically promoted and implemented so as not to jeopardise people's health during a pandemic, Márquez's protagonist enforces distancing so as not to jeopardise love, even though love itself might likewise take a toll on the condition of the lovers' bodies. This strategy of the protagonist points to two framings of his action. First, it can be framed as a wily application of the law, i.e. of appropriating the law for one's own ends at one's own individual discretion. Second, it can be framed as a conventional interpretation of the modern narrative of romance which holds that love is experienced at its ›purest‹ through the exclusion of any contextual interference from society. This second framing raises the question, however, of whether the application of any narrative – especially a globally accepted narrative – does not in fact serve to highlight the *intrusion* of society per se. Indeed, I would argue that this socio-semiotic approach is all the more interesting when the narrative itself, as in the case of romance, is based on the opposite of societal intrusion. On the one hand, Márquez's novel inspires us to expand such possible associations between love and a plague. On the other hand, and in addition to addressing the seemingly obvious impacts of emergency policies such as physical distancing measures on love-related practices, it is also relevant to consider the cultural concept of romantic love itself and the crucial impacts of this model on the performance of love regardless of whether there is a pandemic. For while romance as a concept is hardly likely to be abandoned due to the introduction of new legal and social policies, practices of performing love are always subject to social change. Accepting that such practices are fluid certainly does not render any analysis of love in the time of a pandemic any easier, however; hence I will limit myself in this essay to what I

---

[1] Cf. Peters: Love and Social Distancing in the Time of Covid-19, p. 758.

think is the primary challenge in discussing the rather complex topic of love in a time of plague. Rather than prematurely assuming that the crisis has changed *everything*, I opt instead to reflect on some important premises that need to be considered when analysing love from an experiential perspective.

1. Is There Really an Old Normal and a New Normal of Love?

Romantic love relationships are particularly interesting in that they are at once deeply enmeshed in the trajectory of Modernity while at the same time love is commonly regarded as a phenomenon that emerges ›naturally‹ and without intentional human agency. By contrast and from the viewpoint of social theory, empirical love relationships are regarded as being highly influenced by social contexts, including prevailing cultural narratives about love, though obviously such cultural narratives need to be *practically* (re)produced to have any effect on the trajectory of social life. It is in the constant interplay between the application and adaptation of cultural narratives within social contexts, i.e. in the same interplay by which every social interaction and communication is framed, that an understanding can be gained to discerning the fluidity of love relationships. The practical reproduction of the prevailing cultural model of romance entails that love be performed and experienced by sensual bodies and as a corporeally perceived dimension of a person's individuality. Anthony Giddens[2] sees a manifestation of the cultural narrative of romance in the extent to which romance is so deeply enmeshed in modern biographies, albeit any reference to the trajectory of Modernity is unacknowledged by modern individuals. Given that the narrative of romance is so crucially integrated in life-worlds, it would seem quite reasonable to assume that rapid changes would occur in practices of romantic love when life-worlds ›collapse‹ (as suggested in the heading of this part of the present volume). It also seems probable, however, that long-standing narratives and concepts will *persist* even when life-worlds are undergoing rapid change, lingering ›in the background‹ of now partially scattered life-worlds, enduring for some time within the ›new normal‹ that emerges from these changes. When analysing any social change, there are good grounds for assuming that a certain *inertia* applies in the case of cultural concepts. After all, even during revolutions not *everything* is changed or can easily be changed at an abrupt pace. Accordingly, I argue, it is generally more fruitful to proceed on the basis of there being a specific *entanglement* between any purported *old* and *new* normal. Most recent studies on love

---

[2] Cf. Giddens: Transformation of Intimacy.

relationships nonetheless apparently find that a one-way shift has taken place in such relationships over the course of the current pandemic, triggered above all by the sudden enforcement of distancing measures to prevent the spread of the virus. These studies typically emphasise the extent to which the consequences stemming from the *containment* of love relationships, romance, intimacy and sexual encounters, particularly during lockdowns of major parts of social life, have become a crucial aspect of the life-worlds of many individuals. In a recent article on *Online Dating Habits amid Covid-19*, for example, Annabelle Winking emphasises the health issues associated with such restrictions for those who engage in dating. The imposition of quarantines and physical distancing measures means that »dating as we know it has changed,« she argues, stressing that »it is crucial to understand these changes since forming intimate connections has a substantial impact on the mental and physical health of individuals«.[3] At the same time, of course, it is also pointed to a strong moral demand to comply with distancing measures. As Myles, Duguay and Dietzel have highlighted in their study on the use of dating apps during the pandemic: »Staying home was likened to a social responsibility or even a civic duty that responds to public health and societal imperatives, thus making dating or flirting while distancing seem like a heroic or political act.«[4]

For the epidemiologist Joan Soriano, it is specifically a human need for love that we necessarily have to cope with the risk of contagious infection: »This is not our first epidemic. It is the toll we have to pay for living in society and in cities. [...] Yet humans are emotional, social animals and beyond our species *Homo sapiens*, scholars say we are of *emotionalis* subspecies. As human animals we are not meant to live alone, or die alone, or in solitude.«[5]

The same importance of *copresent* human contacts is extended by scholars to the conditions in which love relationships are practised. Maxime Felder has proposed that urban environments lose their *urbanity* through the containment of physical contacts, since urbanity is inextricably connected with haphazardly meeting numerous people in the streets and stores or when using public transport.[6] This purported decline of modern social life can be further extended to the cultural narrative of romance as another product of Modernity and likewise it could be asked whether love relationships necessarily lose their romantic quality in the absence of physical contacts. The answer to this question is not quite clear according to recent studies. In depicting love during the pandemic, such studies often include the claim that copresent contacts are apparently quite *easily* substituted by communication at a distance, using digital technology as a matter of

---

[3] Winking: Online Dating Habits Amid Covid-19, p. 1.
[4] Cf. Myles/Duguay/Dietzel: #DATINGWHILEDISTANCING, p. 84.
[5] Soriano: Humanistic Epidemiology, p. 324.
[6] Cf. Felder: Die abgeschottete Stadt, p. 131.

course: »Those who do not have a partner or partners […] must find alternatives to meeting potential partners in person […] Dating apps are a way to safely maintain contact while social distancing, and therefore crucial to both maintaining contact and slowing the spread of Covid-19.«[7] In their overview of media discourses during the pandemic, Döring and Walter find that in spite of a »strong sensitization regarding certain restrictions on sexual and reproductive self-determination«, there has been a distinctly *moral* framing of requests and demands to replace physical encounters with online communications. Indeed, the authors detect a predominantly »very sex-positive« attitude in this discourse that evinces an »almost glorifying appreciation of solo and online sex« and which is »commercially friendly« towards the technology that facilitates such practices.[8] Digital technologies thus appear to be even more highly appreciated when romance is basically seen as a communicative practice. As Dibble and McDaniel have pointed out:

»Scholars have described communication to be the currency, if not the lifeblood, of human relationships in general and romantic relationships more specifically […] With a centuries-long history of intertwining between communication mediums and pursuit of romance [therefore] it was no surprise when the Internet and digital technologies became coopted for love and sexual expression.«[9]

Another consequence of these demands on distancing, intentions of performing love, and the use of technologies to replace physical copresence is that the hitherto somewhat dubious image of commercial dating apps has been able to be successfully altered. According to Myles, Duguay and Dietzel, for example:

»Dating app companies can also be understood as digital health actors because they normalise online dating cultures and practices in ways that can impact the physical, mental and sexual health of their users […] they have become new moral authorities that participate in shaping attitudes and behaviours in matters of human sexuality, romance, flirting, partnering and socialisation.«[10]

The new role of these companies has contributed greatly to their expanded commercial success as yet another side-effect of the pandemic. This is all the more the case insofar as policies of distancing, and above all impending lockdowns of social life, have triggered a desire to establish at least one ›intimate‹ relationship. According to Portolan and McAlister, for example: »The pandemic, and its accompanying promise of lockdown, sent many people searching frantically for the security offered by the romantic masterplot, including many who had not hitherto

---

[7] Winking: Online Dating Habits amid Covid-19, p. 86.
[8] Cf. Döring/Roberto: Wie verändert die COVID-19-Pandemie unsere Sexualitäten?
[9] Dibble/McDaniel: Romance and Dating in the Digital Age, p. 1.
[10] Myles/Duguay/Dietzel: #DATINGWHILEDISTANCING, p. 85.

used dating apps in this way.«[11] While doubt may be cast on the claim as to the *suddenness* of the popularity of the *romantic masterplot* resulting from the pandemic, the authors usefully allude to the cultural narrative of romance in their explanation of the increasing success of dating apps.

Overall, then, these quite diverse attempts to depict changes related to love in the time of the Covid pandemic do suggest that it is fruitful to look at more aspects of this phenomenon than merely the restrictions imposed on physical contact. I shall argue here that the ›old‹ normal of romantic love was already based on policies and practices of *distancing*, on a *specific* role assigned to the human body, and simultaneously on the importance of material technology in facilitating *intimate* communications. Proceeding from a delineation of these traits of the old normal in this way provides an analytical framework for fruitfully connecting the old with the new normal. Before elaborating further on this connection of the old and the new, therefore, I will first more generally address the overarching entanglement of love, the body, and mediated communications. This entanglement can best be made clear by describing three distinct strands: social distancing throughout Modernity; embodied practices of love; and digital communication technologies.

2. Social Distancing throughout Modernity

Theories of Modernity, above all classical theories, have long identified and analysed the development of increased ›distancing‹ in modern society as a distinctive change in social practices from those of pre-modern society. In this larger sense of distancing, as Sascha Dickel[12] has pointed out, the term *social distancing* now popularly introduced in reference to spatial measures against the spread of coronavirus is quite inaccurate insofar as these measures exclusively target physical distancing. For Dickel, this misnomer evidences the assumption that society is *run* predominantly on the basis of communications in physical copresence – an assumption that has clearly been rendered insupportable since the widespread adoption and implementation of digital technology. Connection made between physical and social distancing was already in place throughout Modernity and encompasses many more technological media than those that are today referred to and understood as *digital* technologies. At the turn of the twentieth century, for example, Georg Simmel[13] identified social distancing as the pivotal premise and defining characteristic of modern life. Simmel wrote extensively on the entangled

---

[11] Portolan/McAlister: Jagged Love, p. 7.
[12] Cf. Dickel: Gesellschaft funktioniert auch ohne anwesende Körper, p. 80.
[13] Cf. Simmel: The Philosophy of Money.

process whereby social life had become increasingly formalised and distantiated applying this concept both to contacts at a physical distance and contacts in physical copresence. The organisation of modern distancing was engendered in practice through the implementation of material and immaterial infrastructures of formalisation. Simmel's primary example was that of money and the money economy, including the credit system, which has enabled the spatial expansion of business activities and temporal extension of payments options without any physical contacts among business partners, thereby generating and facilitating ever greater distantiation within the economy. Most importantly, the activities and communications mediated by money technology and the environments surrounding this technology, including the digital logic of numerical, quantifying and calculable systems, have further served to introduce and amplify social distance in those encounters and activities that do still take place in physical copresence. Indeed it is precisely the relative abstractness of these physical contacts that allows for the effectiveness and potentially *unlimited* range of business transactions. Moreover, these affordances of the modern money economy are necessarily based not only on distant but also »ephemeral«[14] social contacts. This ephemerality arises because each single economic transaction now counts as a stand-alone activity, with sequences of such activities performed among the same individuals no longer involving any joint commitment to future business activities. At the same time, the sum of all these abstractly calculated and fleeting activities are nonetheless permanently recorded. The existence of such records, as being less ephemeral than physical contacts, affords the possibility of continuous contact-tracing of data and individuals and long-term access for interpreters of such data. This tracing is undertaken quite invisibly, remotely and anonymously, unnoticed by the individuals surveilled. Today, these same characteristics of the money economy apply especially to communications via digital apps, including apps newly introduced for contact-tracing of infected people or potential dating partners. The consequences of these distantiating attributes also include a widely perceived asset of modern life in the form of greater individual freedoms.

As Simmel elucidated, within the money economy, for example, there is the freedom to engage in business activities without the need for the prior establishment of any personal or physical contact with others. This freedom was initially facilitated and expanded through urbanisation and has more recently been greatly amplified through the World Wide Web. Urban contexts have further afforded individuals the freedom to mingle with *masses* of people without much social control, presenting them with an abundant variety of consumption choices at numerous stores, as well as ample opportunities for easy and rapid corporeal movement by means of transport to and from urban nodes (e. g. train stations), thereby

---

[14] Weber: Economy and Society, p. 637.

interconnecting a large network of otherwise physically more or less isolated and remote spaces. (Many such physical movements in order to get in contact with others, it should be noted, have since been even rendered potentially obsolete by the Internet, including our increased use of digital communication apps during the pandemic).

It was these urban environments, the icons of Modernity at the turn of the twentieth century, that produced modern relationships. Characterised by a weakening of social ties with the majority of copresent others, they also entail – as Durkheim famously noted – impersonal and distantiated dependencies enforced through formal institutions.[15] This development was also greatly supported by the emergence of bourgeois culture which gave rise to the widespread acceptance of the modern concept of romance and the practical introduction of love relationships. Similar to people's appreciation of the modern *freedoms* afforded by the ephemerality of social relationships, those who enjoyed the resources available within bourgeois life-worlds – often in strong contrast to the resources available to the working class – also developed a positive approach to *self-isolation*. The new bourgeois form of self-isolation involved creating and maintaining a distinct form of privacy in various ways. Spatially, for example, this included the creation and maintenance of a quite secluded and comfortably large residence with separate rooms for each individual. Temporally, meanwhile, a strong distinction was now drawn between *work time* and *leisure time*, with the latter periods often spent engaged in self-referential activities such as reading, combined with reflections on one's own life course. Socially, maintaining such isolation entailed securing a continuous input of sufficient money to afford this elaborate life-style without the need to fear the imposition of any *incalculabilities* on one's life course by others. And while withdrawing into such privacy does *not* in fact mitigate the dependencies imposed by modern institutions and their implemented formalisms, it did support the emergence of a concept of a lifestyle unencumbered by *society*. Furthermore, it was this context of individualising practices and experiences throughout Modernity which gradually fostered the idea that the concept of romantic love should be practically implemented into these life-worlds of designed self-isolation. This is largely because the predominantly literary concept of romance that had hitherto prevailed had also entailed both exclusivity and selectivity and was thus well-suited to the lifestyle of bourgeois privacy.

In sum, it was specifically the distantiating practices of bourgeois culture, both individually appreciated and collectively enforced, that engendered the desire for and expectations of romantic love to be included in one's biography – a biography that was now understood as individually designed. Social distancing and performing love thus both constitute eminent products of Modernity and are connected in

---

[15] Cf. Durkheim: The Division of Labor in Society.

a quite specific way. The culture of social distancing simultaneously highlights the importance of successively experiencing exclusive and intimate relationships with other individuals.[16] From this we can see that the interconnection between social distancing and performing love is by no means merely a disruptive innovation introduced in a time of plague but is rather quite consistent with key features of the purportedly *old* normal of modern life.

3. Embodied Practices of Love

Implementing the initially literary concept of love within modern lifestyle routine was inevitably accompanied by a stronger emphasis on embodied practices. While pre-modern and early modern practices of mating, at least among the educated and better-off classes, had often involved communications at a distance, including letter-writing, telegramming, telephoning, and the use of commercial ads and human mediators, Günter Burkart[17] has interestingly pointed out that embodied practices of communication first emerged as a feature of working-class culture in the United States, becoming ever more widely adopted from the beginning of the 1920s onwards until it eventually came to be accepted by all social classes throughout much of the world. Within the context of modern urban environments, mating came to be based on rituals of pronounced embodied practices through the introduction of sequences of copresent encounters called dating. This dating system crucially reflected and depended upon a specific urban infrastructure around the turn of the twentieth century, necessarily requiring the existence of a pool of individuals as yet totally unknown to one another. Such dating practices further assumed that urban singles, by dint of being mostly detached from social ties due to prior work-related migration, were now able to select freely from the pool of possible matches, i. e. without needing to worry about incurring any socially imposed obligations through making such matches. (Such freedom was in sharp contrast with practices surrounding the formation of matches in previous times, of course, as well as with enduring practices in rural areas.) As a consequence of copresent dating practices, the bodily performances came to seem of the utmost importance. Such practices of dating, involving the careful selection of dates and the scheduling of encounters with them, retrospectively help to explain the distinction between physically dating and formally securing opportunities for such dates – a distinction that is still fundamentally upheld by (the use of) dating apps. The embodied practice of dating as a new cultural prerequisite

---

[16] Cf. Hahn: Romantische Liebe als Phänomen der Moderne.
[17] Cf. Burkart: Soziologie der Paarbeziehung, pp. 105 f.

for mating also corresponded by chance with a feature of the previously purely literary model of romance.

The romantic model envisaged that love should be experienced in a sensual way and *avant la lettre*, i.e. before it is explicitly and mutually acknowledged by the lovers. This model implies that love is experienced *speechlessly*, i.e. primarily by bodily signs rather than verbally negotiated by arguments. Indeed, Burkart[18] has argued that a love relationship is an activity defined precisely by its contrast with communication based on cognitive reasoning. According to such a model, only bodily signs are often interpreted and valued as signifiers of *true* love. This seemingly clear contrast between the significance of purely embodied and purely cognitive signifiers does not render the experience of *love* unambiguous, however, since embodied signifiers are interpreted cognitively, and cognitive signifiers in turn are interpreted sensually and emotionally. A longstanding philosophical notion involves the metaphor of incomplete human bodies in a constant quest for uniting with their other *missing* halves. Heterosexual practices of intercourse, in particular, are interpreted from this perspective as being based on *complementary* performances and as physical evidence of the proper *fit* between the otherwise incomplete segments of two bodies – a fit that also hints at the possibility of an emotionally *right* match.[19] Another influential perspective on the connection of body and mind accompanying romantic love is based on erotic attraction. As Günther Dux[20] contends, erotic emerges from the *augmented* perception of being together in the same physical space with another body, though an augmentation engendered by a prior communicative bond. Here it is implicitly taken as understood that such practices of love are necessarily based on physical copresence. Notions surrounding distinctions between the body and mind, however, are generally subject to changing cultural thought systems. For example, while the ways in which a body signifies *something* and the sensations that trigger such bodily expressions have not been considered as arbitrary, spoken language has indeed consistently been understood as based on a culturally developed code that is cognitively controllable by speakers since the end of the 18th century. By contrasting the body with this ability and thus highlighting the incapacity of the body to control the signs it produces, including an inability to disguise the mind's intentions and thoughts, this perspective designates the body as the primary signifier for *true* love.[21] However, this also implies that *the mind* needs to figure out how to properly express love through embodied performances.[22] Overall, these cultural concepts present the body as a medium that specifically authenticates love

---

[18] Cf. Burkart: Auf dem Weg zu einer Soziologie der Liebe, p. 41.
[19] Cf. Krebs: Zwischen Ich und Du, p. 26.
[20] Cf. Dux: Geschlecht und Gesellschaft, p. 85.
[21] Cf. Kyora: Wahre Liebe.
[22] Cf. Hahn: Die Repräsentation des »authentischen« Körpers.

by rendering bodily signifiers of love readable to others. As I shall elaborate below (section 5), this idea of the importance of copresence in love relationships now potentially poses a problem for the users of dating apps, and one which such users have indeed themselves reported in interviews.

4. Digital Technologies of Communication

The term *romance* etymologically alludes to Romance languages and then Romantic verse styles and narrative themes, which itself indicates that the invention of romantic love was not originally mediated by performances of the human body. And while language-based representations of love do use descriptions of the body when referring to signifiers of love, *written* language in particular has played a major role in developing the cultural model of romantic love. Writing obviously already represents a certain level of abstraction as compared to embodied practices as a form of communication. Moreover, this abstraction has further given rise to enduring reflections by readers on romantic literature, in turn leading to even more cognitive reasoning about love. This is because representing love and love relationships through language, most often written language, necessarily relies on symbols whose reproduction and interpretation render them more and more conventionalized over time. In his study of the historical development of love throughout Modernity, Niklas Luhmann[23] famously showed that it was the gradual codification of signs that led to the widespread acceptance and practice of romance and simultaneously harnessed the perceived *uncontrolled* corporeal performance of passion. In this way, the codification of love did not initially emerge so much through the performative reproduction of codes in everyday life but rather through literature and the visual arts. From the early twentieth century onwards, films became especially influential in representations of romantic love relationships, ultimately at a global level. As Sabine Kyora[24] has shown, film producers further contributed to the codification of seemingly *involuntary* bodily expressions as signifiers for love because specifically embodied expressions were the most impressive and vivid means of visually illustrating love to film audiences. Given the extent to which social norms have excluded practices of performing love from the public eye, moreover, it is all the more plausible that audiences should have learned how to detect, reveal and perform love in their own lives from these fictional and codified representations.[25]

---

23 Cf. Luhmann: Love as passion.
24 Cf. Kyora: Wahre Liebe, p. 99.
25 Cf. Hahn: Liebe im Film.

With their global audiences, such representations of love have been highly effective in further implementing a specific cultural model of romantic love in everyday life, especially in cultures in which certain practices of performing love, including dating, had previously been unknown or unacceptable. At the same time, these representations tend to further conventionalise and standardise practices of performing love, to some extent *inverting* the ideal of the concept of romance. The classical version of this ideal, developed throughout the age of what was later termed *Romanticism*, held that romantic love relationships are constituted by individual communicative forms among lovers that lead to what Simmel described as their changed *relation to the world*.[26] Friedrich Schlegel, the famous German writer of Romanticism, even more radically depicted (the understanding of) romantic love in his novel *Lucinde* (1799) as the lovers' experience to *being each other's world*. In contrast to these views implicitly emphasising the creation of an individual meaning system by the lovers, codifications of love rather shape a type of relationship that is constituted by the application of social conventions. Instead of connecting lovers to each other by establishing their own *society among two* (Georg Simmel, referring to the form of a couple of lovers), codifications rather connect lovers to the world as it is represented by these conventions. Applying this analysis to the contemporary use of digital platforms and applications reveals a further paradox. For while the capacity of such technology to extend or maximise potential contacts and relationships spatially, temporarily and socially would seem to provide the perfect conditions for practising dating, the use of this technology also inevitably further codifies and formalises all communications. However, this does not mean that such communication is necessarily *perceived* as conventionalized by the users of (digital) technology; rather it suggests that these users' communication is necessarily attached to conventionalised systems and that they would need additional efforts in order to reframe such communication as being *individualised* and *romantic*.

5. Does Hoisting the Yellow Flag Already Do the Trick? On Researching Love in Times of Plague

While one might expect to find at least some obvious parallels between Márquez's novel and today's love stories in a time of plague, such parallels are in fact most likely to be quite limited, since any analysis needs to consider the social contexts of phenomena more specifically. Moreover, considering the pandemic and the policies introduced to mitigate infection as a kind of overarching context per se

---

[26] Cf. Hahn: Liebe.

is not yet sufficient to fully capture current love relationships. For example, contemporary relationships are not influenced only by policies of physical distancing. They are rather influenced by complex sets of practices, experiences and perceptions, especially by the set based on the intertwined social and physical distances entailed in the prevailing cultural concept of romance. As elucidated above, this concept comprises complementary practices of social distancing and establishing intimacy, complementary experiences of sensual non-cognitive signifiers, and experiences of signifiers mediated by codified conventions. Last but not least, this cultural concept includes complementary perceptions of copresence, the physical closeness of bodies, and communications at a physical distance mediated by different technologies, from letters to digital apps. Even at a time of the emergence of a seemingly *new normal* induced by a global pandemic, this complex set of practices, experiences and perceptions still produces multiple empirical variations in love relationships. Márquez' protagonist, for example, combines technology and policies designed to stop the spread of infectious disease with the opportunity to create an intertwined physical/social intimacy. Hoisting the yellow flag to indicate a case of contagious disease on board allows him to signal to any observer that the ship's movement needs to be framed in the context of a state of crisis, thereby making it necessary to suspend the usual legal policies regarding the ship's navigation. These policies of the ›old normal‹ before the proclamation of a crisis held that the ship must comply with scheduled harbour stops and thus refrain from *free* navigation. Navigating the ship freely was technically never impossible, however, and could even be done in compliance with the legal policies after the *context* of the ship's movement was actively re-framed. Likewise, and in accordance with recent social theory of digitalisation,[27] we can assume that it is not primarily the policies of physical distancing but the set of practices, experiences and perceptions mediating distances and proximity by the specific uses of digital technology that rather shape a combined form of the old and the new normal.

In what follows, therefore, I look at the old/new normal of copresence in order to better illustrate my argument that any analysis of changes in love relationships – indeed in any type of relationship – should address the entanglement of the old and the new normal. The use of digital technology during the pandemic has not exactly *replaced* communications otherwise intended to solely occur in copresence. Rather our use of digital technology is influenced not only by the *prohibition* of physical contacts but by the prevailing concept of romance itself. For example, this concept already includes the selection processes of *dates* and dating schedules being based on more or less *gradually* overcoming physical and social distances while establishing individualised communications. Though these constitutive components of love relationships do exist independently of digital tech-

---

[27] Cf. Hahn: Social Digitalisation.

nology, the technology currently at hand in the midst of the Covid pandemic is particularly well suited to meeting these demands included in the prevailing concept of romance, which goes some way to explain the increased use of communications based on mailing, texting, and videoconferencing. The features of such contemporary communications are actually quite comparable to the classic *romantic* practices of writing and reading love letters.

In contrast to dating in copresence, technology has ›brought back‹ extensive options for the intensive contemplation of (visual) texts, for storing such (visual) text for further reference, and for making (visual) text available to a wider audience. Importantly, our prior experiences of communicating via digital apps inevitably influence our first-time and subsequent copresent contacts with potential dates. Indeed, these experiences contribute to our interpretation of *all* subsequent communications, whether such communication takes place in copresence or not. Literally in-dividual, meaning indivisible, experiences (or biographical experiences, if seen from the perspective of a whole life-course) cannot be divided into two distinct categories of experience, i. e. between experiences involving physical copresence and those without physical copresence. If communication via (dating) apps has come to be the main form of communicating with each other, then actually being with somebody in physical copresence increasingly counts for an extraordinary situation inasmuch as it has become an *unusual* circumstance. The consequences of this extraordinariness are ambivalent, since such a situation might be characterized either as pleasant or unpleasant or both, depending on, for example, whether the sensual richness of copresence is perceived as a pleasant erotic augmentation or whether the lack of formal *data* about the other person(s) within spontaneous copresent encounters is perceived as unpleasantly depriving the interpreter of the wherewithal to *properly* frame the communication and situation. This problem might increase when more and more communications are operated via apps in a codified and conventionalized form. For example, Portolan and McAlister have concluded from the narrative interviews they conducted with users of dating apps: »There was a strong desire for romance to be *organic*, but also a strong sense that they were not the kind of person who could find romance without using the apps to explicitly seek it out.«[28] Seeking out romance may now involve a preference for situations which include signifiers that are *not* corporeally presented and/or which do not require an instant reaction/response.

In addition, the particular signifiers that are regarded as necessary when it comes to mating will obviously depend on social context and how these signifiers are specifically interpreted. In contrast, as indicated by matrimonial advertisements in the context of the nineteenth and early twentieth century there was apparently a stronger preference for knowing some ›data‹ on financial assets of

---

[28] Portolan/McAlister: Jagged Love, p. 12.

potential dating partners prior to dating them.[29] Likewise, but on an even more elaborate basis, representations of individuals conveyed through social media accounts – including their social status and body – are today often considered quite indispensable information that needs to be made public in order to attract potential dates.

All kind of experiences inevitably contribute both to what it means for an interpreter to communicate in copresence rather than at a physical distance and to how interpreters perceive the difference between copresent and non-copresent communications. These perceptions can obviously vary greatly, further supporting the point that it is not material technology itself that determines the significance of transmitted signs. For example, dating apps designed to ›seek and find‹ are apparently not unambiguously perceived as a tool to aid in precisely this task. From her interviews with users of these apps, Andrea Newerla[30] has concluded that some of the interviewees who had succeeded in finding a match had dissolved their relationships after a short while because they felt that the technically supported selection process could not have created a *romantic* match by definition. This contrasts with the findings of an earlier study that showed how some users of dating apps, despite having taken a very active and conscious role in the process of selecting digitally presented choices of dates, eventually came to romanticize the technological medium itself as a kind of »amor ex machina«.[31] Apparently seeking to frame their technologically supported dating process as being aligned with the belief that romantic matches should be encountered haphazardly or by faith, these users described meeting each other through the perceived unpredictable outcome of the app service as *magical*. From this it seems no longer self-evident whether falling in love while navigating Internet or falling in love at first copresent sight (or over the course of more copresent sightings) counts for a greater degree of contingency – with such contingency apparently remaining the gold standard of romantic meeting. In addition to the elaborate coding of closeness/distances according to the prevailing model of romance, all of these experiences induced by digital technology ultimately shape an increasingly complicated mixture of copresent and non-copresent communications, signifiers and coding systems.

The new need for interpreters to develop the capacities required to make sense of this mixture may eventually take the gradual ›escalation‹ of love and intimacy to a new level. However, this new level of entanglement of the concept of romance, practices of sensual embodiment and distancing, and codified communications via digital apps, does not seem to mean that falling in love or establishing love relationships has been made any easier or faster. The most recent empirical findings

---

[29] Cf. Carrington: Love at Last Sight.
[30] Cf. Newerla: Love Struggles.
[31] Cf. Hahn/Schmidl: Intim werden.

regarding practices of performing love during the Covid pandemic point to some interesting variants. These include temporal variants arising due to the rhythm of embodied/copresent and distantiated/non copresent practices, a social variant in which a relationship is carefully selected and exclusive but is not perceived as *romantic*, and the most obvious spatial variant of enforced physical proximity during strict lockdowns. An example of a temporal variant identified in the literature is what Portolan and McAlister have termed *jagged love*, defined by alternating between increased use of dating apps and explicit avoidance of these apps:

»This is the beginning of what we term the jagged love cycle, where the majority of participants became trapped in a cyclical loop. This involved downloading dating apps (sometimes multiple apps), vigorously swiping, matching, starting multiple chats (with low level personal investment), becoming quickly bored or exhausted with the process and their matches, deleting the dating apps, and then after approximately two weeks of experiencing FOMO (Fear of Missing Out) and loneliness, re-downloading the apps.«[32]

Such cyclical use of digital apps is clearly not intentionally induced by the form of the material technology itself or the marketing strategies adopted by the tech companies, since most business models would generally prefer to retain customers and achieve continuous purchases of their services. Rather this use of digital apps only becomes fully comprehensible when we consider it in relation to the concept of romance, as in the following explanation offered by Portolan and McAlister: »While this pattern [of cyclical use] was not necessarily markedly different to the ways in which people used dating apps in the past, it was heightened and accelerated by the pandemic, as people desperately sought the certainty offered by the romantic masterplot.«[33] In referring to the »certainty offered by the romantic masterplot«, the authors allude to people's attraction to a sequence of specific events (or a variation of this sequence), traditionally framed as »you meet someone, you fall in love, you marry, you have children, you live happily ever after«.[34]

Here the quest for such certainty is associated with an attempt to *balance* the uncertainties shaped by the pandemic with *normal* social life. However, this rhythmic use of dating apps also suggests that users might at least intermittently harbour doubts as to whether the dating app tool is really useful in helping them cope with the impacts of the pandemic on their lives. An example of a social variant is the emergence of *Corona buddies*. This phenomenon has been explored by Andrea Newerla,[35] who defines a Corona buddy as a partner who is carefully selected via dating apps from among a pool of potential matches in order to pursue

---

[32] Portolan/McAlister: Jagged Love, p. 13.
[33] Ibid., p. 2.
[34] Ibid., p. 2.
[35] Cf. Newerla: Intime Beziehungen und physische Nähe im Covid-19-Krisenkontext, p. 4.

an exclusive and committed relationship, i. e. a relationship that is intended to be close, that includes sexual intercourse, and is limited to one person. While these are traits equally aligned with the concept of romance, this type of relationship deviates from a romantic relationship in that the interview respondents expressly defined it as non-romantic. Similar to the findings of Portolan and McAlister, Newerla concludes that choosing a non-romantic Corona buddy (in the absence of a *romantic* mate) represents a *pragmatic* way in which to endure lockdowns, i. e. of undergoing this experience not as a *lonely* single but still in compliance with pandemic-related restrictions. Given that Newerla's respondents typically stated a preference for non-monogamous relationships and simultaneous dating with more than one person, however, this specific practice of social distancing can also be seen as representing at least a partial *return* to the concept of romance. This is all the more plausible if selecting a Corona buddy is likewise interpreted as a way of actually reproducing some of the certainties comprised within »the romantic masterplot«. Interestingly, the spatial variant defined by compulsory spatial proximity due to lockdowns is apparently *not* found empirically in practice. In this regard, Portolan and McAlister reflect on the ›locked-up‹ version of ›meet cute‹ scenes in popular movies presenting love relationships. Quoting Jessica Avery, the authors describe how the genre of romantic comedy in particular often entails »»any plot point that forces the two main characters to spend time together (whether they want to or not)‹«: »This trope often manifests in texts where people are snowed in together, stranded on a desert island, locked together in a safe house, or find themselves sharing a room for a night in which there is only one bed.«[36] In these films, love is depicted as being induced by a sudden breakdown of *normal* physical and, therefore, social distancing. While film producers might understandably perceive this crisis of reduced distancing as a genuinely appropriate way to visually illustrate practices of falling in love, what we learn from the data produced on and during Covid-related lockdowns is that this scenario is not actually the case in social reality. In other words, the condition of instant copresence is not (or no longer) the predominant trigger for love. That Márquez himself had some notion of this development seems quite likely, since it is only after having separately reflected on their relationship for fifty years that his fictional couple is finally self-quarantining on their locked-up love trip by hoisting the ship's yellow flag.

---

[36] Portolan/McAlister: Jagged Love, p. 13.

References

Burkart, Günter: Auf dem Weg zu einer Soziologie der Liebe, in: Kornelia Hahn/Günter Burkart (eds.): Liebe am Ende des 20. Jahrhunderts. Studien zur Soziologie intimer Beziehungen, Opladen 1998, pp. 15–49.

Burkart, Günter: Soziologie der Paarbeziehung. Eine Einführung, Wiesbaden 2018, p. 105–106.

Carrington, Tyler: Love at Last Sight. Dating, Intimacy and Risk in Turn-of-the-Century, Berlin/Oxford 2018.

Dibble, Jayson L./Brandon T. McDaniel: Romance and Dating in the Digital Age: Impacts of Computer-Mediated Communication and a Global Pandemic, in: Cyberpsychology, Behavior, and Social Networking, 24(7), 2021, pp. 1–2.

Dickel, Sascha: Gesellschaft funktioniert auch ohne anwesende Körper. Die Krise der Interaktion und die Routinen mediatisierter Sozialität, in: Michael Volkmer/Karin Werner (eds.): Die Corona-Gesellschaft: Analysen zur Lage und Perspektiven für die Zukunft, Bielefeld 2020, pp. 79–86.

Döring, Nicola/Walter Roberto: Wie verändert die COVID-19-Pandemie unsere Sexualitäten?, in: Z Sexualforschung, 33, 2020, pp. 65–75.

Durkheim, Émile: The Division of Labor in Society. Glencoe/Ill, 1933.

Dux, Günther: Geschlecht und Gesellschaft – Warum wir lieben. Die romantische Liebe nach dem Verlust der Welt, Wiesbaden 2018.

Felder, Maxime: Die abgeschottete Stadt, in: Fiorenza Gamba/Marco Nardone/Toni Ricciardi/Sandro Cattacin (eds.): COVID-19. Eine sozialwissenschaftliche Perspektive, Zürich/Genf 2020, pp. 131–140.

Giddens, Anthony: Transformation of Intimacy: Sexuality, Love and Eroticism in Modern Societies, Cambridge 1992.

Hahn, Kornelia: Liebe im Film. Fiktionale Modelle intimer Beziehungen?, in: Kornelia Hahn/Günter Burkart (eds.): Liebe am Ende des 20. Jahrhunderts. Studien zur Soziologie intimer Beziehungen, Opladen 1998, pp. 154–174.

Hahn, Kornelia: Die Repräsentation des »authentischen« Körpers, in: Kornelia Hahn/M. Meuser (eds.), Körperrepräsentationen, Konstanz 2002, pp. 279–302.

Hahn, Kornelia: Romantische Liebe als Phänomen der Moderne. Anmerkungen zur Soziologie intimer Beziehungen, in: Yvonne Niekrenz/Dirk Villányi (eds.): LiebesErklärungen. Intimbeziehungen aus soziologischer Perspektive, Wiesbaden 2008, pp. 40–49.

Hahn, Kornelia/Alexander Schmidl: Intim werden. Annäherungsgeschichten intrakulturell erzählt, in: Kornelia Hahn (ed.): E>3Motion. Intimität in Medienkulturen, Wiesbaden 2012, pp. 169–185.

Hahn, Kornelia: Liebe, in: H.-P. Müller/T. Reitz (eds.): Simmel-Handbuch. Begriffe, Hauptwerke, Aktualität, Frankfurt am Main 2018, pp. 361–365.

Hahn, Kornelia: Social Digitalisation. Persistent transformations Beyond Digital Technology, London 2021.

Krebs, Angelika: Zwischen Ich und Du. Eine dialogische Philosophie der Liebe, Berlin 2015.

Kyora, Sabine: Wahre Liebe. Die Zeichen des Körpers und ihre Inszenierung, in: Zeitschrift für Germanistik, Neue Folge, 12(1), 2002, pp. 99–111.

Luhmann, Niklas: Love as Passion. The Codification of Intimacy, Cambridge/Massachusetts 1986.

Márquez, Gabriel García: Love in the Time of Cholera, New York 2016.

Myles, David/Stefanie Duguay/Christopher Dietzel: #DATINGWHILEDISTANCING. Dating Apps as Digital Health Technologies During the COVID-19 Pandemic, in: Deborah Lupton/Karen Willis (eds.): The Covid-19 Crisis. Social Perspectives, London/New York 2021, pp. 79–89.

Newerla, Andrea: Love Struggles. Intime Beziehungen in Zeiten mobilen Datings, in: Michael Wutzler/Jaqueline Klesse (eds.): Paarbeziehungen heute. Kontinuität und Wandel, Weinheim/Basel 2021, pp. 46–72.

Newerla, Andrea: Intime Beziehungen und physische Nähe im Covid-19-Krisenkontext. Über Coronogamie, Dating und pragmatische Lösungen, in: Kornelia Hahn/Andreas Langenohl (eds.): »Öffentliches Leben«. Gesellschaftsdiagnose Covid-19, Wiesbaden 2022.

Peters, Michael A.: Love and Social Distancing in the Time of Covid-19: The Philosophy and Literature of Pandemics, in: Educational Philosophy and Theory, 53(8), 2021, pp. 755–759.

Portolan, Lisa/Jodi McAlister: Jagged Love. Narratives of Romance on Dating Apps During COVID-19, in: Sexuality & Culture, July 20, 2021, https://link.springer.com/article/10.1007%2fs12119-021-09896-9; last accessed September 05, 2021.

Simmel, Georg: The Philosophy of Money, London/New York 1978.

Soriano, Joan B.: Humanistic Epidemiology. Love in the Time of Cholera, COVID-19 and Other Outbreaks, in: European Journal of Epidemiology, 35(4), 2020, pp. 321–324.

Weber, Max: Economy and Society. An Outline in Interpretive Sociology, Berkeley/Los Angeles/London 1978.

Winking, Annabelle R.: Online Dating Habits Amid Covid-19, in: Anthós, 10(1), 2021, pp. 86–93.

Angela Condello

Justice and (Sexual) Difference. Questioning Gender Inequality from a Feminist Perspective

1. The Crisis within the Crisis

In 2020, a few months after the pandemic had become a global issue everywhere discussed and theorized, we were invited by Werner Gephart to sketch a first series of reflections on the contingency that we were going through.[1] The majority of the authors, including myself, focused on the *exceptional* nature of the crisis caused by the pandemic. Caught by surprise, we were interpellated by the extraordinary nature of the situation we were living, and such situation did require specific analysis on the forms and conditions of the *Corona Normativities*, for example on the new balance (or better: imbalance) caused by the pandemic at various levels.

One and a half years have passed. We are currently questioned by a new set of issues, mainly ascribable to the persistence of the situation emerged in the beginning of 2020. In this second collection, what we are asked to reflect upon is no longer exceptional or extraordinary; it is, instead, wide and it requires complex analysis. It is not one single problem or one single process we are going through, but a conundrum of problems and processes altogether. Also, reflecting on the persistence entails the observation of a situation which is now more or less stable, though permanently mutating, hence requiring a different theoretical effort. The *Persistence of the Exception* entails more data, more individual and collective experience(s), more elaboration(s). Yet, the doubts persist, and the precedent questions are amplified on the one hand by the resistance of some issues and, on the other, by the recurrence of older ones. The present text deals specifically with the repetition of a problem, namely gender inequality, which can be certainly traced back decades (if not, obviously, centuries) earlier than the explosion of the Covid-19 pandemic. And yet, it is a problem that – as we shall see – has gone through a dangerous acceleration in the last months.

I am hence opting to focus on a new question, and namely how has the pandemic exacerbated preexisting aspects of injustice – especially as far as gender equality is concerned – to what extent, and why. I am driven by one, sharp, ques-

---

[1] Cf. Gephart (ed.): In the Realm of Corona Normativities.

tion: how is it possible that the crisis of rights caused by the pandemic has worsened the condition of the female subject, also in contexts such as western democracies, where gender equality had been conceived, for decades, as a priority? The preliminary response to such question is that – probably – what appeared to be a stable and uncontroversial aspect of our societies, i. e., gender equality, is either a) unrealized, or b) it has been achieved under criteria that have led to cause some sort of new *crisis within the (current) crisis*.

How come, for instance, that Covid-19 pandemic has been termed a »disaster for feminism«?[2] The pandemic has indeed worsened, where not canceled, the progresses made in decades of struggles for gender equality. It is now evident that the pandemic has *radically worsened* the disparities between men and women from many perspectives, one of which is undoubtedly the disparity in the management of the workload consequent to the frequent and persistent presence of all members of families within the walls of houses and apartments. Schools and other public institutions in charge of care work were often shutting down, and then reopening irregularly, in addition to periods of lockdown causing problems with ordinary daily timetables for families with children, elderly people and in general with subjects requiring care work and time. It has been underlined, and then constantly confirmed by documents such as the Report of the Commission on the Status of Women (New York, 2020), as well as by the Technical Brief of the United Nations Population Fund and by recent declarations on the UN Sustainable Development Goals (especially Goal n. 5, *Gender Equality*), that the coronavirus outbreak has radically worsened the disparity between men and women, and consequently the progress of gender equality and the effectiveness of antidiscrimination protocols. What has been judged as striking is the accelerated falling back of rights and guarantees that had been taken for granted, without a particular differentiation between countries and geographic areas. Indeed, according to the reports there is not one country where full and harmonious equality between genders has been realized. In the *Policy Brief »The Impact of Covid-19 on Women«*[3], classical themes connected to the gender gap such as retribution, the balance between care work and profession, and mental load – are all back in the discourse as if the decades between 1970 and 2020 had not passed at all. Mental load, again? Care work, again?

Indeed, the pandemic has exacerbated the load of preoccupation already falling upon the shoulders of women. Inequality, furthermore, is persistent and the

---

[2] Lewis: The Coronavirus is a Disaster for Feminism. The opening lines of the article present a meaningful critique to all those that had underlined the great potentialities of smart working and lockdowns: »enough already. When people try to be cheerful about social distancing and working from home, noting that William Shakespeare and Isaac Newton did some of their best work while England was ravaged by the plague, there is an obvious response: *neither of them had child-care responsibilities*« (ibid.).

[3] United Nations: Policy Brief.

pandemic has worked as a litmus paper, showing more and better what was already there. How come that the progress achieved has proved so vulnerable? It has been noted that the current crisis has basically hastened a situation already critical. Hence, we could infer that the persistence of the exception – in this case for instance the loss of jobs due to inequalities in terms of access to health care, and unemployment benefits – basically reflects an unequal social system that has collapsed under the pressure of a crisis. The limited progresses in gender equality made since the 1995 Beijing Platform for Action are now at risk of being rolled back as the pandemic deepens precedent inequalities.[4]

The crisis of gender equality, within the larger socio-economic crisis caused by the pandemic, is mainly ascribable to the sudden growth of unpaid care responsibilities: Covid-19 closed schools, overwhelmed health services, and worsened the needs of weak and old people. These sudden changes have burdened women more than usual and have exposed the fragility of their roles in the job market.[5] Interestingly, early in 2020, when the pandemic had just emerged as a global issue, Covid-19 was considered as a potential *great equalizer*: the dangers of the virus could impact anyone regardless of their social position and everyone was forced to respect newly created rules. Further on, during 2020 and then also in the first half of 2021, what was supposed to function as an *equalizer* turned into the *source of larger inequalities* for the abovementioned reasons. Women perform most of the unpaid and underpaid care work: women's so-called *second shift* – the work at home after the working hours – has been exacerbated by the pandemic (e. g., with activities such as homeschooling, cooking, cleaning, and performing tasks like grocery shopping or bringing food and medicines to elder relatives). The last one and a half years have laid bare the structural inequalities that exist (and persist) in our society. A puzzling and uncertain socio-economic model emerged from the crisis and such model has clearly undervalued care work in favor of other values (consumption, efficiency: to name a few). Against this background, voices from the feminist movements have raised, claiming that what we are going through should push us towards sharing values of solidarity, care and respect, concepts that urgently need to be re-signified. Since the exceptionality of the context seems to resist in time, in the following considerations I intend to question some aspects characterizing the conceptualization of gender equality.

---

[4] Cf. United Nations: Policy Brief; Berkhout/Richardson: Identity, Politics, and the Pandemic.
[5] Cf. Power: The COVID-19 Pandemic Has Increased the Care Burden of Women and Families.

2. Untangling the Reasons of the Persistence

The previous, brief, preliminary data and remarks seem to lead our thoughts towards one basic assumption: if we are to untangle the reasons of the persistence here at stake, what must be questioned is the way equality and nondiscrimination have been imagined and realized. It is otherwise hard to believe that it suffices to suddenly enter a crisis to erase decades of achievements. How can that even be possible? Are antidiscrimination policies capable of valuing the point of view of the singular existence or their universalizing codes risk to become counter-productive? Difference feminism has developed these questions in the name of a new conceptualization of what should mean to be *equal*, valuing the aspects that constitute the feminine as a discourse which does not develop from the masculine, but that has instead its own logic, code, imaginary.[6]

Difference feminism differs from other streams in feminism, especially from so-called *equality feminism*. Although both streams desire a more *just* world, on the one hand, equality feminism is associated with politics of sameness between men and women: the main goal for this conceptualization of feminism is a model (usually: androgynous) in which men and women are equal partners. In terms of relationship and family, such conceptualization would manifest in the symmetrical division of care work and domestic labor.

Difference feminism, on the other hand, claims that men and women are fundamentally different, by bringing different values and qualities to relationships and family life, especially for what concerns parenting. From this point of view, men and women just achieve different tasks and are naturally inclined to do (or do not) something. Hence, policies that aim at neutralizing the figures of man and woman within society, in particular the neoliberal policies in labor law that tend to treat female and male subjects exactly as *the same*, when *they are not the same*, might have fractured, in time, the originally worthy objectives of equality policies.

The universal language of international protocols, for instance, in its typically general attitude (such that the protocols can be as inclusive as possible) can be too neutral and thus, in critical situations, this language could let unjust balances emerge. Human relationships are, on the contrary, everything but neutral: often, for example, one subject could represent the intersection of race, gender, economic position, and migration.[7] Normative systems overlap – hence, injustices can

---

[6] Sources that cannot be neglected are: De Beauvoir: The Second Sex; Irigaray: Speculum of the Other Woman; Irigaray: This Sex Which Is not One; Héritier: Masculin/Féminin; Difference feminism widely developed in Italy, as well, with authors like Luisa Muraro, Lia Cigarini and Adriana Cavarero (the main experiences developed starting from the mid-Sixties were Diotima, a philosophical circle, and La Libreria delle donne di Milano). For a recent synthesis, especially in relation to legal science, see Boiano/Condello/Simone: Femminismo giuridico.

[7] Cf. Crenshaw: Mapping the Margins. On intersectionality, cf. Cho/Crenshaw/McCall: Toward a Field of Intersectionality Studies.

be based on gender, but also on race, ethnicity, sexuality, economic background, (dis)ability, religion.

The crisis caused by Covid-19 has clearly shown that in all social units (larger or smaller) there are balances which are hard to dismantle, since they are based on traditions, and inclinations, passed down generation after generation. If, on the one hand, antidiscrimination law is *made of* norms and principles oriented towards equal treatment for those who might be discriminated, it is nevertheless (on the other hand) important that the project of equality is based on a clear and *just* model of society. Let us for instance consider, again, antidiscrimination policies in labor law, often providing equal payment, equal treatment, and equal conditions for male and female workers. Such neutralization of the figures of the female and the male worker reflects the logic of equality feminism: *women should be treated like men*. Indirectly, such logic translates the principle that *women should be like men*. Hence, from the point of view of such logic, care work becomes an obstacle to the realization of perfect equality between women and men. Care work, from this point of view, is undervalued and – in the difficult balance between working life and domestic life – it is often domestic life that should be sacrificed for the higher value, which in this model reflects the idea that ideally, women (just like men) should be mainly or mostly workers, and that everything else might create flaws in their professional life. Quite evidently, if the exemplary subject considered as the *measuring stick* to produce subjectivities is the middle-class, working, family man, then antidiscrimination policies might risk flattening the differences to pursue a unique and monolithic model, which does not represent diverse types of subjects, but only those who are numerically prevailing or anyways prevailing for other reasons.[8]

3. The Flaw in the Model

What emerges from this crisis is thus a mindset with a clear hierarchy, where capitalist values such as consumption and production prevail over care work and other activities not convertible into cash (unless they are *treated like* work). Behind this mindset, lies the idea that to men and women should correspond the same social roles. Yet, the current crisis has indeed shown that there are clear differences between male and female subjects and such differences can be either undone or pre-

---

[8] In many of her works, for example Niccolai: Non siamo tutti uguali; Niccolai: »Comprendere le ragioni dei mutamenti«, Prof. Silvia Niccolai (Constitutional Law, University of Cagliari) has argued that a mere request for equality without a concrete social and political project behind might risk to conceal an economic project (often based on the principles of neoliberalism).

served. In this second case, the sexual difference theorized by intellectuals such as De Beauvoir, Irigaray, Young, Héritier, and the Italian feminists, could indicate a way to conceptualize antidiscrimination in general, as well as antidiscrimination law. A feminist thinker, Carol Smart, underlined how law is often sexist, male, and gendered:[9] the rights of women (and hence, also those deriving from antidiscriminatory laws) should be designed on individual experiences since each life is unique and each subject has singular, unique, needs.

Let us return on the Sustainable Development Goal n. 5 of the United Nations (for 2030), devoted to gender equality, where we read:

»Women do 2.6 times more unpaid care and domestic work than men. While families, societies and economies depend on this work, for women, it leads lower earnings and less time to engage in non-work activities. In addition to equal distribution of economic resources, which is not only a right, but accelerates development in multiple areas, there needs to be a fair balance of responsibility for unpaid care work between men and women.«[10]

The comment on the Goal underlines the importance of a just distribution of the *invisible* work between men and women, on the one hand; on the other hand, it stresses on the damage produced until now by the unequal distribution of care work and, even if not explicitly, to the poor amount of resources destinated to welfare plans. Data on unpaid care work show that, on average, the economic value of unpaid care work amounts to 40 % of GDP;[11] and that, on average again, women dedicate 3.2 times more hours (every day) to unpaid care work than men. In Asia and in the Pacific area, moreover, they dedicate 4.1 times more hours per day.[12]

In high-income countries, as women have increased their paid work, the gender gap in unpaid work has narrowed slightly but not closed: women still do the bulk of routine housework and caring for family members. Interestingly, moreover, more recent data show that the more likely a wife's income exceeds her husband's, the more probable that she takes on a larger share of home production.[13] There is not yet one country in the world that has achieved equal share of unpaid care work and the progress in reducing such work has been too slow. Covid-19 has shown a detail that confirms how much of the mental load still falls as a burden on the shoulders of women: men are more involved in household activities like shopping, house repairs – that is to say, in quite exceptional tasks if compared to daily tasks such as childcare, grocery shopping or cooking and cleaning. To these daily do-

---

[9] Cf. Smart: Feminism and the Power of Law; Smart: The Woman of the Legal Discourse.
[10] UN Women: SDG 5.
[11] Cf. Dugarov: Unpaid Care Work in Times of the Covid-19 Crisis.
[12] Cf. International Labour Organization: Women Do 4 Times More Unpaid Care Work than Men in Asia and the Pacific.
[13] Cf. Kabeer / Razavi / van der Meulen Rodgers: Feminist Economic Perspectives on the Covid-19 Pandemic.

mestic tasks, Covid-19 added homeschooling.[14] Data, therefore, prove that unpaid care work has had unprecedented impact on gender inequality, especially considering the consequences on women's productivity and potential on the job market.

The flaws in the model have hence exacerbated the situation and the pandemic has not at all worked as a *great leveler*: on the contrary, it has shown that we are not all equally vulnerable across the lines of gender, race, and class.[15] Social privileges have protected the advantaged from suffering the worst consequences of the pandemic but that was not possible for the most socially vulnerable, who have also suffered from the so-called *loss of ethical goods* such as friendship, human connections, good relationships with family and partners, romantic attachments. Such losses have often been related to *pandemic parenting* and the disequilibrium in the division of care work.

Among the main issues emerging from this situation, we should mention the sudden contingency of plans: adults with care work responsibilities have often experienced no guarantee that they will have any protected alone time, apart from children, to work or to take care of themselves. On top of this, parents have often experienced the imperative to manage their own families' risks in the absence of consistent plans from governments and authorities. These effects testify of how Covid-19 has exposed the *toxic* effects of a system that has for far too long dominated many aspects of our societies, i.e., neoliberalism – an economic ideology based on the principle of capitalism that has often turned healthcare and education structures into profit-driven businesses. Again, as abovementioned, the reason for this transformation is a shift in the hierarchy of values governing contemporary societies, where care is less meaningful than consumption and gain.

Hence, the global fallout of the pandemic is deeply connected with the kinds of issues that feminist economists have long explored and investigated: the pandemic has developed into (and persists to be) *both a health and a socioeconomic crisis*, with very different outcomes by gender.[16] The model has, thus, shown, flaws: and the crisis has exacerbated them. Without a more inclusive economic paradigm, that values care and makes visible what the market-driven paradigm renders invisible or unimportant, any analyses of the pandemic and proposed responses to it are incomplete.

---

[14] The problem of mental load is a classic topic of feminist debates. The mental load, also called *cognitive labor*, refers to the non-tangible tasks involved in running a household. If one partner must constantly remind the other to uphold their end of the bargain, make to-do lists for them, or maintain a chore chart, that's still *work*. A journalist on the New York Times has commented recently on how to make a man aware of what it means to be in charge (cf. Grose: A Modest Proposal for Equalizing the Mental Load.).

[15] Cf. Hay: How Privilege Structures Pandemic Narratives.

[16] Cf. Kabeer/Razavi/van der Meulen Rodgers: Feminist Economic Perspectives on the Covid-19 Pandemic.

Care work, in other words, should *count as* work. It is work, and not something else: it is ontologically an activity requiring energies, efforts, sacrifices, concentration. A feminist perspective might afford a deeper understanding of the crisis, especially the interconnected gender dynamics of work, agency, and well-being. Such perspective could also build more resilient and gender-equal economies that support the flourishing of individuals lives, i.e., more *just*, proportioned, and balanced economies. If the system, the *model* as we have named it, is flawed, this does not entail that nothing could change.

Problems and contrasts have not only been produced by neoliberal policies at a normative level (e.g., in labor law like mentioned above), but also at the level of frameworks used to support and transform gender equality. An interesting example is the Athena Swan Charter.[17] This Charter was established to encourage the commitment of institutions such as Universities to advance the careers of women in various fields. The objective of the program is hence completely praiseworthy, since it aims at recognizing and celebrate good practices in higher education and research institutions towards the advancement of gender equality in terms of representation and progression.

Systems like these, though, follow the logic of constant evaluation of results and products of the research, where the task is to make it possible for women to reach as many prestigious positions as men, hence working long hours, also on weekends, etc. Weird circular dynamics are established by similar systems and the reason lies in the complete overcoming of differences between the two sexes. Initiatives like Athena Swan are based on hard data, which are crucial for credibility and accountability. Yet, all too often, these data focus on women as a homogenous group and so overlook intersecting patterns of disadvantage faced by women of color, early-career researchers, and sexual minorities. For example, compared with white women, female academics of color still report limited access to mentoring and higher rates of feeling isolated, excluded, discounted, and not belonging.

We could here reverberate the (rhetorical) questions asked by feminists in the Sixties and Seventies: what is the cake that we want? Do we want half of it, even if it is poisoned and makes us feel bad? What if, instead, we opted for a subversion of the order of values since *that is not our cake*?

Often, contemporary economic models lead us to please certain types of lifestyles, prioritizing values that have been imposed to us (let us think of the image *We can do it!*, showing a woman that can handle all aspects of her life). Perhaps, we do not want to do it, we do not want to live a life that resembles a box-ticking exercise.

---

[17] Advance HE: Athena Swan Charter.

4. The Exception and the Rule

These brief remarks were aimed at reading critically a situation we are still experiencing. As it is known, everyone can have opinions on the present, but it is hard to grasp the correct lines of analysis that can lead to thorough and exact understanding. The problems at stake are a conundrum: I took the liberty to bridge data, presumptions, theories developed in dishomogeneous phases, places, and fields of knowledge. The main objective of these remarks was reflecting on the *persistence of the exception* as an occasion to observe, critically, the socio-economic model dominating the present. The persistence of the exception indeed testifies of how the crisis has become (since it already was) *structural*. Such *exception*, and its *persistence*, could have been foreseen as endemic within contemporary society, given the frequent tendency to reduce social justice (and hence also gender justice, and gender equality) to distributive justice.[18] We must question, therefore, what is the *exception* and what has become the *rule*, in this system, as far as impartiality and formal equality are concerned. Following the theoretical framework of difference feminism, normative theories and public policies should *affirm* rather than *suppress* social groups differences.[19]

Many feminist theories are complex theories of justice and not only theories of gender oppression in culture, as it is often reiterated; in other words, theories deriving from difference feminism are centered around the female-sexed or female-embodied social subject, »whose constitution and whose modes of social and subjective existence include most obviously sex and gender, but also – and at times more prominently – race, class, ethnicity, and any other significant sociocultural divisions and representations thereof; a developing theory of the female-embodied social subject that is based on its specific, emergent, and conflictual history«.[20] Feminists who work on gender justice have elaborated different ideas on what goals and paradigms of justice are actually viable to assess the situation of women, especially in times of crisis.[21] In those specific times, in fact, different models of justice clash: some are oriented towards the distribution of resources, others towards the affirmation of the feminine subject. It is thus difficult to establish if a system is just or unjust since it might be just for some criteria and unjust for others. Different paradigms of justice prioritize different values and so those using them may often disagree as to whether a given policy or situation is just or unjust.

Often, as we have seen with the example of Athena Swan, there are women's empowerment projects and human rights demands that are based on capitalist

---

[18] Cf. Young: Justice and the Politics of Difference.
[19] See the special issue of Critical Inquiry dedicated to reflections on the pandemic: Scotch: Posts from the Pandemic.
[20] de Lauretis: Feminism and Its Differences.
[21] Cf. Ferguson: Feminist Paradigms of Solidarity and Justice.

values: neoliberals argue that political and civil liberties are best promoted by giving individuals strong property rights and economic independence. The opposite political traditions argue that the social and economic rights necessary for the minimal equality of citizens and their freedom require a welfare state that provides minimal safety nets, that can guarantee an adequate standard of living, health care, housing, and education for all. The concept of *sexual difference* as developed by feminist thinkers suggests understanding justice as equity, as a shifting and adaptable measure or proportion and not as a definite standard, aimed to treat equally cases that are equal, and differently cases that are different (such thesis is confirmed by more recent works by feminist theorists such as I. M. Young and N. Fraser).[22] Equality, in other words, is also (maybe: only) just only when it promotes one's freedom to develop one's own capabilities and to engage in active participation.

Conclusively, against the background of the persistence of the exception, and as far as gender equality is concerned, difference feminism seems to offer a way of »upsetting an applecart« and of rethinking the balance between genders, in terms of the different logics governing the spheres of the feminine and of the masculine. An upsetting code, that of feminism, that could re-position each subject within her unique character, inside a story that is unmatched and unparalleled. The rehabilitation of the principle of sexual difference, though it might sound out of date, restores a thought of the *singularity*: the only space where *right* and *just* can encounter each other.

References

Advance HE: Athena Swan Charter, https://www.advance-he.ac.uk/equality-charters/athena-swan-charter; last accessed August 26, 2021.
Berkhout, Suze G. / Lisa Richardson: Identity, Politics, and the Pandemic: Why Is COVID-19 a Disaster for Feminism(s)?, in: History and Philosophy of the Life Sciences, 42(4), 2020.
Cho, Sumi / Kimberlé Crenshaw / Leslie McCall: Toward a Field of Intersectionality Studies: Theory, Applications, and Praxis, in: Signs, 38(4), pp. 785–810, 2013.
Crenshaw, Kimberlé: Mapping the Margins: Intersectionality, Identity Politics, and Violence against Women of Color, in: Stanford Law Review, 43(6), pp. 1241–1299, 1991.
de Beauvoir, Simone: The Second Sex, Paris 1949.

---

[22] Cf. Young: Justice and the Politics of Difference; Fraser: Justice Interruptus.

de Lauretis, Teresa: Feminism and Its Differences, in: Pacific Coast Philology, 25(1), 1990, pp. 24–30.

Dugarova, Esuna: Unpaid Care Work in Times of the Covid-19, June 18, 2020, https://www.un.org/development/desa/family/wp-content/uploads/sites/23/2020/06/Unpaid-care-work-in-times-of-the-COVID-19-crisis.Duragova.pdf; last accessed August 26, 2021.

Ferguson, Ann: Feminist Paradigms of Solidarity and Justice, in: Philosophical Topics, 37(2), 2009, pp. 161–177.

Fraser, Nancy: Justice Interruptus: Critical Reflections on the »Post-Socialist« Condition, New York 1997.

Gephart, Werner (ed.): In the Realm of Corona-Normativities. A Momentary Snapshot of a Dynamic Discourse, Frankfurt 2020.

Grose, Jessica: A Modest Proposal for Equalizing the Mental Load, in: The New York Times, June 11, 2019, https://www.nytimes.com/2019/06/11/parenting/mental-load.html); last accessed August 26, 2021.

Hay, Carol: How Privilege Structures Pandemic Narratives, in: American Philosophical Association Newsletter on Feminism and Philosophy, 20(1), 2020, pp. 7–12.

Héritier, Francoise: Masculin/Féminin. La pensée de la difference, Paris 1996.

International Labour Organization: Women Do 4 Times More Unpaid Care Work than Men in Asia and the Pacific, June 27, 2018, https://www.ilo.org/asia/media-centre/news/WCMS_633284/lang--en/index.htm; last accessed August 26, 2021.

Irigaray, Luce: Speculum of the Other Woman, Minuit 1984.

Irigaray, Luce: This Sex Which Is Not One, Cornell 1985.

Kabeer, Naila / Shahra Razavi / Yana van der Meulen Rodgers: Feminist Economic Perspectives on the Covid-19 Pandemic, in: Feminist Economics, 27(1), pp. 1–29, 2021.

Lewis, Helen: The Coronavirus Is a Disaster for Feminism, in: The Atlantic, March 19, 2020, https://www.theatlantic.com/international/archive/2020/03/feminism-womens-rights-coronavirus-covid19/608302/; last accessed August 08, 2021.

Niccolai, Silvia: Non siamo tutti uguali: con l'universalismo è lei che ci perde, in: Morena Piccoli (ed.): Gestazione per altri. Pensieri che aiutano a trovare il proprio pensiero, 2017, pp. 157–183.

Niccolai, Silvia: »Comprendere le ragioni dei mutamenti«: il costituzionalismo, la new governance e l'ascolto della differenza di genere, in: Ales, Edoardo / Marzia Barbera / FaustinaGuarriello: Lavoro, welfare e democrazia deliberative, 2010, pp. 81–128.

Power, Kate: The COVID-19 Pandemic Has Increased the Care Burden of Women and Families, in: Sustainability: Science, Practice and Policy, 16(1), 2020, p. 67–73.

Scotch, Hank: Posts from the Pandemic, in: Critical Inquiry, 47(2), 2021.
Simone, Anna / Angela Condello / Ilaria Boiano: Femminismo giuridico. Teorie e problem, Milano 2019.
Smart, Carol: Feminism and the Power of Law, London 1989.
Smart, Carol: The Woman of Legal Discourse, in: Social & Legal Studies, 1(1), 1992, pp. 29–44.
United Nations: Policy Brief: The Impact of Covid-19 on Women, April 09, 2020, https://www.un.org/sites/un2.un.org/files/policy_brief_on_covid_impact_on_women_9_apr_2020_updated.pdf.; last accessed August 26, 2021.
UN Women: SDG 5: Achieve Gender Equality and Empower All Women and Girls, https://www.unwomen.org/en/news/in-focus/women-and-the-sdgs/sdg-5-gender-equality; last accessed August 26, 2021.
Young, Iris Marion: Justice and the Politics of Difference, Princeton 2012.

Brigitte Nerlich

The Coronavirus and Covid-19: Verbal and Visual Metaphors

Introduction

In December 2019, eighteen years after the outbreak of SARS, or Severe Acute Respiratory Syndrome, a new SARS-like virus began to circulate in China. On January 12th, 2020, the World Health Organisation (WHO) confirmed that a novel coronavirus, SARS-CoV-2, or Severe Acute Respiratory Syndrome Corona Virus 2, had caused a new respiratory illness. This was first called 2019-nCoV, with nCoV standing for new Corona Virus or coronavirus. On February 11th, 2020 the WHO announced *Covid-19* as the name of this new disease. On January 30th it was declared a Public Health Emergency of International concern and recognised as a pandemic on March 11th, 2020.[1]

One country after another went into *lockdown*, some closed borders, all implemented public health measures such as social distancing, self-isolation or quarantine, and, some belatedly, the wearing of masks in order to contain and control the new virus. In the midst of this turmoil, and a day after the United Kingdom went into lockdown, the science writer Philip Ball wrote an article entitled »Shot of hope: inside the *race* for a coronavirus vaccine«.[2] A year later the race was *won*, not by a single vaccine but by numerous vaccines. Millions of people have been vaccinated, mostly in rich countries. But still, in the meantime, between the spring of 2020 and the spring of 2021 millions of people have died world-wide and many more will continue to die, especially in countries that don't have access to vaccines. We need a *tsunami* of vaccines to counteract the tsunami unleashed by the SARS-CoV-2 virus.

While waiting for vaccines, governments have waged *war* on the virus with non-pharmaceutical public health measures such as distancing and isolation, which have come to warp space and time. Social and physical space between people has changed and perceptions of the passing of time have become distorted. Language has changed as well. New words have been coined, from *covidiot* to *vaxxie* (selfie taken while being vaccinated), but, most importantly, metaphors

---

[1] Cf. Zinn: Introduction: Towards a Sociology of Pandemics.
[2] Ball: Shot of Hope.

have emerged. As readers will have noticed, when describing this pandemic, I have used or cited metaphors of hope and, mostly, metaphors of fear – race, lockdown, tsunami, war etc. Metaphors are everywhere during this pandemic, and in this chapter, I will explore some metaphorical patterns and imagery that emerged early on in the pandemic – words and images that became metaphors we lived and still live by, for good or for ill.

The metaphors used during the pandemic are *generative metaphors* to use a term coined by Donald Schön in the 1970s. Such metaphors influence »how we think about things, make sense of reality, and set the problems we later try to solve. In this [...] sense, ›metaphor‹ refers both to a certain kind of product – a perspective or frame, a way of looking at things – and to a certain kind of process – a process by which new perspectives on the world come into existence.«[3] In an early key paper, Schön argued that »the essential difficulties in social policy have more to do with problem setting than with problem solving, more to do with ways in which we frame the purposes to be achieved than with the selection of optimal means for achieving them.«[4] In the following we shall see that all too often metaphors were used to frame political purposes to be achieved rather than trying to find the optimal means to solve the problems of the pandemic. Indeed, they mostly hid or exacerbated existing social problems and distracted from dealing with them in humane and responsible ways.

1. Metaphors and Meaning

Why look at metaphors in the time of coronavirus? Metaphors create meaning. They have been tools for meaning making as long as humans have been able to talk to each other. They are essential for the development of language, cognition and culture. They also play an important role in how we think and talk about health, illness and medicine and they shape how we act, individually and collectively.

The impact of metaphors in particular and social representations in general on thinking, talking and acting in the context of emerging infectious diseases, has been studied systematically by social scientists and communication scholars from Susan Sontag's work on illness as metaphor onwards, starting with AIDS in the 1980s,[5] followed by Ebola in the 1990s,[6] foot and mouth disease,[7]

[3] Schön: Generative Metaphor.
[4] Ibid.
[5] Cf. Sontag: AIDS and Its Metaphors.
[6] Cf. Ungar: Hot Crises and Media Reassurance; Joffe/Haarhoff: Representations of Far-Flung Illnesses.
[7] Cf. Nerlich/Hamilton/Rowe: Conceptualising Foot and Mouth Disease; Nerlich: War on Foot and Mouth Disease in the UK; Larson/Nerlich/Wallis: Metaphors and Biorisks.

SARS,[8] avian/bird flu/influenza,[9] swine flu,[10] Zika[11] and many more. Lorenzo Servitje has recently explored how the war metaphor became part and parcel of Victorian literature and culture,[12] and Alex de Waal has written a book on how the modern world adopted a martial script to deal with epidemic disease threats.[13] Covid metaphors are now also being studied by linguists and other experts.[14] This chapter is an eclectic contribution to this emerging trend. I collected the metaphors and images that I discuss here between March and November 2020 – and there are many many more out there. This is a rather serendipitous and random collection, but it might provide some insights into the early effervescence of imagery and become an illuminating by-product of the rather dark times we lived in, shedding light on the use and misuse of metaphors in a context where science and society and science and politics became entangled in ways rarely seen before.

2. War Metaphors

A core metaphor used during the pandemic, especially in its early stage was the metaphor *Managing an epidemic is war*, a metaphor that has been with us for a very long time. Expressions relating to this overall conceptual metaphor, such as fight, battle, combat, attack, defend and defeat, as well as enemy, especially invisible enemy, and hero, for example, came out in force when the outbreak of Covid-19 started in China. In country after country metaphors also turned into reality when the army joined the *war effort* in fighting Covid. It should be stressed however, that this mapping of one conceptual domain, war, onto another, management of disease, mostly happens at a rather superficial level, with little knowledge or understanding of *real war*.

This is quite common in conceptual mapping processes and in storytelling. In his book *Frankenstein's Footsteps* Turney has explored the role of popular culture in helping to shape and express public attitudes.[15] He suggests that just the title of a cultural reference, such as *Frankenstein* can evoke an entire story or *script*, which can be used as an interpretative frame. This frame then structures the way we think and talk about the social consequences of biotechnology, for example.

---

8   Cf. Wallis/Nerlich: Disease Metaphors in New Epidemics.
9   Cf. Nerlich/Halliday: Avian Flu; Brown/Nerlich/Crawford/Koteyko/Carter: Hygiene and Biosecurity.
10 Cf. Nerlich/Koteyko: Crying Wolf?
11 Cf. Ribeiro/Hartley/Nerlich/Jaspal: Media Coverage of the Zika Crisis in Brazil.
12 Cf. Servitje: Medicine Is War.
13 Cf. de Waal: New Pandemics, Old Politics.
14 Cf. Semino: »Not Soldiers but Fire-fighters«; cf. Wicke/Bolognesi: Framing Covid-19.
15 Cf. Turney: Frankenstein's Footsteps.

Frankenstein evokes the script of the mad scientist who invents an individual human monster, whereas *Brave New World* evokes the script of the state-managed production of copies of human beings on assembly lines.

We know the outlines of these scripts, even though we might never have read *Frankenstein* or *Brave New World*. In the same sense, *war* evokes rather a skeletal script of heroism and sacrifice through which people like me understand the phenomenon of a global pandemic and vaguely know how we are supposed to act. We might not know what war really is, but we know that script from previous exposures to it during many other illnesses, epidemics and even pandemics. Those who have lived through or are living through actual wars will, of course, bring different experiences to this common understanding.[16]

Here is one prominent example of the war metaphor: »President Xi Jinping has vowed to wage a ›people's war‹ against the Covid-19 epidemic. Judging by the draconian measures that have been introduced to quarantine tens of millions of people, restrict the return to work after the Chinese New Year, and shutter much of the Chinese economy, he was certainly not understating his determination.«[17] There are thousands more used by leaders all over the world. However, there are cultural differences in the use of war metaphors. For example, in Germany, at least at the beginning of the pandemic, the focus has been less on war and more on science, investigation, testing and research,[18] while in New Zealand the focus was on compassion,[19] community,[20] and collaboration, indeed teamwork, a strategy that seems to have worked much better *in bringing the virus under control*.

War metaphors also marched into the UK discourse, once the government announced its action or *battle plan*. One headline in *The Sun* brought many aspects of the war metaphor together when it declared: »Army on standby as Boris declares war on coronavirus with battle plan to kill the deadly virus«.[21] Franziska Kohlt has dissected this war discourse in some detail in her article entitled *Over by Christmas*.[22]

Some people opposed the war metaphor, and rightly so. Simon Jenkins wrote in *The Guardian*: »Never, ever, should a government use war as a metaphor in a time of peace. Britain is not at war with coronavirus. The phrase and its cognates should be banned. Those who exploit them to heighten panic and win obedience

---

[16] Cf. in this volume Krumeich: Corona und Krieg.

[17] Magnus: China and Covid-19.

[18] Cf. Jaworska: Is the War Rhetoric Around Covid-19 an Anglo-American Thing?; cf. Paulus: How Politicians Talk About Coronavirus in Germany, Where War Metaphors Are Avoided.

[19] Cf. Flanagan: Lead with Compassion and Ditch the Wartime Metaphors.

[20] Cf. Vowles: Want, Want, Want: How Boris Johnson's Choice of Language Failed to Bring the UK Together.

[21] Clark/Brown: Army on Standby as Boris Declares War on Coronavirus with Battle Plan to Kill Off Deadly Bug.

[22] Cf. Kohlt: »Over by Christmas«.

to authority should be dismissed from public office.«²³ Similarly, Simon Tisdall asked people to »lay off the war metaphors«.²⁴

A French article summarises the issue with the war metaphor well, highlighting instead the importance of care and solidarity: »Les mots ont un sens. Nous ne sommes pas en guerre. Nous sommes en pandémie. Nous ne sommes pas des soldats, mais des citoyennes et citoyens. Nous ne voulons pas être gouvernés comme en temps de guerre, mais comme en temps de pandémie. La solidarité et le soin doivent être institués comme les principes cardinaux de nos vies. La solidarité et le soin. Pas les valeurs martiales et belliqueuses.«²⁵

The metaphorical framing of *frontline* healthcare workers as *heroes* in the United Kingdom was especially egregious, as it set them up to be sacrificed. This is the opposite to solidarity and care. Similarly, the metaphors of the virus as the *invisible enemy* or the *invisible mugger* by Donald Trump and Boris Johnson respectively, were counterproductive, even dangerous in the context of populist governments.²⁶ Framing the coronavirus as an »invisible enemy«²⁷ in the context of an anti-immigration policy stance does not set up the optimal means for solving the problem of Covid-19. Equally, framing it as an »unexpected mugger«²⁸ in a context where a government repeatedly delayed action on Covid-19 does not provide the optimal means for dealing with the pandemic. In both cases this framing may well have contributed to the loss of lives. Explaining challenges plainly and communicating science well, while also appealing to community, compassion and solidarity, seems to work better.

War framing diverts attention away from government responsibilities and focuses instead on individual responsibilities, individuals who are asked to handwash and social distance, to not *flood* parks and beaches or crowd together in protest marches.²⁹ It diverts attention away from the impacts of austerity and ingrained inequalities,³⁰ from critically underfunded healthcare systems, and from the hostile environments for migrants and people of colour. Most importantly, it diverts attention away from our common humanity.³¹

---

23 Jenkins: Why I'm Taking the Coronavirus Hype with a Pinch of Salt.
24 Tisdall: Lay Off those War Metaphors; Sanderson/Meade: Pandemic Metaphors; Serhan: The Case against Waging ›War‹ on the Coronavirus; an article against the war metaphor illustrated with a cartoon showing a tank whose track system is made up of coronaviruses.
25 Combes: Non, nous ne sommes pas on guerre, nous sommes en pandemie.
26 Cf. Shafer: Behind Trump's Strange ›Invisible Enemy‹ Rhetoric; Shariatmadari: Muggers and Invisible Enemies.
27 Ibid.
28 Ibid.
29 Cf. Nerlich/Jaspal: Social Representations of ›Social Distancing‹ in Response to Covid-19 in the UK Media.
30 Cf. in this volume Spranz: Celebreties in Coronaland.
31 Cf. Sanderson/Meade: Unimaginable Times.

3. Elementary Metaphors

Once the coronavirus pandemic began to *sweep* around the world, people started to talk about it in rather elementary ways, using stock metaphors – linked to the classical elements: Air, fire, earth and water. The pandemic is *the perfect storm*, there is a *tsunami of cases*, and, of course, the fear of being swamped by cases, of a *second/third etc. wave*, even, as some Germans said, a *Dauerwelle* or permanent wave/perm, is forever with us; there are *flare-ups* and *hotspots*; the pandemic spreads like *wildfire* and we have to introduce *fire-breaks*.

The use of such elementary metaphors has advantages and disadvantages. Let's look briefly at the *perfect storm* metaphor. It focuses our attention, but, as Brandt and Botelho pointed out in *The New England Journal of Medicine*: »the perfect-storm metaphor may misdirect our concepts of – and therefore our approach to addressing – emerging pandemics. This language creates a public health discourse that seems reactive rather than proactive, reductive rather than holistic, disempowering rather than empowering«.[32]

What about fire metaphors? One could probably write a whole book about fire metaphors, from *burning embers* to *devastating wildfire* ... Elena Semino, an expert on metaphors, has recently written a defence of fire metaphors. She points out: »Even out of context, forest fires are a suitable area of experience for metaphorical exploitation. They are vivid, or image-rich; they are familiar, even when not experienced directly; they have multiple elements (trees, fire-fighters, arsonists, victims, etc.); and they have strong evaluative and emotional associations.«[33] She goes on to explain that in the specific data she collected, »fire metaphors are used flexibly and creatively for multiple purposes, particularly to: convey danger and urgency; distinguish between different phases of the pandemic; explain how contagion happens and the role of individuals within that; justify measures for reducing contagion; portray the role of health workers; connect the pandemic with health inequalities and other problems; and outline post-pandemic futures«.[34]

I want to add to this list of flexible uses of fire metaphors one more and that is: contestation of pandemic policies. As one resident of New York said after the outbreak was brought under control there: »Just because the fire was put out doesn't mean the house wasn't burned down.«[35] In an article for *The Guardian*, the epidemiologist William Hanage, reacting to the UK government's misconceived plans to manage the pandemic, said: »Your house is on fire, and the people whom you have trusted with your care are not trying to put it out. Even though they knew

---

[32] Brandt/Botelho: Not a Perfect Storm.
[33] Semino: ›A Fire Raging‹. See also Semino: »Not Soldiers but Fire-fighters«.
[34] Ibid.
[35] Dean: Twitter-Post from July 21, 2020,

it was coming, and could see what happened to the neighbours as they were overwhelmed with terrifying speed, the UK government has inexplicably chosen to encourage the flames, in the misguided notion that somehow they will be able to control them.«[36]

There are also ways of using the fire metaphor to demand new ways of acting on pandemics in the future, anticipating a fire rather than fanning it. As Professor Peter Piot, who contributed to the discovery of the Ebola virus, wrote: »I hope the lesson will really be that we can't afford to recreate the fire brigade when the house is on fire, we need the fire brigade ready all the time, hoping that it never has to be deployed.«[37] Such anticipatory action might also have been useful in another disastrously mismanaged aspect of earthly life, namely climate change – which, by the way, might contribute to more zoonotic events in the future.

And finally, earth – are there any metaphors relating to this element? There are geological ones like *eruption* but mostly landscape ones of *mountains* and *peaks*, *valleys* and *plateaus* through which we and the virus journey in the real world but also in mathematical space, and where we and the virus move and encounter *obstacles* and *barriers* and where we also, more positively, might erect *walls* of vaccines to stop the virus in its tracks. In a recent blog post Grant Jacobs, a bioinformation, wrote about the spread of a new virus variant, Delta, and noted that: »An over-arching pattern may be that the transmissibility of new variants leaves little room for weaknesses in control measures. The wall needed to protect against Delta needs to be higher and tighter-packed than for Alpha.«[38] And if you read the blog post you'll see a neat little illustration of the two types of wall, the Alpha wall and the Delta wall.[39]

In the middle of the first period of the pandemic in the UK, just after our Prime Minister had himself recovered from the virus and the country was recovering too, he used landscape metaphors extensively and even introduced a tunnel to the landscape: »We've come through the peak, or rather, we've come under what could have been a vast peak, as though we've been going through some huge Alpine tunnel. And we can now see the sunlight and the pasture ahead of us. And so, it is vital that we do not now lose control and run slap into a second and even bigger mountain.«[40] He also said that we are »on a downward slope«.[41] As a reporter for *Politico* quipped: »Boris Johnson is back and he has metaphors.«[42]

---

[36] Hanage: I'm an Epidemiologist.
[37] Hamill: Millions Could Be Left with Health Complications.
[38] Jacobs: Covid-19 and the Rise and Rise of Delta.
[39] Cf. Ibid.
[40] Johnson: Prime Minister's Statement on Coronavirus (Covid-19).
[41] Ibid.
[42] Cooper: Boris Is Back.

The pandemic brought about an explosion of metaphors through which we, ordinary people, health officials and politicians all tried to make sense of the new world we live in. But what about images, literal and metaphorical ones? What role did they play in the pandemic of a virus that nobody had heard about before and that was invisible to the human eye?

4. From Words to Images and from Science to Politics

When did I first hear the word *coronavirus*? That must have been during the outbreak of SARS in 2003, but I had surely forgotten. Then I heard it again in January 2020. Now it is a word we use every day. When it was used more and more frequently in early 2020, I began to wonder who researched and named the coronavirus first? To find out, I looked at the science publication database *Scopus* and found that the first article to use it was published in the 1950s and related to coronavirus in turkeys. Another early article dealt with infectious bronchitis. Then the term lay relatively dormant until it exploded into the academic publishing scene in 2004 after SARS and in 2020 it went supernova and became part of ordinary language all over the world.

I also looked at what the *Oxford English Dictionary* had to say. Its definition under *virology* is: »Any member of the genus Coronavirus of enveloped, single-stranded RNA viruses which have prominent projections from the envelope and are pathogens of humans, other mammals, and birds, typically causing gastrointestinal, respiratory, or neurological disease.«[43] *Projections from the envelope* – what we now call *spikes*. The *OED*'s first attestation is for a 1968 article in *Nature*: »In the opinion of the eight virologists, these viruses are members of a previously unrecognised group which they suggest should be called the coronaviruses, to recall the characteristic appearance [sc. recalling the solar corona] by which these viruses are identified in the electron microscope.«[44]

So, etymologically *coronavirus* is rooted in the word *corona*, Latin for *crown*, but more immediately in the metaphorically named solar corona that is to say, as the *OED* entry for *corona* points out: »A small circle or disc of light (usually prismatically coloured) appearing round the sun or moon.«[45] This does not quite explain the characteristic spikes of the coronavirus, which make it really what it is. As an article in *New Scientist* explains: »Coronavirus particles are surrounded by a fatty outer layer called an envelope and usually appear spherical, as seen under

---

[43] OED: Coronavirus.
[44] Ibid.
[45] OED: Corona.

an electron microscope, with a crown or ›corona‹ of club-shaped spikes on their surface.«[46] Or to be more precise »The name refers to the characteristic appearance of virions (the infective form of the virus) by electron microscopy, which have a fringe of large, bulbous surface projections creating an image reminiscent of a crown or of a solar corona. This morphology is created by the viral spike peplomers, which are proteins on the surface of the virus.«[47]

If you want to see how our novel coronavirus looks under a scanning electron microscope you can admire some great images published in the *Daily Mail* (of all places).[48] Not only did the word *coronavirus* become commonplace this year, so did images of the virus with its characteristic ball or globe-shaped body and bulbous spikes sticking out of it. There were thousands of different scientific images, many artistic images and corona-inspired artworks, as well as political cartoons that exploited the coronavirus as a visual metaphorical source domain. In the following I shall only be able to give a brief overview of this explosion of imagery.

There has been an explosion not only of scientific images, from renditions of the virus to innumerable infographics, but also of artistic renditions, such as David Goodsell's wonderful paintings,[49] as well as cartoons and satirical explorations of the virus. Artists like David Goodsell became involved in communicating the virus, in making the invisible visible. One rendition stood out for me and that was a beautiful glass sculpture by Luke Jerram. Jerram said about it: »Helping to communicate the form of the virus to the public, the artwork has been created as an alternative representation to the artificially coloured imagery received through the media. In fact, viruses have no colour as they are smaller than the wavelength of light.«[50] Janus and Sons Art Lab produced a more satirical and virtual glass sculpture of the virus where the spikes are replaced by the necks of corona beer bottles (David Steinman, p.c.).[51] And here we transcend scientific images and even artistic images of the virus and enter the political and satirical scene.

Let's now have a look at some of the ways these shapes shaped not only the scientific imagination but also the political imagination. What we see is a sort of semantic infection from corona (crown, wreath) which is transferred metaphorically to corona of the sun which is metaphorically transferred to a virus which then through its shape and function inspires/infects many more metaphors and images. Here are some random examples. Many images homed in on the ball shape of the virus, the globe, and highlighted global issues by superimposing the virus globe onto our earthly one. One image, for example, showed the virus as the

---

[46] Liverpool: Coronavirus.
[47] Wikipedia: Coronavirus.
[48] Cf. Enoch: The ›Invisible‹ Enemy Unmasked.
[49] Goodsell: Molecular Landscapes.
[50] Jerram: Coronavirus Glass Sculpture.
[51] Cf. Janus and Sons Art Lab: Facebook Post of an Artwork by Valentine Panchin.

earth suspended in space with the spikes depicting industrial production of food and thinking about global responsibility. Another image on the front page of *The Guardian* was published when the UK went into *lockdown*. It depicts the earth with the virus cut in half and the two halves enveloping the earth from the top and the bottom, gradually covering it and shutting it in like a two-ended butter dish.

The virus was not only used to visually think about global problems, but also focused on issues that nations had with the pandemic. One article on science, politics and values was illustrated by an image in which the dome of the White House is rendered as half a virus globe, for example. There are, naturally, also images that go from the world to the White House and from there to those inside the White House, namely, during the early pandemic, Donald Trump, the then president of the United States; and here many of the images focus on the metaphor of the crown underlying the images of spheres and spikes. There are innumerable images that play with the corona-crown and former President Donald Trump's hair and head. There is even an image where the spikes of the virus are rendered as MAGA hats... And of course, the virus itself can be depicted satirically, for example, as a green or red blob with an evil grinning face.[52]

The virus seems to be indeed an inexhaustible reservoir of political satire all over the world. Often the images exploit cultural icons, like the bindi in India, in an image of a woman in which the bindi has been replaced by the coronavirus (Ahmed Abdel-Raheem, p.c.); or, in a merger of myth and reality, Sisyphus pushing a spiked ball up a steep mountain slope, a slope that is actually part of curve on a graph (and there are many versions of this). The same happens to other iconic images of the pandemic, like the vaccine syringes and, indeed, masks which merge with cultural icons, as, for example in an image of the Eiffel Tower wearing a mask, the Mona Lisa wearing a mask, the American Presidents on Mount Rushmore wearing masks and much more.

This political use of pandemic icons as metaphorical source domains to explore many political target domains, from Donald Trump to the Israel-Palestine conflict has been extensively explored by Abdel-Raheem.[53] As we have seen, our knowledge of war can be used to think about the pandemic. Here we have a mapping from a familiar societal source domain, war, to an unfamiliar medical or scientific target domain, the coronavirus and its management. What is perhaps less well-known is that the pandemic and all its associated icons like the virus, the vaccine etc., which have now become quite familiar to us, can also be used, as Abdel-Raheem points out, a as a science/medical source domain to talk about emerging societal target domains, including wars between countries. The pandemic shapes the way we see the world.

---

[52] Cf. Joubert/Wasserman: Spikey Blobs with Evil Grins.
[53] Cf. Abdel-Raheem: Reality Bites.

To give only one example: Shortly after the mass shooting at a FedEx facility in Indianapolis on Friday 16th of April, 2021, Brazilian cartoonist Carlos Latuff tweeted a cartoon that shows a syringe (symbolising a vaccine) labelled »gun control« and a blood-soaked gun bearing the letters »NRA« (which stands for the National Rifle Association). The word »Cure« also floats in the air above the syringe, and the word »Disease« above the smoking gun.[54] The cartoon is captioned: »The country [i. e. the US] has been plagued by two diseases: the coronavirus and the gun. In both cases, there's a vaccine.«[55] The cartoon's message is that gun control, the vaccine, will end gun violence, the disease.[56] Corona, politics and culture become intertwined.

5. Corona as a Cultural Phenomenon

At the beginning of the pandemic I was doing my daily allowed walk up and down the neighbouring streets, when I happened to glance into a driveway and saw chalked on the pavement not a hopscotch pattern but a huge coronavirus smiling at me in the mode of the song *the sun has got his hat on* ... This brought me up short and I began to think how much this virus has begun to permeate our thinking and acting, that of children as much as of adults. This was the time when clapping or applause for health and other key workers, for example, became for a while a collective practice – a practice that over time turned into a rather hollow gesture. The singing and sharing of music from balcony to balcony, from street to street and on the internet was a more positive development, as well as the sharing of poetry.[57] The novel coronavirus has become a truly social and cultural phenomenon. It has spread into our bodies, societies, into science and art, into popular culture, into languages and minds. Amongst all the anxiety and destruction and despite divisive and derogatory metaphors used by some politicians, there is also hope. »The shared experience and interconnectedness of being human has been brought sharply into focus. Our health is inextricably linked to the health of our neighbours. Our resilience is community resilience. In the face of this crisis to cooperate and collaborate is not a choice, it is the only way to respond.«[58]

Cooperation, and global cooperation at that, is still badly needed, now that we can manufacture vaccines, potentially for the whole world. But the virus has exploited not only weaknesses in human bodies but also weaknesses in the global

---

[54] Cf. Latuff: Cure for Gun Violence.
[55] Ibid.
[56] Abdel-Raheem: How the Pandemic Is Shaping Worldviews.
[57] Nerlich/Döring/Jørgensen: Silence, Songs and Solace.
[58] Sanderson/Meade: Unimaginable Times.

body politic. As Laurie Penny said in a *Wired* article: »Stopping an outbreak is never just a fight with nature. It's also a fight with culture.«[59] And: »A bug or a virus will exploit any weakness in the body politic. Cholera became a huge problem when human beings started moving to cities in huge numbers. It stayed a problem until we worked out new ways of building large-scale public sewage systems, which involved a lot of money and manpower. Because of diseases like cholera, we literally figured out how to handle our shit.«[60]

Let's see whether the Covid-19 outbreak makes us figure out how to handle living together in an interconnected global world threatened by climate change. We have verbal and visual power and imagination at our fingertips, but, unfortunately, that power can too easily be misused by people, especially politicians whose only aim is to gain more power over people.

References

Abdel-Raheem, Ahmed: Reality Bites: How the Pandemic Has Begun to Shape the Way We, Metaphorically, See the World, in: Discourse & Society, 32(5), 2021, pp. 1–23.

Abdel-Raheem, Ahmed: How the Pandemic Is Shaping Worldviews, in: Making Science Public Blog, April 23, 2021: https://blogs.nottingham.ac.uk/makingsciencepublic/2021/04/23/how-the-pandemic-is-shaping-worldviews/; last accessed July 14, 2021.

Ball, Philip: Shot of Hope: Inside the Race for a Coronavirus Vaccine, in: Prospect Magazine, March 24, 2021, https://www.prospectmagazine.co.uk/magazine/when-will-there-be-vaccine-coronavirus-progress; last accessed July 14, 2021.

Brandt, Allan / Alyssa Botelho: Not a Perfect Storm – Covid-19 and the Importance of Language, in: New England Journal of Medicine, 382(16), 2020, pp. 1493–1495.

Brown, Brian / Brigitte Nerlich / Paul Crawford / Nelya Koteyko / Ronald Carter: Hygiene and Biosecurity: The Language and Politics of Risk in an Era of Emerging Infectious Diseases, in: Sociology Compass, 3(5), 2020, pp. 811–823.

Clark, Natasha / Alexander Brown: Army on Standby as Boris Declares War on Coronavirus with Battle Plan to Kill Off Deadly Bug, in: The Sun, https://flipboard.com/@TheSunOnline/army-on-standby-as-boris-declares-war-on-coronavirus-with-battle-plan-to-kill-of/a-utABvDPtTQmkQXaoNv6pfw%3Aa%3A2533536023-d3145d3b99%2fco.uk; last accessed July 14, 2021.

---

[59] Penny: Panic, Pandemic, and the Body Politic.
[60] Ibid.

Combes, Maxime: Non, nous ne sommes pas on guerre, nous sommes en pandemie, et c'est bien assez, in: Mediapart, March 20, 2021, https://blogs.mediapart.fr/maxime-combes/blog/200320/non-nous-ne-sommes-pas-en-guerre-nous-sommes-en-pandemie-et-cest-bien-assez; last accessed July 14, 2021.

Cooper, Charlie: Boris Is Back, in: Politico, April 30, 2021, https://www.politico.eu/newsletter/london-playbook/politico-london-playbook-pm-boris-is-back-alpine-tunnel-all-about-the-r/; last accessed July 14, 2021.

de Waal, Anton: New Pandemics, Old Politics: Two Hundred Years of War on Disease and its Alternatives, 2021.

Dean, Janice: Twitter-Post, July 21, 2020, https://twitter.com/JaniceDean/status/1285518403650883584?s=20; last accessed July 14, 2021.

Enoch, Nick: The ›Invisible‹ Enemy Unmasked: Chilling Microscope Images Reveal the Reality of Coronavirus as It Erupts Out from the Surface of a Human Cell, in: DailyMail, March 19, 2021, https://www.dailymail.co.uk/news/article-8132325/Coronavirus-chillingly-seen-scanning-electron-microscope.html; last accessed July 14, 2021.

Flanagan, Mark: Lead with Compassion and Ditch the Wartime Metaphors, in: The Article, May 07, 2021, https://www.thearticle.com/lead-with-compassion-and-ditch-the-wartime-metaphors; last accessed July 14, 2021.

Goodsell, David: Molecular Landscapes, https://pdb101.rcsb.org/sci-art/goodsell-gallery/coronavirus; last accessed July 14, 2021.

Hamill, Jasper; Millions Could Be Left with Health Complications, in: Herald Scotland, May 21, 2020, https://www.heraldscotland.com/news/18467082.coronavirus-millions-left-health-complications-vaccine-may-never-found-scientist-warns/; last accessed July 14, 2021.

Hanage, William: I'm an Epidemiologist. When I Heard about Britain's ›Herd Immunity‹ Coronavirus Plan, I Thought It Was Satire, in: The Guardian, March 15, 2021, https://www.theguardian.com/commentisfree/2020/mar/15/epidemiologist-britain-herd-immunity-coronavirus-covid-19; last accessed July 14, 2021.

Jacobs, Grant: COVID-19 and the Rise and Rise of Delta, in: Sciblogs, June 22, 2021, https://sciblogs.co.nz/code-for-life/2021/06/22/covid-19-the-rise-and-rise-of-delta/; last accessed July 14, 2021.

Janus and Sons Art Lab: Facebook Post of an Artwork by Valentine Panchin, March 26, 2020, https://www.facebook.com/janusandsons/photos/a.106315350839238/155432955927477/?type=3&theater; last accessed July 14, 2021.

Jaworska, Sylvia: Is the War Rhetoric around COVID-19 an Anglo-American Thing?, in: Viral Discourse, April 13, 2020, https://viraldiscourse.com/2020/04/13/is-the-war-rhetoric-around-covid-19-an-anglo-american-thing/; last accessed July 14, 2021.

Jenkins, Simon: Why I'm Taking the Coronavirus Hype with a Pinch of Salt, in: The Guardian, March 06, 2020, https://www.theguardian.com/comment

isfree/2020/mar/06/coronavirus-hype-crisis-predictions-sars-swine-flu-panics; last accessed July 14, 2021.

Jerram, Luke: Coronavirus Glass Sculpture: https://www.lukejerram.com/glass/gallery/coronavirus-covid-19; last accessed July 14, 2021.

Joffe, Hélène / Georgina Haarhoff: Representations of Far-Flung Illnesses: The Case of Ebola in Britain, in: Social Science & Medicine, 54(6), 2002, pp. 955–969.

Johnson, Boris: Prime Minister's Statement on Coronavirus (Covid-19), in: Government of the United Kingdom, April 30, 2020; https://www.gov.uk/government/news/prime-ministers-statement-on-coronavirus-covid-19-30-april-2020; last accessed July 14, 2021.

Joubert, Marina / Herman Wasserman: Spikey Blobs with Evil Grins: Understanding Portrayals of the Coronavirus in South African Newspaper Cartoons in Relation to the Public Communication of Science, in: Journal of Science Communication, December 14, 2020, https://jcom.sissa.it/archive/19/07/JCOM_1907_2020_A08; last accessed July 14, 2021.

Kohlt, Franziska: »Over by Christmas«: The Impact of War-Metaphors and Other Science-Religion Narratives on Science Communication Environments during the COVID-19 Crisis, November 09, 2020, https://osf.io/preprints/socarxiv/z5s6a/; last accessed July 14, 2021

Larson, Brendon / Brigitte Nerlich / Patrick Wallis: Metaphors and Biorisks: The War on Infectious Diseases and Invasive Species, in: Science Communication, 26(3), 2005, pp. 243–268.

Latuff, Carlos [@LatuffCartoons]: Cure for Gun Violence, Twitter, April 16, 2021, https://twitter.com/LatuffCartoons/status/1383009077014454272/photo/1; last accessed July 14, 2021.

Liverpool, Layal: Coronavirus, in: New Scientist, January 08, 2021, https://www.newscientist.com/definition/coronavirus/#ixzz6HyuGgOOQ; last accessed July 14, 2021.

Magnus, Georg: China and COVID-19: A Shock to Its Economy. A Metaphor for Its Development, in: LSE Ideas, February 25, 2020, https://lseideas.medium.com/china-and-covid-19-a-shock-to-its-economy-a-metaphor-for-its-development-11b1e31e643c; last accessed July 14, 2021.

Nerlich, Brigitte: War on Foot and Mouth Disease in the UK, 2001: Towards a Cultural Understanding of Agriculture, in: Agriculture and Human Values, 21(1), 2004, pp. 15–25.

Nerlich, Brigitte / Christopher Halliday: Avian Flu: The Creation of Expectations in the Interplay between Science and the Media, in: Sociology of Health & Illness, 29(1), 2007, pp. 46–65.

Nerlich, Brigitte / Nelya Koteyko: Crying Wolf? Biosecurity and Metacommunication in the Context of the 2009 Swine Flu Pandemic, in: Health & Place, 18(4), 2012, pp. 710–717.

Nerlich, Brigitte / Rusi Jaspal: Social Representations of ›Social Distancing‹ in Response to COVID-19 in the UK Media, in: Current Sociology Monograph, 69(4), 2021, pp. 566–583.

Nerlich, Brigitte / Craig Hamilton / Victoria Rowe: Conceptualising Foot and Mouth Disease: The Socio-Cultural Role of Metaphors, Frames and Narratives, in: Metaphorik.de, 2, 2002, pp. 90–108.

Nerlich, Brigitte / Martin Döring / Pernille Jørgensen: Silence, Songs and Solace: Music in the Times of Coronavirus, in: University of Nottingham Blog, February 27, 2020, https://blogs.nottingham.ac.uk/makingsciencepublic/2020/03/27/silence-songs-and-solace-music-in-the-time-of-coronavirus/; last accessed July 14, 2021.

Oxford English Dictionary: Coronavirus, in: OED online, https://www.oed.com/view/Entry/266178?rskey=SSgjny&result=20#eid42789674; last accessed July 14, 2021.

Oxford English Dictionary: Corona, in: OED online, https://www.oed.com/view/Entry/41771?rskey=9ZQG5B&result=1&isAdvanced=false#eid; last accessed July 14, 2021.

Paulus, Dagmar: How Politicians Talk About Coronavirus in Germany. Where War Metaphors Are Avoided, in: The Conversation, May 22, 2020, https://theconversation.com/how-politicians-talk-about-coronavirus-in-germany-where-war-metaphors-are-avoided-137427; last accessed July 14, 2021.

Penny, Laurie: Panic, Pandemic, and the Body Politic, in: Wired, March 14, 2020, https://www.wired.com/story/what-coronavirus-pandemic-says-about-society/; last accessed July 14, 2021.

Ribeiro, Barbara / Sarah Hartley / Brigitte Nerlich / Rusi Jaspal: Media Coverage of the Zika Crisis in Brazil: The Construction of a ›War‹ Frame That Masked Social and Gender Inequalities, in: Social Science & Medicine, 200, 2018, pp. 137–144.

Sanderson, Bec / Dora Meade: Pandemic Metaphors, in: Public Interest, March 26, 2020, https://publicinterest.org.uk/part-4-metaphors/#more-11066; last accessed July 14, 2021.

Sanderson, Bec / Dora Meade: Unimaginable Times, in: Public Interest, March 20, 2020, https://publicinterest.org.uk/part-1-unimaginable-times/; last accessed July 14, 2021.

Schön, Donald A.: Generative Metaphor: A Perspective on Problem-Setting in Social Policy, in: Andrew Ortony (ed): Metaphor and Thought, Cambridge 1979, pp. 137–163.

Semino, Elena: ›A Fire Raging‹: Why Fire Metaphors Truly Fan the Flames of Covid-19, in: Lancaster University, August 10, 2020, https://www.lancaster.ac.uk/news/a-fire-raging-why-fire-metaphors-truly-fan-the-flames-of-covid-19; last accessed July 14, 2021.

Semino, Elena: »Not Soldiers but Fire-fighters« – Metaphors and Covid-19, in: Health Communication, 36(1), 2021, pp. 50–58.

Serhan, Yasmeen: The Case against Waging ›War‹ on the Coronavirus, in: The Atlantic, March 31, 2021, https://www.theatlantic.com/international/archive/2020/03/war-metaphor-coronavirus/609049; last accessed July 14, 2021.

Servitje, Lorenzo: Medicine Is War: The Martial Metaphor in Victorian Literature and Culture, New York 2021.

Shafer, Jack: Behind Trump's Strange ›Invisible Enemy‹ Rhetoric, in: Politico, September 04, 2020, https://www.politico.com/news/magazine/2020/04/09/trump-coronavirus-invisible-enemy-177894; last accessed July 14, 2021.

Shariatmadari, David: Muggers and Invisible Enemies: How Boris Johnson's Language Hints at His Thinking, in: The Guardian, April 27, 2020, https://www.theguardian.com/politics/2020/apr/27/muggers-and-invisible-enemies-how-boris-johnsons-metaphors-reveals-his-thinking; last accessed July 14, 2021.

Sontag, Susan: Illness as Metaphor, London 1979.

Sontag, Susan: AIDS and Its Metaphors, London 1989.

Tisdall, Simon: Lay Off Those War Metaphors, in: The Guardian, March 21, 2020, https://www.theguardian.com/commentisfree/2020/mar/21/donald-trump-boris-johnson-coronavirus; last accessed July 14, 2021.

Turney, Jon: Frankenstein's Footsteps: Sscience, Genetics and Popular Culture, London 1998.

Ungar, Sheldon: Global Bird Flu Communication: Hot Crisis and Media Reassurance, in: Science communication, 29(4), 2008, pp. 472–497.

Ungar, Sheldon: Hot Crises and Media Reassurance: A Comparison of Emerging Diseases and Ebola Zaire, in: British Journal of Sociology, 1998, pp. 36–56.

Joffe, Hélène / Georgina Haarhoff: Representations of Far-Flung Illnesses: The Case of Ebola in Britain. Social Science & Medicine, 54(6), 2002, pp. 955–969.

Vowles, Neil: Want, Want, Want: How Boris Johnson's Choice of Language Failed to Bring the UK Together, in: University of Sussex Broadcast, July 10, 2020, http://www.sussex.ac.uk/broadcast/read/52112; last accessed July 14, 2021.

Wallis, Patrick / Brigitte Nerlich: Disease Metaphors in New Epidemics: The UK Media Framing Of the 2003 Sars Epidemic, in: Social Science & Medicine, 60(11), 2005, pp. 2629–2639.

Wicke, Philipp / Marianna M. Bolognesi: Framing Covid-19: How We Conceptualize and Discuss the Pandemic on Twitter. PLOS ONE, 15(9), 2020, pp. 1–24.

Wikipedia: Coronavirus, https://en.wikipedia.org/wiki/Coronavirus; last accessed October 12, 2020.

Zinn, Jens O.: Introduction: Towards a Sociology of Pandemics, in: Current Sociology, 69(4), 2021, pp. 435–452.

Theresa Strombach

From *Verbot* to *Gebot*? – A Linguistic View on Legal Phrasing in Infection Protection Law

From today's perspective (June 2021) there are fifty-six of them: Fifty-six protection ordinances, in German: *Coronaschutzverordnungen*[1] (CoronaSchV), which have passed the state cabinet of only North Rhine-Westphalia since the start of the pandemic in 2020. A legal text has maybe never been subject to so many changes in such a (relatively) short period of time. – Or the other way around: People have maybe never been subject to such a fast changing and thereby challenging legal situation, not only affecting certain recipients under certain circumstances, but instead: everyone in everyday life.

With regard to their overall relevance, these ordinances should ideally be as accessible as possible, leading us to an almost ancient topos, that should actually be even more en vogue at the moment than is the case: the (in-)comprehensibility of legal texts.[2] Of course, there are lots of sheets and tables with the most important – and above all: currently valid – facts and rules; there are even rules in easy language (so-called *Leichte Sprache*),[3] clearly stressing an immediate correlation between current incidences and the strictness of rules:

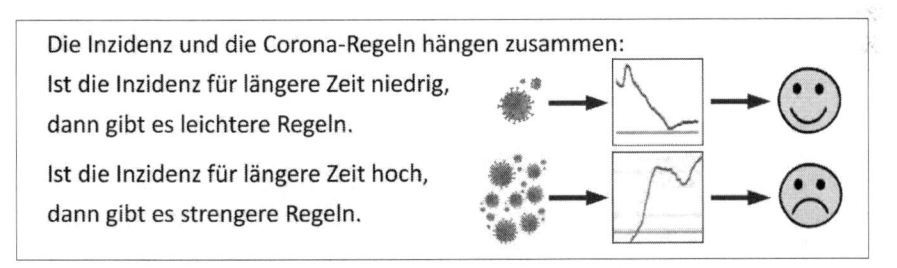

> Die Inzidenz und die Corona-Regeln hängen zusammen:
> Ist die Inzidenz für längere Zeit niedrig, dann gibt es leichtere Regeln.
>
> Ist die Inzidenz für längere Zeit hoch, dann gibt es strengere Regeln.

Fig. 1: Covid-19-Rules in easy language, June 05, 2021.

---

[1] In addition, there are dozens of other ordinances dealing with other priorities like care (*Coronabetreuungsverordnung*), entry (*Coronaeinreiseverordnung*), testing and quarantine (*Corona-Test-und-Quarantäneverordnung*).

[2] Cf. in particular: Lerch's Anthology: Recht verstehen; Eichhoff-Cyrus/Antos: Verständlichkeit als Bürgerrecht; Busse: Verständlichkeit von Gesetzestexten, etc.

[3] See the latest version, at least applicable in June (or more exactly: from June 5, 2021 to June 24, 2021).

From a linguistic point of view, it is particularly interesting to have a look at, how these correlations are phrased. In this case, we can identify unintroduced subordinate clauses with the finite verb (*Ist* ...) in first position (so-called V1-clauses), taken up by a correlate ([...], *dann* ...) in the main clause. As it is quite ordinary for a legal text to contain unintroduced V1-clauses,[4] it is rather extraordinary for a text in easy language, because subordinate clauses are traditionally avoided — due to their presupposed unintelligibility and although recent studies show: One subordinate clause is not just like another.[5] If drafting a text in easy language can be seen with Jakobson (1959)[6] as a form of intralingual translation[7] — an assumption, which is quite obvious, but not without controversy[8] — there should be at least a corresponding construction in the original text. The only problem is: There is no (visible) original text in this case.[9] Whether there had been a template or not,[10] the underlying correlation between incidence and rule should be found in a legally binding version, for example: in the latest ordinance on protection against new infections with Covid-19.[11] But before having a closer look at phrasing strategies on the level of ordinances, it might seem necessary to take a step back, or rather: upwards in the hierarchy of norms, leading us to § 28b *Infektionsschutzgesetz* (IfSG), better known as the so-called *Bundesnotbremse* (›federal emergency brake‹). The scope of these nationwide protective measures aiming to prevent the spreading of Covid-19 is bound by a *special* occurrence of infection (Bundesweit einheitliche Schutzmaßnahmen zur Verhinderung der Verbreitung der Coronavirus-Krankheit-2019 (Covid-19) *bei besonderem Infektionsgeschehen*). That is to say: The measures apply, if a certain threshold, in this case: a 7-day incidence of 100, is exceeded.

Until now, we could observe two different strategies to express a conditional relation between incidence and rule: 1. unintroduced V1-clauses[12] (e. g. *Ist* [...], *dann*/*so* [...].) and 2. prepositional phrases (e. g. *bei* [...], see above). These observations basically correspond to the findings for conditional expressions in various

---

[4] Cf. e. g.: Heller: Prinzipien der Textgestaltung; Soffritti: Diatopische Unterschiede im Ausdruck von Bedingungen; Strombach: Ohne *wenn* und *aber*.

[5] Cf. Bock: Leichte Sprache, pp. 48 ff.

[6] Cf. Jakobson: On Linguistic Aspects of Translation.

[7] Cf. Rink: Rechtskommunikation und Barrierefreiheit; Maaß / Rink / Zehrer: Leichte Sprache in der Sprach- und Übersetzungswissenschaft, pp. 55 ff.

[8] Cf. e. g.: Stephan: Leichte Sprache und der Übersetzungsaspekt.

[9] It is simply recalled, that the text is *made* by the Ministry of Labour, Health and Social Affairs and *translated* by an agency for accessibility (Agentur Barrierefrei NRW).

[10] »Texte in Leichter Sprache können als solche konzipiert sein, in diesem Falle liegt kein Ausgangstext vor.« (Maaß / Rink / Zehrer: Leichte Sprache, p. 55).

[11] The following remarks refer, unless otherwise specified, to the Coronaschutzverordnung of May 26, 2021, in a version applicable from June 12, 2021.

[12] For another example, see below: § 28b IfSG I.

legal texts.[13] However, it remains questionable how a legal text may be adapted to (sometimes daily[14]) changing conditions – how it can possibly stay precise and flexible at the same time?

The answer could be: There is another type of clause, which is equally characteristic for legal texts and which is – at the same time – able to express complex conditional relations with fine shades of meaning and (partly) various restrictions, namely: 3. subjunctionally introduced clauses, like in the following section:

§ 28b I Nr. 1, 2 IfSG

Überschreitet in einem Landkreis oder einer kreisfreien Stadt an drei aufeinander folgenden Tagen die durch das Robert Koch-Institut veröffentlichte Anzahl der Neuinfektionen mit dem Coronavirus SARS-CoV-2 je 100 000 Einwohner innerhalb von sieben Tagen (Sieben-Tage-Inzidenz) den Schwellenwert von 100, so[15] gelten dort ab dem übernächsten Tag die folgenden Maßnahmen:
1. private Zusammenkünfte im öffentlichen oder privaten Raum sind **nur** *gestattet*, **wenn** an ihnen höchstens die Angehörigen eines Haushalts und eine weitere Person einschließlich der zu ihrem Haushalt gehörenden Kinder bis zur Vollendung des 14. Lebensjahres teilnehmen; […].
2. der Aufenthalt von Personen außerhalb einer Wohnung oder einer Unterkunft und dem jeweils dazugehörigen befriedeten Besitztum ist von 22 Uhr bis 5 Uhr des Folgetags *untersagt*; […].

According to the eponymous title »Genau *wenn* oder nur *insoweit*?«[16], we could basically distinguish between hypothetical conditionals (e.g. introduced by *wenn* or *falls*) and restrictive conditionals (particularly introduced by *soweit*[17]); in this case (*nur* […], *wenn*), the restrictive effect is mainly caused by inserting the particle *nur* (*only*) as a corresponding element in the main clause.[18] A clause like the above might be labeled as some kind of ›restrictive permission‹: Private meetings are *only* permitted, *if* members of the same household and not more than one additional person participate. But of course, a message is not solely transported by its syntactic structure per se, but also, maybe even predominantly by its lexical units: Thus, it makes a (not inconsiderable) difference, whether something is only

---

13   Cf. Fn. 4.
14   In June 2021, I could detect three different protection ordinances in four days (June 9, June 10, June 12).
15   Concerning a potential difference between *so* and *dann* as correlates cf. Strombach: Ohne *wenn* und *aber*.
16   Cf. Soffritti: Einschränkende Bedingungen.
17   It is disputed whether *sofern* should as well be classified as a restrictive subjunction (as done in the *Handbuch der Rechtsförmlichkeit*, marginal no. 89) or as a conditional subjunction (in the strict sense, cf. Duden: Die Grammatik, marginal no. 1772; Zifonun et al.: Grammatik der deutschen Sprache, p. 2280).
18   Cf. ibid., pp. 58 ff.; Visconti: A Textual Approach to Legal Drafting and Translation, pp. 111 ff.

permitted (*gestattet*) or only *prohibited* (*untersagt*), if a certain condition applies, even though it is possible to construe an almost analogical provision (b) based on § 28b I Nr. 1 IfSG (a):

(a) Private Zusammenkünfte im öffentlichen oder privaten Raum sind **nur** *gestattet*, **wenn** an ihnen <u>höchstens</u> die Angehörigen eines Haushalts und eine weitere Person [...] teilnehmen.

(b) Private Zusammenkünfte im öffentlichen oder privaten Raum sind **nur** *untersagt*, **wenn** an ihnen <u>mehr als</u> die Angehörigen eines Haushalts und eine weitere Person [...] teilnehmen.

The subjacent difference is: In (a), private meetings are principally prohibited, but permitted, if the subsequent condition applies; in (b), private meetings are principally permitted, but prohibited, if the subsequent condition applies. Hence, we could say, that version (a), as currently set in § 28b I Nr. 1 IfSG, may be classified both: as a ›restrictive permission‹ and as an ›implicit prohibition‹. This observation leads us back to a somewhat visionary claim, made about one year ago,[19] according to which life *with* Covid-19 should rather not consist of prohibitions (*Verbote*), but of requirements (*Gebote*)[20] – in the long run. Has this prognosis come true until now? We can at least identify the use of (peripheral) modal verb constructions, here: with *zu*-infinitives, verbalizing some kind of requirement, which has to be met in order to be covered by an exception (*ausgenommen*) to a general prohibition (*untersagt*):

§ 28b I Nr. 4 IfSG
4. die Öffnung von Ladengeschäften und Märkten mit Kundenverkehr für Handelsangebote ist *untersagt*; wobei der Lebensmittelhandel einschließlich der Direktvermarktung [...] mit den Maßgaben *ausgenommen* sind, dass
 a) – b) [...]
 c) in geschlossenen Räumen von jeder Kundin und jedem Kunden eine Atemschutzmaske (FFP2 oder vergleichbar) oder eine medizinische Gesichtsmaske (Mund-Nase-Schutz) zu *tragen ist*; [...]

While modal verbs tend to be used in legal texts in order to express different subcategories of deontic modality[21] – like permission and prohibition, it might be worthwhile to have a look at their frequency in a text type, that seems to be even closer to life *with* Covid-19.

---

[19] Cf. Strombach: Stay (At) Home; Jaeger: Gebote statt Verbote.
[20] For various dichotomies in legal language see Bukovčan: Verbot vs. Gebot.
[21] Cf. Heller/Engberg: Verwendungskonventionen deontischer Modalmarker; Goletiani: Zur Übersetzung deontischer Modalmarker, p. 272.

From *Verbot* to *Gebot*? 323

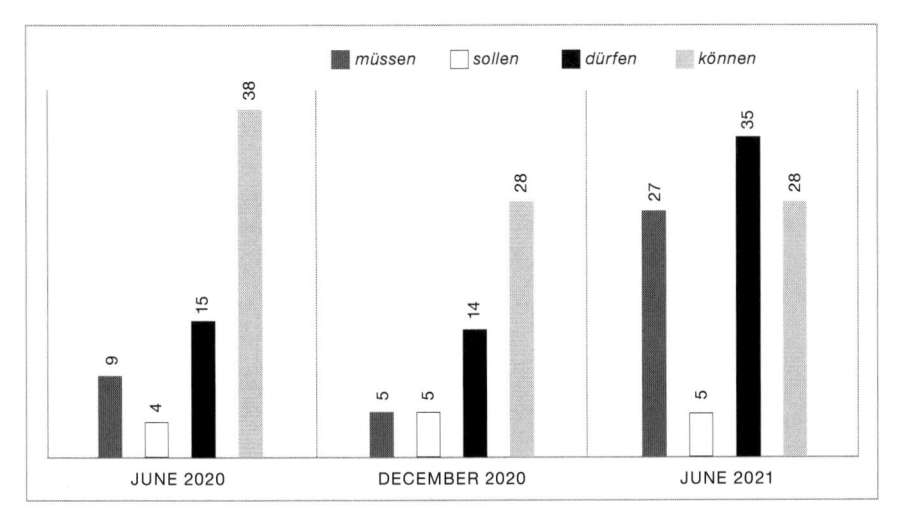

Fig. 2: Absolute occurrences of modal verbs in the *Coronaschutzverordnung* (own diagram).

The diagram (fig. 2) compares the absolute[22] occurrences of four modal verbs (*müssen, sollen, dürfen, können*) in three different versions[23] of the *Coronaschutzverordnung*: At first, we can observe, that *sollen* – as a prototypic marker of deontic modality – stagnates on a quite low level. In comparison of June 2020 and 2021, it is just as striking and unexpected, that the use of *müssen* increases, whereas the use of *können* decreases: Due to a flattened infection curve during the last weeks, one might have expected the rules to become rather less binding, to include more and more permissions – and the latter might actually be confirmed with regard to the frequency of *dürfen*. But in fact, a glance at the texts suggests another assumption: It reveals that the rules have become more decisive, more uncompromising – the provisions in question *cannot*, but *must* apply.

§ 2 IV CoronaSchV (June 2020)
(4) Die nach dem Landesrecht für Schutzmaßnahmen nach § 28 Absatz 1 des Infektionsschutzgesetzes zuständigen Behörden *können* für bestimmte Bereiche des öffentlichen Raums, in denen das Abstandsgebot nicht sicher eingehalten werden kann, aufgrund örtlicher Erfordernisse (räumliche Situation, lokales Infektionsgeschehen usw.) die Geltung der vorstehenden Regelungen zusätzlich anordnen.

---

[22] It must be kept in mind that the three versions differ with regard to their extent; thus, quantitative observations have to be treated with caution.

[23] June 2020: *Coronaschutzverordnung* in a version applicable from June 15, 2020; December 2020: *Coronaschutzverordnung* of November 30, 2020, in a version applicable from December 16, 2020; June 2021: *Coronaschutzverordnung* of May 26, 2021, in a version applicable from June 12, 2021.

§ 13 V CoronaSchV (June 2021)
(5) Für Theater- und Tanzdarstellungen, bei denen die Darstellenden Mindestabstand und Maskenpflicht nicht einhalten können, sind unabhängig von der Inzidenzstufe besondere Hygienekonzepte zu erarbeiten und umzusetzen. Diese *müssen* neben dem Erfordernis eines Negativtestnachweises an jedem Aufführungstag vor allem die besondere Beachtung der allgemeinen Hygieneregelungen und die größtmögliche Umsetzung der Mindestabstände enthalten und sind der zuständigen Behörde auf Verlangen vorzulegen.

What can be said for sure, however, is that the examined ordinances show a wild mix of different phrasing strategies, effectively concealing the crucial correlation between incidence and rule, that becomes immediately overt in easy language (see fig. 1). Recently, those responsible try to remedy the lack of transparency and traceability by assigning three levels of incidence (*Inzidenzstufe 1, 2, 3*). So, when it comes to rules for a life *with* Covid-19, there is at least one constant: the number three – because there have always been three rules to remember, going from AHA (*Abstand, Hygiene, Alltagsmaske*) to GGG (*Geimpft, Genesen, Getestet*). We will be eagerly expecting the next trio, while hoping, that there is none to expect.

References

Bock, Bettina M.: »Leichte Sprache« – Kein Regelwerk. Sprachwissenschaftliche Ergebnisse und Praxisempfehlungen aus dem LeiSA-Projekt, Berlin 2019.

Bukovčan, Dragica: Verbot vs. Gebot: Dichotomien und Gegensatzpaare in der Rechtssprache, in: Linguistica, 53(2), 2013, pp. 115–126.

Busse, Dietrich: Verständlichkeit von Gesetzestexten – ein Problem der Formulierungstechnik?, in: LeGes 5(2), 1994, pp. 29–47.

Eichhoff-Cyrus, Karin M. / Gerd Antos (eds.): Verständlichkeit als Bürgerrecht? Die Rechts- und Verwaltungssprache in der öffentlichen Diskussion (Thema Deutsch 9), Mannheim et al. 2008.

Goletiani, Liana: Zur Übersetzung deontischer Modalmarker ins Ukrainische: eine korpusgestützte Untersuchung anhand von EU-Richtlinien, in: Zeitschrift für Slawistik 60(2), 2015, pp. 269–293.

Heller, Dorothee: Prinzipien der Textgestaltung und der Gebrauch von Konditionalsätzen im deutschen Schiedsverfahrensrecht, in: Vijay K. Bhatia / Jan Engberg / Maurizio Gotti / Dorothee Heller (eds.): Vagueness in Normative Texts (Linguistic Insights 23), Bern 2005, pp. 357–378.

Heller, Dorothee / Jan Engberg: Verwendungskonventionen deontischer Modalmarker im deutschen Schiedsverfahrensrecht, in: Maurizio Gotti / Dorothee

Heller / Marina Dossena (eds.): Conflict and Negotiation in Specialized Texts, Bern 2002, pp. 165–188.

Jacobson, Roman: On Linguistic Aspects of Translation, in: Reuben A. Brower (ed.): On Translation, Cambridge 1959, pp. 232–239.

Jaeger, Mona: Gebote statt Verbote, in: Frankfurter Allgemeine Zeitung, May 24, 2020, https://www.faz.net/aktuell/politik/inland/ramelow-macht-tempo-gibes-bald-gebote-statt-verbote-16783935.html; last accessed June 15, 2021.

Lerch, Kent D. (ed.): Recht verstehen. Verständlichkeit, Missverständlichkeit und Unverständlichkeit von Recht (Die Sprache des Rechts 1), Berlin / New York 2004.

Maaß, Christiane / Isabel Rink / Christiane Zehrer: Leichte Sprache in der Sprach- und Übersetzungswissenschaft, in: Klaus Schubert / Heike E. Jüngst / Susanne Jekat / Claudia Villiger (eds.): Sprache barrierefrei gestalten. Perspektiven aus der Angewandten Linguistik, Berlin 2014, pp. 53–85.

Rink, Isabel: Rechtskommunikation und Barrierefreiheit. Zur Übersetzung juristischer Informations- und Interaktionstexte in Leichte Sprache, Berlin 2020.

Soffritti, Marcello: Bedingung und Zeitangabe – *wenn* und verwandte Ausdrucksformen in deutschsprachigen Gesetzbüchern für Südtirol, in: Piergiulio Taino / Marina Brambilla / Tobias Briest (eds.): Eindeutig uneindeutig: Fachsprachen – ihre Didaktik, ihre Übersetzung (Deutsche Sprachwissenschaft international 7), Frankfurt 2009, pp. 27–37.

Soffritti, Marcello: Diatopische Unterschiede im Ausdruck von Bedingungen in deutschsprachigen Gesetzestexten, in: Marina Brambilla / Joachim Gerdes / Chiara Messina (eds.): Diatopische Variation in der deutschen Rechtssprache (Forum für Fachsprachenforschung 113), Berlin 2013, pp. 29–52.

Stephan, Alea: Leichte Sprache und der Übersetzungsaspekt. Lassen sich Fachtexte in Leichte Sprache übersetzen? Ist ein Leichte-Sprache-Text überhaupt eine Übersetzung?, in: Stiftung Universität Hildesheim, October 22, 2014, https://hildok.bsz-bw.de/frontdoor/index/index/docId/243; last accessed June 14, 2021.

Strombach, Theresa: Ohne *wenn* und *aber*. Zur Verwendung und ›Verständlichkeit‹ von (un-)eingeleiteten Adverbialsätzen in deutschsprachigen Gesetzestexten (Master's thesis, unpublished manuscript), Bonn 2020.

Strombach, Theresa: Stay (At) Home – A Linguistic View on Imperatives in Times of Crisis, in: Werner Gephart (ed.): In the Realm of Corona Normativities. A Momentary Snapshot of a Dynamic Discourse, Frankfurt am Main 2020, pp. 209–213.

Visconti, Jacqueline: A Textual Approach to Legal Drafting and Translation, in: Gianmaria Ajani / Ginevra Peruginelli / Giovanni Sartor / Daniela Tiscornia (eds.): The Multilanguage Complexity of European Law. Methodologies in Comparison, Florenz 2007, pp. 107–132.

Zifonun, Gisela / Ludger Hoffmann / Bruno Strecker: Grammatik der deutschen Sprache, Vol. 3 (Schriften des Instituts für Deutsche Sprache 7.3), Berlin/New York 1997.

List of Figures

Fig. 1: Covid-19-Rules in easy language, June 05, 2021, Image detail from: Ministerium für Arbeit, Gesundheit und Soziales (Nordrhein-Westfalen): Corona-Regeln in NRW vom 05. bis 24. Juni 2021, https://www.land.nrw/sites/default/files/asset/document/corona-regeln_leicht_2021-06-09_bf_web.pdf; last accessed June 30, 2021.

Fig. 2: Absolute occurrences of modal verbs in the *Coronaschutzverordnung*, Diagram by the author.

Helga María Lell

Persona, the Mask and the Anomic Person

1. Persona and Anomie

When the pandemics arrived to Argentina, in March 2020, the *dumb anomie* (also called the *Argentinean anomie* by Nino) was a useful concept to explain the behavior of certain people who disobeyed rules intentionally taking advantage from the context in which all the other citizens or the majority of them would comply.[1] The problem with this kind of anomie is not that rules are contradictory or unclear, but that there is an individual that despises them. For example, there was a famous case in the country, the one of the *surfer*, a man who during the first lockdown travelled to Brazil to surf and returned just circulating without the due permission, avoided to do the quarantine (he went to visit his parents) and complained about the police controls. The fact that other people would respect the lockdown provided a faster way home, without traffic jams but, above all, in a safer way: if nobody else was out there, the risk of contagion was lower or null. If everybody would have done the same as he did, the measure would have been completely useless. The *dumb* factor comes from the fact that the subject acts with »viveza criolla«[2], the individual believes that he/she is smarter than the others, but his/her action degrades social order. As Fucito explained, Argentina has a long background on disobeying laws and a strong historical tendency to dissociate the law in force with the law that is lived (in the way that Ehrlich would understand it).[3]

In this paper I do not focus on this kind of anomie although there are many and very interesting examples. My aim here is to provide some ideas on how a more traditional way of understanding the anomie (if there is such a traditional way) impacts on the conception of person in law during the Corona crisis. Durkheim explained the relevance of normativity to create a social order. The contrary, when this order is not in force or cannot regulate individuals' behavior, the loss of sense

---

[1] Cf. Nino: Un país al margen de la ley, pp. 17–42.
[2] In Argentina, to make oneself »el vivo/la viva« is to behave in a certain way in order to take advantage of an opportunity, sometimes violating rules, for selfish interests and depreciating the common good or social wellbeing (cf. Academia Argentina de Letras: Diccionario del habla de los argentinos, p. 634).
[3] Cf. Fucito: La crisis del derecho en la argentina y sus antecedentes literarios, pp. 16–20. On Ehrlich, see his »Fundamental Principles of the Sociology of Law«.

and of stability derive in social disintegration.[4] Not only that, individuals are not complete and can lose, in some way to say, their identity. The heterogeneity that characterizes Modernity involves interdependence of people that distribute work and may complement themselves.[5] Also, from a structuralism-based perspective, we could think that complex modern societies define individuals always in relation to others. For example, Saussure's identity principle is to be what the others are not. The coexistence and articulation of all components together allow every part to be what they are: what the others are not.[6] Merton adds that anomie can be grounded on discrepancies between means and ends[7] and Parsons explains the link between individual expectations and actions and economic cycles and social abrupt changes.[8] These ideas that in a global world that has changed completely and has subverted the order of rights and concerns in just a few months but for a long term get to be particularly enlightening.

The political, economic, sociological and legal chaos that the Covid experience has brought up implies a deep break of paradigms in social lives and, derived from this, in the way of producing, interpreting and obeying/disobeying rules. As Gadebusch-Bondio and Marloth commented in 2020, abrupt changes in political decision makers are an evidence of how much we ignore about the pathogen. Examples of this are the erratic and contrasting measures that vary from trivializing the illness to accepting the danger, from pursuing herd immunity to total lockdowns.[9]

The case that I present in the following pages points out that this crisis provokes: a) law losing its capacity to force conducts, b) increasing difficulties for law to generate courses of actions perceived as legitimate and binding; and c) challenges to law in order to create new ways of achieving widespread social complying to legal rules.[10] In the frame of the law as culture paradigm, thinking about normativity requires considering factors such as religion, historical institutions, rituals and costumes, communication acts and forms, aesthetics, etc.[11] In this case I will refer to the Argentinean context during the emergency of Covid-19 as a breaking moment in which, although the society is used to economic, political and sanitary crisis, normativity and social bonds have been especially destroyed.

---

[4] Cf. Durkheim: El suicidio.
[5] Cf. Durkheim: La división del trabajo social.
[6] Saussure explains this to define the linguistic sign. See Saussure: Curso de lingüística general.
[7] Cf. Merton: Teoría y estructura sociales.
[8] Cf. Parsons: The Structure of Social Action; and Parsons: El sistema social.
[9] Cf. Gadebusch-Bondio/Marloth: Clinical Trials in Pandemic Settings: How Corona Unbinds Science, p. 30.
[10] This idea is based on Fucito: La crisis del derecho en la argentina y sus antecedentes literarios, p. 18.
[11] On the different elements of the law as culture paradigm and the Corona Crisis, see Gephart: Introduction, pp. 13–16.

My thesis here is that when normativity, particularly legal normativity, gets to be fuzzy and uncertain, individuals cannot perform as persons in legal scene. The risk is that the narration of law on how persons can and should be considered does not work anymore and then social order (or some part of it) disappears, social control gets weaker and fear increases.

2. Persons and Masks

The legal concept of person is built on a metaphor, the one that links the subject that acts in the legal scene to the ancient masks in Rome and Greek theaters. The masks were not the actors themselves but the tool that allowed the human being behind to perform a character, to show an emotion, to play a specific role and to be heard according to the script. The narrative context of the story that was told provided a meaning to what the performing actor that carried a mask was doing. The actor itself was not enough to create an effect, but a complex framework of story, auditorium, expectations, dialogues, masks, social reactions, performances, etc. was. So, nowadays, the concept of person in legal scene implies to perform a role created by law according to legal rules and social expectations in a believable way and to be known as such a legal character/person in a legal relation. The lesson of this metaphor is that a person to law is a ›status function‹: as money is not just a piece of paper or a metal, a person is more than its physical structure. It is the functions assigned, played and recognized as well interpreted.[12]

The Corona crisis has changed completely the way legal relationships are understood. The traditional ways of performing roles have changed abruptly (not only changes have been fast but also have been profound). Let's think of an example. Before the pandemics, to play the role of a minor's parent would imply to live with the child and take care of him/her. If the parents would have been divorced, then, the family coexistence would have been part-time according to the agreements between the former couple. After the pandemic, living with the minor is not the rule, it actually depends on where the child was the day the lockdown began – of course, this is in case there is a lockdown – and on whether there is or not a permission to circulate in order to pick up the daughter or son. In this case, we can notice that the role is completely different: one needs a permission in order to live with or to visit one's child or children.

The idea of a person in law, then, comes from playing roles that determine rights and duties. However, in a crisis context, where the narratives that provide

---

[12] The idea of status functions has been explained by Searle: The Normative Structure of Human Civilization, pp. 21–31.

meaning to facts and that create social expectation and symbolic dimensions to interpret reality, the rights and duties that constitute a legal person are absolutely unclear. In consequence the person becomes also unclear. How to play a role when the rules are changing? What to expect from the scene and from the story if we have never lived something like this? Where is the promised and expected security and certainty that law should provide to citizenship?

3. Anomic Persons

The regulations of the emergency context and the speed of new regulations towards a new normality that comes and goes has provoked legal uncertainty and individuals are unclear about what to expect from their actions in the legal sphere. One of the main expectations on law is that it should provide certainty about the consequences of our own conducts and about what other people might do or not. If legal positive rules change too fast and sometimes without a clear logic, the expectations cannot be fulfilled. Let's see some examples about this.

If we check the web page of the National Government's announces about the Covid-19 in Argentina, we can see that there is a report on which decisions have been ruled to face this crisis. The list includes only those measures that have been carried out by the National Executive Branch. During the period from February 26, 2020 to April 4, 2021, 396 rules (decrees, resolutions and dispositions) have been ruled.[13] This is, in average, 0.99 per day. This number excludes laws or other judicial dispositions. So, if someone wants to catch up with what the national government is doing needs to check one rule per day (and should do the same task with the Judicial and the Legislative Powers). However, since Argentina is a federal country, in order to be aware of what is forbidden, allowed or mandatory, checking out what the national government has stated is not enough. People should also check out what the provincial government is ruling. During the period from January 1, 2020 to April 4, 2021, the Governor of La Pampa (just the Governor, this does not include other kind of dispositions such as those of Ministers or Directors) has ruled 4517 decrees which is around 9.8 decrees per day.[14] Of course, not all of them are related to the pandemics, but certainly many of them. The bad news is that many of those Covid-19 related and that regulate permissions change in a very short period establishing what can be done or not and in which hours. That is

---

[13] Ministerio de Salud (Argentina): ¿Qué medidas está tomando el gobierno?
[14] This number is the result of the addition between the decrees of 2020 and those of 2021 until April, 4, according to the Official Bulletin. See Boletín Oficial de la provincia de La Pampa n° 3447 and Boletín Oficial de la provincia de La Pampa n° 3460.

not all, people should also check which laws are in force or not. For example, just in the province of La Pampa, during April and May 2021, there have been four different limit hours to circulate: until 1am; until 11pm; until 9 pm; until 6 pm. In three weeks, gyms were allowed with many protocols; then, with limited people (10 persons), then they had to exercise in open air spaces and then were forbidden.

Even more, if someone wants to travel to another province, he or she should check what is in force over there: if we count how many provincial laws and decrees were ruled during the period March 3, 2020[15] to April 4, 2021, there is an average of 4.18 rules coming in force per day.[16] And things may change surprisingly too. For example, during the »long-weekend« of 22–25 May 2021,[17] in just one week the holiday of the 24th May was on, then it was suspended so that people would not travel. Finally, the holiday came back so that people would stay at home during strong restrictions (lockdown) but in a way that employees would not lose their payment. Also, the tourism permissions certificates were suspended and, after many people travelled for holidays, it was announced that it would be punished to go back home before May 31st 2021 (there was a strict lockdown until that date). So, it is hard to be aware of what the legal system is ruling and it is absolutely impossible to know what the system will rule in a very short term. Certainty is a fiction perhaps now more that in the pre-Coronavirus era.

Kelsen defined the person as a center of rights and duties imputation.[18] If legislation gets to be so confusing as it is now, then, the person gets to be fuzzy too. The identity facing law and according to law vanishes. Today a person is equal to some rights and duties but tomorrow will be a whole different catalog of norms: he or she will be a completely different person. If the concept of person in law provides an identity as a character in legal scene, nowadays this aim is broken.

Even more, this sort of anomic persons is not only a problem when it comes to define it but also when individuals need to decide what to do or not in order to violate rules or to have their conducts guided by them. Anomie is a problem since legal security is absent. Uncertainty produces two kind of problems: on one hand, there is a crisis on civic values about taking responsibility for other people's lives, and, on the other, the lack of certainty and the sometimes contradictory regulations weaken social tights and produce chaos. The fact that everyone is a risk to others plus that there is a feeling of continuous threaten and unsafety make persons socially uncomfortable. What to expect from others, what to do, what to

---

[15] When the first case of Covid-19 was confirmed in Argentina.

[16] There is a margin of statistical error due to the fact that the search engine that provides this information may not have all the recent rules or some of the relevant rules may not be detected by the engine because of the »Covid« key word (they may include other key words or synonyms).

[17] May 25th is a patriotic holiday due to the May Revolution of 1810. May 24th was a holiday for touristic reasons; it is what is known as a »bridge holiday«.

[18] Cf. Kelsen: Teoría pura del derecho.

claim, which are the risks of doing an activity, are hard to make decisions in an unclear normativity context.

While the idea that every citizen should have a good behavior in order to take care of the others (*social responsibility*) is still binding, relaxing is becoming a tendency. For example, during January (summer vacations), it seems that around 8 million people travelled as intern tourists in the country, this is the 17.77 % of the population.[19] Although *stay at home* was, at that time, no longer the main applied strategy against Coronavirus, going out just for what it is needed and obeying protocols are still rules that seem to be derogated by costume.

The circulating hours change constantly, the allowance of private gatherings and the amount of people that can share a space variate, the activities widen up but protocols come and go, everyday less people use facemasks properly, etc. Anomie is a result that can be easily expected in a society that has been changing abruptly, not only locally but also globally, that is under pressure and that works in a system of cultural, economic and political relations that are unstable due to the pandemics.

4. Confusing Times for Being a Person

Not only the speed of rules' changes influences the anomie but also that the role of legal sphere is going beyond what it used to be, it is regulating phenomena that are strange to be payed attention to. For example, before 2020, it would have been ridiculous to think that a rule would state the way in which an individual should cough. However, nowadays there is a decree that states that coughing in the elbow crease is mandatory. Not sharing lunch in working spaces, how to ventilate an office, not to share the mate and washing hands are regulated conducts. A year ago, it would have been conceived as an excess of power but in current crimes public health and the global crisis legitimate these regulations.[20]

Pre-Coronacrisis law in Argentina would hardly state how to show ourselves in public (except for some specific cases such as firemen, people working in labs or at hospitals with very contagious diseases or for ID photos)[21]. Nowadays the facemask is mandatory, and not wearing it is punished. Just standing somewhere

---

[19] The data was extracted from Ministerio de Turismo y Deportes (Argentina): Verano 2021.

[20] Examples of this measures can be find in National Decree 520/20 Social, Preventive and Mandatory Distancing; National Decree 67/21. Social, Preventive and Mandatory Distancing and Social Preventive and Mandatory Isolation. Even more, we can see in the official webpage of the National Government a tutorial to wash our hands: Ministerio de Salud (Argentina): ¿Cómo debemos lavarnos las manos?

[21] Dreier: Law and Images, p. 155.

is not a random conduct anymore: one cannot stand next to other person without constituting a risk for his/her health and public health. Two meters or three according to circumstances is the *new normal* distance in order not to threaten the other. If one has travelled abroad or to another province, a quarantine might be an obligation or a recommendation in order not to be a risk to others. If someone is a contact of a positive case, then, quarantine is mandatory and in some provinces the contact of the contact should be isolated. The *contact* issue implies a new symbolic way of considering people's relations: being in presence of another person is potentially the way of becoming a community risk. The remedy of such a consideration is isolation. After 14 days the positive cases and their contacts and contacts of contacts will acquire the legal redemption.

Some other regulations are contested because they contradict relevant constitutional principles that have been conquered along political history. As Dreier affirmed, during the crisis rapid solutions that do not provide the same level of detail are needed and the urgency does not let decision makers to weight rights and interests with the same care they would have done it in normal circumstances.[22] The emergency has required to create a new order of things and it is a complicated issue to force rules compliance when the exception is the new normality. For example, freedom to circulate is a constitutional principle that has been part of society in an explicit way since 1811.[23] However, nowadays in order to get out of home it is necessary to check out in which hours that is allowed and to have a permission to do so according to the task to execute (for example, being an essential worker or just going to supermarket). Another constitutional principle that has an historical root back in 1813 is the equality one. Vaccination, for example, is a process that is based on hierarchies of people: according to the role in society (essential persons) or their conditions of vulnerability (sick or elderly persons). Those categories have been socially accepted since equality is understood as *equal in equal circumstances*. However, recently the country witnessed a big scandal due to *VIP vaccination*: journalist, politicians, family of politicians, etc. got their vaccines before the essential or the vulnerable persons. The discredit on the process of vaccinating the population was the result: not only we are unequal but there is no faith in the solidarity value that inspires the priorities. That is when the door for the *dumb anomie* opens.

Finally, anomie takes place when contradictions arise. For example, during 2020, funerals of deceased people because of Covid-19 could not take place. For those who died of other causes, funerals did take place but with protocols and strictly with the closest family and for around half an hour. However, when Diego Maradona passed away, the funeral was organized by the National Government

---

[22] Cf. Dreier: Law as Culture in Times of Corona, p. 43.
[23] Argentinia: Decree of Individual Security (October 26, 1811).

and in the Pink House (the main Government's building). Around a million of people travelled from the whole country and got together outside the building making a line to get in. The controls of social distances and facemasks were inefficient. There was an entire day (and the night before) destined for this. The mourning of a beloved one is a sensitive moment. The limits to it demand a strong and solid argumentation that is not only in discourse but also in coherent facts. Contradictions, such as the one of this case, cause discredit and weakens the force of law. Should a person act according to law or according to what those who create rules do?

5. To Sum Up

Anomie is a result but also a process that is built in a two directions process: from the State that regulates conducts and from citizens that act. Expectations of regulations and of compliance are part of decisions. The major crisis that is going on due to Coronavirus is provoking a dissolution of the old normality towards a new one. Although we tend to call the current state of things *the new normality*, we can only see chaos. The lack of certainty impacts on how people behave in society. Social bonds are damaged and individuals cannot play roles correctly because they are undetermined. Old narratives are invalid, new ones do not last more than days, weeks or, in the best cases, a few months. Rules are weak, have new logics that are strange to the usual institutions, and the proliferation of legal decisions is impossible to keep up with.

Though we talk about a *new normality*, we cannot describe it or, if we do, we know that it will be provisory without even imagining for how long: the description might be accurate for just a few days or even less. Everything depends on how many infections per day there are, on how hospitals can help, etc. If this is the case, we cannot define concretely what a person is: only the abstract *center of imputation* definition may work. However: which rights and duties? Can we think of persons that are defined for around ten times a day with new rules? Is the abstract definition enough? How can a person prevent being a risk to others if she/he is unable to know the rules that regulate her/his actions? What can anybody expect from other when the allowed, forbidden or mandatory actions are absolutely unclear?

If the person in the legal field is defined by the rights and duties that it has and if the certainty that law provides is a defining factor for its performance in the scenarios in which it performs, then, the context of this crisis has led to persons that are fuzzy. Persons cannot act in a scene that changes the way of performing constantly. The anomic persons are those that result in this critical context. Their main characteristic is not to know which their rights or duties are, not to know how they will perform tomorrow or how to recognize the role they are playing.

The anomic person is the actor/actress that performs while the former scenario is no longer there and the future scenario has not come yet.[24] In this way, it is constituted by a contradiction: as Derrida would notice, the anomic person does not coincide with itself: it is the remains of the past norms that are not available as they used to be and it is an anticipation of a future order that is not here.[25]

References

Academia Argentina de Letras: »Vivo/va«, in: Diccionario del habla de los argentinos, Buenos Aires 2008, pp. 634.
Argentina: Decree of Individual Security (October 26, 1811), in: Estatutos, Reglamentos y Constituciones Argentinas (1811–1898), Buenos Aires 1956, pp. 28–31.
Boletin Oficial de la provincia de La Pampa n° 3447, December 12, 2020 [Argentina].
Boletín Oficial de la provincia de La Pampa n° 3460, March 31, 2021 [Argentina].
Davignaud, Jean: Herejía y subversión. Ensayos sobre la anomia, Barcelona 1990.
Derrida, Jacques: De la gramatología, Buenos Aires/México 2005.
Dreier, Thomas: Law and Images. Normative Models of Representation and Abstraction, in: Werner Gephart/Jure Leko (eds.): Law and the Arts. Elective Affinities and Relationships of Tensions, Frankfurt am Main 2017, pp. 155–175.
Dreier, Thomas: Law as Culture in Times of Corona, in: Werner Gephart (ed.): In the Realm of Corona Normativities. A Momentary Snapshot of a Dynamic Discourse, Frankfurt am Main 2020, pp. 41–59.
Durkheim, Émile: El suicidio. Un estudio de sociología, Madrid 2012.
Durkheim, Émile: La división del trabajo social, Madrid 2001.
Duvignaud, Jean: La sociología. Guía alfabética, Barcelona 1974.
Ehrlich, Eugen: Fundamental Principles of the Sociology of Law, New Jersey 2009.
Fucito, Felipe: La crisis del derecho en la Argentina y sus antecedentes literarios. Un enfoque sociológico, Buenos Aires 2010.
Gadebusch-Bondio, Mariacarla/Maria Marloth: Clinical Trials in Pandemic Settings: How Corona Unbinds Science, in: Werner Gephart (ed.): In the Realm of

---

[24] This idea is inspired on the definition that Duvignaud provides of anomie as a situation between the society that is still not dead and the society that is still not born. Cf. Duvignaud: La sociología. Also Davignaud refers to the anomic personality in Davignaud: Herejía y subversion, pp. 71–93.
[25] This is an adapted idea from Derrida: De la Gramatología.

Corona Normativities. A Momentary Snapshot of a Dynamic Discourse, Frankfurt am Main 2020, pp. 30–40.

Gephart, Werner: Introduction: The Corona Crisis in the Light of the Law as Culture Paradigm, in: Werner Gephart (éd.): In the Realm of Corona Normativities. A Momentary Snapshot of a Dynamic Discourse, Frankfurt am Main 2020, pp. 11–25.

Kelsen, Hans: Teoría pura del derecho, México 1982.

Merton, Robert: Teoría y estructura sociales, México 2002.

Ministerio de Salud (Argentina): ¿Cómo debemos lavarnos las manos?, https://www.argentina.gob.ar/coronavirus/lavar-manos?gclid=EAIaIQobChMIpcaNkvzn7wIVNPC1Ch2txQAFEAAYASAAEgLuBPD_BwE; last accessed May 28, 2021.

Ministerio de Salud (Argentina): ¿Qué medidas está tomando el gobierno?, https://www.argentina.gob.ar/coronavirus/medidas-gobierno; last accessed May 28, 2021.

Ministerio de Turismo y Deportes (Argentina): Verano 2021: 8 millones de turistas ya se movilizaron por los destinos del país, February 01, 2021, https://www.argentina.gob.ar/noticias/verano-2021-8-millones-de-turistas-ya-se-movilizaron-por-los-destinos-del-pais; last accessed May 28, 2021.

Nino, Carlos Santiago: Un país al margen de la ley. Estudio de la anomia como componente del subdesarrollo argentino, Buenos Aires 1992.

Parsons, Talcott: The Structure of Social Action, New York 1968.

Parsons, Talcott: El sistema social, Madrid 1984.

Saussure, Ferdinand de: Curso de lingüística general, Buenos Aires 1945.

Searle, John: The Normative Structure of Human Civilization, in: Werner Gephart/Jan Suntrup (eds.): The Normative Structure of Human Civilization. Readings in John Searle's Social Ontology, Frankfurt am Main 2016, pp. 21–31.

Valérie Hayaert
Pestis and Anomia*

>»Strange new illnesses produce strange new doctors.«
>Petrus Severinus

Since the discovery of the first cases of Covid-19 in Wuhan in December 2020, a continuous search for causation, symptoms and *signs* has posed a wide number of issues. The definition of the Covid-19 syndrome as described by virologists has certainly evolved, but a list of significant signs taken together (coughing, fever, difficulty in breathing, parosmia etc.) is now believed to eliminate all possibility of ambiguity. Since the revolution of genomic sequencing, medical science has radically transformed the core principles of our medical knowledge, its means of conveying and disseminating information. It also had a profound impact on the relationship between disciplines and scholarships. The recent development of genome sequencing is one mark of the growing prestige of medical science, but, at the same time the effects of Covid-19 on communities has caused disastrous damages and inequities unleashed on the social world, due to promiscuous dwellings and general frustration about distancing rules. If one looks at the early links between the notion of *pestis* and the origins of history, Thucydides' view of the fall of Athens, his interpretation of the disintegration of that *polis* helps us to root the historical understanding of a disease understood as a paradigm, which resulted into a complete shift of moral values, a mere rejection of the *nomoi*.[1] The current pandemic unmasks how the emergence of *pestis* may trigger *anomia*.

Much in the same way that the French sixteenth-century jurist François Hotman describes a legal rule as producing a polyphonic harmony,[2] medical science is able to discern the meaning of these signs, producing a method to define a disease. The new deal we have experienced since the beginning of this outbreak raises key issues of certainty and uncertainty, ambiguity and conjecture. It profoundly changes our ways of reasoning, it is often associated with the vexed question of biopolitics, as this semiological uncertainty pervades almost every sphere of knowledge. Not only are anamnesis, diagnosis and prognosis given expert oversight of

---

* I wish to thank Peter Goodrich for revising my English and for his careful reading of this brief note.
[1] Cf. Mittelstadt: From *Nomos* to *Anomia* in Thucydides' History, pp. 187–198.
[2] Cf. Hotman: Commentarius de Verbis iuris, p. 324.

our daily lives, but our semiotic beings are also affected as this pandemic reveals in a broad context how the world of learning and the transmission of knowledge are at stake.

A central issue which throws light on this ongoing crisis is that of the definition of time. The high value placed on an unprecedented transnational circulation of virological knowledge, especially in the medical field, has paved the way for historians to reconsider the history of past pandemics. In a conference held recently via zoom at the Paris Institute of Advanced Studies, Patrick Boucheron highlighted the fundamental difference between past phenomena, variously defined as *calamité*, *fléau*, and *peste*.[3] Plague itself is a paradigm, and announces the possibility of *anomia* (lawlessness). Before mastering the technology of pathogen agent sequencing, observers of past pandemics had absolutely no clue as to how to explain and understand a contagious disease transmitted by contact. The actual Covid-19 pandemic may thus be used as a historiographical laboratory in order to reflect on two major parameters: on one hand, illness is always caused by a pathogen agent *pestis*; on the other hand, an archaic fear, which sees in plague a possibility of *anomia* is also reflected in the enhanced awareness of risk, emergency claims, including the aesthetic responses to new types of mourning the dead.

1. Pestis

Circa 1460, the feminine substantive *peste* is borrowed from the Latin *pestis* (contagious disease, pandemic, plague, destruction).[4] According to virologist Thierry Wirth, an historical perspective should take into account the genetics of pathogen agents themselves: More than 5000 years ago, plague was a pulmonary disease, it then became bubonic.[5] The medical reality covered by the word *pestis* is thus a paradigm, reflecting the essential need for fundamental research into the ambit of medical science as it contributes to the development of natural science as a whole. Today, the renewed interest in medical discourses about zoonosis is accompanied by a greater focus on the dialogue between the humanities, arts and sciences. This contribution will address some of the aesthetic responses to the disruptive state of *anomia* we are now experiencing.

---

[3] Cf. Boucheron/Wirth: Histoire des pandémie.
[4] Cf. Trésor de la Langue Française informatisé: Peste.
[5] Cf. Boucheron/Wirth: Histoire des pandémie.

2. The Plague Paradigm as the Origin of History and Language

Thucydides once provided an acute analysis of the state of *anomia*, i. e. the weakening of social bonds, customary practices and conventional religious beliefs, including the destruction of death rituals. When the *nomoi* lose their binding force, anarchy, chaos, along with the suffering of the entire community, the political system is itself threatened.[6] His treatment of the Great Plague of 430 BC[7] provides a typical model, as his historical work (the *History*) is meant to serve as a tool for posterity and an instrument for predictability, so as to avoid the tragic disintegration of the *polis*.[8] Beyond *oikonomia* (effective management) and *isonomia* (equality under the law), the *unwritten laws* protecting the weak are safeguarded by civic responsibility, calm deliberation before action, and a wide array of moral values shared by volunteer members of an ideal *polis*.[9] According to the Greek historian, Athens owed to the plague an unthinkable state of *anomia*, where in a short timespan, bonds of honor dissolved, desperate people would heave the corpses of their own kin onto funeral pyres. The death of Pericles facilitated the empowerment of demagogues and the advent of ochlocracy (the disintegration of democracy). The new illness gave rise to the reign of self-interest and increasing ruthlessness, as the use of language itself was distorted in manifold ways.[10]

3. In Search for the Epitome of a Common Soldier?

Our biopolitical current state of political affairs is often explained through Foucault's understanding of bio-power. In a quite literal way, Foucault's 1970s lectures[11] strike a chord with the new discovery of Covid-19, the first *global* pathogen, after tuberculosis, malaria or Aids. The exceptional speed of propagation of the Covid-19 outbreak gave added weight to the explanation of disease as an occasion for rehearsing a caricatural reading of Michel Foucault's influential works.[12] What is rather new is an open-access to scientific publications, and this new era of global attention to medical knowledge gives rise to unorthodox medical thinking, not yet peer-reviewed, sometimes used by unscrupulous journalists in non-ethical ways.

---

6 Cf. Mittelstadt: From *Nomos* to *Anomia* in Thucydides' *History*, p. 189.
7 Thucydides: Historiae, II, 47–53.
8 Cf. Mittelstadt: From *Nomos* to *Anomia* in Thucydides' *History*, pp. 189 f.
9 Cf. ibid., p. 191.
10 Cf. ibid., p. 192.
11 See for example his remarkable 1978–1979 lectures on this topic (cf. Foucault: The Birth of Biopolitics).
12 Cf. Suntrup: Corona, pp. 137–145.

In a more nuanced and compelling way, Didier Fassin has brought to the fore the necessity of pin-pointing the novelty of a redefinition of bio-politics: today, a democratic polity has no other choice than to safeguard the unconditional value of life. This is what Fassin calls »bio-légitimité«[13]. Now that panic, distrust and *anomia* have caused major disruptions in our daily lives, it seems pertinent to take a look at some aesthetic responses to the disintegration of mourning rituals. What could serve nowadays as an equivalent to past funerary tombs or death rituals? It seems that a new type of invisible war has discarded the possibility of representing the brunt of the horrors, the banalities of anomic behaviors, execrable indignities triggered by a new type of apartheid. In such a context, what sort of monuments to the dead are yet desirable? The former epitome of the monument to the Common Soldier, as a visible mooring point of rallying affects and as a condensation or *punctum* for communal mourning rituals seems to illustrate our inability to sanction the powerful drives of zoonoses. If the rational is overpowered in each outbreak, a new focus on time-span, a new sense of duration (in Bergsonian parlance) is now desirable. *Anomia* being a figure of chaos, it brings the necessity for artists to invent new forms, new artistic languages, new ways of memorializing death.

4. Fabienne Verdier and the *Isenheim Altarpiece*: An Artistic Response to the Pandemic

One example will be particularly developed here as this is the one context in which a visual panel devoted to an ancient *pestis* serves as a point of departure for the creation of a new symbolic act. Late medieval religious art is particularly telling as it displays the signs of suffering on the face of God the Father, as well as on his son.[14] Hans Belting has studied in depth the ways in which Christian art takes suffering into account, including its inscription in anatomy and nosology.[15] The *Isenheim Altarpiece* (1512–1516) is a polyptych of articulated wooden oil panels which each showed a different scene according to the liturgical calendar. The whole work includes depictions of the *Annunciation*, the *Nativity*, the *Crucifixion* and the *Resurrection*. The Altarpiece is attributed to two artists: Mathis Gothart Nithart, called Grünewald (* Würzburg, circa 1475/1480, † Halle (Saale), 1528) and Niklaus von Hagenau (quoted in Strasbourg from 1485 to 1526).[16] It was created to

---

[13] Fassin: »Le corps exposé. Essai d'économie morale de l'illégitimité«, p. 242.
[14] Cf. Boespflug/Cunneen: The Compassion of God the Father in Western Art, pp. 489–499.
[15] Cf. ibid., p. 489. See also on this topic: Belting: Das Bild und sein Publikum im Mittelalter.
[16] Cf. Heck: De Nicolas de Haguenau à Grünewald, pp. 223–237.

Fig. 1: Matthias Grünewald, Isenheim Altarpiece (first view),
Saint Sebastian, Crucifixion, Saint Anthony & Lamentation, ca. 1512–1516.

adorn the main altar of the Church of the Antonite Hospital, in Isenheim, a little town located 20 km from Colmar (Alsace).[17]

Alsace, a major epicenter of the Covid-19 outbreak in March 2020, has been particularly hit by the first wave of the pandemic, as intensive care units were then overstretched in Haut-Rhin. Helicopters for the military health service transferred seriously ill people to other hospitals.

Grünewald's crucified figure represents (fig. 1), allegedly, the summit of cruel realism; the contrasts between agony and hope, the vivid colors and lurid imagery are particularly striking.[18] Contemporary viewers of the panel would have appreciated departures from the norm (here Christ's distress is excruciating), just as they recognize the norm of God's traditional depiction. Usually, restraint is the rule. The particular taste of the German schools for the pathetic is thus to be noted. God's distress serves as an appeal to compassion, as God sends his compas-

---

[17] See also for general information on the Isenheim altarpiece the articles collected in the following anthology: Heck (ed.): Le Retable d'Issenheim et la sculpture au nord des Alpes à la fin du moyen-âge.
[18] Cf. Boespflug/Cunneen: The Compassion of God the Father in Western Art, p. 489.

Fig. 2: Matthias Grünewald, Isenheim Altarpiece (second view), The Resurrection of Christ, ca. 1512–1516.

sion forth to humanity.[19] One may see the triptych as a manifestation of new forms of devotional practices, in relation to funerals. But the *Isenheim Altarpiece* is well known for the extreme variety of his usages. The religious order of the Antonites was dedicated to cure those who suffered from the illness of Saint Anthony's fire (*mal des ardents*) and those who were diagnosed with this illness were brought by the Antonites in front of the triptych inside the Church choir where they were administered a remedy: a beverage made of wine and soothing botanical extracts where the sacred relics of Saint Anthony had been plunged.[20]

Seventeenth century medical authorities will later link the signs and symptoms of this illness with the rye ergot: a parasite of this cereal whose ingestion provoked vasoconstriction causing gangrene or convulsions.[21]

In *The Resurrection of Christ* (fig. 2), Grünewald invented a new formal language. The body of the crucified man becomes light, carried away in an ascent defying the laws of weight, while the shroud that contained the corpse, subjected to an analogous transfiguration, blazes with all the colors of the rainbow. This

---

[19] Cf. ibid., pp. 499–502.
[20] Cf. Clementz: Die Isenheimer Antoniter, pp. 161–169.
[21] Cf. Bauer: Das Antonius-Feuer in Kunst und Medizin, pp. 7–11.

supernatural scene contrasts with the heavy, frozen bodies of the guards, whose military garb inscribes them in the specific historical period of the painter.

In her forthcoming exhibition (2022) at the Unterlinden Museum, the French contemporary artist Fabienne Verdier has crafted a new symbolism for contemporary post-Covid-19 crisis survivors. Facing a recognizable difficulty in her attempt to abstract a pictorial canon of post-Covid-19 death values, trying to extract the *should* or the *ought* of the Christian visual paradigm from the *is*, she focused on the optical notion of *aberration*, the other perceptual space of a new way of expressing time, cosmos, and restoration after anomia. Using the *Isenheim Altarpiece* as a source of inspiration, she has painted a polyphony of circles born from her conversation with Covid-19 patients.[22] Unique in its cosmological form, the painting of an optical *aberration de peinture* serves as a prelude to new ways of mourning the deceased, using art as a silent companion to our innermost human feelings. If lessons of virologists were most likely learnt through experimental methods driven by sociology (think of the great book by Bruno Latour, sociologist of the Pastorian revolution[23], which is so useful these days), our ideal *polis* is now haunted by the lost images of past illnesses. Artistic responses to the challenge of memorializing Covid-19 deaths have only just begun.

References

Bauer, Veit Harold: Das Antonius-Feuer in Kunst und Medizin (Sitzungsberichte der Heidelberger Akademie der Wissenschaften. Mathematisch-naturwissenschaftliche Klasse. Supplement zum Jahrgang 1973), Berlin/Heidelberg/New York 1973.

Belting, Hans: Das Bild und sein Publikum im Mittelalter. Form und Funktion früher Bildtafeln der Passion, Berlin 1995.

Boespflug, François/Joseph Cunneen: The Compassion of God the Father in Western Art, in: CrossCurrents 42 (4), 1992, pp. 487–503.

Boucheron, Patrick/Thierry Wirth: Histoire des pandémié. Peut-on apprendre des pandémié du passé?, April 14, 2021, https://www.agirentempsdecrise.fr/histoire-des-pandemies; last accessed August 17, 2021.

Clementz, Elisabeth: Die Isenheimer Antoniter: Kontinuität vom Spätmittelalter bis in die Frühneuzeit?, in: Matheus, Michael (ed.): Funktions- und Strukturwandel spätmittelalterlicher Hospitäler im europäischen Vergleich (Geschichtliche Landeskunde 56), Stuttgart 2005, pp. 161–174.

---

[22] Cf. Giuliani: Fabienne Verdier: »Ma dévotion à la peinture brûle, éprouve«.
[23] Cf. Latour: Les microbes: guerre et paix suivi de irréductions.

Fassin, Didier: »Le corps exposé. Essai d'économie morale de l'illégitimité«, in: Didier Fassin / Dominique Memmi (ed.): Le gouvernement des corps, Paris, Éditions de l'EHESS, 2004, p. 237–266.

Giuliani, Emmanuelle: Fabienne Verdier: »Ma dévotion à la peinture brûle, éprouve«, in: La Croix L'Hebdo, June 30, 2020, https://www.la-croix.com/Culture/Expositions/Fabienne-Verdier-Ma-devotion-peinture-brule-eprouve-2020-06-30-1201102636; last accessed August 17, 2021.

Heck, Christian (ed.): Le Retable d'Issenheim et la sculpture au nord des Alpes à la fin du moyen-âge : Actes du colloque de Colmar (2–3 novembre 1987) (Bulletin de la Société Schongauer de Colmar), Colmar 1989.

Heck, Christian: De Nicolas de Haguenau à Grünewald: origine et structure du retable d'Issenheim, in: Krohm, Hartmut (ed.): Flügelaltäre des späten Mittelalters. Die Beiträge des Internationalen Colloquiums »Forschung zum Flügelaltar des Späten Mittelalters«, veranstaltet vom 1. bis 3. Oktober 1990 in Münnerstadt in Unterfranken, pp. 223–237.

Hotman, François: Commentarius de verbis iuris, Lyon 1569.

Latour, Bruno: Les microbes: guerre et paix suivi de irréductions. Paris 1984.

Maclean, Ian: Logics, Signs and Nature in the Renaissance. The Case of Learned Medicine, Cambridge 2002.

Mittelstadt, Michael C.: From Nomos to Anomia in Thucydides' History: The Moral and Political Context, in: The Journal of Value Inquiry 30(1–2), 1996, pp. 187–198.

Rey, Alain (ed.): Dictionnaire culturel en langue française, Vol. 3, Paris 2005.

Suntrup, Jan Christoph: Corona: Biopolitical Models and the Hygiene of Tact, in: Werner Gephart (ed.): In the Realm of Corona Normativities. A Momentary Snapshot of a Dynamic Discourse, Frankfurt am Main 2020, pp. 137–145.

Trésor de la Langue Française informatisé: Peste, in: ATILF – CNRS & Université de Lorraine, http://stella.atilf.fr/Dendien/scripts/tlfiv5/advanced.exe?8;s=2022144900; last accessed August 17, 2021.

List of Figures

Fig. 1: Matthias Grünewald, Isenheim Altarpiece (first view), Saint Sebastian, Crucifixion, Saint Anthony & Lamentation, ca. 1512–1516, Image: Gzen92 / Wikimedia Commons, CC BY-SA 4.0.

Fig. 2: Matthias Grünewald, Isenheim Altarpiece (second view), The Resurrection of Christ, ca. 1512–1516, Reproduced with permission of the copyright owner: Unterlinden museum.

Sergio Genovesi

Digital Rights in Times of Pandemic

After a year and a half of pandemic, the global community developed many resources to face the virus and avoid its spread. Of course, vaccines are without doubt one of the most powerful ones. The debate around their delivery and fair distribution is monopolizing the mediatic attention in the global north and the increase of the share of population fully vaccinated is giving a new hope to those people who had to sacrifice fundamental rights such as freedom of movement and freedom of assembly to stop the infections. However, another powerful resource already allowed countries such as China, Vietnam, South Korea and Taiwan to set their citizens free to move and gather again even before starting the immunization campaign. The solution was the combination of targeted quarantine measures and accurate tracking of the spread of infections among the population through digital applications. The use of digital tracing apps has been seen by many observers as very critical and, in many countries where it was not mandatory to install a so-called Corona-App, the majority of the citizens did not download the app since they distrusted either its technical robustness or the use of data that the government and the app provider would have done. One of the major concerns that fuelled the debate was that Corona-Apps would infringe fundamental rights such as privacy.[1] In this way, the introduction of digital tools to prevent the spread of the virus further complicated the difficult justification process of the suspension of fundamental rights for the sake of a greater good – that is, saving lives. In addition to the limitations to the freedom of movement and gathering, what is at stake is the control of digital data produced by the citizens and their possible misuse by different public or private stakeholders.

Observing how much critical attention was gathered around the case of the Corona-Apps allowed to mark an asymmetry in the public opinion in the consideration of other apps, such as those harvesting our data for commercial purposes powered by Facebook and Google.[2] This asymmetry looks even more remarkable if we take into account that many commercial apps recommend content that promotes disinformation or misinformation to entertain their users. This is another important issue widely discussed in the public and scientific debate of the last years and recently put in the spotlight by the spread of Covid-19. After framing

---

[1] Cf. Sweeney: Tracking the Debate on Covid-19 Surveillance Tools.
[2] Haggag et al.: Covid-19 vs. Social Media Apps.

the discussion around privacy, I will focus on protection against mis- and disinformation as a digital right and show in conclusion how raising awareness about objective facts concerning the virus and the digital tools to prevent its spread could ease information sharing in a privacy preserving scenario.

1. Privacy and Data Protection

According to the *Charter of Fundamental Rights of the European Union*, respect for private and family life (art. 7) and protection of personal data (art. 8) are fundamental rights of the human being.[3] Moreover, article 12 of the *Universal Declaration of Human Rights* of the United Nations may be interpreted as assuming privacy as a fundamental right in the statement: »No one shall be subjected to arbitrary interference with his privacy, family, home or correspondence, nor to attacks upon his honour and reputation.«[4] Since the introduction of digital applications working with a large amount of data generated by their users, worries about privacy intrusion and misuse of data harvested for commercial purposes have been increasing. Indeed, user generated data can potentially be related to personal data allowing an accurate profiling of individuals. The introduction of the *General Data Protection Regulation* (GDPR) of the European Union in 2018 – which, according to the GDPR website, is »the toughest privacy and security law in the world«[5] – can be seen as a reaction to the danger represented by unregulated data collection and processing. That this danger is real and should be taken seriously was showed by episodes such as the Facebook and Cambridge Analytica data scandal (before GDPR)[6] or the Google+ data breach scandal (after GDPR).[7]

Depending on the quality and quantity of data that are collected by Corona-Apps, data leaks or misuse could represent a great threat to privacy and other basic freedoms. Many Corona-Apps just use Bluetooth technology matching users when their devices are close to each other's and save the data on the user's device in a decentralized way, destructing the data after a short period of time (e. g. two weeks). This is the most privacy-preserving option since localization tools are not used and data is not saved on a central server owned by a private stakeholder or a controlling authority. However, other Corona Apps such as the Chinese one use

---

[3] Cf. European Union: Charter of Fundamental Rights of the European Union.
[4] Cf. United Nations: Universal Declaration of Human Rights.
[5] Cf. Wolford: What is GDPR.
[6] Cf. Cadwalladr/Graham-Harrison: 50 Million Facebook Profiles Harvested for Cambridge Analytica.
[7] MacMillan/McMillan: Google Exposed User Data, Feared Repercussions of Disclosing to Public.

geolocalization, mine data from other apps, save data on centralized servers and do not destroy them afterwards.[8] Many observers have seen these procedures in a very critical way since they enable the government to control people's movements and habits, enacting a surveillance mechanism that can undermine the free expression of opinions and beliefs. Scholars referred to this phenomenon as »digital authoritarianism«.[9]

Another example of data misuse and betrayal of citizen trust can be found in Singapore. As well as in China, downloading the local Corona-App *TraceTogether* is mandatory in Singapore. However, the government originally ensured that the data would have been accessed only by the ministry of health for pandemic containment purposes and deleted after 25 days. Unfortunately, this was not the case. On January 4th, 2021, the minister of the interior Desmond Tan announced that data gathered by *TraceTogether* were also used for criminal investigations, changing the terms of use of the app. This fact provoked the reaction of many data rights activists, who claimed that in many countries the pandemic control was used as a pretext to increase digital surveillance.[10] Also the contact tracing strategy of South Korea was highly criticized because of the not consensual data collection procedures that combined information from security camera footages, financial transactions and cell phone location data.[11]

Despite these cases, an effective pandemic containment through digital tools is not necessarily to be associated with digital surveillance and/or authoritarianism. Vietnam is worldwide acknowledged as one of the most successful countries in the pandemic containment. Together with an early response to the pandemic outbreak and rigid, targeted quarantine measures, Vietnam excelled in contact tracing through digital tools.[12] Even though Vietnam was criticized too for using social media posts to track contacts, the Corona App *Bluezone* is one of the most downloaded among the not-mandatory ones: in March 2021 it exceeded 30 million downloads.[13] This data matches well the results of a survey by the Institute of Global Health Innovation according to which people in Vietnam are more willing to provide contact information to fight the pandemic than in other nations: only 4 % of participants in Vietnam said that they would not provide this information,

---

[8] O'Neill et al.: A Flood of Coronavirus Apps.
[9] Cf. Dragu / Lupu: Digital Authoritarianism and the Future of Human Rights; Polyakova / Meserole: Exporting Digital Authoritarianism.
[10] Cf. Holz: Singapur gebrochenes Versprechen.
[11] Cf. Covid-19 National Emergency Response Center: Contact Transmission of Covid-19 in South Korea; Kleinman / Merkel: Digital Contact Tracing for Covid-19.
[12] Cf. Holz: Der Erfolg Vietnams im Kampf gegen das Virus; Matheis / Pye: Covid-19-Strategien in Südostasien.
[13] Cf. Kiet: Bluezone Covid-19 Tracking App Exceeds 30 Million Downloads.

while in the United States and Germany the proportion was 21 %, and in France it was 25 %.[14]

The more citizens download the national Corona-App, the better the local health institutions can trace contacts with infected people. In scenarios where downloading the app is not mandatory, people's belief in the trustworthiness of the national apps and their willingness to share their personal contact information is the key to a wide coverage and a better functioning of this digital resource. While the health institutions should gain the citizen's trust by ensuring protection of their privacy, awareness about the important social role that Corona-Apps play by tracing contacts and avoiding new infections should be risen. As a matter of fact, personal and user generated data are nowadays a universal good of exchange to access digital services such as entertainment, news, messaging, etc. It has been shown that social media apps such as Facebook, Instagram or TikTok access and process personal and user generated data in a larger extent than many Corona Apps using just Bluetooth and saving data in a decentralized way such as the German *Corona WarnApp* or the Italian *Immuni*. Using social media apps leads therefore to more critical privacy issues than in the case of many Corona-Apps.[15] Nevertheless, while many people expressed privacy and ethical concerns about using Corona-Apps, social media apps were voluntarily used at a significantly higher rate during the pandemic without similar privacy concerns compared with the former.[16] In other words, many more people were ready to exchange their user generated data and personal information for entertainment and communication on social media (while also being targeted with personalized advertising) than people willing to share a smaller amount of anonymized information to prevent new infections and save lives. This asymmetry is particularly remarkable if one considers that social media in some way eased the spread of disinformation about the coronavirus and its medical treatments.

2. Misinformation and Disinformation

Social Media apps are not designed to spread misinformation and fake news, but just to engage users recommending content they might like. On the news feed of a social media app, a recommender system shows different kinds of posts based on the available data on the user that allow to calculate the probability a certain content matches their interests. However, a content does not need to be trustworthy

---

[14] Cf. Institute of Global Health Innovation: Covid-19; Lewis: Covid Contact-Tracing.
[15] Haggag et al.: Covid-19 vs. Social Media Apps.
[16] Ibid.

to be entertaining. During the past years, this led many social media users to be exposed to false or misleading information without any disclaimer on its trustworthiness, with severe implications for democratic processes, mental health and society at large.[17] A decade after the spread of recommender systems in every aspect of our everyday life, it has become clear that the use of this AI-powered tools deeply affects our digital life and represents great ethical challenges.[18]

Protection from misinformation and fake news is increasingly being considered a digital right and to prevent the spread of misleading content online both tech companies and legislators are taking radical measures such as advertising control, introduction of fake news detection algorithms and immediate ban of content flagged as illegal – measures that sometimes even raised censorship concerns.[19] From 2019 on Facebook and Instagram introduced a fake news label for content detected as misleading.[20] TikTok started this year.[21] In 2020 Twitter introduced an *ad hoc* label for misleading information related to Covid-19.[22] However, if not paired with digital literacy, these measures are not truly effective to prevent the spread of misinformation. A study published on the American Journal of Tropical Medicine and Hygiene stated that the so-called »infodemic«, that is the uncontrolled spread of rumours, fake news and conspiracy theories about the pandemic, led to hundreds of deaths.[23]

The Austrian Ministry of Social Affairs, Health, Care and Consumer Protection addressed in a report the most spread rumours and conspiracy theories about Covid-19 and vaccination. Among others, reported circulating fake news were: masks do not protect against infections, 5G mobile networks are spreading the virus, hot peppers heal and protect against Covid-19, spraying bleacher on the body protects against Covid-19, Corona-tests can provoke brain damages, vaccines cause sterility, vaccines cause immunosuppression.[24] It goes without saying that social media are the perfect platform for the rapid spread of such content since, despite their engagement in fighting fake news, they tend to set users in so-called »eco chambers« where content assumed to be interesting for the user is likely to be reproposed again and again.[25] That means that not all users are exposed to fake

---

[17] Cf. Pariser: The Filter Bubble; Bozdag/Van den Hoven: Breaking the Filter Bubble.
[18] Cf. Milano et al.: Recommender Systems and Their Ethical Challenges.
[19] Cf. Henley: Global Crackdown on Fake News Raises Censorship Concerns.
[20] Cf. Instagram: Combatting Misinformation on Instagram; Facebook: Taking Action Against Misinformation Across Our Apps.
[21] Cf. Entrepreneur Europe: TikTok Introduces Warning Label to Combat Fake News.
[22] Cf. Twitter: Updating our Approach to Misleading Information.
[23] Cf. Islam et al.: Covid-19-Related Infodemic and Its Impact on Public Health; Silk: Spread of Coronavirus Fake News Causes Hundreds of Deaths.
[24] Cf. Bundesministerium für Soziales, Gesundheit, Pflege und Konsumentenschutz: Corona Fake-News.
[25] Cf. Cinelli et al.: The Echo Chamber Effect on Social Media.

news in the same way since the ones who are more likely to see misleading content on their news feed are those who are more likely to keep following discussion threads about conspiracy theories and rumours. This mechanism penalizes in an unfair way those who have worse digital literacy skills and, paired with other complex social factors, may lead to a dangerous radicalization of opinion.[26]

If recognized and granted as a digital right, protection against mis- and disinformation could, in times of pandemic, help containing the spread of scepticism and mistrust towards the scientific community and the official measures against the rise of infections, such as wearing masks, social distancing and getting vaccinated.

Conclusion

After the events of the last year and a half, the public discourse about the right to freedom and its limitation for a greater good has been influenced by the many deaths that could have been avoided if only more effective measures to contain the virus were adopted. As well as in the case of the ecological crisis and climate change, it is becoming clear that the enjoyment of many freedoms should not be unrestricted and should also take into account the right to freedom of other human beings living in the present and in the future – a principle that the philosopher Hans Jonas called »principle of responsibility«.[27] During the pandemic, many people showed solidarity and responsibility by accepting limitations to their freedom of movement and gathering. To be prepared to face new epidemics in a digitalized society, politics and public discourse should also thematize digital rights, their improvement, and the limits and extent of their possible restriction in the event of a pandemic.

In the case of digital data protection, some measures can be taken to encourage the citizens sharing contact information – which may be seen as a limitation to the right to privacy – to prevent the spread of the virus. On the one hand, designing applications that preserve the users' privacy as much as possible by minimizing the amount of data collected, anonymizing the data, and saving them only the user's device – as already happened in many countries – avoids the threat of digital surveillance. On the other hand, a transparent communication concerning the use made of the collected data and raising awareness on their importance to contain infections could encourage people cooperating in the shared effort to contain the pandemic and create a virtuous circle of trust. Fighting fake news and providing

---

[26] Cf. Baumann et al.: Modeling Echo Chambers and Polarization Dynamics in Social Networks; Ribeiro et al.: Misinformation, Radicalization and Hate Through the Lens of Users.

[27] Cf. Jonas: Das Prinzip Verantwortung.

tools to unmask disinformation sources should be part of this operation of clarification and explanation, allowing to cement a core of objective knowledge at the basis of the public debate about the measures to be taken to face the current and future pandemics.

References

Baumann, Fabian: Modeling Echo Chambers and Polarization Dynamics in Social Networks, in: Physical Review Letters, 124, 2020; last accessed June 06, 2021.

Bozdag, Engin / Jeroen Van den Hoven: Breaking the Filter Bubble: Democracy and Design, in: Ethics and Information Technology, 17, 2015, pp. 249–265.

Bundesministerium für Soziales, Gesundheit, Pflege und Konsumentenschutz: Corona Fake-News, Presseunterlage, https://www.sozialministerium.at/dam/jcr:4cf0bab9-22dd-4dbd-88b7-83337c62cc1e/PU_Corona-Fake_News.pdf; last accessed June 06, 2021.

Cadwalladr, Carole / Emma Graham-Harrison: Revealed: 50 Million Facebook Profiles Harvested for Cambridge Analytica in Major Data Breach, in: The Guardian, March 17, 2018, https://www.theguardian.com/news/2018/mar/17/cambridge-analytica-facebook-influence-us-election; last accessed June 06, 2021.

Cinelli, M.: The Echo Chamber Effect on Social Media, in: Proceedings of the National Academy of Science, 118(9), 2021.

Covid-19 National Emergency Response Center, Epidemiology & Case Management Team: Korea Centers for Disease Control & Prevention Contact transmission of Covid-19 in South Korea: Novel Investigation Techniques for Tracing Contacts, in: Osong Public Health Res Perspect, 11(1), 2020, pp. 60–63.

Dragu, Tiberiu / Yonatan Lupu: Digital Authoritarianism and The Future of Human Rights, in: International Organization, February 09, 2021, pp. 1–27.

Entrepreneur Europe: TikTok Introduces Warning Label to Combat Fake News, in: Entrepreneur Europe, February 04, 2021, https://www.entrepreneur.com/article/364767; last accessed June 06, 2021.

European Union: Charter of Fundamental Rights of the European Union, December 12, 2012, 2012/C 326/02, https://www.refworld.org/docid/3ae6b3b70.html; last accessed July 20, 2021.

Facebook: Taking Action Against Misinformation Across Our Apps, https://www.facebook.com/combating-misinfo; last accessed June 06, 2021.

Haggag, Omar / Sherif Haggag / John Grundy / Mohamed Abdelrazek: Covid-19 vs. Social Media Apps: Does Privacy Really Matter?, in: 2021 IEEE/ACM 43rd International Conference on Software Engineering: Software Engineering in Society (ICSE-SEIS), March 01, 2021, pp. 48–57.

Henley, Jon: Global Crackdown on Fake News Raises Censorship Concerns, in: The Guardian, April 24, 2018, https://www.theguardian.com/media/2018/apr/24/global-crackdown-on-fake-news-raises-censorship-concerns; last accessed June 06, 2021.

Holz, Julia: Der Erfolg Vietnams im Kampf gegen das Virus, in: Südostasien, February 16, 2021, https://suedostasien.net/der-erfolg-vietnams-im-kampf-gegen-das-virus/; last accessed June 06, 2021.

Holz, Julia: Singapurs gebrochenes Versprechen, in: Südostasien, February 25, 2021, https://suedostasien.net/singapurs-gebrochenes-versprechen/; last accessed June 06, 2021.

Instagram: Combatting Misinformation on Instagram, December 16, 2019, https://about.instagram.com/blog/announcements/combatting-misinformation-on-instagram; last accessed June 06, 2021.

Institute of Global Health Innovation: Covid-19: Perceptions of Contact Tracing. Global Report (IGHI, 2020), August 07, 2020, https://www.imperial.ac.uk/media/imperial-college/institute-of-global-health-innovation/Global_ICL-YouGov-Covid-19-Behaviour-Tracker_contact-tracing_20200821_vF%5B1%5D.pdf; last accessed June 06, 2021.

Islam, Saiful/Tonmoy Sarkar/Sazzad Hossain Khan/Abu-Hena Mostofa Kamal/S. M. Murshid Hasan/Alamgir Kabir/Dalia Yeasmin/Mohammad Ariful Islam/Kamal Ibne Amin Chowdhury/Kazi Selim Anwar/Abrar Ahmad Chughtai/Holly Seale: Covid-19 – Related Infodemic and Its Impact on Public Health: A Global Social Media Analysis, in: The American Journal of Tropical Medicine and Hygiene, 103(4), 2020, pp. 1621–1629.

Jonas, Hans: Das Prinzip Verantwortung: Versuch einer Ethik für die technologische Zivilisation, Frankfurt am Main 1979.

Kiet, Ahn: Bluezone Covid-19 TrackingAapp exceeds 30 Million Downloads, in: Hanoi Times, March 03, 2021, http://hanoitimes.vn/bluezone-covid-19-tracking-app-exceeds-30-million-downloads-316516.html; last accessed June 06, 2021.

Kleinman, Robert/Colin Merkel: Digital Contact Tracing for Covid-19, in: CMAJ, 192(24), 2020, pp. E653–E656.

Lewis, Dyani: Why Many Countries Failed at Covid Contact-Tracing – but Some Got It Right, in: Nature, 588, 2020, pp. 384–387.

MacMillan, Douglas/Robert McMillan: Google Exposed User Data, Feared Repercussions of Disclosing to Public, in: The Wall Street journal, October 08, 2018, https://www.wsj.com/articles/google-exposed-user-data-feared-repercussions-of-disclosing-to-public-1539017194; last accessed June 06, 2021.

Matheis, Tanja/Oliver Pye: Lehren aus Covid-19-Strategien in Südostasien, in: Sudostasien, May 03, 2021, https://suedostasien.net/lehren-aus-covid-19-strategien-in-suedostasien/; last accessed June 06, 2021.

Milano, Silvia / Mariarosaria Taddeo / Luciano Floridi: Recommender Systems and Their Ethical Challenges, in: AI & SOCIETY, 35, 2020, pp. 957–967.

O'Neill, Patrick / Tate Ryan-Mosley / Bobbie Johnson: A Flood of Coronavirus Apps Are Tracking Us. Now It's Time to Keep Track of Them, in: Technology Review, May 07, 2020, https://www.technologyreview.com/2020/05/07/1000961/launching-mittr-covid-tracing-tracker/; last accessed June 06, 2021.

Pariser, Eli: The Filter Bubble: How the New Personalized Web Is Changing What We Read and How We Think, New York 2011.

Polyakova, Alina / Chris Meserole: Exporting Digital Authoritarianism. The Russian and Chinese Models, in: Brookings Policy Brief, August 2020, https://www.brookings.edu/research/exporting-digital-authoritarianism/; last accessed June 06, 2021.

Ribeiro, Manoel Horta: Misinformation. Radicalization and Hate Through the Lens of Users, in: Sociedade Brasileira de Computação (ed.): Anais do XXXIII Concurso de Teses e Dissertações, Porto Alegre 2020, pp. 79–84.

Silk, John: Spread of Coronavirus Fake News Causes Hundreds of Deaths, in: Deutsche Welle, August 11, 2020, https://www.dw.com/en/coronavirus-misinformation/a-54529310; last accessed June 06, 2021.

Sweeney, Yann.: Tracking the Debate on Covid-19 Surveillance Tools, in: Nature Machine Intelligence, 2, 2020, pp. 301–304.

United Nations: Universal Declaration of Human Rights, December 10, 1948, 217 A (III), https://www.refworld.org/docid/3ae6b3712c.html; last accessed June 06, 2021.

Wolford, Ben: What is GDPR, the EU's New Data Protection Law?, in: GDPR.EU, https://gdpr.eu/what-is-gdpr/; last accessed July 20, 2021.

Francesca Caroccia

The Principle of Solidarity as Relational Dimension of the (Informed) Consent: The Case of Covid-19 Vaccines

1. In a juridical perspective, the pandemic crisis is a giant laboratory for testing the effectiveness and the extent of the right to health. In the past months, right to health has been analysed in terms of public/private healthcare system, in terms of liability and compensation for damages, in terms of respect of human dignity, and has been constantly balanced with other fundamental rights, namely with individual freedom. This is nothing new by itself: the novelty obviously lies in the context in which such a balancing was inserted, as well as the way in which individual freedom was intended. The first year after the WHO's pandemic declaration was dominated by a reflection on the relationship between collective health and personal freedom, mainly intended as freedom of movement, while this second year is announced to shift the focus on the individual freedom as right to self-determination. During this second phase of the pandemic crisis, the need to reach high vaccination coverage compels us to return to the eternal question of the definition of the limits of private autonomy, when the defence of public health is at stake.

2. In western legal tradition, the relationship between individuals and their own body is essentially conceived as a private matter. Free and responsible persons have been allowed to make choices, according to their personal, religious, political convictions. At the beginning of the XX century, this was the absolute prevailing model, clearly codified in the article 5 of the Italian civil code (dated 1942), following which everyone may dispose of parts of its own body, with the only limits of permanent damage to physical integrity or violation of public order or decency. Private autonomy covered all aspects of human life. Quite paradoxically, in the same years, the approach to human health was dominated by a paternalistic trend.[1]

Within the described frame, the right to health was completely absent. Such a circumstance could be explained in the light of three factors, at least. Firstly, the application of the liberal individualistic model to human body allowed individuals

[1] Cf. Childress: Who Should Decide?

to make choices, which remain confined to their private sphere; secondly, health was conceived as a highly and merely technical question, which only qualified experts could understand. Thus, only physicians were allowed to take decisions on the behalf of patients. Lastly, the paradigm of nature dominated and limited the power of self-determination.

In the second half of the XX century, such an approach experienced an interesting transformation.[2] Private autonomy and self-determination began to be accompanied by the concept of consent, which could be conceived as the relational dimension of self-determination, usually related both to personal freedom and human dignity and to the right to health, this last finally appearing on the scene.[3] By this means, individuals transmit to others their choices concerning their own body and, at the same time, they prevent possible intrusions in their private bodily sphere. Moreover, if humans are autonomous moral agents who make decisions freely and are held morally responsible for the consequences of their actions, then the agent needs to have accurate information in order to make a decision.[4] Consent becomes Informed Consent and any unconsented physical intrusion becomes a human rights violation.[5] In a relatively short time, the model of the (informed) consent became the absolute prevailing paradigm, as it was believed to guarantee the highest level of both protection of private autonomy and freedom of choice.

A combination of different factors contributed to this assumption about the centrality of informed consent, »including the awareness of past abuses and controversial cases, the growth of the patients' rights movement and perhaps a growing consumerist attitude to medicine«.[6] Three among these factors could be expressly mentioned, at least. From an historical point of view, in the second half of the XX century the informed consent represented the most efficient answer to the acceleration of technological innovation. In the last decades, scientific progress created unknown as well as wide decision spaces. As never before, human health, human life and even death could be conditioned and controlled. Individuals were requested to determine opportunities and limits of the application of new techniques, while professionals were called to explain as clearly as possible consequences, risks and benefits of any treatment. The involved person – namely the patient – was identified as the only subject entitled to determine the boundaries of invasive procedures and therapeutic interventions. Moreover, it is not a

---

[2] Cf. Zatti: Verso un diritto per la bioetica.

[3] Cf. Perlingieri: Il diritto alla salute quale diritto della personalità.

[4] Cf. Faden/Beauchamp: A History and Theory of Informed Consent; Engelhardt: The Foundations of Bioethics.

[5] »Conscious that the misuse of biology and medicine may lead to acts endangering human dignity« (Preamble of the Convention for the Protection of Human Rights and Dignity of the Human Being with Regard to the Application of Biology and Medicine: Convention on Human Rights and Biomedicine).

[6] Messer: Professional-Patient Realtionships and Informed Consent, p. 277.

case if this theory was developed between the 1950s and the 1960s in the United States, also as a consequence of the growing attention for personal freedoms and the claim for civil rights.[7] Oversimplifying, it is possible to affirm that science allowed people to have a certain control over their health, life and death, just when law was discovering a new dimension for individual's rights.

A third element, which contributes to explain the success of the paradigm of consent, is the fact that the consent itself is more a moral, than a technical question. The moral foundations for informed consent have been largely explored by doctrine and have been essentially linked to two dimensions: one describing an autonomous authorisation action by a subject, incorporating the concepts of understanding, voluntariness, and intention; and the other considering a set of rules of public policy, with such concepts as disclosure and competence.[8] Such a moral nature of the choice that the patient is called to make, deeply influenced the juridical consideration of the problem. It is certainly true that technological information is crucial, when making a decision; but »in its essence the therapeutical choice is based on a judgment of compatibility and coherence of the medical proposal with the moral structure of the patient, with the representation of his humanity, with his self-image [...] in a word – we could say – with his dignity«.[9] Hence, it is reasonable that the same subject that will get the treatment becomes the holder of the right of choice.

3. In sum, as it has already been said, in recent decades informed consent has become the absolutely dominant paradigm.[10] It has been conceived as the expression of the fundamental rights of individuals, in accordance with a common constitutional culture, »whose conceptual core is shared by the whole society and which consists of fundamental rights to self determination *and* to health«.[11] In concrete terms, and at a national level, the discipline has been built following two basic trends: »the prevailingly permissive one and the prevailingly impositive one, neither one of them allowing for extreme solutions (such as the right to die or the duty to be kept artificially alive beyond one's own idea of human dignity)«.[12] In other words, the Western Legal Tradition model seems to be essentially characterised by three elements. Firstly, it recognises a fairly broad space of individual freedom. Conversely, it does not grant to individuals an absolute and unconditioned right

---

[7] Cf. Casonato: Il consenso informato.
[8] Cf. Faden/Beauchamp: History and Theory.
[9] Casonato: Il consenso informato, p. 2.
[10] Cf. Calò: Il ritorno della volontà; Graziadei: Il consenso informato e i suoi limiti; Calderai: Consenso informato.
[11] Santosuosso/Sellaroli: Informed Consent, Self-Determination and Rights to Freedom in Jurisprudence, p. 154. See also, in more general terms: Rodotà: La vita e le regole.
[12] Following the distinction proposed by Casonato: Il consenso informato, pp. 4 ff.

on their own body (better: on their biological sphere, including life and death). Finally, it still provides the State the power to impose some compulsory medical treatments, notably when it is necessary to protect public health. Thus, it seems possible to affirm that personal freedom, self-determination and even the right to health should be balanced with other subjective situations, recognised as worthy of protection.

However, it shall be noted that this last element and its logical consequences have been quite neglected. The semantic of the consent has been almost exclusively developed in the light of individuality and personhood. The collective public dimension of the right to health has been essentially omitted. Generally speaking, it is possible to affirm that, in the last 30–40 years, the debate on the relationship between right to health and right to self-determination registered a decisive turn in favour of the second term of this binomial, and the informed consent has been simply defined as »a process of shared decision making based on mutual respect and participation«[13], which guarantees the respect, the protection and the promotion of *individual autonomy*. The collective dimension of the right to health, the duties of solidarity, the Other, are nothing more than invisible spirits.

4. Within such a context, vaccines represent a relevant exception. They are a rare example of compulsory medical treatment, admitted in western democracies, as such as, for instance, involuntary commitments applied to psychiatric patients. However, the most evident trait distinguishing vaccines from any other compulsory treatment is the number of involved persons. Whereas the largest part of medical treatments are effective even if they are applied to single persons, vaccines require a high rate of immunized, in order to achieve the *herd immunity*.

Hence, they constitute a particularly difficult challenge for the Law, as they dare to deny the freedom of choice to entire categories of people, if not to the whole population. Nevertheless, a large number of western governments have not hesitated to make vaccinations compulsory: United States, Australia, and approximately half of European countries have mandatory vaccination requirements.[14] Since 1905, the U.S. Supreme Court ruled that the federal government has the power of requiring adults and children to receive an approved vaccine, with regard to a case involving the smallpox vaccine in a period where smallpox was having a devastating effect on the population.[15] One century later, in 2017, the Italian government has made vaccines against 10 diseases compulsory for children enrolling in state-run schools.

---

[13] President's Commission for the Study of Ethical Problems in Medicine and Biomedical and Behavioural Research: Making Health Care Decisions, p. 2.

[14] Cf. Salmon/MacIntyre/Omer: Making Mandatory Vaccination Truly Compulsory.

[15] Cf. The Harvard Law Review: Towards a Twenty-First-Century, Jacobson vs. Massachusetts.

The liberal paradigm of the sovereignty of individual freedom seems to be limited by the collective exigency of safety. It should also be noted that, in a first time, in Western countries this requirement (that is, mandatory vaccination) was not often accompanied by a juridical sanction. In rare cases, there were obviously some exceptions, as the payment of a fine, but generally speaking compliance with the duty could not be physically enforced. But even so, it is possible to affirm that a large part of the population accepted to get vaccination and the goal of the herd immunity was widely achieved. The practice of immunization outlined a zone where the *collective* still prevailed over the *individual*, quite easily.

In the last decades, however, something has changed. The number of persons refusing vaccines dramatically increased, not only for medical, but also for religious or moral reasons. The negative impact of such a trend is augmented because of the dynamically changing social situation associated with migrations and the popularity of anti-vaccine movements.[16] Ever more frequently, scientists warned population and governments about such a growing danger and called for adoption of strategies to compel adults and children to get vaccines. In 2019, the WHO named hesitancy to vaccinate as one of the ten gravest threats to global health. A wide range of strategies had been proposed and the governments' answer was not completely absent. However, quite paradoxically, while the solution seems to be relatively defined with regard to minors, the idea of forcing adults to accept medical treatment still is extremely disturbing from a juridical point of view. In the name of the *best interests of the child*, between 2015 and 2019, legislators in Australia, France and Italy (*inter alia*) have restricted school access for children who had not received the country's recommended panel of vaccinations. Some US states removed the ability for parents to legally refuse vaccines for non-medical reasons. There is also a significant body, both of national and supranational case law, stating that the best interests of the child, and also those of the children as a group, must be placed at the centre of all decisions affecting their health and development: when it comes to immunization, the aim should be that every child is protected against serious diseases.[17] In 2014, e.g., the Constitutional Court of North Macedonia ruled that it is justified to deny the parents' freedom to refuse vaccination, since the right of the child to health prevails over the parents' right to choose.[18] In 2020, in UK, in the case EWCA Civ. 664, the Court of Appeal ruled that »parental views regarding immunisation must always be taken into account but the matter is not to be determined by the strength of the parental view unless the view has a real bearing on the child's welfare«.[19] Finally, on April 8th, 2021,

---

[16] Cf. Patryn/Zagaja: Vaccinations, pp. 2204 f.
[17] See for example: European Court of Human Rights: Vavrička and Others vs. the Czech Republic, par. 288.
[18] Cf. Constitutional Court of the Republic of the North Macedonia: Resolution U.no. 30/2014.
[19] Court of Appeal (Civil Division): Parental Responsibility: Vaccination, par. 104.

the European Court of Human Rights clearly stated that compulsory vaccinations would not contravene human rights law, and may be necessary in democratic societies.[20] The case concerned Czech families who had been fined, or whose children had been refused access to schools for failing to comply with their legal vaccination duty. In the Court's opinion, compulsory vaccination, as an involuntary medical intervention, interferes with physical integrity, thus it concerns the right to respect for private life under Article 8 of the European Convention of Human Rights. However, this interference did not entail a violation of Article 8, since it was »in accordance with the law« and pursued a legitimate aim. In fact, on the one hand, vaccination is considered effective and safe by the scientific community and strongly recommended by medical authorities; on the other hand, it protects both those who receive it and those who cannot be vaccinated for medical reasons. Also in this case, judges emphasise that in all decisions concerning children, their interests must be »of paramount importance«.[21] But, when the question involved adults, mandates were not perceived as an efficient solution: from a strictly juridical point of view, it is difficult to find arguments against the rhetoric of individual freedoms and the self-determination.[22] The same idea of a mandatory medical treatment dramatically evokes the phantom of totalitarianism.

5. What about the described theoretical apparatus, when faced with the SARS/Covid-19 pandemic? What we called *the second phase of the crisis*, which imposes the necessity of balancing the theory of consent with the need to protect the entire population through the imposition of a medical treatment, forces us to review some assumptions. The easier way to do so could be to reaffirm the said collective dimension of the right to health. Following the reasoning of *Jacobson vs. Massachusetts*, »The liberty secured by the Constitution [...] does not import an absolute right in each person to be [...] wholly freed from restraint. There are manifold restraints to which every person is necessarily subject for the *common good* [...]«. Hence, there is »a sphere within which the individual may assert the supremacy of his own will and rightfully dispute the authority of any human government, [...]. But it is equally true that in every well-ordered society charged with the duty of conserving the safety of its members the rights of the individual in respect of his liberty may at times, under the pressure of great dangers, be subjected to such restraint, to be enforced by reasonable regulations, as the safety of the general

---

[20] Cf. European Court of Human Rights: Vavrička and Others vs. the Czech Republic.
[21] European Court of Human Rights: Vavrička and Others vs. the Czech Republic, par. 286.
[22] Where the term »rhetoric« is not necessarily assumed in its negative meaning; Cf. Ruotolo: L'onere dei test anti-aids per i soggetti che svolgono attività a rischio; Romboli: I limiti alla libertà di disporre del proprio corpo nel suo aspetto attivo ed in quello passivo; Modugno: Trattamenti sanitari »non obbligatori« e Costituzione; Vincenzi Amato: Sub Art. 32.

public may demand«.²³ In the judges' words, »*Real* liberty« does not exist without the respect that may be given to others. Thus, as vaccination tends to prevent the transmission or the spread of dangerous and contagious diseases, making them compulsory constitutes »a reasonable and proper exercise of the police power«. This argument was sustained in 1905, but it is not so far from the position recently taken by the ECHR, in the case Vavrička, following which »where the view is taken that a policy of voluntary vaccination is not sufficient to achieve and maintain herd immunity, or herd immunity is not relevant to the nature of the disease, domestic authorities may reasonably introduce a compulsory vaccination policy in order to achieve an appropriate level of protection against serious diseases«.²⁴ In this light, a relevant difference has been proposed »between laws that are intended to prevent a person from harming other people, which can be a justified exercise of police power, and laws that are intended to protect only the health of the individual herself, which are unjustified violations of liberty«.²⁵ Furthermore, a second condition is requested, granting the safety of the recipient.²⁶

Such an opinion had been resumed by the Italian Constitutional Court, ruling that a law imposing a health-related treatment is not incompatible with the Constitution if: »the treatment was intended not only to improve or maintain the health of the recipient, but also to preserve the health of others; the treatment was not expected to have a negative impact on the health of the recipient, with the exclusive exception of those consequences that normally arose and, as such, were tolerable; and, in the event of further injury, the payment of just compensation to the injured party was provided for, separate and apart from any damages to which they might be entitled«.²⁷ The power of the state is safe, the individuals' health too, and monetary compensation seems to become the price for individual freedom.²⁸

Such a doctrine could plainly be applied to Covid-19 vaccines: a number of medical authorities have confirmed that they are safe and their positive impact

---

23 Harvard Law Review: Towards a Twenty-First-Century, Jacobson vs. Massachusetts, p. 29.
24 European Court of Human Rights: Vavrička and Others vs. the Czech Republic, par. 288.
25 Mariner/Annas/Glantz: Jacobson vs. Massachusetts.
26 Cf. Rossi: Consenso informato.
27 See also Italian Constitutional Court, June 22, 1990, n. 307 and April 15–18, 1996, n. 118, where the Court underlined that health in constitutional law has two aspects: the individual and subjective aspect concerning a fundamental right of the individual; and the societal and objective aspect concerning health as a public interest. The risk of damage to an individual's health could not be completely avoided. The legislature had therefore struck a balance, giving precedence to the collective aspect of health. Yet nobody could be asked to sacrifice their health to preserve that of others without being granted just compensation for damage caused by medical treatment. In 2018 (Italian Constitutional Court, December 14, 2017, no. 268), the same Court observed that there was no qualitative difference between compulsory and recommended vaccinations, the key issue being the essential objective of preventing infectious diseases that was pursued by both types. Accordingly, the exclusion of compensation was contrary to the Constitution.
28 A variant of such a »monetary« approach is represented by the proposal of introducing financial responsibility for refusing vaccinations (Patryn/Zagaja: Vaccinations).

on the population is self-evident. At the same time, however, the idea of imposing a medical treatment attracts criticism on several counts.[29]

6. Not surprisingly, in order to prevent those criticisms, national government opted for a different strategy. To be accepted, the prevalence of the *collective* over the *individual* should be in some degree englobed in what we could call *the rhetoric of the consent*. Therefore, on the one hand, national governments did not mandate the receipt of Covid-19 vaccines. Yet, on the other hand, they introduced or reaffirmed or at least considered *socio-juridical* sanctions. A variety of incentives and penalties have been employed, with differing levels of enforcement. For example, a certificate of vaccination might be requested for traveling, accessing the gym, being admitted to school, working both in public offices and in private businesses. Vaccinated consumers could be preferred (as well as the unvaccinated could be excluded). In this perspective, Italy approved an emergency decree on April 1st, stating that health professionals who refuse to have the vaccine will have the option to be transferred to duties where they do not risk spreading the virus or to be suspended without pay for as much as one year. In other words, people who refuse consent do not pay a fine nor are physically forced, but are excluded from the collective dynamics and their social life is severely limited. Personal freedom is formally safeguarded, but practically emptied of meaning. Or, if preferred, the juridical existence of individuals is undamaged, but the exercise of their social relationships is subject to the acceptance of the medical treatment.

7. There is a third governmental strategy, which can be discerned. It is based on concepts as *truth*, *trust* and *confidence*, and supported by communication campaigns as well as incentives. The basic idea is that *people are more likely to trust officials who protect their personal liberty*, and that the *public will support reasonable public health interventions if they trust public health officials to make sensible recommendations that are based on science*. Hence, »21st-century public health depends on good science, good communication and trust in public health officials to tell the truth.«[30] The Italian deputy vice-president of the National Bioethics Committee officially declared that »vaccines are an ethical obligation for health professionals: their professional duty to treat the sick obliges them to avoid transmitting the infection, to operate in safe conditions, and to provide reliable infor-

---

[29] For example, it is not surprising if Jacobson was cited by the same Supreme Court as support for the general principle that public welfare is sufficient to justify involuntary sterilization: see United States Supreme Court: Buck vs. Bell: 274 US 200 (1927): »Society can prevent those who are manifestly unfit from continuing their kind. The principle that sustains compulsory vaccination is broad enough to cover cutting the Fallopian tubes [Jacobson vs. Massachusetts: 197 US 11]. Three generations of imbeciles are enough«.

[30] Mariner/Annas/Glantz: Jacobson vs. Massachusetts.

mation on the significance of vaccines for the protection of public health.«[31] *Ethical*, not *Juridical*. But the message is, *you are not an authentic physician, if you don't get the vaccine*. Similarly, numerous politicians have shown that they think the vaccine is safe by publicly getting it themselves. Social media have shown triumphant pictures of doctors, nurses, and people getting inoculated.[32] The State of New York launched an incentive program, which provides free tickets for popular attractions, gift cards and free metro-cards.

This third way seems to be the most convincing, as human rights and personal freedoms are apparently untouched and the punitive side is completely absent. However, it has been proved that the improvement of the quality of public immunisation services and communication campaigns is not sufficient to have a positive impact over the vaccine diffusion.[33] Moreover, communication strategies in XXI century are sophisticated as much as powerful: it is legitimate to ask if the consent would be actually free. The risk of a *Big Brother* effect is real.

8. Once again, the question of consent deserves further attention. Until now, (informed) consent has been conceived as the *external* result of an *internal* process of self-determination. The sequence will-decision-communication is apparently linear. Yet, the decision-making process actually has a relational dimension, which cannot be omitted. Such a relational aspect can be considered and/or addressed into two different directions. On the one hand, it can be regarded from the point of view of the medical relation between patients and physicians. On the other hand, the relational dimension of the consent should be regarded in the light of the relation between individual and the Collective. The first direction has been widely explored. As we said, the question of the informed consent has been morally founded on concepts as disclosure and competence and legally subsumed under the contractual theory. In its most traditional and diffused formulation, the doctrine of consent »requires a health care provider to make the relevant information available, then to adopt a stance of non-interference in the patient's decision making. In short, information plus non-interference is necessary and sufficient to secure an agent's free and autonomous choice«.[34] Several authors investigated some limits of this doctrine. For instance, it has been proposed that a relational concept of autonomy should be adopted, in order to take into account, the social conditions that affect patients' capacities for an autonomous reasoning.[35] It has been also observed that, in practice, consent was often used mainly to protect physicians from

---

[31] Paterlini: Covid-19: Italy Makes Vaccination Mandatory for Healthcare Workers; Paterlini: On the Front Lines of Coronavirus.
[32] Cf. Freeman/Engstrom/Meyers: Coronavirus Vaccines and the Law.
[33] Cf. D'Ancona/D'Amari: The Law on Compulsory Vaccination in Italy.
[34] Stoliar: Informed Consent and Relational Conceptions of Autonomy, pp. 375 f.
[35] Cf. ibid.

financial liability. The necessity of strictly linking medical practice to human rights and human dignity was reasserted since the »complexity of power of medical science and technology has increased the patient's vulnerability«.[36] However, these criticisms did not discuss the *model* of the informed consent, as they rather contributed to redefine its *content*, with the aim of ensuring a most complete, adequate, effective and personalised communication between patient and physician (and a most conscious patient's decision).

The second profile, that is, the relation individual/collective, has been essentially viewed in the light of the right to health. Following Article 32 of the Italian Constitution, »[t]he Republic safeguards health as a fundamental *right of the individual* and as a *collective interest*«.[37] It is significant that the principle of therapeutic self-determination, which does not have a textual recognition in the Italian Constitution, has been affirmed in the Italian legal system properly *in the shadow* of the constitutional right to health.[38] Yet, such an approach reduces the question to a *fight* among fundamental rights, whose battlefield is the human body, and does not prevent accuse of tyranny.

There is a further perspective, from which the question of the (informed) consent can be considered, confined until now at the peripheries of the scientific debate.[39] Such a perspective was the relational character of consent in its collective/individual meaning could be strictly linked to the duty of solidarity. The question of (informed) consent actually might be seen not simply as the alternative between a model which guarantees personal freedom and a model that denies it, but as the output of a complex process, in which the individual will is faced with, crosses, and encounters, the Other. Informed consent is not the external dimension of an internal process of self-determination, but rather the point where the individual *meets* the collective. In this light, self-determination has no limits, while the limit of the consent are the rights and freedoms of others. Consent becomes the external *measure* of the internal will, as it drafts the limits of self-determination, in function of our collective living. In other words, the process of forming consent necessarily involves the social dimension of individuals and their capacity/necessity of living with others. By this way, our understanding of individual rights is shaped both by juridical duties and shared social practices, and by the consciousness of the authentic sense of living together. It was suggested that protection of rights *and* the maintenance of social solidarity as a rationale for (health) regulation could be theoretically supported by the work of Durkheim and Duguit and the concept

---

[36] Crawley: Ethics Committees and Informed Consent: Locating Responsibility in Clinical Trials, p. 259.
[37] See at least Luciani: Salute; Principato: Il diritto costituzionale alla salute.
[38] Cf. Graziadei: Il consenso informato e i suoi limiti.
[39] With rare exceptions: see for example: Prainsack: The »We« in the »Me«; Prainsack/Buyx: Solidarity.

of public service.[40] But the same rationale could be found in the strictly juridical discourse, by considering solidarity as one of the pillars of the legal regulation of the fundamental rights. To neglect such a solidarity-based sense of personhood not only may cause many practical problems (e.g. organ donation, data management for medical research), but also may contradict the deep meaning of the western constitutional foundations of common existence.

References

Vincenzi Amato, D.: Sub Art. 32, 2° comma, in: Guiseppe Branca (ed.): Commentario della Costituzione, Bologna Roma, 1976.

Barbara Prainsack: The »We« in the »Me«: Solidarity and Health Care in the Era of Personalized Medicine, in: Science, Technology and Human Values, October 19, 2017, pp. 21–44.

Calderai, Valentina: Consenso informato, in: Annali dell'enciclopedia del diritto, VIII, Milan 2015, pp. 225–263.

Calò, Emanuele: Il ritorno della volontà. Bioetica, nuovi diritti e autonomia privata, Milan 1999.

Casonato, Carlo: Il consenso informato. Profili di diritto comparato, in: Corte Costituzionale, July 09, 2019, https://www.cortecostituzionale.it/documenti/convegni_seminari/Consenso_informato_Casonato.pdf., https://www.cortecostituzionale.it/documenti/convegni_seminari/Consenso_informato_Casonato.pdf; last accessed June 15, 2021.

Childress, James F.: Who Should Decide? Paternalism in Health Care, in: Perspectives in Biology and Medicine, 28(3), 1985, pp. 452–456.

Constitutional Court of the Republic of the North Macedonia: Case U No. 30/2014, October 08, 2014, http://ustavensud.mk/?p=12442&lang=en; last accessed June 15, 2021.

Council of Europe: The Preamble of the Convention for the Protection of Human Rights and Dignity of the Human Being with Regard to the Application of Biology and Medicine: Convention on Human Rights and Biomedicine, in: Council of Europe (COE), April 04, 1997, https://www.coe.int/en/web/conventions/full-list/-/conventions/treaty/164?module=treaty-detail&treatynum=164; last accessed June 06, 2021.

Court of Appeal UK (Civil Division): On Appeal of The High Court of Justice (Family Division): McCombe, King and Peter Jackson LJJ: Re H (A Child): Parental Responsibility: Vaccination, May 22, 2020, [2020] EWCA Civ. 664.

---

[40] Prosser: Regulation and Social Solidarity.

Crawley, Francis P.: Ethics Committees and Informed Consent: Locating Responsibility in Clinical Trials, in: Tokai Journal of Experimental and Clinical Medicine, 22(6), 1996, pp. 259–265.

D'Ancona, Fortunato / Claudio D'Amario / Francesco Maraglino / Giovanni Rezza / Stefania Iannazzo: The Law on Compulsory Vaccination in Italy: An Update 2 Years after the Introduction, in: Euro Surveill, 24(26), 2019.

Engelhardt, H.Tristam: The Foundations of Bioethics, in: Oxford University Press, New York 1996.

European Court of Human Rights (ECHR): Case of Vavrička and Others vs. the Czech Republic, ECHR 116 (2021), April 08, 2021, Strasbourg; http://hudoc.echr.coe.int/fre?i=001-209039; last accessed June 20, 2021.

Faden, Ruth R. / Tom L. Beauchamp: A History and Theory of Informed Consent, in: Oxford University Press, New York 1986.

Freeman Engstrom, Nora / Meyers, Peter H.: Coronavirus Vaccines and the Law, in: Stanford Law School, December 22, 2020, https://law.stanford.edu/2020/12/22/coronavirus-vaccines-and-the-law/; last accessed June 15, 2021.

Graziadei, Michele, Il consenso informato e i suoi limiti, in: Paolo Zatti / Leonardo Lenti / Elisabetta Palermo Fabris: Trattato di biodiritto. I diritti in medicina, Milan 2011, pp. 191–288.

Harvard Law Review: Towards a Twenty-First-Century, Jacobson vs. Massachusetts (197 U.S. 11 1905), The Harvard Law Review Association, 121(7), 2008, pp. 1820–1841.

Italian Constitutional Court: Sentenza No. 307, in: Corte Costituzionale, June 22, 1990, cortecostituzionale.it/actionSchedaPronuncia.do?anno=1990&numero= 307; last accessed September 30, 2021.

Italian Constitutional Court: Sentenza No. 118, in: Corte Costituzionale, April 18, 1996, cortecostituzionale.it/actionSchedaPronuncia.do?anno=1996&numero= 118; last accessed September 30, 2021.

Italian Constitutional Court: Sentenza No. 5, in: Corte Costituzionale, November 22, 2017, cortecostituzionale.it/actionSchedaPronuncia.do?anno=2017&numero =5; last accessed September 30, 2021.

Luciani, Massimo: Salute. Diritto alla salute – Diritto costituzionale, in: Enciclopedia giuridica Treccani, XXVII, Roma, 1991.

Mariner, Wendy K. / George J Annas / Leonard H Glantz: Jacobson vs. Massachusetts: It's Not Your Great-Great-Grandfather's Public Health Law, in: American Journal of Public Health, 95(4), 2005, pp. 581–590.

Messer, Neil: Professional-Patient Realtionships and Informed Consent, in: Postgraduate Medical Journal, 80(943), 2004, pp. 277–283.

Modugno, Franco: Trattamenti sanitari »non obbligatori« e Costituzione, in: Diritto e società, 1982, pp. 303–334.

Paterlini, Marta: Covid-19: Italy Makes Vaccination Mandatory for Healthcare Workers, in: The BMJ, 373, 2021, n905.

Paterlini, Marta: On the Front Lines of Coronavirus: The Italian Response to Covid-19, in: The BMJ, 368, 2020.

Patryn, Rafal K./Anna Zagaja: Vaccinations – Between Free Will and Coercion, in: Human Vaccines Immunother, 12(8), 2016, pp. 2204–2205.

Perlingieri, Pietro: Il diritto alla salute quale diritto della personalità, in: Rassegna di diritto civile, 4, 1982, pp. 1035–1065.

Prainsack, Barbara/Alena Buyx: Solidarity: Reflections on an Emerging Concept, Swindon (Wiltshire) 2011.

President's Commission for the Study of Ethical Problems in Medicine and Biomedical and Behavioural Research: Making Health Care Decisions: A Report on the Ethical and Legal Implications of Informed Consent in the Patient-Pratictioner Relationship, Vol. I: Report, Washington, DC, 1982, https://repository.library.georgetown.edu/bitstream/handle/10822/559354/makinghealthcaredecisions.pdf?sequence=1&isAllowed=y; last accessed June 15, 2021.

Principato, Luigi: Il diritto costituzionale alla salute: molteplici facoltà più o meno disponibili da parte del legislatore o differenti situazioni giuridiche soggettive?, in: Giurisprudenza Costituzionale, 1999, IV, pp. 2508–2518.

Prosser, Tony: Regulation and Social Solidarity, in: Journal of Law and Society, 33(3), 2006, pp. 364–387.

Rodotà, Stefano: La vita e le regole. Tra diritto e non diritto, Milan 2006.

Romboli, Roberto: I limiti alla libertà di disporre del proprio corpo nel suo aspetto attivo ed in quello passivo, in: Foro italiano, 1991, pp. 15–21.

Rossi, Stefano: Consenso informato (il), in: Digesto delle discipline privatistiche, sezione civile, Appendice di aggiornamento VII, Torino, 2012, pp. 177–215.

Ruotolo, Marco: L'onere dei test anti-aids per i soggetti che svolgono attività a rischio: violazione del diritto alla riservatezza o ragionevole bilanciamento degli interessi in gioco?, in: Giurisprudenza Italiana, 1, 1995, pp. 637–642.

Salmon, Daniel/C. Raina MacIntyre/Saad B. Omer: Making Mandatory Vaccination Truly Compulsory: Well Intentioned but Ill Conceived, in: The Lancet Infectious Diseases, 15(8), 2015, p. 872–873.

Santosuosso, Amedeo/Valentina Sellaroli: Informed Consent, Self-Determination and Rights to Freedom in Jurisprudence, in: Salute e società, 3, 2012, pp. 154–178.

Stoliar, Natalie: Informed Consent and Relational Conceptions of Autonomy, in: Journal of Medicine and Philosophy, 36(4), August 08, 2011, pp. 1–10.

United States Supreme Court: Buck vs. Bell: 274 US 200, 1927.

United States Supreme Court: Jacobson vs. Massachusetts: 197 US 11, 1905.

Zatti, Paolo: Verso un diritto per la bioetica: Risorse e Limiti Del Discorso Giuridico, in: Rivista di diritto civile, 1, 1995, pp. 43–57.

Christoph Antons

Intellectual Property Policies and *Vaccine Diplomacy* in Asia

Introduction

When the Covid-19 crisis hit in early 2020 and the feverish search for vaccines began, it was foreseeable that the long running debate between the pharmaceutical industry and consumer organizations about the extent of patent protection for pharmaceuticals would go into another round. Although many were hoping that the pandemic would lead governments to reassess patent protection under such exceptional circumstances, it soon turned out that the old arguments would simply be repeated. The pharmaceutical industry and supportive governments argue that the patent system is indispensable for innovation in this field and that the current crisis is not the right time to think about restrictions to the system.[1] This indispensable role, however has long been questioned from the perspective of consumer welfare[2] and human rights.[3] Vaccines in particular have been included among categories of health innovation, for which patents under normal circumstances fail to provide adequate incentives because of weakness in private demand.[4] It has also been pointed out in the case of the United States that most drug breakthroughs are due to academic and federal government rather than industry research and development efforts.[5] With the enormous government subsidies paid for Covid-19 research, taxpayers then have to pay twice for vaccines developed with government funding and then purchased by governments at high costs. Hence, India and South Africa's proposal at the World Trade Organization (WTO) for a waiver of relevant intellectual property rights and the debate it has triggered.[6]

The present contribution does not seek to add to the substantive literature on the pros and cons of patent protection for pharmaceuticals but will place this dis-

---

[1] Cf. the statements of U.S., EU and UK representatives quoted in Prabhala et al.: Want Vaccines Fast?; Office of the United States Trade Representative: 2021 Special 301 Report.
[2] Cf. Mazzucato/Momenghalibaf: Drug Companies Will Make a Killing.
[3] Cf. the literature in Helfer/Austin: Human Rights and Intellectual Property, pp. 90–170.
[4] Cf. Eisenberg: Intellectual Property and Public Health, pp. 933–938.
[5] Cf. Landes/Posner: The Economic Structure of Intellectual Property Law, p. 313 (fn. 31).
[6] For contrasting views see, for example Prabhala et al.: Want Vaccines Fast?; Hilty et al.: Covid-19 and the Role of Intellectual Property.

cussion into the context of *vaccine diplomacy* and international relations in Asia during the Covid-19 pandemic. The focus will be on East, South and Southeast Asia. The context of these parts of Asia is important for several reasons. First, after decades of celebrating the economic development achievements of many countries from this part of Asia moving (according to one of its leaders) »From Third World to First«[7] in academic literature and international policy circles,[8] tensions within the various sub-regions of Asia have recently been increasing. Second, there is the continuing debate about the origins of the virus and the reactions of the Chinese government in the early days of the crisis. Third, India had for many years patent legislation that allowed it to become the major supplier of generic medicines to other developing countries and this role is now under threat. Fourth, there is a strategic competition between India and China as models of economic development and effective governance for other countries in the region and between the United States and China as powers in the region. Fifth, Chinese and Russian vaccines have been adopted by countries in the region and are competing with those produced in India, Europe and the United States. Sixth, in terms of intellectual property policies related to pharmaceuticals, this part of Asia is home to drug exporting countries with a high level of intellectual property protection such as Japan, large developing countries with manufacturing capacity for drugs criticized for their intellectual property systems such as India and China,[9] as well as least developed countries with no drug manufacturing capacity of their own. The contribution will show the expansion of intellectual property law in the public health sector in the region and the problems this expansion is creating. It will then examine the vaccine diplomacy of regional powers, in particular of China, the United States and India and the reactions to that diplomacy. It will finally ask in how far the Covid-19 crisis challenges the global value chains and supply networks, which had developed as a result of globalization and how they will be transformed as a result of the crisis and the increasing strategic competition between major powers in the region.

---

[7] Lee: From Third World to First.
[8] Most notably in World Bank: The East Asian Miracle.
[9] Cf. Office of the United States Trade Representative: 2021 Special 301 Report.

1. A Short History of Intellectual Property and Public Health in Asia

From the 1970s onwards, East Asian models of economic development were much discussed in the academic and policy literature as »Asian developmental states«[10] finding »pathways from the periphery«[11]. Their apparent success in development provided counterarguments to the gloomy picture of potential deindustrialization as a result of incorporation into the world economy presented by the then popular dependency theory[12] and Immanuel Wallerstein's world-system theory.[13] A common feature in the early stages of the Asian development model was a certain disregard of intellectual property rights.[14] This began to concern American and European governments from the 1980s onwards, when US legislation began to tie import privileges under the GATT (General Agreement on Tariffs and Trade) to the prevention of *unjustifiable or unreasonable trade practices*, including intellectual property violations.[15] With the new concept of *trade-related intellectual property rights*, international negotiations shifted from the specialized World Intellectual Property Organization (WIPO) to the GATT and then to the newly formed Word Trade Organization (WTO). The outcome was the Agreement on Trade-related Aspects of Intellectual Property Rights (TRIPS), a specific agreement within the bundle of agreements establishing the WTO.[16] It has since provided the minimum standards of intellectual property protection for WTO member states, although higher levels of protection have been negotiated and agreed upon in bilateral and multilateral Free Trade and Economic Partnership Agreements.[17] Prominent among the industries lobbying for and informing the discussions about the TRIPS agreement was the pharmaceutical industry. Peter Drahos has explained how Pfizer executives in particular were influential on the U.S. Advisory Committee on Trade Negotiations and how this committee during the 1980s worked closely with the U.S. Trade Representative (USTR) to shape the trade-related intellectual property rights agenda of this period.[18] Pharmaceutical companies had long been

---

[10] Woo-Cumings: Introduction.
[11] Haggard: Pathways from the Periphery.
[12] Cf. Blomstrom/Hettne: Development Theory in Transition.
[13] Cf. Wallerstein: The Modern World-System III, pp. 127–189.
[14] Japan is a partial exception here, because the country's initial modernization policy occurred prior to the conclusion of the major intellectual property treaties of the late 19th century (cf. Ganea/Nagaoka: Japan, p. 132).
[15] On the important role of section 301 of the US Omnibus Trade and Competitiveness Act of 1988 and the preceding Tariff and Trade Act of 1984 see Antons: Intellectual Property Law in ASEAN, p. 78; Cornish/Liddell: The Origins and Structure of the TRIPS Agreement, pp. 16 ff.
[16] Cf. Cornish/Liddell: The Origins and Structure of the TRIPS Agreement, p. 27.
[17] For such agreements in the Asia-Pacific region cf. Antons/Hilty: Intellectual Property and Free Trade Agreements.
[18] Cf. Drahos: »IP World«, pp. 205–208.

concerned about generic manufacturing in countries such as India.[19] During the 1980s, the USTR criticized countries like the Philippines for weakening the patent protection for pharmaceuticals and threatened to use section 301 of the Omnibus Trade Act 1988 against Thailand for excluding pharmaceuticals from patent protection.[20] Prior to the WTO TRIPS agreement, Thailand's approach was by no means exceptional. At the start of the Uruguay round of the General Agreement on Tariffs and Trade (GATT), which led to the formation of the WTO and the adoption of TRIPS, some 50 countries did not grant protection to pharmaceutical products and some also excluded pharmaceutical processes from protection.[21] India protected pharmaceutical processes only, but not products, and this allowed Indian generic drug manufacturers to flourish.[22] Indian generic manufacturers became important suppliers for the health sector in many other developing countries, which did not have drug manufacturing capacity of their own and could not afford paying for patented drugs from US American or European manufacturers. As a result, the country developed a reputation as the »pharmacy of the developing world«,[23] which is now under threat.[24]

TRIPS was a major victory for multinational companies in the pharmaceutical sector. Article 27.1 prescribed that WTO member states had to make patents available for »any inventions, whether products or processes, in all fields of technology«.[25] Thus, the carrot of WTO membership and access to markets came combined with the stick of patent protection in controversial fields such as pharmaceuticals. There were transitional periods for the full introduction of such protection for developing country and least-developed country members. For the least-developed country members, this transitional period has been extended three times, most recently to July 1, 2034. For pharmaceuticals in particular, the current deadline for implementation in least developed countries is 2033.[26] Following the conclusion of TRIPS, the discussion shifted almost immediately to the remaining flexibilities that governments could use in the interest of public health policies, most importantly compulsory licensing and government use of patent protected inventions in situations of health emergencies. TRIPS narrowed the conditions for such measures, but they remained possible. Nevertheless, instances of such overriding

---

[19] Cf. ibid., p. 206.
[20] Cf. Antons: Intellectual Property Law in ASEAN, pp. 82 f.
[21] Cf. United Nations Conference on Trade and Development (UNCTAD) / International Centre on Trade and Sustainable Development (ICTSD): Resource Book on TRIPS and Development, p. 353.
[22] Cf. Dhar / Gopakumar: Post-2005 TRIPS Scenario in Patent Protection in the Pharmaceutical Sector, p. 30.
[23] Bazzle: Pharmacy of the Developing World.
[24] Cf. Prabhala / Menghaney: The World's Poorest Countries.
[25] WTO: TRIPS, Article 27.1.
[26] Cf. United Nations, LDC Portal: WTO Drugs Patent Waiver for LDCCs Extended.

of the interests of the patent owners could trigger diplomatic and trade frictions and countries did not take such steps lightly.

The Doha WTO Declaration on the TRIPS Agreement and Public Health was adopted in 2001 after a period of considerable controversy over the health implications of the TRIPS provision for developing and least developed countries. The perhaps most widely published case was that of South Africa that had amended its Medicine and Related Substances Control Act to provide for parallel importation and compulsory licensing. Pharmaceutical corporations and the Pharmaceutical Manufacturers Association of South Africa subsequently sued the government but drew severe criticism in view of the AIDS crisis in the country. They withdrew the case in 2001.[27] The Declaration reconfirms the right of members to grant compulsory licences and the freedom to determine the grounds upon which such licences are granted. Members are also free to determine what constitutes a national emergency or other circumstances of extreme urgency and it is understood that public health crises often will represent such a national emergency. Countries further remain free to allow for parallel importation.[28] While most of these provisions only reaffirm the flexibilities of the TRIPS Agreement, they are nevertheless important in encouraging countries to exploit these flexibilities. At a diplomatic and negotiation level, it is harder for industry representatives and governments of industrialised countries to criticise such measures if they are taken.

The Doha declaration in paragraph 6 also instructed the TRIPS Council to find an expeditious solution for the problems of countries with insufficient or no manufacturing capacities in using compulsory licensing mechanisms. A decision in 2003 introduced the system and links up countries with no or insufficient manufacturing capacity as eligible importing members with countries as exporting members that do have such a capacity. It allows such countries to give effect to the compulsory licensing mechanisms of TRIPS by using the cooperation and services of foreign generics manufacturers and by waiving Article 31 (f) TRIPS which stipulates that any use without authorization of the right holder must be predominantly for the supply of the domestic market.[29] The system requires the granting of compulsory licenses at both ends, in the importing and in the exporting country and the entire amount necessary to meet the demands of the importing country making the request must be exported by the exporting country, so there can be no additional production for the local market of the exporting country. In 2005, the general Council decided to amend the TRIPS Agreement in line with the Doha declaration and the subsequent Council decision of 2003 and to insert Article 31*bis*. that repeats the major features of the 2003 Council decision on the implementation

---

[27] Cf. Shashikant: The Doha Declaration on TRIPS and Public Health, pp. 143 f.
[28] Cf. ibid., pp. 148 f.
[29] Cf. WTO: TRIPS, Article 31 (f).

of the Doha declaration. After ratification by two thirds of the WTO members, this amendment came into force in 2017.

While least developed country members are automatically entitled to use the system, other countries have to notify the TRIPS Council of their intention to become importers or exporters. Until recently, the only notification was from Canada and Rwanda for export of AIDS medicine from Canada to Rwanda. After the onset of the Covid-19 pandemic, they were joined by declarations as importers from Bolivia and Antigua and Barbuda. Developed country WTO members (US, Japan, Switzerland, Norway, Iceland, Canada, Australia and the EU countries) notified the TRIPS Council in 2003 that they will not use the system. A further group of developing countries has restricted their use only to national emergencies and cases of extreme urgency. Apart from Mexico, all of these countries are in Asia: China, Korea, Israel, Singapore, Taiwan, Turkey, Kuwait, Qatar and the United Arab Emirates. Although the Council Decision of 2003 and the amendment of the TRIPS Agreement seemed to offer a solution for countries with no or insufficient manufacturing capacity, Article 31bis has been criticized as a failure among other reasons due to the administrative burden placed on importing countries, pharmaceutical challenges and conflicts with so-called TRIPS-plus provisions, which have meanwhile been included in regional and bilateral Free Trade Agreements.[30] As for TRIPS conform compulsory licenses more generally and specifically for India, Gopalakrishnan and Anand concluded that »the uncertain meanings, evidentiary requirements, and considerable expenses with little prospect of gauging the possible success of an application are factors that may discourage a potential applicant.«[31] They further point to the ineffectiveness of many such licenses if relevant technological know-how is not transferred as well. Another important factor is the increasing interconnectedness and collaboration of Indian pharmaceutical companies with multinational partners, which may prevent them from taking any steps that could disturb this collaboration.[32]

Thus, with TRIPS flexibilities remaining cumbersome and the Covid-19 crisis raging, India and South Africa in October 2020 proposed a waiver of the obligation of WTO members to implement certain sections of the TRIPS Agreement in relation to prevention, containment or treatment of Covid-19 to ensure »rapid access to affordable medical products«.[33] Although the proposal has support from over 100 countries,[34] former Heads of State and Nobel Laureates[35] as well as an impressive

---

[30] Cf. Vincent: Triping-Up.
[31] Gopalakrishnan/Anand: Compulsory Licence Under Indian Patent Law, p. 40.
[32] Cf. Gopakumar/Santhosh: An Unhealthy Future.
[33] WTO: Waiver from Certain Provisions of the TRIPS Agreement.
[34] Cf. Zarocostas: What Next for a Covid-19 Intellectual Property Waiver?
[35] Cf. People's Vaccine Alliance: Open Letter: Former Heads of State and Nobel Laureates Call on President Biden.

number of civil society organizations, especially from the global South,[36] it was initially rejected by Australia, Brazil, Canada, the EU, Japan, Norway, Singapore, Switzerland, Taiwan, the UK and the US.[37] On May 5, 2021, the Biden administration expressed support for WTO negotiations on waiving intellectual property rights for Covid-19 vaccines. This shift in position was immediately supported by Australia but opposed by Germany with the position of the EU still unclear.[38]

2. The Geo-Politics of Covid-19 and Vaccine Diplomacy in the *Indo-Pacific Region*

The discussion about pharmaceuticals and intellectual property in Asia and the most appropriate way to address the Covid-19 crisis must also be seen against the background of geo-political rivalry in Asia as well as the national politics of individual Asian governments. This political context is too often missing from an analysis that focuses on scientific or legal problems only. The Director General of the World Health Organization, Tedros Adhanom Ghebreyesus, has pointed to the problems of vaccine nationalism, the hoarding of excessive amounts of vaccine by a small number of rich countries, as well as vaccine diplomacy, which he defines as »bilateral donations for reasons that have more to do with geopolitical goals than public health«.[39] At the core of the latter issue in Asia is the strategic competition between the United States and some of its allies and China. Former President Obama's administration announced a *pivot to Asia* policy in 2011, explained as a rebalancing of foreign policy attention toward the Asia-Pacific region.[40] Around the same time, government circles in several countries began to speak of an *Indo-Pacific* region expanding the previously used concept of the *Asia Pacific* westwards. This new discourse has been criticized in China and Russia as a U.S. led attempt to contain geopolitical rivals.[41] Although such regional constructs have been frequently criticized for their artificiality,[42] political scientists and international relations experts point out that there are no »natural« regions,[43] and that material realities and political choices in this regard are recursively shaped.[44] The Indo-Pacific concept was first used by Japanese Prime Minister Shinzo Abe dur-

---

36 Cf. Civil Society Letter.
37 Cf. Zarocostas: What Next for a Covid-19 Intellectual Property Waiver?
38 Cf. Borger/Wintour: US-Germany Rift as Berlin Opposes Plan.
39 Ghebreyesus: I run the W.H.O.
40 Cf. Davidson: The U.S. »Pivot to Asia«.
41 Cf. Denisov et al.: Russia, China and the Concept of the Indo-Pacific.
42 Cf. Dirlik: What Is in a Rim?
43 Hettne: Beyond the ›New Regionalism‹, p. 544.
44 Cf. Medcalf: The Indo-Pacific.

ing a visit to India in 2007, when he proposed a closer alignment of the previously separate regional concepts focused on the Indian Ocean and the Pacific respectively.[45] It then became an increasingly common reference in media reports and policy documents, such as Australia's Defence White Paper of 2013.[46] The envisaged Indo-Pacific cooperation has also a focus on shared security issues, in addition to the economic and trade linkages that were traditionally promoted by the Asia Pacific concept.[47]

After the combination of openly confrontational policies on trade with simultaneous disengagement from regional Free Trade Agreements under President Trump, recent reports conclude from key appointments in the Biden administration that it is likely that there will be a return to the »pivot to Asia« policies of the Obama era.[48] Two recent developments are particularly interesting in this context. The first is the passing in the US Senate of an Industrial Policy Bill to channel money into strategic industries[49] after a debate that according to media reports was »laced with cold war references and warning that a failure to act would leave the United States perilously dependent on its biggest geopolitical adversary«, by which they meant China.[50] They pointed out how remarkably similar the choice of funded projects in the Industrial Policy Bill is to China's »Made in China 2025« program announced six years ago.[51] The second interesting development is the list of guest nations invited to the Group of 7 meeting in Cornwall, UK. With the exception of South Africa, all were from the Indo-Pacific region: India, South Korea, Australia as well as Brunei as the current chair of the Association of South East Asian Nations (ASEAN).[52] Analysts suggest that the inclusion of the key agenda item »defending democratic values and open societies« shows a change in emphasis of the G7 meeting from shared economic interests to common values.[53] At this meeting, the US President announced the donation of 500 million doses of the Pfizer-BioNTech vaccine to 100 nations. While the President said that the donation came with »no strings attached«, his aides elaborated that it was a powerful demonstration that democracies rather than China or Russia were able to respond

---

[45] Cf. Denisov et al.: Russia, China and the Concept of the Indo-Pacific, pp. 72 f.
[46] Cf. Medcalf: In Defence of the Indo-Pacific.
[47] Cf. Denisov et al.: Russia, China, and the Concept of the Indo-Pacific.
[48] Deutsche Welle: Can President Joe Biden Return the US Pivot to Asia? Views that see a certain disengagement from Asia during the Trump administration can be contrasted with those seeing a continuity of the »pivot to Asia« with an »adjusted course« (cf. Denisov et al.: Russia, China, and the concept of the Indo-Pacific, p. 74). The same researchers also note, however, at p. 78 the lack of high-ranking representation of the U.S. at the East Asia Summit in November 2019 and of ASEAN countries at the U.S.-ASEAN summit.
[49] Cf. Edmonton: Senate Overwhelmingly Passes Bill.
[50] Sanger et al.: Senate Poised to Pass Huge Industrial Policy Bill.
[51] Ibid.
[52] Cf. Crowley: Blinken and G7 Allies.
[53] Ibid.

to crises faster and more effectively.⁵⁴ In fact, this donation and the earlier announcement to support an intellectual property waiver came after foreign policy experts in the US, including former ambassadors and diplomats had warned that Russia and China were well ahead in vaccine diplomacy.⁵⁵ While both decisions have been welcomed, the Vaccine Alliance Gavi, WHO officials and public health advocates have pointed out that new manufacturing capability is needed and that it remains important that relevant technologies and know-how are transferred to as many qualified manufacturers as possible.⁵⁶

In the regional vaccine diplomacy, China and Russia became early suppliers of developing nations. This was possible, because they had been cutting corners in the approval process and had started inoculating some of their citizens without results from Phase 3 clinical trials. Public health activists acknowledge this fact but point out that the same is true for the development of India's Covaxin.⁵⁷ India and China then became competitors in vaccine supply to countries where they were battling each other for influence such as Nepal and Sri Lanka.⁵⁸ However, in 2021 following the massive outbreak in India, ›the pharmacy of the developing world‹ urgently needed the vaccines for its own population and had to delay its supply of other nations.⁵⁹ Because rich countries at the same time were buying and stockpiling over 75 percent of the supply of the major vaccines,⁶⁰ Asian countries turned in particular to China for vaccine supply.⁶¹

What are the reactions of countries in Asia at the receiving end of donations to the vaccine diplomacy and rivalry of the major powers in the region? The invitation of the chair of ASEAN to the G7 meeting shows the importance of ASEAN and its centrality to any regional constructs such as the Indo-Pacific,⁶² so this chapter will concentrate on the reactions in these countries. ASEAN's 2019 strategy paper »ASEAN outlook on the Indo-Pacific« speaks of »avoiding the deepening of mistrust«, an »Indo-Pacific region of dialogue and cooperation instead of rivalry« and of ASEAN's role as »an honest broker within the strategic environment of competing interests«.⁶³ This language shows little appetite to come out strongly on one side or the other of what appears to be an emerging strategic and geopo-

---

54 Sanger/Shear: Eighty Years Later, Biden and Johnson Revise the Atlantic Charter.
55 Cf. Smith: Russia and China Are Beating the U.S. at Vaccine Diplomacy.
56 Cf. Zarocostas: What Next for a Covid-19 Intellectual Property Waiver; LaFraniere et al.: Biden to Send 500 Million Doses of Pfizer Vaccine.
57 Cf. Prabhala/Chee: It's Time to Trust China's and Russia's Vaccines.
58 Cf. Mashal/Yee: The Newest Diplomatic Currency.
59 Cf. Wallen/Newey: The Pharmacy of the Developing World Shuts Its Doors; Prabhala/Menghaney: The World's Poorest Countries Are at India's Mercy.
60 Cf. Grullón Paz: This Week in Covid-19 News: Global Inequities.
61 Cf. Wee: From Asia to Africa, China Promotes Its Vaccines.
62 Cf. Medcalf: In Defence of the Indo-Pacific, p. 475; Denisov et al.: Russia, China and the Concept of the Indo-Pacific, p. 77.
63 ASEAN: Outlook on the Indo-Pacific.

litical divide. Regional analysts have further pointed to meetings between China and ASEAN on the Covid-19 crisis as early as February 2020,[64] ASEAN benefitting from the U.S.-China trade war because of companies relocating to the region and the fact that ASEAN has become China's largest trading partner.[65] ASEAN is an organization that includes democracies, socialist countries, countries ruled by military governments and an Islamic monarchy. They share a developmentalist outlook placing at least in international relations economic development over political ideology, which is reserved for the domestic level. A survey of media reports on vaccine use in ASEAN countries shows that they are using the Chinese vaccines Sinovac and Sinopharm in addition to Astra Zeneca, Pfizer and Moderna vaccines. Vietnam, a country with historically the most tensed relationship with China, initially relied on Astra Zeneca and the Russian Sputnik vaccine, but was forced to add Sinopharm to its arsenal after the recent Covid-19 outbreak in the country.[66] In some countries, such as Indonesia and Cambodia, Chinese vaccines are clearly dominant in the vaccination strategy.[67]

Conclusion: Lessons from the Pandemic and the Future of Globalization

The use of several vaccines simultaneously by ASEAN governments shows that they were happy to take whatever they could get, but also that they were wary of supply bottlenecks, either because companies would not be able to deliver fast enough or because prices could be too high. The G7 nations agreed at the Cornwall meeting on the Carbis Bay Health Declaration[68] based on the »100 Days Mission to respond to future pandemic threats« report.[69] This report does not problematize intellectual property rights but acknowledges that government research funding may be needed where there is a lack of commercial opportunity, or the market is not responding fast enough.[70] It also recommends that governments should build in conditions into their funding arrangements with industry to ensure access of Low and Lower-Middle-Income Countries at not for profit and scale, once the WHO declares a Public Health Emergency.[71] This is meant to ad-

---

[64] Cf. Blanco Pitlo: China, ASEAN Band Together.
[65] Cf. Kaneti: ASEAN Must Make the Best of Its New Centrality.
[66] Cf. Strangio: Vietnam Approves Chinese COVID-19-19 Vaccine.
[67] Cf. Hung: Indonesia's Sinovac Rollout Sets High Stakes for China's Vaccine Diplomacy.
[68] Cf. United Kingdom Government: G7 Leaders to Agree Landmark Global Health Declaration.
[69] Cf. United Kingdom Government: 100 Days Mission to Respond to Future Pandemic Threats.
[70] Cf. Paragraph 80, p. 48.
[71] Cf. Paragraph 84, p. 49.

dress one of the main criticisms of government reactions after the onset of the crisis that they provided massive public funding for research without using their leverage on industry to secure better public access, including in lower income countries.[72] It is doubtful, however, whether government in countries most affected by the devastating impact of this current pandemic will be content to wait and see whether their interests will be better accounted for on another occasion. As Oxfam has pointed out, the current crisis continues, and infection rates are still soaring in many countries.[73] Oxfam proposes in the alternative »a publicly funded and managed network of vaccine manufacturers around the world, free from the constraints of intellectual property.«[74] Finally, vaccine distribution has also partly been affected by a disruption of global supply chains that has prompted political scientists to wonder whether the Covid-19 crisis combined with the rising US-China rivalry signals the end of globalization. They predict that multinational corporations will increasingly organise global value chains around national security agendas and geo-economic concerns.[75] The current public health diplomacy is then unlikely to end with the current crisis. Different global actors will continue to offer different models of procuring pharmaceuticals in competition with each other, in which the role of intellectual property law and the most beneficial balance of public and private funding in medical research will remain contested.

References

Antons, Christoph: Intellectual Property Law in ASEAN Countries: A Survey, in: European Intellectual Property Review 13(3), 1991, pp. 78–84.

Antons, Christoph / Reto M. Hilty (eds.): Intellectual Property and Free Trade Agreements in the Asia-Pacific Region, Heidelberg / New York / Dordrecht / London 2015.

Association of Southeast Asian Nations (ASEAN): ASEAN Outlook on the Indo-Pacific, June 23, 2019, https://asean.org/storage/2019/06/ASEAN-Outlook-on-the-Indo-Pacific_FINAL_22062019.pdf; last accessed June 12, 2021.

Bazzle, Timothy: Pharmacy of the Developing World: Reconciling Intellectual Property Rights in India with the Right to Health: TRIPS, India's Patent System and Essential Medicines, in: Georgetown Journal of International Law, 42, 2011, pp. 785–815.

---

[72] Cf. Prabhala / Menghaney: The World's Poorest Countries Are at India's Mercy; Gebrekidan / Apuzzo: Rich Countries Signed Away a Chance.
[73] Cf. Oxfam: Oxfam Reaction to G7 Leaders Agreeing ›Carbis Bay Declaration‹.
[74] Ibid.
[75] Cf. Hameiri: COVID-19: Is This the End of Globalization?

Blanco Pitlo, Lucio: China, ASEAN Band Together in the Fight Against Coronavirus, in: The Diplomat, March 04, 2020, https://thediplomat.com/2020/03/china-asean-band-together-in-the-fight-against-coronavirus/; last accessed June 22, 2021.

Blomstrom, Magnus/Björn Hettne: Development theory in transition: the dependency debate and beyond: Third World responses, London 1984.

Borger, Julian/Patrick Wintour: US-Germany rift as Berlin opposes plan to ditch Covid-19 vaccine patents, in: The Guardian, May 07, 2021, https://www.theguardian.com/world/2021/may/06/us-germany-rift-Covid-19-vaccine-patent-waivers; last accessed June 21, 2021.

Civil Society Letter Supporting Proposal by India and South Africa on Waiver from Certain Provisions of the TRIPS Agreement for the Prevention, Containment and Treatment of COVID-19, available at https://twn.my/announcement/signonletter/CSOLetter_SupportingWaiverFinal.pdf; last accessed December 13, 2021.

Cornish, William/Kathleen Liddell: The Origins and Structure of the TRIPS Agreement, in: Hanns Ullrich/Reto M. Hilty/Matthias Lamping/Josef Drexl (eds.): TRIPS plus 20: From Trade Rules to Market Principles, Heidelberg/New York/Dordrecht/London 2016, pp. 3–51.

Crowley, Michael: Blinken and G7 Allies Turn their Focus to ›Democratic Values‹, in: The New York Times, May 04, 2021, https://www.nytimes.com/2021/05/04/world/europe/blinken-G-7-china-russia.html; last accessed, June 22, 2021.

Davidson, Janine: The U.S. »Pivot to Asia«, in: American Journal of Chinese Studies, 21(77), 2014, pp. 77–82.

Denisov, Igor/Oleg Paramonov/Ekaterina Arapova/Ivan Safranchuk: Russia, China, and the concept of Indo-Pacific, in: Journal of Eurasian Studies, 12(1), 2021, pp. 72–85.

Deutsche Welle: Can President Joe Biden Return the US Pivot to Asia?, January 25, 2021, https://www.dw.com/en/can-president-joe-biden-return-the-us-pivot-to-asia/a-56337037; last accessed June 04, 2021.

Dhar, Biswajit/K. M. Gopakumar: Post-2005 TRIPS Scenario in Patent Protection in the Pharmaceutical Sector: The Case of the Generic Pharmaceutical Industry in India, November 2006, https://unctad.org/system/files/official-document/ictsd-idrc2006d2_en.pdf; last accessed June 03, 2021.

Dirlik, Arif: What Is in a Rim? Critical perspectives on the Pacific region idea, Boulder/Colorado/London 1993.

Drahos, Peter: »IP World« – Made by TNC Inc., in: Gaëlle Krikorian/Amy Kapczynski (eds.): Access to Knowledge in the Age of Intellectual Property, New York 2010, pp. 197–235.

Edmonton, Catie: Senate Overwhelmingly Passes Bill to Bolster Competitiveness with China, in: The New York Times, June 08, 2021, https://www.ny

times.com/2021/06/08/us/politics/china-bill-passes.html; last accessed June 22, 2021.

Eisenberg, Rebecca S.: Intellectual Property and Public Health, in: Rochelle C. Dreyfuss/Justine Pila (eds.): The Oxford Handbook of Intellectual Property Law, Oxford 2018, pp. 931–957.

Ganea, Peter/Sadao Nagaoka: Japan, in: Paul Goldstein/Joseph Straus (eds.): Intellectual Property in Asia: Law, Economics, History and Politics, Berlin/Heidelberg 2009.

Gebrekidan, Selam/Matt Apuzzo: Rich Countries Signed Away a Chance to Vaccinate the World, in: The New York Times, March 21, 2021, https://www.nytimes.com/2021/03/21/world/vaccine-patents-us-eu.html; last accessed June 22, 2021.

Ghebreyesus, Tedros Adhanom: I Run the W.H.O., and I Know That Rich Countries Must Make a Choice, in: The New York Times, April 22, 2021, https://www.nytimes.com/2021/04/22/opinion/who-Covid-19-vaccines.html; last accessed June 22, 2021.

Gopakumar, K. M./M. R. Santhosh: An unhealthy future for the Indian pharmaceutical industry? in: Third World Resurgence, No. 259, https://www.twn.my/title2/resurgence/2012/259/cover03.htm; last accessed June 08, 2021.

Gopalakrishnan, N. S./Madhuri Anand: Compulsory Licence Under Indian Patent Law, in: Reto M. Hilty/Kung-Chung Liu (eds.): Compulsory Licensing: Practical Experiences and Ways Forward, Berlin/Heidelberg 2015, pp. 11–42.

Grullón Paz, Isabella: This Week in Covid-19 News: Global Inequity in Vaccine Doses, in: The New York Times, April 3, 2021, https://www.nytimes.com/2021/04/03/world/this-week-in-Covid-19-news-global-inequities-in-vaccine-doses-travel-advice-from-the-cdc-and-cuomos-book.html; last accessed June 22, 2021.

Haggard, Stephan: Pathways from the Periphery: The Politics of Growth in the Newly Industrializing Countries, Ithaca, New York 1990.

Hameiri, Shahar: COVID-19-19: Is This the End of Globalization? in: International Journal, 76(1), 2021, pp. 30–41.

Helfer, Laurence R./Graeme W. Austin: Human Rights and Intellectual Property: Mapping the Global Interface, New York 2011.

Hettne, Björn: Beyond the ›New‹ Regionalism, in: New Political Economy, 10(4), 2005, pp. 543–571.

Hilty, Reto M./Pedro Henrique D. Batista/Suelen Carls/Daria Kim/Matthias Lamping/Peter R. Slowinski: COVID-19 and the Role of Intellectual Property, Position Statement of the Max Planck Institute for Innovation and Competition of 7 May 2021, https://www.ip.mpg.de/fileadmin/ipmpg/content/stellungnahmen/2021_05_25_Position_statement_Covid-19_IP_waiver.pdf; last accessed June 15, 2021.

Hung, Jason: Indonesia's Sinovac rollout sets high stakes for China's vaccine diplomacy, in: East Asia Forum, 06.02.2021, https://www.eastasiaforum.

org/2021/02/06/indonesias-sinovac-rollout-sets-high-stakes-for-chinas-vaccine-diplomacy/; last accessed June 15, 2021.

Kaneti, Marina: ASEAN Must Make the Best of Its New Centrality in China's Diplomacy, in: The Diplomat, June 04, 2020, https://thediplomat.com/2020/06/asean-must-make-the-best-of-its-new-centrality-in-chinas-diplomacy/; last accessed June 22, 2021.

LaFraniere, Sharon / Sheryl Gay Stolberg / Noah Weiland: Biden to Send 500 Million Doses of Pfizer Vaccine to 100 Countries Over a Year, in: The New York Times, June 09, 2021, https://www.nytimes.com/2021/06/09/us/politics/biden-pfizer-vaccine-doses.html; last accessed June 22, 2021.

Landes, William M. / Richard A. Posner: The Economic Structure of Intellectual Property Law, Cambridge, Massachusetts and London 2003.

Lee Kuan Yew: From Third World to First – The Singapore Story: 1965–2000, New York 2000.

Mashal, Mujib / Vivian Yee: The Newest Diplomatic Currency: Covid-19 Vaccines, in: The New York Times, February 11, 2021, https://www.nytimes.com/2021/02/11/world/asia/vaccine-diplomacy-india-china.html, last accessed June 22, 2021.

Mazzucato, Mariana / Azzi Momenghalibaf: Drug Companies Will Make a Killing from Coronavirus, in: The New York Times, March 18, 2020, https://www.nytimes.com/2020/03/18/opinion/coronavirus-vaccine-cost.html; last accessed June 21, 2021.

Medcalf, Rory: In Defence of the Indo-Pacific: Australia's New Strategic Map, in: Australian Journal of International Affairs, 68(4), 2014, pp. 470–483.

Medcalf, Rory: The Indo-Pacific: what's in a name? in: American Interest, 9:2, October 10, 2013, https://www.the-american-interest.com/2013/10/10/the-indo-pacific-whats-in-a-name/; last accessed June 07, 2021.

Office of the United States Trade Representative: 2021 Special 301 Report, April 2021, https://ustr.gov/sites/default/files/files/reports/2021/2021%20Special%20301%20Report%20(final).pdf; last accessed June 13, 2021.

Oxfam: Oxfam reaction to G7 leaders agreeing a ›Carbis Bay Declaration‹ to end future pandemics faster, June 11, 2021, https://www.oxfam.org/en/press-releases/oxfam-reaction-g7-leaders-agreeing-carbis-bay-declaration-end-future-pandemics; last accessed June 13, 2021.

People's Vaccine Alliance: Open Letter: Former Heads of State and Nobel Laureates Call on President Biden To Waive Intellectual Property Rules for COVID Vaccines, April 10, 2021, https://peoplesvaccinealliance.medium.com/open-letter-former-heads-of-state-and-nobel-laureates-call-on-president-biden-to-waive-e0589edd5704; last accessed June 15, 2021.

Prabhala, Achal / Arjun Jayadev / Dean Baker: Want Vaccines Fast? Suspend Intellectual Property Rights, in: The New York Times, December 07, 2020, https://

www.nytimes.com/2020/12/07/opinion/Covid-vaccines-patents.html; last accessed June 22, 2021.

Prabhala, Achal / Chee Yoke Ling: It's Time to Trust China's and Russia's Vaccines, in: The New York Times, February 05, 2021, https://www.nytimes.com/2021/02/05/opinion/Covid-vaccines-china-russia.html; last accessed June 22, 2021.

Prabhala, Achal / Leena Menghaney: The world's poorest countries are at India's mercy for vaccines. It's unsustainable, in: The Guardian, April 02, 2021, https://www.theguardian.com/commentisfree/2021/apr/02/india-in-charge-of-developing-world-Covid-vaccine-supply-unsustainable; last accessed June 22, 2021.

Sanger, David E. / Michael Shear: Eighty Years Later, Biden and Johnson Revise the Atlantic Charter for a New Era, in: The New York Times, June 10, 2021, https://www.nytimes.com/2021/06/10/world/europe/biden-johnson-atlantic-charter.html; last accessed June 24, 2021.

Sanger, David E. / Catie Edmondson / David McCabe / Thomas Kaplan: Senate Poised to Pass Huge Industrial Policy Bill to Counter China, in: The New York Times, June 08, 2021, https://www.nytimes.com/2021/06/07/us/politics/senate-china-semiconductors.html; last accessed June 22, 2021.

Shashikant, Sangeeta: The Doha Declaration on TRIPS and Public Health: An Impetus for Access to Medicines, in: Gaëlle Krikorian/Amy Kapczynski (eds.): Access to Knowledge in the Age of Intellectual Property, New York 2010, pp. 141–159.

Smith, Anthony: Russia and China are beating the U.S. at vaccine diplomacy, experts say, in: NBC News, April 2, 2021, https://www.nbcnews.com/news/world/russia-china-are-beating-u-s-vaccine-diplomacy-experts-say-n1262742; last accessed June 11, 2021.

Strangio, Sebastian: Vietnam Approves Chinese COVID-19 Vaccine, Reluctantly, in: The Diplomat, June 09, 2021, https://thediplomat.com/2021/06/vietnam-approves-chinese-Covid-19-vaccine-reluctantly/; last accessed June 24, 2021.

United Kingdom Government: G7 leaders to agree landmark global health declaration, June 11, 2021, https://www.g7uk.org/g7-leaders-to-agree-landmark-global-health-declaration/; last accessed June 13, 2021.

United Kingdom Government: 100 Days Mission to respond to future pandemic threats, A report to the G7 by the pandemic preparedness partnership, June 12, 2021, https://assets.publishing.service.gov.uk/government/uploads/system/uploads/attachment_data/file/992762/100_Days_Mission_to_respond_to_future_pandemic_threats__3_.pdf; last accessed June 13, 2021.

United Nations Conference on Trade and Development (UNCTAD)/International Centre for Trade and Sustainable Development (ICTSD): Resource Book on TRIPS and Development, Cambridge 2005.

United Nations, LDC Portal: WTO drugs patent waiver for LDCs extended until 2033, https://www.un.org/ldcportal/wto-drugs-patent-waiver-for-ldcs-extended-until-2033/; last accessed June 13, 2021.

Vincent, Nicholas G.: Triping-Up: The Failure of TRIPS Article 31bis, in: Gonzaga Journal of International Law, 24(1), 2020, pp. 1–38.

Wallen, Joe / Sarah Newey: ›The pharmacy of the developing world shuts its doors‹: India stockpiles Oxford-AstraZeneca vaccine, in: The Telegraph, January 04, 2021, https://www.telegraph.co.uk/global-health/science-and-disease/pharmacy-developing-world-shuts-doors-india-stockpiles-oxford/; last accessed June 24, 2021.

Wallerstein, Immanuel: The Modern World-System III: The Second Era of Great Expansion of the Capitalist World-Economy, 1730s-1840s, Berkeley / Los Angeles / London 2011.

Wee, Sui Lee: From Asia to Africa, China Promotes Its Vaccines to Win Friends, in: The New York Times, September 11, 2020, https://www.nytimes.com/2020/09/11/business/china-vaccine-diplomacy.html; last accessed June 24, 2021.

Woo-Cumings, Meredith: Introduction: Chalmers Johnson and the Politics of Nationalism and Development, in Meredith Woo-Cumings (ed.) The Developmental State, Ithaca, New York 1999, pp. 1–31.

World Bank: The East Asian Miracle: Economic Growth and Public Policy, Oxford / New York 1993.

World Trade Organization, Council for Trade-Related Aspects of Intellectual Property Rights: Waiver From Certain Provisions of the Trade-related Aspects of Intellectual Property Rights Agreement (TRIPS) For the Prevention, Containment and Treatment of COVID-19, Communication from India and South Africa, Doc. IP/C/W/669, October 02, 2020, https://docs.wto.org/dol2fe/Pages/SS/directdoc.aspx?filename=q:/IP/C/W669.pdf&Open=True; last accessed June 13, 2021.

Zarocostas, John: What next for a Covid-19 intellectual property waiver? in: The Lancet, 397(10288), 2021, pp. 1871–1872.

Jonas Grutzpalk

»Le réel c'est le cogne?«
Über die Wechselwirkung von Corona-Virus und polizeilichem Sanktionsregime

Der französische Psychoanalytiker und Philosoph Jacques Lacan wird gerne mit dem Satz zitiert, das Reale sei dann zu erkennen, wenn man sich daran stößt – »*le réel c'est quand on se cogne*«.[1] Die Formulierung hat im Zusammenhang dieses Beitrags, der sich mit dem Sanktionsregime der Polizei in der Corona-Krise beschäftigt, eine merkwürdige Ironie, weil *cogne* zugleich auch der vulgärfranzösische Ausdruck für Polizist ist – also letztlich: *Bulle*. Daher der vielleicht etwas gewagte Titel dieses Beitrages.

Zugleich dürften sich diejenigen Polizist*innen für Lacans Definition des Realen durchaus begeistern, die von sich sagen: »Wir beschäftigen uns mit realitätsnahen Dingen und weniger mit was wäre wenn.«[2] Letzteres Zitat stammt aus einer Befragung zum Selbstbild angehender Polizeibeamter und beschreibt deutlich, dass es den jungen Leuten, die sich für den Polizeiberuf entschieden haben, häufig nicht um intellektuelle Finessen geht. Formulierungen wie die, in der *Flachdachschule* lerne man gar nicht all das, was man im realen Leben als Polizist*in so braucht, mögen mit der Zeit weniger energisch vorgetragen werden und der vormals bei der Polizei durchaus verbreitete »naturburschenhafte Anti-Intellektualismus«[3] einem breiteren Bildungsinteresse weichen, aber dass es der Polizei und genau jenes *Reale* geht, das man daran erkennt, dass es Widerstand leistet würde vermutlich noch jeder Polizist unterschreiben.

Dieser polizeiliche Bezug zum Realen hat schon sehr früh in der intellektuellen Welt der Moderne Wellen geschlagen. Friedrich Schiller hat Fragmente eines Theaterstückes mit dem Titel *Die Polizey* hinterlassen und der Aufklärer Louis Sébastien Mercier forderte gar, die Philosophen sollten bei der Polizei in die Schule gehen und dort etwas über die Wirklichkeit lernen.[4] Auch Antonio

---

1 Der tatsächlich formulierte Satz ist – wie wäre es anders zu erwarten gewesen? – komplizierter, läuft aber inhaltlich auf das Gleiche hinaus: »Il n'y a pas d'autre définition possible du réel que: c'est l'impossible quand quelque chose se trouve caractérisé de l'impossible, c'est là seulement le réel; quand on se cogne, le réel, c'est l'impossible à pénétrer« (Lacan: Conférance au MIT, S. 53).
2 Dübbers/Grutzpalk: Wenn nicht wir, wer dann?
3 Mohler: Vorwort.
4 Cf. Siegert: The Horrifying Ties.

Gramscis unverhüllte Begeisterung für Kriminalromane ist bekannt.[5] Man sollte mit der Begeisterung für das polizeilich Reale aber vorsichtig sein – die Polizei ist durchaus in der Lage, tatsächliche – statistisch nachvollziehbare – Entwicklungen zu ignorieren, wenn es ihr passt. So gehört es seit Jahrzehnten zur Folklore der Polizeigewerkschaften, der Gesellschaft ein Ansteigen der Gewalt zu attestieren, ohne, dass sich klären ließe, ob das tatsächlich stattfindet.[6] Der polizeiliche Realismus ist eben doch auch eine Frage des Standpunktes.

Aber eines ist für die Soziologie am polizeilichen Realismus sicherlich dennoch interessant: Polizei verfügt über Sanktionsgewalt und trägt damit nicht unbedeutend dazu bei, das sichtbar zu machen, was man in der Disziplin seit Emile Durkheim den »moralischen Tatbestand« (»*fait moral*«) nennt. Die Sanktion ist ihm zufolge *eines* der Erkennungsmerkmale gesellschaftlich anerkannter Regeln. Eine Sanktion macht dem außenstehenden Beobachter sichtbar, was der sonst nur erahnen kann: dass es ein Regelsystem gibt, dem zu folgen alle verpflichtet sind.[7] Wer das Regelsystem verletzt, wird entweder von außen sanktioniert oder reagiert selbst auf den Fehltritt – z. B. durch Erröten.

Dieser Text geht der Frage nach, wie die Polizei, mit der durch den Covid-19-Virus neu in das Leben getretenen Realität umgegangen ist. Das ist in erster Linie eine rechtliche Frage, denn bei solchen Realitätsbeschreibungen ist die Polizei selbstverständlich nicht allein, sondern sie ist auf die Zuarbeiten des Gesetzgebers angewiesen, damit sie die Beschreibung der Realität in der Sprache des Rechts anwenden kann.[8] Vor dem Hintergrund der Feststellung Karl W. Deutschs, Macht sei die *»ability to afford not to learn«*[9] schauen wir außerdem auf die Lernprozesse, die der Polizei durch Corona aufgezwungen wurden, denn auch das Virus selbst führt ein Sanktionsregime – indem es Zuwiderhandlungen gegen seine Existenz bestraft. Inwieweit sich das auf die Polizei ausgewirkt hat, werden wir uns ansehen. Dann werden wir das Vorgehen der Polizei als realitätssetzende Instanz genauer analysieren. Interessant ist dabei, dass die Polizei die Realität des Virus im Gespräch mit dem, was man so gerne das *polizeiliche Gegenüber* nennt, kommunizieren muss. Gerade die englische Polizei-Strategie der vier E (*»Engage, Explain, Encourage, Enforce«*), zeigt, dass Polizei nicht nur ein reines Sanktionierungsinstrument der Gesellschaft ist, sondern auch in der Lage sein muss zu erklären, was ein unsichtbarer Virus tut. In gewisser Hinsicht ruft sie dadurch das Virus kommunikativ ins soziale Leben.

[5] Cf. Gramsci: Sherlock Holmes & Padre Brown.
[6] Cf. Görgen / Hunold: Gewalt durch und gegen Polizistinnen und Polizisten.
[7] »On appelle fait moral normal pour une espèce sociale donnée, considéré à une phase déterminé de son développement, toute règle de conduite à laquelle une sanction répressive diffuse est attaché dans la moyenne des sociétés de cette espèce, considéré à la même période de leur évolution« (Durkheim: La division du travail social, S. 37 f.).
[8] Cf. Luhmann: Rechtssoziologie, S. 94 ff.
[9] Deutsch: The Nerves of Government.

1. Das staatliche Sanktionsregime und die *Philosophie in Echtzeit*

Eine Virus-Pandemie ist eine Realität *sui generis*, die sich nicht darum schert, was wir Menschen von ihr halten. Vielmehr ist es unter »den für pandemische Krankheitserreger günstigen Bedingungen der modernen Welt«[10] nur eine Frage der Zeit, bis sie uns heimsucht. Über die Wucht, mit der der Corona-Virus zuschlug herrschte anfangs Entsetzen – hatte sich doch eine Letalität von bis zu 4 % für wahrscheinlich erwiesen und das bei einem Verbreitungs-Faktor (der berühmte R-Wert) von 2,2. Das hätte in Deutschland nach Schätzung zu zwischen 278.000 und einer Million Todesopfer führen können. Hinzu kamen Erschöpfungssyndrome bei damals 40 % der Genesenen.[11]

Die von der Pandemie betroffenen Staaten mussten *Philosophie in Echtzeit* (Mukerji/Mannino) betreiben und binnen extrem kurzer Fristen ihre ersten Antworten auf das Virus festlegen. Dabei zeigten sich die erwartbaren weltanschauliche Differenzen. Während der chinesische Präsident Xi Jinping z. B. einen *Volkskrieg* gegen das Virus ausrief, tweetete US-Präsident Donald Trump am 22.03.2020: »*We cannot let the cure be worse than the problem itself*«[12]. Auf der Abwägungs-Skala, der zwischen individuellen Freiheitsrechten und kollektivistischer Verantwortung, war seit dem Frühjahr 2020 viel Bewegung. Die polizeiliche Sanktionsmacht wurde zum lokalen Indikator der nationalen politische Reaktion auf das Virus.

Sébastian Roché hat besonders intensiv zu der staatlichen Reaktion auf das Auftreten der Corona-Pandemie geforscht und seine Ergebnisse (die in Zusammenarbeit mit verschiedenen Wissenschaftler*innen zusammengetragen wurden), lassen aufhorchen. So zeigt sich ein aus kultursoziologischer Sicht besonders interessanter Aspekt, der sich wie folgt zusammenfassen lässt: die Heftigkeit der staatlichen Reaktion auf das Virus korreliert kaum mit mangelnden Bettenkapazitäten oder höheren Inzidenzzahlen, sondern vielmehr mit der kulturellen Vorstellungswelt der politischen Eliten. Während in einigen Ländern wie Frankreich *vom Krieg gegen einen unsichtbaren Feind* gesprochen wurde, redete man in Neuseeland von *Teamarbeit*, bei der das Virus mit allem beworfen werde, was man gerade zur Hand habe.

»Ainsi le recours à l'exception, la décision de suspendre l'état de droit dans le cadre d'une politique publique de santé, ne trouve pas sa source dans une lecture directe des ›données‹ ni dans ›la science‹, mais bien dans une représentation de ce que gouverner veut dire. Chaque gouvernement décide de ce qui fait exception et permet de s'écarter des règles qui garantissent son contrôle et des valeurs de liberté. La culture politique des élites dirigeantes nous

---

[10] Mukerji/Mannino: Covid-19, S. 27.
[11] Cf. ibid., S. 32–37.
[12] Trump: Facebook Post.

semble d'autant plus susceptible d'orienter les décisions que les gouvernements ne savaient pas à quel degré les mesures dont ils décidaient la mise en œuvre seraient efficaces.«[13]

Die polizeiliche Sanktionsmacht war sich offensichtlich nicht immer sicher, welche Bedeutung das Krisenreglement für sie hatte. Es kam zu Reaktionen seitens der Polizei, die als zu weitgehend eingeschätzt wurden, die aber zugleich auch zeigen, dass eine gewisse Unsicherheit über die rechtspositivistische Bedeutung der Maßnahmen herrschte. So fand die Durchsuchung einer Einkaufstasche durch einen englischen Polizisten breitere Aufmerksamkeit. Er wollte sich vergewissern, dass, wie unter dem damals geltenden Lockdown-Reglement geltend – auch wirklich nur das Nötigste gekauft worden sei. Ebenso bekannt wurde der Einsatz von Drohnen im Peak District, um dort befindliche Urlauber auf den Lockdown hinzuweisen.[14]

Ein Forscherteam im internationalen PolStop-Forschungsverband hat ein Whitepaper herausgegeben, das sich mit dem Polizieren der Pandemie beschäftigt. Hier wird u. a. die Not der Polizei aufgezeigt, sich zwischen verschiedenen Logiken, die auf sie einprasselten, so zu bewegen, dass ihr Verhalten jeweils als *angemessen* wahrgenommen würde:

»As the lockdown has gradually been relaxed, it has become harder for the police and the public to understand what is and is not acceptable behaviour. All the data points to a growing reluctance to Enforce. As beaches opened up and as demonstrations over #blacklivesmatter have taken place, the police have found themselves caught between competing and contradictory expectations. Politically, they find themselves caught between a Home Secretary and others demanding tough action against illegal parties and #blacklivesmatter protests as if they are the same policing problem.«[15]

Auch in Deutschland zeigte sich das Problem, Maßnahmen jeweils polizeilich klug zwischen Rechtspositivismus und Deeskalation abzuwägen, wie sich aus folgendem Zitat, aus einem Interview zu einem Forschungsprojekt zum Wissensmanagement der Polizei (s. u.) folgern lässt: »Wenn man immer wieder Leute aufmerksam machen muss, setzt eure Maske auf. Dann wollen sie das natürlich oft auch nicht. Dann muss man gucken, was ziehen wir für Konsequenzen.«[16]

Ähnliche Probleme haben sich da aufgezeigt, wo einerseits tausende selbsternannte *Querdenker* unter Verzicht auf Corona-Schutzmaßnahmen demonstrierten und dabei von Polizei begleitet wurden,[17] andererseits Jugendliche verfolgt wurden, wenn sie mit Verstößen gegen dieselben Schutzmaßnahmen auffielen.[18]

---

[13] Roché: Le coronavirus.
[14] Cf. Aston et al.: Policing the Pandemic.
[15] Ibid.
[16] Anastasiadis/Bergmann/Grutzpalk: Polizeiliches Professionswissen.
[17] Bilger: Warum die Polizei nicht hart eingeschritten ist.
[18] Cf. Norddeutscher Rundfunk: Verfolgungsjagd im Jenischpark.

Es hatte den Anschein, als habe die Polizei hier bereits bestehende Vorstellungen über die *üblichen Verdächtigen* bzw. die *üblichen Unverdächtigen* weiter verfestigt. So sprach der Einsatzleiter, der den Stuttgarter Querdenker-Umzug polizeilich begleitete von Menschen aus der bürgerlichen Mitte, gegen die ein Einsatz unmittelbaren Zwanges *unverhältnismäßig* gewesen wäre. Sébastian Roché und Jan Terpstra (2021) haben umgekehrt beobachtet, dass sich das Corona-Regime in erster Linie bei den sozialen Gruppen ausgewirkt hat, die ohnehin schon unter besonderer Aufmerksamkeit der Polizei standen:

»The data made available by the Paris Prefecture of Police show a higher number of checks and reports in departements with a lot of deprived areas. ... It appears that the proportion of stops ending in a fine has substantial territorial variability. In Paris itself, with a wealthy core of 2 million, the number of stops is the highest, but the ratio is of six fines per 100 stops. Around Paris, in the most well-off départements of greater Paris (département 92), the ratio rises to 8.7 fines per 100 stops, then 13.7 (département 94), and reaches a maximum of 17 fines per 100 stops in Seine Saint-Denis (département 93), the poorest area of greater Paris. This is almost three times as many as in inner-city Paris.«[19]

Das deutet auf die Fortsetzung einer Routine hin, die Didier Fassin schon zuvor als ethnologischer Begleiter von Polizeistreifen durch die Pariser Banlieus beobachtet hatte und die eine höhere Toleranz bei privilegierten Schichten erkennen lässt und eine ungeduldigere Intoleranz bei Zugewanderten und sozial Randständigen.[20] Gleichzeitig zeigt sich im polizeilichen Sanktionsregime der Polizei eine enorme Unsicherheit – es fällt Polizei schwer, ihre Routinen abzurufen, dem *polizeilichen Riecher* zu vertrauen und ihre *Schweine am Gang* zu erkennen.[21] Das notorische Pendeln zwischen Routine und pragmatischer Kreativität in der Polizei, das Astrid Jacobsen als Spezifikum polizeilicher Rationalität erkannt hat wurde durch die Pandemie sicherlich in Richtung Pragmatismus/Durchwurschteln/Bricolage verschoben.[22]

2. Das virale Sanktionsregime: Polizeiliches Lernen

Es lässt sich also nicht nur ein polizeiliches, sondern auch eine Art Sanktionsregime seitens des Virus der Polizei gegenüber erkennen. Der französische Philosoph Bruno Latour vergleicht das Virus mit einem strengen Lehrer, der der Menschheit erklärt, worauf sie sich mit Blick auf die kommende Klima-Krise einzustellen habe. Er wiederhole eins ums andere Mal seine Botschaft, dass wir

---

[19] Roché et al.: Policing the Corona Crisis.
[20] Cf. Fassin: Die Politik des Ermessensspielraums.
[21] Cf. Grutzpalk/Hoppe: Polizeiliches Handlungswissen.
[22] Cf. Jacobsen: Die gesellschaftliche Wirklichkeit der Polizei; Mensching: Gelebte Hierarchien.

uns zu verändern haben.[23] In diese strenge Schule muss nun auch die Polizei gehen und steht`also vor der Frage, was sie selbst aus der Corona-Krise gelernt hat. Dabei zeigt sich, dass die Digitalisierung mancherorts weite Sprünge macht und große Teile der Lehre und der beratenden Polizeiarbeit tatsächlich online stattfinden kann.[24]

Im Rahmen eines Forschungsprojektes, das Stephanos Anastasiadis, Jens Bergmann (Polizeiakademie Niedersachsen) und Jonas Grutzpalk (Hochschule für Polizei und öffentliche Verwaltung NRW) zum Wissensmanagement der Polizei durchführen, wurden 28 Interviews zu Wissen, Lernen und Vergessen bei der Polizei durchgeführt.[25] Gefragt wurden angehende Polizist*innen genauso wie Polizeibeamte im Dienst, in der Führung oder in der Lehre. Unter anderem wurden sie auch gefragt, welche Lernprozesse sie bei der Polizei erkennen könnten, die durch die Corona-Krise ausgelöst worden seien. Ihre Antworten lassen sich in fünf Kategorien einordnen:

2.1 Polizei wusste schon vorher von den unsichtbaren Gefahren

In einem ethnographischen Bericht über das Wissensmanagement der Polizei berichtet Jonas Grutzpalk, wie im Wach- und Wechseldienst immer wieder »kleine Fläschchen mit Desinfektionscreme die Runde«[26] machen. Die Gefahr, die von Bakterien, Viren und ähnlichen unsichtbaren Feinden ausgeht war der Polizei also schon seit Langem bekannt. Nun freut man sich über eine Anerkennung und Bestätigung dieser Weltwahrnehmung:

»Ich habe mir ganz oft die Hände desinfiziert, vor Corona auch schon. Irgendjemand, der auf der Straße lebt und sich seit Wochen nicht geduscht hat, möchte man halt auch eigentlich nicht unbedingt anfassen. Aber wenn der Hilfe braucht, müssen wir es halt machen, ne. Und deswegen sind grundsätzlich, glaube ich, Beamtinnen und Beamte in Sachen Desinfektion durchaus auch, finden das gut, wenn man einen gewissen Schutz bekommt und damit schützt uns der Dienstherr ja auch mit unseren Masken und mit Desinfektionsmitteln und so weiter.«[27]

---

[23] Cf. Latour: Interview in der Sendung »La table ronde« auf France Culture am 25.01.2021.
[24] Das zumindest ist das Bild, das sich auf der Cepol Online-Tagung Pandemic Effects on Law Enforcement Training & Practice« vom 05.05. bis zum 07.05.2021 zeigte.
[25] Anastasiadis/Bergmann/Grutzpalk: Polizeiliches Professionswissen.
[26] Cf. Grutzpalk: Die Erforschung des Wissensmanagements in Sicherheitsbehörden.
[27] Anastasiadis/Bergmann/Grutzpalk: Polizeiliches Professionswissen.

2.2 Polizist*innen vermissen das informelle Netzwerk

Polizei ist ein sehr kommunikativer Beruf – »Polizisten lieben Geschichten« ist eine Formel, die das ganz gut auf den Punkt bringt.[28] Dabei spielt das Zusammensitzen eine wichtige Rolle, und auch wenn aus dienstrechtlichen Gründen das Feierabendbier nur noch in der Erzählung der Alten eine Rolle spielt, so ist doch das ortsnahe Beieinandersein ein wichtiger Bestandteil polizeilicher Kultur.[29] Der von Peter Sloterdijk beschriebene Kampf zweier Erzähltraditionen um die Vorherrschaft in der antiken Philosophie – die mündliche der Rhapsoden und die schriftliche der Philosophen[30] – findet sein Pendant im polizeilichen Wissensmanagement. Hier werden auch Informationen ausgetauscht, die man aus verschiedenen Gründen glaubt, nur mündlich weitergeben zu können. Auch deswegen fiebert man bei der Polizei einem Ende der Pandemie entgegen: »Ich glaube die freuen sich alle da drauf, wenn das wieder anders herum geht, weil ich denke, dass die meisten ja doch eher gesellig sind und in anderen Teams auch mal arbeiten wollen.«[31]

2.3 Der Kontakt mit dem »polizeilichen Gegenüber« wird schwieriger

Polizei ist ein kontaktreicher Beruf. Die Formulierung »das Wort ist die wichtigste Waffe des Polizisten« mag mitunter zur Floskel verstauben, doch ist die gelungene Kommunikation mit dem, was in der Polizeisprache das *polizeiliche Gegenüber* heißt immer wieder entscheidend für Erfolg oder Misserfolg einer polizeilichen Mission. Die Befragten erleben die Corona-Richtlinien als eher hemmend für diesen Aspekt der polizeilichen Arbeit.

Die Masken sind im Weg, Mimik ist nicht richtig zu erkennen, bei einem selbst nicht und nicht beim Gegenüber und die Wahrnehmung der kommunikativen Aufgabe wird erschwert. Zudem kommen immer weniger Menschen auf die Polizei zu, weil sie die Maßnahmen auf der Wache für zu kompliziert halten und sie unsicher sind, ob sie nach wie vor mit ihren Anliegen Gehör finden: »Gerade in der kleinen Station, da kommen ja ganz oft ältere Herren oder Damen vorbei, die haben den Schlüssel verloren oder die Schubkarre im Garten ist weg und die kommen dann halt gar nicht mehr.«[32]

---

28 Grutzpalk: Die Erforschung des Wissensmanagements in Sicherheitsbehörden, S. 16.
29 Cf. Grutzpalk/Hoppe: Polizeiliches Handlungswissen.
30 Cf. Sloterdijk: Philosophische Temperamente, S. 21.
31 Anastasiadis/Bergmann/Grutzpalk: Polizeiliches Professionswissen.
32 Ibid.

2.4 Zweifel an der Gefährlichkeit des Virus und dem politischen Handling der Krise

Auch wenn ein Großteil der Befragten keinerlei Zweifel an der Gefahr durch den Virus und die pandemische Lage geäußert haben, gab es auch einige Polizist*innen, die sich mit der Aussage »Jetzt mit Corona/ich weiß es nicht, also ist jetzt so übertrieben«[33] durchaus anfreunden konnten. Bei diesen Beamten zeigte sich eine Skepsis, ob die politische Führung die Lage richtig eingeschätzt habe. Diese Skepsis wiederum machte es ihnen schwer, die angeordneten Maßnahmen durchzusetzen:

»Und dass es, glaube ich, für viele Kollegen dann auch schwierig wird, ihre Aufgabe gelungen und gut auszuführen, weil sie vielleicht ganz andere Meinungen dazu haben, wie es eigentlich laufen sollte. Und wenn man dann gegen Corona Verstöße vorgehen muss, aber eigentlich innen drin denkt, was soll der Schwachsinn hier alles? Dann ist es, glaube ich, schwierig, dass diese beiden Pole in einem vereint sind.«[34]

2.5 Polizei macht weiter wie zuvor

Es deutet sich hier eine gewisse Latenz im Umgang der Polizei mit der Corona-Krise an, die sich auch in zahlreichen Aussagen der Befragten bestätigt. Als Beispiel sei auf folgende Aussage eines dienstälteren Beamten verwiesen: »Ich glaube tatsächlich, dass die Polizei durch die Corona-Krise kaum was gelernt hat. Ich glaube, die macht eher so das was irgendwie alle machen, aber dann in abgespeckter Form und wie es gerade so passt.«[35] Als Grund für die Zurückhaltung Veränderungsprozessen gegenüber wird zum einen darauf verwiesen, dass Polizei ein sozialer Beruf sei und Heimarbeit deswegen kontraproduktiv sei und zum anderen, dass Polizeiarbeit im Kern immer noch papierzentriert sei und deswegen nur zum Teil über Computernetzwerke gesteuert werden könne.

In gewissen Hinsicht kann dieses Ergebnis als Beispiel für das Präventionsparadox herhalten: Gerade weil die gesundheitspolitische Reaktion des deutschen Staates so erfolgreich war, ist die Polizei in Deutschland nicht durch die gleiche harte Schule gegangen wie in Frankreich oder Großbritannien. Zugleich macht Bruno Latour im zitierten Interview darauf aufmerksam, dass die Lernerfolge nicht sprunghaft zu erkennen sein werden, sondern sich sukzessiv in die bestehenden Weltwahrnehmungen einschleichen werden. Insofern ist es beim aktuellen Stand zu früh, um pessimistisch zu sein – es ist nicht auszuschließen, dass das

---

[33] Ibid.
[34] Ibid.
[35] Ibid.

virale Sanktionsregime durchaus seine Spuren in der Polizei hinterlässt. In der Ausbildung, in der man lange Zeit online-Unterricht für eine absolute Ausnahme wahrgenommen hatte, ist das tatsächlich schon passiert, ohne, dass darüber viele Worte verloren worden wären.

3. Das Polizieren des Unsichtbaren

Polizei hält sich, das hatten wir gesehen, einen gesunden Realismus zugute, von dem sie sagt, dass er sich vom spekulativen Erfahren der Welt abgrenzt. Die Corona-Lage stellt diesen Realismus nun dahingehend auf die Probe, als dass hier ein unsichtbarer Akteur in Erscheinung tritt, der nicht zuletzt mit Hilfe polizeilicher Maßnahmen bekämpft wird. Ein Virus ist selbst unter einem normalen Mikroskop nicht zu sehen – er hat damit für Menschen, die kein Rasterelektronenmikroskop zur Verfügung haben, im Prinzip unsichtbar.

Grundsätzlich hat die Polizei mit dem Unsichtbaren kein Problem. Ein Beamter berichtete beispielsweise, dass er es geschafft habe, einen aufgebrachten Bürger zu beruhigen, indem er seine neun unsichtbaren Kinder zu Bett brachte.[36] Aber wenn der polizeiliche Auftrag ist, etwas Unsichtbares sozial verbindlich zu erklären, dann kommt die Polizei doch in Schwierigkeiten, weil die Aufgabe letztlich sehr umfassend ist und den Bereich des Mathematischen und vielleicht sogar des Metaphysischen berührt.

Die Polizei in Großbritannien verfolgt nun die Policy der »Vier E's«: »Engage. Explain. Encourage. Enforce.«[37] Es obliegt also der Polizei zu erklären, was es mit dem Virus auf sich hat und warum ein bestimmtes Reglement gilt. Wie sich gezeigt hat, verstecken sich Viele dabei hinter einem gewissen *ich-habe-die-Regeln-nicht-gemacht*-Rechtspositivismus. Sie erklären somit die staatlich gesetzten Regeln, aber nicht das Virus, das mit Hilfe der Regeln eingegrenzt werden soll. Dass solch ein Positivismus nicht ausreichen kann, um zu beschreiben, was es mit der Corona-Pandemie auf sich hat, hat sich schon recht frühzeitig nach ihrem Ausbruch gezeigt. Brigitte Nerlich von der University of Nottingham hat eine wunderbare Sammlung von Metaphern angelegt, die zur Beschreibung des Virus und der von ihm ausgelösten Pandemie genutzt wurden.[38] Sie zeigt, wie phantasievoll sprachlich auf die Pandemie reagiert wurde.

Für Sozialwissenschaftler*innen steckt eine gewisse Verlockung darin, sich nicht objektive Tatsachen anzuschauen, sondern zu prüfen, inwieweit Metaphern,

---

36 Cf. Grutzpalk/Hoppe: Polizeiliches Handlungswissen.
37 Police UK: Coronavirus (Covid-19) Police Powers.
38 Nerlich: Metaphors in the Time of Coronavirus.

die wir uns von Tatsachen machen, handlungsauslösend sein können. So hat Andreas Pettenkofer in seiner soziologischen Geschichte der Grünen die Bedeutung *starker Metaphern* wie *Atomtod* zur Beschreibung von Radioaktivität herausgearbeitet.[39] Andernorts wurde überprüft, ob sich die soziale Bedeutung *unsichtbarer Aktanten* anhand der Metaphern beschreiben lässt, die zu ihrer Beschreibung verwandt werden.[40] Eine solche Forschung zur Polizei steht noch aus, wäre aber sicherlich auch aus religionssoziologischer Sicht interessant. Denn hier ist ja u. a. auch die Frage, wie unsichtbare Aktanten soziale Wirklichkeit entfalten können. Max Webers ironische Betitelung des Polizisten als »Stellvertreter Gottes auf Erden«[41] könnte zu neuer Bedeutung finden – nämlich dann, wenn im Polizeiberuf ein gesellschaftliches Feld erkannt wird, das unsichtbarer Aktanten sozial sichtbar macht.

Fazit

Der Staat betreibt Pandemie-Philosophie in Echtzeit und die wird polizeilich in Form eines spezifischen Sanktionsregimes umgesetzt. Beim genaueren Blick auf dieses Regime zeigt sich, dass die Polizei bei dessen Durchsetzung einerseits auf Routinen zurückgreift, denen sie schon vorher gefolgt ist und andererseits selbst verunsichert ist, was denn nun tatsächlich gültig ist und welche Umsetzung in ihrem Sinne ist. Die Pandemie perpetuiert also polizeiliche Verhaltensmuster und irritiert die Polizei zugleich hinreichend, so dass sie sich vor das Problem gestellt sieht, aus der aktuellen Lage zu lernen.

Das virale Sanktionsregime des Corona-Virus stellt die Polizei als Institution also vor eine harte Herausforderung, die sie (zurzeit noch) mit einer deutlichen Latenz beantwortet. Es ist noch nicht klar, welche Lehren sie letztlich aus dieser Schule mitnimmt. Es deutet sich an, dass diese Lehre in erster Linie im Bereich der online-Kommunikation zum Durchschlag kommen wird. Sowohl für Pessimismus als auch für Optimismus angesichts weiterer Lernerfolge scheint es derzeit noch zu früh.

Dass die Polizei dem unsichtbaren Aktanten Corona-Virus soziale Wirksamkeit verschafft lässt sich nicht bestreiten. Wie genau sie das tut, muss allerdings erst noch erforscht werden.

---

[39] Cf. Pettenkofer: Die Entstehung der grünen Politik.
[40] Cf. O'Neill/Grutzpalk: How Is Corona Being Perceived and Described?
[41] »Es führt ein stetiger Weg von der bloß sakralen oder bloß schiedsrichterlichen Beeinflussung der Blutfehde, welche die Rechts- und Sicherheitsgarantie für den Einzelnen gänzlich auf die Eideshilfe- und Rachepflicht seiner Sippegenossen legt, zu der heutigen Stellung des Polizisten als des ›Stellvertreters Gottes auf Erden‹« (Weber: Wirtschaft und Gesellschaft, S. 561).

Einen wichtigen Punkt zur Polizei haben wir bis hierher ausgespart. Es betrifft die Frage, wie sich Polizei überhaupt definieren lässt. Das ist verblüffend schwierig, denn nicht überall, wo *Polizei* draufsteht, ist Polizei drin. Und nicht jede Körperschaft, die polizeiliche Aufgaben versieht heißt auch *Polizei*. Die International Police Association (IPA) überlässt wohl vor dem Hintergrund dieser Beobachtung die Definition derer, die zur Mitgliedschaft bei ihr berechtigt sind ihren Mitgliedssektionen in den verschiedenen Ländern.[42] So darf in Deutschland nur jemand, der *polizeiliche Aufgaben* versieht Mitglied der IPA werden. In Italien hingegen steht die Mitgliedschaft auch Feuerwehrleuten und Gefängniswärtern offen.

Das sollte man nicht als Beliebigkeit missdeuten. Vielmehr scheint das Problem der begrifflichen Erfassung von Polizei ähnlich gelagert zu sein wie das, was Zygmunt Bauman zur soziologischen Beschäftigung mit Gewalt festgestellt hat: »So gut wie alle Autoren, die sich mit dem Phänomen Gewalt auseinandersetzen, müssen erkennen, dass der Begriff entweder zu vage oder zu strikt formuliert definiert wird – oder beides.«[43] Ähnliches lässt sich für die Polizei feststellen, die sich je nach Blickpunkt als bewaffnete Verwaltung (z. B. in den verschiedenen munizipalen Polizeien) oder als verwaltende Waffengattung (z. B. in den verschiedenen Varianten der Gendarmerie) verstehen lässt. Dazwischen ist eine ganze Menge Spielraum für jeweils sehr unterschiedlich gewachsene Polizeien.

Wenn aber, wie hier von einer allgemeinen Alltags-Begrifflichkeit von Polizei in hypermodernen Gesellschaften die Rede ist, dann speist sich diese aus drei wesentlichen disparaten Quellen:

»erstens: aus einem in staats- und verwaltungsrechtlichen Setzungen verankerten und codierten Diskurs, der im Zweifelsfall nichtsdestotrotz einem regierungspraktischen Primat unterworfen bleibt; zweitens: einer mächtigen, von unablässig sprudelnden medialen Quellen gespeisten fiktiv-dokumentarischen Wimmelbildwelt uniformierter, fallösender, behelmt-bewaffneter Akteure; und drittens: einem verästelten, zunehmend weniger marginalisierten akademischen Diskurs, der versucht, die verschiedenen Aspekte und Erscheinungsformen der Institution und ihres Handelns empirisch einzufangen, zu analysieren, und, falls möglich, auf den theoretisch wie anleitungpraktisch relevanten Punkt zu bringen.«[44]

Einer der vielleicht unerwarteten Effekte der Corona-Krise könnte nun sein, diese Begriffsbestimmung der Polizei zu verdichten. Es könnte gerade das diffuse Sanktionsregime der Corona-Pandemie sein, dass sie sich tatsächlich als die Lehrerin herausstellt, als die Bruno Latour sie beschrieben hat. Ihre Lehre könnte auch

---

42 Cf. International Police Association: Why Become a Member?
43 Bauman: Gewalt, S. 12.
44 Nogala: Von der Policey zur PolizAI.

dazu führen, dass die Polizei zunehmend als Teil des Netzwerkes verstanden wird (und sich selbst so versteht), was man *faute de mieux* Gesellschaft nennt. Polizei wäre somit keine äußere Kraft, die in der Gesellschaft *aufräumt*, sondern Teil einer Gesamtheit, die sich durch gegenseitige Abhängigkeit auszeichnet und die lernen muss, sich dauerhaft im Raumschiff Erde einzurichten.[45]

Literatur

Anastasiadis, Stephanos / Jens Bergmann / Jonas Grutzpalk: Polizeiliches Professionswissen: Rollenverständnis und Generationswechsel, Polizeiakademie Niedersachsen, Projektlaufzeit 2020–2026.

Aston, Liz / José A. Brandariz / Dorota Czerwinska / Sofie De Kimpe / Jacques de Maillard / Istvan Hoffman / Megan O'Neil / Mike Rowe / Randi Solhjell: Policing the Pandemic, https://polstops.eu/wp-content/uploads/2020/10/White-Paper-Policing-the-Pandemic.pdf; letzter Zugriff am 22.07.2021.

Bauman, Zygmunt: Gewalt – modern und postmodern, in: Max Miller / Hans-Georg Soeffner (Hrsg.): Modernität und Barbarei. Soziologische Zeitdiagnose am Ende des 20. Jahrhunderts, Frankfurt am Main 1996, S. 36–67.

Bilger, Christine: Warum die Polizei nicht hart eingeschritten ist, in: Stuttgarter Zeitung, 04.04.2021, https://www.stuttgarter-nachrichten.de/inhalt.polizeieinsatz-bei-demo-in-stuttgart-polizei-es-sollte-kein-zweites-kassel-geben.obef88 79-dfed-4c69-b3aa-dfe199267883.html; letzter Zugriff am 26.06.2021.

Cepol Research and Science Conference 2021: Pandemic Effects on Law Enforcement Training and Practice: Taking Early Stock from a Research Perspective, https://www.cepol.europa.eu/science-research/conferences/2021; letzter Zugriff am 26.06.2021.

Deutsch, Karl W.: The Nerves of Government: Models of Political Communication and Control, New York 1963.

Dübbers, Carsten / Jonas Grutzpalk: Wenn nicht wir, wer dann? Das polizeiliche Wir bei Anfängern im PVD-Studiengang, in: Polizei & Wissenschaft, 2017, pp. 29–37.

Durkheim, Emile: La division du travail social, Paris 1893.

Fassin, Didier: Die Politik des Ermessensspielraums. Der »graue Scheck« und der Polizeistaat, in: Daniel Loick (Hrsg.): Kritik der Polizei, Frankfurt am Main 2018, S. 135–164.

Görgen, Thomas / Daniela Hunold: Gewalt durch und gegen Polizistinnen und Polizisten, in: Bundeszentrale für Politische Bildung, https://www.bpb.de/po

---

[45] Cf. Sloterdijk et al.: Das Raumschiff Erde hat keinen Notausgang.

litik/innenpolitik/innere-sicherheit/321874/gewalt-durch-und-gegen-polizistinnen-und-polizisten; letzter Zugriff am 26.06.2021.

Gramsci, Antonio: Sherlock Holmes & Padre Brown. Note sul romanzo poliziesco, Bologna 2019.

Grutzpalk, Jonas: Die Erforschung des Wissensmanagements in Sicherheitsbehörden mit Hilfe der Akteurs-Netzwerk-Theorie, in: Jonas Grutzpalk (Hrsg.): Polizeiliches Wissen. Formen, Austausch, Hierarchien, Frankfurt am Main 2016, S. 15–49.

Grutzpalk, Jonas / Rolf-Peter Hoppe: Polizeiliches Handlungswissen: Eine mehrstufige Untersuchung des Wissensbedarfs und Wissenstransfers in Kreispolizeibehörden, in: Polizei & Wissenschaft, Vol. 4, Frankfurt 2018, S. 13–22.

International Police Association: Why Become a Member, https://www.ipa-international.org/Join-the-IPA; letzter Zugriff am 26.06.2021.

Jacobsen, Astrid: Die gesellschaftliche Wirklichkeit der Polizei. Eine empirische Untersuchung zur Rationalität polizeilichen Handelns, Dissertation Universität Bielefeld 2001.

Lacan, Jacques: Conférences dans les universités nord-américaines: le 2 décembre 1975 au Massachusetts Institute of Technology, in: Scilicet, 6–7, 1975, S. 53–63.

Latour, Bruno: Interview in der Sendung »La table ronde« auf France Culture am 25.01.2021, https://www.franceculture.fr/emissions/la-grande-table-idees/redevenir-terrestres-avec-bruno-latour; letzter Zugriff am 26.06.2021.

Luhmann, Niklas: Rechtssoziologie, 2 Bände. Reinbek 1972.

Mensching, Anja: Gelebte Hierarchien. Mikropolitische Arrangements und organisationskulturelle Praktiken am Beispiel der Polizei, Wiesbaden 2008.

Mohler, Armin: Vorwort, in: Alain de Benoist: Kulturrevolution von rechts, Krefeld 1985, S. 9–12.

Mukerji, Nikil / Adriano Mannino: Covid-19. Was in der Krise zählt. Über Philosophie in Echtzeit, Ditzingen 2020.

Nerlich, Brigitte: Metaphors in the Time of Coronavirus, in: University of Nottingham Blog, 17.03.2020, https://blogs.nottingham.ac.uk/makingsciencepublic/2020/03/17/metaphors-in-the-time-of-coronavirus/; letzter Zugriff am 26.06.2021.

Norddeutscher Rundfunk: Verfolgungsjagd im Jenischpark: Ermittlungen gegen Polizisten, 08.03.2021, https://www.ndr.de/nachrichten/hamburg/Verfolgungsjagd-im-Jenischpark-Ermittlungen-gegen-Polizisten-,verfolgungsjagd452.html; letzter Zugriff am 26.06.2021.

Nogala, Detlef: Von der Policey zur PolizAI. Vorüberlegungen zur weiteren Aufklärung eines zukunftsfesten Polizeibegriffs, in: Kilchling, Michael (Hrsg.): Festschrift zu Ehren von Prof. Dr. Dr. h.c. mult. Hans-Jörg Albrecht, Berlin 2021.

O'Neill, Megan / Jonas Grutzpalk: How Is Corona Being Perceived and Described? The Social Impact of the Virus on Policing, in: Corona Soziologie Blog,

06.05.2021, https://coronasoziologie.blog.wzb.eu/podcast/megan-oneill-and-jonas-grutzpalk-how-is-corona-being-perceived-and-described-the-social-impact-of-the-virus-on-policing/; letzter Zugriff am 26.06.2021.

Pettenkofer, Andreas: Die Entstehung der grünen Politik: Kultursoziologie der westdeutschen Umweltbewegung, Frankfurt am Main 2014.

Police UK: Coronavirus (Covid-19) Police Powers, www.police.uk/advice/advice-and-information/c19/coronavirus-covid-19/coronavirus-covid-19-police-powers/; letzter Zugriff am 26.06.2021.

Roché, Sébastian: Le coronavirus, l'exception et la culture politique des élites, in: Esprit May, https://esprit.presse.fr/actualites/sebastian-roche/le-coronavirus-l-exception-et-la-culture-politique-des-elites-42766; letzter Zugriff am 22.07.2021.

Roché, Sebastian/Jan Terpstra/Jacques de Mailland/Renze Salet: Policing the Corona Crisis: A Comparison Between France and the Netherlands, in: International Journal of Police Science & Management, 2021, S. 1–14.

Siegert, Bernhard: »The Horrifying Ties, From Which the Public Order Originates«. The Police in Schiller and Mercier, in: Clifford Siskin/William Warner (Hrsg.): This Is the Enlightenment, Chicago 2010, S. 357–367.

Sloterdijk, Peter: Philosophische Temperamente. Von Platon bis Foucault, München 2009.

Sloterdijk, Peter/Paul Crutzen/Mike Davis/Michael D. Mastrandrea/Stephen H. Schneider: Das Raumschiff Erde hat keinen Notausgang, Berlin 2011.

Trump, Donald: Facebook Post, 23.02.2020, https://de-de.facebook.com/Donald Trump/posts/we-cannot-let-the-cure-be-worse-than-the-problem-itself-at-the-end-of-the-15-day/10164267660280725/; letzter Zugriff 21.07.2021.

Weber, Max: Wirtschaft und Gesellschaft, Tübingen 1988.

IV. Cultural Meaning of the Pandemic Crisis

Stefan Finger

Corona ist nicht das Ende

Es gehört zu den Besonderheiten der Corona-Pandemie, dass sie für viele verschiedene Gruppierungen und ›Glaubensrichtungen‹ interessante Ansatzpunkte bietet. Verschwörungstheoretiker kommen ebenso auf ihre Kosten wie Impfgegner, Technologieskeptiker sowie Feinde der freiheitlich-demokratischen Grundordnung und des politischen Systems der Bundesrepublik Deutschland. Auch Kapitalismus- und Globalisierungsgegner fühlen sich bestärkt und bestätigt. »Bedeutet Corona das Ende der Globalisierung?« lautet eine häufig zu lesende Schlagzeile der vergangenen eineinhalb Jahre.[1] Die Antwort lautet: Selbstverständlich nicht, denn im Kern hat der Prozess der Globalisierung bereits vor über 2.000 Jahren mit dem Aufbau des Imperium Romanum, spätestens jedoch im 15. Jahrhundert mit der Entdeckung Amerikas begonnen und wird sich während und nach der Corona-Krise unvermindert fortsetzen. Allein das im November 2020, also mitten in der weltweiten Covid-19-Pandemie beschlossene Asiatische Freihandelsabkommen umfasst 15 Staaten, rund 2,2 Milliarden Menschen und ein Drittel des Welthandels. Dank der Abwahl von US-Präsident Donald Trump wird nun von mancher Seite eine Neuaufnahme der TTIP-Verhandlungen gefordert. Die vor einigen Jahren gescheiterte Transatlantische Handels- und Investitionspartnerschaft solle künftig vor allem die stetig anwachsende wirtschaftliche Macht Chinas begrenzen. Ja, antikapitalistische Träumereien von einer Post-Corona-Ära, in der die Menschen Mutter Erde endlich schonen, ihren Konsum reduzieren, die weltweiten Warenströme eindämmen, den Tourismus begrenzen und überwiegend auf regionale Produkte setzen, mögen gutherzig und romantisch sein – realistisch sind sie nicht.

1. Der Staat ist ein lausiger Unternehmer

Im Gegenteil wird sich die Corona-Pandemie nur mit den Mitteln kapitalistisch orientierter Wirtschaftssysteme, globaler Lieferketten und schneller Transportsysteme überwinden lassen. So stammen die ersten und bislang besten Impfstoffe von BioNTech, einem Nasdaq-notierten Biotechnologieunternehmen, und

---

[1] Bundeszentrale für Politische Bildung: Bedeutet Corona das Ende der Globalisierung?

Pfizer, einem weltweit vertretenen Pharmakonzern mit Hauptsitz in New York City, zudem von Moderna, einem ebenfalls börsennotierten privatwirtschaftlichen Unternehmen. Es sind dieselben Flugzeuge, Schiffe und Lastkraftwagen, die die Impfstoffe zu den Menschen in aller Welt bringen, die zuvor die Handelswaren und Virenüberträger von Kontinent zu Kontinent brachten. Selbst aus jenen politischen Lagern, die seit geraumer Zeit vehemente Kapitalismus- und Globalisierungskritik äußern und die globale Verflechtung sowie grenzüberschreitenden Warenverkehr reduzieren wollen, wird eine möglichst schnelle globale Verteilung des Impfstoffes gefordert – einer von vielen ermüdenden Widersprüchen in einer Zeit, in der so viele Anti-Autobahn-Demonstranten mit dem Auto zur Demo im Dannenröder Forst fuhren, dass vor Ort keine Parkplätze mehr verfügbar waren.[2] Es ist nicht die Privatwirtschaft, die in der Bekämpfung der Corona-Pandemie bislang kläglich versagt hat, es sind auch nicht die freien marktwirtschaftlichen Systeme, sondern, wie so oft, die Allianz aus Politik und staatlicher Bürokratie. »Der Staat ist ein lausiger Unternehmer«[3], titelte das Handelsblatt im Herbst 2020. Beispiele gibt es zu Genüge: der Berliner Großflughafen BER, Stuttgart 21, die Hamburger Elbphilharmonie, die Beethovenhalle in Bonn – und am dramatischsten, weil gesundheitsgefährdend und in vieltausendfacher Weise tödlich: die schwerwiegenden Versäumnisse bei der Bestellung ausreichender Mengen an Impfstoffen. Ja, Corona legt alle systemischen Schwachstellen schonungslos offen, nicht nur jene im Gesundheits- und Bildungssystem, zeigt zugleich aber eindeutig: freies Unternehmertum, wenngleich vereinzelt als Auslöser der »kapitalistischen Pandemie«[4] diffamiert, funktioniert schnell, zielgerichtet und effizient, der Staat als planwirtschaftlicher Organisator hingegen nicht. Nicht bei der flächendeckenden Beschaffung von Schutzmasken oder Schnelltests, nicht bei der Ertüchtigung der Gesundheitsämter zur Infektionskettennachverfolgung, nicht bei der (frühzeitigen) Einführung eines digitalen Impfnachweises und vor allem nicht bei der Ausstattung der Schulen mit Raumluftreinigern oder stabilen IT-Systemen. Es gelingt dem Staat ja nicht einmal, die schriftliche Benachrichtigung der Impfberechtigten zu organisieren. Während 80-jährige Jubilare vom Bürgermeister per Post eine Gratulation erhalten, können 80-jährige Impfberechtigte leider nicht auf direktem Wege von den lokalen Behörden und Meldeämtern informiert werden. Aus Gründen des Datenschutzes, wie es heißt. Die Weitergabe von personenbezogenen Daten an den ARD-ZDF-Deutschlandradio-Beitragsservice hingegen stellt kein Problem dar. Kaum ist man umgezogen, da liegt auch schon der Gebührenbescheid im Briefkasten. Anderes Beispiel gefällig? Kein Problem: Jüngst entschied das Oberlandesgericht Koblenz rechtskräftig, dass Meldeämter

---

[2] Vgl. Europäisches Institut für Klima & Energie: Keine Parkplätze bei Öko-Demo mehr.
[3] Greive: Der Staat ist ein lausiger Unternehmer.
[4] taz: Die kapitalistische Pandemie.

Pass- oder Personalausweisfotos herausgeben dürften, um fotografierte Temposünder zu identifizieren.[5] Beim Geldeintreiben kennt der Staat keine administrativen Hürden, beim Auszahlen von Hilfsgeldern und der behördlichen Organisation lebensrettender Impftermine hingegen schon. Zu denjenigen, die vor den mangelnden organisatorischen und unternehmerischen Fähigkeiten von Staat und Politik die Augen verschließen und weiterhin von einer zentral gelenkten Kommando- oder Planwirtschaft träumen, gehört beispielsweise Bernd Riexinger von der Linkspartei, der meint, die Regierung halte an Markt und Wettbewerb fest, »obwohl sie Leben kostet und Gesundheit gefährdet«[6]. Dabei habe sich, so Riexinger, doch überdeutlich gezeigt: »Der Markt regelt nichts. Wir müssen den Markt regeln.«[7] Der Kabarettist Dieter Nuhr kann solchen Vorschlägen sogar etwas abgewinnen. Augenzwinkernd regte er in seiner Sendung *Nuhr im Ersten* vom 29.01.2021 an: »Wenn wir den Staat mit der Covid-19-Verbreitung beauftragen würden, wenn der Staat versuchen würde, die Ansteckung zu organisieren, dass wir sagen: Ansteckung ist Staatsaufgabe, dann wäre Covid wahrscheinlich in vier Wochen verschwunden.«[8] Etwas ernsthafter aber nicht minder meinungsstark formulierte es Christian Reiermann im SPIEGEL: »Untergangspropheten sehen in der Coronakrise mal wieder ein Zeichen für das Ende unserer Wirtschaftsordnung. Sie irren sich – wie immer.«[9]

2. Neid ist keine Leistung

Ähnlich ideologiegesteuert sind auch die Forderungen nach Sonderabgaben für Krisengewinner wie dem Online-Handel und den Supermärkten, denn während viele Unternehmen und Gewerbetreibende um ihre Existenz kämpfen, klingelt bei den Pandemie-Profiteuren die Kasse. Das weckt Neidgefühle und verschleiert den Blick dafür, dass es der Online-Handel und die Supermärkte waren, die die Menschen trotz der Krise mit einem breiten Angebot an Lebensmitteln und sonstigen Waren versorgt haben. Man stelle sich vor, es hätte während der Lockdowns keine Bestellportale und auch keine geöffneten Bau-, Garten- und Supermärkte, sondern nur eine bezugsscheinregulierte Essensausgabe oder vom Militär eingerichtete Suppenküchen gegeben – und sonst gar nichts. Man muss vermuten, dass es dann nach wenigen Wochen zu einem Volksaufstand gekommen wäre. Ja,

---

[5] Siehe AutoBild: Jagd auf Raser mit Passfotos vom Amt.
[6] Zweites Deutsches Fernsehen: Linke fordert »sozial-ökologische Wende«.
[7] Ibid.
[8] Arbeitsgemeinschaft der öffentlich-rechtlichen Rundfunkanstalten der Bundesrepublik Deutschland: Nuhr im Ersten.
[9] Reiermann: Seine besten Alternativen produziert der Kapitalismus selbst.

bestimmte Branchen haben an den Lockdowns besonders gut verdient, aber sie haben im Gegenzug trotz aller Widrigkeiten nicht nur die Versorgung der Bevölkerung sichergestellt, sondern auch, was nicht zu unterschätzen ist, während der stubenarrestähnlichen Wochen und Monate für Zeitvertreib und Unterhaltung gesorgt. Da Ausflüge, Reisen und Verwandtschaftsbesuche nicht möglich waren, haben sich Millionen von Menschen damit beschäftigt, Haus und Garten zu verschönern. Es wurde gestrichen und tapeziert, umgebaut und renoviert, neu eingerichtet und dekoriert, getopft und gepflanzt, und nicht wenige haben sich im Internet sogar Swimming-Pools für Garten oder Terrasse bestellt. Andere haben sich mit Unterhaltungselektronik eingedeckt, haben online neue Fernseher, Videospiele und Surround-Sound-Anlagen geordert. Wieder andere ließen sich Fitnessgeräte oder Gesellschaftsspiele zur Familienunterhaltung kommen. Das übergeordnete Ziel war immer dasselbe: die Zeit der Kontaktbeschränkungen erträglicher zu gestalten. Viele mussten zu Beginn des ersten Lockdowns zudem dafür sorgen, die nötigen Voraussetzungen für die verordnete Home-Office-Tätigkeit zu schaffen, und bestellten – natürlich online – Monitore, Mousepads, Webcams und PC-Speaker, manche gar Schreibtische und Bürostühle. Dass irgendjemand daran verdienen muss, dürfte auf der Hand liegen. Doch es scheint zu den Zeichen der Zeit zu gehören, Neiddebatten zu schüren statt Leistung zu honorieren.[10] Übrigens war es während des zweiten Lockdowns im Frühjahr 2021 der Discounter ALDI, dem es als erster gelang, die Bevölkerung flächendeckend mit Corona-Selbsttests zu versorgen. Kurz darauf folgte Lidl. Die von der Bundesregierung für den 1. März 2021 angekündigte staatliche Beschaffung von Schnelltests musste überraschend verschoben werden – aus organisatorischen Gründen. Freilich kosten die Tests bei ALDI Geld, anderenfalls gäbe es sie gar nicht. Und auch keine Masken. Und auch keine Impfstoffe. Es gäbe überhaupt nur sehr wenig, wenn die Wirtschaft nach staatlichen Plänen organisiert würde. Die Geschichte kennt einige Beispiele solcher gescheiterten Experimente.

3. Planetarische Immunreaktionen

Zu den vielfältigen Thesen und Diskursen, die das Corona-Jahr 2020 hervorbrachte, gehörte auch die Überlegung, das Corona-Virus könne als eine Art Immunreaktion des Planeten gegen den parasitären Befall mit knapp acht Milliarden Individuen der Gattung *Homo sapiens* verstanden werden. Ein spannender ge-

---

[10] Zu berücksichtigen ist auch, dass manche der vermeintlichen Pandemieprofiteure zugleich auch Pandemieverlierer waren. So hat beispielsweise die REWE-Gruppe seit März 2020 zwar in seiner Lebensmittelsparte besonders gut verdient, dafür aber in seiner Reisesparte kräftig verloren.

danklicher Ansatz, der jedoch außer Acht lässt, dass es Viren und Mikroben schon lange vor den hochentwickelten Vielzellern gab, zu denen der Mensch gehört. Der Wissenschaft sind heute fünf große Massenaussterben bekannt: das Ordovizische Massenaussterben vor 444 Millionen Jahren, das sogenannte Kellwasser-Ereignis im Oberdevon vor 372 Mio. Jahren, ein weiteres Massenaussterben an der Perm-Trias-Grenze vor 252 Mio. Jahren, die Krisenzeit an der Trias-Jura-Grenze vor 201 Mio. Jahren und das Massenaussterben an der Kreide-Paläogen-Grenze vor 66 Mio. Jahren. Mutter Erde muss also schon öfter versucht haben, die Läuse in ihrem Pelz loszuwerden, zuletzt mit Hilfe kosmischer Artillerie. Erfolglos, und sie wird auch diesmal scheitern. Vermutlich ist es dem Menschen bestimmt, sich selbst auszulöschen, entweder mit seinen eigenen nuklearen Waffen oder einer momentan in den Grundzügen befindlichen Kombination aus Robotik und künstlicher Intelligenz, die bei ausreichender Rechenleistung eines Tages entscheiden könnte, gegen ihre Erbauer vorzugehen. Immerhin befürchten sogar die Vereinten Nationen, die Welt könne durch Entwicklungen u. a. auf dem Gebiet der Kampf- und Militärroboter destabilisiert werden.[11] Noch wahrscheinlicher ist aber, dass die Menschheit ganz banal an sich selbst ersticken wird, wenn zehn, 15 oder noch mehr Milliarden Erdenbewohner sich ihre eigenen Lebensgrundlagen nachhaltig entzogen haben. Nach dem Ende der Corona-Pandemie sollte daher einmal grundlegend überdacht werden, ob staatliche Reproduktionsförderungen wie beispielsweise Kindergeld, Elternzeit, Elterngeld und Steuervorteile für Eltern überhaupt noch zeitgemäß sind. Immerhin zielen sie darauf ab, die Weltbevölkerung noch weiter zu vergrößern. Das Auftreten und die Verbreitung des Corona-Virus ist jedenfalls kein neues Phänomen. Die diversen Pestwellen der vergangenen Jahrhunderte brachen in ähnlicher Art und Weise über die Menschheit herein, nämlich als eine vom Tier auf den Menschen übertragene Krankheit, die mit Segelschiffen grenzüberschreitend weiterverbreitet wurde. Nicht ganz so schnell wie mit modernen Containerschiffen und Flugzeugen, aber ähnlich effektiv. Die als *Schwarzer Tod* bezeichnete Pandemie der Jahre 1346 bis 1352 zählt zu den verheerendsten Seuchenereignissen der Weltgeschichte und forderte geschätzte 25 Millionen Todesopfer – ein Drittel der damaligen Bevölkerung Europas. Noch schlimmer wüteten die in die *Neue Welt* eingeschleppten Infektionskrankheiten. Im Verlauf von nur 100 Jahren nach der Entdeckung Amerikas wurden schätzungsweise 90 Prozent der dortigen Ureinwohner von Grippe-, Masern- und Pocken-Erregern, gegen die sie keine Abwehrkräfte aufbieten konnten, dahingerafft. Das rücksichtslose Auftreten der Eroberer tat ein Übriges. Die Zahlen schwanken, aber es muss sich um viele Millionen Menschen gehandelt haben, die in kürzester Zeit den Tod fanden. Einige Theorien gehen davon aus, dass dieses Massensterben, das gelegentlich

---

11 Vgl. Boffey: Robots Could Destabilise World through War and Unemployment, Says UN.

sogar als »Amerikanischer Holocaust«[12] bezeichnet wird, zu einem drastischen Rückgang des Ackerbaus und damit zu einer rasanten Ausbreitung einstmals gerodeter Wälder führte. Hierdurch sollen große Mengen an CO_2 gebunden worden sein, woraufhin sich die globale Durchschnittstemperatur absenkte und die sogenannte *kleine Eiszeit* ausgelöst wurde, welche vom 16. bis etwa zur Mitte des 19. Jahrhunderts andauerte. Ein von Menschen gemachter Klimawandel mit umgekehrten Vorzeichen also. Es mag sogar sein, dass jene Kälteperiode bereits einige Jahrhunderte zuvor begann, als Ergebnis der ersten Pestwellen in Europa und Asien, und zwar aus denselben Gründen, nämlich dem Tod von Millionen von Menschen, deren Äcker sich daraufhin schnell bewaldeten. Die Hungersnöte des 18. Jahrhunderts, die schlussendlich zusammen mit verschiedenen anderen Faktoren zur Französischen Revolution führten, können also im Zusammenhang mit einem menschengemachten Klimawandel gesehen werden, ausgelöst von Entdeckungen, Eroberungen und der globalen Verbreitung von Waren und Viren.

4. Globalisierung – Ein neues altes Phänomen

Ist es nicht vielleicht auch eine Form von Hybris, zu glauben, ein Phänomen namens Globalisierung gäbe es erst seit rund 70 Jahren und träfe die gegenwärtigen Generationen besonders hart? Immerhin ist dies der Standpunkt zahlreicher Politik-, Wirtschafts- und Sozialwissenschaftler, da seit dem Ende des Zweiten Weltkrieges grenzüberschreitende Kräfte in zunehmender Weise nationale Kompetenzen erodieren ließen und es einigen Unternehmen sogar gelang, mehr Finanz- und Wirtschaftskraft und damit mehr politischen Einfluss zu kumulieren als manche Staaten. Aber nein, auch das ist im Grunde nichts Neues, denn schon Jakob Fugger, ein europaweit agierender Unternehmer, vermochte es im frühen 16. Jahrhundert, sich einen Kaiser zu kaufen. Ohne Fuggers Reichtum wäre Karl V. wohl niemals deutscher Kaiser geworden. Dass Fugger hernach in ähnlicher Weise auf die Politik Karls V. Einfluss nehmen konnte wie die deutsche Autoindustrie dereinst, das heißt vor den Abgas-Skandalen, auf die Bundesregierung, versteht sich von selbst. Auch die weltweiten wirtschaftlichen Verflechtungen sind im Grunde ein alter Hut, wie Timothy Brook in seinem beeindruckenden Werk *Vermeers Hut: das 17. Jahrhundert und der Beginn der globalen Welt* darlegt: Auf einem der Gemälde Vermeers ist ein Hut eines Offiziers zu sehen, der aus Biberfell gemacht wurde, das europäische Händler von nordamerikanischen Ureinwohnern im Austausch gegen Waffen erhielten. Die Biberpelze finanzierten die Reisen von Seeleuten nach China, wo sie mit Silber Porzellanwaren und Gewürze kauften, die sie nach

---

[12] Patata: Der Holocaust an den nordamerikanischen Indianern.

Europa brachten, um großen Profit daraus zu schlagen. Das Silber und sonstige Bodenschätze, die bald in den weltweiten Handel eingebracht wurden, waren in südamerikanischen Kolonien zunächst von der einheimischen Bevölkerung, später dann auch von importierten, genauer: von versklavten und aus Afrika verschleppten Menschen gewonnen worden.[13] Wenn das keine Globalisierung, keine Verflechtung von Interessen, Geld- und Warenströmen, kein internationales, ja globales Netzwerk zum Transport von Menschen und Produkten war, was soll man dann unter diesem Begriff verstehen? Zugegeben, die Globalisierungsphänomene des 20. und 21. Jahrhunderts zeichnen sich durch die enormen Mengen und Geschwindigkeiten des Personen-, Waren- und Datenverkehrs und der allgegenwärtigen Echtzeitkommunikation aus, die grundlegenden Prinzipien weltweiter Vernetzung und globaler Tauschgeschäfte sind jedoch bereits seit Jahrhunderten etabliert und erprobt. Fabian Dittrich, Professor für Betriebswirtschaftslehre an der Fachhochschule Dortmund, bringt es auf den Punkt:

»›Wir leben im Zeitalter der Globalisierung! Die Welt ist zusammengerückt und eng verflochten. Wirtschaft, Politik, Kultur – alles spielt sich im internationalen Kontext ab.‹ So könnte ein römischer Senator seine Grundsatzrede begonnen haben. Denn Globalisierung ist so alt wie die Menschheit. Handel, Völkerwanderungen und Kriege haben schon immer für einen regen Austausch zwischen den Kulturen gesorgt. So verkauften die Römer nicht nur Oliven in den Orient und bekamen dafür Gewürze, sogar blonde Haare aus dem Norden waren eine Zeit lang der letzte Schrei.«[14]

Auch Spekulationsblasen sind nichts Neues, denn die ersten Börsencrahs gab es bereits vor rund 400 Jahren, basierend auf dem Marktsegment der Tulpenzwiebel, das sich bald zu einer Tulpenmanie und infolgedessen zu einer Tulpenblase überhitzte. In der Hochphase des *Tulpenfiebers* kostete eine einzelne Zwiebel in den Niederlanden so viel wie ein stattliches Haus im Zentrum von Amsterdam. Spekulativer Irrsinn ist also kein neuzeitliches Phänomen, auch wenn die historische Bildung mancher Globalisierungsgegner nur bis zur amerikanischen Immobilienkrise von 2008 oder allenfalls noch bis zur Dotcom-Blase des Jahres 2000 reicht. Auch der internationale Tourismus, der ja ebenfalls gerne als modernes Globalisierungsphänomen verleumdet wird, kann auf eine lange Geschichte zurückblicken. Der bekannte französische Romancier Alexandre Dumas der Ältere fuhr bereits im Jahr 1856 mit Ausflugsdampfern über den Rhein, bestaunte die vorüberziehende Loreley und beklagte sich über das scheußliche Essen und den sauren Wein.[15] Es mag zunächst verwunderlich erscheinen, dass solche Vergnü-

---

[13] Vgl. Brook: Vermeers Hut.
[14] Dittrich: Was ich im BWL-Studium hätte lernen sollen; vgl. insb. auch S. 231–305.
[15] Vgl. Dumas: Ein Liebesabenteuer (Titel der französischen Ausgabe: »Une aventure d'amour«, 1860).

gungsreisen schon vor über 160 Jahren möglich waren – doch wohl nur, wenn man touristische Fernreisen für eine Erfindung des 20. Jahrhunderts hält. Ja, die Technik ist heute weiter, die Taktung höher, die Anzahl der Reisenden größer, das Grundprinzip ist jedoch dasselbe. Und immer noch stellt das Reisen eine Mischung aus Vergnügen und Strapaze dar, auch wenn die Passagiere heute nicht mehr aussteigen müssen, um die überladene Kutsche über steile Hügel zu schieben, so wie einst Dumas bei seinen Fahrten durch deutsche Lande. Übrigens: Für mehrere Generationen ist die gegenwärtige Corona-Krise bereits die zweite Pandemie, die sie erleben. Allerdings ist die vorletzte Seuche, die sich weltweit verbreitete, allgemein fast in Vergessenheit geraten, obwohl sie nie vollständig besiegt und überwunden werden konnte: die Humane Immundefizienz-Virus (HIV)- bzw. acquired immune deficiency syndrome (AIDS)-Pandemie. So lag die Zahl der in Deutschland lebenden Menschen mit einer HIV-Infektion im März 2021 immer noch höher als jene der Corona-Toten. Weltweit starben 2018 – also über 30 Jahre nachdem diese Krankheit allgemein bekannt wurde – rund 770.000 Menschen[16] an AIDS. Und bis heute gibt es keine Impfung! Die wichtigsten Empfehlungen bei der HIV-Bekämpfung entsprechen übrigens im Prinzip weitgehend den Anti-Corona-Maßnahmen: Kontakte vermeiden, Hygienemaßnahmen beachten, Testmöglichkeiten nutzen, Nachverfolgung vornehmen. Und Maske tragen – wenn auch nicht im Gesicht.

Abb. 1: Abstand halten als neues altes Mittel des Infektionsschutzes, Neunkirchen-Seelscheid (Deutschland), 20.05.2020.

---

[16] AIDS-Hilfe Deutschland: HIV-Statistik in Deutschland und weltweit.

5. Some Are More Equal – As Always.

Wie zu erwarten war, dauerte es im Corona-Frühjahr 2020 nicht lange, bis das Pandemiegeschehen ideologisch und philosophisch gedeutet und überhöht wurde. Die parteipolitisch oder gar religiös geprägte Sehnsucht mancher Beobachter nach indifferenter Gleichmacherei bescherte der von vieltausendfachen Infektions- und Todesfällen schockierten Öffentlichkeit die These, vor dem Virus seien alle Menschen gleich. Dass diese Behauptung biologisch und medizinisch wenig durchdacht war, da viele Betroffenen ihre Infektion kaum spüren während andere qualvoll sterben, sei an dieser Stelle vernachlässigt. Entscheidender ist, dass bislang kaum bemerkt oder zumindest nicht öffentlich diskutiert wurde, dass verhältnismäßig wenig Wohlhabende und Prominente an dem Virus erkranken und versterben. Dies hat einen einfachen Grund: gut betuchte Menschen können sich auf ihre Landgüter zurückziehen oder die Virus-Pandemie auf ihren Anwesen auf Hawaii oder den Fidschis verschlafen, während die allermeisten anderen Tag für Tag mit Bus und Bahn zur Arbeit fahren müssen und sich somit zwangsläufig besonderen Risiken aussetzen. Die Superreichen fliegen derweil mit Privatjets zu ihren gigantischen Yachten und können sich, von Tankstopps und Lebensmittelanlieferungen abgesehen, vom virusgeplagten Festland fernhalten. Zumindest aber brauchen sie nicht tagtäglich zur Arbeit zu gehen, um ihren Lebensunterhalt zu sichern. Kim Kardashian West mietete sich aus Langeweile eigens eine Insel und gönnte sich mitten in der Pandemie und ihren Freunden eine exaltierte Party unter Palmen.[17] Zumindest für kurze Zeit habe man so tun wollen, als sei alles normal, ließ die Initiatorin verlauten. Kein Problem für Superreiche, die sich zur Vorbereitung auf solch eine Inselparty problemlos einer freiwilligen Quarantäne in einer ihrer Luxusvillen mit 50 Zimmern, Schwimmbad und Tennisplatz unterziehen können, während Otto Normalverbraucher, Odette Toulemonde und Joe Average in ihren 50-Quadratmeter-Wohnungen ohne Balkon oder Terrasse einem Käfigkoller erliegen. Manche Spitzenverdiener haben von der Krise sogar profitiert und konnten ihren Reichtum obendrein noch mehren.[18] Doch selbst bei durchschnittlichen Arbeitnehmerinnen und Arbeitnehmern gibt es Unterschiede, denn längst nicht jede und jeder genießt die Privilegien des Home-Office. Und längst nicht für jede und jeden stellt das Home-Office ein Privileg dar – voll berufstätige Eltern mit schulpflichtigen Kindern wissen, was gemeint ist. Wer also tatsächlich glaubt, das Virus mache alle Menschen gleich, der möchte das glauben, weil dies gut zum Weltbild, oder besser, zum Wunschdenken passt. In Wirklichkeit sind auch vor dem Virus manche Menschen *more equal than others*. Selbiges gilt für die von Millionen, eigentlich sogar von Milliarden von Menschen sehn-

---

17 Vgl. Scheer: Egotrip auf der Insel.
18 Vgl. Zweites Deutsches Fernsehen: Superreiche werden noch reicher.

lichst erwarteten Impfungen. »›Impf-Urlaub‹ für Superreiche«, so meldete die Bild, wird seit Januar 2021 von Firmen angeboten, die sich auf exklusive Luxusreisen für schwerreiche Menschen spezialisiert haben.[19] Ein Monat *Impf-Urlaub* in Dubai beispielsweise ist ab 45.000 Euro pro Person buchbar, mit schöner Villa, Pool, Koch und Personal. Nach der Landung gibt es die erste Spritze, drei Wochen später die zweite. In der Zwischenzeit lässt man es sich im Luxus-Resort gut gehen. Während die Wohlhabenden Wellness-Anwendungen genießen, leiden die Ärmsten der Armen in aller Herren und Frauen Länder in besonders schlimmer Weise unter der Pandemie und ihren wirtschaftlichen und gesellschaftlichen Auswirkungen. Ein Blick auf die Wanderarbeiter in Indien genügt, um dies zu erkennen. »Corona macht arme Länder noch ärmer«, prophezeit die Weltbank und befürchtet zudem »generationenumspannende Auswirkungen« der Pandemie.[20] Kurzum, vor dem Corona-Virus sind definitiv nicht alle Menschen gleich! Dass sich prominente Spitzenpolitiker und -verdiener wie Boris Johnson, Emmanuel Macron oder – wer's glauben mag – Donald Trump trotzdem angesteckt haben, stellt keinen Widerspruch dar. Staats- und Regierungschefs mögen mächtig und mitunter auch wohlhabend sein, aber sie können sich gerade nicht zurückziehen oder gar verstecken. Ihre Pflicht ist es, präsent und sichtbar zu bleiben, an der Lösung der Probleme zu arbeiten, Zuversicht zu verbreiten und die Gesellschaft zusammenzuhalten – sofern das überhaupt noch möglich ist.

6. Corona als Gesellschaftskrise

Zu den erschreckendsten Begleiterscheinungen der Covid-19-Pandemie gehört die *gesellschaftliche Pandemie*, also die nicht nur in Deutschland tagtäglich zu beobachtende Erosion des Vertrauens in den Staat und seine Organe, in wissenschaftliche Erkenntnisse und in die Berichterstattung der Medien. Dem öffentlich-rechtlichen Rundfunk wird dabei von Teilen der Bevölkerung ebenso misstraut wie den privaten Sendern, die tagesaktuell über die Anzahl an Infizierten und Verstorbenen sowie über Ursache und Verlauf der Erkrankung berichten. Die Skeptiker als *Covidioten* abzutun, greift zu kurz, die Ursachen liegen tiefer. Viel tiefer, als an dieser Stelle eruiert werden könnte. Nur so viel sei erwähnt: es war in den vergangenen Jahren und Jahrzehnten sicherlich nicht vertrauensfördernd, dem Wahlvolk zahlreiche Zusagen und Versprechungen zu geben, die schlussendlich nicht eingehalten wurden. »Der Solidaritätszuschlag ist bis Ende 1999 endgültig weg«, versprach Helmut Kohl dereinst. Über zwanzig Jahre später ist er immer noch da,

---

[19] Bild: Vier Wochen Piks-Urlaub in Dubai, S. 6.
[20] Bundesverband deutscher Banken: Weltbank: Corona macht arme Länder noch ärmer.

und er wird bleiben, denn auch künftig soll etwa die Hälfte des Aufkommens eingetrieben werden, und zwar von jenen, die ohnehin stets den größten Soli-Anteil aufbrachten. Die Entscheider bezeichnen es als »sozial gerecht«, dass diejenigen, die mehrere Jahrzehnte die größte Last getragen haben, diese auch weiterhin tragen sollen. Ein anderes Beispiel: Vor der Bundestagswahl 2005 sprach sich eine der beiden (damaligen) großen Volksparteien für eine Anhebung der Mehrwertsteuer von 16 auf 18 Prozent aus, die andere große Volkspartei war strikt dagegen. Nach der Wahl einigte man sich auf eine große Koalition und eine Erhöhung der Mehrwertsteuer auf 19 Prozent und verkaufte dies als »Kompromiss«. Ein Kommentar hierzu erübrigt sich. Ein weiteres Beispiel: Das völlig eindeutige und absolut unmissverständliche Versprechen, mit ihr werde es auf deutschen Autobahnen keine PKW-Maut geben, wurde schlussendlich nicht von Bundeskanzlerin Angela Merkel, sondern vom Europäischen Gerichtshof gehalten, der 2019 feststellte, die geplante und kurz vor dem Startschuss stehende deutsche PKW-Maut sei mit EU-Recht nicht vereinbar. Anderenfalls wäre inzwischen längst eingeführt worden, was die Regierungschefin im Wahlkampf noch kategorisch ausgeschlossen hatte. Und auch der allgemeinhin als ›Lockerungsinzidenz‹ verstandene Wert von 50 Neuinfektionen pro 100.000 Einwohner innerhalb von sieben Tagen wurde im Februar 2021, als er endlich in Reichweite zu liegen schien, plötzlich einkassiert und durch eine niedrigere und weit schwieriger zu erreichende 35er-Inzidenz ersetzt, die dann kurz darauf Teil eines völlig undurchsichtigen Stufenplans wurde, den FDP-Chef Christian Lindner als Öffnungs-Fata-Morgana bezeichnete, also als eine Art Mogelpackung, die mehr Öffnung versprach als enthielt. Im Mai 2021 gab Bundesgesundheitsminister Jens Spahn dann ein neues Ziel aus, nämlich eine Inzidenz von unter 20 als Zielmarke für weitreichende Lockerungen. Während die strengen Kontaktbeschränkungen für Privatpersonen aufrechterhalten wurden, tagten rund einhundert CDU-Delegierte Ende Februar in Dessau trotz einer 88er-Landesinzidenz dicht an dicht, ohne Maske, Trennwände und teilweise ohne Sicherheitsabstand. »Das Signal des Parteitags an die deutsche Öffentlichkeit: Die CDU darf trotz erhöhter Inzidenz unter Auflagen mit Hundert Delegierten tagen. Restaurants, Kinos und der Einzelhandel müssen dicht bleiben!«[21] Die SPD in Sachsen-Anhalt verhielt sich übrigens fast zeitgleich ähnlich unsensibel, sorgte aber zumindest dafür, dass alle Delegierten eines Parteitags in Magdeburg Einzeltische hatten und außerhalb ihres Platzes und des Rednerpultes eine FFP2-Maske trugen. Und trotzdem: Wasser predigen und Wein trinken unterminiert die Glaubwürdigkeit, denn wenn sich auf einem Parteitag Hundert Menschen mit Hygienekonzept in einem Raum aufhalten dürfen, dann sollte dies auch für den Einzelhandel und die Gastronomie gelten. Doch der Vertrauensverlust in die Sinnhaftigkeit, Berechenbarkeit und Gerechtigkeit, ja gar Rechtmäßigkeit von

---

21 Bild: So tagte die Partei der Corona-Verbote, S. 2.

politischen Zusagen und Entscheidungen ist nur ein Aspekt von vielen. Wie eingangs angedeutet, bedürfte es einer großangelegten interdisziplinären Untersuchung, um den Ursachen jener Proteste und Demonstrationen auf den Grund zu gehen, die sich zu einem Sammelbecken von Corona-Leugnern, Verschwörungstheoretikern, 5G-Gegnern, Rechtsradikalen, Wut- und Reichsbürgern sowie anderen Gruppen und Grüppchen entwickelt haben. Es wäre zu untersuchen, weshalb so viele Menschen das Vertrauen in den Staat verloren haben und die Demokratie längst nicht mehr als die beste Staatsform ansehen – oder eher noch, wieso die große Mehrheit der Bürgerinnen und Bürger trotz wachsendem Verdruss an der »Demokratie als Staatsform des Imperfekten«[22] festhalten will. Hierbei wäre auch die Rolle der Wissenschaft zu untersuchen, denn im Februar 2021 erhob Michael Esfeld, Professor für Wirtschaftsphilosophie und Mitglied der Nationalen Akademie der Wissenschaften, schwere Vorwürfe gegen die Bundesregierung und die Leopoldina selbst. Seiner Einschätzung nach ziehe die Regierung »vor allem jene Wissenschaftler zu Rate, die bereit sind zu sagen, was die Regierung auch hören will«.[23] Der Infektiologe Matthias Schrappe ging noch einen Schritt weiter: Zwar würde er die Kanzlerin sehr gerne beraten, doch Angela Merkel habe sich in einen Tunnel vergraben. »In der Risikoforschung nennt man das Kuba-Syndrom, wenn sich eine Führungsgruppe nur mit Menschen umgibt, die alle der gleichen Meinung sind.«[24] So könne es nur die Fortsetzung der Fehler geben. Dies, so führt Michael Esfeld aus, schade »massiv der Reputation der Wissenschaft«, führe »zu einer populistischen Gegenreaktion gegen die Wissenschaft als ganze«[25]. Man dürfe sich »nicht wundern, dass viele Menschen sich deshalb von der Wissenschaft abwenden und anfangen, ganz grundlegende Fakten zu leugnen«[26].

7. Quis custodiet ipsos custodes?

Zu den Folgen der Corona-Pandemie gehört auch die Anpassung und Ausweitung der jeweiligen Sanktionskultur. Um die Menschen vor Ansteckung, Erkrankung und einem vermeidbaren Covid-19-Tod zu schützen, sollen sie Abstand halten, Maske tragen, unnötige Kontakte vermeiden und verschiedene andere Regelungen befolgen. Auch hier ist festzustellen: die jeweiligen Maßnahmen sind neu, das Prinzip ist alt. So wurde in Deutschland bereits im Jahr 1976 die Gurtpflicht auf den Vordersitzen von Kraftfahrzeugen eingeführt, 1984 auch für die Rückbank,

---

[22] Politik & Kommunikation: Die Demokratie ist die Staatsform des Imperfekten.
[23] Bild: Regierung spannt Experten für Corona-Propaganda ein!
[24] Majurani: »Missbrauch von Wissenschaft!«.
[25] Bild: Regierung spannt Experten für Corona-Propaganda ein!
[26] Ibid.

um Menschen bei einem Verkehrsunfall zu schützen und schwere Verletzungen sowie Todesfälle möglichst zu vermeiden. Selbiges gilt auch für die Helmpflicht bei Zweirädern und vielen anderen Vorschriften, Verordnungen und Gesetzen, deren Nichteinhaltung entsprechend sanktioniert wird, denn es gehört zu den zentralen Aufgaben des Staates, die Sicherheit seiner Bürgerinnen und Bürger zu schützen.[27] Daraus lässt sich allerdings nicht ableiten, dass die Vorgaben zum Eigen- und Fremdschutz und die damit verbundenen Sanktionen stets sinnvoll und nachvollziehbar sein müssten. So ist es in Italien Menschen aus zwei Haushalten nur dann gestattet, gemeinsam in einem Auto zu sitzen, wenn der Beifahrersitz frei bleibt und in jeder Sitzreihe nur Personen aus demselben Haushalt sitzen. Wenn also vier Personen aus zwei Haushalten – zum Beispiel ein Ehepaar mit den Schwiegereltern des Ehemannes – nach Italien in den Urlaub fahren wollen, wird ein Fahrzeug mit mindestens drei Sitzreihen benötigt.[28] Wer hat das schon, und wozu soll das gut sein? Als ob sich dadurch eine Ansteckung in einem Fahrzeug, in dem die Luft immer von vorne nach hinten strömt, vermeiden ließe. Allerdings können auch hier Menschen mit etwas dickerer Brieftasche der jeweiligen Sanktionskultur entkommen, indem sie einfach mehr Geld für ihren Urlaub ausgeben und einen Leihwagen mit drei Sitzreihen anmieten – in der Urlaubssaison mitunter recht kostspielig und besonders ärgerlich, weil zum Zweck der Corona-Bekämpfung vollkommen unwirksam. In solchen Fällen sind es nicht die Vernunft und die Einsicht der Menschen, die zu regelkonformen Verhaltensweisen führen, sondern allein die Furcht vor Strafen und Sanktionen. Dieses und andere Beispiele zeigen, dass der Souverän stets wachsam bleiben und sich zumindest bis zur nächsten Wahl ein gutes Erinnerungsvermögen bewahren sollte, damit die Ausnahme nicht zur Regel, die Sondersituation nicht zur Gewohnheit wird. Denn die Versuchung, in Corona-Zeiten die Gunst der Stunde zu nutzen und politisches Kapital aus dem Ausnahmezustand zu schlagen, scheint für manche Entscheider und Gestalter äußerst verlockend zu sein. Als der erste Lockdown im Frühjahr 2020 angeordnet wurde, vermittelten die politisch Verantwortlichen den Eindruck, es handele sich hierbei um eine Maßnahme allein zum Zwecke des Infektionsschutzes und der Pandemiebekämpfung, die vollständig aufgehoben werde, sobald die Ziele, nämlich die Reduzierung der Neuinfektionen und Todeszahlen, erreicht und die intensivmedizinischen Einrichtungen ertüchtigt seien. Die betroffenen Menschen und Unternehmen würden während und nach der Krise bestmöglich unterstützt, um hernach die nun kurzzeitig unterbrochenen Tätigkeiten fortsetzen zu können. Ein vorübergehender Ausnahmezustand also, ähnlich einer Unterbrechung in einem Fußballspiel wegen starken Niederschlags. Doch die Auszeit währte noch nicht lange, als einige Spitzenpolitikerinnen und Spitzen-

---

27 Vgl. Bundesregierung der Bundesrepublik Deutschland: Sicherheit für die Bürger.
28 Vgl. Allgemeiner Deutscher Automobil-Club: Italien-Urlaub in Corona-Zeiten.

politiker die Chance witterten, die Situation zu ihrem Vorteil zu nutzen und mithilfe des Ausnahmezustandes lang ersehnte ideologisch und politisch motivierte Ziele zu erreichen – genau so, wie es manche Verschwörungstheoretiker befürchtet hatten. So formierte sich schnell eine überparteilich zusammengesetzte Gruppierung von Abgeordneten, die forderte, die günstige Gelegenheit zu nutzen und das vorübergehende Verbot von Prostitution und Sexarbeit auf ewig zu verstetigen. Andere machten sich dafür stark, nach dem Lockdown nur solche Unternehmen zu unterstützen, die ökologisch einwandfrei operierten. Wieder andere knüpften finanzielle Unterstützungen von Betrieben an die Bedingung einer akzeptablen Frauenquote in den Führungsetagen. »Keine Corona-Hilfen für Macho-Betriebe«, lautete eine Schlagzeile vom 30.05.2020. »Die Familienministerin will die Frauenförderung zur Bedingung machen, damit Betriebe Geld aus dem Konjunkturprogramm bekommen.«[29] Auch die Umverteilungsbefürworter aus dem linken Spektrum meldeten sich zu Wort und forderten eine Vermögensabgabe für die finanzielle Bewältigung der Corona-Krise, nachdem sie sich zuvor über viele Jahre hinweg mit dem Wunsch nach einer Reichen- und Vermögenssteuer nicht hatten durchsetzen können. Die Liste der Beispiele ließe sich fortsetzen, denn die angeordnete Zwangspause galt offensichtlich nicht für die üblichen parteipolitischen Taktiereien derjenigen, die ihre Ziele im freiheitlich-demokratischen Normalzustand bislang nicht hatten erreichen können – der Ausnahmezustand als Fortsetzung der Politik mit anderen Mitteln also. Joseph Schumpeter würde heute vielleicht sagen, eher legt sich ein Mops einen Wurstvorrat an, als dass eine Regierung den Ausnahmezustand ungenutzt verstreichen lässt. Und Juvenal bemerkte bereits vor fast zweitausend Jahren sorgenvoll: *Quis custodiet ipsos custodes?* Seinerzeit Satiriker und Sittenrichter, würde Decimus Iunius Iuvenalis seine kritischen Fragen heutzutage vermutlich als Journalist oder Kabarettist stellen und per live-stream Lokalpolitiker kritisieren, die sich eine zufällig übrig gebliebene Impfdosis spritzen ließen, obwohl sie längst noch nicht an der Reihe waren. As said: *some are more equal than others!* Im April 2021 gingen Kurs und Kompass der Pandemiebekämpfung in der Bundesrepublik Deutschland dann endgültig verloren. Mitten in der Nacht gefasste Beschlüsse mussten einen Tag später wieder zurückgenommen werden. Eine Arbeitsweise, die an Udo Lindenberg erinnert. Seine Liedtexte, so erzählte er dem Publikum auf einem Konzert in der Kölner Lanxess-Arena am 28.06.2019, habe er zumeist »nachts breit geschrieben und tagsüber nüchtern gegengelesen«. Als Sänger und Musiker kann man mit solchen oder ähnlichen Methoden sehr erfolgreich sein, verantwortliche Politikerinnen und Politiker sollten umsichtiger agieren und wichtige Sitzungen früher am Tag ansetzen. Es geht schließlich um Menschenleben! Dies wäre übrigens auch zu berücksichtigen gewesen, als die Bundesregierung im Frühsommer 2020 die

---

[29] Hellemann/Block: Keine Corona-Hilfen für Macho-Betriebe.

Impfstoffbeschaffung an die Europäische Union abtrat und damit den Schutz und die Sicherheit der in Deutschland lebenden Menschen hinfort delegierte, obgleich es zu den wichtigsten Aufgaben des Staates gehört – ja vielleicht sogar seine oberste Pflicht ist –, seine Bürgerinnen und Bürger zu schützen. Wie viele Menschen bereits erkrankt und gestorben sind, deren Leben hätte gerettet werden können, wenn der Bundesgesundheitsminister auf seiner Zuständigkeit für die Gesundheit der Bundesbürger*innen insistiert hätte, ist nicht ermittelbar. Sicher ist jedoch, bei einer früheren und größeren Vakzin-Bestellung wären zu jedem Zeitpunkt des Jahres 2021 mehr Menschen geimpft gewesen als dies nun der Fall ist. In diesem Sinne hat Volker Erb, Strafrechtsprofessor an der Johannes-Gutenberg-Universität in Mainz, die Bundesregierung bereits eindringlich gewarnt und in einer gutachterlichen Stellungnahme darauf hingewiesen, dass sie sich bei der Impfstoffbeschaffung möglicherweise strafbar gemacht haben könnte.[30] Die mögliche »Strafbarkeit des Unterlassens einer maximalen Beschleunigung der Covid-19-Impfungen durch die Bundesregierung« begründet sich laut Erb damit, dass zahlreiche Menschen aufgrund einer Coronavirus-Infektion verstorben oder langfristig erkrankt sind bzw. noch erkranken und versterben werden, obwohl sie längst hätten geimpft und damit geschützt sein können, wenn Angela Merkel und Jens Spahn gemäß ihres Amtseides gehandelt hätten, der sie dazu verpflichtet, Schaden vom deutschen Volk abzuwenden.[31] Immerhin habe Jens Spahn öffentlich eingeräumt, »dass schnelleres Impfen Leben rettet«. Insofern hätte die schnellstmögliche Beschaffung größtmöglicher Mengen an Impfstoffen oberste Priorität haben müssen. Offensichtlich jedoch wurde die Vermeidung eines sogenannten Impfnationalismus höher priorisiert als die Rettung von Menschen im eigenen Lande. Den Preis dafür zahlen die Long-Covid-Erkrankten, die Corona-Toten und deren Angehörige. Inzwischen trauen immer weniger EU-Mitgliedsstaaten Brüssel die nötige Kompetenz und Entschlossenheit zu, die weitere Impfstoffbeschaffung erfolgversprechend für ganz Europa zu koordinieren. Während Österreich und Dänemark mit Israel eine Impfstoffallianz schmieden wollen, streben unter anderem Spanien, Italien und auch Bayern den Kauf von Sputnik V an, einem russischen Impfstoff, an dessen Wirksamkeit und Qualität Zweifel bestehen.[32] Die Corona-Krise droht damit ein weiterer Sargnagel der Europäischen Union zu werden, nach der Banken-, Finanz-, Wirtschafts- und Flüchtlingskrise. Doch bei aller berechtigten Kritik an der langsamen und überbürokratisierten Vorgehensweise

---

30 Vgl. Serif: Jura-Professor warnt Angela Merkel und Jens Spahn vor Strafbarkeit.
31 Der Amtseid für Bundeskanzler und Bundesminister lautet gemäß Art. 56 GG bzw. Art. 64 GG: »Ich schwöre, daß ich meine Kraft dem Wohle des deutschen Volkes widmen, seinen Nutzen mehren, Schaden von ihm wenden, das Grundgesetz und die Gesetze des Bundes wahren und verteidigen, meine Pflichten gewissenhaft erfüllen und Gerechtigkeit gegen jedermann üben werde. So wahr mir Gott helfe.«
32 Stand April 2021.

in Deutschland und Europa: wer in Rechtsstaaten und Demokratien westlicher Prägung lebt, kann sich glücklich schätzen, auch wenn manche asiatische Staaten dem Anschein nach besser und schneller auf die pandemische Bedrohung reagieren konnten. China beispielsweise stehen Mittel und Wege zur Verfügung, die im Kampf gegen das Virus effektiv sein mögen, dafür aber an Unmenschlichkeit und Brutalität weltweit ihresgleichen suchen: »Die Menschen essen aus der Not heraus sogar ihre eigenen Haustiere«[33], berichtete nicht nur RTL, sondern auch der STERN und ARTE. »Corona-Total-Lockdown in Tonghua: Ausgänge werden versperrt, Türen zugeschweißt. ›Wir brauchen was zu essen‹, schreien Menschen aus ihren Fenstern eines mehrstöckigen Wohnkomplexes. Ein Mitarbeiter des Nachbarschaftskomitees in Schutzausrüstung brüllt zurück: Seid still. Schnauze, und dann geht seine Wortwahl noch weiter unter die Gürtellinie. Die Situation steht stellvertretend für den Umgang mit den Menschen in Tonghua in diesen Tagen. Von heute auf morgen wurde die Stadt abgeriegelt. 400.000 Menschen dürfen ihre Häuser und Wohnungen nicht verlassen. Jede einzelne Wohnungstür wurde versiegelt – berichten die Bewohner im Internet.«[34] Mit solchen Methoden lässt sich freilich effektiv gegen das Virus vorgehen. Den Preis dafür zahlen die Betroffenen, denen keinerlei Rechtsmittel zur Verfügung stehen.

8. Verbote und Privilegien

Im April 2021 nahm die Bundesregierung zur Wissenschaft eine neue Haltung ein. Hatte sie sich zuvor, wie bereits erwähnt, vornehmlich von Wissenschaftler*innen beraten lassen, die zum Dauerlockdown rieten, wurde nun der Nutzen wissenschaftlicher Diskussionen grundsätzlich in Frage gestellt. So bezeichnete es Vize-Kanzler Olaf Scholz am 14.04.2021 mit Blick auf die sogenannte Bundesnotbremse als »unverantwortlich«, jetzt »eine ganz lange wissenschaftliche Debatte darüber zu führen, was man alles auch anders machen könnte, ohne zu handeln«[35]. Eine bemerkenswerte Haltung für einen Kanzlerkandidaten einer seriösen Partei: Wissenschaftliche Debatten und somit auch wissenschaftliche Erkenntnisse sowie fundierte wissenschaftliche Beratung waren offenkundig nicht länger erwünscht. Medizin, Naturwissenschaften, Sozialwissenschaften, Rechtswissenschaft – alles irrelevant, sofern der Regierungspolitik situativ nicht zuträglich. Eine erschreckende, aber nicht verwunderliche Offenbarung, denn

---

[33] RTL interactive GmbH: »Die Menschen essen aus der Not heraus sogar ihre eigenen Haustiere«.
[34] Ibid.
[35] Brenner: Scholz gegen »lange wissenschaftliche Debatte« um Notbremse.

Olaf Scholz und auch Angela Merkel, die Initiatorin der Bundesnotbremse, wussten genau: wissenschaftliche Erkenntnisse, die Stubenarrest für mündige Bürgerinnen und Bürger nach 21 oder 22 oder 24 Uhr rechtfertigen würden, gibt es nicht. Einsame oder auch zweisame Abendspaziergänge durch leere Straßen, durch den Wald oder über weite Felder haben keinen Effekt auf das Pandemiegeschehen. Eine Fahrt ins Autokino oder zum nächsten Drive-In-Schnellrestaurant auch nicht. Da kamen die neuesten wissenschaftlichen Erkenntnisse von Aerosolforschern freilich recht ungelegen. »Tatsächlich sind sich die meisten Experten darin einig, dass es sehr unwahrscheinlich ist, sich im Freien anzustecken«[36], wurde am 12.04.2021 bekannt – einen Tag bevor Olaf Scholz weitere wissenschaftliche Debatten als »unverantwortlich«[37] bezeichnete und sich für eine unverzügliche Anpassung und Erweiterung des Infektionsschutzgesetzes aussprach. Demnach sollten selbst geimpfte Personen ihre Häuser und Wohnungen in den Abend- und Nachtstunden nicht mehr verlassen dürfen, wenn die Inzidenz in der jeweiligen Stadt oder im Landkreis einen bestimmten Wert überschreitet. Dass viele Kreisgebiete im Wesentlichen aus locker gruppierten Dörfern und Orten bestehen und es völlig unbegründet wäre, beispielsweise die Menschen im östlichen Rhein-Sieg-Kreis einzusperren, weil Ausbrüche in einer fünfzig Kilometer entfernten Ortschaft im westlichen Rhein-Sieg-Kreis die Inzidenz hochtreiben, blieb unberücksichtigt. Helgoland, eine Null-Inzidenz-Insel, die einsam vor der norddeutschen Küste liegt, aber administrativ zum Kreis Pinneberg gehört, bekam das zu spüren. Und inwiefern es für die Pandemiebekämpfung sinnvoll und notwendig sein soll, den Besuch bei Freund oder Freundin vor statt nach 21 Uhr zu beenden, um rechtzeitig zum Beginn der Ausgangssperre daheim zu sein, bleibt unergründlich. Die Vermutung ist beklemmend: weil Ausgangssperren in der Regel nicht dem Schutz der Bevölkerung dienen, sondern ihre Kontrolle und Überwachung erleichtern. Dieser Logik folgend, räumte Bundeskanzlerin Angela Merkel am 16.04.2021 im Deutschen Bundestag ein: »Ich höre sehr wohl, wenn manche Aerosolforscher darauf hinweisen, dass man sich im Freien sehr viel weniger ansteckt als in geschlossenen Räumen. Aber bei der Ausgangsbeschränkung geht es ja um etwas anderes. Es geht darum, abendliche Besuchsbewegungen von einem Ort zum anderen im Übrigen auch unter Benutzung des Öffentlichen Personennahverkehrs zu reduzieren.«[38] Damit gab die Regierungschefin offen zu, auch diejenigen allabendlich einsperren zu wollen, von denen nachweislich keine Gefahr ausgeht und die sich zudem an alle Regeln und Vorschriften halten. Nicht einmal für die zum Zeitpunkt jener Bundestagsrede von Angela Merkel bereits vollständig immunisierten Personen, immerhin rund fünf Millionen Menschen,

---

[36] Westdeutscher Rundfunk Köln: Aerosol-Forscher: Ansteckungsgefahr im Freien überschätzt.
[37] Brenner: Scholz gegen »lange wissenschaftliche Debatte« um Notbremse.
[38] Merkel: Rede im Deutschen Bundestag am 16.04.2021.

sollte es Ausnahmen geben, nur um anderenorts Kontakte und Neuinfektionen zu vermeiden – eine Art Kollektivhaftung also, eine unzulässige Bestrafung oder Benachteiligung einer Personengruppe wie z. B. der Bewohner*innen einer Stadt oder eines Landkreises aufgrund verallgemeinernder Schuldzuweisungen für das Fehlverhalten Einzelner bzw. dessen Vermeidung. Besorgniserregend, denn Kollektivhaftung und Kollektivschuld widersprechen eindeutig der aufgeklärten Grundhaltung europäischer Kulturtradition, wonach jeder und jede für seine bzw. ihre Taten eine individuelle Verantwortung trägt.[39] Im April des Jahres 2021 flammte erneut eine Diskussion auf, die bereits zu Beginn der Impfkampagne im Januar die Gemüter erregt hatte, nun aber neue Nahrung erhielt, als Studien zu dem Ergebnis kamen, dass geimpfte Personen nach etwa vierzehntägiger Wartezeit keine nennenswerte Corona-Gefahr mehr für sich und andere darstellen.[40] Den vielstimmig vorgetragenen Forderungen, die Grundrechtseinschränkungen für immunisierte Personen aufzuheben, wurde das Scheinargument entgegengehalten, »Privilegien für Geimpfte« dürfe es nicht geben. Dies würde zu einer Zwei-Klassen-Gesellschaft und somit zu einer Spaltung derselben führen. Mitunter wurde sogar argumentiert, Geimpfte seien ja schon privilegiert, da sie durch die Impfung vor Covid-19-Erkrankung und Corona-Tod geschützt seien – da dürfe es nun keine »doppelte Privilegierung« geben, der Impfausweis dürfe nicht zum Reisepass oder zur Eintrittskarte für Kinos, Konzerte, Theater und Restaurants werden. Eine eigentümliche, von Neid und Missgunst geprägte Sichtweise, die außer Acht lässt, dass Grundrechte keine Privilegien sind. Berufsfreiheit, Reisefreiheit, Versammlungsfreiheit und andere wesentliche Freiheitsrechte sind im Grundgesetz verbrieft. Allein aufgrund der Bedrohung durch das Corona-Virus war es erforderlich, diese Grundrechte zum Schutz der Bevölkerung vorläufig auszusetzen. Sobald aber eine vollständig geimpfte Person nach zweiwöchiger Wartezeit keine nennenswerte Corona-Gefahr mehr für sich und andere darstellt, gibt es keinerlei Begründung mehr für die Suspendierung der Grund- und Freiheitsrechte.[41] Die Aufhebung dieser Suspendierung stellt kein Privileg dar, so wie es auch kein Privileg darstellt, nach Verbüßung einer Gefängnisstrafe wieder in die Freiheit entlassen zu werden. Die von manchen Politikerinnen und Politikern vorgetragene oder vorgeschobene Sorge, Nicht-Geimpfte könnten Neidgefühle entwickeln, ist kein ausreichender Grund, die Freiheitsrechte von Immunisierten weiterhin auszusetzen. Im Gegenteil wäre es unverantwortlich, älteren Menschen weiterhin den persönlichen Umgang mit ihren Angehörigen zu verwehren, wirt-

---

[39] Im FOCUS vom 15.05.2021 kam der Virologe Hendrik Streeck sogar zu dem Ergebnis: »Es gab vielleicht sogar ein Lockdownparadoxon, dass sich das Virus gerade in sozialen Brennpunktvierteln zuletzt eher ausbreitete, weil die Leute nachts nicht auf die Straße durften. Also traf man sich eben zu Hause mit Freunden.« Vgl. hierzu: FOCUS Nr. 20/2021, S. 86.
[40] Wildermuth: Können Geimpfte andere Menschen weiter anstecken?
[41] Gemäß Kenntnisstand im Mai 2021.

schaftliche Existenzen zu vernichten und noch mehr Menschen in die Depression zu treiben, nur weil sich manche Nicht-Geimpfte nicht solidarisch mit denjenigen zeigen wollen, denen sie eigentlich Solidarität schuldig wären: den Älteren, den Vorerkrankten, den Krankenpflegerinnen und -pflegern, den Ordnungskräften und überhaupt all jenen, die nun mal früher an der Reihe sind. Verdrehte Vorstellungen, wonach sich Geimpfte mit den noch nicht Geimpften zu solidarisieren und auf ihre Grundrechte zu verzichten hätten, bis allen ein Impfangebot gemacht worden sei, lassen einen zentralen Punkt unberücksichtigt, nämlich wie wichtig es für Wirtschaft und Gesellschaft und letztlich für uns alle wäre, wenn nun täglich mehr und mehr Geimpfte wieder unbehelligt in Restaurants, Geschäfte, Theater, Kinos und Reisebüros gehen könnten, denn dies würde die Chance erhöhen, dass diese Einrichtungen und Unternehmen überhaupt noch existieren, wenn eines Tages die angestrebte Herdenimmunität erreicht ist. Wem nützt es denn, wenn der immunisierte 80-jährige nicht ins Dorfrestaurant gehen kann, nur weil der 30-jährige von Nebenan noch nicht geimpft wurde? Nützt das etwa dem 30-jährigen, weil dieser dann nicht auf seinen Nachbarn neidisch zu sein braucht? Eines ist klar, dem Restaurant nützt das jedenfalls nicht, und der Allgemeinheit auch nicht. Denn je schneller die Wirtschaft wieder den Staat finanzieren kann und der Staat nicht mehr die Wirtschaft bezuschussen muss, desto geringer fällt das zusätzliche Wachstum des ohnehin bereits immensen Schuldenberges aus, der von uns allen abgetragen werden muss, vor allem von den jüngeren Generationen. Doch Missgunst und Egoismus sind keine guten Ratgeber und verstellen manches Mal den Blick dafür, dass vieles, was dem Gemeinwesen nutzt, über kurz oder lang auch dem Individuum zum Vorteil gereicht, selbst wenn es zunächst hintanstehen muss.

9. Corona ist nicht das Ende!

Die Covid-19-Pandemie birgt viele Schrecken, doch Corona ist nicht das Ende! Im Grunde ist es nur ein weiteres gravierendes Ereignis in einer langen Kette von gravierenden Ereignissen. In der Rückschau wird sichtbar: seit mindestens einhundert Jahren hatte jedes Jahrzehnt wenigstens eine unliebsame Überraschung im Gepäck. Jede Generation seit 1900 hatte schwere Zeiten mit teilweise drastischen Einschränkungen, herben Verlusten und schmerzlichen Langzeitfolgen zu überstehen. Selbst bei einem flüchtigen Blick auf die deutsche Geschichte wird fraglich, ob es jemals eine Jugend gab, die völlig unbeschwert und sorglos in die Zukunft schauen konnte, insbesondere im sogenannten »kurzen 20. Jahrhundert«, das mit dem fürchterlichen ersten Weltkrieg (1914–1918) begann, gefolgt von der unruhigen Weimarer Republik mit Hyperinflation (1923), Weltwirtschaftskrise

(1929/30) und offenen Straßenschlachten von Links- und Rechtsextremisten. Keine schönen Jahre, weder für Junge, noch für Alte. Die Schreckensherrschaft der Nationalsozialisten währte bis zum Ende des grauenhaften zweiten Weltkrieges im Jahr 1945, dann folgten die Besatzungszeit (1945–1949), der mühselige Wiederaufbau und die Integration von rund 14 Millionen (!) Heimatvertriebenen aus den ehemaligen deutschen Ostgebieten, sodann die deutsche Teilung und der Mauerbau (1961). Zwischenzeitlich wurde u. a. der Versuch unternommen, eine halbe Stadt auszuhungern (Berlin-Blockade 1948/49). Die Dokumentation der Verbrechen, die vom SED-Regime bis zum Fall der Mauer (1989) an den Menschen in der DDR verübt wurden, füllt ganze Archive. Wer unerlaubt in den Westen wollte, musste Todesstreifen und Selbstschussanlagen überwinden. Über hundert Menschen bezahlten ihren Wunsch nach Freiheit mit dem Leben, Tausende saßen unschuldig in Stasi-Foltergefängnissen ein. Während die Kuba-Krise (1962) die Welt an den Rand eines Atomkrieges brachte, lösten die Ölkrisen der 1970er Jahre, der blutrünstige RAF-Terrorismus, insb. der Deutsche Herbst 1977, sowie der saure Regen und das große Waldsterben der 1980er Jahre tiefgreifende Zukunftsängste aus. »Praktisch denken – Särge schenken« lautete das Motto der No-Future-Generation, die in den frühen 80ern jede Hoffnung verloren hatte. Die frühe Form der Digitalisierung der Arbeitswelt mit Computern und Industrierobotern tat ein Übriges – unzählige Arbeitsplätze wurden wegrationalisiert, der Mensch wurde zur Nummer, zu einem Datensatz, ja zu einem Störfaktor im automatisierten Produktionsprozess. Derweil wurde der kalte Krieg erneut heiß, denn am 26. September 1983 hätte die Sowjetunion aufgrund eines Fehlalarms beinahe ihre Atomraketen gestartet. Nur zwei Monate später stand die menschliche Zivilisation erneut kurz vor ihrer Vernichtung, denn das NATO-Manöver »Able Archer« im November 1983 vermittelte Moskau den Eindruck, ein atomarer Angriff des Westens auf die UdSSR stehe unmittelbar bevor. Nur dank eines gut informierten Doppelagenten konnte der Weltuntergang in letzter Minute verhindert werden. Nach dem Ende des Ost-West-Konflikts begannen die Balkankriege, die von 1991 bis 2001 auf dem Gebiet des ehemaligen Jugoslawiens wüteten. Es waren die ersten kriegerischen Auseinandersetzungen in Europa seit 1945. Neben zahlreichen Todesopfern waren auch Massenvergewaltigungen von Tausenden Frauen und Kindern zu beklagen. Auch Männer wurden Opfer sexualisierter Gewalt, die wie eine Kriegswaffe eingesetzt wurde – im Europa der 1990er Jahre. Im gleichen Jahrzehnt tauchte plötzlich eine neue Bedrohung auf: riesige Ozonlöcher hatten sich über dem Nord- und dem Südpol aufgetan und ließen die Strahlung der Sonne weitgehend ungefiltert hindurch. Augenschäden und Hautkrebserkrankungen waren die Folge, auch bei jungen Menschen. »Heute rot, morgen tot«, wurde gewarnt. Die Menschen hatten Angst, ungeschützt ins Freie zu gehen, und fürchteten zeitweilig, eines Tages ihre Häuser gar nicht mehr verlassen zu können. Danach folgte die Millennium-Panik, da man annahm, der Datumswechsel könnte veraltete Computerchips mit zweistelliger Jahreszählung irritieren, der Umsprung von *99* auf *00* statt von *1999* auf *2000* würde die halbe Welt lahmlegen und die Atomraketen starten lassen. Eine schon damals übertriebene Sorge, die nach den schrecklichen Terroranschlägen vom 11. September 2001 schnell vergessen war. In der Rückschau scheint es, als habe das 21. Jahrhundert erst mit 9/11 begonnen, geprägt von der Prophezeiung: »Nichts wird mehr so sein, wie es war!« Ein finsterer Auftakt für das neue Jahrtausend. Es folgten mehrere Kriege in aller Welt, die Weltfinanzkrise (ab 2007/8), die Weltwirtschaftskrise (ab 2008/9), die Flüchtlingskrise (ab 2015) sowie einige Jahre IS-Terror mit barbarischen Akten der Grausamkeit innerhalb und außerhalb von Europa. All diese Krisen und Ereignisse mit der Corona-Pandemie zu vergleichen, mag müßig sein, doch es gehört zur Ehrlichkeit und Vollständigkeit dazu, zumindest zu erwähnen, dass frühere Generationen ebenfalls vor großen Herausforderungen standen und allein an den Folgen zweier Weltkriege viele Jahrzehnte zu tragen hatten. Selbst die friedliche Wiedervereinigung Deutschlands ist immer noch nicht abbezahlt – mehr als drei Jahrzehnte nach dem Fall der Mauer. Ergo: keine Dekade ohne Krieg oder Krise, ohne Bedrohung oder Terror, ohne Unrecht oder Verlust, ohne Angst oder Sorge. »*You have stolen my dreams and my childhood*«, hätte auch schon die Mutter des Verfassers dieses Beitrages sagen können, besonders nach dem großen Luftangriff vom 18.10.1944 auf Bonn, damals gerade erst acht Jahre alt und ausgebombt.[42] Und voller Angst vor der Zukunft. Doch zurück zu Covid-19, -20, -21 ff. Was wird *unsere* Zukunft bringen? Wird Corona den vielbeschworenen *Niedergang des Westens* beschleunigen, oder, ganz im Gegenteil, gar aufhalten und umkehren? Wird das *amerikanische Jahrhundert* jetzt noch schneller von einem *chinesischen Zeitalter* abgelöst? Oder wird es nun unter Joe Biden, dem 46. Präsidenten der Vereinigten Staaten, neue Impulse für eine *atlantische Zivilisation* in Europa und Amerika geben? Wird Geopolitik künftig von Impfstofflieferungen bestimmt werden? Erste Ansätze hierzu gibt es leider schon. Wird das Ansehen von Forschung und Technik nach erfolgreicher Bekämpfung des Virus wachsen, oder werden Corona-, Fakten- und Wissenschaftsleugner, Schamanisten und Verschwörungstheoretiker die Oberhand und Deutungshoheit gewinnen? Wird man den Pioniergeist und das Durchhaltevermögen der mRNA-Impfstoffentwickler würdigen oder ihnen zum Dank die Patente stehlen? Werden die Corona-Beschränkungen als Blaupause für eine CO_2-Diktatur dienen, in der Produktion, Handel, Konsum und Mobilität zur Bewältigung der Klimakrise heruntergefahren werden müssen? Ausgangssperren und Fahrverbote zum Zwecke der Emmissionsreduzierung? Schließung aller Geschäfte, die nicht zur Deckung

---

[42] Für jüngere Leser: »ausgebombt« bedeutet, Haus oder Wohnung wurde durch Luftangriffe zerstört. Die Opfer hatten zumeist ihr gesamtes Hab und Gut verloren und waren obdachlos, mussten bei Verwandten unterkommen oder im Luftschutzbunker schlafen. Eine Gerechtigkeitsdiskussion zwischen Ausgebombten und Nicht-Ausgebombten so wie heute zwischen Geimpften und Nicht-Geimpften gab es zu jener Zeit übrigens nicht.

des täglichen Bedarfs dienen, um Energie und Ressourcen zu schonen? Klima- statt Corona-Shutdown? Einen *Dicken-Pulli-Tag*, an dem die Heizung für den Klimaschutz selbst in öffentlichen Gebäuden wie bspw. Schulen heruntergedreht wird, gibt es bereits.[43] In jedem Fall müssen wir darauf gefasst sein, dass die Covid-Seuche nur eine globale Plage von vielen weiteren ist, die schon sehr bald folgen werden. Schließlich wächst die Menschheit ungehemmt weiter. Die Überfischung der Meere und die Bevölkerungsexplosionen in Asien und Afrika führen zu einer weiteren Verschärfung der Nahrungsmittelknappheit. In manchen Regionen kann man nicht wählerisch sein: Fledermäuse, Hunde, Gürteltiere, Affen, Insekten – es wird alles verzehrt, was verfügbar ist. Ideale Voraussetzungen für Viren aller Art, vom Tier auf den Menschen überzuspringen. Die europäische Massentierhaltung mit ihrem intensiven Antibiotikaeinsatz ist kaum besser. Die Städte wachsen wie Krebsgeschwüre in die letzten verbliebenen Wälder und Naturlandschaften hinein, jedoch nicht aufgrund kapitalistischer Habgier, sondern als Folge ungehemmter Fortpflanzung. Um den damit einhergehenden, wachsenden Bedarf unter anderem an Rindfleisch und Palmöl zu decken, werden die letzten Regenwälder in immer größerem Tempo abgeholzt. Zugleich sind weltweit viele hundert neue Kohlekraftwerke in Planung oder bereits im Bau. China plant obendrein, in den nächsten 15 Jahren über zweihundert neue Flughäfen zu bauen[44]. Das relativiert nicht nur die Bedeutung des Dannenröder Forstes für den globalen Klimaschutz, sondern wirft auch die Frage auf, ob nicht gerade erst die Voraussetzungen für die Verbreitung von weiteren, schnelleren, größeren und dramatischeren Pestwellen geschaffen werden, die Covid-19 eines Tages in einen finsteren Schatten stellen und wie einen Auftakt für ein neues Zeitalter erscheinen lassen: das Zeitalter der Pandemien.

Literatur

AIDS-Hilfe Deutschland: HIV-Statistik in Deutschland und weltweit, https://www.aidshilfe.de/hiv-statistik-deutschland-weltweit; letzter Zugriff am 10.04.2021.

Allgemeiner Deutscher Automobil-Club: Italien-Urlaub in Corona-Zeiten. Einreise für Touristen erschwert, 09.04.2021, https://www.adac.de/news/italien-urlaub-corona/; letzter Zugriff am 10.04.2021.

Arbeitsgemeinschaft der öffentlich-rechtlichen Rundfunkanstalten der Bundesre-

---

[43] Vgl. Internetseite »Dicker-Pulli-Tag«.
[44] German.China.Org.Cn: China braucht 216 neue Flughäfen bis zum Jahr 2035; ZEIT ONLINE: Treibhausgase: China überholt alle Industrieländer zusammen.

publik Deutschland – Mediathek: Nuhr im Ersten (03/20), 29.01.2021, https://www.ardmediathek.de/ard/video/comedy-one/nuhr-im-ersten-03-20/one/Y3JpZDovL3dkci5kZS9CZWlocmFnLWJhZjFlYmM2LTMoN2QtNGFhMS1hZTA3LTNhNTAoMGQzMDlhZQ/; letzter Zugriff am 11.04.2021.
AutoBild: Jagd auf Raser mit Passfotos vom Amt, in: AutoBild Nr. 7 vom 18.02.2021.
Bild: Regierung spannt Experten für Corona-Propaganda ein!, 14.02.2021, https://www.bild.de/bild-plus/politik/inland/politik-inland/leopoldina-professor-experten-fuer-corona-propaganda-eingespannt-75366018,view=conversion ToLogin.bild.html; letzter Zugriff am 10.04.2021.
Bild: So tagte die Partei der Corona-Verbote, in: BILD-Zeitung vom 22.02.2021, S. 2.
Bild: Vier Wochen Piks-Urlaub in Dubai, in: BILD-Zeitung vom 25.01.2021, S. 6.
Boffey, Daniel: Robots Could Destabilise World through War and Unemployment, Says UN, in: The Guardian, 27.09.2017, https://www.theguardian.com/technology/2017/sep/27/robots-destabilise-world-war-unemployment-un?CMP=share_btn_tw; letzter Zugriff am 10.04.2021.
Brenner, Ulrich: Scholz gegen »lange wissenschaftliche Debatte« um Notbremse, in: Saarbrücker Zeitung (Online), 14.04.2021, https://www.saarbruecker-zeitung.de/saarland/landespolitik/corona-olaf-scholz-verteidigt-inzidenz-wert-bei-ausgangsperre-und-notbremse_aid-57329789; letzter Zugriff am 11.04.2021.
Brook, Timothy: Vermeers Hut. Das 17. Jahrhundert und der Beginn der globalen Welt, Berlin 2009.
Bundesregierung der Bundesrepublik Deutschland: Sicherheit für die Bürger, https://www.bundesregierung.de/breg-de/themen/viii-sicherheit-fuer-die-buerger-457468; letzter Zugriff am 10.04.2021.
Bundesverband deutscher Banken: Weltbank: Corona macht arme Länder noch ärmer, 09.11.2020, https://bankenverband.de/blog/weltbank-corona-arme-lander-noch-armer/; letzter Zugriff am 11.04.2021.
Bundeszentrale für Politische Bildung: Bedeutet Corona das Ende der Globalisierung?, 19.11.2020, https://www.bpb.de/politik/wirtschaft/schuldenkrise/318378/bedeutet-corona-das-ende-der-globalisierung; letzter Zugriff am 10.04.2021.
Dicker-Pulli-Tag, https://www.dicker-pulli-tag-bonn.de/; letzter Zugriff am 18.04.2021.
Dittrich, Fabian: Was ich im BWL-Studium hätte lernen sollen. Betriebswirtschaftslehre für Berufseinsteiger, Wiesbaden 2020.
Dumas, Alexandre: Ein Liebesabenteuer, Zürich 2014 (Titel der französischen Ausgabe: »Une aventure d'amour«, 1860).
Europäisches Institut für Klima & Energie: Keine Parkplätze bei Öko-Demo mehr – Luxus-Demonstranten im Dannenröder Forst, 13.10.2020, https://www.eike-klima-energie.eu/2020/10/13/keine-parkplaetze-bei-oeko-demo-mehr-luxus-demonstranten-im-dannenroeder-forst/; letzter Zugriff am 10.04.2021.

FOCUS: Corona ist nicht weg. Interview mit Hendrik Streeck, in: Focus Nr. 20/2021 vom 15.05.2021, S. 86.

German.China.Org.Cn: China braucht 216 neue Flughäfen bis zum Jahr 2035, 12.12.2018, http://german.china.org.cn/txt/2018-12/12/content_74266759.htm; letzter Zugriff am 10.04.2021.

Greive, Martin: Der Staat ist ein lausiger Unternehmer, in: Handelsblatt, 28.09.2020, https://www.handelsblatt.com/meinung/kommentare/kommentar-der-staat-ist-ein-lausiger-unternehmer/26222164.html?ticket=ST-9668980-Diyy6X4hvbdbXNF7YP5f-ap3; letzter Zugriff am 10.04.2021.

Hellemann, Angelika / Thomas Block: Keine Corona-Hilfen für Macho-Betriebe, in: BILD-Zeitung, 30.05.2020, https://www.bild.de/bild-plus/politik/inland/politik-inland/franziska-giffey-keine-corona-hilfen-fur-macho-betriebe-70968082,view=conversionToLogin.bild.html; letzter Zugriff am 10.04.2021.

Majurani, Mayls: »Missbrauch von Wissenschaft!« Experten wettern gegen Merkels Corona-Plan – »Man nennt es Kuba-Syndrom«, in: Merkur, 18.02.2021, https://www.merkur.de/politik/corona-angela-merkel-soeder-deutschland-wissenschaft-leopoldina-lockdown-kuba-syndrom-aktuell-90204364.html; letzter Zugriff am 13.04.2021.

Merkel, Angela: Rede von Bundeskanzlerin Angela Merkel vor dem Deutschen Bundestag, 16.04.2021, https://www.bundeskanzlerin.de/bkin-de/aktuelles/rede-von-bundeskanzlerin-merkel-im-deutschen-bundestag-am-16-april-2021-1891424; letzter Zugriff am 20.04.2021.

Patata, Alberto: Der Holocaust an den nordamerikanischen Indianern. Eine ethnografische Studie, Leussow 2013.

Politik & Kommunikation – Deutschlands Fachportal für politische Kommunikation: Die Demokratie ist die Staatsform des Imperfekten, 02.06.2020, https://www.politik-kommunikation.de/ressorts/artikel/die-demokratie-ist-die-staatsform-des-imperfekten-1534780218; letzter Zugriff am 16.04.2021.

RTL interactive GmbH: »Die Menschen essen aus der Not heraus sogar ihre eigenen Haustiere«, 03.02.2021, https://www.rtl.de/cms/extreme-corona-abriegelung-in-china-menschen-essen-aus-der-not-heraus-sogar-ihre-eigenen-haustiere-4694214.html; letzter Zugriff am 15.04.2021.

Reiermann, Christian: Seine besten Alternativen produziert der Kapitalismus selbst, in: DER SPIEGEL, 05.06.2020, https://www.spiegel.de/wirtschaft/wirtschaft-nach-corona-der-kapitalismus-ist-nicht-kaputt-zu-kriegen-a-00000000-0002-0001-0000-000171426714; letzter Zugriff am 16.04.2021.

Scheer, Ursula: Egotrip auf der Insel, in: Frankfurter Allgemeine Zeitung, 29.10.2020, https://www.faz.net/aktuell/feuilleton/kim-kardashian-feiert-trotz-corona-egotrip-auf-der-insel-17024496.html; letzter Zugriff am 14.04.2021.

Serif, Moritz: Jura-Professor warnt Angela Merkel und Jens Spahn vor Strafbarkeit, in: Frankfurter Rundschau, 04.02.2021, https://www.fr.de/politik/

impfstoff-deutschland-jura-professor-volker-erb-mainz-angela-merkel-jens-spahn-corona-virus-beschaffung-strafbar-90188830.html; letzter Zugriff am 13.04.2021.
taz: Die kapitalistische Pandemie, https://taz.de/Wirtschaftsweise-und-Corona-virus/!5733918/; letzter Zugriff am 10.04.2021.
Westdeutscher Rundfunk Köln: Aerosol-Forscher: Ansteckungsgefahr im Freien überschätzt, 12.04.2021, https://www1.wdr.de/nachrichten/themen/coronavirus/corona-aerosole-risiko-draussen-100.html; letzter Zugriff am 14.04.2021.
Wildermuth, Volkart: Können Geimpfte andere Menschen weiter anstecken?, in: Deutschlandfunk, 06.04.2021, https://www.deutschlandfunk.de/corona-impfungen-koennen-geimpfte-andere-menschen-weiter.709.de.html?dram:article_id=495266; letzter Zugriff am 15.04.2021.
ZEIT ONLINE: Treibhausgase. China überholt alle Industrieländer zusammen, 07.05.2021, https://www.zeit.de/news/2021-05/07/treibhausgase-china-ueberholt-alle-industrielaender-zusammen; letzter Zugriff am 13.04.2021.
Zweites Deutsches Fernsehen: Linke fordert »sozial-ökologische Wende«, 10.01.2021, https://www.zdf.de/nachrichten/politik/linke-riexinger-kipping-corona-100.html; letzter Zugriff am 15.04.2021.
Zweites Deutsches Fernsehen: Trotz Coronakrise. Superreiche werden noch reicher, 07.10.2020, https://www.zdf.de/nachrichten/wirtschaft/corona-milliardaere-reichtum-100.html; letzter Zugriff am 10.04.2021.

Bildnachweis

Abb. 1: Abstand halten als neues altes Mittel des Infektionsschutzes, fotografiert von Stefan Finger in Neunkirchen-Seelscheid (Deutschland), 20.05.2020.

Anne-Marie Bonnet

Art and Life in Pandemic Times*

> »Corona has slowed down the hamster wheel of life,
> yet we are more restless.«
>
> Hartmut Rosa

1. The Pandemic Is No Metaphor

While a year ago in a state of shock everything seemed magnified as well the positive as the negative aspects, the sudden consciousness of our fragility and exposure to contingency had to be *digested*. It generated a sense of hypersensitivity, in which state the feeling of impotence in and for the »lock-downed« arts was acute.[1] In the meantime, a kind of habituation and dullness has taken over, even though we realize that the pandemic is no metaphor: »The corona virus is more than a pathogenic/disease agent. It penetrates all areas of society because it changes the social behavior. It is not only a biologic problem of the body, but it also infects/affects the psyche, dreams. consciousness and the subconscious.«[2] Through a disturbing anthropological experience, we have come to the realize how diverging the ›pandemic experience‹ is and will be lived/sublimated/interpreted by the various parts of our social body. Because, »an event becomes such as it is interpreted. Only as it is appropriated in and through a cultural scheme does it acquire historical significance.«[3] Never has it become more obvious how diverging the *cultural schemes* in our society have become. Whereas at the beginning, one could make puns about the profusion of so-called *conspiracy theories*, we now must learn to take them seriously as a part of our sociopolitical *mental state*.

---

* Once again, the assignment to reflect on art in times of pandemic did not lead to a scientific debate, but to a sharpened diagnosis of the present. The essay endeavours to grasp the current constitution of the arts from the perspective of a Central European who, however, follows art events inter- and transnationally through the media. The guiding questions were: What does the pandemic teach me about art and what does art teach me about the present? Thanks to Heather Sheehan for her editing of the English version of this text as a native speaker.

1 Cf. Bonnet: Aren't So-Called Conspiracy Theories the Most Influential Art of Our Time?
2 Magenau: Das Abendland geht ohne Abschied, p. 19.
3 Sahlins: Islands of History.

2. Shadow Boxing

After a year in the pandemic, life continues to be shaped by the securing of one's private space, the avoiding of closeness, evasion and physical *distancing*, which not infrequently also lead(s) to a so-called *social* one. We move in public and in closed spaces according to the dubious choreographies of distancing. Never has there been so much awareness of the close connection between spatial, physical and social dimensions since in the late 1950s, when the Situationists had, for this reason, invented »Psychogeography« and developed, ofttimes urbanist, visions of a more humane modern, social existence. What was once the body language of encounters has mutated into the shadow boxing of evasion and spatial dislocation. Physical and mental spaces are now increasingly joined within digital spaces, the psychosocial properties and effects of which are only gradually coming to be more consciously recognized. Whereas in the 1990s, after an initial intensifying of the problem of spatial experience, one gave consideration to places and non-places, and the differences between space and place, today, it is important to think about how real the digital spaces are and how they affect our psychosocial balance. It is no coincidence that there is a boom in thoughts on *immersion* or that devices are emerging which promise *augmented reality*. In other words, the paradox that digitally simulated spaces/realities should convey more reality than real spaces and spatial experience. What is augmented? What does the electronic simulation convey that makes the virtual experience superior to the real one? Is it something one lives or just an experience one has?

3. Digital Reality?

Has the pandemic placed a filter between us and life? Wouldn't we prefer to wander around as if sheltered in a transparent bubble/protective shell? To transfer, as it were, the *bubble*, as digital space is categorized, to join us in physical life. Convictions gained from the net do not bother to be checked against real facts: people complain that one is no longer allowed to express a free opinion, while every day there is a controversial argument that pervades the media and even the most outlandish thesis can be made public, even under the assurance of police protection. Apparently, even the perception of physical facts is now so massively predetermined by ideological prejudices that the possibility of expressing any opinion, no matter how nonsensical, is experienced and condemned as the behavior of a *dictatorship*. Did the pandemic and the associated life-threatening insecurities intensify these radicalizations and ideologizations or rather, is the fact that the use of digital space has increased more than ever before? Is there no longer a *common sense* option in the digital age, but only *sense communities*?

4. Reality and Fictionality

Much, if not everything, has been said on the subject of reality/truth and fiction since the Trump era, which is accredited the concepts of *alternative reality* or *fake news*, in spite of the fact that it has not led to a more differentiated culture overall. The increasingly permeable boundaries between fiction and reality also lead to interesting side effects. For example, representatives of the art of acting, who are identified with the characters they portray to such an extent, especially those who play »villains«, no longer feel their lives in the »real« are safe.[4] The bubbles of mass hysteria in the so-called social media play a significant role in this. These new public spheres, while welcome alternatives as refuge from the currently contaminated analogue world, are increasingly having a very real effect outside the supposedly virtual world of the www. The relation between cause and effect, in any case, questions the separation between the so-called virtual/digital and real/analogue world. This paradigm shift has numerous consequences, the extent of which we are not yet fully aware. It has already altered the relationship between art and irony, as the failure of the art action, »#allesdichtmachen«, in April 2021, demonstrated. Ironic commentaries on the current pandemic situation in Germany, in short video clips by, and with, actors and actresses were responded to/misunderstood so strongly that there were threats and even calls for professional bans and censorship. The constitutional protections of the freedom of the arts does not exist or is suspended in the uninhibited *steam bubbles* of the net. In the visual arts, too, positions that deal with the topic of AI, including the role of avatars are on the rise.[5] The field of the humanities are being expanded into the *digital humanities*, while what this ultimately means remains to be seen. In this shift from *digital human* to *digital humanities* and the increasing confrontation with digitized representations of our world that this entails, Olivier Séguret wonders: »Whether between either curing us of the world, or making it better, it's ›actually‹ about saying goodbye to its reality?«[6] Do the arts remain a field in which other approaches and interpretations of the world are still possible? To what extent does the power/potential of the arts depend on the way its producers are perceived?

---

4   Cf. Kniebe: Die Bullshit-Maschine.
5   Cf. Kröner: Digital. Virtuell. Posthuman?
6   »Nous guérir du monde ou le rendre meilleur revient-il á faire le deuil de sa réalité?« (Séguret: L'intelligence virtuelle ne rève pas; transl. by the author).

5. Un-Freedom(s) of the Arts/Artists?

The violation of the self-esteem of the arts/artists by the official classification of art and culture as a »leisure activity« is accepted in different ways and leads, for example, to a public conflict between the president and some members of the Bavarian Academy of Fine Arts.[7] The members do not see the freedom of culture as being threatened and do not want cultural workers to be given greater privileges than other fellow citizens. They denounce the president for speaking on their behalf without consulting them. They go on to state that everyone suffers equally from the pandemic and that artists are not entitled to special treatment. The lack of hierarchical elitism and the empathetic solidarity they express for all humankind is so remarkable that I would like to acknowledge it. In the opinion of these members of the Bavarian Academy, other laws apply in situations of existential and physical threat. Art/culture have no special need or claim to preferential consideration. In the meantime, the Academy has become strangely quiet about the debates fiercely fought in the first year of the pandemic over ›system relevance‹. Nevertheless, questions remain as to how the demand for and the situation of art/culture will develop once the pandemic subsides.

6. Comfort in Uncertainty?

On Sunday, March 14, 2021, NTV/Panorama puts out a report under the title »What about the future of the museums?«[8] After the second so-called lockdown, the museums have just reopened, causing them to garner the media's attention. This interest in art, however, is met with scepticism. The author of the article continues: »It seems as if there is a great longing for culture after the lockdown. Experts, however, assess the situation differently.«[9] This is followed by voices that do not fully believe in the impactful power of the aura of the original, but rather in the convenience of online museum visits habitually practised throughout the pandemic. It should not go unmentioned that museums must already struggle with the diminished social and cultural diversity of their *core audience*. The pandemic has only heightened awareness of this problem. Hanno Rauterberg, on the other hand, observes, in the ZEIT of the same week, on the occasion of a visit to the current Caspar David Friedrich exhibition in Düsseldorf: »The view of art is

---

[7] Mitglieder der Bayerische Akademie der Schönen Künste: In welcher Gesellschaft lebt Herr Nerdinger.
[8] Sommer: Das Museum, p. 4.
[9] Driessen: Wie steht es um die Zukunft der Museen.

now different.«¹⁰ Recognizing a new preference for the uncertain and the ambiguous, he diagnoses: »The openness of his pictures, their abstraction, their idea of a promising indeterminacy, all this now seems modern. And has a comforting effect relevant to this day.«¹¹ Leaving aside how consensual Rauterberg's Friedrich understanding is, I doubt that the majority of our contemporaries are presently enjoying »how beautiful the uncertain can be« as the pandemic confronts most with serious economic, psychosocial and personal challenges whose uncertain outcome is likely to be anything but comforting. Rauterberg's statement speaks rather to a certain detachment or indolence of the art world in the face of the disruptions of contingency. This somewhat idiosyncratic attitude is contradicted by the Munich members of the Bavarian Academy of Fine Arts, who emphasize that they are merely one part of a threatened and suffering majority. But what about the significance of their actions?

7. What Does the Absence of Art Do to Society?¹²

In a discourse on the situation of the arts after a year of pandemic, it is stated that attempts were made to support culture financially, but this happened: »without really helping the individuals – the content, the power, the social dimension of art is being betrayed«.¹³ In the discussion, they defend themselves against the disqualification of culture as merely a *leisure activity* and discuss its *added value for social interaction*. They also plead for a *commitment to art by society as a whole* and wonder why the public did not protest more vehemently or show solidarity. The pandemic has repeatedly proved to be a litmus test that reveals the fractures of current social interaction in the digital late modern age. This includes the realization/awareness that art and culture do not belong to the so-called »system-relevant« aspects of late-modern liberal democratic capitalist society.¹⁴ Here are the *usual* arguments put forward for the role of art in and for society: In offering us alternative perspectives on the world, they cannot improve it, but may illuminate it differently. The way we deal with and access the world in everyday life is instrumental, whether economically or politically conditioned or justified. Media and imagery are largely focused on promoting a materialistic orientation – produce more consume more. In fact, literature, theatre, music and the visual arts offer the only alternative interpretations and representations. Therefore, the declassi-

10 Rauterberg: Ins Offene!
11 Ibid.
12 Lemke-Matwey: Echtzeit! Langsamkeit! Aura!
13 Ibid.
14 Cf. e. g. Reckwitz: Die Gesellschaft der Singularitäten.

fication of the arts to that of a leisure activity presents itself de facto as the elimination of critical and alternative resonant spaces. Should not the role of art and the significance of its producers be separated? Perhaps a change of consciousness is in the offing, one that recognizes and accepts a shift in »values of relevance«?[15] The presence and cultivation of art and culture in Western societies to date is still predominantly shaped by a bourgeois canon from the 19th century. The extent to which this still corresponds to today's social realities and needs has not even been rudimentarily discussed. The crisis of the interpretive sovereignty of museums, theatres and opera houses that has been taken for granted up to now is only a symptom of forthcoming fundamental revisions. Proven to be an accelerant for social injustices, the pandemic may accelerate these processes as well.

8. Live Art under Epidemic Conditions

In March 2021, an experiment was made in Berlin to enable the enjoyment of art in real presence under heightened safety conditions (tests, distance, registration). In his review of a concert held under this new constellation, critic Reinhard J. Brembeck speculates on the motivation for this experiment, which he euphorically describes as a miracle. Aside from his intended context, he formulates an idea of art: »the rare miracle of many people coming together to experience live art, so that they can get through the times better with an expanded heart and a sharpened imagination«.[16] Art is once again praised as »life enhancement« and consolation. Yet, under the current experimental conditions, two determining factors are added: Real Presence and Communal Enjoyment. If art is thereby categorized as an occasion for shared aesthetic enjoyment, does this become a necessary ingredient when defining art? Is it not often those who live their lives largely shielded by headphones, wandering zombie-like through cities, who then long for the noise of crowds and club nights? What does live, shared experience means in the age of competition for individuality? Concepts/ideas and the reality of what is *communal* are up for discussion or redefinition. Can a communal visit to a museum or an opera be compared to a football game or a night at Berghain? Do all the participants of a communal experience actually share the same experience? Not even the pandemic experience was able to generate sustainable communities of solidarity, making way for a new field of sociology and a revision of the fundamental assumptions on social interaction.

---

[15] Schütz/Luckmann: Strukturen der Lebenswelt.
[16] Brembeck: Das Glück sitzt im Auditorium.

9. Lif/ve – Real Presence

Is it not already significant or disturbing to have to speak of *real presence*? The semantic change of our vocabulary in the time of digital late (?) modernity is correspondingly accelerated by the *forced digitalization* of the pandemic. With all its subtle and implicit hidden dimensions (innumerable invisible nets of algorithmic captures) and levels, we have not yet truly realized the ›structural change of the public sphere‹ of our epoch with which life under pandemic conditions confronts/challenges us. Being with/for oneself? Self-image? World-image? Perception? Private? Public? When are these (still) self-determined? When are they imposed? Is the way we deal with art and the arts a marginal phenomenon or a litmus test of our contemporary constitution(s)? The most recent European Song Contest 2021 offered a picture of inter/transnational, digitally overwhelming fireworks that left any previous notions of song or national musical cultures buried in its ashes.

10. A New Nowness?

What is the present?[17] What does it counter? In Dutch, *tegen* means *against* and also *toward*, so the present can be felt less as an obstacle than something leading to the future. »What if the ›now‹ were the new future?« This question, that came up in a recent conversation, continues to reverberate.

At the beginning of the pandemic, the thesis was put forward that being trapped in the now had robbed us of the future, because we cannot plan, and that »credit on the future« with which we have hitherto lived unreflectively, has, as a matter of course, been taken away from us.[18]

This strange situation of being caught in the now and simultaneously feeling as if we are out of time: what does this mean for individuals and social life? Occasionally, one discovers works on instagram in the midst of the so-called lockdown that explore new dimensions of intimacy. For example, the work of photographer Joan Braun.[19] The body fragments she offers to the gaze are not surrendered, but gently caught and at the same time, denied us. Here, proximity and distance are mapped anew. The encounter with these images on instagram, which provides

---

17 In German *present* is called *Gegenwart*; *gegen* means *against*. This leads to a possible *pun* in connection with Dutch connotations: The present not as something one is faced with (one hast to *counter*), but rather something one is driven to (*towards*).

18 Cf. Bonnet: Aren't So-Called Conspiracy Theories the Most Influential Art of Our Time?

19 Cf. Braun: »Friendly Bodies« (Series in which Joan Braun photographs her friends in a series of body fragments showing nudity, each without a face and in a way as if to rediscover and re-map the female body from all the exploitation by the male gaze).

a completely different visual experience than a visit to an exhibition, proves to be an ideal format. Instead of the usual maximally optimised *instagramability* presence, here, a discreet casualness is staged. Braun succeeds in making positive capital out of a predicament. While there are traditions that attribute creative potential to the darker sides of the human condition, such as *melancholy*, which today would probably be diagnosed as *depression*, it is often the negative aspects of forced pandemic heteronomy that are mainly emphasized.

11. Melancholy 2.0

In daily life and within the lack of support in the parallel universes of the www, is the contemporary form of melancholy, what is generally called *corona blues*, a paraphrasing of »paranoid hyperlocality«?[20] How long will the *forced deceleration* also be attributed positive effects? For how long does it foster positive self-contemplation? At what point does it accelerate private frustrations or apparent indifference (lateral thinking[21])? There were times when *ennui* – refined boredom – became a catalyst to creativity or when melancholy was considered the conditio sine qua non of creativity. In the 1980s, Jürgen Klauke still found his way to the *formalization of boredom* and stylized it as the »queen of affects«: »After Samuel Beckett, is it not the last provocation that manages to transcend the triviality of life [...] A lack of intensity is intensely demonstrated. Art is no longer an interpretation of the world, but stares into the meaning of nothingness. This does not create a depressed state, but rather, poetry. Ennui gives us a foothold.«[22] In the current digital late modernity, there have been only a few brief appreciations of possible boredom at the beginning of the pandemic. Although cultural life appeared to have come to an uncreative standstill, it seemed to affect the producers most of all, the art market quickly expanded its digital capacities. Fairs, galleries, auction houses and magazines continued to flourish.

---

[20] Roelstraete: Thinktank.
[21] »Lateral thinking« (Querdenken) might have had positive connotations of creativity in the past, since the pandemic in Germany it is associated to adepts of conspirative so called theories and corona deniers.
[22] Borchhardt-Birbaumer: Jürgen Klaukes Fotografien der Langeweile.

12. Perpetuum Mobile

By April 2021, one year into the pandemic, the art magazines continue to publish and are full of advertisements for upcoming exhibitions, even if one cannot ever know whether the next so-called lockdown threatens. Art and cultural institutions have been officially de-/declared/graded to that of pursuits of leisure and their activities, prevented or frozen, have shifted as best as possible to the digital, to so-called *online viewing rooms*, if these electronic substitute worlds can be considered a *substitute* at all. Here forth, one struggles with the slight feeling of dizziness, the confused, unsteady seasickness of wandering through groundless rooms, disoriented following the so-called user interface of the *cursor*. Apparently, the only thing that has not been interrupted and continues to flourish is the art market, especially the so-called secondary market and auction system. New categories of works are even being invented, such as the so-called NFT (non-fungible tokens), which are generating a euphoric market success in the time of digital quarantine. The extent to which they affect the notion of art and art works – beyond their functioning within the art market – cannot yet be adequately reflected upon. The market creates facts whose effects and resonances cannot yet be measured, yet should not be ignored. It seems to be the only indestructible dimension quick in adapting any situation The shift to the digital which the pandemic has forced may have accelerated these developments and altered perceptions.

13. State of Emergency?

In real life, as well as in digital life – which is no less real, as it can be experienced in the moment on a daily basis – we are currently living in a state of emergency. Have we become accustomed to its rhetoric?[23] As a result of the pandemic, industry (pharmacological business) and technology suddenly joined the natural sciences (virologists) as co-responsible parties in making political decisions. Surprisingly, this has not led to increased credibility, but rather, has contributed to the ›intellectual – and elite-bashing‹ that has blossomed especially in the so-called ›social media‹. Although the rapid development of vaccines and their mass distribution must be acknowledged as remarkable, the politician's handling of medical care and social preventative measures is viewed critically by the majority. The restriction of individual needs due to the pandemic state of emergency generates numerous criticisms, even massive expressions of displeasure. When the addressing of

---

23 For so-called *digital natives*, something is only real when it has been *posted* on a so-called social network.

these needs does not appear to be of political interest, it only gives rise to further articulations of individual dissatisfaction. The extent to which the reactions to the imposed state of emergency remain apolitical, sounding far more like rhetoric than sensitivity, became apparent on the occasion of the artistic protest action: #allesdichtmachen.[24] Is art failing in the face of the pandemic?

14. Pandemic Art? Art in/to/and the Pandemic

As the art market and auctions continue to thrive, with some galleries doing better than others, attempts continue to be made to operate digitally or within the few gaps of permitted accessibility. Various sectors, especially the performative ones, are affected differently, but when some join together for an artistic action (#allesdichtmachen) to criticize the way politics deals with preventive measures, ironically addressing the repressive aspects, the artistic was misjudged, ignored or denied. Irony, it seems, is the wrong tool in pandemic times. Is an action an act of art because it is carried out by artists? Because it is declared so? Does a pandemic relativize the artistic? Its scope? Its methods? Is art supposed to illustrate the pandemic? Distract us from it? Process it productively? Apparently, art has yet to find its own way to deal with it. A first theatre play dealing with the pandemic evidently fails due to its inability to orchestrate a heightened vision of the grotesqueness of pandemic reality.[25]

15. Post-ironic Age?

Has the pandemic incited the beginning of a post-ironic age? Not only in the case of the unsuccessful #allesdichtmachen action does the new consideration of the unpredictability of *the excitement factor* within the extended public sphere of the so-called *social media* make itself strongly felt. The so-called *cancel culture* or the possibility of articulating previously unheard segments of the public is also increasingly changing ideas and perceptions in the world of art and public institutions such as museums and exhibition halls. Beyond the decision of whether

---

[24] Cf. e. g. Soboczynski: Es geht nicht darum, wer recht hat; DIE ZEIT: Schauspieler sorgen mit der Aktion »Alles dicht machen« für Aufsehen; Di Lorenzo / Parnack: Ich wurde immer meschuggener.

[25] »The public discussion of crisis management in the media, parliament and social networks has always been at its most Jelinekian; it simply could not be any more grotesque than reality itself« (Jessen: So grotesk wie Anne Will).

something is art or irony, it is now necessary to constantly be reconsidering prejudices and discriminations. While exhibition and playhouses stood still, the very structures and hierarchies of the museums and theatre/opera houses were pulled under the microscope of #metoo and the postcolonial turn of consciousness, exposing countless grievances to scrutiny. The formerly unquestioned strongholds of bourgeois high culture face a crisis of legitimacy that will only exacerbate and deepen what was first perceived as a humiliation suffered by their declassification as *leisure*. Educational and cultural institutions that previously imparted or provided knowledge from above must transform themselves into places of participation, exchange and true democratization.

16. Heteropatriarchal Twilight?

The hitherto imagined superiority and exemplariness of Western ideas (so-called *enlightenment, progress, modernity*) is increasingly being critically examined as a colonial hegemonic heteropatriarchal ideology of oppression. The postcolonial turn in consciousness is accelerated by digital presence and platforms for discussion. For example, due to the »Decolonize the museum« movement, far more voices than ever before make themselves heard. Thus, on the one hand, the pandemic prevents many experiences and participation in and with art in real life, but on the other hand, it has created multiple forums in which far more aspects come to light than ever before. Formerly unquestioned sovereignties of thought, especially in the field of art and culture, are now caught in the crossfire of very diverse, awake (*woke*) publics – just think of the *unfortunate* Humboldt Forum in Berlin. Is Seeßlen's diagnosis of the doctrine of the pandemic, correct? »There is a lot of bad in the crisis, and there is a lot of good. There's only one catch: the good shows up individually, episodically, humanly and apolitically, but the bad works its way into the structural, organizational, the powerful and political.«[26]

17. Sobering Up

The defenselessness and helplessness among those working in the cultural sector in the face of being classified as *leisure activity*, on the one hand, and the lack of creative reaction to changed *relevance value system*, on the other, has sobered

---

26 Seeßlen: Coronakontrolle.

self-perceptions.²⁷ The aforementioned conflict within the Bavarian Academy of Fine Arts sparked, among other things, by the disdain for art in the president's complaint which was experienced by some as »conceit«.²⁸ This could be the beginning of a reorientation and recalibration, especially of Western supposed *self-evident facts* and self-assessments/overestimations. The increasing openness to other concepts of art (e.g. The Collective Ruangrupa at the next documenta 2022) can be of support to creatively use the awareness of our own boundaries. Just as the pandemic has taught us the dark side of globalization, the relativization of our significance and the fragility of what is supposedly tried and tested, it could sharpen our awareness of what has changed and what needs to be changed. Although the impression prevails that it is primarily the power of the market that has survived the pandemic crisis, there are also signs of increasing self-reflection and a new politicization, or questioning of the social place and role of artistic activity.²⁹

18. »Back to Real Life?«³⁰

This is the title of the weekly magazine, DIE ZEIT, at the end of May 2021, as the so-called incidence levels in the FRG gradually fall and the so-called lockdown is relaxed, and the main concern seems to be whether *one* can plan a summer holiday. Interestingly, the title question backed by George Seurat's famous pointillist painting *Bathers at Asnière*, is accompanied by the caption, »Finally back among people, finally away from the screen. On the beach, in the restaurant and in the theatre, people see each other again. But are they still the same?« Apart from the fact that the question ignores a large part of the fellow citizens who have worked consistently throughout this time despite difficult conditions and have all along been exposed to *the people*, it implies that leisure time is now a priority. Interestingly, not a contemporary image but an idyllic painting from the end of the 19th century was chosen as suitable illustration. Neither was an impressionist picture chosen, one which would capture a sparkling summer atmosphere, but rather one that attempts to freeze the moment, to make it Egyptian (Seurat's words), i.e., to

---

²⁷ Printed pandemic diaries provide a mix of contemporary diagnostics and prose on states of mind from the perspective of the privileged. The numerous forums of the net, on the other hand, offer insights into heterogeneous and sometimes abstruse models of explaining the world, in which one puts one's own spin on the world; Cf. e.g. Bronfen: Angesteckt; Czollek: Gegenwartsbewältigung; Lieske/Zeh: Emcke.

²⁸ Cf. Mitglieder der Bayerische Akademie der Schönen Künste: In welcher Gesellschaft lebt Herr Nerdinger.

²⁹ Cf. KUNSTFORUM International: Utopia; Tempest: On Connection; Architektur Biennale Venedig: Wie wollen wir leben?

³⁰ DIE ZEIT: Zurück ins echte Leben; transl. by the author.

make it last. Yet, exemplified by the sitter amid the pale, recovering protagonists against an industrial backdrop, a seemingly disillusioned dullness is conveyed at the same time. Might this have been what inspired the layout artist? The question, however, would be: What can already/still/again be called *real* life today? The fairly isolated life with a predominance of solely online contacts to the outdoors and to other people was/is also experienced/lived as intensely *real*. The answer to last question, whether people are still *the same* after the pandemic, remains to be seen. How will immediate life be experienced after all the media mediation?

19. ImMEDIAcy

The pandemic has often placed a filter between us and life. It has taught us a new calibration of closeness and distance, middle and immediacy. Unfortunately, Georg Seeßlen, a fine seismograph for social developments, has been able to show quite convincingly that this also leads to certain forms of de-socialization, instilling more fear than the disease itself.[31] At the same time that they demonstrate against the attempts of politics to cope with the crisis in a medically rational way, people often polemicize against democracy. The motives, however, are most often merely expressions of a desire for subjective freedom in leisure and work. At so-called *hygiene demos*, the absurd rationality as basis for social communication and understanding can be experienced. In addition to the scepticism of the global South against the legacy of the Enlightenment, there is also a cultivated anti-rationalism and *intellectual bashing* promoted in the agitation communities of the internet and by populist movements. Since hardly any direct negotiation remains, but rather that of a predominantly digital, via online, media whose algorithmic manipulability is known, there is currently no hope in sight. We live in a *medi/a/ocrit/cy* that has apparently not yet found an appropriate or convincing stance against the »strange mixture of aggressiveness and esotericism, conspiracy belief, anti-science and political agitation, cynicism, superstition and genuine existential despair«.[32] Interestingly, however, one artist — Sebastian Jung, for example — is able to capture the complex present better than any reportage with his very minimalist, almost elementary style of drawing.[33] Remarkably, it is possible to offer a more differentiated image of the present by means of a medium of

---

[31] Cf. Seeßlen: Coronakontrolle.

[32] Nedo: Krisengebiet vor der Haustür.

[33] In cooperation with the Thuringian office of the Friedrich Ebert Foundation, the artist has set up his own website: hotspotsociety.com, where he publishes his drawn diagnosis of the present, accompanied by scientific texts on the sociology of culture.

artistic expression still with us from the past – the pencil drawing – than with all the digital media available.

Thus, if the arts currently find itself in an in-between realm, with the multitude of digital offerings as stopgap/substitute solutions experienced more as ›rites de passage‹, it cannot be ruled out that new kinds of experiences and their expression will be distilled from them. Whether, in the long run, they will lead to new dimensions remains to be seen. In any case, they do sound out the new ›being-mediated‹ of our current being-here-and-being-there. The pandemic challenge is experienced as a catalyst and magnifying glass for the fragility of our Anthropocene condition. This generates, as illustrated here, the irrational reactions or populist, supposed solutions. The self-questioning of the arts as a seismograph seems to me to be more productive and diverse, and so, I would like to conclude with a confident and positive perspective by referring to Kae Tempest's recent work »On Connection« in which she argues for a politics of compassion and creativity: »Where loneliness and isolation are rampant, art and culture can be uniquely community-building.«[34] Creativity is seen as a means of fostering our need for connection; a thesis that has become all the more compelling since the pandemic generated lockdowns. Meanwhile, in their mediation, the arts develop new qualities in their media, like Joe Braun, Sebastian Jung and Kae Tempest, to name just a few. The immediacy of the experience of difference in these artistic ways of negotiating the present may immediately recapture something of our sensual self- and world-assurance.

References

Bonnet, Anne-Marie S.: Aren't So-Called Conspiracy Theories the Most Influential Art of Our Time?, in: Werner Gephart (ed.): In the Realm of Corona Normativities, A Momentary Snapshot of a Dynamic Discourse, pp. 355–368.
Borchhardt-Birbaumer, Brigitte: Jürgen Klaukes Fotografien der Langeweile, in: Wiener Zeitung, February 04, 2021, https://www.wienerzeitung.at/nachrichten/kultur/kunst/2091475-Juergen-Klaukes-Fotografien-der-Langeweile.html; last accessed July 20, 2021.
Braun, Joan [joan_braun]: »Friendly Bodies«, Instagram, https://www.instagram.com/joan_braun/?hl=de; last accessed July 01, 2021.
Brembeck, Reinhard J.: Das Glück sitzt im Auditorium, in: Süddeutsche Zeitung, March 21, 2021, https://www.sueddeutsche.de/kultur/klassik-berliner-philharmoniker-kirill-petrenko-konzert-1.5242413; last accessed July 20, 2021.

---

[34] Tempest: On Connection.

Bronfen, Elisabeth: Angesteckt. Zeitgenössisches über Pandemie und Kultur, Basel 2020.

Czollek, Max: Gegenwartsbewältigung, München 2020.

Di Lorenzo, Giovanni / Charlotte Parnack: Ich wurde immer meschuggener. Streitgespräch zwischen dem Schauspieler Jan Josef Liefers und Bundesgesundheitsminister Jens Spahn, in: DIE ZEIT, April 28, 2021, https://www.zeit.de/2021/18/jan-josef-liefers-jens-spahn-allesdichtmachen-corona-kritik; last accessed July 20, 2021.

DIE ZEIT: Zurück ins echte Leben, 22, 2021, May 27, 2021, Title.

Driessen, Christoph: Wie steht es um die Zukunft der Museen, in: n-tv, March 14, 2021, https://www.n-tv.de/panorama/Wie-steht-es-um-die-Zukunft-der-Museen-article22423771.html; last accessed March 14, 2021.

Jessen, Jens: So grotesk wie Anne Will. Das Hamburger Schauspielhaus eröffnet die Post-Corona-Saison mit einer Uraufführung von Elfriede Jelinek, in: DIE ZEIT, June 09, 2021, https://www.zeit.de/2021/24/hamburger-schauspielhaus-saison-eroeffnung-urauffuehrung-elfriede-jelinek; last accessed July 01, 2021.

Kniebe, Tobias: Die Bullshit Maschine, in: Süddeutsche Zeitung, April 27, 2021, https://www.sueddeutsche.de/kultur/oscars-alles-dicht-machen-film-1.5276633?reduced=true; last accessed July 01, 2021.

Kröner, Magdalena: Digital. Virtuell. Posthuman? Neue Körper in der Kunst, in: KUNSTFORUM International, 265, 2019, pp. 47–48.

KUNSTFORUM International: Utopia, Weltentwürfe und Möglichkeitsräume in der Kunst, 275, 2021.

Lemke-Matwey: Echtzeit! Langsamkeit! Aura!, in: DIE ZEIT, March 17, 2021, https://www.zeit.de/2021/12/matthias-goerne-matthias-schulz-kulturbranche-corona-kulturmanager-gesellschaft; last accessed July 01, 2021.

Lieske, Tanya / Miriam Zeh: Caroline Emke: Journal: Tagebuch in Zeiten der Pandemie, in: Deutschlandfunk, March 11, 2021, https://www.deutschlandfunk.de/carolin-emcke-journal-tagebuch-in-zeiten-der-pandemie.700.de.html?dram:article_id=493877; last accessed March 14, 2021.

Magenau, Jörg: Das Abendland geht ohne Abschied, in: Süddeutsche Zeitung, June 12, 2021, https://www.sueddeutsche.de/kultur/volker-braun-grosse-fuge-lyrik-literatur-rezension-1.5319085; last accessed July 20, 2021.

Mitglieder der Bayerischen Akademie der Schönen Künste: In welcher Gesellschaft lebt Herr Nerdinger. Widerspruch aus der Akademie, in: Frankfurter Allgemeine Zeitung, May 11, 2021, https://www.faz.net/aktuell/feuilleton/debatten/mitglieder-der-bayerischen-akademie-widersprechen-nerdinger-17335391.html; last accessed July 20, 2021.

Nedo, Kito: Krisengebiet vor der Haustür. Künstler Sebastian Jung im Porträt, in: Süddeutsche Zeitung, May 28, 2021, https://www.sueddeutsche.de/kultur/

kunst-corona-querdenker-demonstration-sebastian-jung-1.5305468; last accessed July 20, 2021.

Rauterberg, Hanno: Ins Offene! Caspar David Friedrich, in: DIE ZEIT, https://www.zeit.de/2021/11/caspar-david-friedrich-museum-corona-oeffnung-kunst-malerei; last accessed July 20, 2021.

Reckwitz, Andreas: Die Gesellschaft der Singularitäten. Zum Strukturwandel der Moderne, Berlin 2017.

Roelstraete, Dieter: Thinktank, in: Monopol, 05, 2021, p. 138.

Rosa, Hartmut: Die Umwege fehlen jetzt, in: Die Tageszeitung, April 24, 2021, https://taz.de/Soziologe-Hartmut-Rosa-im-Gespraech/!5763329/; last accessed June 30, 2021.

Sahlins, Marshall: Islands of History, Chicago 1985.

Schauspieler sorgen mit der Aktion »Alles dicht machen« für Aufsehen, in: DIE ZEIT, April 23, 2021, https://www.zeit.de/gesellschaft/zeitgeschehen/2021-04/coronapolitik-internet-kampagne-allesdichtmachen-lockdown-schauspieler; last accessed July 20, 2021.

Schütz, Alfred / Thomas Luckmann: Strukturen der Lebenswelt, Konstanz / München 2017.

Seeßlen, Georg: Coronakontrolle, oder: Nach der Krise ist vor der Katastrophe, Wien 2020.

Séguret, Olivier: L'intelligence virtuelle ne rêve pas. Nous sommes déjá entrain de fabriquer des avatars humains en série. Les ›digital humains‹ sont-ils une menace pour le réel, in: VANITYFAIR France, October 22, 2020, p. 129.

Soboczynski, Adam: »Es geht nicht darum, wer recht hat«, in: DIE ZEIT, April 28, 2021, https://www.zeit.de/2021/18/corona-politik-juli-zeh-thea-dorn-daniel-kehlmann; last accessed July 20, 2021.

Sommer, Tim: Das Museum, in: art, das Kunstmagazin, 12, 2020, p. 4.

Tempest, Kae: On Connection, London 2021.

Katja Spranz

Celebrities in Coronaland

Es soll schon Kleider gegeben haben, die direkt vom roten Teppich aus im Alleingang Technikgeschichte geschrieben haben. Nachdem Jennifer Lopez in einem Hauch von Versace-Kleid in Meerestönen bei den *Grammys* im Jahre 2000 gesichtet wurde, registrierten *Google*-Mitarbeiter die populärste Suchanfrage seit Existenz der Suchmaschine. Eric Schmidt, damaliger *Google*-CEO, erkannte, was die Leute sehen wollten: »J-Lo wearing that dress.« Man wollte mehr als nur Text, oder vielmehr gar keinen Text, und das Unternehmen reagierte schnell: »*Google Image Search* was born.«[1]

Celebrities erzählen sich und ihre Geschichte gerne auf glamourösen Veranstaltungen. Es geht hier nicht nur um die Insignien des Privilegs, teure Kleider, Juwelen, und Schönheit (mindestens bei weiblichen Stars untrennbar verbunden mit dem »Dünnsein«) – die Gesellschaft, in der sie sich auf diesen Veranstaltungen bewegen, ist existentiell für die Relevanz: Die Kontaktbeschränkungen, die durch das Coronavirus lebensnotwendig und in vielen Ländern zum Gesetz wurden, zog ihnen allerdings den roten Teppich unter den Füßen weg. Celebrities werden wie folgt charakterisiert: »A unique persona made widely known to the public via media coverage, and whose life is publicly consumed as dramatic entertainment, and whose commercial brand is made profitable for those who exploit their popularity, and perhaps also for themselves.«[2] Es gibt ein Portrait über Frank Sinatra, es gilt als eine der besten *non-fiction stories* aller Zeiten: *Frank Sinatra has a cold*, von Gay Talese, im April 1966 im *Esquire* veröffentlicht. Ohne den Entertainer persönlich interviewt zu haben, schrieb der Journalist seine Geschichte. Sinatra stand in Verdacht, Verbindungen zur Mafia zu haben und fürchtete wohl auch, nicht mehr zeitgemäß zu sein und in der Bedeutungslosigkeit zu versinken: Es wurde ein Portrait über Sinatra, über Celebrity-Kultur und Amerika an sich; die *entourage* ist omnipresent in seinem Leben – seine *hangers-on* beschützen ihn, bewundern ihn, fürchten ihn, sie sind das sichtbare Symbol seiner Bedeutsamkeit: Fast immer bewegt er sich »within dozens of people who work for him, drink with him, love him, depend on him for their own welfare and stability.«[3] Der Autor beschreibt Begegnungen, wie er ihn beobachtet, im Club und beim Konzert: Niemals durften

---

1 Schmidt.: The Tinkerer's Apprentice.
2 Jenner: Dead Famous.
3 Talese: Frank Sinatra Has a Cold.

die Zuschauer fehlen, Sinatra pflegte sein öffentliches Image. Doch mit Corona, wo ist diese Bühne, von der das Star-System lebt? Keine Premieren, keine Konzerte, keine Sportveranstaltungen und keine Reisen an exotische Orte, die Zeugnis ablegen von einem unangestrengten Reichtum. Chris Rojek unterschied drei Formen: »ascribed« (z. B. einige Mitglieder der britischen Königsfamilie), »achieved« (der Status, der auf Talent beruht, z. B. Sportstars wie Ronaldo oder SchauspielerInnen wie Angelina Jolie) und »attributed« celebrity (Berühmtheit als mediale Fabrikation, z. B. Reality-TV-Stars wie Kim Kardashian).[4] Ist diese Unterscheidung noch aktuell? Die Wiederverwertungsmaschinerie der Reality-TV-Shows kann heute Celebrities hervorbringen: Gelegentlich sogar für länger als 15 Minuten. Während am Anfang der Pandemie einige Film- und Fernsehproduktionen für einige Zeit stoppten, liefen viele Reality-Sendungen weiter: Das *Dschungelcamp* in Australien wurde zur *Dschungelshow* in Hürth, die *Big Brother*-Editionen in Deutschland, Kanada und Brasilien fingen an, bevor die Lage als ernst wahrgenommen wurde: Einige BewohnerInnen wurden vor laufender Kamera über die Lage der Welt informiert.[5] Andere Sendungen wie *Love Island* oder *The Bachelor* spielten weiter leichtbekleidete Normalität vor: Die MacherInnen versicherten stets, dass alle MitarbeiterInnen und TeilnehmerInnen zwei Wochen isoliert und getestet wurden. Gerade während der Pandemie boten diese Shows eine willkommene Ablenkung. In der *fiction* hielt das Virus nach einer Beobachtungsphase in manchen Geschichten Einzug: Die Krankenhausserie *Grey's Anatomy* machte es über mehrere Folgen hinweg zu dem zentralen Thema, auch im *Tatort* hatte es Auftritte.

1. Gleiches Virus für Alle?

Schon im Juni 2020 beschrieb Werner Gephart die »Gemeinschaftskrise«[6], die durch die Ausnahmesituation der Pandemie entstanden ist, normative Ordnungen, die selbstverständlich schienen, waren nunmehr in Unordnung. Betraf das die Stars gleichermaßen? Die Normalität der Stars bedeutet, dass sie sich feiern lassen, während ihr Publikum eskapistische Träume träumt – aber diese machen nur Sinn, wenn es wenigstens eine Möglichkeit gibt, dass diese für Jeden Realität werden könnten: Sonst bliebe nur der pure Neid. Doch das Coronavirus hat diese Illusion zunichte gemacht, was bleibt den Celebrities ohne Events und die richtigen Freunde unter den »Reichen und Schönen«? Es gab Stimmen, die sagten, es sei ein »demokratisches Virus«, Sängerin Madonna nannte es gar »the great

---

[4] Drake/Miah: The Cultural Politics of Celebrity, p. 51.
[5] Harrison: Coronavirus.
[6] Gephart: Introduction, p. 16.

equalizer«: »It doesn't care about how rich you are, how famous you are, how funny you are, how smart you are, where you live, how old you are, what amazing stories you can tell.«[7] Doch die Zahlen widersprechen dieser Aussage: Das Virus »interessiert« sich sehr dafür, wie alt man ist, wie arm oder reich man ist[8], wo man lebt (im nationalen[9] und globalen[10] Vergleich). Inzwischen ist dieser Post von ihrer *Instagram*-Seite verschwunden ... Schon in ihren Anfängen legte die Pandemie die Ungleichheit in der Welt offen: Wie einige Zeitungen schrieben, schien es – im März 2020 – für Menschen, die reich/berühmt/gut vernetzt waren, sehr viel einfacher zu sein, sich testen zu lassen, während es an Corona-Testkits besonders in den Hotspots mangelte, sogar in den Krankenhäusern.[11] Heidi Klum berichtete, sie und ihr Mann Tom Kaulitz – welcher einige Tage zuvor von seiner Tour zurückgekehrt war – haben sich nun »endlich« testen können, man wolle ja mit gutem Beispiel vorangehen. Sie hatten sich ein paar Tage voneinander isoliert: »We don't want to spread germs and risk others getting sicker ... even each other!« Man sieht die beiden küssend, durch eine Glastür getrennt.[12] Dem Rest der Welt blieb lediglich die Vorsichtsmaßnahme, sich bei Unwohlsein die vollen zwei Wochen bis zur Gewissheit zu isolieren: Tests waren kaum zu bekommen. Naomi Campbell zeigt sich im März 2020 auf Reisen, gekleidet in voller – offenbar medizinischer – Schutzmontur (»Safety First NEXT LEVEL.«). Auch hier blieben die negativen Kommentare nicht aus: Sie solle die Schutzkleidung doch lieber dem medizinischen Personal überlassen, in Krankenhäusern fehle es momentan an Allem.[13] In vielen Ländern kam der Lockdown: Die Ungleichheit beschränkte sich nicht nur auf die medizinische Versorgung, auch wurde offensichtlich, dass die *self-isolation* in einer Villa mit Garten angenehmer ist als in einer Plattenbauwohnung – Ellen deGeneres verglich die Isolation in ihrer Millionenvilla gar mit *being in jail*. Die Kritik an dieser Aussage ließ nicht lange auf sich warten.[14] Außerdem ermöglichte ein ländlicher Zweitwohnsitz eine willkommene Abwechslung zu dem Trubel der Großstadt. Schnell war klar, dass man während der Pandemie Menschenmassen meiden sollte: »The City That Never Sleeps« wurde zu einem Hotspot. Viele Reiche, die New York angeblich so lieben, flohen: Jeder Mitmensch wurde zu einem potentiellen Todesengel; wer es sich leisten konnte, floh also lieber in die Hamptons.[15] Der schottische »Celebrity Chef« Gordon Ramsay zog mitsamt

---

7 Owoseje: Coronavirus is ›The Great Equalizer‹, Madonna tells Fans from her Bathtub.
8 Pitzke et al.: Coronavirus Spread Lays Bare Underlying Inequalities.
9 Achermann/Daum: Das Leiden der anderen.
10 United Nations: COVID-19 to Worsen Poverty in 47 Poorest Nations.
11 Eder/Stein/Twohey: Need a Coronavirus Test?; Clymer: If You're a Celebrity Who's Mysteriously Found a Coronavirus Test Despite.
12 Klum: Instagram-Post, 15.03.2020.
13 Campbell: Instagram-Post, 11.03.2020.
14 Lee: Ellen DeGeneres Sparks Backlash after Joking that Self-Quarantine is like ›Being in Jail‹.
15 Bellafante: The Rich Have a Coronavirus Cure.

Familie von London nach Cornwall: Den Zweitwohnsitz für den Lockdown zu wählen, war erlaubt, pendeln sollte aber vermieden werden. Trotzdem blieb für viele eine Irritation angesichts der Entrücktheit seiner Aussage: Ramsay beschrieb sein Isolations-Leben mit Frau und Kindern in der kornischen Strandvilla als »living nightmare«.[16] Die britische Boulevardpresse – berüchtigt für ihre Obsession mit Immobilienpreisen[17] – vergaß nicht zu erwähnen, dass sich einige *locals* über die Ferienhausbesitzer ärgerten, sie brächten Corona aus der City nach Cornwall und hielten sich nicht an die Regeln: Außerdem solle sich Ramsay in seiner 4-Millionen-Pfund-Villa nicht beschweren.[18] Arnold Schwarzenegger ermutigte die Menschen – in seinem Outdoor-Whirlpool Zigarre rauchend – ebenfalls, zu Hause zu bleiben: Er mache das schließlich auch.[19] Dann kam der erste Impfstoff, und es häuften sich die Berichte über Impftourismus, auch dieser war den Wohlhabenden vorbehalten.[20]

2. Die Abwesenheit der *audience*

Aber nun gehören zu einem Star auch die Zuschauer, die ihn/sie bewundern, zu Celebrities gehört ein Publikum, das sie feiert. Mit der Pandemie wurde aber auch die Selbstdarstellung der Stars auf die immer gleichen Bilder reduziert: Zwar war oft mehr Reichtum sichtbar, aber glamourös waren die Bilder nicht mehr. Corona ist zwar nicht für alle eine gleich große Gefahr, und trotzdem wusste man, dass die Gefolgschaft nun sogar den Stars fehlte: Interessante Geschehnisse konnte es nicht wirklich geben. Ohne Auftritte bei der *Oscar*-Verleihung, bei der VIP-Preview der *ArtBaselMiamiBeach*, oder »heimliche« Küsse auf einer Yacht vor St. Tropez, was bleibt dann noch? Was bedeutet schon ein Rockstarleben ohne Zeugen? Das Virus verwandelte die Welt in ein globales Dorf der Aussätzigen, denen man die Krankheit aber oft nicht anmerkte, eine unsichtbare Gefahr also. Die Sozialen Medien scheinen bei einigen Stars den Glauben zu erwecken, sie könnten ihr eigenes Narrativ kontrollieren – doch so sehr sie auch bewundert werden, bevormunden lassen möchte sich das Publikum nicht. Die Geschichte hinter dem proklamierten Eigenbild wird oft die bessere Story. Meghan Markle betont bei Oprah Winfrey, *her own truth* erzählen zu wollen, und da zeigt sich das Missverständnis, die »Untertanen« gängeln zu können. Doch eine Celebrity ist eine solche nur durch Publikums Gnade; offenbar war die Schauspielerin aus der

---

[16] Pike: Gordon Ramsay Angers Locals.
[17] Greenslade: Why Are Papers like The Daily Mail Obsessed with House Prices?
[18] Chester: Gordon Ramsay and His Family.
[19] Schwarzenegger: Stay at Home.
[20] Ledsom: Covid-19 Vaccine Tourism Takes Off.

zweiten Riege ausgezogen, um eine zweite Lady Di zu werden. Diana galt als die meistfotografierte Frau der Welt, noch heute werden ihre Looks diskutiert, denen manchmal gar ein eigenes Bewusstsein zugeschrieben wird: So gilt sie als erste Trägerin des *Revenge-Dresses* (*show him what he's missing*). Nachdem Charles im Fernsehen seine Affäre gestanden hatte, sicherte sich Diana einige Tage später die Titelseiten der *tabloids*. In einem sehr knappen schwarzen Kleid erschien sie zum Sommerfest der *Serpentine Gallery*: »The Thrilla He Left To Woo Camilla«, ächzte The Sun.[21] Diana wurde zur Figur eines »Medienmärchens«, der es gelang, »eine aus dem Hochadel stammende Blaublütige als Aschenputtel zu inszenieren«[22] – welches sich dann emanzipierte und das Glück außerhalb des goldenen Käfigs suchte, die selbsternannte *Königin der Herzen*, die jetzt ihre *story* erzählen wollte, erzählte diese meist durch makellose Auftritte. Doch das öffentliche Bild ist nicht kontrollierbar: Der Vorstandsvorsitzende von *Axel Springer*, Mathias Döpfner, sagte 2006 in einem Gespräch mit Günther Grass den berühmten Satz: »Für die Bild-Zeitung gilt das Prinzip: Wer mit ihr im Aufzug nach oben fährt, der fährt auch mit ihr im Aufzug nach unten.«[23] Während der Pandemie kann so niemand richtig mit im Fahrstuhl fahren. Meghan Markle arbeitet noch an ihrer Inszenierung als Heiligenfigur, in Großbritannien ist ihr das nicht gelungen, sie floh mit ihrem Prinzen nach Kalifornien für mehr »Privatsphäre«, um dann allerdings ständig in der Öffentlichkeit aufzutreten.[24]

3. Celebrities als Simulakren

Celebrity ist ein Status, und der ist von Zeichen abhängig und von der Rezeption derselben: Bilder und Zeichen sind in ihrer ersten Phase eine Landkarte, die ein Territorium, eine Realität beschreiben sollen. Ein Simulakrum aber ist die letzte Phase des Bildes als Simulation und wird von Jean Baudrillard als Bild ohne Ursprung oder Realität charakterisiert – Letztere wird auf dieser Stufe nicht mehr imitiert, sondern durch Zeichen substituiert. Das Simulakrum zirkuliert in sich selbst, ohne Referenz und Umfang.[25] Berühmtheit ist – auch durch die Sozialen Medien – nicht mehr abhängig von einem bestimmten Talent: *Famous for being famous* ist ein Zustand, der sich selbst bestätigt und bestätigt werden muss, am besten durch Zuspruch von andern Menschen, die auch zu den »Reichen und Schö-

---

[21] Pithers: From Princess Diana to Jennifer Aniston, These Are the Ultimate Revenge Looks.
[22] Gephart: Die Märchenprinzessin Diana. Eine Heiligenfigur der Mediengesellschaft? Medien-Mythos?, S. 157.
[23] Von Schirach: Die Menschen bei »Bild« sind doch nicht so schlimm.
[24] Ellen: Will Harry and Meghan Learn the A-list Art of Saying Nothing At All?
[25] Baudrillard: Agonie des Realen, p. 7 ff.

nen« gehören, auch dieser Begriff bezeichnet ein Simulakrum, eine imaginierte Clique, deren Mitglieder alle bestimmte Merkmalen haben und untereinander vernetzt zu sein scheinen. Der »internationale Jetset« war mit Covid-19 aber nun auch an das das eigene Zuhause gebunden, alle Menschen wurden zu digitalen Nomaden im Live-Stream, ohne aber Nomaden in der Welt sein zu können. Die Familie Kardashian-Jenner gilt als ein Beispiel für ungerechtfertigten Celebrity-Status: Ob nun echte Milliardärinnen oder nicht[26] – wer weiß das schon. Fest steht: Kim Kardashian und Kyle Jenner haben mehrere hundert Millionen Follower auf *Instagram*, sind häufig unter den Top 10 der beliebtesten Accounts gelistet:[27] Das ist die Währung der Social Media, die Anzahl der Follower und der Likes, eine Beliebtheit, die ab einer bestimmten Anzahl zu barem Geld gemacht werden kann.[28] Es ist ein Clan, der nur aus Frauen zu bestehen scheint. Es gab zwei Männer, die eine Rolle gespielt haben (die übrigen scheinen zu kommen und zu gehen). Einer der Väter, Bruce Jenner – Goldmedaillengewinner im Zehnkampf –, ist nunmehr zur Frau geworden: Caitlyn.[29] Der andere, Robert Kardashian, ist verstorben: Auch er war schon ein großer Geschichtenerzähler – er erzählte seine Geschichten nicht auf *Instagram*, sondern vor Gericht. Er war Teil des Anwaltsteams, welches O. J. Simpson vor der Jury zum Vorkämpfer der Schwarzen stilisierte (eine Rolle, die dieser nie hatte; er hatte im Gegenteil zuvor des Öfteren betont, dass er überhaupt nicht über seine Hautfarbe definiert werden wolle) und u. a. mit dieser Strategie dessen Freispruch erwirkte. Kardashian war schon lange mit Simpson befreundet und reaktivierte eigens für dessen Prozess seine Zulassung zur Rechtsanwaltschaft.[30] Der Prozess als Simulakrum[31], es gab keine Referenz mehr in der Wirklichkeit, der Prozess drehte sich um Rassismus in der US-amerikanischen Gesellschaft. Es ging nicht mehr um das Tötungsdelikt. Auch hier spielte der Celebrity-Status – eines schwarzen Sportlers, der im »weißen Establishment« angekommen war – eine Rolle.[32] Besonders wenn man *famous for being famous* ist, ist ein Merkmal existentiell: stay relevant! Filme wurden irgendwann wieder gedreht, aber es gab keine Premieren, Konzerte hatten keine Zuschauer; und am wichtigsten: Die *audience* fand eben auch nicht mehr statt.

---

[26] Berg/Peterson-Withorn: Inside Kylie Jenner's Web Of Lies.
[27] Statista: Top-10 Instagram Accounts mit den meisten Followern weltweit.
[28] Barker: How to Make Money off Your Instagram Account.
[29] Bissinger: Caitlyn Jenner.
[30] Shuster: Kardashian-Simpson Bond Stands Test of Time, Trouble.
[31] Baudrillard: Agonie des Realen, S. 7 ff.
[32] Edelmann: O. J. – Made in America.

4. Die Pandemie als soziales Laboratorium

Ohne Referenz-Territorium wurde die Leere einiger Celebrities und der sie umgebenen Zeichen offenbar – einerseits geben sie ein Versprechen von einem Leben, die Illusion der Unsterblichkeit; doch das ist eigentlich nur verlockend, wenn es für Jedermann als eine Möglichkeit wenigstens *träumbar* ist. Diese Möglichkeit ist durch Castingshows, die schnellen Ruhm versprechen, scheinbar für alle in greifbare Nähe gerückt. Mit X-Factor und/oder Instagram kann jetzt jeder nach den Sternen greifen! Doch das hat seinen Preis, denn es gibt in der Regel einen Unterschied zwischen privatem Ich und öffentlichem Ich: Auf der einen Seite gibt es Bewunderung, und dann gibt es die Schadenfreude, wenn etwas schiefläuft. Brechen überirdisch perfekte Patchwork-Familien wie die Familie Jolie-Pitt auseinander, oder scheint es gar hinter der Fassade dunkle Geheimnisse zu geben, heißt das für das Publikum gegebenenfalls Schadenfreude ohne Schuldgefühle. Es hat etwas Tröstliches, dass man sich mit Geld, Macht und Schönheit eben doch nicht alles kaufen kann. Das deutsche Wort Schadenfreude wird als Notion besonders gerne benutzt, wenn Celebrities scheitern. So geschehen in Bezug auf das *Fyre Festival* (als »Fyre: The Greatest Party That Never Happened«, als Dokumentarfilm 2019 verewigt). Es sollte ein gigantisches Festival auf den Bahamas stattfinden, mit den besten Acts, dem feinsten Essen, und alle wollten sie kommen, die Hadids, die Jenners, die Kardashians (die Tickets kosteten bis zu 12.000 US-Dollar): Statt Gourmet-Catering gab es trockene Sandwiches in Schaumstoffbehältern, statt »Glamping« gab es Flüchtlingszelte, bei der Verteilung der knappen Schlafplätze kam es zu Tumulten, außerdem hatte es zuvor in Strömen geregnet. Die Headliner hatten schon im Vorfeld abgesagt, nachdem Gerüchte über die Undurchführbarkeit des Festivals laut geworden waren – eine Gruppe lokaler Musiker spielte für einige Stunden, bis das Festival erst einmal abgesagt wurde und die Besucher, die es bis zur Insel geschafft hatten, nach langen Wartezeiten nach Miami zurückgebracht werden konnten: »Schadenfreude is the emotion that defines our times«, vermutete gar eine Autorin in *The Guardian*.[33] Auch die Corona-Pandemie hatte schon ziemlich am Anfang ihre ganz eigenes »Schadenfreude-Event« zu verzeichnen: Stars wie Will Ferrell, Gal Gadot und Jimmy Fallon wollten die Welt retten, durch den engelsgleichen Zauber ihrer Stimme – heraus kam eine bemerkenswert atonale Version von John Lennons »Imagine«[34]. »Doesn't matter who you are, where you're from. We're all in this together«. Die Reaktion war praktisch einstimmig: »So Bad It Can Bring Us All Together in Hatred.«[35]

---

[33] Mahdawi: From the Fyre Festival to Brexit.
[34] Caramanica: This »Imagine« Cover Is No Heaven.
[35] Schwedel: A Video of Celebrities Singing »Imagine« So Bad It Can Bring Us All Together in Hatred, Slate.

Das Wort »viral« hatte wieder seine ursprüngliche Bedeutung und bezeichnete hier nicht ein erfolgreiches Internetphänomen, sondern etwas, was »durch einen Virus verursacht« ist. Manche Stars schreiben mit derartigen Showmomente Geschichte, andere überschätzen die Macht der Geschichten, die sie dem Publikum erzählen: Beeinflusst Celebrity-Kultur Kultur wirklich? Was bewirken Influencer eigentlich auf der Ebene der Tatsachen? Es bleibt schwierig, eine belastbare Analyse durchzuführen, die einen Kausaleffekt beschreibt, also herauszufinden, ob Celebrities wirklich einen Einfluss auf das Denken und Handeln ihres Publikums haben. Bei der US-Wahl 2016 scheint die Promi-Unterstützung für Hillary Clinton eher einen schädigenden Effekt gehabt zu haben.[36] Bei Obama gab es damals den Oprah-Effekt; Oprah Winfrey unterstütze ihn eifrig bei ihren Auftritten. Doch sie scheint eine Glaubhaftigkeit zu besitzen, die anderen Celebrities fehlt. Der normale Wähler möchte sich nicht von fachfremden Sternchen über Politik belehren lassen.[37] Es ist unwahrscheinlich, dass es nach Corona keine Celebrities mehr gibt, auch wenn es sein kann, dass einige sich durch ihre Äußerungen selbst zu Fall gebracht haben: Doch sind sie deswegen für immer entzaubert? Und außerdem: Will das Publikum eine Entzauberung überhaupt? Es gab auch unerwartete Heldenreisen und es fanden neue Zuordnungen während der Pandemie statt, zum Beispiel in Bezug auf Britney Spears, die sich im Dokumentarfilm *Framing Britney Spears*[38] als würdevolle Protagonistin inmitten misogyner Angriffe behauptet. Sie sang keine Lieder, um Corona zu vertreiben, sie befahl den Menschen nicht, »auch« in ihrem eigenen Garten zu bleiben. Sie hatte einen ganz pragmatischen Ansatz, sie wollte drei Fans finanziell helfen: »DM me and I will help you out«, seien es nun Lebensmittel oder Windeln für das Kind.[39] Die britische und amerikanische Linke feiert die Sängerin gar als eine neu gewonnene Genossin, denn schließlich bekenne sie sich nunmehr vor ihren 23,7 Millionen Followern zu ur-sozialistischen Ideen: »We will feed each other, re-distribute wealth, strike«, außerdem schmückte sie einen Kommentar mit Rosen-Emojis,[40] ein Symbol der amerikanischen Sozialdemokraten. Sie habe die Macht des Streikes erkannt, und die Macht des Volkes läge ja in der Tat in der Verweigerung der eigenen Arbeitskraft, jubelten die Genossinnen und Genossen: »Comrade Britney Spears, We Salute You«!.[41]

---

36 Drake/Miah: The Cultural Politics of Celebrity.
37 Bryant: Did Celebrity Endorsements Contribute to Hillary Clinton's Presidential Upset?
38 Day: The Handling of Britney Spears.
39 Spears: Instagram-Post, 21.03.2021.
40 Spears: Instagram-Post, 23.03.2021.
41 Foster: Comrade Britney Spears, We Salute You.

Literatur

Achermann, Barbara / Matthias Daum: Das Leiden der anderen, in: DIE ZEIT, 17.01.2021, https://www.zeit.de/2021/03/corona-armut-soziale-ungleichheit-homeoffice-job-gesundheit; letzter Zugriff am 28.05.2021.

Barker, Shane: How To Make Money off Your Instagram Account, in: Forbes, 20.11.2017, https://www.forbes.com/sites/forbescoachescouncil/2017/11/20/how-to-make-money-off-your-instagram-account/?sh=3200b9da6af0; letzter Zugriff am 31.05.2021.

Baudrillard, Jean: Agonie des Realen, Berlin 1978.

Bellafante, Ginia: The Rich Have a Coronavirus Cure: Escape From New York, in: The New York Times, 14.03.2020, https://www.nytimes.com/2020/03/14/nyregion/Coronavirus-nyc-rich-wealthy-residents.html; letzter Zugriff 19.06.2021.

Berg, Madeline / Chase Peterson-Withorn: Inside Kylie Jenner's Web Of Lies – And Why She's No Longer A Billionaire, in: Forbes, 01.01.2020, https://www.forbes.com/sites/chasewithorn/2020/05/29/inside-kylie-jennerss-web-of-lies-and-why-shes-no-longer-a-billionaire/?sh=10e6802025f7; letzter Zugriff am 31.05.2021.

Bissinger, Buzz: Caitlyn Jenner: The Full Story, in: Vanity Fair, 25.06.2015, https://www.vanityfair.com/hollywood/2015/06/caitlyn-jenner-bruce-cover-annie-leibovitz; letzter Zugriff am 31.05.2021.

Bryant, Kenzie: Did Celebrity Endorsements Contribute to Hillary Clinton's Presidential Upset?, 21.11.2016 in: Vanity Fair; https://www.vanityfair.com/style/2016/11/celebrity-endorsements-donald-trump-hillary-clinton; letzter Zugriff am 18.05.2021.

Caramanica, Jon: This »Imagine« Cover Is No Heaven, in: The New York Times, 20.03.2020, https://www.nytimes.com/2020/03/20/arts/music/coronavirus-gal-gadot-imagine.html; letzter Zugriff am 18.05.2021.

Chester, Jason: Gordon Ramsay and his Family Risk Further Outrage from Cornish Locals on a Beach Walk After Chef was Warned for Flouting Lockdown Rules, in: MailOnline, 04.05.2020; https://www.dailymail.co.uk/tvshowbiz/article-8285323/Gordon-Ramsay-family-risk-outrage-Cornish-locals.html; letzter Zugriff am 09.06.2021.

Clymer, Charlotte: If You're a Celebrity Who's Mysteriously Found a Coronavirus Test Despite the Shortage, I Need You to Read This, in: The Independent, 19.03.2020, https://www.independent.co.uk/voices/coronavirus-test-covid19-celebrities-influencer-heidi-klum-arielle-charnas-nba-golden-state-warriors-a9411971.html; letzter Zugriff am 04.06.2021.

Day, Liz.: The Handling of Britney Spears, in: The New York Times, 05.02.2021, https://www.nytimes.com/2021/02/05/insider/britney-spears-father-documentary.html; letzter Zugriff am 10.06.2021.

Drake, Philip / Andy Miah: The Cultural Politics of Celebrity, in: Cultural Politics, Volume 6(1), UK 2010, pp. 49–64.

Edelmann, Ezra: O. J. – Made in America, ESPN FILMS 2016.

Eder, Steve / Marc Stein / Megan Twohey: Need a Coronavirus Test? Being Rich and Famous May Help, in: The New York Times, 18.03.2020, https://www.nytimes.com/2020/03/18/us/coronavirus-testing-elite.html; letzter Zugriff am 04.06.2021.

Ellen, Barbara: Will Harry and Meghan Learn the A-list Art of Saying Nothing At All? in: The Guardian; 20.03.2021; https://www.theguardian.com/commentisfree/2021/mar/20/pipe-down-harry-and-meghan-if-you-want-to-hang-with-a-listers; letzter Zugriff am 10.06.2021.

Foster, Dawn: Comrade Britney Spears, We Salute You, in: JACOBIN, 25.03.2020, https://jacobinmag.com/2020/03/britney-spears-coronavirus-strike; letzter Zugriff am 10.09.2021.

Gephart, Werner: Die Märchenprinzessin Diana. Eine Heiligenfigur der Mediengesellschaft?, in: Miriam Meckel / Klaus Kamps / Patrick Rössler / Werner Gephart (Hrsg.): Medien-Mythos? Die Inszenierung von Prominenz und Schicksal am Beispiel von Diana Spencer, Wiesbaden 1999, S. 157–158.

Gephart, Werner: Introduction: The Corona Crisis in the Light of the Law as Culture Paradigm, in: Werner Gephart (Hrsg.): In the Realm of Corona Normativities. A Momentary Snapshot of a Dynamic Discourse, Frankfurt am Main 2020.

Greenslade, Roy: Why Are Papers like the Daily Mail Obsessed with House Prices?, in: The Guardian, 21.04.2011, https://www.theguardian.com/media/greenslade/2011/apr/21/dailymail-national-newspapers; letzter Zugriff am 14.06.2021.

Harrison, Ellie: Coronavirus: Big Brother Contestants around the World Left Unaware of Pandemic, in: The Independent, 17.03.2020, https://www.independent.co.uk/arts-entertainment/tv/news/coronavirus-big-brother-contestants-house-germany-brazil-canada-isolation-pandemic-a9405581.html; letzter Zugriff am 14.06.2021.

Spears, Britney: Instagram-Post, 21.03.2020, https://www.instagram.com/p/B9-VuoaAXU7/?utm_source=ig_embed; letzter Zugriff am 10.06.2021.

Spears, Britney: Instagram-Post, 23.03.2021, https://www.instagram.com/p/B-FppKxAFxm/?utm_source=ig_embed; letzter Zugriff am 10.06.2021.

Klum, Heidi: Instagram-Post, 15.03.2020, https://www.instagram.com/p/B9vJ3QvJy1c/; letzter Zugriff am 04.06.2020.

Campbell, Naomi: Instagram-Post, 11.03.2020, https://www.instagram.com/p/B9kwcbPnFP0/; letzter Zugriff am 04.06.2020.

Jenner, Greg: Dead Famous: An Unexpected History of Celebrity from Bronze Age to Silver Screen, London 2020.

Ledsom, Alex: ›Shot Trips‹ To Dubai, Florida, Tel Aviv, Havana: Covid-19 Vaccine Tourism Takes Off, in: Forbes, 14.02.2021, https://www.forbes.com/sites/alex

ledsom/2021/02/14/shot-trips-to-dubai-florida-tel-aviv-havana-covid-19-vaccine-tourism-takes-off/?sh=605e3f6e199c; letzter Zugriff am 10.06.2021.

Lee, Alicia: Ellen Degeneres Sparks Backlash after Joking That Self-Quarantine Is Like ›Being in Jail‹, in: CNN, 09.04.2020, https://edition.cnn.com/2020/04/08/entertainment/ellen-degeneres-quarantine-jail-trnd/index.html; letzter Zugriff am 04.06.2021.

Mahdawi, Arwa: From the Fyre Festival to Brexit, Schadenfreude Is the Emotion That Defines Our Times, in: The Guardian, 02.05.2017, https://www.theguardian.com/commentisfree/2017/may/02/fyre-festival-brexit-schadenfreude-emotion-defines-times; letzter Zugriff am 21.04.2021.

Owoseje, Toyin: Coronavirus is ›The Great Equalizer,‹ Madonna Tells Fans from her Bathtub, in: CNN, 23.03.2020, https://edition.cnn.com/2020/03/23/entertainment/madonna-coronavirus-video-intl-scli/index.html; letzter Zugriff am 10.06.2021.

Pike, Molly: Gordon Ordon Ramsay Angers Locals Who Threaten to Chase Him Out of £4 million Second Home in Cornwall, in: Daily Mirror, 08.04.2020, https://www.mirror.co.uk/3am/celebrity-news/gordon-ramsay-angers-locals-who-21831729; letzter Zugriff am 09.06.2021.

Pithers, Ellie: From Princess Diana to Jennifer Aniston, These Are the Ultimate Revenge Looks, in: VOGUE, 27.05.2020, https://www.vogue.co.uk/fashion/gallery/revenge-dressing; letzter Zugriff am 14.06.2021.

Pitzke, Marc / Britta Sandberg / Fritz Schaap / Jörg Schindler: Coronavirus Spread Lays Bare Underlying Inequalities, in: DER SPIEGEL, 05.06.2020, https://www.spiegel.de/international/world/the-corona-class-wars-a-pandemic-fueled-by-inequality-a-685b2edf-6f20-489e-a18f-932b89091b4b; letzter Zugriff am 21.04.2021.

Schmidt, Eric: The Tinkerer's Apprentice, in: Project Syndicate, 19.01.2015, https://www.project-syndicate.org/onpoint/google-european-commission-and-disruptive-technological-change-by-eric-schmidt-2015-01; letzter Zugriff am 18.05.2021.

Schwarzenegger, Arnold: Stay at Home. Even If You're Young. Even If You're on Spring Break, https://www.youtube.com/watch?v=a4tIomQ4ZdI; letzter Zugriff am 28.05.2021.

Schwedel, Heather: A Video of Celebrities Singing »Imagine« So Bad It Can Bring Us All Together in Hatred, in: Slate; https://slate.com/culture/2020/03/celebrities-singing-imagine-video-explained.html; letzter Zugriff am 10.06.2021.

Shuster, Beth: Kardashian-Simpson Bond Stands Test of Time, Trouble, in: Los Angeles Times, 06.07.1994, https://www.latimes.com/archives/la-xpm-1994-07-06-mn-12500-story.html; letzter Zugriff am 07.06.2021.

Talese, Gay: Frank Sinatra Has a Cold, in: Esquire, https://www.esquire.com/news-politics/a638/frank-sinatra-has-a-cold-gay-talese/; letzter Zugriff am 19.05.2021.

United Nations: COVID-19 to Worsen Poverty in 47 Poorest Nations, in: Deutsche Welle, 03.12.2020, https://www.dw.com/en/un-covid-19-to-worsen-poverty-in-47-poorest-nations/a-55799928; letzter Zugriff am 28.05.2021.

Von Schirach, Ferdinand: Die Menschen bei »Bild« sind doch nicht so schlimm, in: Die Welt, 24.06.2012, https://www.welt.de/kultur/article106639177/Die-Menschen-bei-Bild-sind-doch-nicht-so-schlimm.html; letzter Zugriff am 14.06.2021.

Hanne Petersen

Re-Evaluation/Value of Nature under Conditions of Social Lock Down?

> »*Like all pandemics, COVID-19 is not an accidental or random event. Epidemics afflict societies through the specific vulnerabilities people have created by their relationship with the environment, other species and each other.*«
>
> Frank M. Snowden

In 1994, the book *Le nouvel ordre écologique* from 1992 by French philosopher and politician, Luc Ferry, was translated into Danish. I read it then and I have been thinking of this book recently during the corona pandemics. I remembered that he mentioned the existence of a link between religious affiliation – indirectly Protestantism – and care for nature.[1] When I revisited the book, I noticed that he called for a more in depths investigation between this link, which seemed to be less pronounced in Catholic countries of the European south. His book is mainly a critique of the ideological roots of *deep ecology*, which he wrote had become the refuge both of nostalgic counterrevolutionaries and of leftist illusions: »The human species is no longer at the center of the world, but subject to a new god called Nature.« He particularly criticized philosophers from the Anglo-Saxon and German parts of the world, who supported *deep ecology*. One of the most important Nordic philosophers involved with deep ecology was Norwegian philosopher, Arne Næss.

1. *Open Nature* During Lock Down (?)

The focus of this article is on Denmark, where people have been encouraged to visit nature, which has still been *open* during the pandemic.[2] The Nordic countries have had somewhat different approaches to the pandemic, with Sweden being the most liberal introducing the fewest and least radical restrictions.[3] All Nordic coun-

---

[1] Cf. Ferry: Den nye økologiske orden, p. 26 (compare for the English edition: Ferry: The New Ecological order).
[2] Thanks to research student Djellza Fetahi for finding material and for comments and suggestions on this article.
[3] Cf. Pickett: Sweden's Pandemic Experiment.

tries have small populations – below 10 million, and especially Norway, Sweden and Finland are thinly populated. The Nordic governments have not introduced curfews during the lockdown. In May 2020, the Danish Ministry of Environmental Affairs informed that the population was using nature more during the crisis, especially young people between 18 and 35 years old. While 25 % had visited a nature area they had not visited before, 34 % had stayed more in nature, than they usually would. In nature areas around bigger cities, the number of registered visitors increased from 70–160 % from March 15 – May 1, 2020, while fewer people visited areas far away. Minister of the Environment, Lea Wermelin said »Nature is our common breathing space in a difficult period. I am glad that many are taking to forests and coastal areas. Everybody is welcome in state owned nature, and I urge everybody, who has the opportunity to find alternatives to visiting the very well-known and visited nature areas. There are many small pearls out there, and the more we are spreading the easier it is for everybody to keep the necessary distance.[4] Denmark is still an agricultural country, where privately owned monoculture and (often) industrial farming, occupies around two thirds of all area. Around one fourth of the area in Denmark consists of nature areas such as forest and heath as well as a minor part of lakes, meadows and moors. Private individuals, associations, businesses and private actors own 74 % of this one fourth. The state and municipalities own the other 26 %. The total nature areas owned by both state and municipalities thus make up around 6 % of *all* nature areas in the country.[5] One really has to look for the *small* pearls. The ministry linked to a number of websites with information on nature guides, trails, camping possibilities and descriptions, one of them by the Danish Outdoor Council (Friluftsrådet), an umbrella organization for about 85 primarily non-profit and non-governmental organizations focusing upon many different types of outdoor life. The head of this organization said in May 2020 that: »The corona crisis has opened the eyes of many people for what outdoor life may offer. This year many of us will take vacations in other ways than we used to, and here Danish nature areas have a lot to offer. The organizations will make sure to draw attention to the many possibilities out there.«[6] Danish Outdoor Council had a five-point strategy for 2018–2020 covering the following fields: Access to nature; nature and physical planning; the importance of outdoor life for health; outdoor life for children and youth, and finally the conditions of member organizations. A survey in March 2021 showed a further general increase to 40 % of the population, who would use nature areas – as well as a generational and a gender divide. Especially women and young people had taken to nature.

---

[4] Cf. Miljøministeriet/Naturstyrelsen: Vi bruger naturen mere under coronakrisen.
[5] Cf. Statistics Denmark Analysis: Størstedelen af de danske naturarealer er ejet af private [Majority of Danish Nature Areas Privately Owned].
[6] Ibid.; cf. Miljøministeriet/Naturstyrelsen.

45 % of women had spent more time outdoor than before the crisis, and in the age group of 18–35 years old almost half of both gender had been outdoor more than normally. Nine out of ten, who used nature more in 2020 expected to continue using nature much. Furthermore, especially the younger age group had discovered the outdoor as a social meeting space, be it for birthday parties, get together, or meeting friends within the last three months.[7]

Denmark has a very long coastline. In practice, the country is an archipelago of more than 400 islands, a few linked by bridges, several still linked by ferries and the smallest only by private boats. There are many summerhouses and secondary homes for rent or private use, and the market has been overheated since March 2020, when it was no longer possible to travel outside of Denmark.[8] During the summer period of 2020 the Danish minority government (Social Democrats) supported by a broad number of parties – left and right – decided on a *summer package* making it cheaper to travel in all of the country, to rent out summerhouses (less taxation) and providing discount for cultural and sports activities. Internal ferry transportation between islands became free for hikers and cyclists, and other prices were reduced for ferries to small islands. Free travel passes for 8-day travels with public transport as well as increased numbers of cheaper train tickets were amongst the most important initiatives.[9] These pandemic initiatives combined an increased health induced use of nature with a legally, economically and practically facilitated access. To some extent, this supported emerging and already changing practices and customs of the population in relation to nature, especially in the case of the younger age groups. In 2019, Swedish teenage schoolgirl Greta Thunberg and other young European leaders – often female – led climate strikes by teenagers and sometimes their parents and grandparents – founding the powerful and sometimes contested *Fridays for Future* in all of Europe. These strikes influenced the elections to the European Parliament in May 2019 and the move towards a European Green Deal. In Denmark, it brought the present Social Democratic government into power after elections on Constitution Day, June 05, 2019 on a quite ambitious climate agenda – which has so far not materialized strongly. An influential part of this age group – notably Greta Thunberg herself – had already changed travel and consumption patterns before corona – to less or no air travel, less meat consumption, more recycling of resources etc. Even if the pandemic ended the physical demonstrations by teenagers without voting rights, it may also have supported this trend to a perhaps broader extent. In January 2019 a major Danish newspaper, Politiken, changed its travel section to become more

---

[7] Cf. Arildsen: Corona-krise: Vi bruger naturen meget mere.
[8] Cf. Nørgaard: Ferie i krisetider.
[9] Cf. Ministry of Trade: COVID-19: Sommerpakke skal sætte skub i dansk sommerøkonomi.

climate friendly by focusing more on train, bicycle and hiking holidays.[10] For many years, many Danes have undertaken international vacation traveling, but in 2020 the pandemic contributed to a further change of this pattern. However, many people have not been used to spending that much time in nature, leading to conflicts between different users of nature.[11] The pandemic has also shown that new interactions between human and non-human species require new knowledge and that learning has to take place, and is already happening.

2. Property Regimes, Access, Conflicts and Health – Changing Social, Urban and Legal Cultures Over Time?

With the transition to a constitutional monarchy and democracy, royal ownership of land, certain roads and many forests were transferred from royal to state ownership in Denmark after 1849. The walls and gates of Copenhagen were abandoned after the Cholera epidemic in 1853 had killed 5000 people in the poor and overcrowded parts of the city, where hygiene was at a very low level. The new quarters for the industrial workers coming from the countryside were subsequently built outside the medieval military protection walls. In 1872, a law on *Mark- & Vejfred* [Peace of Field and Road) was enacted mainly dealing with responsibility for damages done by cattle to other people's land or animals, which is still in power in an updated version from 1953 – but still primarily dealing with animals. The regulation of access to land, (public and private) forests, roads and paths and sea territory is complicated and contested and reflects the changes of society, customs, regulations and legal culture as well as the relation to nature.[12] Nineteenth century historical conflicts regarding customary use and access relate to agriculture and (competing) owners of domestic cattle. In the late 19th and early 20th centuries, tuberculosis was an epidemic treated by recreational stays in nature expected to increase healing – particularly for the affluent classes. Many of the tuberculosis sanatoria were placed in beautiful surroundings including the first Danish sanatorium at Vejlefjord opened in 1900, which has now become a treatment center for brain damage as well as a spa and recreation resort. Medical historian Frank M. Snowden notes that tuberculosis was, however, »above all a social disease that disproportionately afflicted the ›dangerous classes‹ – working men and women and the urban poor.«[13] Propelled by a sense that »tuberculosis was a national emergency

---

[10] Cf. Bevar Jordforbindelsen: Nyt og mere klimavenligt rejse tillæg i Politiken.
[11] Cf. Schuldt: Han må aflive dyr efter invasion af skovgæster.
[12] Cf. Baaner: Friluftsliv og regelsammenstød, pp. 25–36.
[13] Snowden: Epidemics and Society, p. 297.

on grounds that were at once humanitarian, sanitarian, patriotic, and economic, powerful interests throughout the industrial world launched a series of *wars against tuberculosis*«[14]. Sanatoria were intentionally paternalistic and hierarchical[15] and »the war on tuberculosis proclaimed a new imperative – that an unquestioned authority by physicians over their patients was essential to recovery,« writes Snowden.[16] To some extent this also resonates with today's treatment of COVID-19. Interestingly, Snowden also speculates whether »this long war on tuberculosis was one of the factors that prepared the way for the establishment of the ›social state‹ that was constructed in western Europe after World War II.«[17] This development was particularly strong in the Nordic countries. Most early twentieth century conflicts regarding land and nature areas seem to concern use and conservation of land, reflecting a changing (elite) view of nature. National and international regulation on nature conservation was introduced in the early part of the 20th century, and given the long tradition in Denmark for establishment of organizations of all sorts, the Danish Association of Nature Conservation (from 1911) had an important influence in relation to the first law from 1918. Almost a century later, the organization now notes that due to the centralization and commercialization of agriculture about half of earlier field roads and private common paths have been abolished and access has been made more difficult during the last half century.[18] The (dangerous) working class grew more urbanized and fought for and achieved shorter working weeks and more spare time. This increased recreational needs and growing demand for access to nature close to urban areas. It created conflicts with private owners of agricultural land and roads, as well as of forests and property close to the sea territory (where there was historically quite open access for the public). The Danish Outdoor Council was established in 1942 in an industrial society, where workers needed access to nature in a way different from the conditions in agricultural society. During the same period, Sweden legally secured The Right of Public Access to nature or *Allemansrätten* as did Norway and Finland. Denmark, probably due to its smaller size, intensive use of land for agriculture and a higher population density did not introduce such a right. It is not a coincidence that the first element of the present strategy of the Danish Outdoor Council is *access to nature*. As the 1950s and 1960s witnessed an increased demand for access to nature by urban populations, the role of nature in relation to *social peace* began to change from a focus on tort and legal responsibility to access to recreational space. Urbanization has increased considerably all over the world for the last many decades, causing housing, health, environmental and economic problems amongst others.

[14] Ibid., p. 301.
[15] Cf. ibid., p. 312.
[16] Ibid., p. 323.
[17] Ibid., p. 326.
[18] Cf. Eigaard: Adgang til naturen.

About one third of the Danish population now lives in the greater Copenhagen area, which is a city of the young and old – students and retired persons, and increasingly a very affluent upper middle class. As in all other capitals and metropoles housing prices have increased leaving a substantial and less well off part of the lower middle class, young people and retired people with low pensions (often female) without the means to acquire adequate condominiums or cooperative apartments. This happens during a period where precarious working and wage conditions are on the rise undermining the security of paid work. Changing family forms and increase of single lifestyle means that women dominate the housing market in several big cities including Copenhagen. Statistics Denmark estimates that while men own two thirds of the urbanized areas in Denmark, the situation differs in bigger cities. Here and in certain municipalities in Northern Zealand, the part owned by women is higher and in municipalities in and around Copenhagen women own more than 45 % of urbanized areas. Around 1.9 mio. persons corresponding to 44 % of the population above 20 years own built property. However, ownership is divided very unevenly amongst generations. In the youngest generation from 20–29, only 4 % own property, while about one third of those aged 30–39 own property. The age group from 50–59 dominates ownership of built property with 60 %.[19] Even if it is not mentioned in the statistics about growing use of nature during corona, there is most likely a correlation between the groups which are economically least well off, the young and a group of (single) women, and the increased use of (and conflicts about) the *free and open nature*. The first months of 2021 have seen an example of such conflicts of interests regarding nature, culture, generations and gender. During several years the use and construction of an area called Amager Fælled [Amager Commons] has given rise to conflicts. The island, Amager, south of central Copenhagen was originally inhabited by Dutch immigrants. It has been used for grazing areas, execution and garbage dumps. Absolutist kings used it as a military area after 1660. From the beginning of the 20th century, decades of landfill based on waste of different kinds expanded the island. In 1964, it was abandoned as a military area, became protected by acts of nature conservation, and was opened to the public and used for recreational purposes. The Øresund Bridge to Sweden was opened in 2000. Legislation from 1992 enabled the development of a new expansion of the city of Copenhagen including the so-called *Ørestad*, and a new (very expensive) metro for the whole city. The intention was to finance this major project and especially the metro by sale of building plots, which has also happened for great parts of the area. There have however, been constant demonstrations regarding some of these construction plans involving parts of the protected areas since 2016. After municipal elections in 2017 the city government gave up earlier construction and development plans for an

---

[19] Cf. Statistics Denmark Analysis: Hvem ejer de bebyggede områder i Danmark?

unprotected old area, *Strandengen*, (Beach Meadow) with considerable biodiversity after public pressure and demonstrations and relocated them to an area called *Lærkesletten*, the *Lark Plain*, a former landfill site and garbage dump until 1974, however under conservation protection. In 2019, the conservation protection of the Lark Plain was lifted with the intention to enable further financing of the costs for the metro. This long drawn out process has given rise to years of demonstrations, and actions by the Danish Association of Nature Conservation, Friends of the Amager Commons and lately activists involved in Extinction Rebellion. Although 76 % of the population of Copenhagen is reported to be against the project, a political majority of the Copenhagen municipal council, which has so far had a Social Democratic mayor since 1903, supported the construction projects of a residential area consisting of 2000 housing entities.[20] The Copenhagen municipal council took this decision in February 2021, and the site will be sold to private investors for development of the area. Demonstrations have continued up until now including physical and zoom-demonstrations and blocking of construction in the spring of 2021.[21] They seem to be informed by a combination of green concerns about lifting of nature conservation for the purpose of construction, increased awareness about biodiversity and perhaps social considerations and a concern about construction for profit, which will not allow ordinary wage earners to live in Copenhagen. The story about the Lark Plain is also a story about changing perceptions of *constructed nature* in an increasingly urbanized world, something that artists have also been dealing with during some years.[22] In the twenty-first century, the pandemic and the subsequent social lockdown have created an increased social, recreational and health motivated demand for access to nature. The political encouragement to use nature may thus produce a situation, where a broader particularly urban and younger public demands a wider and more general access to (non-urban and sometimes ›reconstructed‹) nature, as well as more urban green spaces. This will no doubt conflict with both private property rights and certain public economic interests. Interestingly, the issue of (responsibility for) animals has also surfaced again, as the number of pets among urban populations – of whom many are single – has grown in general and particularly during the pandemic the demand for pets has grown considerably. In 2000, the Danish Ministry of the Environment

---

20 Cf. Brandt: Aktivister blokerer byggeri på Amager Fælled; Dansk Naturfredningsforening: Byggeri jager lærker væk fra Lærkesletten på Amager Fælled; Waaben: Aktivister kæmper mod byggeri på Lærkesletten: »I politibilen på vej til arresten sad vi og sang.«

21 Note by Djellza Fetahi April 2021.

22 See for instance the group exhibition »Langt Ude i Skoven« [Far Away in the Forest«, transl. by the author] by eight Nordic and European artists Rune Bosse, Stefanie Bühler, Marjolijn Dijkman & Toril Johannessen, Tue Greenfort, Sanna Kannisto, Anders Moseholm and Marika Seidler in Skovhuset Art & Nature (April 21 – June 13, 2021). The exhibition deals with the relationship between contemporary art and nature in order to investigate the actual conditions of nature and climate through art.

and Energy established a Council for Nature which in its report dealt with the role of *urban nature* and its growing importance in contemporary society, where views of nature have been changing, and demands for more and different recreational space has grown. *Urban nature* may be understood as breathing spaces improving climate.[23] The chapter on *Urban nature* also mentions a growing demand for *wilder nature* in cities, which was in May 2021 also expressed at an art exhibition in Amager *PRIVACY (wilding)*, which addressed the changing norms for urban gardens in areas of detached housing.[24] Articles dealing with the consequences of the pandemic for urban life and public space are beginning to appear.[25] In an article on *The Impact of COVID-19 on Public Space: A Review of the Emerging Questions*[26], the group of authors ask questions concerning three categories of emerging questions in regard to a) urban design, b) perceptions, use and behavior in public space and c) inequities and exclusions in relation to public space. The general design questions concern the future of large public spaces, the need for a new typology and whether public space will be re-designed and temporary transformations will lead to permanent changes. Further, whether health criteria will become a mainstream part in design, and whether green space planning will need new designs, uses and practices as well as the impacts on public transit and micro-mobility. The questions about the category of ›perceptions, use and behavior‹ concern the amount of people, who will be using public space in the future, what we will do in public and whether our *intuitive carrying capacity* for public spaces will decrease. They further deal with legal questions regarding use and regulations of public spaces, infringement on civil liberties as well as our perceptions of public space. The final category about *inequities and exclusions* deals with the needs of vulnerable groups such as women, racial minorities, immigrants, low-income residents, the elderly, children and the homeless and how they will be accounted for in future public space designs, practices and rules. It asks whether cities in the Global South will attempt to constrain or regulate the informal street economy, and whether the pandemic will permanently regulate the informal street economy. In the same way, a Norwegian article discusses issues of recreational use of urban nature during the pandemic,[27] and a Swedish article discusses »Urban nature as a source of resilience during social distancing amidst the coronavirus pandemic.«[28]

---

[23] Cf. Delling: Bynatur, p. 211.
[24] Cf. Art catalogue PRIVACY (wilding) (2021) produced in relation to an exhibition by artist Asmund Havsteen Mikkelsen. The exhibition is associated with a Research Centre of Excellence at UCPH on PRIVACY and includes several theoretical articles, reflections and manifestos related to urban nature.
[25] Cf. Rocha: Post-Pandemic Urbanism for Small Cities.
[26] Cf. Honey-Rosés et al.: The Impact of COVID-19 on Public Space, p. 4.
[27] Cf. Venter et al.: Urban Nature in a Time of Crisis.
[28] Samuelsson et al.: Urban Nature as a Source of Resilience.

3. Gender and Nature? The Permanence of the Exception?

In *The New Ecological Order*, Luc Ferry wrote a section called *In praise of diversity or the transformation of left radicalism. The case of Ecofeminism*,[29] where he clearly distanced himself from this radical ecofeminism. This section ends with a sentence saying the »The demand for diversity becomes undemocratic the moment it is prolonged to a demand for a difference in relation to law.[30] During the pandemic, Denmark's second female prime minister, Mette Frederiksen, has led the Social Democratic Danish minority government, which also has a female minister of the Environment. None of them could fairly be described as declared feminists or ecofeminists. There are nonetheless quite a number of significant democratically elected female politicians maybe all over the world, who have dealt with environmental issues and who have influenced and to some extent changed both politics and law in this field. They include Gro Harlem Brundtland, medical doctor and the first female Nordic prime minister. She also became the head of the UN Commission which in 1987 produced the report *Our Common Future* (in the Nordic countries mostly called the Brundtland report). The report made the term *sustainability* a household term in the decades to come. Another famous example is Germany's first female chancellor for 16 years, Angela Merkel, who started her career in the Ministry of Family affairs and went on to become minister of Environmental issues. Danish minister of the environment (2004–2007) Connie Hedegaard subsequently became the country's first minister of climate and energy (2007–2009), and went on to become the first ever EU commissioner of climate in 2010. In the Nordic countries three countries out of five (Norway, Finland and Denmark) have been under female leadership during the pandemic. The center-right very fragmented opposition has criticized the Danish prime minister for being far too headstrong and authoritarian – although neither for being an Iron Lady nor an Ice Queen or a female Leviathan. In November 2020, all mink farms in Denmark were closed and all animals slaughtered to limit contamination and spread of the virus. At subsequent demonstrations by farmers and mink producers, the prime minister was portrayed with caricatures showing her in dominatrix outfit and with swastikas. The termination of mink farms is now under investigation for being unconstitutional. Mette Frederiksen was initially very popular, and she has continued to enjoy a considerable support – as has been the case for many political leaders during the pandemic. However, there is no doubt that the population has become ever more exhausted during the repeated openings and recurring lockdown periods. If nature had not been *open*, social life might not have been as peaceful. The centre-right opposition has been very

---

[29] Cf. Ferry: Den nye økologiske orden, p. 162 f.; transl. by the author.
[30] Cf. ibid., p. 183.

keen about a return to *normal life*, and its commercialized consumption patterns especially in the entertainment industry, which has been hardest hit by the pandemic. Women have always been considered closer to nature – mostly due to their ability to bear offspring – and Western legal cultures have tended to devalue both women and non-human nature. This has led to an exclusion and denigration of both women and nature in modern industrial societies and their legal cultures. I touched upon this relation in a book chapter from 1997 on *Gender and Nature in Comparative Legal Cultures*[31], where I discussed two issues, which characterize western legal culture, the devaluation of female/human gender and non-human nature. One consequence of this devaluation has been an exclusion and denigration of both women and nature in the law of *modern industrial societies.* During the pandemic, all societies in the world have had a great demand for a workforce which could care for the sick, the elderly and the dying. Traditionally, such care work has been carried out by women. The job as a (traditionally female) nurse has often been low paid in many countries. Over the last decades, the dominant neoliberal New Public Management regime has led to cutting costs in a strained welfare state, which has (in Denmark) for half a century been staffed by a primarily female workforce. Many female nurses and midwives had already left the public health sector before the pandemic due to intolerable working and wage conditions after an unsuccessful general strike in 2008. During collective negotiations in the spring of 2021, Danish nurses rejected the meager agreement, which was the result of the collective bargaining process, and again threatened to go on strike. Not surprisingly, the strike was postponed by the (female) Conciliator. A combined devaluation of (female) care for humans and (human) care for nature may well contribute to difficulties in withstanding this (as well as future) pandemics. In Denmark as in other countries, spontaneous Black Lives Matter demonstrations took place in June 2020. Perhaps this pandemic experience will raise questions about whose lives and work matter as well as which relations between human nature and non-human nature matter and how. The pandemic and the concomitant crisis is clearly also a crisis for the political and legal systems, for the institutions and regulations as well as for an anthropocentric and often androcentric legal culture. We may not want the present exceptions to become permanent, but it may not be viable either to return to the attitudes, norms and values, which dominated the perceptions of *permanence* before the pandemic.

---

[31] Cf. Petersen: Gender and Nature in Comparative Legal Cultures.

References

Arildsen, Søren: Corona-krise: Vi bruger naturen meget mere, in: sn.dk, March 29, 2021, https://sn.dk/Lev-sundt/Corona-krise-Vi-bruger-naturen-meget-mere/artikel/1423836; last accessed April 12, 2021.

Baaner, Lasse: Friluftsliv og regelsammenstød [Outdoor Life and Conflict of Laws], in: Juristen 1, 2019, pp. 25–36.

Bevar Jordforbindelsen: Nyt og mere klimavenligt rejse tillæg i Politiken [A New and More Climate Friendly Travel Section], January 08, 2019, https://bevarjordforbindelsen.dk/velkommen-til-et-nyt-og-mere-klimavenligt-rejser-politiken/; last accessed May 03, 2021.

Brandt, Kasper Bruun Vindum: Aktivister blokerer byggeri på Amager Fælled. »Vi er naturens stemmer« [Activists Block Contruction at Amager Commons: »We Are the Voices of Nature«], in: TV2 Lorry, February 21, 2021, https://www.tv2lorry.dk/koebenhavn/aktivister-blokerer-byggeri-paa-amager-faelled-vi-er-naturens-stemmer; last accessed May 04, 2021.

Dansk Naturfredningsforening: Byggeri jager lærker væk fra Lærkesletten på Amager Fælled [Construction Chases Away Larks From the Lark Plain at Amager Commons], March 10, 2021, https://www.dn.dk/nyheder/byggeri-jager-laerker-vaek-fra-laerkesletten-pa-amager-faelled/; last accessed May 04, 2021.

Delling, Dieter: Bynatur, in: John Holten-Andersen/Hanne Stensen Christensen/Thomas Nicolai Pedersen/Sanni Manninen (eds.): Dansk naturpolitik – viden og vurderinger, Naturrådet, Temarapport 1, 2000, pp. 204–217.

Eigaard, Annette: Adgang til naturen, Danmarks Naturfredningsforening, https://aktiv.dn.dk/sagsarbejde/natur/adgang-til-naturen/; last accessed April 27, 2021.

Ferry, Luc: Den nye økologiske orden. Træet, Dyret og Mennesket, Munksgaard/Rosinante, Copenhagen 1994.

Ferry, Luc: The New Ecological Order, Chicago 1995.

Honey-Rosés, Jordi et al.: The Impact of COVID-19 on Public Space: A Review of the Emerging Questions, April 21, 2020, https://doi.org/10.31219/osf.io/rf7xa, p. 4; last accessed April 27, 2021.

Miljøministeriet Naturstyrelsen: Vi bruger naturen mere under coronakrisen, May 10, 2020, https://naturstyrelsen.dk/nyheder/2020/maj/vi-bruger-naturen-mere-under-coronakrisen/; last accessed April 12, 2021.

Ministry of Trade: COVID-19: Sommerpakke skal sætte skub i dansk sommerøkonomi. https://em.dk/nyhedsarkiv/2020/juni/covid-19-sommerpakke-skal-saette-skub-i-dansk-sommeroekonomi/; last accessed April 12, 2021.

Nørgaard, Tom: Ferie i krisetider: Corona sender efterspørgslen på sommerhuse i naturen i top [Vacation in Crisis Times Boosts Demand for Summerhouses in Nature], Finans, February 10, 2021, https://finans.dk/privatokonomi/

ECE12735084/ferie-i-krisetider-corona-sender-eftersjoergslen-paa-sommer huse-i-naturen-i-top/?ctxref=ext; last accessed April 12, 2021.

Petersen, Hanne: Gender and Nature in Comparative Legal Cultures, in: David Nelken (ed.): Comparing Legal Cultures, Dartmouth 1997, pp. 135–154.

Pickett, Mallory: Sweden's Pandemic Experiment, The New Yorker, April 06, 2021.

Rocha, Ricardo: Post-Pandemic Urbanism for Small Cities: Density Versus Green (Private) Areas, in: Academia Letters, Article 667, 2021, https://doi.org/10.20935/AL667.

Samuelsson, Karl et al.: Urban Nature as a Source of Resilience During Social Distancing Amidst the Coronavirus Pandemic, April 18, 2020, https://osf.io/3wx5a/; last accessed April 27, 2021.

Schuldt, Laura Kongsmark: Han må aflive dyr efter invasion af skovgæster: »Folk aner ikke, hvordan de skal opføre sig i skoven« [He Must Put Animals to Death After an Invasion of People in the Forest.« People Have No Clue About How to Behave in the Forest«], Berlingske, February 22, 2021, https://www.berlingske.dk/hovedstaden/han-maa-aflive-dyr-efter-invasion-af-skovgaester-folk-aner-ikke; last accessed April 12, 2021.

Snowden, Frank M.: Epidemics and Society. From the Black Death to the Present, New Haven 2020.

Statistics Denmark Analysis: Størstedelen af de danske naturarealer er ejet af private [Majority of Danish Nature Areas Privately Owned], 2017:14, October 31, 2017, https://www.dst.dk/Site/Dst/Udgivelser/nyt/GetAnalyse.aspx?cid=29460; last accessed May 03, 2021.

Statistics Denmark Analysis: Hvem ejer de bebyggede områder i Danmark? [Who Owns Built Areas in Denmark?], October 08, 2018, https://www.dst.dk/Site/Dst/Udgivelser/nyt/GetAnalyse.aspx?cid=31405; last accessed May 04, 2021.

Venter, Zander S. et al.: Urban Nature in a Time of Crisis: Recreational Use of Green Space Increases During the COVID-19 Outbreak in Oslo, Norway, in: Environ. Res. Lett. 15, 2020.

Waaben, Line: Aktivister kæmper mod byggeri på Lærkesletten: »I politibilen på vej til arresten sad vi og sang.« [Activists Fight Against Construction at the Lark Plain. »We Sat and Sang in the Police Car on the Way to Confinement«], in: Information, March 20, 2021, https://www.information.dk/moti/2021/03/aktivist-kaemper-byggeri-paa-laerkesletten-politibilen-paa-vej-arresten-sad-sang; last accessed May 04, 2021.

Maurizio Ferraris

Coronavirus and the Education of Homo Sapiens

Unlike the Lisbon earthquake of 1755, the pandemic has only rarely raised the question of theodicy, that is, the justification of a God who, while being omniscient, omnipotent and – above all – good, allows evil to take place. Where was God when the pandemic started? Where was God when Trump was elected? To this second question one can answer that indeed God was there, except the postmodern God is not a bearded old man, but mother nature wounded by human greed. Rousseau blamed the deadliness of the Lisbon earthquake on the civilization that had led humans to build seven-story houses. And if the plagues of Egypt were to occur again today, it is predictable that, in defiance of secularization, we would interpret them as ecological reprisals: what can an invasion of locusts or frogs, the rain of fire and hail and darkness mean, if not a revolt of nature against our abuses? It should be noted that here nature is not seen as the work of God, but *as God*, precisely after the manner of Spinoza: *Deus, sive natura, God, that is, nature*. The bat or the pangolin, in this view, are the emissaries of a virus bearing the annunciation of the environmental crisis.

1. Nature

The path of theism is not the most traveled, but it is not entirely deserted either. A personal God is sending us a message, some say, yet they do not examine the concrete possibility that the message might be *go to hell*. Some suggest, biblical evidence in hand, that the pandemic is part of a divine providential plan, and that the only solid rock to cling to is Jesus Christ. Thus, it is said, not all evil comes to harm: the virus has actually reminded us of the misery of life without God, it has knocked down our hybris and reopened the paths of salvation. Christ thus appears to be the way not only to make sense of the pandemic, but also to find hope amidst the stormy sea, preluding to a re-qualification of Catholicism as an alternative globalization. Of course, one can seek hope in texts other than the Gospels, such as the Talmudic tradition or the Kabbalah; or else, one may draw the conclusion that the world is coming to an end. Whatever the case, reading these texts one has the impression of being faced with the end of an era, a bit like in the *Rape of Proserpina* put into verse by Claudian: the personal God has other things to do than send messages to his largely unbelieving subjects. Now that the God of Abraham, Isaac and Jacob has gone, what remains is the God of philosophers: the secularized self-awareness thanks to which, in the face of the virus, people have not taken refuge in churches or gathered in contagious processions – a sign that a new God, science, has taken hold of humankind. In his prayer of March 27, 2020, interpreted by some, perhaps with excessive emphasis, as a watershed for humanity, the Pope was able to develop alternative strategies of strong visual and spiritual impact. These strategies, after all, refer to a debilitating virus: the virus reminds us of our fragility and invites us to discard our misplaced pride, he said. Few have spoken of *punishment*, as this is not the Middle Ages; however, many have referred to that eve of punishment which is warning. For example, the virus brings to the fore the thought of death, rescuing it from the state of mere abstraction – it might force us to adopt unusual funeral rites, but it certainly brings us together in our common fate. And since the viral pandemic is intertwined with the racist pandemic, it is on this ground that we find the challenges awaiting the post-pandemic Church. And similar conclusions can also be reached within a secular horizon: by disrupting the linguistic games of postmodernism, the virus forces us to surrender to the harshness of reality, or even the (*Lacanian*) Real. Conversely, the harshness of reality reminds us of the demands of the spirit, and enjoins us to abandon the dream of an immune society without evil – notwithstanding the possibility of an Übervirus forcing humanity to make ruthless choices between those who have and do not have a ventilator or, reversing the perspective, discriminates the strong from the weak, the brave from the fearful. Since the alleged secularization is not the death of God, but simply a struggle between the old and the new gods, the real turning point is precisely the handover from the Bearded Old Man to Mother Nature. However, the pantheistic virus appeals not to a Spinozian vision, but to the romantic perspective of a long-suffering and finally rebellious world-soul, akin to Native Americans in reservations. As a result, it is said, the class struggle today is fought by animals, plants, and the environment, the only effective medicine against the virus is ecomedicine, and the final solution can only come from a completely new global and environmental economy and a Green New Deal. In this framework, some argue that ecological knowledge can allow us to predict and moderate pandemics, which are accelerated precisely by the reduction of biodiversity. However, not only the virus is a vigorous proof of biodiversity as such, but its propensity to variants is a further dimension of this biodiversity: life has never been so powerful and triumphant as during the pandemic, and never has nature shown its power as much as in the last two years. In short, let's not forget this: the virus is part of nature, and we are its environment, so any attempt to defend ourselves from the virus should be considered as an attack against the environment. And if it is true, as someone observed, that global warming, deforestation and increased air traffic are the first clues as to the genesis of the coronavirus, then jets, deforestation, and global warming empower nature more than any ecological procession. The truth is that we do not and cannot have any correct idea of nature *per se*, nature being a concept, therefore a human and necessarily anthropocentric construct (meaning, of course, not its beings, its ontology, but its epistemology, the theories with which we glamorize and interpret it). On closer inspection, therefore, the handover did not take place between the Bearded God and Mother Nature, but, according to the norms of secularization, from God to Man, who considers himself omnipotent and created, according to the norms of fetishism, the imaginary of an aching and abused Nature. Yet this alleged human omnipotence appears as a paranoid fantasy. An Italian pop singer, claiming that humans are the cause of the slaughter of dinosaurs, expressed a conviction shared by many: »Man has killed the dinosaurs, of course he will destroy this little worm, this microbe, called coronavirus«.[1] This paternalistic and wishful attitude whereby we feel responsible for nature as if it were our own backyard has shown its absurdity with the pandemic, even if the major premise of the most anti-Socratic syllogism should have already warned us that, except for unforeseen events, we are subject to the laws of nature like any other living being. Let us imagine the worst case scenario: unexpectedly, the virus is not tamed but strengthened, and with each wave it reappears more aggressively and violently. After a long struggle, the virus prevails and humanity disappears. Has nature disappeared? Of course not. One can easily imagine a planet devoid of humans and in perfect health, provided that this anthropomorphic term can be applied to a planet. Let us now think of an alternative dystopian scenario: humanity defeats this and other viruses, reasserts its belief that it is the master of nature, proceeds to a systematic destruction of the environment making human life on the planet impossible, and disappears. Has the planet disappeared? Of course not. So, let us sit back and reflect on our powers and responsibilities. What does it mean to be a slave to nature? Many things, from suffering from gout to not being able to go skiing if there is no snow, to being stranded on an island because of a storm, to crashing in an airplane, to being swept away by an avalanche, to blowing up because of a defect in the gas pipes (gas is nature, and even pipes are not supernatural), to being victims of food poisoning. And, even if we manage to escape all these possibilities, being slaves to nature means that sooner or later we all die. Given that the modest slowdown in global warming has been caused by the pandemic, it would be better, if we care about the planet more than humanity (as implied by the logic of this position), to hope for further and more deadly pandemics.

---

[1] Al Bano cit. in Caruso: Da Al Bano a Madonna.

2. Technology

So, we are not masters of nature – that's the bad news. The good news is that we are masters of technology, even if, for less than a century, we have chosen to think of ourselves as exactly the opposite, namely masters of nature and slaves to technology. I have no idea when this misunderstanding will come to an end, but I have a very precise theory about when it began: the self-defence of Albert Speer, the German Minister of Armaments, at Nuremberg, where he pleaded guilty but blamed his crimes on technology. Speer's speech inaugurated the idea of the non-responsibility of technicians that still prevails in common sense (think of the absolution and impoliticity presupposed by the syntagm *technical government*), and at the same time made it possible to achieve a kind of *Metropolis*-style dystopia, according to which humans, in the *age of technology* (a strange expression, given that technology has accompanied and defined humanity since its origins) would be reduced to automatons, and enslaved by the machines they themselves have produced. It is not surprising that Speer's speech set the standard, and his greatest, albeit perhaps unwitting, megaphone was no less than Heidegger himself. I am not talking about the Heidegger of *Being and Time*, but of the post-war Heidegger, of the so-called *second Heidegger* who transmitted a fundamental and widely received message: nature has been forgotten and ravaged (this is the meaning behind the *oblivion of being*), and humans take pride in their triumphs, which are however only apparent, since the technology they claim to dominate actually dominates them. Thus, paradigmatically, in *Das Gestell, the framework*, a lecture delivered in Bremen in 1949, Heidegger inaugurated a long period of complaints and excuses about the *Gestell* annihilating everything and governing our every action, depriving us of any initiative. If you want to know the full list of *Gestell*-induced pathologies, just scroll through Byung-Chul Han's bibliography. To indulge these diagnoses of imaginary pathologies without treatment is to feed an old ghost: machines will take over, something we ourselves have built will eventually rule us. This narrative is already found in many notions: the Golden Calf, the idol that we manufacture and to which we submit; the magical helpers (wands, swords in the stone and the like) that save us but make us dependent on them; the Golem, the fake Adam who rebels against the sorcerer's apprentice; or humans reduced to machines by other machines, on assembly lines, and then surrounded, even outside the factory, by the machines they have built. This goes all the way to the ultimate spectre, that of an artificial intelligence fed up with being controlled by stupid natural intelligences. Not to mention that the spectre itself is a kind of machine, automaton or zombie: something that looks human but is not, and is superior to humanity because it cannot die, and therefore has no fear of death. Ghost stories have always been popular, and today we have legions of ideologues ready to say that technology dehumanises and governs us, thereby absolving us of our duties and responsibilities as humans, that is, as agents endowed with reason and above all with will and intentions that machines do not and never will possess. This is because they are mechanisms and not organisms, and therefore know nothing of hunger, thirst, desires, fears and hopes. More precisely, the more sophisticated a machine is, the less interested it is in taking over, not only because it is difficult to imagine a machine interested in anything, but because the more complex a machine is, the more dependent it is on humans. A rudimentary technology, like the prehistoric chipping of a flint to make a scraper, makes the human an appendage of the machine. The same happens with compounds of the human – the plough and the ox – or with the assembly lines of the twentieth century. Moreover, in a primitive technology, the instrument enjoys some autonomy: think of how many possible uses there are for a stick. On the other hand, once we have ruled out the use of a mobile phone as a projectile object, there is only one possible use for it, in which the machine is totally dependent on the human, without whom it would be useless. And the result of our interactions with mobile phones, smartwatches and computers – i.e., artificial intelligence – is not a demonic machination that rules over us, a Golem that rebels and annihilates us, but simply the slavish recording of human life-forms, which become valuable capital because that tireless archival activity is what makes automation possible. *Automation*, in fact, means just that: enabling a machine to act as a human: to do so, it is necessary to record and reproduce the human. To whoever fears the dictatorship of machines, I object that, if one can very well conceive of a humanity without the Web (that was my own case, for a good part of my life, as well as anyone of my generation and all the infinite generations that have come before us), one cannot conceive of a Web without humanity. So it is we who, to use a technological metaphor, have the whip hand. Like all machines, the Web was made in our image and likeness and exists to serve our needs (not those of a virus, a beaver, or any other machine, for that matter). Any dystopia where humans are reduced to automatons is only the outcome of imperfect automation. In such situations, machines not only record, imitate and reproduce our life-forms but, firstly due to energy shortages (water and wind are less efficient energy resources than steam or electricity), then due to automation shortcomings (lawnmowers long required someone to operate them) turn humans into momentary, insufficient and intolerant prostheses of the machines themselves. If it is so, it is indeed strange to fear that machines will take over, or that algorithms will rule us: if it is far-fetched to blame Caesar's death on the conspirators' daggers and the fall of cable cars on brackets, it is even more far-fetched to blame our mistakes (let alone our sins) on the mobile phone. Rather, it is a useful argument in a court of law if you are accused of crimes against humanity or other crimes large or small, but it remains false there and everywhere else. There, as everywhere else, algorithms tell us what to do only if we are willing to obey them, just as we are governed by the laws of the state or moral commandments

– which can also be violated – by the books we read, by our good and bad habits and so forth. As a 65-year-old man rooted in his habits and convictions, which are not heaven-sent, but result from thousands of hours of experience, and therefore of exposure to influences and conditioning of all kinds, I am convinced that I am the one who governs the algorithms that concern me, for example when I search for books that reflect my stubbornness and surrender to my pigheadedness and mistakes. Feeling that you are responsible for your own mistakes and stubbornness is not a great feeling, I admit, but it is better than blaming it on technology.

3. Politics

The combination of our alleged domination of nature and our alleged enslavement to technology is biopolitics, which provides the reasonable foundation for the unreasonableness of conspiracy theories. Judging humans against apes is as unfair to both, but the fact remains that had it not been for the idea that the modern state exercises its power through the control of life and not, for example, through the collection of taxes, such rubbish would never have been printed. We have seen and still see very few states that are primarily concerned with the lives of their citizens (one of the few examples that comes to mind is the Third Reich in its early days, but certainly not in its epilogue), while we have seen and still see a great many states preoccupied with a thousand other useful, futile or even harmful affairs, and there is no reason to see biopolitics as the *Shibboleth* of modern governmentality. Some say that the decision-making virus has imposed a state of exception and recourse to a single leader. In the Italian case, the tyrant would have been Giuseppe Conte, and there are good reasons to doubt the seriousness of the allegation. To speak of a *universal attack* means attributing intentionality to the virus, and to think that a virus can infect democracy is a slippery metaphor. Few reflect on the fact that the greatest restriction on freedom experienced in the pandemic was the ban on dinners, happy hours and nightlife. Indeed, distribution chains have changed as a result of the shift from restaurants to home dining. Now, a power that prohibits social gatherings is not a power that prohibits all freedoms, as we keep being told: it simply limits one specific freedom – which for decades has been used for recreational purposes rather than political ones, as the latter are now taken over by social media. Of course, for many people the problem is not giving up aperitifs, but access to food. And again, the ability of criminal organizations to provide food to the underprivileged, as has been the case in many places in Mexico, cannot but make one wonder. In the light of this circumstance, however, some would argue that the real problem is not the state of exception, but that when the nightlife freedoms are restored, many venues will have been bought by the mafia. More generally, to our knowledge, it is the mafias that effectively increased their control by taking advantage of the state of emergency. This contradicts the paradigm of the panoptic state of biopolitics, and suggests rather a sieve-like state. If, as everyone can see, the reactions of governments have varied radically, the question arises as to how biopolitics could impose itself. And above all, how local measures and strategies can be used as universal (and indicative of the characteristics of humanity as a whole). The question also arises as to what biopolitical strategy could have led to the inefficiencies that can be observed in all liberal states. Rather, there is a clear contradiction between biopolitics and liberalism: the former aims at control, the latter at profit, and it is not at all clear how these opposing interests can be reconciled. Indeed, it is worth noting that the countries at greatest risk of authoritarianism, such as Trump's United States and Bolsonaro's Brazil, have been the most lax when it comes to anti-virus measures, and that the countries, such as China, that have managed the crisis in an authoritarian way were authoritarian regardless. The unfortunate affair of covid-related apps, in Italy and Europe, shows that authoritarianism cannot be improvised with a virus. At the same time, it demonstrates the complete inability of states to govern — for this is the opposite objection, which yet is not perceived as contradictory to the first. Also, contrary to many negationist claims, it is by no means true that jihadism has been silenced by the pandemic: the international chessboard, from Washington to Moscow via Istanbul, is being repositioned precisely *in function of* jihadism, while a headless jihadism is bursting out in France and Austria. In fact, why shouldn't the jihadists take advantage of the opportunity, instead of (as others suggest) retreating offended because the pandemic is competing for their headlines? Finally, claiming that modern power, unlike that of older times, is life power rather than death power means overlooking three circumstances: first, having power of life is conceptually identical with having power of death, meaning that biopolitics is also thanatopolitics; second, from this point of view the legitimate monopoly of violence as a characteristic of the modern state is, therefore, to all intents and purposes, a biopolitical power. Finally, expressions such as *your money or your life* or Brenno's answer to the Romans as to what remained to them after the dispossession they had undergone, namely *life!*, was a biopolitical answer without Brenno having read a single line of Foucault. It is natural that today's governments should involve science and health, just as in old times that we do not regret it involved tradition, religion and race. What has changed is not power, but medicine, which is much more effective, as demonstrated by the impressive increase in average life expectancy. Yet, a glance at Marc Bloch's *The Royal Touch: Monarchy and Miracles in France and England* (the original is dated 1924, two years before Foucault was born) shows that power has always played the biopolitical card, albeit in a thaumaturgical rather than surgical capacity. There is also an argument to the contrary: the Nero order with which, in March 1945, Hitler ordered the destruction of Germany's industrial apparatus – in the belief that the Germans did not deserve to live because they were inferior to the *strong races of the East* – is considered neither tanatopolitical nor biopolitical, but simply insane, and no one remarked on this.

4. Resilience

Let us change perspective. Political subjects are not necessarily victims, and when they are, it might very well be their own fault. Not to mention that the most interesting political subjects are the winners, unless one cares to write a history of victimhood that puts Salièri before Mozart in music, Carlo Pisacane before Lenin in politics, and Silvio Pellico before Kafka in literature. The idea is very simple: instead of putting everyone in a position to lament the common evil, which seems to be by far the prevailing activity of victimhood, let us try to build a future humanity in which everyone's a winner, without prejudice to the inalienable right to fail again and to fail better, if that is what we wish. Consider this point. After a few months of the pandemic, some clever person decided to digitize the paper magazine found on the seats of high-speed trains, spreading the virus with greater efficacy than a handshake. Indeed, as soon as they were seated, people would move it to the hatbox, from where it would be moved back to the seat for the next journey by the attendants. That person was not the only thoughtful one, nor the only resilient one. After all resilience, understood as vital obstinacy, is already a serious objection to biopolitics: is there resilience, say, in the family businesses linked to tourism? As soon as we ask ourselves this question, we are already outside the Panopticon, because the question actually is: will people go back on holiday or not? Life, in fact, is not only the alleged object of domination by a moloch that, in its mythological representation of Power, Palace and Capital, simply does not exist. It is also the *raison d'être* of every power, every palace and every capital – indeed, no such things would exist without the drive of human needs, of our infinite and illogical necessities that today, stored on the web, produce enormous wealth. This wealth must be understood in its genesis and conceptualised in its structure, and this has never been more evident than after these last two years we all spent on Internet platforms. The crisis we are witnessing must teach us how to create healthier, sustainable, fairer and more resilient food systems, generating a nutritional virus that would prevent us from getting fat during confinement. The other side of this concern is that the virus is a serious candidate, in the face of happy degrowth, for creating disasters through food shortages, reviving problems that we had gladly forgotten about – at least at our latitudes. Of course, the virus may well open up brand new problems: what food producers need to know in order to comply with pandemic regulations; how to deal effectively with the new regulations introduced by the pandemic and by financial support measures, according to German, French, Spanish, Italian and EU legislation; how to build an anti-pandemic hospital in no time, etc. Transcendental philosophy or shamanism can be used to promote resilience and, if necessary, to provide more readily available instructions for problems of various kinds: recovery from post-traumatic stress; the silent tragedy and social regression of confined adolescents; the depression of the elderly who cannot receive visits from relatives and who are socially ostracised. Anxiety needs to be quelled by answering questions such as: what information should I trust? What should I tell the children? How can I not panic? In the variety of advice and manuals we get a broad view of something that is very real and yet rarely thought of: how to grieve and appreciate the life we are given. Think of the two ladies, mother and daughter, who lost their husbands 41 days apart on the eve of the pandemic and found themselves grieving in full lockdown. And the list of questions goes on. How to calm children and allay their fears during the pandemic. Conversation and consolation manuals for anxious parents and worried children. How to invest wisely in the age of Covid. How to make your business flourish in a pandemic. How to rebuild social solidarity. How to prevent remote working from becoming non-stop, endless labour. How to take advantage, with communication strategies (but is it really just communication?), of the pandemic situation that has linked us even more to Internet platforms. How the crisis has affected and changed management. How to protect oneself, one's family and loved ones, from a medical and psychological point of view; how to protect oneself from anxiety, especially among young people, and from stress, if not angst, by remaining impassive in an unpredictable and threatening world. How to manage dream life in the time of pandemic, noting the similarities and differences between nine thousand pandemic dreams and the stress of Kuwaitis during the Iraqi occupation, prisoners in Nazi camps, and Middle Eastern populations during the Islamic Spring.

5. Experience

Coercive resilience makes us immune to experience. This is also true of coercive residence, amidst diaries of theologians, psychoanalysts, and memories of good old-fashioned travel when the only possible journey is around one's own room. Despite appearances, the lockdown had nothing Pascalian about it. *Forgetfulness of the world and of everything except God*, Pascal wrote after the mystical crisis that, on November 23, 1654, ended a process of conversion that dated back to 1646. From that moment on, Pascal would only measure himself against the God of wrath and mercy, convinced, as the Jansenist he was, that man cannot save himself by his own deeds but is totally at the mercy of the Almighty, and therefore of predestination and grace. The fact that the pandemic-induced loneliness did not provoke mass conversions (as some expected, not without naivety), notwithstanding the possibility of still believing for those who already did, is therefore not surprising. The experience we are dealing with is of a different kind, and, in a certain sense, even more interesting – indeed, I would say, more promising. The pandemic has shown how a society can be transformed overnight. Perhaps not completely, but certainly to a great extent, and there is no reason to limit the change to the green revolution. Rather than the weakness of nature, the virus reveals the weakness of humans without a welfare state that promotes public health, public education, public nature, and fair taxation. Well, it is hard to deny that. But where should we start? From labour, or rather from a mobilisation that we do not recognise as labour but which produces much more value than toil in fields and factories. One might say that, by a strange trick of reason, while satisfying their desires, humans work for their unemployment: this is undoubtedly a misfortune, but only until we recognise that this working for one's unemployment is the only activity in which no machine can ever replace a human being. What we need is a radical change in the concept of labour, so that we no longer see it as the (automatable) production of goods and services, but as the production of value, which is to be understood in two senses. All the goods that are produced and all the services that are provided would have no value without humans, who are therefore the positive, non-subordinate pole of automation. A world of machines without humans is inconceivable, while a world of humans without machines would just be very inconvenient. If we understand this, we will realise that in the struggle with the machine, the human is always the master, not the slave. Hence the change of perspective needed to transform shock into experience and not simply resilience. Humans are the only organisms that defer death by means of technology, and for this very reason they are the masters of technology, which without them would have no meaning or purpose. Once it is understood that machines depend on humans, and that such dependence is all the greater the higher the degree of complexity of the automaton, we can relaunch a master-slave dialectic in which humans recognise their superiority over machines. When the head of Google's search sector states: »16 to 20 % of queries that get asked every day have never been asked before«[2] he seems to treat us like little brats driving mum crazy (last year Google's algorithm changed 4.887 times, how much patience it takes to keep up with you!), but his statement actually shows the total subordination of the automaton to the souls that make it work. On its own, the machine wouldn't do anything, the Web would fall into absolute lethargy, into an endless stand-by state, because the machine has no ur-

---

[2] Mitchell: How Google Search Really Works.

gency or need, doesn't get tired, doesn't get hungry, and doesn't die, so it has no temporality, no finality, no will, and no responsibility: it has no reason to search anything on the Web.

6. Rejuvenation

»Standing, now, on an immense sort of terrace of Elsinore that stretches from Basel to Cologne, bordered by the sands of Nieuport, the marshes of the Somme, the limestone of Champagne, the granites of Alsace [...] our Hamlet of Europe is watching millions of ghosts. But he is an intellectual Hamlet, meditating on the life and death of truths; for ghosts, he has all the subjects of our controversies; for remorse, all the titles of our fame. [...] Every skull he picks up is an illustrious skull. This one was Leonardo. [...] And that other skull was Leibnitz, who dreamed of universal peace. And this one was Kant ... and Kant begat Hegel, and Hegel begat Marx, and Marx begat [...]. Hamlet hardly knows what to make of so many skulls. But suppose he forgets them! Will he still be himself?«[3]

This is what Valéry wrote exactly one hundred years before the virus radically changed our lives in Wuhan. The war had taught him that civilisations are mortal, he concluded. I do not share his view: civilisations do not turn out to be mortal, if anything they die in their sleep or *of* sleep. What comes forward in times of crisis is rather the feeling of an old age of the world that prevents us from seeing what is good and new despite the catastrophe. As I write these lines, the fourth wave is creeping forward, and it is now twenty months since the first hints of a strange virus in a remote Chinese town. Will it ever end? Will vaccines, waves, green passes, *revanchisms* and rebellions continue to occupy our thoughts and transform our lives? The only prediction I can hazard is that the virus will not wipe out our species. I write this in a much lighter spirit because not only if I am wrong, no one will survive to hold this miscalculation against me, but above all because the carnage will bring about the triumph of the environment and the final crisis of capitalism which seemed to be the main concern of large parts of humanity in recent decades. One often has the impression that, for some people, disenchantment with the world, i.e. human progress, is a negative event because it sets the stage for the destruction of the environment. But there is no continuity from disenchantment with the world to the environmental disaster. It would therefore be illusory to think that re-enchanting nature and introducing superstitious and animistic attitudes is the ideological precondition for environmental protection. On the contrary, if we do so, we will continue to ravage the environment, and we will only make it worse, because we will not be sustained by the

[3] Valéry: An Anthology, pp. 99 f.

light of reason and technical and scientific awareness, and on top of that we will go back to burning witches. And are we sure that the West believes in the myth of infinite progress? It seems to me that this has long been a minority Faustianism, whereas the prevailing ideology by far is – in theory, of course, in practice it is a different kettle of fish – that of skimping, limiting, renouncing. However, we can be certain of one thing: growth can never be infinite, because not only every human being, but humanity as a whole, is mortal. So, raising the problem of the limits of development in general is a reflection of the Promethean attitude whose problematic nature we have already seen. Given that we will not last indefinitely, what we can try to do is to rejuvenate the world by introducing (and this is precisely what the history of our relations with technology teaches us) elements of continuous regeneration. People tend to underestimate the present, and often consider it the worst of all possible worlds and times, simply because they do not bother to compare it with the past. If we go back a hundred years from now, what do we find? A humanity freshly emerged from two catastrophes without common measure. First, the Spanish flu (which spread in a time without the web, globalisation, etc.): then, there was no such thing as intensive care units in hospitals; no such issue as testing tourists returning from their holidays; no such matter as a world market brought to its knees by the crisis, and so on. And, above all, there was a much bigger problem: the First World War, an organised extermination in which it was considered right and patriotic to send thousands of young people to die. In a single day at Verdun or on the Somme a far greater number of young people died than all the elderly people who died in Lombardy due to Covid, and, what's worse, these young people died because someone sent them to die. All this seems totally inconceivable at present. Are we denying that 2021 is a preferable time to 1921? To the unconvinced who might find some cause for nostalgia for the lives of our great-grandparents, I suggest we go back to 1621. Europe is ravaged by the plague and torn apart by the Thirty Years' War. Shall we go back to 1521? On August 13 of that year Cortes finally expelled Tenochtitlán, at least two hundred thousand Aztecs died of starvation during the siege, and soon nine-tenths of Mexico's population would die, mainly from a flu brought by the immunised Conquistadores. The only effective way to counter conspiracy theories is to mitigate the unhappiness, the frustrations, the injustices that drive humans to console themselves with such views. But in doing so, one must be aware that even in this case, now that humanity is increasingly free of need and suffering, there will always be some who say that we are dealing with a neo-liberal conspiracy to dull our consciousness.

If history makes sense, it is because reason moves forward; if it went backwards, history would not only be depressing but would be a careless fable that forecloses the possibility of a future. The history of humankind involves progressive settlement, of which confinement – which was forced but only accelerated an ongoing process that coincides with human civilisation – is simply a stage. Of course, when the pandemic is hopefully over, this will not prevent us from enjoying the pleasure of physical contact and the freedom to go wherever we like. Only, it will be a pleasure, not a necessity: I may well walk on a beach or in a forest, but my livelihood does not depend on catching fish with a spear gun, nor does my life expectancy depend on my ability to fight Grizzly bears. Catastrophism lends a spiritual quality even to the face of a lunatic. Enlightenment, the belief in progress, has the opposite effect: it exposes every idea to the accusation of superficiality, connivance and stupidity. What is ironic, if I may say so, is that this catastrophism is taking place at a time when it is possible to think of a humanity finally freed from work, having freed itself from the systematic use of war and from the idea that some human beings are naturally destined to slavery. The fact is that pessimism is an easy attitude to adopt, which exempts the pessimist from fighting for themselves and for humanity in the name of a better world. Moreover, pessimists do not take any responsibility, since progress goes on anyway, whereas progressives, if they are really such, have to take charge of the conceptual understanding and political governance of progress. This is why I consider optimism to be a moral duty, because if we were really convinced that nothing we do can improve the lot of humankind, or that whatever we do will only make it worse, then we should have the courage to shut up shop, pack up our bags, and turn off the lights.

7. Labour

Why do I say that we are more and more free? Paradoxical as it may seem, I base this view on experience. Consider the fifty liras coin that was in circulation in the Italian Republic for much of the twentieth century. It depicted a *homo faber* – a naked man who did not cause scandal only because he represented Hephaestus. He was represented beating on an anvil with a hammer, and I doubt that he was doing it to burn calories: in those days, humankind did not have the issue of fitness because it was often engaged in hard, harmful and exhausting work. Is beating on an anvil without even a pair of trousers and a shirt somehow noble? It depends. Rather than lying on the floor with the sole company of bad liquor, it is better to go and bang on an anvil with a hammer in order to get something to sustain oneself and one's family. But it would be even better if a machine were beating on the anvil, and the human merely controlled the production process: the evolution of the industrial economy has gone precisely in that direction. And once we have artificial intelligence systems that make it unnecessary to control the production process, and perhaps also the distribution process, is there any point in regretting the good old days when we stood in the forge hammering on red-hot iron? For years I woke up at five o'clock to write, and I still tend to do so, strength permitting. But I would never go for a run: I believe that the essence of human beings does not lie in exertion, otherwise a convict at Lepanto would be the happiest of men. I believe there is satisfaction in completing a task, and more radically in fulfilling a duty, and this is properly human, but nowhere does it say that the task ahead of us must be an imperfect imitation of a machine, as was the case for the worker in Modern Times. The pandemic produced much unemployment, but at the same time it confirmed that it is not by chasing the past that we can solve the problems of the present, let alone generate a desirable future. Galleys used to be pushed by chained and whipped rowers; then, for centuries, we have used engines, and now, seeing that they pollute, we use nuclear submarines that pollute less. The fields used to be worked by thousands of farmers, now just a few machines are needed for the job and the harvest is bigger. And, let's not forget, washing machines were also a great liberation. The way has been known and mapped out since an early ingenious ancestor used fire, a wheel and a stick to perform tasks that would have been far more tiring and alienating with his bare hands. A man »Who works in mud / Who knows no peace / Who fights for a crust of bread / Who dies by a yes or no«[4] is much less human than someone who spends their time on a mobile phone, and is much closer to homo faber than homo sapiens. The slogan »work sets you free«, found on the gate of Auschwitz, is not only tragically ironic, but also an epitaph on the era of work, which we can leave behind just as we did with the age of military glory: as long as the dignity of the human being is recognised in doing rather than in knowing, humanity will appear as a fragile construct that is far removed from the wisdom we presume to have. The lockdown has taught us that a form of human life can take place, albeit with limitations, through the mediation of technical devices. What we need to reflect on is that without technology there can be no human beings, but only particularly disadvantaged animals; above all, without human beings there can be no technology.

8. Consumption

I can imagine an obvious objection: *Automation may well be the grand thing you say it is, but it will still take our jobs away*. I would reply that what cannot be automated is consumption, and all the production in the world cannot take place without consumption. For this reason, humanity has a great opportunity, which it must understand and orientate politically: it must no longer be a producer or distributor of goods, i.e. an appendage of machines, but a producer of values. As

---

[4] Levi: Survival in Auschwitz.

long as there are humans carrying out tasks that, like a large part of logistics, distribution and production, can be automated, the door will always be open for tragedies like the death of Luana D'Orazio or Adil Belakhdim. It is certainly necessary, for the time being, to safeguard and protect these jobs, and first and foremost these people, but the aim of a humanity worthy of the name is to make such jobs disappear, obviously by guaranteeing alternative occupations for those who currently perform them. We are familiar with the dystopia of a world of outcasts, in which machines have replaced humans in every way, perhaps even in consumption. But to seriously believe this means not understanding what automation is and what consumption is. Let us think about this for a moment. Automation is the answer to human needs that cannot be automated; therefore, the more automation grows, the more dependent machines become on humans. Now, a machine can do anything except consume, in the sense that if it runs out of energy, it does not die, as organisms do, but only stops working and resumes as soon as the electricity comes back. Unique among all other organisms, humans have deployed an impressive number of technologies, from fire to writing to culture in general, precisely because they are driven by consumption, by the vital urge which obviously also turns into a spiritual urge. Inversely, machines exist only in function of humans, of their needs, of their mortality, and this applies first of all to the universal machine that is artificial intelligence. Useless as appendages to spades, lathes, and typewriters, humans are irreplaceable as appendages to knives and forks, to movies, concerts, novels, and of course many other less commendable but exclusively human entertainments. The problem with the last few decades leading up to the virus – which is often reduced to the failure to provide leaders that are as smart as the person making the complaint – points in spite of everything to a world beyond capital or beyond neo-liberalism, exploiting the social capital of solidarity produced by the pandemic and the new sense of responsibility dictated by the crisis. All of these things, when laid out plainly, turn out to be wishful thinking. But a conceptual effort can be made to make sense of them. The communist utopia exalts labour, for reasons that can be explained historically but which are out of date today, and remains chained (to use a fitting expression) to an industrial society. As for the Bible, it is the fruit of a peasant and pastoral civilisation; I doubt that the expulsion from Eden or the birth of labour would have been conceivable for a society of hunter-gatherers (the one represented by Cain), i.e. for the largest part of human history by far. Leaving aside the myths of the industrial and agricultural society, and without upholding the virtuous but limiting poverty of hunter-gatherers (what would a hospital, a library or a concert hall look like in a world of hunter-gatherers?), I think the most desirable option is to conceive a new era – the one that has opened up through the Internet. Indeed, what is the present? It's a time when work in the traditional sense, born with agriculture and continued with industry, is occupying less and less of our lives. This is how we must try to understand the present in order to squeeze out of it the sweetness of life attributed to the myth of the good savage, just as (and with stronger reasons) Talleyrand regretted the Ancien Régime. We can have those good things without the side effects of a life in the bush or of unacceptable social injustices. Labour, in a progressive sense, is anything that produces value, even if it is not intentional or born of the purpose of generating value, but simply of consuming and responding to needs. This was not the case until recently, but today, with the web recording our consumption and turning it into the capital of artificial intelligence, it is the simple truth. If we manage to redistribute this capital with political wisdom, we will be as happy as bushmen without missing out on sources of well-being and culture to which we have become accustomed and which I doubt we will be able to forget. Humans will be able to cease all activity as producers of goods, but without losing an ounce of weight in the production of goods, first and foremost by creating value. This transformation is not due to the acceleration of production processes resulting from the exploitation of human workforce, but rather to the *automation* of production processes made possible by the exploitation of human consumption and mobilisation which, recorded on the web, are transformed into artificial intelligence. The latter is the faithful, and therefore rarely flattering, record of what we are and what we want. Now, since it is not only imperturbable but also patient and untiring, artificial intelligence can take things that would otherwise go to waste for lack of documents, time and energy and turn them into a resource to capitalise on. Who would sit at a person's bedside and measure their biorhythm? Yet if this person gets a smartwatch, they will produce value even while sleeping (because biorhythms are useful). Not to mention what we do when we are awake: the dictation mechanism I am using right now is recording the words I say, which in turn will make the system of transforming speech into writing more effective; and this also applies to automatic translators and an infinite number of tools. Humans are now only the largely unwitting instructors, while machines are becoming the increasingly autonomous executors. This is the point that must drive our reflection: when we no longer need to be the prostheses of machines, two conditions are created. On the one hand, we wonder what we will do, now that we have now lost that sense of purpose that came from performing a job. Well, we need to understand that we, all of humanity – children, the elderly, the unemployed, the otherwise employed – produce value on the Internet because for the first time in the history of the world consumption is systematically recorded and then transformed into value through a process of capitalisation. For the first time in the history of the world, living *as such* is value production. Now humans can act as humans, not as tools or energy reserves. And acting as a human means manifesting desires and exercising consumption, which is the one thing that can never be automated. I can automate production, and that is undoubtedly intelligent; I can automate distribution, and that is also very intelligent. But there is nothing more senseless than automating desires and consumption, because the purpose and meaning of production and distribution is precisely to satisfy desires and consumption. If Internet platforms achieve such tremendous benefits, it is simply because they are factories relying on an immense number of unpaid workers. Yet it would be absurd for workers to complain of any alienation whatsoever, since access to the web is voluntary and satisfies our needs. But one must not forget that without those needs, Internet platforms would die in the space of a morning. When humans are no longer an appendage of a technical apparatus that can do without their contribution — namely, toil and boredom — they do not disappear from the economic horizon, but take on their essential function, which no machine can ever replace. Human labour becomes the work of the spirit, which does not consist in composing verses or conceiving sublime doctrines (this can still be done, but not by everyone or all day long), but in consuming, under the drive of organic needs and their social metamorphoses. It consists in manifesting interests, desires, even follies and rivalries, and all the variety of the human life form that remains absolutely impermeable and incomprehensible to a machine. The work of the spirit, thus, consists in unfolding the biosphere as the *raison d'être* of the docusphere (there would be no acts if there were no living organisms embedded in a social context) and of the infosphere — the tip of the iceberg that, however, is only accessible to a few, who possess the means of recording and interpretation, i.e. the platforms.

9. Webfare

I can already hear a second objection: who is going to pay for all this? Well, here's a narrative to consider: the worsening inequality triggered by the virus is fuelled by an economic model that has allowed some of the world's biggest corporations to give billionaire dividends to shareholders, further enriching the world's top billionaires, namely a small group of mostly white men. At the same time, it has made workers and women pay the price of the crisis. We must take advantage of the pandemic to remedy these injustices (though it seems bizarre to ask the virus of inequality to turn into the virus of equality). In short, the common good must be put back at the forefront. Yet somehow, this common-sense principle is often interpreted in the punitive terms of misery loves company. Perhaps this is because it is not clear what the good in question is: a virus that is a precursor of communism or commonism? In these terms it may sound like capitalist *captatio benevolentiae*, or ideological wishful thinking, but it actually makes sense if we consider that here, too, we are dealing with the acceleration of ongoing processes. And here is another narrative, which I am more inclined to believe and hope in.

Internet platforms have gained enormous wealth during the pandemic. Indeed, one would be surprised otherwise, as they have undoubtedly provided us with valuable services. But why did they get *so* rich? Because of the production of value that humanity has delivered, for free, by mobilising itself for the most diverse reasons (consumerism, work, entertainment, sociality) on said platforms. How many pictures of us are stored by surveillance cameras? How much data do we produce every time we search the Web? Compared to this data, our fears about the panopticon and the biopolitical state are not so much misguided as exaggerated, since Internet platforms (at least in the West) are interested in our money, not our ideas or our personal lives. And more than exaggerated, they are misguided, because worrying about privacy hides much bigger problems, and above all great opportunities. While we are busy fearing that Alexa might be spying on us, we do not realise that we are working for free for Alexa and her colleagues, generating unparalleled wealth that, if its origin were recognised, could be distributed and generate a new welfare system. It is therefore necessary to recognise the documedia surplus value, i.e. the unfair exchange between platforms and users. Platforms, as opposed to users, have not only data, but metadata (access to the docusphere); they have proprietary documents (primary accumulation); and finally they have capitalisable documents (as they are interpretable, exploitable, and sellable). For this reason, I propose conceptualising recorded mobilisation as production of value, i.e. as huge invisible labour performed by the young and the old, by the employed and the unemployed. I propose recognising the asymmetry of the exchange between users and platforms (the latter collect much more data, own it, can compare it with the data of many other users, and can sell it like any other commodity). Finally, I propose redistributing the surplus value generated by this asymmetry through a European taxation that would generate what I call Webfare: digital welfare that would allow us to deal in a progressive way with the problems generated by automation and its acceleration in the time of pandemic. It has been said that the pandemic is the so-called darkest hour that distinguishes good leaders from the bad; that it has tested us and revealed our weaknesses, and at the same time that it has brought out a civil society that has proved more robust than the state. Now, I have my doubts about the desirability of this, because the prototypical expression of civil society is precisely found in Internet platforms. Indeed, it has been rightly observed that the dynamic accelerated – and not inaugurated – by the pandemic, consists of a growth of the imperial state, which is anything but unitary, contrary to what was wrongly believed. This imperial state is centralised and controlled in China, decentralised and liberal (or, seen from the Chinese perspective, disharmonious and nihilistic) in the United States, and largely ghost-like in the European Union, which is neither an empire nor an agglomeration of regional sovereign states such as Russia, Turkey, Iran, India or Israel, it being unclear what role to ascribe to what remains of the United Kingdom.

However, if there is one field in which the European Union has undoubtedly shown its usefulness, it has been governance in the pandemic. This is where we should take action, following two directions. The first is the establishment of a European approach to welfare, based on platform taxation. The second is the constitution of a European army which, centralizing under a single command the essential prerogative of the state over capital, i.e. the monopoly of the legitimate use of force, can finally answer the question of who is ultimately in charge of decision-making in the European Union: not simply a general, of course, but a general reporting to a politician or a council, which would therefore be defined as a last-resort determination of political decision-making. As I have no idea how to develop this second course of action, I will only make a few suggestions on the first. It is not so much a question of regretting jobs that in the pandemic turned out to be fragile, but of recognising the relentless production of value, i.e. the enormous invisible labour, that humanity performs by connecting to the web — whenever we do so, we are enriching the platforms instead of ourselves, simply because we are not aware that we are working. Hence my political proposal: instead of dreaming of wealth taxation or blaming platforms for their wealth (it is obvious that a factory that does not pay its workers can only get richer), let us try to redistribute it through fair taxation, initiating a Webfare system for which the pandemic has laid the foundations in terms of technological acceleration, but which must be understood conceptually and oriented politically. The pandemic crisis is a stress test for welfare. There is no doubt about it: we have lost the old welfare, and nothing can give it back to us. There is little point in simply relaunching Keynes or proposing (to whom?) a new social pact. What can be done, however, is create a completely new one. What kind? There is one issue that old welfare could not see, and which the welfare of the future is based on. Ninety years ago Keynes prophesied that today automation would make it enough to work fifteen hours a week, and that we would have to think about how to occupy that enormous amount of free time. The prophecy has been fulfilled in a peculiar way, because many people do not work at all, since automation has taken away their jobs, but spend fifteen hours *a day* on the computer, producing value. Where does that feeling of over-employment come from if we are not working or are unemployed? If we want to avoid people unwittingly fighting for their own unemployment by feeding artificial intelligence, we need to reconceptualise labour. Instead of regretting, I do not know how sincerely and certainly not very sensibly, the fields and factories, let us consider that now, thanks to the Web, something very important is happening, namely the fact that consumption automatically translates into the production of value. If we manage to overcome the narrow and ephemeral concept of humans as producers of goods instead of values, if we manage to recognise them also as consumers and as bearers of bodiliness as well as, obviously, of creativity, then we will see that the fundamental activity that humans carry out is care, for themselves and for others. Indeed, this situation is not exactly unprecedented, as it presents significant analogies with life in late antiquity: in Rome and Constantinople, enormous masses of consumers lived without productive necessity, since functions that are now performed by automation were then fulfilled by the slave economy. The urban masses of consumers, however, had only marginal economic utility, as they produced political consensus. The documedia revolution, on the other hand, made it possible to transform consumption into not just a political but an economic value, laying the foundations for a taxation system capable of restarting humanity as such, supporting it in its needs and making it flourish. This is something that has been impossible for millennia and that we can and must do today, throwing away, together with homo faber, the saddest law of the sad science of economics: the one that says *nothing is ever for free*.

10. Education

I can imagine a final objection, which is not as naive or futile as some would be inclined to think: i.e.m »without work we will be bored«. Well, it depends on the work. Boredom, this delicate monster, condemns jobs that were once bearable and secure (typist, bank clerk, town clerk), and makes them not only undesirable *de facto* (they no longer exist) but also *de iure* (even if they did exist, no one would be willing to do them). Let us think about it. The true machine-doctor is the GP, not the one who, assisted by machines, takes over the management of human relations. Today, those who reproach artists for not working hard, for exhibiting works *that we could make ourselves* or, worse still, that we could buy at a much more reasonable price in a supermarket, are considered petty bourgeois and uneducated. But why should supposedly non-artists have to endure either the inconveniences of an artist's life, i.e. the risk, uncertainty and evanescence that have become the rule of life in a post-industrial society — or a return to a life of toil, manual labour, industriality without industriousness, alienation and boredom? And, conversely, why should a platform owner be the lowest rank of humanity, while the conceptual (or lazy) artist the highest? They both invent things; they both generate value where there was none; they both earn more than we think is legitimate. But while artists exploit the desire for consumption of the rich, and once paid, nothing can be demanded of them, platform owners exploit the desire for consumption of all and, by offering services and not objects, are more exposed to retaliation: *if you don't give us back a part of your profits, we will stop using you, and you are done.* If Baudelaire had worked in a furnace he would not have said that working is less boring than having fun. And certainly writing the *Fleurs du Mal* is a job that automation will not steal from anyone, and it is a much more effective response to the *delicate monster* of boredom than the life of Bartleby the scrivener, secured but boring, or that of the Wolf of Wall Street, not boring but harmful to himself and others. Without consumption — that is, without the spring of human mobilisation that drove our ancestors to hunt, then to cultivate, finally to produce industrially, and which today leads us to spend our lives on the web both to meet needs and to keep boredom at bay — the history I have described so far would not have taken place. Except — and this is the point we must not miss — the web has introduced a qualitative leap in this progression: traditionally, consumption left no trace, apart from skins, bones or tins. Today, instead, material and spiritual consumption — i.e. all forms of human life poured onto the web — is recorded and produces value: data is collected and systematised by platforms that turn it into automation, distribution, knowledge, and wealth. In the light of what has been said, it is clear that the fundamental character of the human being is consumption. Of course, this is not to be confused with consumerism, though unfortunately it is not always apparent. Consumption is not simply a matter of pulling out *some Fritos corn chips Dr. Pepper and an Ole Moon Pie waiting for a junk food high* as Larry Groce used to sing, but also consists in reading, educating oneself, enjoying the pleasures of the spirit, in other words getting ever closer to *homo sapiens* — which is not a starting point, but a point of arrival. Consumption, too often seen as the burden of the white, capitalist man, is therefore the destiny of homo sapiens: it means doing things that are beyond the reach of a machine, i.e. growing up as a human being by consuming books and education, deliberating politically like the Roman senators who enjoyed the perfect but inhumane automation of slavery. Of course, nothing perfectly straight can be made out of the crooked wood of humanity, but the human is the only animal that can be educated. If I teach a horse to do tricks in a circus, I turn it into a clown; if I teach a child to read, to write, to respect others and to know the world, I offer it much more than if I teach it to sew footballs, when a machine can do it. How did Leibniz put it?

»If someone looks attentively at more pictures of plants and animals than another person, and at more diagrams of machines and descriptions and depictions of houses and fortresses, and if he reads more imaginative novels and listens to more strange stories, then he can be said to have more knowledge than the other, even if there is not a word of truth in all that he has seen and heard. That is because the practice he has had in portraying in his mind a great many actual, explicit conceptions and ideas makes him better able to conceive what is put to him. He will certainly be better educated, better trained, and more capable than someone who has seen and read and heard nothing — provided that he takes nothing in these stories and pictures to be true which really is not so, and that these impressions do not prevent him in other contexts from distinguishing the real from the imaginary, the existent from the possible«.[5]

---

5   Leibniz: New Essays on Human Understanding, p. 355.

What Leibniz describes to us, against Cartesian asceticism, is a consumer crapula linked to the spirit, i. e. the education of *homo sapiens*.

11. Value

Remember aphorism 211 from *Beyond Good and Evil*, contained in the section on the *free spirit*? Nietzsche writes, among other things:

»true philosophers are commanders and legislators: they say ›That is how it should be!‹ they are the ones who first determine the ›where to?‹ and ›what for?‹ of people, which puts at their disposal the preliminary labor of all philosophical laborers, all those who overwhelm the past. True philosophers reach for the future with a creative hand and everything that is and was becomes a means, a tool, a hammer for them. Their ›knowing‹ is creating, their creating is a legislating, their will to truth is – will to power. – Are there philosophers like this today? Have there ever been philosophers like this? Won't there have to be philosophers like this?«.[6]

Fortunately, no. To think that the determination of our values should be in the hands of someone like Nietzsche gives one the creeps, and it would not be too reassuring if even the most judicious philosopher were to take his place. However, this aphorism says something not about philosophers, but about humanity. Indeed, workers, not in philosophy but of any other kind, are disappearing, in a slow but irreversible process. Instead of regretting the past, let us ask ourselves if it is not possible to give to every human being the function of value creation that Nietzsche ascribed to philosophers. To do so, I have three suggestions. The first is to abandon the idea that the only way to qualify as a political subject is to be a victim, because victimhood is just resignation: you don't help migrants or delivery riders by sympathising with them, but by creating a different world. To do so, it is useless to restore some Spartacist morality drawn from the class struggle, which has ended along with the productive cycle that made it possible. Instead, we should think of the present moment not as a terminal phase of the revolutionary cycle that began in 1789, but as a new age, similar to that which led from feudal anarchy to the genesis of the sovereign state. In the historical example we all know, the king summoned the feudal lords to Versailles and made them his dependents; in the history we are yet to write, the European Union should subordinate the new dukes and barons, i. e. the platforms, to the higher ends of the common good, taxing their surplus value, the fruit of the labour of all humanity, and redistributing it in terms of welfare. This brings us to the second suggestion, namely that

---

[6] Nietzsche: Basic Writings, p. 324.

we have entered a new era of labour. If, as has traditionally been the case in situations of rudimentary automation, the purpose of labour is to perform actions that can be better performed by machines, it is evident that the growth of automation infallibly coincides with the disappearance of labour, because, all things being equal, a machine is always more profitable than a human. This is for very good reasons: a machine never gets tired, it never dies, it has no rights and it does not retire. But, fortunately, labour is not just that. No longer an appendage of the machine, today we can work as human beings, i.e. first and foremost as bearers of needs that a machine will never have; of goals (a machine can well go to Mars, but only if we ask it to); and of interests, (we decide whether a machine is useful or not). No longer interesting or useful as a producer of goods, humankind finds a different focal point as a producer of data, that is, as a producer of value. The third suggestion may seem paradoxical, but it follows directly from the previous ones. The labour of homo faber deserves to be mourned only if we do not consider that its end will usher in the universalisation of the only work worthy of a human being: the work of the spirit, the work of *homo sapiens*, the manifestation of freedom instead of necessity. In 1919, in the aftermath of a crisis compared to which ours is laughable, Keynes wrote *The Economic Consequences of the Peace*, in which, unheeded, he warned against the harshness of the conditions imposed on the defeated, and laid the foundations for the Marshall Plan. Today I would be happy if a revived Keynes wrote *The Economic Consequences of Freedom*. Many would argue that China, which has nationalised the platforms by implementing welfare but also establishing the most perfect surveillance state in history, will be the next world empire. I doubt it. The spirit is free by definition, without necessarily being wise, good, or intelligent. And if freedom is an obstacle for the planned economy, in the platform economy there is nothing more profitable than freedom as an expression of the infinite and often irrational forms of human life. That is why the platform economy was born in the United States, and China has merely rationalised it. Europe, if it is able to do so, may have the task of transforming it into a liberal welfare proposal.

References

Caruso, Paola: Da Al Bano a Madonna: il coronavirus e gli scivoloni dei vip, in: Corriere della Sera, July 30, 2020, https://www.corriere.it/moda/cards/da-bano-madonna-coronavirus-scivoloni-vip/al-bano.shtml; last accessed August 12, 2021.

Leibniz, Gottfried Wilhelm: New Essays on Human Understanding, Cambridge 1996.

Levi, Primo: Survival in Auschwitz, New York 1995.
Mitchell, Jon: How Google Search Really Works, in: Readwrite, February 29, 2012, https://readwrite.com/2012/02/29/interview_changing_engines_mid-flight_qa_with_goog/; last accessed August 12, 2021.
Nietzsche, Friedrich: Basic Writings, New York 2000.
Valéry, Paul: An Anthology, Princeton 1977.

Volker Kronenberg and Christopher Prinz

Politics and Science: Greater, More Ambitious. Countering the Temptations of (Post-)Pandemic Politics*

On June 14th, 2021, as these lines were written, Johns Hopkins University's *Covid-19 Dashboard* – whose updates over the past one and a half years have been followed with a sense of hope and not infrequently dread not just by virologists, epidemiologists, and infectious disease specialists but by some members of the general public as well – reported a mere 101 new SARS-CoV-2 infections in Germany, the lowest number since August 2nd of the previous year.[1] On the same day, more than 40 million people in Germany, or about 48.7 percent of the total population, had received at least one dose of their Covid-19 vaccines. Having gotten off to a slow start compared to some other Western nations and receiving a fair bit of warranted criticism, more than 800,000 people (roughly one percent of the country's total population) were being vaccinated in Germany on a daily basis by June of 2021[2] against this »mysterious lung disease«[3], which first appeared on the world stage at the end of 2019. There is no doubt that, as has been the case with so many viruses we have learned to live with over time, this novel coronavirus is unlikely to simply disappear. And yet, life *after* Covid or *with* Covid will resemble its *pre-*Covid normalcy in several areas, as is already evident today. Certainly, many of the things we have learned and adopted during the pandemic – especially those that have proven useful in our daily lives, such as video conferences when the schedule does not allow for physical face-to-face meetings – are changes we probably *want* to embrace permanently. However, this may apply even more so to the *regained* physical closeness with our loved ones, a previously integral part of our lives and of vital importance to our mental *and* physical health, especially to the elderly, whose loss many feared – and quite a few had to mourn. At this stage of the pan-

---

* The authors would like to give a special thanks to Dr. Philipp Adorf for translating the manuscript of this essay.
1 Cf. Johns Hopkins University: Covid-19 Dashboard by the Center for Systems Science and Engineering.
2 Cf. Bundesministerium für Gesundheit: Aktueller Impfstatus.
3 Cf. DER SPIEGEL: Zentralchina meldet mysteriöse Lungenkrankheit.

demic, it seems appropriate to undertake a few, almost retrospective, fundamental reflections on two — by no means novel — phenomena that in recent months have once again become the focus of politics, society, and science as well.

1. The Authoritarian Temptation

While immediately invoking Carl Schmitt's dictum would serve no purpose but to simply state the obvious, it would nonetheless border on negligence to underestimate the socio-psychological significance of the state of emergency that both politics and society have operated in for the past 14 months: As Chancellor Angela Merkel already noted in her now historic televised address on March 18th, 2020, this was indeed the first such state of emergency since the end of World War II,[4] affecting the *entirety* of the population and subjecting it to government measures that deeply and, above all, *tangibly* intervened in their daily private lives. In light of their extensive and seemingly expanding consequences, it is not scientifically unsavory but rather almost necessary to interpret the measures meant to »combat«[5] the Covid pandemic — this bellicose formulation alone can serve as justification — through the analytical application of the *state of exception*, as it was (re)popularized during the interwar period:

>»The rule of law presupposes the existence of a stable and predictable world. But events never unfold in a perfectly smooth and repetitive way. To the contrary, they are often complicated by the sudden appearance of the unexpected. It is exactly this that justifies granting executive power, conceived as distinct in its character and purpose from legislative power, its own sphere of application. [...] But once the particular case assumes an extreme form, as an unforeseen and imminent danger, and the normal rhythms of public life are disrupted by extraordinary circumstances, the need to act promptly and forcefully becomes inescapable.«[6]

In fact, the pandemic created an environment not dissimilar to »when armed conflict breaks out or catastrophe strikes«[7] that is *characteristic* of the ideal type of a state of exception/emergency, in which the »abruptness of the moment condenses and precipitates events«[8], leading to the aforementioned necessity for prompt

---

[4] Cf. Presse- und Informationsamt der Bundesregierung: Fernsehansprache von Bundeskanzlerin Angela Merkel.

[5] Along with numerous similar statements by leading actors across a variety of governmental levels, the bellicose rhetoric of *pandemic policy* has extended to the naming of corresponding legal ordinances within the states (cf. Erste Coronabekämpfungsverordnung Rheinland-Pfalz (1. CoBeVo), p. 73).

[6] Rosanvallon: Good Government, pp. 65 f.

[7] Ibid., p. 66.

[8] Ibid.

and forceful action that results in »the supremacy of the executive inevitably impos[ing] itself«[9] as its measures take on the role of veritable life-or-death decisions. In particular during the first few days and weeks during the pandemic as well as in the midst of the so-called *second* and *third waves* in the winter of 2020 and in the spring of 2021, the overarching objective of avoiding excess deaths seemed to often guide the thought-process and actions of both individuals and political decision-makers.[10] As a result, it was not only the pandemic with its spread of the virus, but the extensive measures to contain it as well, which constituted a brutal rupture in the lives of those who were particularly affected by them. This not only impacted the elderly and people dependent on special assistance in nursing homes and care facilities – many of whom were towards the tail end of their twilight years – who spent months in isolation not only from the outside world, but from each other as well. One must, moreover and above all, remember the toll on children and young people. Along with doctors, nurses, and grocery store employees, they bore the brunt of containing the pandemic. The long-term impact of daycare and school closures, their lack of adequate alternatives as well as the inability to grow up in the presence of other adolescents is still being underestimated. This not only pertains to the consequences regarding the mental health of children and adolescents along with their *individual* educational and professional opportunities, but also its impact on society *in general*, which will have to absorb a *Covid Generation* whose emergence politicians of all political stripes had sworn to prevent.[11] This crisis may, however, also contain a seemingly paradoxical spark of hope for the political cultures of the West's liberal democracies, whose capacities to react and strategize are being challenged by Chinese-style digital totalitarianism. Having felt subjected at times to, in reference to Ernst Fraenkel, a state of measures instead of a state of norms,[12] it is the adolescents and young adults of the *Covid Generation* whose experiences may engender a greater appreciation of civil liberties.

9   Ibid.
10 In the public debate on the pandemic, Bundestag president Wolfgang Schäuble (Christian Democratic Union of Germany, CDU) was quick to criticize the notion that the protection of life should take precedence over everything else: »[W]hen I hear that everything else has to take a back seat to the protection of life, then I have to say: This is not correct in such an absolute sense. Fundamental rights constrain one another. If there even is an absolute value in the Basic Law at all, it is human dignity. It is inviolable. But it does not eliminate the fact that we have to die« (Birnbaum / Ismar: Schäuble will dem Schutz des Lebens nicht alles unterordnen).
11 As the federal labor minister Hubertus Heil (Social Democratic Party of Germany, SPD) reminded everyone, »[w]e must do everything to prevent a Covid Generation« (Specht: Die Sorgen der »Generation Corona«). In a similar vein, CDU chairman and state premier of North Rhine-Westphalia, Armin Laschet, said in mid-May of 2021: »The losses the young generation has had to contend with over the past one-and-a-half years, [...] this is something we need to make up for with giant strides« (Süddeutsche Zeitung: Laschet unterrichtet zu Perspektiven für Kinder nach Corona).
12 Cf. Fraenkel: Der Doppelstaat. Of course, even under the conditions of the policies to combat the Covid pandemic, Germany cannot be classified as a »state of measures« in the Fraenkelian sense. The conceptual duo of the »state of measures« and »state of norms« referred to the ambivalent – to put

Especially against the backdrop of the undisputed challenges posed by climate change and the strain placed on the planet's limited capacities by a still growing world population, some scientists motivated by climate and environmental policy concerns already saw post-growth policies as the sole solution for overcoming these daunting problems before the advent of the Covid era – with *post-* or even *de*-growth strategies constituting political stipulations whose implementation probably runs counter to the preferences of democratic majorities.[13] They therefore seemed to succumb to an »authoritarian ecological temptation«[14], in which a »*logic of restrictions*«[15] – comprised of restraint and prohibitions – »appears morally unassailable and necessary«[16], as »democracy [...] becomes a luxury we can no longer afford«[17] and »freedom [...] is reduced to the acceptance of ecological necessities.«[18] One can tacitly hope that while the generation *burned* by Covid may not be *immunized* against political currents that demand the harsh imposition of restrictions, no matter how noble the intentions behind them purport to be, it will nonetheless be more critical of them. A similar effect could also occur regarding the faith placed in the state by German citizens in particular, even beyond crisis situations: Although a national pandemic plan drawn up by the country's disease control and prevention agency (Robert Koch Institute) had been in place since 2005 (having been updated in 2017)[19] with an additional risk analysis based on the spread of a (then still) fictional new SARS virus drafted in 2012 explicitly warning that in the event of such a pandemic »[t]he personnel and material capacities«[20] of the health care system »would not be sufficient to maintain the usual level of care,«[21] it is hard to shake the impression of Germany having been inadequately prepared for this pandemic. *Could* a better level of preparation have been achieved? Certainly. What would have been the impact, however, on the *day-to-day* capacity to act of a state that prepares for a »once every 100 to 1,000 years«[22] crisis event – as the risk analysis itself stated concerning a possible

---

it kindly – »legal« environment of the Third Reich. Nevertheless, the terminological pair, »stripped« of its role in the analysis of Nazi Germany's legal practice, can certainly be converted into a sensible criterion for the political science analysis of »policies to combat« Covid-19. Political scientist Claus Leggewie warned, for example, as early as March of 2020 of a long-term »danger that we are now willingly or unwillingly growing used to an authoritarian state of measures [...]« (Koldehoff: »Gefahr, dass wir uns an autoritären Maßnahmenstaat gewöhnen«).

13 Cf. Paech: Der »grüne« Fortschritt ist gescheitert, pp. 217 ff.
14 Fücks: Ökologie und Freiheit, p. 18.
15 Ibid.
16 Ibid.
17 Ibid., p. 19.
18 Ibid.
19 Cf. Robert-Koch-Institut: Nationaler Pandemieplan Teil I; Robert-Koch-Institut: Nationaler Pandemieplan Teil II.
20 Deutscher Bundestag: Bericht zur Risikoanalyse im Bevölkerungsschutz 2012, p. 73.
21 Ibid.
22 Ibid., p. 56.

new SARS pandemic – with the constant specter of a state of emergency looming over both the state and society? Especially within the increasingly secular societies of Western Europe, we continue to appear incapable of finding an appropriate conduct concerning the concept of contingency, which – this is not really a new insight either – decisively (co-)determines our entire private and public life while largely escaping our control and general predictability. And yet, it has been kind to us in the context of the Covid pandemic: Had the 2012 models come true during the 2020/21 crisis, the safe haven of a vaccine would still be well beyond the horizon.[23] These considerations lead to the second phenomenon that – once again – became apparent during the crisis.

2. The Technocratic Temptation

According to historian Pierre Rosanvallon, by the end of the 19th century in France and the United States, the »ideal of competence«[24] began to assume a dominant position in the public discourse and, above all, in the intellectual assessment of the *politics* of democratic political systems. What might not appear particularly objectionable at first glance, was an attempt, however, to legitimize a »technological view of reason as a progressive form of social generality by comparison with the unruly emotions of the masses«[25] – in other words, the sentiments of the democratic majority. This culminated in the notion that »[b]y narrowing the scope for political influence«[26] – and thereby ridding democracy of its »partisan poison«[27] along with its inherent traits of weighing conflicting interests, negotiation, as well as its regularly maligned compromises – »it would once again become possible to promote the general interest, only now more effectively than before.«[28] Shortly after the end of World War I, the term *technocracy* would enter political dictionaries, depicted by its proponents as a system »in which the resources of the nation were marshaled and deployed by experts for the common good.«[29]

While some voices in that particular era sang the praises of a supposedly neutral *administrative* elite holding the reins of power, in our day calls demanding *science* to influence if not outright determine political decisions in all spheres of public life have become more vocal – a trend whose fashionability preceded the

---

23 Cf. ibid., p. 61.
24 Rosanvallon: Good Government, p. 62.
25 Ibid.
26 Ibid., p. 64.
27 Ibid.
28 Ibid.
29 Ibid.

pandemic. This is illustrated by the »Listen to the science!« slogan of the *Fridays for Future* movement, a mantra that also gained widespread popularity in the pandemic policy context.[30] However: Not only the first, but all demands of this kind – translating supposedly neutral scientific findings, not exclusively but in particular within the fields of virology and climatology, into policy – fundamentally contradict not only liberal democracy as a political order, but also run counter to its enlightened scientific paradigm, which deliberately contests the existence of any *final* knowledge settling scientific questions once and for all. Whereas the state on the one hand should avoid giving the impression of possessing the absolute capacity to plan and control everyday life and guarantee a maximum of risk minimization, all those in the world of science who strive for progress in their respective fields would be equally well advised to not idolize progress in research as the ultimate truth. What, if not a generalized skepticism, according to which »every scientific fact is nothing more than a lie, which has not yet been recognized as such«[31], should instead constitute the driving force behind science? In this regard, Max Weber already demonstrated a better understanding more than a century ago than those who consider the future to be no more than a mere »extrapolation of the present.«[32] In simple yet impressive words, he pointed out that »[e]very one of us in science is aware that whatever he has worked on will be obsolete in 10, 20, 50 years. That is the fate, indeed: that is the *meaning* of scientific work.«[33]

Scientific findings should undoubtedly be incorporated into political decisions and form a *part* of the foundations they rest on. And political decisions are indeed often taken in opposition to the prevailing mood of public opinion, the democratic majority of the day. However, when on the one hand scientists actually profess to be the voice of indisputable scientific conclusions, embracing labels that the media has bestowed upon them due to the necessity of condensing complex questions, while *politics* is, on the other hand, reduced to the simple implementation of merely preliminary and, moreover, subject-specific scientific findings, both cease to be what they are, both lose their social function within the structure of a liberal democracy. Science and politics are both greater and more than this, more complex, more ambitious.

---

[30] Cf. Stokowski: Hört. Auf. Die. Wissenschaft.
[31] Kany: Die soziale Funktion der Wissenschaft. p. 29.
[32] Laurin: Wirtschaftstheorie aus dem braun-grünen Sumpf.
[33] Weber: Wissenschaft als Beruf, p. 85.

References

Birnbaum, Robert / Georg Ismar: Schäuble will dem Schutz des Lebens nicht alles unterordnen, in: Tagesspiegel, April 26, 2020, https://www.tagesspiegel.de/politik/bundestagspraesident-zur-corona-krise-schaeuble-will-dem-schutz-des-lebens-nicht-alles-unterordnen/25770466.html; last accessed June 17, 2021.

Bundesministerium für Gesundheit: Aktueller Impfstatus, June 15, 2021, https://impfdashboard.de/; last accessed June 15, 2021.

DER SPIEGEL: Zentralchina meldet mysteriöse Lungenkrankheit, https://www.spiegel.de/gesundheit/diagnose/wuhan-zentralchina-meldet-mysterioese-lungenkrankheit-a-1303225.html; last accessed June 15, 2021.

Deutscher Bundestag: Unterrichtung durch die Bundesregierung: Bericht zur Risikoanalyse im Bevölkerungsschutz 2012, Drucksache 17/12051, January 03, 2013.

Fraenkel, Ernst: Der Doppelstaat, Hamburg 2001.

Fücks, Ralf: Ökologie und Freiheit. Wie wir Klimaschutz, Demokratie und Marktwirtschaft unter einen Hut bekommen, in: Ralf Fücks/Thomas Köhler (eds.): Soziale Marktwirtschaft ökologisch erneuern. Ökologische Innovationen, wirtschaftliche Chancen und soziale Teilhabe in Zeiten des Klimawandels, Berlin 2019, pp. 15–27.

Johns Hopkins University: Covid-19 Dashboard by the Center for Systems Science and Engineering, https://www.arcgis.com/apps/dashboards/bda7594740fd40299423467b48e9ecf6; last accessed June 15, 2021.

Kany, Jens: Die soziale Funktion der Wissenschaft. Wiederaufnahme eines Forschungsprogramms, Heidelberg 2016.

Koldehoff, Stefan: »Gefahr, dass wir uns an autoritären Maßnahmenstaat gewöhnen«, in: Deutschlandfunk, March 25, 2021, https://www.deutschlandfunk.de/coronakrise-und-grundrechte-gefahr-dass-wir-uns-an.691.de.html?dram:article_id=473298; last accessed June 17, 2021.

Laurin, Stefan: Wirtschaftstheorie aus dem braun-grünen Sumpf, in: Salonkolumnisten, January 13, 2017, https://www.salonkolumnisten.com/niko-paechs-postwachstumsoekonomie-wirtschaftstheorie-aus-dem-braun-gruenen-sumpf/; last accessed June 18, 2021.

Paech, Niko: Der »grüne« Fortschritt ist gescheitert. Nachhaltige Transformation und die Wachstumsfrage, in: Maja Göpel / Heike Leitschuh / Achim Brunnengräber / Pierre Ibisch / Reinhard Loske / Michael Müller / Jörg Sommer / Ernst Ulrich von Weizsäcker (eds.): »Leitkultur« Ökologie? Was war, was ist, was kommt?, Stuttgart 2018, pp. 207–220.

Presse- und Informationsamt der Bundesregierung: Fernsehansprache von Bundeskanzlerin Angela Merkel, in: Die Bundesregierung, March 18, 2020, https://www.bundeskanzlerin.de/bkin-de/aktuelles/fernsehansprache-von-bundeskanzlerin-angela-merkel-1732134; last accessed June 19, 2021.

Robert-Koch-Institut: Nationaler Pandemieplan Teil I. Strukturen und Maßnahmen, Berlin 2017.

Robert-Koch-Institut: Nationaler Pandemieplan Teil II. Wissenschaftliche Grundlagen, Berlin 2017.

Rosanvallon, Pierre: Good Government. Democracy Beyond Elections, Cambridge/London 2018.

Specht, Frank: Die Sorgen der »Generation Corona«, in: Handelsblatt, April 29, 2021, https://www.handelsblatt.com/politik/deutschland/ausbildung-die-sorgen-der-generation-corona/27140756.html?ticket=ST-14792163-E4P4d7sCecHMrlPiDht4-ap4; last accessed June 17, 2021.

Stokowski, Margarete: Hört. Auf. Die. Wissenschaft, in: DER SPIEGEL, April 06, 2021, https://www.spiegel.de/kultur/corona-politik-hoert-auf-die-wissenschaft-kolumne-a-7f2a0621-54b5-41e0-859d-a2b9b5bcbe08; last accessed June 18, 2021.

Süddeutsche Zeitung: Laschet unterrichtet zu Perspektiven für Kinder nach Corona, May 18, 2021, https://www.sueddeutsche.de/politik/landtag-duesseldorf-laschet-unterrichtet-zu-perspektiven-fuer-kinder-nach-corona-dpa.urn-newsml-dpa-com-20090101-210518-99-647117; last accessed June 17, 2021.

Weber, Max: Wissenschaft als Beruf (Max Weber-Gesamtausgabe: Volume I/17 Wissenschaft als Beruf/Politik als Beruf; edited by Wolfgang J. Mommsen/Wolfgang Schuchter/Brigitte Morgenbrod) Tübingen 1992.

About the Authors

Christoph Antons, Prof. Dr., is a professor at the Macquarie Law School, Macquarie University (Sydney). He has published extensively on intellectual property law and law and society in Asia. Professor Antons was a Fellow at the Käte Hamburger Center for Advanced Study in the Humanities »Law as Culture« from October 2020 to March 2021. His recent book publications include *Intellectual Property, Cultural Property and Intangible Cultural Heritage* (co-edited with W. Logan); *The Routledge Handbook of Asian Law*; and *Intellectual Property and Free Trade Agreements in the Asia-Pacific Region* (co-edited with R. M. Hilty).

Beatriz Barreiro Carril, Assoc. Prof. Dr., is a legal scholar and Associate Professor of International Law and International Relations at Rey Juan Carlos University (Madrid). She was a visiting researcher at the Max Planck Institute for Social Anthropology (Halle), the Institute for International and European Law at the University of Göttingen, the Centre for Ethics at the University of Toronto, and the Centre of Socio-Legal Studies at Oxford University. Furthermore, she is an observer of the UNESCO Committee for Cultural Diversity and a member of the University of Fribourg's Observatory for Diversity and Cultural Rights. She was a Fellow at the Käte Hamburger Center for Advanced Study in the Humanities »Law as Culture« from June to August 2020.

Upendra Baxi, Prof. em. Dr. h.c. mult., is one of the most renowned contemporary Indian legal scholars. His academic career has led him to universities in Delhi, Durham (Duke University), Sydney, Surat, New York, Toronto, and Warwick. He was a Fellow at the Käte Hamburger Center for Advanced Study in the Humanities »Law as Culture« from April to November 2011 and from July to December 2012.

Anne-Marie Bonnet, Senior Prof. Dr., is Professor of Renaissance, Modern, and Contemporary Art at the University of Bonn's Department of Art History. Since 1999 she has also played an active role in various commissions, executive boards, and foundations, including the Kunstverein Bonn since 2005 and the Federal Commission on the Acquisition of Contemporary Art for the Art Collection of Germany from 2007 to 2011. Since 2020 she is member of the Curatorium of the Cultural Foundation of the German States. She was a Fellow at the Käte Hamburger Center for Advanced Study in the Humanities »Law as Culture« from October 2018 to March 2019.

Pierre Brunet, Prof. Dr., is a legal scholar. He is a professor at the University of Paris I (Panthéon Sorbonne), where he also serves as Director of the LL.M. de droit français et droit européen and the Double LL.M. Sorbonne-Queen Mary programs. He is a co-editor and member of several editorial boards for French and foreign journals, such as *Droit et Société* (LGDJ). Moreover, he was a visiting professor at universities in Brazil, Italy, Japan, the United States, and Argentina. He was a Fellow at the Käte Hamburger Center for Advanced Study in the Humanities »Law as Culture« from May to September 2020.

Marta Bucholc, Prof. Dr., is a sociologist, legal scholar, and philosopher. She works at the Faculty of Sociology at the University of Warsaw. Until 2020 she was a research professor at the Käte Hamburger Center for Advanced Study in the Humanities »Law as Culture«. Her research focuses on historical sociology, the history of social theory, the sociology of law, the sociology of economy, and the sociology of knowledge. Her recent journal publications include *Law and Liberal Pedagogy in a Post-Socialist Society: The Case of Poland, Schengen and the Rosary. Catholic Religions and the Postcolonial Syndrome in Polish National Habitus*, and *Die PiS, das Virus und die Macht. Wahlen in Zeiten der Pandemie*.

Francesca Caroccia, Prof. Dr., is a legal scholar. She is a professor at the University of L'Aquila (Italy) and coordinates the Conference of the Italian Rectors' Commission on Gender Questions. She has published extensively on questions of legal interpretation, contract, and tort, notably from the perspective of the intersection between private autonomy and judicial power. Among her main publications are *Ordine pubblico. La gestione dei conflitti culturali nel diritto privato*, *L'interpretazione del contratto* and *Il paradigma della condizione e le dinamiche negoziali*. She was a Fellow at the Käte Hamburger Center for Advanced Study in the Humanities »Law as Culture« from July to December 2013 and from May to September 2016.

Angela Condello, Asst. Prof. Dr. iur., Ph.D., is a legal scholar and philosopher. She is Tenure-Track Assistant Professor of Legal Philosophy at the University of Messina (Italy) and Adjunct Professor at the University of Turin (Italy), where she held a Jean Monnet module on human rights and critical legal thinking within European legal culture until 2020. She has published four monographs, including *Money, Social and Law* (with J. R. Searle and M. Ferraris), edited various journal issues and contributed to numerous volumes (i. e. *Sensing the Nation's Law: Historical Inquiries into the Aesthetics of Democratic Legitimacy, Post-Truth, Philosophy and Law, Law, Labour and the Humanities*). She was a Fellow at the Käte Hamburger Center for Advanced Study in the Humanities »Law as Culture« from January to December 2014.

About the Authors

Katharina C. Cramer, Dr., is a research fellow for the Chair of International Relations and Global Politics of Technology in Bonn. She studied Political Science at the Universities of Bonn, Luxembourg, and Istanbul. She received her doctorate in History from the University of Konstanz with the thesis *A Political History of Big Science: The Other Europe*. Her research interests include various aspects of the history and politics of research infrastructures in the 20th and 21st centuries; the role of knowledge, innovation, and technology in global contexts; and feminist perspectives on international relations and the history of science. Katharina C. Cramer is co-editor of *Big Science and Research Infrastructures in Europe* and co-founder of the Network for Big Science and Research Infrastructures (BSRI).

Hanna Eklund, Asst. Prof. Dr., is a European Union lawyer. She is Assistant Professor of Constitutional Law at the University of Copenhagen, where she is affiliated with the Centre for European and Comparative Legal Studies and the Saxo Institute. She was previously a postdoctoral researcher at the Sciences Po Law School and holds a Ph.D. from the European Union Institute. She is interested in and has published on the ways in which EU law relates to politics and society. She is currently working on her Marie Skłodowska-Curie Fellowship project entitled *An Ever Closer Union Among the Peoples of Europe: A Critical Legal History*, which deals with colonialism and socio-economic stratification in European integration.

Maurizio Ferraris, Prof. Dr. Dr. h.c. mult., is a philosopher. He is Professor of Philosophy at the University of Turin (Italy), where he is also President of the LabOnt – Center for Ontology. He is Directeur de Recherche at the Collège d'Études Mondiales (Paris) and Director of Rivista di Estetica. He has worked in the fields of aesthetics, hermeneutics, and social ontology, attaching his name to the theory of documentality and contemporary new realism. He was a Fellow at the Käte Hamburger Center for Advanced Study in the Humanities »Law as Culture« from June 2013 to July 2014, and since September 2017 he has been member of the Center's Scientific Advisory Board. He is the author of *Manifest des Neuen Realismus* in the series »Law as Culture« (ed. by Werner Gephart).

Stefan Finger, Dr., is Managing Director of the Käte Hamburger Center for Advanced Study in the Humanities »Law as Culture« in Bonn. After studying History and Social Sciences at the University of Bonn from 1994 to 2000, he completed his first state examination for teaching in secondary schools. In 2005, Finger was awarded his doctorate degree (Dr. phil.) by the Faculty of Philosophy at the University of Bonn. He was later entrusted with organizing a Master's programme »German and European Politics«. Since December 2009, he has coordinated the reintroduction of the Social Sciences teaching degree program at the University of Bonn's Institute for Political Science and Sociology.

Mariacarla Gadebusch-Bondio, Prof. Dr. phil. Dr. rer. med. habil., has led the Institute of Medical Humanities at the University of Bonn's Hospital since 2017. She is currently a guest professor at the University of Uppsala's Department of History of Science and Ideas (sponsored the Alexander von Humboldt Foundation and the Stiftelsen Riksbankens Jubileumsfond (29th Swedish Prize Award 2020)). Her main research interests lie in the following areas: intersections between medicine and philosophy, norms and deviance in medical discourses, medical fallibility, ethical dimensions of predictive knowledge in medicine, patient narratives, and ethics and cancer.

Sergio Genovesi, Dr. des., is a postdoc researcher at the Center for Science and Thought of the University of Bonn. His current research focuses on the ethics and philosophy of AI. He obtained his Ph.D. from the University of Bonn. In his thesis, he analyzed the contemporary debate on the philosophy of events. He has been a research associate at the Käte Hamburger Center for Advanced Study in the Humanities »Law as Culture« from 2019 until 2021. His research interests also include contemporary ontology, epistemology, and aesthetics.

Werner Gephart, Prof. Dr. jur. Dr. h.c., is a legal scholar, sociologist, and artist. He is Founding Director of the Käte Hamburger Center for Advanced Study in the Humanities »Law as Culture«, and he has additionally held numerous visiting professorships around the world. In 2019 he was appointed as President of the Jury Senior of the Institut Universitaire de France (IUF). He is the publisher of the series »Law as Culture« and co-editor of the volume *Recht*, which was part of the *Max Weber Gesamtausgabe (MWG I/22-3)*. His publications are centered on the cultural analysis of law, the sociology of religion, and aesthetics. He is co-editor of the international journal *Brill Research Perspectives in Art and Law*. In 2014 he, along with German artist Amselm Kiefer, was awarded an honorary doctorate in Philosophy by the University of Turin. Since 1988 he has held numerous exhibits in cities including Paris, Düsseldorf, Cologne, Bonn, St. Louis, Houston, Bloomington, Minneapolis, Tunis, New Delhi, and London.

Peter Goodrich, Prof. Dr., is a lawyer and cultural scientist. He was Founding Dean of Birkbeck College's Department of Law and is currently Professor and Director of the Program in Law and Humanities at Cardozo School of Law (New York). He is also a visiting professor of Law at New York University, Abu Dhabi. He is one of the leading representatives of the law and literature movement, as well as the founder and co-editor of *Law and Critique*. He has written numerous books in legal history and theory, law and literature, and semiotics. One of his recent publications is *Schreber's Law: Jurisprudence and Judgment in Transition* and *Imago Decidendi: On the Common Law of Images*. Goodrich is a member of the Scientific Advisory Board for the Käte Hamburger Center for the Humanities »Law as Culture«.

Kevin Grecksch, Dr., is a political scientist and economist. He is Departmental Lecturer and Course Director (M.Sc. in Water Science, Policy, and Management) at the University of Oxford's School of Geography and the Environment. His main research interests include climate change adaptation, water governance, governance of societal transformation processes, and questions of property rights and natural resources. Among his recent publications are *Historic Narratives, Myths and Human Behavior in Times of Climate Change: A Review From Northern Europe's Coastlands* and *Drought and Water Scarcity in the UK. Social Science Perspectives on Governance, Knowledge and Outreach.*

Jonas Grutzpalk, Prof. Dr., is Professor for Sociology and Political Science at the University of Applied Science for Police and Public Administration (HSPV) in Bielefeld, Germany. From 1998 he was a lecturer at the universities of Bonn, Potsdam and Bielefeld, at the Berlin School of Economics and Law (HWR), and in the master's program »Police Management« of the Deutsche Hochschule der Polizei (DHPol). From 2003 to 2009 Grutzpalk worked in public relations for the *Verfassungsschutz* Brandenburg – the interior intelligence service. His research areas are mainly the sociologies of knowledge, religion, and security. He has published on questions of sociological anthropology, police training and security agencies. He is editor of the journal »Polizei.Wissen«, offices as Humanist celebrant and is regular contributor to humanistisch!net.

Kornelia Hahn, Prof. Dr., is Professor for General Sociology and Sociological Theory and Chair of the Department of Sociology at the University of Salzburg, posts she has held since 2010 and 2011, respectively. Her research agenda is primarily focused on cultural dynamics through an interpretive approach that combines material, historical and semiotic perspectives, theorizing these dynamics particularly in the areas of (digital) communication, intimate relationships, the political public sphere, and the embodied service and fashion/garment industries. She received her Ph.D. and her habilitation degree/venia legendi from the University of Bonn, where she was also trained in sociology, modern German literature, and linguistics.

Valérie Hayaert, Dr., is a classicist, historian, and humanist researcher of early modern European tradition. Her particular interest lies in images of justice, judicial rites, and symbolism and its role in contemporary courthouses. She received the European Union Institute Alumni Prize for the best interdisciplinary thesis in 2006. Her first book, ›*Mens emblematica*‹ *et humanisme juridique*, was published in 2008. Her subsequent work looked at the aesthetics of justice in courthouses of the early modern period through today. She was a Fellow at the Käte Hamburger Center for Advanced Study in the Humanities »Law as Culture« from April 2018 to March 2019. She is currently a researcher at the Institut des Hautes Études sur la Justice, Paris and from November, 2021 she will be a Eutopia Science and Innovation Fellow at the Criminal Justice Centre of the University of Warwick.

Volker Kronenberg, Prof. Dr., is Dean of the Faculty of Arts and Professor of Political Science at the Institute for Political Science and Sociology at the University of Bonn. In his research, Kronenberg is particularly concerned with topics relating to the political system, political culture, and political history of the Federal Republic of Germany. His other areas of expertise include political biographies and party research. He is also regularly invited to speak as a political expert on German media outlets including Phoenix, WDR, and Deutschlandfunk. In 2011 and 2012, Kronenberg was involved as an expert in the citizens' dialog initiated by Federal Chancellor Angela Merkel.

Gerd Krumeich, Prof. em. Dr., is one of the most well-known contemporary German war historians and Emeritus Professor of Modern History at the Heinrich Heine University Düsseldorf. In 1996, he was awarded the title Chevalier dans l'Ordre des Palmes Académiques. His research focuses on the First World War and the military history in France in the 19th and 20th centuries. From 2004–2016, he was Head of the Office for the Max Weber Edition in Düsseldorf. Since 2008, he has served as Vice President of the Comité Directeur du Centre de Recherche de l'Historial de la Grande Guerre.

Helga María Lell, Dr., is a legal philosopher. She is a researcher at the National Council of Scientific and Technological Research (CONICET) as well as a research coordinator at the Economic and Legal Sciences Faculty of the National University of La Pampa (Argentina). She has published on questions of semantics in the legal field, citizenship, legal hermeneutics, and political institutions – all from philosophical, sociological, and historical perspectives. She was a Fellow at the Käte Hamburger Center for Advanced Study in the Humanities »Law as Culture« from April to June 2019.

Maximilian Mayer, Prof. Dr., is Junior Professor of International Relations and Global Technology Policy at the University of Bonn. His research interests include the role of science and technology in international relations, China's foreign and energy policies, and global environmental and climate politics. He has published more than 40 scholarly articles and seven books including *China's Energy Thirst: Myth or Reality?*; *Changing Orders: Transdisciplinary analysis of global and local realities* (co-editor); and two volumes on *The Global Politics of Science and Tech-*

nology. Maximilian has been a visiting scholar at the Harvard Kennedy School's program on Science, Technology, and Society, and also served as co-chair of the International Studies Association's Science, Technology, Arts and International Relations (STAIR) branch from 2015 to 2017.

Sabine N. Meyer, Prof. Dr., is Professor of American Studies and Co-director of the North American Studies program at the University Bonn. Her research primarily focuses on Native American writing and law/politics from the 19th century onward; representations of Native Americans/Indigenous people in North American popular culture; and the history/literary representation of social movements, (forced) migration, and processes of identity formation (ethnicity, race, gender) in the United States. Meyer is the author of *We Are What We Drink: The Temperance Battle in Minnesota* and *Native Removal Writing: Narratives of Peoplehood, Politics, and Law*. She has received numerous research grants and scholarships. From April 2015 to March 2016, Meyer was a Fellow at the Käte Hamburger Center for Advanced Study in the Humanities »Law as Culture.«

Birgit Ulrike Münch, Prof. Dr., is a professor at the Institute of Art History and Vice Rector for International Affairs at the University of Bonn. Her research interests include the social history of the (fe)male artist, genre paintings and their art theory and the history of illness and sexuality. Current research projects address the self-portrait up to the selfie and Aby Warburg. Her project in the Cluster of Excellence »Beyond slavery« deals with prostitution in Early Modern Amsterdam and in Dutch colonialism. Currently, she also is planning an exhibit on still life painting as a source of social inequality together with the LVR-Landesmuseum Bonn and the Allard Pierson Museum Amsterdam (2022/2023).

Brigitte Nerlich, Prof. Dr., is Professor Emeritus of Science, Language, and Society at the Institute for Science and Society at the University of Nottingham. She studied French and Philosophy in Germany and gained a Dr. Phil. in French Linguistics in 1985. Her current research focuses on the cultural and political contexts in which metaphors and other framing devices are used in the public, in policy, and in scientific debates about genetics and genomics, climate change and infectious diseases. She has recently written books and articles on the sociology of health and illness and the social study of science and technology. In 2011 the University of Nottingham awarded her a D.Litt. for her research and publications relating to the social study of metaphor.

Chioma Daisy Onyige, Dr., is Senior Lecturer of Criminology at the Department of Sociology, Faculty of Social Sciences, University of Port Harcourt (Nigeria). Currently she is Heinz Heinen Senior Fellow at the Cluster of Excellence »Bonn

Center for Dependency and Slavery Studies« at the University of Bonn. Her research includes gender and crime, environmental sociology, gender and climate change, and cognate issues like conflict and peacebuilding. Her current research is on contemporary slavery, such as human trafficking and the smuggling of women and children. She has held fellowships amongst others at the Graduate Institute of International and Development Studies (Geneva); Commonwealth Fellow at the University of Oxford; the Global Young Academy (GYA) of the German National Academy of Sciences (Leopoldina); and the Käte Hamburger Center for Advanced Study in the Humanities »Law as Culture« (Bonn).

François Ost, Prof. Dr. Dr. h.c. mult., is a lawyer, philosopher and poet. He is a professor and former vice rector of the University Saint-Louis in Brussels and an honorary professor at the University of Geneva. He is a member of the Royal Academy of Belgium and Founding President of the European Academy of Theory of Law. He is President of the Interdisciplinary Seminar of Legal Studies (SIEJ) and Center for the Study of Environmental Law (CEDRE) at Saint-Louis University. He has published 20 books on the theory and philosophy of law, many of which have been translated. He holds honorary doctorates from the Universities of Nantes, Geneva, Montreal, and Montpellier. Ost holds numerous scientific prizes, including the Polignac Prize (Institut de France) and the Grammaticakis-Neumann Prize (Academy of Moral and Political Sciences). He is also President of the Foundation for Future Generations and the author of several plays.

Hanne Petersen, Prof. Dr. jur., is Professor of Legal Culture at the Centre for European and Comparative Legal Studies at the University of Copenhagen. After studying Sociology and Law at the Universities of Copenhagen and Bremen from 1970 to 1978, she received her doctoral degree at the University of Copenhagen in 1991. She was later Jean Monnet Fellow at the European University Institute, Florence. From 1995 to 2018, she held several professorships and visiting professorships at the Universities of Greenland, Copenhagen, Gothenburg, Lund, and Tromsø.

Christopher Prinz, M.A., is a research assistant at the Institute for Political Science and Sociology at the University of Bonn. In his studies, during which Prinz worked for Sabine Bätzing-Lichtenthäler, Member of the State Parliament of Rhineland-Palatinate and then Minister for Social Affairs, Labour, Health and Demography of the State of Rhineland-Palatinate, he has researched on elections and voting behavior, political communication, in particular political campaigns and campaign strategies. His current research interests focus on the political systems and political cultures of and political polarizations in Western democracies as well as non-majoritarian decision-making in the majoritarian institutions of such polities.

Christa Rautenbach, Prof. Dr., is a legal scientist. She is a professor at the Faculty of Law at the North-West University, Potchefstroom Campus (South Africa). She has published extensively on subjects dealing with legal pluralism, customary law, mixed jurisdictions, cultural diversity, judicial comparativism, and family law. She is the editor of *Introduction to Legal Pluralism in South Africa* published and *In the Shade of an African Baobab: Tom Bennett's Legacy*, as well as co-editor of *The Law of Succession in South Africa* and *The Diffusion of Law: The Movement of Laws and Norms Around the World*. She is also editor-in-chief of the peer-reviewed, open-access Potchefstroom Electronic Law Journal.

Katja Spranz, Dott. ssa, is a researcher at the Käte Hamburger Center for Advanced Study in the Humanities »Law as Culture«. She received her degree in Cultural Anthropology at the University La Sapienza in Rome. She subsequently worked as a television editor for German news outlets and reality shows (i. e. *Big Brother* Germany). At the Center, she assists the directorate and is currently working on her doctoral thesis, which focuses on crime TV series in the German Democratic Republic. She also holds seminars about storytelling and popular culture at the Institute for Political Science and Sociology at the University of Bonn.

Theresa Strombach, M.A., works as a researcher at the University of Bonn's Department of German Linguistics. Her main research interests include linguistic cases of doubt, especially concerning case agreement, as well as morphosyntactic features of legal language. In her Master's thesis entitled *Ohne wenn und aber*, she examined both the usage and comprehensibility of (un-)introduced adverbial clauses in German legal texts. She was an assistant at the Käte Hamburger Center for Advanced Study in the Humanities »Law as Culture« from April 2016 until March 2020.

Sam Whimster, Prof. Dr., is Deputy Director of the Global Policy Institute (London) and editor of *Max Weber Studies*. Most recently, he edited *The Oxford Handbook of Max Weber* (with Edith Hanke and Lawrence Scaff). Besides Weber, his research interests lie in historical and comparative sociology, social theory, methods of social research, and social economics. He was a Fellow at the Käte Hamburger Center for Advanced Study in the Humanities »Law as Culture« from October 2011 to January 2013.

Daniel Witte, Dr., is Research Coordinator at the Käte Hamburger Center for Advanced Study in the Humanities »Law as Culture«. From 2019 to 2020, he held an interim professorship for Sociology with special emphasis on Sociological Theory and the History of Social Theory at the Institute of Sociology at Goethe University (Frankfurt/Main). He is a board member of the research committees »Sociology of Law« and »Sociological Theory« of the German Sociological Association (DGS).